T0215813

Lecture Notes in Computer Science 12200

More information about this series at http://www.springer.com/series/7409

Aaron Marcus · Elizabeth Rosenzweig (Eds.)

Design, User Experience, and Usability

Interaction Design

9th International Conference, DUXU 2020
Held as Part of the 22nd HCI International Conference, HCII 2020
Copenhagen, Denmark, July 19–24, 2020
Proceedings, Part I

 Springer

Editors
Aaron Marcus
Aaron Marcus and Associates
Berkeley, CA, USA

Elizabeth Rosenzweig
World Usability Day and Bentley User
Experience Center
Newton Center, MA, USA

ISSN 0302-9743   ISSN 1611-3349   (electronic)
Lecture Notes in Computer Science
ISBN 978-3-030-49712-5   ISBN 978-3-030-49713-2   (eBook)
https://doi.org/10.1007/978-3-030-49713-2

LNCS Sublibrary: SL3 – Information Systems and Applications, incl. Internet/Web, and HCI

This Springer imprint is published by the registered company Springer Nature Switzerland AG
The registered company address is: Gewerbestrasse 11, 6330 Cham, Switzerland

Foreword

The 22nd International Conference on Human-Computer Interaction, HCI International 2020 (HCII 2020), was planned to be held at the AC Bella Sky Hotel and Bella Center, Copenhagen, Denmark, during July 19–24, 2020. Due to the COVID-19 coronavirus pandemic and the resolution of the Danish government not to allow events larger than 500 people to be hosted until September 1, 2020, HCII 2020 had to be held virtually. It incorporated the 21 thematic areas and affiliated conferences listed on the following page.

A total of 6,326 individuals from academia, research institutes, industry, and governmental agencies from 97 countries submitted contributions, and 1,439 papers and 238 posters were included in the conference proceedings. These contributions address the latest research and development efforts and highlight the human aspects of design and use of computing systems. The contributions thoroughly cover the entire field of human-computer interaction, addressing major advances in knowledge and effective use of computers in a variety of application areas. The volumes constituting the full set of the conference proceedings are listed in the following pages.

The HCI International (HCII) conference also offers the option of "late-breaking work" which applies both for papers and posters and the corresponding volume(s) of the proceedings will be published just after the conference. Full papers will be included in the "HCII 2020 - Late Breaking Papers" volume of the proceedings to be published in the Springer LNCS series, while poster extended abstracts will be included as short papers in the "HCII 2020 - Late Breaking Posters" volume to be published in the Springer CCIS series.

I would like to thank the program board chairs and the members of the program boards of all thematic areas and affiliated conferences for their contribution to the highest scientific quality and the overall success of the HCI International 2020 conference.

This conference would not have been possible without the continuous and unwavering support and advice of the founder, Conference General Chair Emeritus and Conference Scientific Advisor Prof. Gavriel Salvendy. For his outstanding efforts, I would like to express my appreciation to the communications chair and editor of HCI International News, Dr. Abbas Moallem.

July 2020   Constantine Stephanidis

Conference Proceedings Volumes Full List

HCI International 2020 Thematic Areas and Affiliated Conferences

Thematic areas:

- HCI 2020: Human-Computer Interaction
- HIMI 2020: Human Interface and the Management of Information

Affiliated conferences:

- EPCE: 17th International Conference on Engineering Psychology and Cognitive Ergonomics
- UAHCI: 14th International Conference on Universal Access in Human-Computer Interaction
- VAMR: 12th International Conference on Virtual, Augmented and Mixed Reality
- CCD: 12th International Conference on Cross-Cultural Design
- SCSM: 12th International Conference on Social Computing and Social Media
- AC: 14th International Conference on Augmented Cognition
- DHM: 11th International Conference on Digital Human Modeling and Applications in Health, Safety, Ergonomics and Risk Management
- DUXU: 9th International Conference on Design, User Experience and Usability
- DAPI: 8th International Conference on Distributed, Ambient and Pervasive Interactions
- HCIBGO: 7th International Conference on HCI in Business, Government and Organizations
- LCT: 7th International Conference on Learning and Collaboration Technologies
- ITAP: 6th International Conference on Human Aspects of IT for the Aged Population
- HCI-CPT: Second International Conference on HCI for Cybersecurity, Privacy and Trust
- HCI-Games: Second International Conference on HCI in Games
- MobiTAS: Second International Conference on HCI in Mobility, Transport and Automotive Systems
- AIS: Second International Conference on Adaptive Instructional Systems
- C&C: 8th International Conference on Culture and Computing
- MOBILE: First International Conference on Design, Operation and Evaluation of Mobile Communications
- AI-HCI: First International Conference on Artificial Intelligence in HCI

38. CCIS 1224, HCI International 2020 Posters - Part I, edited by Constantine Stephanidis and Margherita Antona
39. CCIS 1225, HCI International 2020 Posters - Part II, edited by Constantine Stephanidis and Margherita Antona
40. CCIS 1226, HCI International 2020 Posters - Part III, edited by Constantine Stephanidis and Margherita Antona

http://2020.hci.international/proceedings

9th International Conference on Design, User Experience, and Usability (DUXU 2020)

Program Board Chairs: **Aaron Marcus, Aaron Marcus and Associates, USA, and Elizabeth Rosenzweig, World Usability Day and Bentley User Experience Center, USA**

- Sisira Adikari, Australia
- Claire Ancient, UK
- Silvia de los Rios, Spain
- Marc Fabri, UK
- Juliana J. Ferreira, Brazil
- Josh Halstead, USA
- Chris Hass, USA
- Wei Liu, China
- Martin Maguire, UK
- Judith A. Moldenhauer, USA
- Kerem Rızvanoğlu, Turkey
- Francisco Rebelo, Portugal
- Christine Riedmann-Streitz, Germany
- Patricia Search, USA
- Marcelo M. Soares, China
- Carla G. Spinillo, Brazil
- Virgínia Tiradentes Souto, Brazil

The full list with the Program Board Chairs and the members of the Program Boards of all thematic areas and affiliated conferences is available online at:

http://www.hci.international/board-members-2020.php

HCI International 2021

The 23rd International Conference on Human-Computer Interaction, HCI International 2021 (HCII 2021), will be held jointly with the affiliated conferences in Washington DC, USA, at the Washington Hilton Hotel, July 24–29, 2021. It will cover a broad spectrum of themes related to Human-Computer Interaction (HCI), including theoretical issues, methods, tools, processes, and case studies in HCI design, as well as novel interaction techniques, interfaces, and applications. The proceedings will be published by Springer. More information will be available on the conference website: http://2021.hci.international/.

General Chair
Prof. Constantine Stephanidis
University of Crete and ICS-FORTH
Heraklion, Crete, Greece
Email: general_chair@hcii2021.org

http://2021.hci.international/

Contents – Part I

Interaction Design and Information Visualization

Emotional Design

Contents – Part II

Usability Aspects of Handheld and Mobile Devices

Designing Games and Immersive Experiences

UX Studies in Automotive and Transport

Contents – Part III

UX Design for Health and Well-Being

DUXU for Creativity, Learning and Collaboration

DUXU for Culture and Tourism

UX Design Methods, Tools and Guidelines

Coherent Heuristic Evaluation (CoHE): Toward Increasing the Effectiveness of Heuristic Evaluation for Novice Evaluators

Anas Abulfaraj$^{(\boxtimes)}$ and Adam Steele

College of Computing and Digital Media, DePaul University,
243 South Wabash Avenue, Chicago, IL 60604, USA
Aabulfa2@mail.depaul.edu, Asteele@cs.depaul.edu

Abstract. Heuristic evaluation (HE) is an inspection-based usability evaluation method in which a number of evaluators, typically 3–5, assess the usability of a system based on a set of usability guidelines. HE was first introduced by Nielsen and Molich and then revised by Nielsen. Since its introduction, HE has gained wide popularity among human-computer interaction (HCI) and user experience (UX) practitioners and is now one of the most common usability evaluation methods. A few years after the introduction of HE, some researchers realized that novice evaluators perform poorly on complex systems. This issue, known as the expertise effect, is one of the major challenges of HE; i.e., the more experienced the evaluator is, the better the results of the evaluation. Consequently, some researchers argue that the results of HE are the product of the evaluator's experience rather than the method itself. To address this issue, we interviewed 15 usability experts, all of whom had at least four years of experience and who came from both academia and industry. We analyzed their responses and developed a step-by-step protocol.

Keywords: Usability · Inspection-based methods · Heuristic Evaluation · Novice evaluators

1 Introduction

Technology is found everywhere around us, from smart phones to smart watches to tablets, and is involved in every aspect of our lives, from communication to education to health. It has basically changed the way we live, and any person in the present day must interact with it. This was not the case until two decades ago. Before then, technology was limited to certain groups of tech-savvy people. However, the focus on developing systems that are merely functional is no longer sufficient; systems must be usable enough to be used by ordinary people who are not tech savvy. Usability is one of the main objectives of the field of human-computer interaction (HCI) [1]. To increase the usability of systems, a number of methods have been proposed, one of which is heuristic evaluation (HE). HE is a method in which a number of evaluators, typically 3–5, assess a system based on a set of usability guidelines. HE was first developed and proposed by Nielsen and Molich [2, 3] and then revised by Nielsen [4]. Currently, HE is very popular and is one of the most common usability evaluation

© Springer Nature Switzerland AG 2020
A. Marcus and E. Rosenzweig (Eds.): HCII 2020, LNCS 12200, pp. 3–20, 2020.
https://doi.org/10.1007/978-3-030-49713-2_1

methods [5, 6]. Despite its popularity, HE suffers from multiple problems to the extent that some researchers have started to question its reliability [7]. One of the major issues of HE is the expertise effect [8], which means that the more experienced the evaluator is, the better the results of the evaluation [9]. This issue has led some researchers to say that the results of HE are the product of the evaluator's experience rather than of HE as a method [7]. A potential reason for this problem is that HE is not a structured method [7], which means there is no step-by-step guide on how to perform it. This lack of direction is especially problematic for novice evaluators who have no or very limited experience. Moreover, HCI is a relatively new field, so there is a scarcity of HCI experts. Even in research projects, researchers depend on novice evaluators to perform HE [10, 11]. Even if experts are available, hiring them is usually expensive, which explains why startups and small companies depend on novice evaluators [12]. HCI is a multidisciplinary field, and HCI practitioners come from different backgrounds, such as computer science, psychology, art, and business; some have no formal HCI education [13]. Ideally, potential users should be involved in the development life cycle. However, HCI practitioners are sometimes expected to represent the user [14], which increases the importance of their work. Additionally, HE should ideally be performed by 3–5 evaluators to increase the likelihood of detecting most usability problems. However, some companies hire a single HCI practitioner, as shown in a survey conducted in Malaysia [15]. Poor usability has large economic costs [16] and can lead to serious health and safety risks [17–19]. Therefore, there is a need to develop a step-by-step protocol to guide novice evaluators through HE to improve the quality of their evaluations, thus improving the usability of the systems that they are evaluating. In this study, our aim is to create such a protocol. We interviewed 15 usability experts from both academia and industry about their experience with HE, the difficulties they faced with it, how they overcame these difficulties, and their suggestions on how to improve HE for novices. We coded and synthesized their responses and created a coherent, step-by-step protocol for HE.

2   Related Work

A review of the HE literature indicates four directions. The first direction focuses on producing general usability guidelines. This direction started even before the proposal of HE in 1990 by Nielsen and Molich [2, 3]. For example, in 1987, Shneiderman [20] produced eight golden rules based on his experience in the field; these rules are general guidelines meant to help designers in designing their system and assessing its usability. After Nielsen's proposal of HE and the ten usability heuristics, many researchers and usability experts tried to follow suit by providing their own usability heuristics and guidelines. These guidelines differ; some are more abstract than others, and there are some overlaps between them. However, most of them are driven by experts' experience in the field. To name a few, Tognazzini [21] created a longer list that contains 19 principles, and Gerhardt-Powals [22] produced a list of 10 principles through her work in cognitive science. A less well-known list is Mandel's [23] three golden rules. Due to the abundance of usability guidelines, some researchers began to compare them or even merge them. For example, in [24], the author merged Nielsen's ten heuristics with

Tognazzini's principles to develop a new set of 15 heuristics, and in [25], the author compared Nielsen's ten heuristics to Gerhardt-Powals's 10 principles.

In contrast to the first direction, the second direction focuses on producing domain-specific heuristics. Many researchers believed that the usability guidelines were very general and difficult to implement in certain domains. Therefore, they started to produce heuristics tailored to specific audiences, platforms, disciplines and contexts. Examples are [26], which is a list of 12 usability heuristics for touch-screen mobile devices; [27], which is a list of 18 usability heuristics for automated teller machines (ATMs); [28], which presents 11 sets of heuristics to evaluate usability and the overall user experience (UX) of social networks; and [29], which generated a set of heuristics for mobile learning applications intended to be used by a Malaysian audience. The aforementioned studies are just examples of the work that has been performed in this area, and many other papers have been published with domain-specific heuristics in areas such as healthcare systems, e-government, and video games.

The aforementioned directions focus on developing a set of usability heuristics. However, usability heuristics are only one component of the HE process; HE as a method needs to be enhanced as well. This need has been realized by a number of HCI researchers. Therefore, researchers pursuing the third direction started to re-evaluate the effectiveness of the method and attempt to improve its various elements to help evaluators utilize it better. They worked on improving the understanding of the guidelines, finding better ways to implement them, and enhancing the reporting of usability issues.

Usability heuristics are abstract and relatively vague and can be open to different interpretations. The authors of [30] realized this issue and analyzed two sets of heuristics: Nielsen's heuristics and Shneiderman's principles. They developed a set of principles on how to improve usability guidelines, such as explaining the relevance of each heuristic, changing the language form of some heuristics to be active rather than passive, and simplifying some heuristics that contain more than one concept. When performing HE, the evaluator should identify usability problems that potential users of the system will encounter. To avoid finding false positive usability issues, the authors of [31] suggested including personas in the process of HE. However, when they compared the results of HE with personas with traditional HE, they found no significant difference in the results. Another way to address this issue is to conduct HE based on specific scenarios. Therefore, a method called heuristics walkthrough (HW) was developed and applied in two studies [32, 33]. The two studies compared HW to HE with contradictory results. In the first study, HW outperformed HE, while in the second study, there was no significant difference between HE and HW. The authors of [31–33] aimed to keep potential users in the mind of the evaluator during HE, but in [34], the authors suggested adding real users during the evaluation; they called this method participatory heuristic evaluation (PHE). They did not mean the addition of potential end users but rather a person with experience related to the domain being evaluated. Another technique is the hybrid usability methodology (HUM) proposed in [35], which suggests integrating HE with usability testing (UT). Combining both HE and UT increases the number of usability issues found. Performing HE in one session can be an overwhelming endeavor. The authors of [36] realized this issue and modified traditional HE to a different version called the structured heuristic evaluation method (sHEM).

The idea of sHEM is to break down the heuristic list into smaller categories and then perform the evaluation for each category in a separate session. When sHEM was tested against HE, the results showed that sHEM was superior [37]. Reporting usability issues is an important component of HE. In fact, it is arguably the most important component because it conveys the results of the evaluation. For that reason, the authors of [38] attempted to improve the formatting of the reports. Rather than using the simple format, which includes describing the usability issue and which heuristic it violated, they suggested a new format that is divided into four parts: first, describing the problem, likely/actual difficulties, the specific context and assumed causes; second, stating the discovery resources and methods; third, stating why the problem is related to a certain heuristic; and finally, stating why the problem should be eliminated. The formatting they suggested improved the quality of the usability issues detected.

HCI is a multidisciplinary and relatively new field, and HCI experts are not easily available and are expensive to hire. Therefore, in research and in industry, novice usability evaluators are used to perform HE. However, novice evaluators can produce poor results. Just a few years after the introduction of HE, the authors of [39] realized this was a problem. In their study, novice evaluators found approximately 23% of the usability issues. In an effort to understand what novice evaluators think about HE, the authors of [40] asked 31 students to express their opinion about HE after evaluating two websites. While most of the students thought it was a useful method, they thought it was difficult to implement. The results of this study, along with those of [41], provided valuable insights into the difficulties that novice evaluators face during HE. For example, novice evaluators faced some difficulties linking the usability problems to the correct heuristic. Additionally, writing the final report was considered problematic. Another effort to understand what makes HE difficult for novices is presented in [42]. In this paper, the authors noted that some novice evaluators had difficulty distinguishing between the heuristics. They suggested renaming some of the heuristics to eliminate confusion.

In contrast, expert evaluators can typically identify 74%–87% of usability issues [9], therefore there is a significant difference between the performance of experts and novices. The researchers in [43] attempted to bridge that gap by interviewing four usability experts. They showed the experts Nielsen's heuristics and asked them to talk about the tactics they used for each heuristic. Consequently, they developed a list of 38 tactics, or 3–6 tactics per heuristic. Usually, HE is performed by multiple evaluators, typically 3–5. However, each evaluator performs the evaluation separately, and they then aggregate the results. To improve the quality of HE, a method called collaborative heuristic evaluation (CHE) was developed [44] that enabled the evaluators to perform the evaluation as a group. This method was tailored for novice evaluators by [45] based on the idea of adding an expert to a group of novice evaluators to see whether the inclusion of an expert in the group increased the quality of the evaluations. When the results of the group of novices plus the expert were compared to those of a group of novices and a group of experts, the findings indicated that the results of the group of novices plus the expert were closer to those of the group of experts than to those of the group of novices. In another attempt to increase the quality of novices' evaluations, the authors of [46] suggested adding real potential users to the HE process and proposed two methods: a user exploratory session of heuristic evaluation (UES-HE) and a user review session of heuristic evaluation (URS-HE). In the former method, users were included before the evaluation and allowed to explore the system, after which the evaluator evaluated the system. The latter method involved the opposite approach: the evaluator evaluated the system, and then the users and the evaluator reviewed the system. When UES-HE and URS-HE were compared to HE, both produced better results than HE.

The goal of this paper is to provide a step-by-step protocol on how to perform HE to facilitate the use of HE for novices, reduce the confusion they may experience, and increase the effectiveness of their evaluations. The literature on HE indicates that some researchers are concerned with developing new heuristics or combining existing heuristics, as shown in the first and second directions. However, HE is a process, and usability heuristics are only one part of it. Improving HE is also a concern, as seen in the third and fourth directions; however, most of the papers approached a particular aspect of HE rather than the entire process. Although these papers provided excellent insight, they did not address the overall issue.

3   Methodology

To develop a step-by-step protocol, we interviewed usability experts. Although this work is aimed at novices, we chose to interview usability experts because they once were novices and experienced the difficulties that novices face. Therefore, they have a good understanding of how to overcome these difficulties. To choose the participants, we first had to define an expert because what makes an individual an expert is not well defined in the literature. This lack of a definitive answer occurs not only in HCI but across all disciplines to different degrees. Some fields have higher interrater reliability (for example, weather forecasting has 95% interrater reliability), whereas other fields have lower interrater reliability (for example, clinical psychology has 40% interrater reliability) [47]. One reason for this discrepancy is that validating the outcomes is more difficult in some fields, especially those that deal with human behavior [47].

To the best of our knowledge, little work has been done to define experts in the field of HCI. The only attempt to do so is [48], in which the authors aimed to classify usability practitioners into five categories: novice, beginner, intermediate, senior and expert. They based their work on the famous idea of deliberate practice [49] and suggested that to be a usability expert, an individual should have a master's degree or PhD in the field and at least 10,000 h of usability practice, which equals 10 years of experience. These are somewhat strict criteria and are based on the idea of deliberate practice, which has been criticized. For example, the authors of [50] stated that deliberate practice is important, but alone, it does not explain how an individual becomes an expert. They noted that other important factors are involved in expertise, such as IQ, starting age, and personality.

Since it is difficult to find many usability experts with 10 years of experience and deliberate practice has been criticized, we attempted to follow previous studies in their methods of interviewing experts, particularly the approach used by the authors of [43]. Thus, we consider the minimum experience for an expert to be 4 years of experience in the field.

When choosing the number of experts to interview, interviews should typically be conducted until data saturation is achieved, meaning no new insights are added. In [51], the authors suggested that to reach saturation, 12 interviews are needed. Therefore, we planned to conduct 10–15 interviews and to add more if we did not feel that we had reached saturation. The number of interviews also depended on the availability of usability experts.

We interviewed 15 usability experts from both academia (7 participants) and industry (8 participants). Ten of them were male, and 5 were female. All of them had at least 4 years of experience, and the maximum amount of experience among the experts whom we interviewed was 15 years. The participants from academia had experience teaching HE and greater access to novices; they also should have previously performed HE at least three times. The participants from industry had more hands-on experience with the method, which gave them more knowledge of the actual techniques used. Interviewing people from both academia and industry gave us better insight into both the knowledge and the techniques behind HE because we believe that knowing the techniques without understanding the knowledge behind them would be less effective and vice versa.

The semistructured interviews were held between May 2019 and July 2019. The major items involved asking participants to describe their overall experience with HE, the difficulties they faced and how they overcame them, the detailed process of conducting HE, and how they documented usability problems, mapped usability problems to the heuristics, and estimated the severity of usability problems. They were also asked to suggest how to improve the understandability and the applicability of HE for novices. In addition, the interviewees were given the chance to talk about anything related to the topic to provide more insight. The interviewer asked questions based on the interviewees' responses.

The interviews were conducted either face-to-face (6 interviews) or via conference calls (9 interviews). After the interviewees gave their consent, each interview was audio recorded. During each interview, the interviewer took notes on the major points made by the interviewees. After 13 interviews, we felt that we had reached saturation. However, we continued our interviews to confirm that belief. After all 15 interviews were completed, the interviews were transcribed, and the audio recordings were deleted.

After the interviews, we analyzed the data to derive coherent insights. We started by examining the similarities in the participants' responses and organizing them into categories. Then, we created higher levels of categories. In this process, we focused on two things. First, we focused on the problems that the usability experts faced when they started performing HE or the mistakes they had seen novices make, how to overcome these difficulties, and how to improve HE as a method. Second, we focused on the overall organization of the HE process. Based on the analysis, we developed a step-by-step protocol.

4 Results

4.1 Problems Evaluators Faced, How to Overcome Them and Suggestions to Improve HE

1. Before performing HE, the evaluator should have some knowledge about human abilities and the way people interact with technology. Considering usability heuristics to be standalone guidelines without understanding why we apply them could lead to incorrect judgments. The reason for performing HE is to help users accomplish their goals in the easiest way possible. Therefore, two main aspects should be understood before performing HE. First, how do humans go about accomplishing their goals? Second, what are the usability components, and how will they help? Consequently, the evaluator should understand these two aspects before undertaking HE. Norman created a famous model called the seven stages of action in his book The Design of Everyday Things [52], which explained how humans perform tasks. Usability is a general term that has many definitions, but Nielsen provided a good definition in which he explained its components. After reading and understanding Norman's seven stages of action and Nielsen's definition of usability, the evaluators would have a better understanding of why they are performing HE.

2. Usability heuristics should help users accomplish their goals and should make the means of accomplishing the goal usable and easy. Therefore, the set of heuristics should be mapped to the seven stages of action as well as the usability components. The evaluator should understand how each of these usability heuristics helps in the process of accomplishing the goal and in which steps of the process it plays a role. The same applies to usability: in what components of usability will each heuristic help?

3. The traditional way of representing usability heuristics does not provide an effective understanding of heuristics. Simply providing a label with 2–3 lines of description and an example is not a good way to explain heuristics. There should be more information about each heuristic, and multiple aspects should be addressed:

   - Give examples that are not limited to the interface. To provide a deeper understanding of each heuristic, provide examples of how these heuristics could be used in everyday life in situations outside the interface.
   - For each heuristic, give multiple examples that are related to the interfaces; between 3 and 5 examples would highlight different issues that these heuristics address.
   - When providing examples, present both good and bad examples. Good examples help the evaluators understand what should be done, and bad examples help the evaluators understand what to avoid.
   - Explain the different components of the heuristics. Some of the heuristics deal with complex ideas that have multiple components, and these components should be clearly written. For example, Nielsen's first heuristic, "Visibility of System Status," states that the user should always be informed about the status

of the system. There are three components of this heuristic: first, the existence of the system status; second, the visibility of the system status to the user; and third, making the status visible to the user in a timely manner.

- Explain the different aspects that each heuristic addresses. For example, Nielsen's second heuristic, "Match Between System and the Real World," says that the system should speak the user's language. Clearly, this heuristic deals with multiple aspects, such as the language used, metaphors, and icons.
- Explain the significance of each heuristic. For example, explain in detail why each heuristic is important and the consequences of ignoring it. Supporting these explanations with empirical results and psychological principles will help in emphasizing their importance.
- Explain the applicability of each heuristic. Some evaluators think that if a system violates one of the heuristics, then it automatically indicates a usability issue that needs to be fixed. This is not the case because there are sometimes good reasons for violating the heuristics. This idea should be clear to the evaluators. Therefore, providing them with examples of situations in which violating the usability heuristics is acceptable will help clarify this idea.
- Explain that some of the heuristics deal with more than one related concept. For example, Nielsen's tenth heuristic, "Help and Documentation," deals with two concepts: providing help to users when needed and the existence of documentation for the system. Although these two are closely related, they are not the same. Putting them into one heuristic tends to make the evaluator focus on only one of them. Separating them into two different heuristics forces the evaluator to examine each concept more carefully.
- Some of the heuristics are labeled in a way that does not convey their meaning. Renaming these heuristics not only enhances their understandability but also helps the evaluator remember them later.

4. Deciding how to inspect the system is another issue, and there is more than one way to do so. The system could be inspected page by page, by certain tasks, by certain aspects, etc. Evaluators will sometimes be asked to inspect only one page or a very small part of the system, and in this case, their job is easier. In contrast, inspecting the entire system could be an overwhelming job for novice evaluators. To choose how to perform the inspection, evaluators should know the main services or purposes of the system. On that basis, they can develop a set of goals rather than tasks. Then, the system can be inspected according to these goals. Moreover, specific parts of the system, such as the homepage, the contact page, and the about us page, should be inspected.

5. The timing of the inspection session is yet another problem. Some evaluators inspect the entire system in one session, which may take up to two hours or more in large systems. This might affect the evaluators' mental stamina and cause them to lose their concentration. To overcome this issue, the inspection session should be broken down into smaller sessions with a suggested duration of between 30 and 45 min. If the system is simple and can be evaluated within 30–45 min, then that duration is good. However, if the evaluation will take longer than that amount of time, breaking it down into smaller sessions is preferable.

6. Usually, evaluators are fully alert when performing the inspection, but being very focused and alert might cause some problems. Evaluators might miss certain usability issues because their performance while alert is likely to be superior. Moreover, they could become overly critical because of their strong focus. In both cases, they might report incorrect results. To address this issue, the evaluation should be performed twice so that the evaluators approach each session in a different mood: first, tired or sleepy, to resemble the situation in which real users use the system, and second, fully focused and more critical. The two sessions will help the evaluator detect different usability issues.

7. Novice evaluators tend to think of usability heuristics as a checklist rather than an inspiration. Thus, they become very focused on the heuristics and pay less attention to the system itself. This approach hinders their ability to fully experience the system and might lead them to detect false positive usability problems. On the other hand, once they find a usability issue that is related to a certain heuristic, they may rule out that heuristic and move on to the next even though they may still find other issues that are related to the same heuristic. Therefore, evaluators should perform two separate sessions. The first session should be a free evaluation in which the evaluators examine the system as if they were real users and do not consider the heuristics while performing the inspection. In the second session, the heuristics should be used to ensure that the evaluators did not miss any issues.

8. When examining different systems and websites, we can see that designers make specific mistakes. Providing a list of common mistakes to the evaluators and linking them to the heuristics could help the evaluators inspect the system. This could serve as a double-check procedure in which, after the evaluators finish the inspection, they could look at these mistakes and double-check whether they exist in the system that is being evaluated.

9. While all heuristics are important, some heuristics are associated with more usability issues than others. There is no agreement regarding which heuristics are associated with more usability issues, but there is agreement that there are discrepancies. Moreover, some usability heuristics are associated with more severe issues than others. Analyzing previous evaluations and providing the evaluators with insight into which heuristics require focus could be helpful, especially when the evaluation is performed under pressure to submit the results as quickly as possible. Ideally, the evaluators should focus equally on all the heuristics, but providing such information may be useful when the schedule is tight.

10. When performing the inspection, one session should be performed without depending on the heuristics, and the other session should be based on the heuristics. In the heuristic-based inspection session, the evaluator should go through each heuristic to determine its components, attempt to focus on the aspects that the heuristic addresses, and then inspect it based on whether there is a problem.

11. Assigning usability issues to a specific heuristic is an issue for novice evaluators. While some think that the most important aim is to identify usability problems regardless of whether they are assigned to a certain heuristic, others think that it is important, especially for novice evaluators, to assign such issues to a certain heuristic. The reason is that assigning usability issues to a specific heuristic increases the credibility of novice evaluators and the legitimacy of the report that

they submit to the developers. However, the task is sometimes confusing for two main reasons. First, novice evaluators tend to think that a single usability issue should be assigned to only one heuristic, while in fact, one issue can sometimes violate multiple heuristics. Second, it is difficult to determine how the usability problem is related to any of the heuristics. To facilitate this process, it is necessary to first examine the effect of the usability issue in light of the seven stages of action and usability components. When the stage of action affected by the usability issue is known, a number of heuristics are automatically eliminated. Moreover, when the usability component effected by the usability issue is known, other heuristics can be eliminated as well.

12. Accurately rating the severity of usability issues is a difficulty that novice evaluators face. Sometimes they overestimate the severity of the issue, while at other times, they underestimate it. To facilitate the rating of such issues, evaluators are encouraged to think of them in light of both the usability components and the seven stages of action. This approach will help in accurately rating the severity of an issue.

13. When reporting usability issues, in addition to what others have mentioned in previous studies [31], increasing the credibility and understandability of novice evaluators' reports is an issue. Two main solutions are suggested. First, explain the issue in light of the seven stages of action and how this issue hinders users in accomplishing their goals, and in light of how the issue affects a specific component of usability. Second, research is needed to support such claims with empirical results, similar types of problems, articles, psychological principles, etc.

4.2   Coherent Heuristic Evaluation (CoHE)

We can divide the CoHE process into three stages: understanding, inspecting, and documenting. In the first stage, the goal is to enable the evaluators to understand the main reasons for performing an evaluation and to understand the set of usability heuristics. In the second stage, the goal is to help the evaluators perform the evaluation. The aim of the third stage is to help the evaluators accurately and clearly describe the results of the evaluation.

Understanding

a. Start by reading Norman's seven stages of action to understand how people go about accomplishing their goals.
b. Read the definitions and explanations of the concept of usability, specifically Nielsen's definition of usability.
c. Read the usability heuristics, and for each heuristic, read the description, example from everyday life, examples from the interface, different components, different aspects, significance, and when it is not applicable.
d. Read how the heuristics are related to Norman's seven stages of action to understand the role each one plays in facilitating the accomplishment of the user goals.
e. Read how the heuristics are related to the components of usability to understand the role each one plays in facilitating the usability of the system.

Inspecting

a. Learn about what the system is, what it does and who the target audience is.
b. Define the goals that users would want to accomplish by using the system.
c. Before inspecting the system, allocate 30–45 min for each session. If a session would take more than 45 min, it is better to divide it into smaller sessions.
d. First, inspect the system without referring to the usability heuristics. Attempt to accomplish the predetermined goals on the system. In addition, go to the homepage, try to learn more about the system from the about us page, and try to use the contact us page.
e. Ideally, perform the inspection without the heuristics twice: once when not fully focused (e.g., tired or sleepy) to resemble users in a normal situation and once when fully focused and more critical. It is better to perform the former evaluation first to avoid the learning effect.
f. Write down each usability issue without assigning it to any heuristic, and do not rate its severity.
g. Second, inspect the system based on the heuristics. This time, examine the system, but when accomplishing the goals, examine the aspects that each heuristic addresses to evaluate whether they comply with the heuristic.
h. Write down each usability issue without rating its severity.
i. Finally, review the list of common problems associated with each heuristic and then see whether the system you are evaluating has similar problems. If so, write them down.

Documenting

a. For each usability issue found, start by assigning it to a usability heuristic or to multiple heuristics. To do so, identify which stage of action it affects and then eliminate the heuristics that are not associated with this stage. Then, determine which usability components it affects and eliminate all heuristics that do not deal with these components.
b. For each usability issue, think of it in light of the usability components and the seven stages of action, and determine how it will affect the user in terms of accomplishing the goal and how it will affect the usability components.
c. For each usability issue, write a description of the problem, take screenshots of it, and provide a recommendation on how to fix it.
d. When describing the usability problem, try to explain it in light of the seven stages of action and the usability components.
e. It is recommended that the description be supported by empirical studies, articles and descriptions of similar problems when possible.

The following diagrams (Diagram a, b, c, and d) provide a high-level overview of CoHE:

a. Stages of CoHE

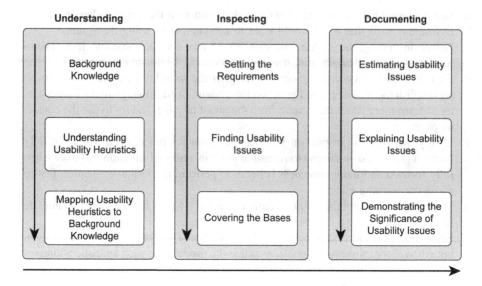

b. The Understanding Stage

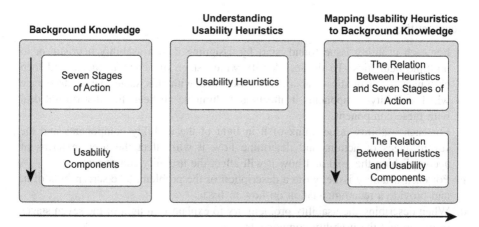

c. The Inspecting Stage

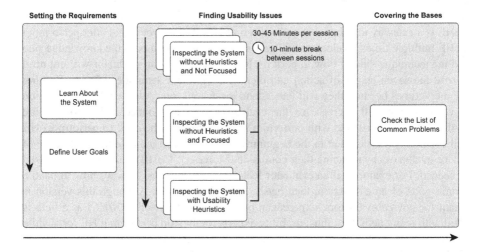

d. The Documenting Stage

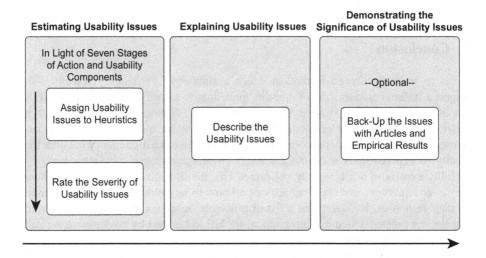

5 Discussion

HE is a discount usability method, meaning that it does not require many resources and is quick to apply. Admittedly, asking evaluators to read more about human ways of accomplishing goals and usability and to perform the evaluation sessions multiple times (based on their mood and on the heuristics) and asking them to put more effort into supporting their results in the report will take more time. However, since novice evaluators tend to produce poor-quality results to the extent that their results are sometimes not very convincing to the developers, the procedure needs improvement. CoHE is a gateway to enhancing and mastering HE. It is expected that after performing CoHE multiple times, evaluators will gain more experience in both the knowledge side and the technique side of how to perform HE. For example, an evaluator will not need to read the seven stages of action and their relation to the heuristics after performing HE a few times because they will understand these concepts. Additionally, the duration of each session will decrease as the evaluators gain experience and become more confident and comfortable with performing HE. Therefore, the need to perform CoHE will eventually subside, but in the beginning, it is needed to increase the confidence of novice evaluators by reducing their confusion. Moreover, CoHE could be partially used as needed. For example, if an evaluator feels that he/she already knows how to handle certain parts of an evaluation, then he/she can skip that part. Although this version is meant for novice evaluators, experts can benefit from it as well. UX/HCI as a field is filled with many activities; thus, usability experts might stop performing HE for a while and then return to it. Therefore, this coherent version could help refresh their memory. CoHE is not based on specific heuristics but is a general step-by-step protocol that can be applied to any set of heuristics, either general heuristics or domain-specific heuristics. However, further work is needed in applying it to a specific set of heuristics and then validating its value.

6 Conclusion

HE is an inspection-based method in which a number of evaluators, typically 3–5, inspect a system based on a set of usability guidelines to identify usability issues. HE is one of the most common usability evaluation methods. Although it is very popular, it suffers from a number of problems. Studies show that the quality of HE when performed by novice evaluators is poor. This means that there is a discrepancy between the quality of expert results and novice results. To bridge that gap, we interviewed 15 usability experts to ask how they performed HE, the difficulties they faced and how they overcame them, and their suggestions on how to improve HE for novices. Based on their responses, we developed a list of problems, solutions and suggestions. From that list, we created a step-by-step protocol for HE to be used by novices that we call coherent heuristic evaluation (CoHE).

In future work, we plan to pursue three directions. First, we will apply CoHE to a specific set of heuristics to map usability problems to heuristics and to Norman's seven stages of action and usability components, explain each heuristic's aspects and components, check for common problems associated with each heuristic, and determine which heuristics detect the most issues. Second, we will validate CoHE by comparing it to traditional HE. Third, we will examine the applicability of CoHE to a wide range of sets of usability heuristics, both general heuristics and domain-specific heuristics.

References

1. Issa, T., Isaias, P.: Usability and human computer interaction (HCI). In: Issa, T., Isaias, P. (eds.) Sustainable Design: HCI, Usability and Environmental Concerns, pp. 19–36. Springer, London (2015). https://doi.org/10.1007/978-1-4471-6753-2_2
2. Molich, R., Nielsen, J.: Improving a human-computer dialogue. Commun. ACM **33**, 338–348 (1990). https://doi.org/10.1145/77481.77486
3. Nielsen, J., Molich, R.: Heuristic evaluation of user interfaces. In: Proceedings of the SIGCHI Conference on Human Factors in Computing Systems, pp. 249–256. Association for Computing Machinery, Seattle (1990). https://doi.org/10.1145/97243.97281
4. Nielsen, J.: Enhancing the explanatory power of usability heuristics. In: Proceedings of the SIGCHI Conference on Human Factors in Computing Systems, pp. 152–158. Association for Computing Machinery, Boston (1994). https://doi.org/10.1145/191666.191729
5. Rosenbaum, S., Rohn, J.A., Humburg, J.: A toolkit for strategic usability: results from workshops, panels, and surveys. In: Proceedings of the SIGCHI Conference on Human Factors in Computing Systems, pp. 337–344. Association for Computing Machinery, The Hague (2000). https://doi.org/10.1145/332040.332454
6. Fernandez, A., Insfran, E., Abrahão, S.: Usability evaluation methods for the web: a systematic mapping study. Inf. Softw. Technol. **53**, 789–817 (2011). https://doi.org/10.1016/j.infsof.2011.02.007
7. Cockton, G., Woolrych, A.: Sale must end: should discount methods be cleared off HCI's shelves? Interactions **9**, 13–18 (2002). https://doi.org/10.1145/566981.566990
8. Hertzum, M., Jacobsen, N.E.: The evaluator effect: a chilling fact about usability evaluation methods. Int. J. Hum. Comput. Interact. **13**, 421–443 (2001). https://doi.org/10.1207/S15327590IJHC1304_05
9. Nielsen, J.: Finding usability problems through heuristic evaluation. In: Proceedings of the SIGCHI Conference on Human Factors in Computing Systems, pp. 373–380. Association for Computing Machinery, Monterey (1992). https://doi.org/10.1145/142750.142834
10. Al-Razgan, M.S., Al-Khalifa, H.S., Al-Shahrani, M.D.: Heuristics for evaluating the usability of mobile launchers for elderly people. In: Marcus, A. (ed.) DUXU 2014. LNCS, vol. 8517, pp. 415–424. Springer, Cham (2014). https://doi.org/10.1007/978-3-319-07668-3_40
11. Paz, F., Paz, F.A., Pow-Sang, J.A.: Experimental case study of new usability heuristics. In: Marcus, A. (ed.) Design, User Experience, and Usability 2015: Design Discourse. LNCS, vol. 9186, pp. 212–223. Springer, Cham (2015). https://doi.org/10.1007/978-3-319-20886-2_21
12. de Salgado, A.L., Amaral, L.A., Freire, A.P., Fortes, R.P.M.: Usability and UX practices in small enterprises: lessons from a survey of the Brazilian context. In: Proceedings of the 34th ACM International Conference on the Design of Communication, pp. 1–9. Association for Computing Machinery, Silver Spring (2016). https://doi.org/10.1145/2987592.2987616
13. Rajanen, D., Clemmensen, T., Iivari, N., Inal, Y., Rızvanoğlu, K., Sivaji, A., Roche, A.: UX professionals' definitions of usability and UX – a comparison between Turkey, Finland, Denmark, France and Malaysia. In: Bernhaupt, R., Dalvi, G., Joshi, A.K., Balkrishan, D., O'Neill, J., Winckler, M. (eds.) INTERACT 2017. LNCS, vol. 10516, pp. 218–239. Springer, Cham (2017). https://doi.org/10.1007/978-3-319-68059-0_14
14. Iivari, N.: Understanding the work of an HCI practitioner. In: Proceedings of the 4th Nordic Conference on Human-Computer Interaction: Changing Roles, pp. 185–194. Association for Computing Machinery, Oslo (2006). https://doi.org/10.1145/1182475.1182495

15. Hussein, I., Mahmud, M., Tap, A.O.M.: A survey of user experience practice: a point of meet between academic and industry. In: 2014 3rd International Conference on User Science and Engineering (i-USEr), pp. 62–67. IEEE, Shah Alam (2014). https://doi.org/10.1109/iuser.2014.7002678

16. Aydin, B., Palikhe, H., Beruvides, M.: The impact of usability on the cost of quality. In: Annual International Conference of the American Society for Engineering Management ASEM, pp. 632–637. ASEM, Virginia (2012)

17. Kushniruk, A.W., Triola, M.M., Borycki, E.M., Stein, B., Kannry, J.L.: Technology induced error and usability: the relationship between usability problems and prescription errors when using a handheld application. Int. J. Med. Inform. **74**, 519–526 (2005). https://doi.org/10.1016/j.ijmedinf.2005.01.003

18. Han, Y.Y., et al.: Unexpected increased mortality after implementation of a commercially sold computerized physician order entry system. Pediatrics **116**, 1506–1512 (2005). https://doi.org/10.1542/peds.2005-1287

19. Sripathi, V., Sandru, V.: Effective usability testing–knowledge of user centered design is a key requirement. Int. J. Emerg. Technol. Adv. Eng. **3**, 627–635 (2013)

20. Shneiderman, B.: Designing the User Interface: Strategies for Effective Human-Computer Interaction. Addison-Wesley Publishing Co., Reading (1987)

21. Tognazzini, B.: First Principles, HCI Design, Human Computer Interaction (HCI), Principles of HCI Design, Usability Testing. http://www.asktog.com/basics/firstPrinciples.html. Accessed 5 Mar 2014

22. Gerhardt-Powals, J.: Cognitive engineering principles for enhancing human-computer performance. Int. J. Hum. Comput. Interact. **8**, 189–211 (1996). https://doi.org/10.1080/10447319609526147

23. Mandel, T.: The golden rules of user interface design. In: Mandel, T. (ed.) The Elements of User Interface Design, pp. 1–28. Wiley, Hoboken (1997)

24. Granollers, T.: Usability evaluation with heuristics. New proposal from integrating two trusted sources. In: Marcus, A., Wang, W. (eds.) DUXU 2018. LNCS, vol. 10918, pp. 396–405. Springer, Cham (2018). https://doi.org/10.1007/978-3-319-91797-9_28

25. Hvannberg, E.T., Law, E.L.-C., Lárusdóttir, M.K.: Heuristic evaluation: comparing ways of finding and reporting usability problems. Interact. Comput. **19**, 225–240 (2007). https://doi.org/10.1016/j.intcom.2006.10.001

26. Inostroza, R., Rusu, C., Roncagliolo, S., Rusu, V.: Usability heuristics for touchscreen-based mobile devices: update. In: Proceedings of the 2013 Chilean Conference on Human - Computer Interaction, pp. 24–29. Association for Computing Machinery, Temuco, Chile (2013). https://doi.org/10.1145/2535597.2535602

27. Chanco, C., Moquillaza, A., Paz, F.: Development and validation of usability heuristics for evaluation of interfaces in ATMs. In: Marcus, A., Wang, W. (eds.) HCII 2019. LNCS, vol. 11586, pp. 3–18. Springer, Cham (2019). https://doi.org/10.1007/978-3-030-23535-2_1

28. Saavedra, M.-J., Rusu, C., Quiñones, D., Roncagliolo, S.: A set of usability and user experience heuristics for social networks. In: Meiselwitz, G. (ed.) HCII 2019. LNCS, vol. 11578, pp. 128–139. Springer, Cham (2019). https://doi.org/10.1007/978-3-030-21902-4_10

29. Ariffin, S.A., Dyson, L.E.: Culturally appropriate design of mobile learning applications in the Malaysian context. In: Rau, P. (eds.) CCD 2015. LNCS, vol. 9181, pp. 3–14. Springer, Cham (2015). https://doi.org/10.1007/978-3-319-20934-0_1

30. Cronholm, S.: The usability of usability guidelines: a proposal for meta-guidelines. In: Proceedings of the 21st Annual Conference of the Australian Computer-Human Interaction Special Interest Group: Design: Open 24/7, pp. 233–240. Association for Computing Machinery, Melbourne (2009). https://doi.org/10.1145/1738826.1738864

31. Friess, E.: Personas in heuristic evaluation: an exploratory study. IEEE Trans. Prof. Commun. **58**, 176–191 (2015). https://doi.org/10.1109/TPC.2015.2429971
32. Po, S., Howard, S., Vetere, F., Skov, M.B.: Heuristic evaluation and mobile usability: bridging the realism gap. In: Brewster, S., Dunlop, M. (eds.) MobileHCI 2004. LNCS, vol. 3160, pp. 49–60. Springer, Berlin (2004). https://doi.org/10.1007/978-3-540-28637-0_5
33. Varsaluoma, J.: Scenarios in the heuristic evaluation of mobile devices: emphasizing the context of use. In: Kurosu, M. (eds.) HCD 2009. LNCS, vol. 5619, pp. 332–341. Springer, Heidelberg (2009). https://doi.org/10.1007/978-3-642-02806-9_38
34. Muller, M.J., Matheson, L., Page, C., Gallup, R.: Methods & tools: participatory heuristic evaluation. Interactions **5**, 13–18 (1998). https://doi.org/10.1145/285213.285219
35. Sivaji, A., Abdullah, M.R., Downe, A.G., Ahmad, W.F.W.: Hybrid usability methodology: integrating heuristic evaluation with laboratory testing across the software development lifecycle. In: 2013 10th International Conference on Information Technology: New Generations, pp. 375–383. IEEE, Las Vegas (2013). https://doi.org/10.1109/itng.2013.60
36. Kurosu, M., Matsuura, S., Sugizaki, M.: Categorical inspection method-structured heuristic evaluation (sHEM). In: 1997 IEEE International Conference on Systems, Man, and Cybernetics. Computational Cybernetics and Simulation, vol. 2613, pp. 2613–2618. IEEE, Orlando (1997). https://doi.org/10.1109/icsmc.1997.635329
37. Kurosu, M., Sugizaki, M., Matsuura, S.: A comparative study of sHEM (structured heuristic evaluation method). In: Proceedings of HCI International (The 8th International Conference on Human-Computer Interaction) on Human-Computer Interaction: Ergonomics and User Interfaces-Volume I, pp. 938–942. L. Erlbaum Associates Inc., Mahwah (1999)
38. Cockton, G., Woolrych, A., Hall, L., Hindmarch, M.: Changing analysts' tunes: the surprising impact of a new instrument for usability inspection method assessment. In: O'Neill, E., Palanque, P., Johnson, P. (eds.) People and Computers XVII—Designing for Society, pp. 145–161. Springer, London (2004). https://doi.org/10.1007/978-1-4471-3754-2_9
39. Slavkovic, A., Cross, K.: Novice heuristic evaluations of a complex interface. In: CHI 1999 Extended Abstracts on Human Factors in Computing Systems, pp. 304–305. Association for Computing Machinery, Pittsburgh (1999). https://doi.org/10.1145/632716.632902
40. Botella, F., Rusu, C., Rusu, V., Quiñones, D.: How novel evaluators perceive their first heuristic evaluation. In: Proceedings of the XIX International Conference on Human Computer Interaction, pp. 1–4. Association for Computing Machinery, Palma (2018). https://doi.org/10.1145/3233824.3233835
41. Rusu, C., Botella, F., Rusu, V., Roncagliolo, S., Quiñones, D.: An online travel agency comparative study: heuristic evaluators perception. In: Meiselwitz, G. (eds.) SCSM 2018. LNCS, vol. 10913, pp. 112–120. Springer, Cham, Switzerland (2018). https://doi.org/10.1007/978-3-319-91521-0_9
42. de Salgado, A.L., de Fortes, R.P.M.: Heuristic evaluation for novice evaluators. In: Marcus, A. (ed.) DUXU 2016. LNCS, vol. 9746, pp. 387–398. Springer, Cham (2016). https://doi.org/10.1007/978-3-319-40409-7_37
43. de Salgado, A.L., de Lara, S.M., Freire, A.P., de Fortes, R.P.M.: What is hidden in a heuristic evaluation: tactics from the experts. In: 13th International Conference on Information Systems & Technology Management - CONTECSI, pp. 2931–2946. CONTECSI, São Paulo (2016). https://doi.org/10.5748/9788599693124-13CONTECSI/PS-4068
44. Petrie, H., Buykx, L.: Collaborative heuristic evaluation: improving the effectiveness of heuristic evaluation. In: Proceedings of UPA 2010 International Conference, Muinch, Germany (2010)
45. Salgado, A.D.: Adaptations to the heuristic evaluation (HE) method for novice evaluators. Master Dissertation. Universidade de São Paulo, São Paulo (2017)

46. Alqurni, J., Alroobaea, R., Alqahtani, M.: Effect of user sessions on the heuristic usability method. Int. J. Open Source Softw. Process. **9**, 62–81 (2018). https://doi.org/10.4018/ijossp.2018010104
47. Thomas, R.P., Lawrence, A.: Assessment of expert performance compared across professional domains. J. Appl. Res. Mem. Cogn. **7**, 167–176 (2018). https://doi.org/10.1016/j.jarmac.2018.03.009
48. Botella, F., Alarcon, E., Peñalver, A.: How to classify to experts in usability evaluation. In: Proceedings of the XV International Conference on Human Computer Interaction, p. Article 25. Association for Computing Machinery, Puerto de la Cruz (2014). https://doi.org/10.1145/2662253.2662278
49. Ericsson, K.A., Prietula, M.J., Cokely, E.T.: The making of an expert. Harv. Bus. Rev. **85**, 114–121, 193 (2007)
50. Hambrick, D.Z., Oswald, F.L., Altmann, E.M., Meinz, E.J., Gobet, F., Campitelli, G.: Deliberate practice: is that all it takes to become an expert? Intelligence **45**, 34–45 (2014). https://doi.org/10.1016/j.intell.2013.04.001
51. Guest, G., Bunce, A., Johnson, L.: How many interviews are enough?: an experiment with data saturation and variability. Field Methods **18**, 59–82 (2006). https://doi.org/10.1177/1525822X05279903
52. Norman, D.A.: The Design of Everyday Things: Revised and Expanded. Basic Books, New York (2013)

House of Prototyping Guidelines: A Framework to Develop Theoretical Prototyping Strategies for Human-Centered Design

Salman Ahmed and H. Onan Demirel$^{(\boxtimes)}$

Oregon State University, Corvallis, OR 97331, USA
{ahmedsal,onan.demirel}@oregonstate.edu

Abstract. Prototyping is one of the most critical and costly steps in the product development process. However, the existing literature lacks in prototyping strategies that are comprehensive and widely accepted. Current prototyping strategies mostly focus on the hands-on activity of building the prototype by relying on the designer's experience. Another limitation is that prototyping strategies often do not address human factors for prototyping human-centered products. This paper introduces a House of Prototyping Guidelines (HOPG) framework, which integrates the existing prototyping guidelines and human factor engineering principles for better prototyping outcomes. The methodology contains four steps. The first step pertains to the state-of-the-art prototyping literature review. The second step consists of filtering the prototyping findings and summarizing the key prototyping findings from Step 1. The third step presents the HOPG conceptual map, which is loosely based on the House of Quality (HOQ) approach. HOPG contains the Prototyping Categories and Prototyping Dimensions, which are similar to Customer Requirement and Engineering Requirement of HOQ, respectively. In the HOPG framework, designers go through the Prototyping Categories to understand the prototyping requirements and then identifies the Prototyping Dimensions to create the prototypes that fit human-centered design needs.

Keywords: Protoyping · Human-centered design · Digital human modeling · Human factors and ergonomics

1 Introduction

Prototyping is one of the most critical aspects of product development [66]. Literature shows that the top 20 companies that are known for their innovative products spend around 142 billion dollars in their research and development (R&D) departments. It is found that around 40 to 46% of R&D resources are spent on products that do not make to the market [19]. For example, it took

© Springer Nature Switzerland AG 2020
A. Marcus and E. Rosenzweig (Eds.): HCII 2020, LNCS 12200, pp. 21–38, 2020.
https://doi.org/10.1007/978-3-030-49713-2_2

about 5,127 prototypes and five years for one of the leading household appliances company to come up with the most successful vacuums on the market [1].

Although prototyping is referred to as the highest sunk cost in the product development [14], there is still a lack of comprehensive and widely accepted prototyping methodology in literature [14,45]. The current prototyping methodologies focus mainly on prototyping activities or hands-on prototyping experiences. Most of the existing prototyping methodologies rely on designers' intuition or experience when building a prototype rather than providing systematic guidelines and best practices to aid designers in their prototyping quest [41,45].

Another limitation associated with current prototyping methodologies is that Human Factor Engineering (HFE) guidelines are not adequately considered [45]. The absence or partial consideration of HFE guidelines causes products or workplaces not to address human needs and limitations. HFE is a multi-discipline that applies theory and practice to optimize human well-being and overall system performance [30,37]. Incorporation of HFE guidelines during product development requires the collection of human-product interactions data, which is often not widely available [29]. Generally, the human-product interaction can be simulated either by creating a physical prototype, computational prototype, or mixed prototype. Physical prototypes are advantageous in representing form and functionality; however, they are time-consuming and costly to build [8,12]. Alternatively, computational prototypes are low-cost and less time-consuming to build, but they lack representing the physical interactions between humans and products, which limit the number of feedback [13,39]. Another concern during prototyping is the amount of interactivity between the user and the product. Duffy (2007) mentioned that if there is a high-level interaction exist between the user and product, then a physical prototype would be a better choice. In contrast, when a low-level interaction exists, the computational prototype is preferable [27]. What level of interactions to consider between the user and product lead designers into the dilemma about the type (physical or virtual), fidelity (low or high), and complexity (low or high) of prototypes to build [27]. Further, Camburn et al. (2015) stated that there are no widely accepted guidelines on prototype building strategies to assist designers [14].

The above limitations found in the prototyping literature provide the primary motivation to undertake the current study. The objective of this study is to create a framework that aids designers in developing theoretical prototyping strategies to evaluate and design human-centered products and workplaces during the conceptual design process by integrating HFE principles. The rest of the paper contains a literature review of prototyping in general and particularly for human-centered products in Sect. 2. Sections 3 and 4 presents the methodology of the framework and the HOPG, respectively. Finally, Sect. 5 presents the discussion, limitations, and future work.

2   Background

2.1   Prototyping

Definitions. Prototyping is referred to as *"An essential part of the product development and manufacturing cycle required for assessing the form, fit, and functionality of a design before significant investment in tooling is made"* [53]. Ulrich et al. (2012) defined prototyping as *"An approximation of the product along one or more dimensions of interest"* [61]. Another definition that can be found in the literature defines prototyping as *"Prototypes are fit, form, or functional design representations which enable designers to communicate test directly, or validate design ideas"* [69]. Further, prototyping is defined as an artifact that approximates a feature (or multiple features) of a product, service, or system [50]. Camburn et al. (2017) listed the common objectives for building prototypes are design refinement, communication, exploration, and active learning [15]. A newly modified prototype definition has been proposed by Lauff et al. (2018) after completing an empirical and industry-based study. Lauff et al. (2018) defined prototyping as *"A prototype is a physical or digital embodiment of critical elements of the intended design, and an iterative tool to enhance communication, enable learning, and inform decision-making at any point in the design process"* [42]. From these definitions, it can be understood that prototyping is used to improve the final design by creating a representation of the final product early in the design process to evaluate and understand the form, fit, and functionality before a considerable investment of resources is made. It can be used for learning, communications, and extracting answers for questions.

Taxonomy. Prototypes have been classified in terms of cost, stage of design, level of abstraction or realism, intended evaluation purpose [50, 51] in the literature. Otto and Wood (2003) classified prototypes based on the evaluation purposes or assessment of the concept. The evaluation can be classified into six classes, which are proof of concept, industrial design, design of experiment, alpha, beta, and pre-production prototypes [50]. Similar to Otto and Wood, Ullman (2002) also classified prototypes based on evaluation purposes [60]. Besides prototyping taxonomy based on the evaluation purposes, taxonomy has been developed based on the exploration of design space. Lim et al. (2008) classified prototypes as filters and the manifestation of design ideas [44]. Prototyping classification is also made based on the process that is used to create the prototype, such as material removal or material addition [73]. The major shortcoming of these classifications is that they are unable to cover and distinguish the entire prototype design space [55]. A recent taxonomy of prototyping based on the concept of Prototype Purpose was proposed by Petrakis et al. (2019) [52]. Petrakis defines the prototyping purpose as as the actual reason for building a prototype in order to achieve explicitly, already set objectives, which then proposes 23 sub-roles of prototyping purpose [52]. It is out of the scope of this report to list all the prototype classifications available and point out the advantages and disadvantages. The classification of prototypes created by Stowe is presented in the document due to its thoroughness and conciseness [55].

It is found that the classification of prototyping is based on variety, complexity, and fidelity [36,55,59]. The first level of classification is in terms of variety, i.e., whether the prototype is physical or non-physical. There is another type of variety of prototype which is not included by Stowe is called a mixed or hybrid prototype [10]. Non- physical prototypes are made using computational tools, such as computer-aided design (CAD), finite element analysis (FEA), or digital sketches [55]. More information about mixed prototyping and computational prototyping is provided in a later section. In the second level of classification, the prototype is divided based on its complexity or, in other words, whether prototypes represent the whole system, a component, or a sub-component. The last level of classification is based on fidelity, where the prototypes are categorized based on the depth of true representation of the final product.

2.2   Prototyping Best Practices and Findings

Physical Prototyping. The development time of physical prototypes usually takes from weeks to months. Hence, industries have limited time and resources to allocate building multiple physical prototypes and build new after each design iteration occurs [53]. Since the mid-1980s, with the arrival of rapid prototyping (RP) technologies, the amount of time that takes to construct a part for prototyping purposes significantly shortened due to automation [53,73]. The fundamental principle behind RP is to create a CAD model of the required design and convert it to a digital file format via Stereo-lithography (SL), where a computer program operates an RP machine based on the CAD file. The fabrication process is done by adding slices of the original model layer upon layer until a physical model is created [73]. This process saves time and cost by around 70% and 90% respectively; hence, designers can create several physical models of their CAD models simultaneously [53,68]. In the literature, RP is broadly classified based on how the prototype is made, i.e., material addition or material removal process. A detailed classification of RP is given in this reference [38]. The various techniques used in rapid prototyping to create prototypes, whether by adding or removing material is described in this reference [53,70].

Computational Prototyping. Computational or virtual prototyping is defined as *"A virtual prototype may be represented as a series of graphical figures or CAD models, in animated or still format, created in the form of mathematical models and stored digitally in computer-usable memory"* [73]. Computational prototyping is about the presentation, testing, and analysis of three-dimensional CAD models before creating any physical prototypes. Similar to physical prototyping, computational prototyping has also been classified in a number of ways in the literature. One of the ways computational prototyping has been classified is based on what computer-aided engineering (CAE) tools are used for creating prototypes. For example, whether the computational prototypes are made to represent a 2D or 3D solid models or made to evaluate performance measures such as fluid dynamics or fatigue. Also, if the computational prototype can be used to analyze and simulate the final product as a whole, then it falls into another category [18]. In another more comprehensive classification, computational prototyping is classified based on (1) visualization, fit, and interference of mechanical assemblies; (2) testing and verification of functions, and performances, evaluation of manufacturing and assembly operations; and (3) human factors analysis [73]. In this paper, only the use of a computational prototype to perform human factors analysis for human-product interactions is reviewed. Hence, the literature review of CAD and CAE is not provided here.

Comparison Between Physical and Computational Prototyping. A designer may favor a computational over a physical prototype if the computational prototype is more advantageous and provides a better alternative than that of a physical prototype. In contrast, designers may prefer computational prototyping over physical prototyping because computational prototyping might be less costly in terms of both finances and time. Despite the high reliability and accuracy of physical prototypes created by computer numerical control (CNC) machines, the longer time and cost could outweigh their benefits [9]. Computational prototypes used during conceptual stage can help to reduce the use of physical prototyping; thus, reducing time and finances [47]. Although physical prototypes made by rapid prototyping are high in accuracy, they often shrink or contain rough surfaces that require further machining operations. Thus, physical prototypes may be dimensionally inaccurate, whereas virtual prototypes do not have this problem [9]. Also, physical prototypes are difficult or impossible to change or require further modifications once they are constructed. This inflexibility also poses a problem when new design ideas need to be prototyped after receiving revisions and feedback [73]. Thus, from the literature, it can be seen that computational prototyping is preferred if greater communication through realistic visualization, shorter lead time, and less cost are desired [73]. However, if the computational prototyping lacks an accurate representation of the final product due to the complexities of the design and incomplete information presented; then, physical prototyping becomes a preferred strategy due to its high fidelity. For example, a recent study compares four different prototyping methods (Physical, Computational, Virtual Reality, and Augmented Reality) by designing an assembly of a corkscrew. It is noted that the majority of designers prefer design by augmented reality. However, the physical prototyping method was most useful for communicating and exploring the function and mechanical aspect of the assembly [20].

High Fidelity or Low Fidelity Prototyping? It is found in the literature that the early use of prototyping has been focused on the physical aspects of design, such as layouts and dimensions. As computer technology developed, prototyping is done with the aid of computers and software tools [32]. One of the main concerns while developing a prototype is whether to build a high or low fidelity prototype [65]. There are different views regarding what type of fidelity to choose in a design process [32,65]. For example, in one study, a low fidelity physical prototype of a domestic lighting controller has been made from cardboard and foam to show that potential problems can be identified from low fidelity prototypes. This approach proved to be a low cost and time-effective strategy. It is reported that 28 problems are identified, and the revised design significantly reduced the number of problems by 70% [32,67]. However, a high fidelity virtual prototype of the same lighting controller has been made, and it revealed an additional 29 (or 100% more) more problems than the original low fidelity strategy approach. It is reported that instant visual feedback and more realistic interaction helped to get more feedback from the user. Thus, high fidelity prototyping reveals more problems but at the expense of a long time and high-cost [32].

Low fidelity prototypes that are quick to make but modeling the main attributes of design is time-consuming in high fidelity prototypes [11]. However, it is also found that low fidelity prototypes might not help designers to evaluate some of the physical attributes such as tactile, auditory, and visual feedback properly [39]. In contrast, a few studies shows that both fidelity levels can help designers during the evaluation of concept ideas. For example, a design study executed in the interface usability domain suggests that low fidelity and high fidelity prototyping are equally good at extracting usability issues [63,65].

Mixed Prototyping. Mixed prototyping is known as a virtualization technique that can blend both the capabilities of physical and computational prototyping by incorporating the advantageous features found at each prototyping type and compensating the limitations by offering a more interactive experience. Bordegoni et al. (2009) defined this technique as *"an integrated and co-located mix of physical and virtual components usually seen using a see-through head-mounted display (HMD)"* [10]. Various studies showed that the key difference in mixed prototyping is not the use of advanced computer-based 3D modeling and projection techniques but the interactive and immersive technologies that enable human-product interaction. Mixed prototyping opens doors to novel venues to create prototyping strategies to add visual realism, auditory realism, tactile realism, and functional realism [10,49]. For example, a study focusing on the development of a novel multi-model interface called Immersive Modeling System (IMM) demonstrated that users wear HMDs to interact with a virtual object while grasping and manipulating the physical object with controllers. In this study, IMM is used to test the usability of a concept MP3 player and a game phone. Although users found that the interface provides more natural, intuitive, and comfortable interactions with the 3D product model within an immersive way, authors reported that within the IMM interface, there could be a dissociation between tactile and auditory realism. Also, limited or poor haptic feedback still causes some of the realism to be disregarded [7,43]. Virtual prototyping offers a highly interactive experience in terms of visibility of the appliance or product, but the accessibility and feedback are still limited. In a different study, Barbieri et al. (2013) evaluated the effectiveness of the mixed prototyping approach within the context of the usability of a washing machine interface. The physical prototype of the washing machine included features that allow users to configure the interface through changing knobs and buttons and allowing them to represent different interface designs rapidly [7]. Although this approach is suitable for a system composed of conventional physical elements such as knobs and buttons, it is limited for digital applications where design interfaces are based on touch screens. Thus, it would become difficult, if not impossible, to represent various interfaces with only one physical prototype [7]. In conclusion, within the human-centered design realm, the majority of the prototyping practices are heavily focusing on the usability testing, and techniques used to build an interaction often vary drastically depending upon the type of interaction (knobs versus touch-displays). Thus, even with the availability of a mixed prototyping approach, what type of interaction method is used or how much of the concept design must be represented physically depends on designers' skill set and expertise. The majority of the prototyping literature does not provide guidance, and even reasoning, regarding the fidelity, type, and at what design stage the mixed prototyping should be applied.

In the next section, we provided a summary of digital human modeling (DHM) research as a computational prototyping technique from a human-centered design perspective, specifically focusing on human factors engineering and ergonomics in product development. DHM is often not covered within the human-centered prototyping publications but mostly treated as an ergonomics evaluation method within the embodiment phase of the product development. However, the real value of the DHM approach is in its capability to represent human attributes with visual realism and biomechanics early in the design phase.

2.3   Prototyping and Digital Human Modeling

There are various definitions of DHM available in the literature. It is defined as *"Digital human modeling is perceived as the digital representation of humans inserted in a simulation or virtual environment to facilitate the prediction of performance or safety of a worker in his/her working condition. DHM includes some visualization of the human musculoskeletal structure as well as the math or science in the background"* [22,23]. Another definition of DHM is *"Digital human modeling technology offers human factors/ergonomics specialists the promise of an efficient means to simulate a large variety of ergonomics issues early in the design of products and manufacturing workstations. It rests on the premise that most products and manufacturing work settings are specified and designed by using sophisticated computer-aided design (CAD) systems. By integrating a computer-rendered avatar (or humonoid) and the CAD-rendered graphics of a prospective workplace, one can simulate issues regarding who can fit, reach, see, manipulate, and so on"* [17]. Ziolek and Kruithof referred to DHM as a mathematical representation of human characteristics or behaviors. The characteristics can include physical attributes such as size and shape, as well as physiological properties, including fatigue [72]. It should also be mentioned here that DHM has two branches where one focuses on the physical aspects, and the other one focuses on the cognition of humans [56].

From the above definitions, it is seen that DHM is a digital representation of a human being inserted in a simulation where the digital human model performs tasks or interacts with a product or a workplace. From these simulations, designers can identify human factors issues by using DHM to improve or explore new design spaces. Hence, DHM can be used to address the ergonomic issues in the early design phase, and it may reduce or even eliminate the need for physical mock-ups and actual human subject testing [6]. Thus, DHM has the potential to do an ergonomic assessment of a given design during the conceptual stage and use the feedback to address ergonomic issues in the final design. Implementation of DHM within digital mock-ups (DMU) or virtual prototyping has the potential to shorten the design time; thus, increasing the number and quality of design options that could be rapidly evaluated by the design team. Incorporation of DHM, digital prototyping, and virtual testing would cause additional cost in the initial stage; however, it leads to an overall reduction in cost and time in the long-run [17,71].

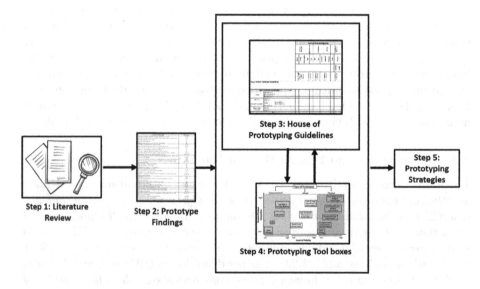

Fig. 1. Flowchart of the prototyping strategy methodology

3   Methodology

It is observed from the literature that there is a common pattern in developing prototyping strategies. In a broader sense, the first step consists of an extensive literature review followed by developing some prototyping guidelines which

Table 1. Step 2: prototyping dimensions and prototyping findings

Prototype dimensions		Summary of findings	References
Type of prototype	Physical	>Provides exploration, refinement, learning, communication of ideas	[12,62]
		>Provides ergonomic assessment for multiple complex physical and/or cognitive task and high human-product interaction	[5] [11]
		>Provides tactile feedback	[8]
		>Requires high resources, i.e. cost and time, less flexibility	[73]
	Computational	>Facilitates communication and transfer of ideas	[13] [21]
		>Facilitates learning and improvement early in the design process	[39,54]
		>For ergonomic assessment of single or few simple physical tasks for low human-product interaction, computational is preferable over physical	[16] [13]
		>Provides ergonomics assessment in a shorter time with less cost	[47]
		>Provides ergonomic assessment where creating a physical prototype is infeasible	[17,33]
		>Multiple task analysis and Cognitive assessment is limited	[28,40,56]
	Mixed	>Provides ergonomic assessment for moderate to simple physical and/or cognitive task	[3,4]
		>Limited tactile feedback	[7]
		>It has some capabilities and limitations of both physical and computational prototype	[7,10]
		>Can be used where a physical prototype is infeasible or unsafe and computational prototype lacks fidelity	[4] [3,15]
Fidelity	High	>Provides accurate ergonomic assessment	[32]
		>Provides feedback of finer details	[32]
		>Requires more resources, i.e. cost and time	[32]

Table 1. (*continued*)

Prototype dimensions		Summary of findings	References
	Low	>Provides rough ergonomic assessment	[11,39]
		>Provides limited tactile, auditory and visual feedback	[39]
		>Requires less cost and time to build	[32,67]
		>Useful for creating quick multiple iterations, reducing design fixation and concept expression and exploration	[15,31,57]
Complexity	Sub-System	>Requires fewer resources	[26]
		>Provides in-depth exploration and focused ergonomic assessment only for a particular sub-system	[19,35]
		>Requires HTA to decide what sub-system to prototype	[2]
	Full System	>Requires more resources	[26]
		>Provides ergonomic assessment for the full system	[19,35]
Scale	Full Scale	>Create full scale prototypes if the budget allow	[19,50]
	Altered	>Create increased/decreased scale prototype for user evaluation	[19]
Iteration	Single	>Provides a fewer number of feedback with less in-depth insight	[25,48]
		>Requires fewer resources	[25,48]
	Multiple	>Useful for refinement, gradual goal accomplishment, higher quality feedback, and the improved end product	[25,48,58]
		>Parallel iteration useful for concept exploration	[24,46]
		>Quick iterations reduce design fixation	[15,64]
		>Cost of new information vs cost of iteration can guide the number of iterations	[57]

are used to create prototypes. For example, Christie et al. (2012) extracted the guidelines from the literature review and named as factors and questions [19]. Similarly, Camburn et al. (2015) extracted heuristics from prototyping literature and created a survey tool [14]. Menold et al. (2017) created specifications, phases and lenses from literature [45]. Lauff et al. (2019) distilled the prototyping literature and extracted three prototyping principles to create prototyping canvas [41].

The proposed methodology to create a prototyping strategy in this study is developed by following the standard approach mentioned above. However, the distinction between this work and previous methodologies is that the focus is on a conceptual prototyping strategy rather than a hands-on prototyping activity. The second distinction is that none of the previous prototyping strategies adequately incorporated HFE guidelines and reviewed usability testing literature, whereas this framework incorporates HFE guidelines. The third distinction is the addition of a prototyping toolbox, which provides the *know-how* and tools to the engineers who lack extensive prototyping experience. The previous prototyping strategies and frameworks do not offer any prototyping toolboxes. The lack of available toolboxes caused wide variations in the final prototype quality, even though designers were using the same prototyping strategy. It is hypothesized that adding a prototyping toolbox can reduce the variance in prototype quality among designers who use the same proposed prototyping strategy.

Figure 1 shows the flowchart of the methodology used to create prototyping strategies for human-centered products during the conceptual design process. Step 1 consists of an extensive literature review of prototype definitions, taxonomy, prototype findings, and framework. A thorough literature review about types of prototypes (i.e., physical, computational and mixed prototype, prototype fidelity, number of iterations) is performed. Step 2 consists of filtering and extracting the prototype findings from Step 1 and presenting them as a list of key prototyping findings. Three filters are used: a) Prototyping findings that are empirically validated, b) Prototyping findings that are repeatable and validated by the scientific community, and c) Prototyping findings that are related to human-centered products. A summary of prototyping findings developed in Step 2 is given in Table 1.

Step 3 presents the theoretical part of the prototyping strategy, i.e., *why?*, and Step 4 presents the practical part (toolbox) of the prototyping strategy, i.e., *how?*. Finally, in Step 5, the theoretical and practical parts are combined to form the prototyping strategy framework. In this paper, we only focus on Step 1 to 3, which provides the theoretical foundations of the prototyping strategy. Step 4 and Step 5 are left out for future work. Step 3 is described in detail in the next section.

4   House of Prototyping Guidelines (HOPG)

The theoretical part of the prototyping strategy in Step 3 is loosely based on the House of Quality (HOQ) [34]. The HOQ has a customer requirement section (What?) and the engineering requirement section (How?). Similarly, the theoretical prototyping strategy named the *House of Prototyping Guidelines* has Prototyping Categories (What?) and Prototyping Dimensions (How?), as shown in

PROTOTYPING DIMENSIONS

	(1) Type of Prototype			(2) Fidelity Level		(3) Complexity		(4) Scale			(5) Number of Iterations		
	Physical	Computational	Mixed	High	Low	Full	Sub	Increased	Same	Decreased	Single	Multiple (Sequential / Parallel)	
	0 = Not Feasible, 1= Feasible, 2= Most Feasible			0 = Not Desired, 1 = Desired		0 = Not Desired, 1 = Desired		0 = Not Desired, 1 = Desired			0 = Not Desired, 1 = Desired		

PROTOTYPING PROBLEM STATEMENT

PROTOTYPING CATEGORIES			Weight														
Purpose	Refinement (0 - 1)																
	Communication (0 - 1)																
	Exploration (0 - 1)																
	Learning (0 - 1)																
Resources	High (0 - 1)																
	Low (0 - 1)																
Ergonomic Assessment	Physical	Single Task (0 - 1)															
		Multiple Task (0 - 1)															
	Cognitive (0 - 1)																
Human Product Interaction	High (0 - 1)																
	Low (0 - 1)																
Sum				0	0	0	0	0	0	0	0	0	0	0	0	0	0

Fig. 2. House of prototyping guidelines

Fig. 2. These Prototyping Categories and Prototyping Dimensions are extracted from the literature review performed in Step 1 and 2. The role of the Prototyping Categories is to identify the purpose of the prototype, i.e., what questions the prototype should answer? What information should the prototype discover? How much budget is available for the prototyping process?. These questions have led us to develop four Prototyping Categories, namely, Purpose of Prototyping, Availability of Resources, Types of Ergonomic Assessment, and the Level of Human-Product Interactions, as shown in Fig. 2. The Prototyping Dimensions are equivalent to the engineering requirement from (HOQ). The Prototyping Dimensions defines the specification of the prototype that can answer the questions and discover the information identified in Prototyping Categories. The prototyping dimensions can affect the quality of the prototype and the end product. Figure 2 shows there are five Prototyping Dimensions, namely, Type of Prototype, Fidelity Level, Complexity, Scale, and Number of Iterations. These six prototype dimensions are adopted from the prototype taxonomy created by Stowe (2008) [55] and Systematic Tool developed by Camburn et al. (2015) [14].

HOPG weaves the Prototyping Categories and Prototyping Dimensions together so that a designer can select the appropriate Prototyping Dimensions corresponding to the prototyping guidelines, as shown in Fig. 2. In HOPG, designers first write down the prototyping problem statement of the product to be prototyped. The problem statement drives the Prototyping Categories. In other words, the Prototyping Categories are derived and weighted as per the problem statement, and the appropriate weights are put in the weight column. For example, in a given prototyping problem statement, if the requirement is to learn about a new function, then the designer should put 1 in the corresponding *Learning* weight column and 0 for the *Refinement, Communication and Exploration.*

Next, the Prototyping Categories drive the selection of Prototyping Dimensions. According to the Prototyping Categories, a designer can rate the corresponding Prototyping Dimensions using the scale given for each Prototyping Dimensions. While rating dimensions, a designer can rate only one of the sub prototyping dimensions or rate all of them as needed. For example, for selecting the *Type of Prototype*, the designer can use the guidelines presented in Table 1 to select whether the *Physical, Computational or Mixed* is appropriate to fulfill the *Purpose of Learning* and then put 0, 1 or 2 in the corresponding boxes of Physical, Computational and Mixed.

The *Sum* can be calculated using the formula below after rating all of the Prototyping Dimensions for each of the Prototyping Categories completed:

Sum = Weight (Prototyping Categories) X Rate (Prototyping Dimensions)

Using HOPG, designers can find out the appropriate Prototyping Dimensions, which can be used as theoretical prototyping guidelines to build prototypes.

5   Discussions

This paper proposes a novel methodology to create theoretical prototyping strategies for human-centered products. It is found in the prototyping literature that the current prototyping strategies focus mostly on hands-on activity and prototyping experience rather than providing the guidelines on how to build a prototype. Hence, success or failure in building a prototype can be mostly attributed to the intuition and experience of the designers. Another gap found in the literature is that none of the existing prototyping strategies focuses on human-centered design. Hence, the proposed methodology addresses these gaps by providing a framework that assists designers in applying prototyping best practices while building a prototype systematically. The prototyping guidelines and the human factor engineering principles are embedded in the framework of HOPG, which ensures that the resulting theoretical prototype can answer the question and discover the information related to human-centered products. The primary outcome of HOPG is a systematic strategy that designers can leverage to build their required prototype. Since HOPG is based on systematic rules and guidelines, designers do not need to be an expert in prototyping and HFE to build a prototype. HOPG can help to reduce the trial and error of building the correct prototype and thus reducing cost and time.

One of the limitations of HOPG is that it does not incorporate all the best practices and guidelines of prototyping. Due to the nature of ever-evolving prototyping literature, it is not possible to incorporate the vast and changing prototyping literature in the framework. Another aspect of the HOPG is that even though the framework is systematic, but the embedded prototyping guidelines are generic. This causes the designers to use their own experience and decisions to a certain degree to interpret the guidelines and select the Prototyping Categories and Dimensions.

6 Future Work

One of the immediate future work that can be added to the theoretical HOPG is related to Step 4 which is shown in Fig. 1. Step 4 is about the practical *know-how* or the fabrication guidelines. Practical *know-how* complements the theoretical framework. This will assist the designer in providing a complete prototyping strategy that has both the theoretical and practical guidelines. The next possible future work is to put the proposed framework (Step 1–4) into a platform that the designers can use to generate prototyping strategies. This is shown in Step 5 in Fig. 1. The platform will help designers to systematically go through the vast number of prototyping guidelines presented in Step 3 (HOPG) and the vast number of tools in Step 4 (toolbox) and create the correct prototyping strategy. Step 5 will help to pair the theoretical guidelines with the correct prototyping tools. Another potential future work is the validation of the proposed framework. The framework can be validated by comparing the prototyping strategies created using designers who use the framework with the prototyping strategies created by designers who do not use the framework and relies on their experience.

References

1. James dyson on his vacuum failure and success. http://nymag.com/vindicated/2016/11/james-dyson-on-5-126-vacuums-that-didnt-work-and-1-that-did.html. Accessed 16 Dec 2019
2. Ahmed, S., Gawand, M.S., Irshad, L., Demirel, H.O.: Exploring the design space using a surrogate model approach with digital human modeling simulations. In: ASME 2018 International Design Engineering Technical Conferences and Computers and Information in Engineering Conference, p. V01BT02A011. American Society of Mechanical Engineers (2018)
3. Ahmed, S., Irshad, L., Demirel, H.O., Tumer, I.Y.: A comparison between virtual reality and digital human modeling for proactive ergonomic design. In: Duffy, V.G. (ed.) HCII 2019. LNCS, vol. 11581, pp. 3–21. Springer, Cham (2019). https://doi.org/10.1007/978-3-030-22216-1_1
4. Ahmed, S., Zhang, J., Demirel, O.: Assessment of types of prototyping in human-centered product design. In: Duffy, V. (ed.) DHM 2018, vol. 10917, pp. 3–18. Springer, Heidelberg (2018). https://doi.org/10.1007/978-3-319-91397-1_1

5. Alexopoulos, K., Mavrikios, D., Chryssolouris, G.: ErgoToolkit: an ergonomic analysis tool in a virtual manufacturing environment. Int. J. Comput. Integr. Manuf. **26**(5), 440–452 (2013)
6. Badler, N.I., Phillips, C.B., Webber, B.L.: Simulating Humans: Computer Graphics Animation and Control. Oxford University Press, Oxford (1993)
7. Barbieri, L., Angilica, A., Bruno, F., Muzzupappa, M.: Mixed prototyping with configurable physical archetype for usability evaluation of product interfaces. Comput. Ind. **64**(3), 310–323 (2013)
8. Bi, Z.: Computer integrated reconfigurable experimental platform for ergonomic study of vehicle body design. Int. J. Comput. Integr. Manuf. **23**(11), 968–978 (2010)
9. Binnard, M.: Design by Composition for Rapid Prototyping, vol. 525. Springer, Heidelberg (2012)
10. Bordegoni, M., Cugini, U., Caruso, G., Polistina, S.: Mixed prototyping for product assessment: a reference framework. Int. J. Interact. Des. Manuf. (IJIDeM) **3**(3), 177–187 (2009)
11. Brereton, M., McGarry, B.: An observational study of how objects support engineering design thinking and communication: implications for the design of tangible media. In: Proceedings of the SIGCHI Conference on Human Factors in Computing Systems, pp. 217–224. ACM (2000)
12. Broek, J.J., Sleijffers, W., Horváth, I., Lennings, A.F.: Using physical models in design. In: Proceedings of CAID/CD'2000 Conference, pp. 155–163 (2000)
13. Bullinger, H.J., Dangelmaier, M.: Virtual prototyping and testing of in-vehicle interfaces. Ergonomics **46**(1–3), 41–51 (2003)
14. Camburn, B., et al.: A systematic method for design prototyping. J. Mech. Des. **137**(8), 081102 (2015)
15. Camburn, B., et al.: Design prototyping methods: state of the art in strategies, techniques, and guidelines. Des. Sci. **3** (2017)
16. Chaffin, D.B.: Some requirements and fundamental issues in digital human modeling. In: Handbook of Digital Human Modeling, pp. 2–1 (2009)
17. Chaffin, D.B., Nelson, C., et al.: Digital Human Modeling for Vehicle and Workplace Design. Society of Automotive Engineers, Warrendale (2001)
18. Chang, K.H., Silva, J., Bryant, I.: Concurrent design and manufacturing for mechanical systems. Concurrent Eng. **7**(4), 290–308 (1999)
19. Christie, E.J., et al.: Prototyping strategies: literature review and identification of critical variables. In: American Society for Engineering Education Conference (2012)
20. Coutts, E.R., Wodehouse, A., Robertson, J.: A comparison of contemporary prototyping methods. In: Proceedings of the Design Society: International Conference on Engineering Design, vol. 1, pp. 1313–1322. Cambridge University Press (2019)
21. Cugini, U., Bordegoni, M., Mana, R.: The role of virtual prototyping and simulation in the fashion sector. Int. J. Interact. Des. Manuf. (IJIDeM) **2**(1), 33–38 (2008)
22. Demirel, H.O., Duffy, V.G.: Applications of digital human modeling in industry. In: Duffy, V.G. (ed.) ICDHM 2007. LNCS, vol. 4561, pp. 824–832. Springer, Heidelberg (2007). https://doi.org/10.1007/978-3-540-73321-8_93
23. Demirel, H.O., Duffy, V.G.: Digital human modeling for product lifecycle management. In: Duffy, V.G. (ed.) ICDHM 2007. LNCS, vol. 4561, pp. 372–381. Springer, Heidelberg (2007). https://doi.org/10.1007/978-3-540-73321-8_43
24. Dow, S.P., Glassco, A., Kass, J., Schwarz, M., Schwartz, D.L., Klemmer, S.R.: Parallel prototyping leads to better design results, more divergence, and increased self-efficacy. ACM Trans. Comput.-Hum. Interact. (TOCHI) **17**(4), 18 (2010)

25. Dow, S.P., Heddleston, K., Klemmer, S.R.: The efficacy of prototyping under time constraints. In: Proceedings of the Seventh ACM Conference on Creativity and Cognition, pp. 165–174. ACM (2009)
26. Drezner, J.A., Huang, M.: On prototyping (2009)
27. Duffy, V.G.: Modified virtual build methodology for computer-aided ergonomics and safety. Hum. Factors Ergon. Manuf. Serv. Ind. **17**(5), 413–422 (2007)
28. Duffy, V.G.: Handbook of Digital Human Modeling: Research for Applied Ergonomics and Human Factors Engineering. CRC Press, Boca Raton (2016)
29. Ferrise, F., Bordegoni, M., Cugini, U.: Interactive virtual prototypes for testing the interaction with new products. Comput.-Aided Des. Appl. **10**(3), 515–525 (2013)
30. Gawron, V.J., Drury, C.G., Fairbanks, R.J., Berger, R.C.: Medical error and human factors engineering: where are we now? Am. J. Med. Qual. **21**(1), 57–67 (2006)
31. Gerber, E., Carroll, M.: The psychological experience of prototyping. Des. Stud. **33**(1), 64–84 (2012)
32. Hall, R.R.: Prototyping for usability of new technology. Int. J. Hum.-Comput. Stud. **55**(4), 485–501 (2001)
33. Hamon, C.L., Green, M.G., Dunlap, B., Camburn, B.A., Crawford, R.H., Jensen, D.D.: Virtual or physical prototypes development and testing of a prototyping planning tool. Technical report, Air Force Academy United States (2014)
34. Hauser, J.R., Clausing, D., et al.: The house of quality (1988)
35. Horváth, I., Du Bois, E.: Using modular abstract prototypes as evolving research means in design inclusive research. In: ASME 2012 International Design Engineering Technical Conferences and Computers and Information in Engineering Conference, pp. 475–486. American Society of Mechanical Engineers (2012)
36. Jönsson, A.: Lean prototyping of multi-body and mechatronic systems. Ph.D. thesis, Blekinge Institute of Technology (2004)
37. Kantowitz, B.H., Sorkin, R.D.: Human factors: understanding people-system relationships. Wiley, Hoboken (1983)
38. Knuth, J.: Material increase manufacturing by rapid prototyping technique. Ann. CIPP **40**(2), 603–604 (1999)
39. Kuutti, K., et al.: Virtual prototypes in usability testing. In: Proceedings of the 34th Annual Hawaii International Conference on System Sciences, p. 7. IEEE (2001)
40. Lämkull, D., Hanson, L., Örtengren, R.: A comparative study of digital human modelling simulation results and their outcomes in reality: a case study within manual assembly of automobiles. Int. J. Ind. Ergon. **39**(2), 428–441 (2009)
41. Lauff, C., Menold, J., Wood, K.L.: Prototyping canvas: design tool for planning purposeful prototypes. In: Proceedings of the Design Society: International Conference on Engineering Design, vol. 1, pp. 1563–1572. Cambridge University Press (2019)
42. Lauff, C.A., Kotys-Schwartz, D., Rentschler, M.E.: What is a prototype? What are the roles of prototypes in companies? J. Mech. Des. **140**(6), 061102 (2018)
43. Lee, Y.G., et al.: Immersive modeling system (IMMS) for personal electronic products using a multi-modal interface. Comput.-Aided Des. **42**(5), 387–401 (2010)
44. Lim, Y.K., Stolterman, E., Tenenberg, J.: The anatomy of prototypes: prototypes as filters, prototypes as manifestations of design ideas. ACM Trans. Comput.-Hum. Interact. (TOCHI) **15**(2), 7 (2008)
45. Menold, J., Jablokow, K., Simpson, T.: Prototype for X (PFX): a holistic framework for structuring prototyping methods to support engineering design. Des. Stud. **50**, 70–112 (2017)

46. Moe, R., Jensen, D.D., Wood, K.L.: Prototype partitioning based on requirement flexibility. In: ASME 2004 International Design Engineering Technical Conferences and Computers and Information in Engineering Conference, pp. 65–77. American Society of Mechanical Engineers (2004)
47. Mutambara, A.G., Durrant-Whyte, H.: Estimation and control for a modular wheeled mobile robot. IEEE Trans. Control Syst. Technol. **8**(1), 35–46 (2000)
48. Neeley, W.L., Lim, K., Zhu, A., Yang, M.C.: Building fast to think faster: exploiting rapid prototyping to accelerate ideation during early stage design. In: ASME 2013 International Design Engineering Technical Conferences and Computers and Information in Engineering Conference, p. V005T06A022. American Society of Mechanical Engineers (2013)
49. Nilsson, S., Johansson, B.: A cognitive systems engineering perspective on the design of mixed reality systems. In: Proceedings of the 13th Eurpoean Conference on Cognitive Ergonomics: Trust and Control in Complex Socio-Technical Systems, pp. 154–161. ACM (2006)
50. Otto, K.N., et al.: Product Design: Techniques in Reverse Engineering and New Product Development. Tsinghua University Press Co., Ltd., Beijing (2003)
51. Pahl, G., Beitz, W.: Engineering Design: A Systematic Approach. Springer, Heidelberg (2013)
52. Petrakis, K., Hird, A., Wodehouse, A.: The concept of purposeful prototyping: towards a new kind of taxonomic classification. In: Proceedings of the Design Society: International Conference on Engineering Design, vol. 1, pp. 1643–1652. Cambridge University Press (2019)
53. Pham, D.T., Gault, R.S.: A comparison of rapid prototyping technologies. Int. J. Mach. Tools Manuf. **38**(10–11), 1257–1287 (1998)
54. Pontonnier, C., Dumont, G., Samani, A., Madeleine, P., Badawi, M.: Designing and evaluating a workstation in real and virtual environment: toward virtual reality based ergonomic design sessions. J. Multimodal User Interfaces **8**(2), 199–208 (2014)
55. Stowe, D.: Investigating the role of prototyping in mechanical design using case study validation (2008)
56. Sundin, A., Örtengren, R.: Digital human modeling for CAE applications. In: Handbook of Human Factors and Ergonomics, pp. 1053–1078 (2006)
57. Thomke, S., Bell, D.E.: Sequential testing in product development. Manag. Sci. **47**(2), 308–323 (2001)
58. Thomke, S.H.: Experimentation Matters: Unlocking the Potential of New Technologies for Innovation. Harvard Business Press, Cambridge (2003)
59. Tseng, M.M., Jiao, J., Su, C.J.: A framework of virtual design for product customization. In: 1997 IEEE 6th International Conference on Emerging Technologies and Factory Automation Proceedings, EFTA 1997, pp. 7–14. IEEE (1997)
60. Ullman, D.G.: The Mechanical Design Process: Part 1. McGraw-Hill, New York (2010)
61. Ulrich, K.T., Eppinger, S.D.: Concept Selection. Product Design and Development, 5th edn., vol. 1, pp. 145–161. McGraw-Hill/Irwin, Philadelphia (2012)
62. Verlinden, J., Horváth, I.: Analyzing opportunities for using interactive augmented prototyping in design practice. AI EDAM **23**(3), 289–303 (2009)
63. Virzi, R.A., Sokolov, J.L., Karis, D.: Usability problem identification using both low-and high-fidelity prototypes. In: Proceedings of the SIGCHI Conference on Human Factors in Computing Systems, pp. 236–243. ACM (1996)
64. Viswanathan, V.K., Linsey, J.S.: Role of sunk cost in engineering idea generation: an experimental investigation. J. Mech. Des. **135**(12), 121002 (2013)

65. Walker, M., Takayama, L., Landay, J.A.: High-fidelity or low-fidelity, paper or computer? Choosing attributes when testing web prototypes. In: Proceedings of the Human Factors and Ergonomics Society Annual Meeting, vol. 46, pp. 661–665. SAGE Publications, Los Angeles (2002)

66. Wall, M.B., Ulrich, K.T., Flowers, W.C.: Evaluating prototyping technologies for product design. Res. Eng. Des. 3(3), 163–177 (1992)

67. Ward, S.: Getting feedback from users early in the design process: a case study. In: Ergonomics: The Fundamental Design Science, Proceedings of the 30th Annual Conference of the Ergonomics Society of Australia, pp. 22–29. The Ergonomics Society of Australia Canberra (1994)

68. Waterman, N.A., Dickens, P.: Rapid product development in the USA, Europe and Japan. World Class Des. Manuf. 1(3), 27–36 (1994)

69. Wickens, C.D., Gordon, S.E., Liu, Y., et al.: An introduction to human factors engineering (1998)

70. Yan, X., Gu, P.: A review of rapid prototyping technologies and systems. Comput.-Aided Des. 28(4), 307–318 (1996)

71. Zhang, X., Chaffin, D.B.: Digital human modeling for computer-aided ergonomics. Handbook of Occupational Ergonomics, pp. 1–20. Taylor & Francis, London (2005)

72. Ziolek, S.A., Kruithof Jr., P.C.: Human modeling & simulation: a primer for practitioners. In: Proceedings of the Human Factors and Ergonomics Society Annual Meeting, vol. 44, pp. 825–827. SAGE Publications, Los Angeles (2000)

73. Zorriassatine, F., Wykes, C., Parkin, R., Gindy, N.: A survey of virtual prototyping techniques for mechanical product development. Proc. Inst. Mech. Eng. Part B: J. Eng. Manuf. 217(4), 513–530 (2003)

Applying Storycraft to Facilitate an Experience-Centric Conceptual Design Process

Berke Atasoy$^{(\boxtimes)}$ and Jean-Bernard Martens

Department of Industrial Design, Eindhoven University of Technology,
P.O. Box 513, 5600 MB Eindhoven, The Netherlands
berkeatasoy@gmail.com, J.B.O.S.Martens@tue.nl

Abstract. The design profession is shifting from designing objects towards designing for experiences, and the main premise of this paper is that designers need strategic guidance in bringing the emotional, contextual, and temporal aspects of experiences into discussion. Existing externalization strategies are not obviously equipped to help incorporate the transient characteristics of experiences into the designer's creative thinking. In this paper, we propose that designers may be able to achieve this by including visual storycraft into their creative process. Storycraft is the skilled practice of generating/building stories. Stories and experiences share a sequential structure with a beginning, middle, and end that can be crafted and influenced through design to evoke and affect the emotions of their experientors. Several activities of designers are already very similar to those of professionals in storycraft, as the tools and techniques used in both domains are aimed at creating emotionally satisfying experiences. While harnessing the power of storycraft to elevate strategies in designing for experiences is an attractive idea, which has been embraced earlier by the design research community, it is not a proposal that can easily be put into practice. We have iteratively designed, evaluated, and improved Storyply as a method that combines 'conceptual design' and 'story planning'. Our studies have confirmed that incorporating storycraft within conceptual design by means of Storyply resonated well with design teams and indeed helped them to discuss and frame ideas in an experience-centric fashion.

Keywords: Design · Design process · UX · User experience · User experience design · Industrial design · Interaction design · Storycraft · Narrative · Design process · Design discussion · Visual meeting · Creativity · Conceptual design · Experience prototyping · Chart and diagram design · Design thinking · Design/evaluation for cross-cultural users · Emotion · Motivation · And persuasion design · Information/knowledge design/visualization · Service design · Storytelling · Fiction · Non-fiction · Comics

1 Introduction

The designer's role in product and service development, and hence also their impact on society, has evolved substantially. This is due to a shift of focus from "making stuff" to "making stuff for people in the context of their lives" [34]. Designing for experiences

© Springer Nature Switzerland AG 2020
A. Marcus and E. Rosenzweig (Eds.): HCII 2020, LNCS 12200, pp. 39–58, 2020.
https://doi.org/10.1007/978-3-030-49713-2_3

requires designers to envision both the 'dynamic qualities of experiences' and the 'constantly changing emotional response to such changes.' They require strategic guidance in bringing the emotional, contextual, and temporal aspects of experiences into discussion [6]. To test, evaluate, and refine ideas, designers also need to externalize and represent ideas into tangibles [8]. Existing externalization strategies are not obviously equipped to incorporate the transient characteristics of experiences into the designer's creative thinking. Designers may need additional methods and tools to envision, sketch, and discuss experiences over time in addition to the existing skills that they have for drawing in 2D and making mock-ups in 3D. In this paper, we suggest that designers may be able to achieve this by including visual storycraft into their creative process. Storycraft is defined here as the skilled practice of generating/building stories. The similarity between the critical properties of a story and an experience is evident.

They are both subjective, context-dependent, and dynamic [26]. They share a sequential structure with a beginning, middle, and end that can be crafted and influenced through design [27]. Both stories and experiences evoke and affect the emotions of their experientors [17]. The activities of designers are already very similar to professional storycrafters since, in both domains, artifacts and services are brought together to interact with people who need to deal with a problem [5].

While harnessing the power of storycraft to elevate strategies in designing for experiences is an attractive idea, which has been embraced earlier by the design research community, it is not a proposal that can easily be put into practice.

In this paper, we propose a conceptual design method called Storyply that aims to merge the skilled practice of generating stories with the competent practice of design. The method includes a set of templates that guide designers by visually organizing their efforts and creative output (see Fig. 1). We have iteratively designed, evaluated, and modified Storyply to assist design teams in discussing and framing ideas in an experience-centric fashion.

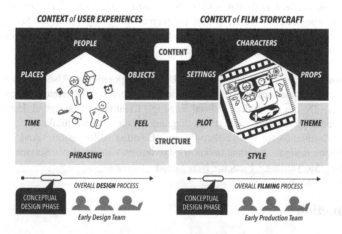

Fig. 1. Designers are conducting very similar activities to professionals in storycraft such as writers and movie-directors. In both domains artifacts and services are brought together to interact with people in order to create emotionally satisfying and meaningful experiences, and tools and methods are needed to discuss these experiences, also in the conceptual design stage.

2 Storyply

Storyply combines 'conceptual design' and 'story planning techniques' to help a design team to discuss and visualize solutions for themselves and the potential audience of their project, such as users, clients, and other stakeholders. A User-centered approach[1] requires designers to place user experiences at the very center of their creative intentions. This is easier said than done since, for decades now, designers have been honing their creative skills to produce tangible products and interactions. So, they need help to re-orient their creative focus from (tangible) objects to (intangible) experiences. Storyply offers useful guidance for that re-orientation and for building confidence in the design for innovative experiences. In this section, we explain how a Storyply session is conducted in several steps and provide a concrete illustration of each step.

2.1 Storyply Toolkit

Storyply provides nine templates to visually organize designers' efforts and creative output by dividing the total effort into more manageable sub-activities, next to offering support for the sub-activities themselves.

There are two decks of pictures to ignite visual imagination. One comes ready-made with the Storyply toolkit, and the other should be prepared by the participating team before the workshop. A reference source called Storyply Tips is available to ground the approach by providing quick access to relevant research findings and best practices. It is a collection of useful tips from design thinking and story crafting disciplines, such as different methods and tools that are widely used by professional designers and storytellers in both industries. There is a procedure to guide the process, which is communicated by the website and/or a facilitator, and supported by on-boarding videos at storyply.nl/videos. These videos also include more details about the example scenario that is used in the next section to explain the Storyply method. The Storyply templates can be obtained upon request through the same website.

2.2 Storyply Method

The Storyply Method distinguishes two types of activities: Backstory[2] and Story & Review (see Fig. 2).

---

[1] User-centered design is a research-led approach that utilizes an "expert mindset to collect, analyze and interpret data in order to develop specifications or principles to guide or inform the design development of products and services. These researchers also apply their tools and methods such as contextual inquiry and lead-user innovation in the evaluation of concepts and prototypes [33].".

[2] In storycraft, a Backstory represents the set of significant events that occurred in the characters' past, and the storyteller utilizes that background information while building the story's progressions [27].

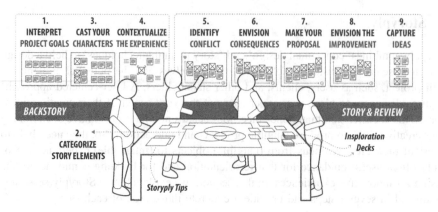

Fig. 2. Storyply supports a visual discussion process using templates, two decks of pictures (Insploration Deck, Project Deck), and a collection of helpful guidelines (Storyply Tips). It consists of two main layers: Backstory and Story & Review. Backstory consists of four steps: Interpret Project Goals, Categorize Story Elements, Cast Your Characters, and Contextualize the Experience. Story & Review consists of five templates: Identify the Conflict, Envision Consequences, Make Your Proposal, Envision the Improvement, and finally Capture Ideas.

Backstory. Is the part to identify and utilize vital information about the background of the project, target user(s), and the context of use while envisioning the experience in general terms. Backstory helps a team with the interpretation of the project requirements and with collecting and organizing material that is potentially useful for identifying the experiences on which to focus. Backstory helps to externalize a fuzzy internal process by steering attention to building blocks that are often taken for granted (such as the project goals) but which tend to create confusion when not being explicitly defined.

Story & Review. Is the part to generates and assesses the content and create alternative approaches that can lead to propositions for new experiences. Story & Review guides the participants in using the outcomes from Backstory, in generating key moments in the experience, and in evaluating how those fit with the emotional needs of potential experientors. This activity helps to envision temporal aspects of an experience and reflect upon the emotional impact of design intentions.

2.3   Storyply Workshop

In this section, we briefly go through the steps of a Storyply workshop (see Fig. 3). As not all details may be sufficiently visible or understandable from the figures provided in this paper, we advise the reader to also consult the onboarding videos at storyply.nl/videos.

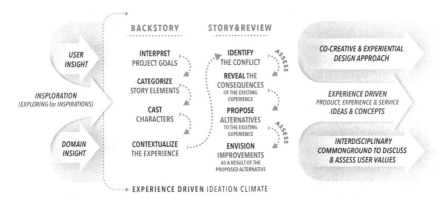

Fig. 3. A conceptual map of how Storyply works as a process: Backstory aims to identify relevant information about the intentions of the project, the target user(s), and the context of use to utilize while envisioning the experience's progression. Story & Review helps to generate and assess the content and creates alternative approaches that can lead to propositions for new experiences.

Step 1-Interpret Project Goals. The first step guides the team to self-reflect by sharing and discussing their interpretation of the project brief. They do so by naming the project and re-writing the goal according to their individual opinions. This step acts as a warming-up exercise and an opportunity to spot 'shared consensus,' 'polarized views' or 'complete lack of direction' from the very beginning of the process.

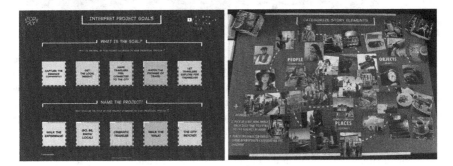

Fig. 4. Step 1: Interpret Project Goals: "What is the goal of this project according to your individual opinion?", "What could be the title of this project according to your individual opinion. Step 2: Categorize Story Elements: Browse the Insploration Decks, pick and choose at least nine images per category (people, places, objects) to be placed on appropriate sections in the diagram.

Step 2-Categorize Story Elements. In this step, the members of the design team browse and pick pictures from the Insploration Decks and organize them in the shared People, Places, and Objects diagram. This acticity prepares the participants for the following steps by inspiring their visual imagination (see Fig. 4). Designers are visual thinkers, so the majority of inspirational material is likely to consist of visuals [22].

There are two decks of pictures. The Storyply Deck comes with the Storyply Toolkit and aims to provide inspirational imagery for all kinds of projects. The Project Deck consists of pictures that the participants should collect by insploring[3] the project domain and bring with them to the session. Browsing and reorganizing the pictures together with all team members allows participants to have a multimodal communication. For instance, placing one card on top of another can indicate priority [31], and that action can possibly trigger a lively discussion.

Step 3-Cast Your Characters. This step allows building believable characters to become the actors in the experience. The goal is to discuss the 'drives' and 'vulnerabilities' of the main character and his/her relationship with supporting characters who could influence the experience under discussion. There is a difference between a Character in Storyply and a Persona[4] as frequently used in design. While a Persona focuses mainly on consuming behavior, the main interest of a Character is the external & internal conflicts that drive the emotional connection of people with their environment (see Fig. 5).

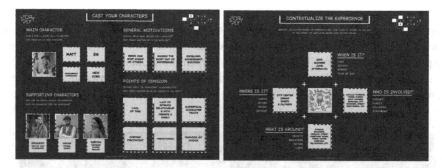

Fig. 5. Step 3: Cast Your Characters has four sections: 1) Main Character: Give a face, a name, age, occupation and location to your character. 2) Supporting Characters: Who are the people around the main character with an influence on the experience? 3) General Motivations of the main character: Discuss about what drives the main character. What wakes him/her up in the morning? and Points of Tension: Discuss about the main characters' vulnerabilities. What keeps him/her up in the middle of the night? Step 4: Contextualize the Experience: "Imagine the setting of experience as vividly as you can following the questions beside each section." The goal is to come up with a simple illustration in the center that shows the character in context.

---

[3] Insploration is an anagram that we came up with to imply exploring inspirations in order to fuel our imagination. Design is a creative endeavor, and designers are explorers of inspiration: Insplorers. Insploration works as a conscious and systematic act of searching for and capturing stimulants that may inspire new ideas [2].

[4] The Latin word 'Persona' means 'Mask' and has its origins in theatrical storycraft to indicate an individual character. In contemporary marketing and design, the same term is used to describe characteristics of a user group to represent the profile of a fictional individual to help companies focus their intentions on their target customers [32].

Step 4-Contextualize the Experience.
The fourth template helps the team to come to a visual agreement in one snapshot about a key moment where the main character interacts with other entities at the location of the experience. The task is to imagine the space where the experience takes place as vividly as possible and to sketch a straightforward visual representation of that scene (see Fig. 5).

Step 5-Identify the Conflict. [5]The fifth template asks the team to describe the existing experience by envisioning probable events that set the experience into motion in the form of five key instances. This step makes participants start thinking about the experience by visually representing how the characters feel throughout the story in terms of key values (see Fig. 6).

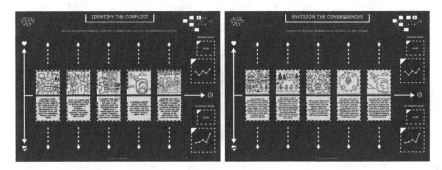

Fig. 6. Step 5: Identify the Conflict: Describe the existing experience, start with a probable event that sets the experience into motion (which is called an 'Inciting Incident' in storycraft). Step 6: Envision the Consequences: Elaborate on the future consequences of events you just imagined (in the previous template). The primary and a secondary value placeholder on the right of both templates are included for assessment purposes.

Step 6-Envision the Consequences. The sixth template guides the team to envision the impact of the conflict *(discovered in the previous step)* on the main character and the consequences on the experience. They do so by imagining five more key frames, that could be triggered by the previous five (see Fig. 6).

Assessing the Experiences in Template 5 and 6. The essential quality that distinguishes experiences from products is their temporal nature. In order to design for experiences, we need a way to think with the same temporal mindset, which requires a temporal interface to play with the instances of the sequence of events. A linear storyboard can only capture the sequence of events that would inform about *'what happens'* or *'what could happen'* and although it might be useful for visual planning, instruction or presenting a user journey, it does not allow us to capture and evaluate how the user feels, and when, why and how that feeling changes over the course of the experience.

---

[5] A **Conflict** is a useful tool that professional story-crafters use to figure out how a story character behaves and decides. A 'Conflict' can be a struggle within the main character (internal conflict) or between the Character and other people, places, and objects (external conflict).

Our goal is to have a discussion about the emotional impact of the experience on specific personal values and make the participants think about the experience while visually emphasizing how people feel throughout that particular story. The goal is to capture changes in emotional intensity on to identify the corresponding *'assessment values'* in order to open them up for discussion. The values *(Primary and Secondary)* represent the positive or negative charge that Characters are exposed to as a result of the choices they make throughout their experience (see Fig. 7). Adding a temporal map where the team discusses not only how events unfold but also how they impact the emotional state of the character throughout the experience opens up a whole new dimension to discuss WHY and WHEN users feel the way they do, and WHAT to do about it.

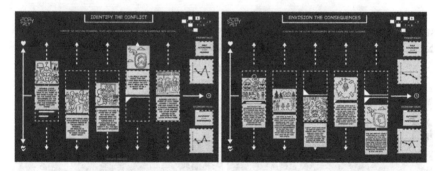

Fig. 7. The Y coordinate with the hearth icons on top and bottom represents the emotional intensity on a scale from negative to positive. The X coordinate with the small clock image at the end represents time. The dashed lines with arrows at each end remind us that the frames can move up and down according to the designated values. To assess the events in terms of assigned values, we ask: "How does the main character feel at each instance? Is it a positive feeling or a negative one?" and to move the keyframes accordingly. In this figure we see that the sequence of events planned in Template 5 & Template 6 are assessed in terms of the Primary Value: Self Actualizing/Meaning and Secondary Value: Autonomy/Independence.

Note that the goal of this chart is not to achieve precise metrics. The goal is to provide an impression of the change as experience arcs that can assist in the discussion. Storyply supports a discussion towards HOW the experience develops with respect to identified project values. These project values can be goals as formulated in Step1 or potential values that start to emerge during the discussion, i.e., any values that help to translate the high-level intentions into meaningful values that can inspire and inform design. During our studies, amongst various alternatives, one reference that proved to be immediately useful was well-known psychological needs as laid out by Hassenzahl [16, 17]. Here is a simplified interpretation of them [Martens, J.B.O.S (2017), private communication]:

- Autonomy *(I can do what I want, the way I want it)*: *independence, freedom, ideals*
- Competency *(I am good at what I do)*: *performance, control, challenge, skills, learning*

- Relatedness *(I feel close to the people I care about)*: *family, romance, presence, emotional expression*
- Stimulation *(I experience new activities)*: *curiosity, mystery, play, coincidence, novelty*
- Popularity *(I have an impact on others)*: *power, status, recognition, fashion, helping*
- Security *(I am safe from threats and uncertainties)*: *order, calmness, familiarity, routine, relaxation*

Step 6a- Assessing the Experiences in TMP 5 and TMP 6 - Primary Value. The team assesses the sequence of instances according to the emotional need that they have adopted as Primary value (see. Fig. 7).

Step 6b- Assessing the Experiences in TMP 5 and TMP 6 - Secondary Value. The team assesses the sequence of instances according to the emotional need that they have adopted as Secondary Value (see. Fig. 7).

Step 7-Make Your Proposal. This stage guides the team to make their proposal using the conflict and the consequences that they have identified in previous stages. The procedure is the same as in Step 5 except that Storyply offers the opportunity to re-tell the story by proposing a more desirable sequence of events that are likely to elevate the experience to a new and more desirable level (see Fig. 8).

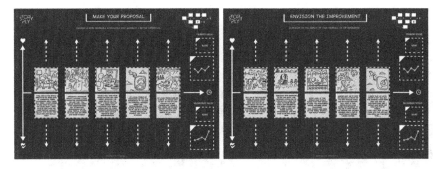

Fig. 8. Step 7: Make Your Proposal: The template prompts participants to "Imagine a more desirable alternative that suggests a better experience." Step 8: Envision the Improvement: Participants are prompted by the message to "Elaborate on the impact of your proposal on the experience." Once again, these templates offer space to express the assessment values on the right.

Step 8-Envision the Improvement. This is the moment to illustrate how the events could unfold with the teams' intervention in mind and also to figure out a resolution[6] within five new frames.

Step8a & 8b-Assessing the Experiences in Template 7 and 8. The team assesses the 10 new frames on the 'Make your Proposal' and 'Envision the Improvement' Templates

---

[6] In storycraft, 'resolution' ties loose-ends of the story, offers a solution rather than an ending and allows people to see the outcome of the main character's decision or actions during the experience [15].

with respect to the same values before. Of course, the intention is to identify improvements in TMP 7 & 8 in comparison to TMP 5 & 6. At first glance, it might look like that we are repeating the whole process all over again as templates TMP 7 & 8 are almost identical to templates TMP 5& 6. However, the objective is distinctly different.

To understand the underlying rationale of this necessity for a substantial number of additional key frames, we need to look at screenwriting. In screenwriting, every newly identified event contributes to a meaningful change into a Characters' life. This change is expressed and experienced in terms of 'Story Values' and achieved through 'Conflict' in order to act as a 'story event' or in other words 'Scene'[7] [27]. Primarily, we need the 3rd and the 4th scene in an experience 'to express the meaningful change' we are introducing into the characters' life inspired by the conflict we established in previous scenes. Moreover, during the workshops, we observed that 10 instances were not sufficient to take the experience to the point it needs to go 'with a degree of perceptible significance,' [27].

Step 9-Capture Ideas & Make Notes. The last step in the Storyply method is to capture initial ideas as a tangible outcome of the process. The assignment is to scribble (quick) visual reminders of the initial ideas and directions that the project may take in the future (Fig. 9).

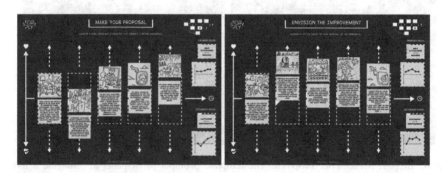

Fig. 9. Step 7: Make Your Proposal: "Imagine a more desirable alternative that suggests a better experience." Step 8: Envision the Improvement: "Elaborate on the impact of your proposal on the experience." Once again, there is space for the assessment values on the right.

The outcome of the whole process includes. (1) A clearly defined, structured and visually recorded brainstorming session. (2) An opportunity to collaboratively re-frame and interpret project requirements. (3) Sophisticated user archetypes who are driven by convincing internal and external conflicts. (4) Visual stories about the impact of emotional values on the user experience. (5) An externalized documentation of the

---

[7] "A SCENE is an action through conflict in more or less continuous time and space that turns the value-charged condition of a character's life on at least one value with a degree of perceptible significance [27]."

shared creative process that is immediately available for external communication purposes. (6) A new design approach to prioritize experiential properties over physical ones. (7) A new interface that allows externalizing ordinarily intangible ingredients such as emotional needs, personal conflicts, and vulnerabilities that could lead to insightful discussions about design directions.

3 Designing and Evaluating Storyply

We have iteratively designed, evaluated and re-designed Storyply over fifteen workshops in Italy, Sweden, Turkey and The Netherlands with 154 participants (63 Professionals and 81Students/Trainees) from diverse backgrounds such as: designers (industrial, product, visual, interaction, service, strategy, software, hardware, UX), researchers, engineers, managers, filmmakers, R&D specialists and CEO's. During the fifteen workshops, the framework evolved and matured into more stable versions of itself. In each version, we built a sequential structure in which the suggested process was open for experimentation, observation, and debate.

3.1 Research Methodology and Procedure

We believe that incorporating storycraft in the conceptual design stage can support a project team's efforts in designing for experiences. This claim can be made more concrete in terms of the following questions and sub-questions:

1. Why do project teams require support in designing for experiences?
   a. Why do we believe that the conceptual design process is the right stage in the design process to introduce storycraft?
   b. What do we mean exactly by the conceptual design stage of design?
   c. What do we mean by storycraft? Why and how can it be useful?
2. How can storycraft be incorporated into the design process?

To explore this latter question, we designed the Storyply method that we presented in the previous section. It started off as an interface to collect user insights and information that would help us to answer research questions and validate claims on the usefulness of storycraft. The interface naturally grew into a framework that produced a physical toolkit. We utilized this design process as our field of data collection with the design iterations providing opportunities to validate or contradict current insights. This process is frequently referred to as a Research Through Design Approach. The Research Through Design Approach involves both a creative and a critically reflective process in which literature survey and case studies are used to discover insights that are subsequently incorporated into the act of designing [1, 12, 14, 25, 40] (Fig 10).

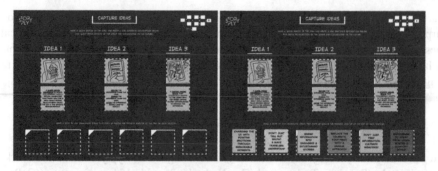

Fig. 10. Template 9-Capture Ideas prompts participants by asking: "Make a quick sketch of the idea and write a one-sentence description below for quick recollection of the ideas and discussions in the future." Additionally, this template offers a section to make notes of significant ideas or discussion topics that feel 'off-track' but relevant during the whole process.

In a Research Through Design approach, the iterative design and evaluation process of the conceptual tools and artifacts plays a crucial role [11]. Storyply is our attempt to generate knowledge on how to enhance design practices by linking theory to practice through investigating the process and tools of thinking and making [25]. Throughout the evaluation process, we were guided by the following research question and sub-questions:

3. Does incorporating storycraft within conceptual design resonate with design teams and provide an improvement in the process of designing for experiences?
   a. Does Storyply help designers to focus on and prioritize the experiential aspects of a design project?
   b. Does Storyply help designers to address the subjective, context-dependent, and temporal nature of experiences?
   c. Does Storyply help designers to envision user experiences in a better (more profound) way?
   d. Does Storyply help to envision better (more profound) user experiences? (Fig 11)

Addressing these questions required a relevant and realistic project context where the value that is generated by the user experience focus could clearly manifest itself *(in order to increase external validity)*. Moreover, to observe real design teams trying the method, we needed a coherent framework and an appropriate setting to apply, observe, and document. In the previous section, we explained the method, workshop, and toolkit, which played a vital role throughout our research-through-design process.

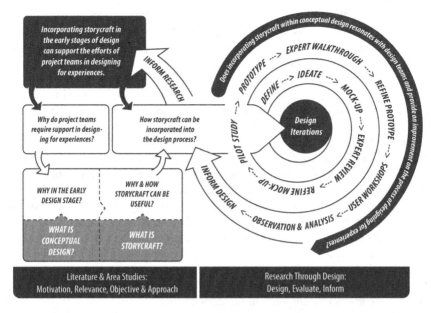

Fig. 11. Research approach to inform the discussion in this paper.

4   Reflections and Conclusions

We started by pointing out the shift of focus from objects to experiences in the design domain and explained the background and implications of this change on how designers operate. We placed the conceptual design phase at the center of our attention and provided an overview of how designers currently cope with the conceptual design process. We proposed storycraft as a means to incorporate the experience into the designer's creative thinking and introduced the practical outcome of our evidencing process as a framework to support our claims. What we learned from the process helped us to produce answers to the research questions which we previously established.

4.1   Informing Research Questions

Why do project teams require support in designing for experiences in the first place? Designing for an experience exceeds the physical product [4, 26, 34] and designers need to consider the time factor, as this is an essential aspect of experiences. We explained the need for a way to assess an emotional experience by discussing and weighing options about situations and events that belongs to a future context long before it becomes an established component of design [6, 8, 23, 25].

- *Why do we think that the early stage of the design process is the right stage in the design process to introduce storycraft?* The Pre-design and Discovery stages of the design development process provide the best opportunity for innovation, opportunity identification and translation of the research into design [6, 8, 21, 23, 30, 34] and hence also to establish an experiential influence over the whole project.

- *What do we mean by the early stage of design?* Designers need to externalize and represent ideas into tangibles in order to test, evaluate and refine ideas at this phase [8, 9, 34]. As explained in detail in *"STORYPLY: Designing for user experiences using storycraft"* [3], we explored the most relevant and widely used tools in the design profession for this purpose and exposed their shortcomings in terms of designing for experiences. We also offered an argumentation for why storycraft offers a potential solution.

- *What do we mean by story craft?* Why and how can it be useful? Methods and tools used in storytelling are believed to be relevant when planning for human experiences [7, 10, 13, 27], as was argued in more detail in "Crafting user experiences by incorporating dramaturgical techniques of storytelling" [2]. Professional storycrafting processes are quite advanced in their explicit awareness and clearly defined strategies to aim at influencing experiences deliberately. Therefore, it is relevant for designers to try and understand the structural strategies behind this craft. This led us to the following question:

- *How can storycraft be incorporated into the design process?* We explored new ways of incorporating storycraft in the design process to ensure that they could be applied in a diversity of design situations. We conducted a Research Through Design Approach as it promotes "creative translation and transformation of precedents from different situations to develop new types of solutions" [37]. We conducted co-creative design workshops. The visual meeting style in these sessions provided clarity and helped our thinking process about how storycraft and the design craft can come together in a structured process. These studies also helped us to understand the requirements of a new interface that allows externalizing intangible ingredients such as emotional needs, personal conflicts, and vulnerabilities that could lead to insightful discussions about design directions. In Sect. 2, we introduced Storyply, as our proposal to remedy the identified deficiency in current design methods. During the evaluation process, we were guided by the following research question and sub-questions:

Does incorporating storycraft within conceptual design resonate with design teams and provide an improvement in the process of designing for experiences? We approached this question by externalizing our own process. We analyzed workshops using the filtering criteria (Flow, Expression, Guidance, Outcome) (see Fig. 12) that we developed with experts from design and storycraft domains. We conducted and analyzed more than a dozen workshops in which we evaluated various iterations of our proposed method and framework. The observations allowed us to conclude that incorporating storycraft within conceptual design most definitely resonated well with design teams.

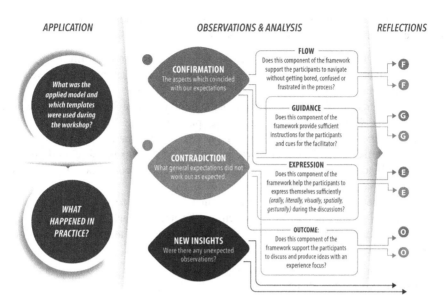

Fig. 12. Four design dimensions emerged as part of our analysis framework and we assigned four descriptors to them: 'The level of friction while navigating (without getting bored, confused or frustrated) within the process' was described as FLOW (Continuity). 'The style and fidelity of expression (orally, literally, visually, spatially, gesturally)' was described as EXPRESSION (Style). 'The descriptiveness and timeliness of instructions and facilitation of the process' was described as GUIDANCE (Instructions & Facilitation). 'The direction of the focus during the discussions' was described as OUTCOME (Focus & Direction).

- *Does Storyply help designers to focus on and prioritize the experiential aspects of a design project?* The participants confirmed that Storyply is perceived as helpful in order to focus their attention and to prioritize the discussion towards experiences. They found this to be a new and valuable approach that facilitated their efforts towards designing for experiences.
- *Does Storyply help designers to address the subjective, context-dependent, and temporal nature of experiences?* The participants confirmed that the suggested structure is indeed empowering, as they felt it helped them to get a concrete handle on otherwise more elusive components of experiences. They appreciated the ability to discuss and play with subjective qualities in concrete terms.
- *Does Storyply help designers to envision user experiences in a better (more pro-found) way?* The participants confirmed that Storyply offers an approach that is an improvement over what they have been using previously for similar purposes. The general tone of the collected comments was that the way we synthesized storycraft with design felt natural and made immediate sense to participants.
- *Does Storyply help to envision better (more profound) user experiences?* The collected comments confirm that Storyply triggers discussions that makes easier for designers to focus on aspects that they had not been so interested in exploring previously.

In summary, the real-time visual mapping of the thinking process under the guidance of story crafting principles offers the following benefits:

- The design team can discuss and iterate new concepts in a platform that offers a structure that allows sketching experiences true to their temporal, emotive, and contextual nature.
- Embedding narrative competence into visual thinking drove the discussion towards experiences. Consequently, the ideas that spin out of such discussions are more likely to serve the purpose of designing for user experiences.
- The ordinarily impenetrable creative process is opened up to the contribution of users and non-designer project stakeholders while the concepts are still under consideration.
- The document which gradually emerges in front of the design team provides a blueprint of the ideation process, which can be iterated back and forth at diverse occasions with various participants who were not present at the time of the generation process.

4.2 Informing Design Practices

While designers are sincerely interested in utilizing stories to create value, without appropriate tools and guidance, this interest can lead to disappointment as this endeavor has proven to be more complicated than advertised.

- **Patience is the key.** Our observations confirm that finding out the intended value of applying storycraft can take longer than expected. Visualizing feelings about a product on a timeline provides an opening towards seeing pain and pleasure points in the course of an experience. However, a visual timeline of events by itself provides only a superficial insight without spending ample time for deliberation on it. In a market where consumer satisfaction relies increasingly on prolonged use, we need tools and methods that allow longitudinal inquiries. One proven approach is to format user feedback in the form of 'experience narratives' that add consistency to the memories that users have [19, 20].
- **The two most relevant alternatives.** The design industry has been quick to embrace 'experience mapping tools' that promise faster gratification with less effort. 'Customer Journey Mapping' is a visual diagram that shows how a customer interacts with a service. Customer Journeys for instance help to illustrate the experience that a customer has with an organization [18]. 'Service Blueprinting' is a multilayered flowchart of the delivery process of a service. Its primary goal is to codify the service delivery process, which was ordinarily perceived as intangible and ephemeral into something that could be documented and systematically improved upon [35]. Currently, service blueprints are used mostly to help visualize, align, and prototype experiences for complex service ecosystems [36]. These tools use similar operational components such as time, flow, actions and "sequencing" in order to prototype new experiences and services [18, 24]. Both tools require little effort to apply and provide a sense of instant accomplishment, which makes them attractive for decision-makers. However, the depth they allow to dig into for insights is equally limited.

- **Output vs. Outcome.** Acritical insight we gained during our studies is the difference between output and outcome. Storyply generates a significant paper trail, but the ultimate objective of using stories is not to only documentation. It is to establish a shared understanding. The focus is not what is on sticky notes, but what we remember when we look at them. Our studies reinforced our conviction, which Patton perfectly formulated as; "Shared documents are not shared understanding." [31, 39]. It is paramount to cultivate an environment and sufficient time to allow the opportunity for a beneficial discussion. The goal is to reach a point where we surpass discussing the 'output' and start to develop an understanding on what is a desirable 'outcome' [31].

- **A trade-off in payoff.** Storycraft has a lot to offer. Nevertheless, designers have to come to terms with the fact that there are no quick recipes which can fast-track you in-front of the line. As in every craft with a reputable value, design-storycraft also requires dedication. Methods and tools can offer helpful guidance, but the expected value requires your trust in the process to collect the payoff. Storyply is no exception. In various workshops, we had at least one participant who is more goal-oriented, asking something like, *"This is all well and good, but I am wondering when we are going to start getting something concrete out of this process?"* The process requires a certain amount of trust in return to the value it provides since the most valuable insights tend to appear after a period of feeling uncertain about the outcome.

4.3   Conclusion

In its current form, Storyply combines 'conceptual design' and 'story planning techniques' to help the design team discuss and visualize solutions for themselves and the potential audience of the project such as users, clients, and other stakeholders. However, Storyply is not primarily intended to generate convincing stories or make good storytellers out of designers. We are interested in adopting strategies from stroycraft that are useful for discussion but not so much in strategies that serve to please an audience. For instance, we are trying to understand the underlying desire that drives a character, but we are not concerned with engaging an audience through dramatic action. We try to pinpoint conflict in a character's life, but we are not trying to escalate conflict for the sake of dramatic intensity. While we encourage "drawing verbs (actions), not nouns (names of things)," we do not expect a good quality of illustration. While we would like to achieve visual clarity to assist in the conversation, we do not worry about the visual composition to direct the attention of the audience like a film director would [13, 27, 38].

In short, we are interested only in the qualities that help designers to empathize with users on an emotional level while visually imagining and discussing experiences to inspire and inform design directions.

Even though we have designed Storyply as a discussion tool for designers, it also aroused an unexpected level of interest amongst decision-makers as a translative tool. Non-designers who work with designers communicated a keen interest in understanding the decision-making within the designers' creative process. Ordinarily, the designers' process is not readily accessible from a management, sales, or engineering point of view. Design is therefore not often recognized as a 'financial performer' that increases revenue and total returns to shareholders [28], despite the fact that the demand for experience-centric design skills is likely to increase in the near future. The UX profession is for instance expected to grow by a factor of 100 between 2017 to 2050, according to the N&N Group [29]. Tools that open up the collaboration between designers and other professionals (and users) are therefore also likely to be beneficial for the design profession itself.

The major obstacle towards a more widespread adoption of storycraft in UX design seems to be the demand on the time investment required, so that scaling down the Storyply method to a more manageable activity (or series of activities) is an obvious direction for further research. Studying the efficiency of the method on repeated use is another aspect that needs further study.

Ultimately, Storyply aims to merge the skilled practice of generating stories with the skilled practice of design. To that end, the insights revealed in this paper can hopefully inspire people who are interested in designing for experiences and services to see storycraft under a new light and tap into its potentials to take their experience design efforts to a new level.

References

1. Archer, B.: The nature of research. Co-Des. J. 2(11), 6–13 (1995)
2. Atasoy, B., Martens, J.B.: Crafting user experiences by incorporating dramaturgical techniques of storytelling. In: Proceedings of the Second Conference on Creativity and Innovation in Design, pp. 91–102. ACM, October 2011
3. Atasoy, B., Martens, J.-B.: STORYPLY: designing for user experiences using storycraft. In: Markopoulos, P., Martens, J.-B., Malins, J., Coninx, K., Liapis, A. (eds.) Collaboration in Creative Design, pp. 181–210. Springer, Cham (2016). https://doi.org/10.1007/978-3-319-29155-0_9
4. Baskinger, M.: From industrial design to user experience: the heritage and evolving role of experience-driven design | UX Magazine. (2012). Uxmag.com. (2010). Accessed 3 Dec 2012. http://uxmag.com/articles/from-industrial-design-to-user-experience
5. Bertolotti, E., Daam, H., Piredda, F., Tassinari, V.: The Pearl Diver. The Designer as Storyteller. DESIS Philosophy Talks-Dipartimento di Design, Politecnico di Milano (2016)
6. Buxton, B.: Sketching User Experiences: Getting the Design Right and the Right Design. Morgan kaufmann, Burlington (2010)
7. Chastain, C.: Experience Themes - boxes and arrows: the design behind the design (2009). http://www.boxesandarrows.com/view/experience-themes. Accessed 06 October 2009
8. Cross, N.: Design Thinking: Understanding How Designers Think and Work. Berg (2011)
9. Dix, A., Gongora, L.: Externalisation and design. In: Proceedings of the Second Conference on Creativity and Innovation in Design, pp. 31–42. ACM, October 2011
10. Duarte, N.: Resonate: Present Visual Stories that Transform Audiences. Wiley, New Jersey (2010)
11. Fallman, D.: Design-oriented human-computer interaction. In: Proceedings of the SIGCHI Conference on Human Factors in Computing Systems, pp. 225–232. ACM, April 2003
12. Gaver, W.: What should we expect from research through design? In: Proceedings of the SIGCHI Conference on Human Factors in Computing Systems, pp. 937–946. ACM, May 2012

13. Glebas, F.: Directing the Story: Professional Storytelling and Storyboarding Techniques for Live Action and Animation. Focal Press, Waltham (2008)
14. Godin, D., Zahedi, M.: Aspects of research through design: a literature review. In: Proceedings of DRS 2014: Design's Big Debates (2014)
15. Hart, J.: Storycraft: The Complete Guide to Writing Narrative Nonfiction. University of Chicago Press, Chicago (2012)
16. Hassenzahl, M.: The hedonic/pragmatic model of user experience. Towards a UX manifesto, October 2007
17. Hassenzahl, M.: Experience design: technology for all the right reasons. Synth. Lect. Hum.-Cent. Inform. 3(1), 1–95 (2010)
18. Kalbach, J.: Mapping Experiences: A Complete Guide to Creating Value Through Journeys, Blueprints, and Diagrams. O'Reilly Media, Inc., Sebastopol (2016)
19. Karapanos, E.: Quantifying diversity in user experience. Doctoral Dissertation, Eindhoven University of Technology (2010)
20. Karapanos, E., Martens, J.B., Hassenzahl, M.: Reconstructing experiences with iScale. Int. J. Hum.-Comput. Stud. 70(11), 849–865 (2012)
21. Takala, R., Keinonen, T., Mantere, J.: Processes of product concepting. In: Keinonen, T., Takala, R. (eds.) Product Concept Design, pp. 57–90. Springer, London (2006). https://doi.org/10.1007/978-1-84628-126-6_3
22. Keller, I.: For inspiration only. In: Michel, R. (ed.) Design Research Now. Board of International Research in Design. pp. 119–132. Birkhäuser Basel (2007). https://doi.org/10.1007/978-3-7643-8472-2_8
23. Lawson, B.: How Designers Think: The Design Process Demystified. Architectural Press-Elsevier, Burlington (2005)
24. Levy, J.: UX Strategy: How to Devise Innovative Digital Products that People Want. O'Reilly Media, Inc., Sebastopol (2015)
25. Marin, B., Hanington, B.: Universal Methods of Design: 100 Ways to Research Complex Problems, Develop Innovative Ideas, and Design Effective Solutions. Rockport Publishers (2012)
26. Moggridge, B.: Designing Interactions. MIT Press, Cambridge (2007)
27. McKee, R.: STORY: Substance, Structure, Style, and the Principles of Screenwriting. HarperCollins, New York (2010)
28. McKinsey & Company: The business value of design (2019). Accessed 10 September 2019. https://www.mckinsey.com/business-functions/mckinsey-design/our-insights/the-business-value-of-design
29. Nielsen, J.: A 100-Year View of User Experience. Nielsen Norman Group (2019). Accessed 10 September 2019. https://www.nngroup.com/articles/100-years-ux/
30. Osterwalder, A.: Business Model Generation. Wiley, Hoboken (2010)
31. Patton, J., Economy, P.: User Story Mapping: Discover the Whole Story, Build the Right Product. O'Reilly Media, Inc., Sebastopol (2014)
32. Pruitt, J., Adlin, T.: The persona lifecycle: keeping people in mind throughout product design. Elsevier (2010)
33. Sanders, E.B.N.: Design research in 2006. Des. Res. Q. 1(1), 1–8 (2006)
34. Sanders, E.B.N., Stappers, P.J.: Convivial Toolbox: Generative Research for the Front End of Design. BIS, Amsterdam (2012)
35. Shostack, L.: Designing services that deliver. Harv. Bus. Rev. 62(1), 133–139 (1984)
36. Stickdorn, M., Hormess, M.E., Lawrence, A., Schneider, J.: This is Service Design Doing: Applying Service Design Thinking in the Real World. O'Reilly Media, Inc., Sebastopol (2018)

37. Swaffield, S., Deming, M.E.: Research strategies in landscape architecture: mapping the terrain. J. Landsc. Archit. **6**(1), 34–45 (2011)
38. Quesenbery, W, Brooks, K.: Storytelling for User Experience: Crafting Stories for Better Design. Rosenfeld Media (2010)
39. Van Dijk, J.: Creating traces, sharing insight; explorations in embodies cognition design. Doctoral Dissertation. Eindhoven university of Technology (2013)
40. Zimmerman, J., Forlizzi, J., Evenson, S.: Research through design as a method for interaction design research in HCI. In: Proceedings of the SIGCHI Conference on Human Factors in Computing Systems, pp. 493–502. ACM, April 2007

Scales for Knowledge Elicitation: An Experimental Comparison Study

Rui Belfort[1]([⊠]), Farley Millano Fernandes[2], and Fábio Campos[1]

[1] Federal University of Pernambuco, Recife 50670-901, Brazil
ruibelfort@gmail.com, fc2005@gmail.com
[2] Unidicom, 1200-649 Lisbon, Portugal
farleymillano@gmail.com

Abstract. This paper was part of a doctoral thesis research and presents a discussion about the importance of selecting right measurement scales for contextual knowledge elicitation and how this contributes to alternative selection (and potentially other phases) in the design process. Four different types were compared, based on the results of two experimental procedures; an open online A/B test, with 294 participants, and a triangulated controlled one, based on test-retest, involving 90 people. The aim is impacting both research and practice, regarding the involvement of users in the designing, a complex and widely discussed matter of the discipline.

Keywords: Design process · Alternative selection · Measurement scales · Knowledge elicitation

1 Introduction

Assess user feedback without manipulating the results is a wide explored problem in the design domain (Roozenburg et al. 1991; Cross 2007), especially alternative selection, that deals with knowledge elicitation (Diaper 1989). The most contemporary concepts of designing propose users as critical participants of the process (Keinonen 2010), that's why this matter is so important.

In past studies (Belfort et al. 2011, 2013, 2015, 2017) evidence were found that principles of experience should be considered when assessing feedback from users. That means elicitation should be real-time, real-context and direct (no intermediation). Skipping any of these factors may lead to weak data collection.

One of the most important part of this process is choosing the correct scale for the data collection. Searching for evidence, experiments have been conducted to compare performances of selected scales (Belfort 2018). First, Likert and Pictorial. Second, Likert (again), Semantic Differential and Opposition. Findings made clear Likert extracted better results, overall.

Also, through these experiments was possible to attest the importance of elicitation design decision making (Stompff 2016). And this depends, among other things, directly on choosing the right scale for each procedure (internal and external validity). In the context of design, this contributes directly with alternative selection and, potentially, other project process phases.

© Springer Nature Switzerland AG 2020
A. Marcus and E. Rosenzweig (Eds.): HCII 2020, LNCS 12200, pp. 59–70, 2020.
https://doi.org/10.1007/978-3-030-49713-2_4

2 Theoretical Basis

First, it's important to state that this research adopts the disciplinary design perspective (Jones 1970); its relationship with the interdependence of problem and solution. Design deals at the same time and similar importance with exploration and construction, seeking transformation by artifacts, projected to meet people's needs and desires. This is still present on its contemporary forms (Sprint 2017) (Fig. 1).

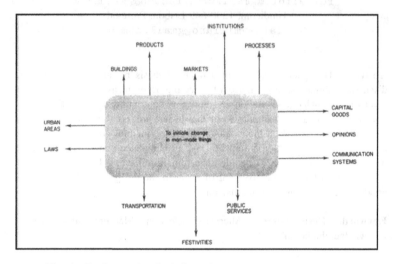

Fig. 1. Design as the discipline of transformation (Jones 1970)

The design process is the greatest feature of its disciplinary form. One of its phases, the alternative selection, deals directly with the objective this study; user (knowledge) elicitation and measurement scales (Micallef 2017). We are working to understand its potential to contribute both academically and commercially, aiming to add value both to research and praxis.

The most contemporary design concepts and approaches consider the involvement of users. In a general way, we have user centered design (projecting for users) (Vredenburg et al. 2002), participatory design (working assessing users in specific touchpoints) (Bødker et al. 2004) and codesign (designing with users) (Steen 2013). That's the context where knowledge elicitation gets important (Fig. 2).

Explaining the concept, knowledge elicitation is the gathering of information from the user (McNeese et al. 2017). Scales have a key function in this. Keeping principles of experience (Belfort et al. 2011) is mandatory: a) situatedness; acting natural; b) realtime; no rationalization; c) direct; without interpretation. This improves continuity (Leont'ev 1978; Festinger 1957; Csíkszentmihályi 1997).

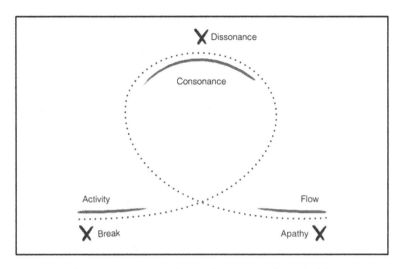

Fig. 2. Experience cycle; continuities and discontinuities

3 Methodology

Methodologically, this is a hypothetic deductive research, with transversal data manipulation (Lakatos et al. 2009). This means, in a general sense, that synchronism is not relevant for hypothesis validation, what allowed the work to be done in two steps; first Experiment 1 and then number 2. To make results comparable, we normalized them in a scale from 0 to 100; this is applicable to other cases.

In Experiment 1, users were presented casually to an online game and asked to use it. During play, he's perceptions was captured with no mediation, in real time and context of use. Avoiding rationalization, the question was "how do you feel?", followed by a 5 point Likert Scale (Kasser et al. 1999) and Pictorial one (Twyman 1985), with 294 participants.

Experiment 2 was a triangulated procedure, involving 90 users, validated with reliability calculation (Lincoln 2012). An online game was also casually presented and throughout experience usage data was collected. After providing feedback (Likert, Semantic Differential and Opposition scales), results were verified by confirmation question; test-retest (Zumpano et al. 2017) and, afterwards, normalized.

In the two experiments' results asynchron comparison, the objective was to generate evidence and determine which scale performed better in capturing user data and analyze methodological framework for future evaluations. This, in the context of design, and more specifically alternative selection, present challenges and opportunities, as detailed in General contributions (Figs. 3 and 4).

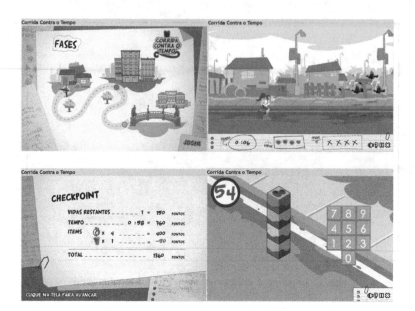

Fig. 3. Running Against Time game screens, from Joystreet (www.joystreet.com.br)

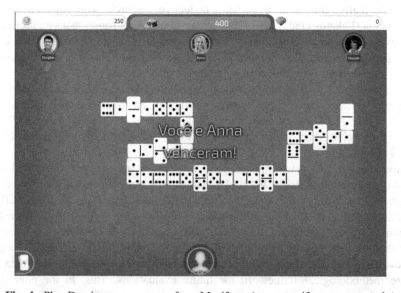

Fig. 4. Play Domino game screen, from Manifesto (www.manifestogames.com.br)

4   Experiments

4.1   Experiment 1

To keep principles of experience contemplated, as described before, we made an A/B test, with a web game, to assess user feedback. 294 participants were assessed immersed on the experience, avoiding rationalization of the responses. Results showed that in terms of engagement and time of response, Likert was a little bit ahead comparing to Pictorial.

In this experiment, the main challenge was, besides its own modeling, partning with a game development company to use a real product as the object. A collaboration was established with Joy Street, that was hugely important to the achieve results presented. Besides authorizing using the game, they implemented the feature of data collection, specially designed to run the experiment (Fig. 5).

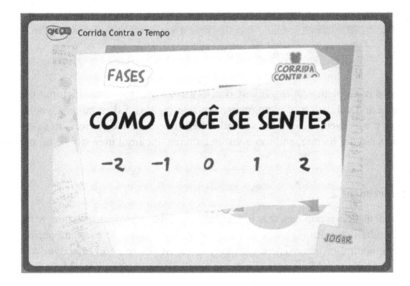

Fig. 5.   Likert scale, Experiment 1

Being online, and spread out like a friend recommendation, made possible to reach a reasonable number of participants, with no use of digital marketing. Starting with two scales was also a good strategy to keep internal and external validity more controlled. A pilot would be helpful if conducted before; this is a lesson learned to be implemented in future experiments (Fig. 6).

Fig. 6. Pictorial scale, Experiment 1

In terms of implementation, Likert is also less time consuming. Pictorial demands the creation and validation of pictograms. Considering this, Likert gains advantage and that's why it was used, also, in the second experiment, described below. In cases when participants are not literate, and more visual cultures, Pictorial may still be an option to be adopted.

4.2   Experiment 2

In Experiment 2, we conducted a triangulated test-retest (repeat question with a different formulation), with 90 users and one online card game, to evaluate performance (consistent, neutral or inconsistent answers) of Likert (more effort effective in the first procedure), Differential Semantic (Snider et al. 1969) and Opposition (Montalván et al. 2017) scales. Principles of experience were, again, preserved.

The challenges of this experiment were, like the first one; finding a game developer to make possible working with commercial games. In this case, Manifesto Studio was kind enough to open their deck of games and collaborate to make the procedure viable. Working with three scales and more criteria was challenging in terms of scientific management (internal and external validity) (Dancey et al. 2013).

In this case, having a pilot was extremely important to enhance the quality of results. Also, test-retest and triangulation were validated as excellent strategies when comparing scales for user elicitation. These two practices can be used in most of all experimental procedures like this. Comparing data transversely with past experiment was also a useful and replicable achieve (Figs. 7 and 8).

Fig. 7. Likert scale, Experiment 2

Fig. 8. Semantic Differential scale, Experiment 2

In the second experiment, results showed that Likert scale could capture more accurate feedback from users, comparing to Semantic Differential and Opposition. This considers engagement and time of response, but also repetition on confirmation question, which adds evidence that Likert is very effective, reinforcing why it's so widely used in scientific and corporative researches (Józsa and Morgan 2017) (Fig. 9).

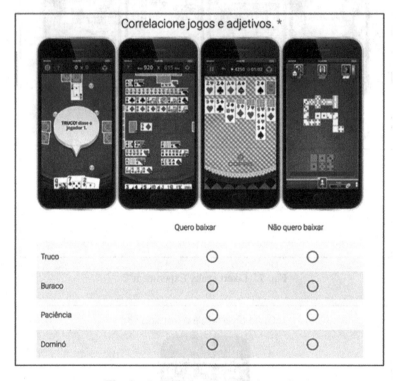

Fig. 9. Opposition scale, Experiment 2

5   General Contributions

With these two experiments, we could better understand the impact of choosing correct scales in the context of user elicitation. Also, Likert type presented better results, in both cases, considering effort to implement, time of response and answer consistency. Additionally, the use of Likert scale with Semantic Differential, and others) seems to be, based on preliminary results, a promising opportunity.

Test-retest and triangulation, as a validation tool of scales consistency, is something to highlight. It is flexible enough to be used in any other comparison, without losing focus on experiment control. These tools can be applied not only for digital products' evaluation, but analog artifacts as well, which enables more research branches and possibilities.

Form this point, we face a potentially endless journey to new comparisons with different scales, in other contexts of use and combined with other elicitation constructs. New hypothesis aroused and the potential contribution was enhanced. Putting this in the scope of design, and more specifically regarding the alternative selection based on knowledge elicitation, seems promising, both academically and commercially.

In a broader perspective, we can benefit by this knowledge in everything related to the involvement of users in design process; which is, as prior mentioned, still an open and controversial topic (Thilo et al. 2017). In this case, we were evaluating alternatives; how should we work from this to generate or select products, for example? Many possibilities come from this question.

6   Procedure Replication

The methodological model, formulated to test the research hypothesis, searching for evidence regarding the comparison of measurement scales for knowledge elicitation, in the context of design alternative selection, is described below. To replicate it, follow steps. Some of the tools used can be replaced for similar alternatives as long as the results provide the necessary validation (Fig. 10).

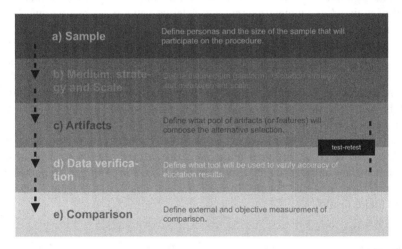

Fig. 10. Opposition scale, Experiment 2

All procedures should answer the following questions: a) What is the elicitation sample?; b) What is the platform, strategy and measurement scale?; c) what alternatives (artifacts or features) are being compared? d) What data verification strategy is going to be applied?; What external objective measure can be used as reference? These are the base for the experimentation.

To illustrate with an example: eliciting c) best confirmation modal for a) e-commerce users b) navigating on a mobile phone e) based on percentile task success d) verified specialist analysis. Many examples like this can be found in recent studies (McNeese et al. 2017; Whitmer et al. 2016; Nguyen and Ricci 2017; Naghiyev et al. 2016).

In this formulation effort is put in habilitating the idea of elicitation design decision making (Stompff 2016), which is a paradigm change still under discussion both in academia and industry. This is an alternative to involve users in the design process, without outsourcing designers' roles and responsibilities. A wide range of possibilities rise from this, pointing future research opportunities.

7   Related and Future Work

As already mentioned, the first (and more obvious) way to extend the research is testing with other scales. There are several (and some yet to be invented). So, this is almost endless journey. Also, we understand as promising testing the combination of scales, as we tried with putting Likert and Differential Semantic together; it makes this an exponential opportunity.

In Experiment 1 and 2, we incremented different experimental constructs, such as piloting, triangulation, test-retest, reliability validation, transversality, normalization, etc. All of it aimed to augment internal and external validity, generating quality data. Extensions of research can aggregate more of these in the future; there is a lot of work, methodological wise, to be done, with correlated potential contributions.

We also understand as a high potential opportunity work with non-digital products and scales. This sets a new and broad variety of problems and opportunities of contribution. Imagine, for example, a furniture business trying to select which product should be included, and which not, in a new line. This would aggregate a lot of value on that alternative selection, based on user (client) feedback.

Lastly, testing achieved constructs in different cultures can reveal more to be worked on and layers of problem mitigation. Both experiments were conducted in Brazil, but we are already planning to carry a third one in Portugal. Hypothetically, results may vary from one country to the other and this may be, again, valuable to enhance future results.

References

Belfort, R.: Elicitação de Conhecimento para Seleção de Alternativas de Design; Um Estudo de Caso aplicado à Gestão de Investimentos em Portfolio de Jogos Mobile. UFPE, Recife (2018)

Belfort, R., Campos, F., Cavalcante, S., Neves, M.: The role of scales in knowledge elicitation. In: PSAM, 2013, Proceedings of PSAM 2013, Tokio (2013)

Belfort, R., Campos, F., Correia, W.: Comparando o desempenho de escalas Likert e Pictórica, para acessar experiência de usuário. In: 5o Congresso Internacional de Design da Informação (Cidi), 2011, Anais do 5o, Congresso Internacional de Design da Informação (Cidi), Santa Catarina (2011)

Belfort, R., Campos, F., Goncalves, J.: User elicitation for cognitive consonance in the design of digital artifacts. In: Proceedings of IHCI 2017 International Conference on Interfaces and Human Computer Interaction, Lisboa (2017)

Belfort, R., Campos, F., Fernandes, W., Neto, E., Correia, W.: Combining principles of experience, traditional heuristics and industry guidelines to evaluate multimodal digital artifacts. In: Marcus, A. (ed.) DUXU 2015. LNCS, vol. 9186, pp. 130–137. Springer, Cham (2015). https://doi.org/10.1007/978-3-319-20886-2_13

Bødker, K., et al.: Participatory IT Design: Designing for Business and Workplace Realities. MIT Press, Cambridge (2004)

Cross, N.: From a design science to a design discipline: understanding designerly ways of knowing and thinking. In: Michel, R. (ed.) Design Research Now. BIRD. Birkhäuser, Basel (2007). https://doi.org/10.1007/978-3-7643-8472-2_3

Csíkszentmihályi, M.: Finding Flow. The Psychology of Engagement with Every Day Life. HarperCollins Publishers, New York (1997)

Dancey, C., et al.: Estatística sem matemática para Psicologia. Penso, Porto Alegre (2013)

Diaper, D.: Knowledge Elicitation: Principles, Techniques and Applications. Elis Horwood Ltd., Chicester (1989)

Eisenberg, B.: Always Be Testing: The Complete Guide to Google Website Optimizer. Wiley Publishing, Indianapolis (2008)

Festinger, L.: A Theory of Cognitive Dissonance. Stanford University Press, Stanford (1957)

Jones, J.C.: Design Methods: Seeds of Human Futures. Wiley & Sons, London (1970)

Józsa, K., Morgan, G.: Reversed Items in Likert Scales: Filtering Out Invalid Responders. JPER, Băile Felix (2017)

Kasser, V., et al.: The relation of psychological needs for autonomy and relatedness to vitality, well-being, and mortality in a nursing home. J. Appl. Soc. Psychol. **29**, 935–954 (1999)

Keinonen, T.: Protect and appreciate - notes on the justification of user-centered design. Int. J. Des. **4**, 17–27 (2010)

Lakatos, E., et al.: Metodologia científica, 5a edn. Atlas, São Paulo (2009)

Leont'ev, A.: Activity, Consciousness, and Personality. Prentice-Hall, Inc., New Jersey (1978)

McNeese, N.J., Cooke, N.J., Gray, R., Fedele, M.: Knowledge elicitation methods for developing insights into team cognition during team sports. In: Salmon, P., Macquet, A.-C. (eds.) Advances in Human Factors in Sports and Outdoor Recreation. AISC, vol. 496, pp. 3–15. Springer, Cham (2017). https://doi.org/10.1007/978-3-319-41953-4_1

Montalván, J., et al.: Adaptation profiles in first-time robot users: towards understanding adaptation patterns and their implications for design. Int. J. Des. **11**, 1–19 (2017)

Naghiyev, A., et al.: Expert Knowledge Elicitation to Generate Human Factors Guidance for Future European Rail Traffic Management System (ERTMS) Train Driving Models. Sage, Thousand Oaks (2016)

Nguyen, T., Ricci, F.: Dynamic Elicitation of User Preferences in a Chat-Based Group Recommender System. ACM, New York (2017)

Roozenburg, N., et al.: Models of the Design Process: Integrating Across Disciplines. Design Studies, New York (1991)

Snider, J., et al.: Semantic Differential Technique: A Sourcebook. Aldine, Chicago (1969)

Sprint, D.: Sprint: How to Solve Big Problems and Test New Ideas in Just Five Days. Simon & Schuster, New York (2017)

Steen, M.: Co-design as a Process of Joint Inquiry and Imagination. Design Issues, Cambridge (2013)

Stompff, G.: Surprises are the Benefits: Reframing in Multidisciplinary Design Teams. Design Studies, New York (2016)

Thilo, F., et al.: Involvement of the End User: Exploration of Older People's Needs and Preferences for a Wearable Fall Detection Device – A Qualitative Descriptive Study. Dove Press, Manchester (2017)

Twyman, M.: Using pictorial language: a discussion of the dimensions. In: Dufty, M., et al. (eds.) Designing Usable Text. Academic Press, Orlando (1985)

Vredenburg, K., et al.: User-Centered Design: An Integrated Approach. Prentice Hall, New Jersey (2002)

Whitmer, D., et al.: Assessing Mental Models of Emergencies Through Two Knowledge Elicitation Tasks. Sage, Thousand Oaks (2016)

The Designer's Creativity Demand&Influence Factor Model Based on Grounded Theory

Ming-hong Chai[(⊠)], Wei Sun, and Xin Lei

Beijing University of Posts and Telecommunications,
Beijing, People's Republic of China
2095857971@qq.com

Abstract. At present, the research of designers' creativity mainly focuses on management level, team level and physiological level. Our research purpose is to study the demand and influence factors in the design creative process at individual level. The significance of this study is that it can help us understand the demand and influence factors of designers. This study also help us understand the present design's situation profoundly. We will learn to take effective measures to improve the creativity of designers effectively, it is very beneficial to strengthen the designer's self-management and designer managers' management. We use Grounded Theory Qualitative Research Method to collect first-hand research data and build theoretical model through three-level coding to get a complete designer's creativity demand&influence factor model. This model can provide pointcut and theoretical guidance for subsequent research. In the process, we also found some interesting phenomena. Design content has obvious moderating effect on the creativity of designers. There is a mismatch between supply and demand of incentive measures in all stages of design process, which makes designers unable to maximize their design creativity. These can be the focus of future research.

Keywords: Grounded theory · Designer's creativity · Demand&Influence factor model

1 Introduction

China's reform and opening up policy has been implemented for more than 30 years. Now China has opened up its own country and is accelerating to the world. After 30 years of rapid development, contemporary China is at a very important historical moment, and the transition from manufacture to creation is imperative. The transformation from Made in China to Created in China is actually an important process of market upgrading, an important measure to solve social problems, and an important step to maximize national interests [1]. China will gain greater benefits in the complex international economic structure. "Creation" can bring new ideas, break the old system, break through the bottleneck of China's economic development, and win dignity through business innovation [2].

But at this stage, the creativity of Chinese designers has not been fully tapped, which can be seen from the functions and appearance of Chinese industrial products.

© Springer Nature Switzerland AG 2020
A. Marcus and E. Rosenzweig (Eds.): HCII 2020, LNCS 12200, pp. 71–82, 2020.
https://doi.org/10.1007/978-3-030-49713-2_5

There are many reasons for this problem, and the following are the most important ones. First of all, the soil of Chinese industrial culture has caused no particularly strong demand for designers' creativity at this stage. China has been a major manufacturing country for many years, and the transition from manufacturing to creation will take time. Manufacturing countries need designers who can complete the employer's ideas. In this process, designers' ability to express themselves is relatively weakened. But now many leading figures in the design industry have realized this problem, and are improving the designer's design cognitive culture from the links of designer education, development and output [3]. Secondly, the education level of designers in China is far from that of foreign countries. The foreign designer industry has developed earlierly and has more categories, which can meet the needs of many industries. China's designer industry started lately [4]. Although the government is vigorously supporting the education of designers, it will take a long time to catch up with foreign education. The complete education chain of foreign designers can ensure that designers have a considerable level of creativity. Finally, people's attention to design is relatively low. Although China's economy has developed rapidly in recent years, it is subject to a large population base, and the improvement of the living standards of ordinary people is very slow [5]. According to Maslow's hierarchy of needs theory, Chinese people's demand for products is changing from basic physiological needs and safety needs to high-level social needs, respect needs, and self-actualization needs [6].

China wants to realize the transformation from "Made in China" to "Created in China", the study of designer creativity is an essential part of it. By studying the creativity of designers, it can have a very positive impact on all aspects of product concept derivation, shaping, research and development, and market launch [7]. Moreover, the effective improvement of designer creativity can promote the awareness of all personnel in the entire industry chain. If the market demand is the source of design, then the creativity of a designer is the brush that describes this source [8]. Designers are more than just employees who can meet the needs of employers. Designers' work is to produce creative products and attract users [9].

2 Model Construction Based on Grounded Theory

2.1 Grounded Theory

Grounded theory is a qualitative research method proposed by Glaser, a famous scholar of sociology at the University of Chicago, and Strauss, a famous sociology scholar at Columbia University in 1967 [10]. The focus of grounded theory is to effectively analyze and summarize the original data, and then sublimate the highly generalized concepts and categories. Then, it is necessary to carry out an association analysis of these concepts and categories. The so-called association analysis is to discover the logical connection between these concepts and categories, and take the research purpose as the main line, so that these concepts and categories are closely spread around the research purpose [11]. The research results are highly focused, compact and logical. After the two scholars proposed this method, they further explained it. New theoretical research results, especially sociology etc., do not necessarily rely entirely on experiments to "discover" or "invent". They can also come from observations of real events and observers' own understanding [12]. These conclusions or understandings may not necessarily be objective, but it is of great significance to understand human behavior, psychology, and form new theories [13]. To eliminate these subjective deviations, you can rely on traditional sociological research methods to seek a transformation from "quantitative change" to "qualitative change".

This research aims to study the influence factors and demand of designers' creativity. In response to this problem, Dr. Zhang once wrote a doctoral dissertation on "Designer Creative Driving Forces: Based on the Perspective of Design Management" [14]. After considerable research, he has found 14 specific factors that drive designers' creativity, which are very representative. These factors played a very important role in constructing the in-depth interview outline in this research. Aiming at the influence factors and demand of designers' creativity, there is no mature theory or theoretical hypothesis, and the grounded theory is very suitable for this kind of research with no hypothesis. The grounded theory is a bottom-up research method, especially in the field of qualitative research, the use of grounded theory will help researchers find general research direction in the early stage, and then carry out purposeful in-depth research [15]. Many topics in the field of design are very suitable to adopt grounded theory, but at present, the frequency of grounded theory in the field of design is at a relatively low level. This research adopts the grounded theory method, because we hope that the factors that really affect the creativity of designers and the real demand of designers to exert their creativity can be discovered from the past experience of designers [16]. In this way, we can find effective incentives which are suitable for designers in the subsequent incentive research.

The research process of grounded theory qualitative research method can be divided into three steps. The first step is to collect raw data, the second step is to perform three-level coding, and the third step is to test theoretical saturation. Collecting the original data and three-level coding needs to be carried out repeatedly. After each repetition, the theoretical saturation test is performed until the constructed theory is completely saturated. At this time, the constructed theory can be regarded as a truly usable conclusion.

1. Collection of raw data: The collection of raw data was carried out using semi-structured in-depth interviews. The outline of the initial in-depth interview is compiled from the literature and has certain objectivity. The advantage of collecting raw data in the form of in-depth interviews is that you can grasp the emotional and psychological changes of the interviewees during the interview process, so that you can adjust the interview strategy in time.
2. Three-level coding: Three-level coding mainly includes open coding, axial coding, and selective coding. Through the three-level coding, the concepts and categories with high generalization can be found in the original data, and the relationship between these factors can be found. Through these connections, it is convenient to build model later. Three-level coding is the most important method in the process of building a pyramidal model.
3. Theoretical saturation test: The theoretical saturation test is performed after collection of raw data and three-level coding. Grounded theory is a gradual approach, and the saturation of the theory is "relative" rather than "absolute" (Fig. 1).

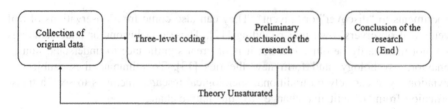

Fig. 1. Grounded theory research flowchart

2.2 Collection of Original Data

The raw data was collected in the form of semi-structured in-depth interviews. Questionnaires, interviews, observations, and other methods are often used when researchers use grounded theory to collect raw data. The advantage of the semi-structured in-depth interview method is that researchers can communicate face-to-face with the interviewees, grasp the interviewees' emotional and psychological changes in real time, and be able to detect the change in the focus of the interview and the interviewee's attitude to some points in time [17]. The initial interview outline was derived from literature analysis. The outline is highly academic, in order to facilitate the understanding of the interviewees, oralization is needed. After each interview, we need to analyze the data immediately, and put the new content in each interview into the outline of the next interview. The sampling principle of the grounded theory is the "saturation theory" principle. Therefore, when a certain number of designers are interviewed, information duplication occurs. When the obtained information starts to repeat continuously, and no new content appears in the interview, At this point, it can be considered that the theory has reached a saturation level, and at this time, there is no need to find new interviewees.

This research mainly studies the creativity of designers. The proposition is relatively broad. When looking for interviewees, the scope of the search is relatively large [18]. The purpose is to describe the influence factors and demand of designers' creativity as accurately as possible. According to the research purpose and the theoretical saturation principle of the grounded theory, this research selects a total of 12 designers through theoretical sampling, including 8 ordinary designers and 4 design managers. These designers cover a wide range from the Internet to State-owned enterprises, from UI design to VI design, and from 7 to 13 years of employment. The selection of samples is quite representative (Table 1).

Before the interview, an outline was prepared in accordance with the documentation. During the semi-structured interview process, the interviewees were encouraged to talk about the design behavior, psychological feelings, other people's influence on themselves, their own evaluation of their design results, etc. in the process of design creation from their real experience as truthfully as possible. We can understand what kind of demand designers will have in the process of design creation, and what factors will have a greater impact on designers' creativity. At the same time, due to the limitation on number of researchers and energy, it is not possible to memorize the content of the interviewees in time. After obtaining the consent of the interviewees, the conversation process is recorded. The time length of each interview is about 50 min. The outline of the initial interview is shown below (Table 2).

Table 1. Interviewees' detailed information

Code	Working years	Gender	Company	Post name
A	7	Male	Byte Dance	Interaction Design
B	7	Male	Meituan	Visual Design
C	8	Female	ICBC	Interaction Design
D	7	Male	Xiaomi	Interaction Design
E	7	Female	Sogou	Visual Design
F	7	Female	China Telecom Research Institute	Interaction Design
G	8	Female	Kugou	Visual Design
H	7	Female	Meituan	Visual Design
I	12	Male	Xiaomi	Visual Design
J	12	Male	Xiaomi	Interaction Design
K	11	Male	Sogou	Interaction Design
L	13	Female	China Telecom Research Institute	Visual Design

Table 2. Interview outline of ordinary designer

Serial number	Question
1	What is your design method or framework?
2	What kind of personality do you think a highly creative designer should have?
3	Can you describe to me the basic personal characteristics of those highly creative designers around you?
4	What factors do you think have a deep impact on your creativity?
5	Do you think the team atmosphere has a great influence on your creativity?
6	What realistic factors do you think will affect your creativity?
7	What do you think you want in design process?
8	Do you think your psychology will have expectations for the design results?
9	Do you actively communicate with other members of the team?
10	What kind of team leader do you like?
...	...

After the interviews is completed, the interview content is converted into text data, and invalid content such as mood words, emotions, etc. are removed from the data. After completing the above work, randomly select 2/3 of the respondents' data as the basis for subsequent coding analysis and model building, and the remaining 1/3 of the data as a sample to test the theoretical saturation of the model (Table 3).

Table 3. Interview outline of design manager

Serial number	Question
1	How would you assign the design work?
2	Do you know the theory of motivation?
3	What considerations do you have when arranging for employees to do some design work?
4	How would you assess the quality of an employee's work?
5	How can you improve the quality of an employee's work
6	Do you have any penalties?
7	Have you communicated with your employees about these rewards and punishments?
8	Do you regularly improve your work environment?
9	What kind of incentive measures do you think are more effective for the creativity of employees?
…	…

2.3   Construct Model Through Three-Level Coding

In the qualitative research method of grounded theory, after collecting the original data, the next step is to construct a model that can pass the theoretical saturation test by a three-level coding method. The so-called three-level coding, the first-level coding is open coding, the second-level coding is axial coding, and the third-level coding is selective coding.

(1) Open coding

Open coding refers to the collation of raw data, the purpose of collation is to achieve conceptualization and categorization. The original data is relatively complex and disordered, and there may be situations where concepts overlap in one piece of data. At this time, researchers need to be able to look at these data comprehensively, systematically, and objectively, and split the statements where concepts cross. In this process, researchers must have excellent logic and inductive ability, be able to accurately capture the main purpose of the original data.

After many detailed analysis by researchers, 34 categories and several concepts were finally sorted out. I want to show the research process to the audience as comprehensively as possible, but due to the limitation of the text space, only show some important categories and their corresponding concepts as examples in the table below (Table 4).

Table 4. Categorization of open coding

Category	Original sentence (Initial Concept)
Knowledge and Skill Level	1. There must be a big difference between undergraduate and doctoral students in doing the same work, because there are too many years of design education difference, undergraduate students should not be as good as doctoral students in some theories. (Knowledge Level Difference)
Thinking Style	1. When I encounter difficulties, I will think for a period of time first. If it doesn't work, I will go to my colleagues for help (Thinking Extroversion)
Personality Factor	1. When I was in school, I was quiet, and gradually became extroverted after work. Communicating with others can really solve many potential problems (Change Character For Work)
Clarity of Design Objectives	1. If it is face-to-face communication, I will confirm clearly with the customer face-to-face for the unclear part in the design goal, so as to avoid rework (Fuzzy Description Delays Time)
The Content of Design Objectives	1. I will spend more time and more effort to achieve design goals which I am interested in (The Mediating Role of Design Content)
The Leadership of Team's Leader	1. A good leader can also bring more design resource (Leadership affects resource support)
Sense of Achievement	1. When I work hard, I hope to hear others' appreciation (Outside Appreciation)
The Freedom of Design Work	1. It would be better if we could form a team freely. I will choose partners to complete this project (Free Organization)
The Reward and Punishment of Design Work	1. Some companies have good fault tolerance mechanisms, which can help designers reduce work pressure, and then designers can boldly create better design products (Flexible System)
The Supply of Design Resource	1. In the design process, if I don't have enough resources to support, I have to give up some good design ideas in favor of a design that can be done within existing resource (Side Effect of Insufficient Design Resource)

(2) Axial coding

Axial coding is secondary coding. On the basis of first coding, inductive analysis is performed again. First-level coding has obtained 34 categories and several concepts. Axial coding is to discover the potential logical connections between these categories, and to maximize the aggregation of categories with high-density logical connections under a main category.

The first-level coding of the previous step has obtained 34 categories. This time, 9 main categories have been found through the second-level coding. These are: design results, individual factors, work factors, organization factors, reality factors, scene factors, and ability demand, psychological demand, basic demand. The nine main categories and their 34 sub-categories and their connotations are in the table below (Table 5).

Table 5. Main and sub-category of axial coding

Main category	Connotation	Sub category
Individual Factor	This category refers to the individual's own factors, which may be innate or acquired. Individual factors are easily recognized by others in the tea	Knowledge and Skill Level
		Thinking Style
		Emotional Factor
		Personality Factor
		Intelligence Factor
Work Factor	This category refers to the factors in the work process. The composition of these factors is complex, and they are also the most relevant factors with creativity	Clarity of Design Objectives
		Feedback of Design Results
		Contents of Design Objectives
		The Supply of Design Resource
		The Difficulty of Design Objectives
		The Reward and Punishment of Design Work
		The Freedom of Design Work
Organization Factor	This category refers to organization factor. Design activities are often carried out in the form of team. As a part of the design team, the quality of all aspects of the design team also affects individual designers, so organization factor is also very important	Shared Mind in Team
		The Level of Team Professional Skills
		Work Assignment in Team
		The Fairness in Team
		Diversified Team Skills
		The Atmosphere of Team
		The Communication of Team
		The Leadership of Team's Leader

(continued)

Table 5. (*continued*)

Main category	Connotation	Sub category
Reality Factor	This category refers to reality factor. Reality factor refers to technical problems that cannot be solved by designers	The Restriction of Technology
Scene Factor	This category refers to scene factor. Scene factor is a collection of factors such as time, place and so on when designers work	The Stability of Work Environment
Ability Demand	This category refers to ability demand. Ability demand is the first condition for designers to survive in the workplace	Manifest The Self-ability
		Improve Design Skills
		Learn Other Work Skills
Psychological Demand	This category refers to psychological demand. Psychological demand is an important support for designers to keep working motivation in work	Sense of Achievement
		Sense of Satisfaction
		Sense of Interest
		Sense of Belonging
Basic Demand	This category refers to basic demand. Basic demand is some demands for designers to ensure their normal survival and life	Economic Reward
		Social contact
		Work Welfare
Design Results	This category refers to design results. The design results is the periodical output of designer's creativity. The design results is a comprehensive result, which has high value in the whole industrial process	Quantity of Design Results
		Quality of Design Results

(3) Selective coding

Selective coding refers to the case where the secondary coding has determined the main category and the sub-category, and it is necessary to further logically summarize all categories, and then select a core category among these categories. The core category should have a leading role, and the core category is the starting point and ending point of other categories. Other categories can be logically linked to the core category. Through the core category, a systematic model can be constructed.

Through generalization and combined with the research purpose mentioned above, the core category was finally defined as "design results". The individual factor, work factor, organization factor, reality factor, scene factor, ability demand, psychological demand, and basic demand are considered to affect the design results. The "design results-design creativity demand-design creativity influence factor "design creativity influence factors and demand model is constructed. In the model, the "design results" includes the quality and quantity of design results, the "design creativity demand" includes ability demand, psychological demand, and basic demand, and the "design creativity influence factor" includes individual factors, organization factor, work factor, reality factor, and scene factor. The demand of design creativity directly affects the quantity and quality of design results, and the influence factors can affect design results directly or indirectly affect the design results through design creativity demand (Fig. 2).

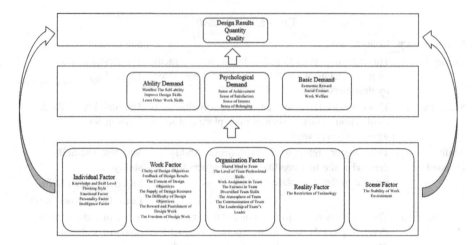

Fig. 2. Designer's creativity demand&influence factor three-layer model

3   Designer's Creativity Demand&Influence Factor Model

We get the model of designer's creativity demand&influence factor shown in the figure below based on previous research (Fig. 3).

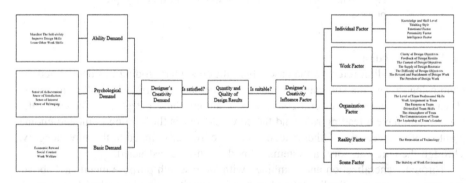

Fig. 3. Designer's creativity demand&influence factor model

In the model, the most important is the design results, the second important thing is the design creativity demand, the third important thing is design creativity influence factor. The "design results" includes the quality and quantity of design results. The "design creativity demand" includes ability demand, psychological demand, and basic demand. The "design creativity influence factor" includes individual factor, organization factor, work factor, reality factor, and scene factor.

(1) Design results

The core part is the design results, which are mainly reflected in the quantity and quality. The number of design results can measure the time and energy invested by the designer, and the quality of the design results can reflect the designer's skill level, knowledge level, and so on.

(2) Design creativity demand

From a macro perspective, the designer's creativity demand is generally in line with Maslow's hierarchy of needs theory [6]. Designers must first solve their own survival problems, and then slowly learn more about design knowledge and skills, and finally want to realize their ideals.

(3) Design creativity influence factor

The factors that influence the designers creativity are very complex, not only at the human level, but also at the scene and reality level. This precisely reflects that the study of designer creativity is a very tedious and long process, and it can also explain that there are no very effective theoretical assumptions on creativity until now.

4 Conclusion

Through this model combined with the interview process, we can know that the order of designer's creativity demand&influence factor are different in each design stage, which means that the incentive measures should change in time to meet the need of designers in each design stage. At the same time, there is a mismatch between supply and demand of incentive measures in all stages of design process, which makes designers unable to maximize their design creativity. It is also very important for designers to find the right team, and suitable team can make designers work at top capacity. At last, the content of design has obvious moderating effect on designers' creativity, so the design manager should pay attention to assign design tasks according to the designers' individual characteristics.

Due to the limitation of time, there are still some shortcomings in this study. If you have different opinions, please write to me to discuss.

References

1. Gao, X.: On the reform and opening-up theory of contemporary china in the perspective of historical development. Econ. Res. Guide (31) (2019)
2. Shu, J.: China's reform and opening up from the perspective of historical materialism. Acad. J. Shanxi Prov. Comm. Party School C.P.C. **42**(4), 21–25 (2019)
3. Sun, M.: Problems and solutions in the development of chinese independent designer brands. Value Eng. **38**(25), 31–34 (2019)
4. Cong, Z., Zhang, F.: Standard disengagement: a crisis study of chinese designers under the domination of consumer logic. In: Art Obs. (11) (2017)
5. Xie, F., Xie, Q., Cheng, D.: Seize the luxury goods market: chinese designers break the cocoon. China Bus. Trad (21) (2011)

6. Niu, L.: Discuss the application of incentive mechanism in management practice. Hum. Res. (18) (2019)
7. AVIC.: Build an innovative designer team. Enterp. Manag. (10) (2018)
8. Qi, X.: Design sketch—creating the potential of industry designer. J. Baoji Univ. Arts Sci. (Nat. Sci. Ed.). **28**(3), 247–249 (2008)
9. Yang, Z.: Quicken up the construction of home-textiles designer system, promote the transformation from "Manufacture" to "Creation". China Text. Leader, (7) (2012)
10. Heinrich, P., Schwabe, G.: Communicating nascent design theories on innovative information systems through multi-grounded design principles. In: Tremblay, M.C., VanderMeer, D., Rothenberger, M., Gupta, A., Yoon, V. (eds.) DESRIST 2014. LNCS, vol. 8463, pp. 148–163. Springer, Cham (2014). https://doi.org/10.1007/978-3-319-06701-8_10
11. Corbin, J.M.: Basics of Qualitative Research: Techniques and Procedures for Developing Grounded Theory. Sage Publications Inc., Thousand Oaks (2014)
12. Glaser, B.G.: The discovery of grounded theory: strategies for qualitative research. Aldine Transaction; Footprint Books Distributor (2009)
13. Xu, M., Wei, H., Wang, J.: Research on development environment of high-level innovation team based on grounded theory. J. Nanjing Tech Univ. (Soc. Sci. Ed.). **18**(6), 101–110 (2019)
14. Zhang, H.: Research on designers' creative driving force—based on the perspective of design management (2014)
15. Jing, M., Yang, Y.: A review of descriptive research methods. Nurs. J. Chin. People's Lib. Army **35**(11), 32–35 (2018)
16. Goldschmidt, G.: Design creativity research: recent developments and future challenges. Int. J. Des. Creat. Innov. (4) (2019)
17. Sun, X.: In-depth interview research: method and techniques. J. Xi'an Jiaotong Univ. (Soc. Sci.) **32**(3), 101–106 (2012)
18. Dong, M.: Research and analysis of sampling standards. China Chem. Trade **11**(20), 255–256 (2019)

Online Interactive Chart Choosers for Novice Visual Designers: Assistance and Restriction

Ching-I Chen[1] and Meng-Cong Zheng[2]

[1] College of Design, National Taipei University of Technology,
Taipei, Taiwan, R.O.C.
zoeychen116@gmail.com
[2] Department of Industrial Design, National University of Technology,
Taipei, Taiwan, R.O.C.
zmcdesign@gmail.com

Abstract. We often need the cooperation of data analysts, statistical professionals, content editors, and visual designers to present a complete and persuasive information visualization project. Even a chart chooser is a tool that designers consult, visual experts with statistical backgrounds think that such a reference tool oversimplifies the process of visualization, and it is easy to guide novice designers to draw the wrong charts. Conversely, some proponents believe that the chart chooser is the primary tool for novice designers to go into the field of information visualization.

Therefore, this study wants to explore the assistance and restriction of online interactive chart choosers for novice visual designers. We collected six online interactive chart choosers from the data visualization community. Ten subjects, 22 to 26-year-old novice designers, were recruited to conduct experiments. They only had a little chart drawing experience. Five subjects referenced the chart choosers in the test, and the other five were free to create charts without reference. Finally, semi-structured interviews and SUS usability evaluation were conducted, and the preferences of the six chart choosers were ranked. The results showed that subjects who did not consult the chart choosers used seven chart types to represent three topics. That is fewer than those with chart choosers used nine different chart types. Subjects who refer to the chart choosers believe that the reference tools do not limit creativity and can assist drawing charts. Moreover, after investigating the preferences of the six chart choosers, we understand what features make designers prefer to use.

Keywords: Online chart chooser · Novice designers · Information visualization · Chart design · Design assistant

1 Introduction

Information visualization is in the form of infographics, dashboards, diagrams, and charts. The development of information visualization has not only been based on data-based facts but also data-driven storytelling (Tong et al. 2018). With the expansion of visualization into applications in different fields, visualization has gradually attached importance to visual narrative (Obie et al. 2019) and aesthetics (Judelman 2004).

© Springer Nature Switzerland AG 2020
A. Marcus and E. Rosenzweig (Eds.): HCII 2020, LNCS 12200, pp. 83–96, 2020.
https://doi.org/10.1007/978-3-030-49713-2_6

Therefore, we often need the cooperation of data analysts, statistical professionals, content editors, and visual designers to present a complete and persuasive information visualization project (Nybro, Skolnik and Makulec 2015).

Nowadays, visualization software or online tools provide more and more diverse, and not all projects have a team with all roles to support each other. In the process of data visualization, a fundamental question often encountered by novice graphic designers is, which type of chart should be used? Graphic designers without statistical training will be confused about the data relationship and the type of chart they correspond to. At this time, assistive tools are essential.

In 2010, Andrew Abela has developed a chart chooser on one page to help users choose what is the best type of chart to use for the specific data relationship. Soon, the page of the diagram was spread to many blogs and visualization communities (Abela 2010). In 2015, Stephen Few wrote an article to oppose Abela's approach (Few 2015). Quoting what Stephen Few wrote in the article, "As data visualization has become increasingly popular during the last decade, efforts to explain it have often become simplistic (i.e., oversimplified) to a harmful degree." Conversely, some proponents believe that the chart chooser is the primary tool for novice designers to go into the field of information visualization. The discussion that followed was positive for the evolution of chart chooser or other assist tools.

Gradually, we can also see more and more data visualization reference guides, e.g., physical cards, posters, and interactive chart choosers published on the internet. These represent the needs of users, and visualization experts are actively developing tools or guides for most people to use.

Even though people have different opinions of chart choosers in the visualization community, there is currently no research on these assist tools for novice designers. We know nothing about novice designers' design processes and strategies when they need to translate a dataset into a visualization story. Therefore, this research wants to know what novice designers themselves think of these chart choosers and understand the following four purposes:

1. Understand the process of novice designers designing data visualization stories;
2. Understand the steps of the novice designer using the chart choosers;
3. The preferences and opinions of the novice designer on the six chart choosers;
4. The usability evaluation of the chart chooser by the novice designer.

2   Prior Work

2.1   Selection of Chart Chooser

The study collected six online interactive chart choosers from the data visualization community: 1) Visual Vocabulary, 2) From Data to Viz, 3) Data Visualisation Catalogue, 4) Interactive Chart Chooser by Depict Data Studio, 5) The Data Viz Project, 6) Juicebox (see Fig. 1).

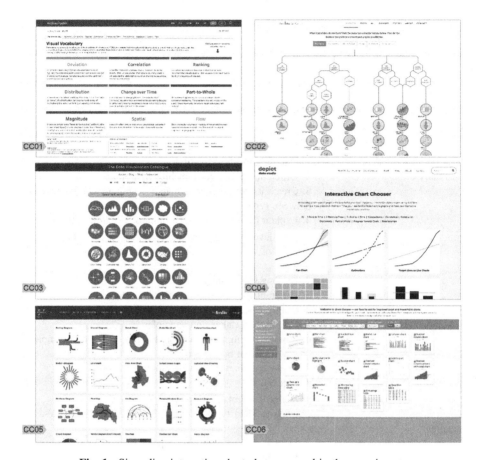

Fig. 1. Six online interactive chart choosers used in the experiment.

"Visual Vocabulary" is developed by Andy Kriebel, and it is inspired by Visual Vocabulary created by Financial Time-FT Graphics Team. It is a static graphic that provides a reference for choosing chart types mapping data relationships. Andy Kriebel developed the interactive "Visual Vocabulary" on Tableau Public and 1,026,109 views as of December 31, 2019.

"From Data to Viz" is created by Conor Healy and Yan Holtz. They obtained KANTAR Information is Beautiful (IIB) Awards 2018. "The Data Visualization Catalogue" is a project developed by Severina Ribecca. It contains both a library of different visualization techniques and a blog. In addition, the website is available in five languages, English, Chinese, Spanish, Russian, and Turkish. The project obtained KANTAR IIB Awards 2014. "The Data Viz Project" is created by Ferdio, which is also the winner in KANTAR IIB Awards 2017.

When searching by the keyword "interactive chart chooser" on Google, we found "Interactive Chart Chooser by Depict Data Studio" listed as the first one on search results. The "Chart Chooser: Juice Labs" listed as the second.

The six online interactive chart choosers are all made by visualization experts. They have the same goal to guide anyone to the most appropriate graphic representation for their given dataset. We made a comparison table (see Table 1) and the operation flow of these chart choosers.

Table 1. Feature comparisons of the six online interactive chart choosers.

OICC	Amount of chart types	features
Visual vocabulary	67	1. Data relationship descriptions 2. Differentiate data relationships by color 3. Create its own interactive chart examples and distinguish between types 4. Explain the timing and precautions of various chart types
From data to viz	39	1. Four levels of data classification: data relationships, number of variables, ordered/not ordered, few points/many points 2. By data story category 3. Differentiate data relationships by color 4. Briefly describe chart types and explain when to use them 5. Common mistakes and examples 6. Provide coding tools to draw this chart type and examples of charts drawn by the tool. 7. Represent chart types with simplified icons. 8. Precautions
Data Visualisation Catalogue	60	1. Define data relationship types as "functions" 2. Classify chart types as graphs/plots, Diagrams, Tables, Other, Maps/geographical 3. Identify various types of graphics by icon or name 4. Provide charts examples, descriptions, functions, and analysis 5. List charts with similar functions 6. List the tools or software that can produce the chart type 7. Example link 8. Video tutorials 9. Downloadable eBook 10. Related product sales 11. Provide other visual resources 12. Five languages available: Chinese, English, Spanish, Russian, and Turkish
Interactive chart chooser	37	1. Chart type icons are large and colorless 2. Guideline 3. Resources 4. Example link

(*continued*)

Table 1. (*continued*)

OICC	Amount of chart types	features
The data viz project	149	1. Classify chart types by Family, Input, Function, Shape 2. Consistent color planning 3. The classification of "Input" is distinguished by the shape of the dataset 4. "Shape" is distinguished by the shape the chart looks like 5. Examples are links to large images, not webpages of the example 6. Include diagrams
Juicebox	17	1. For PowerPoint and Excel users 2. Downloadable examples for use

Furthermore, the operation flows of the six OICC are arranged in Fig. 2.

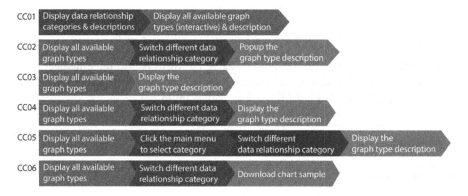

Fig. 2. The operation flows of the six OICC.

2.2 Selection of Datasets

All three datasets are taken from public data. In order not to make the participants feel unfamiliar with the subject and increase time and cognitive load, the data subject is closer to the participants' life and culture. The goal is to expect they can focus on creating and telling stories of data visualization.

The first dataset is "National Referendum Proposition 14: Results." The thematic content is "This is the results of National Referendum Proposition 14: "Do you agree to the protection of same-sex marital rights with marriage as defined in the Civil Code?" The dataset fields contain county/city, vote for/against, invalid/blank, total, registered voters, turnout. The dataset was sourced from Central Election Commission.

The second dataset, "Netflix Original Series (2013–2017)." Data fields include major genre, title, subgenre, premiere year, seasons, status, minimum length, maximum length, episodes and IMDB rating. The dataset was sourced from data world.

The third dataset is "Nomadlist City List." The thematic content is "This is the result of global nomads scored on Nomadlist.com. Data fields include the average scores, the temperature of every city, living cost by month, and network speed." The dataset was sourced from nomadlist.com.

In these three datasets, several data relationships that can be used. Please refer to Table 2.

Table 2. The data relationships in the three datasets.

Dataset subject	Data relationship
National Referendum Proposition 14: Results	Part-to-Whole, Ranking, Magnitude, Spatial, Distribution, Deviation
Netflix Original Series (2013–2017)	Part-to-Whole, Ranking, Magnitude, Correlation, Flow, Change over time
Nomadlist City List	Part-to-Whole, Ranking, Magnitude, Spatial, Distribution, Correlation

The data relationships are partially the same, but there is also the difference. We want to understand what data relationships the participants choose to correspond to the chart type to present the subject of the story they want to tell.

3   Method

3.1   Participants

The 10 participants were all students of the master's class of the School of Design, aged 22 to 26, including four males and six females. The definition of a "novice" designer in this study is a student who is still studying and not yet engaged in design work. This group of participants has a background in graphic design and industrial design but has not received professional training in statistics and data visualization. The average number of times they drew charts in the past six months was four. The purpose of the drawing chart is for course briefings and presentations.

None of the 10 participants had any experience using the six OICC in this study. Those pieces of software they usually use are sorted from the most frequent to Word, Excel, Illustrator, and Keynote. Only two of them chose the chart type according to their own ideas, and the remaining eight always refer to the software suggestion or other references from books. We randomly assigned these 10 participants into two groups. Five participants in Group A referenced the chart choosers in the whole tasks, and the others in Group B were free to create charts without reference, and then let them try the OICC after drawing.

3.2   Task Procedure

This study wanted 10 participants to complete three tasks, draw three charts based on three different datasets, and give textual explanations. The purpose of the task is to understand the steps of data visualization for designers with a non-statistical background. Moreover, we conducted a semi-structured interview after the three tasks to understand whether the OICC limits the creativity of the designers or assist the designers. Besides, we would like to get their opinions on the OICC through interviews.

The tasks and interviews were conducted in the laboratory. We set up a 21-inch iMac to present six OICC. Three datasets were printed on paper. The A4 paper layout used to draw charts was divided into a drawing area and a story area, which were used to describe the chart they draw in text. Tools for drawing were colored pencils and black markers. Please refer to Fig. 3.

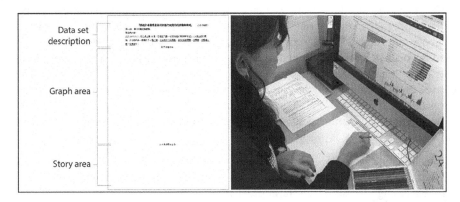

Fig. 3. The left picture is the paper layout for drawing; the photo on the right shows the participant doing the task.

Before the formal experiment, a pilot test was performed, and the time of each task was adjusted to complete within 12 min according to the status of the pilot test. Take a two minutes break between tasks. Therefore, the whole experiment and interview time is about one hour. A timer was used in each task, and the participants were informed of the time remaining when there were five and two minutes remaining. The purpose of this action is mainly to hope that the participants can complete the graph and text required for the task within the time limit.

The first stage was to fill in a questionnaire for personal charting experience; the second stage was to perform three tasks; the third stage was a semi-structured interview. In the final stage, the six OICC are sorted by preference, and the SUS usability assessment scale for the six OICC was filled out. Please refer to the experiment process of Group A and Group B (see Fig. 4).

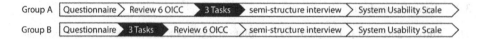

Fig. 4. Comparing the process of Group A and Group B

After introducing the entire experiment and interview process to the participants, the observer read the following instructions to the participants before the task began, "You will see three subjects and datasets later. Please draw a visualization on paper that you think can present the data story. The graph/chart type is not limited, but it must fully express the facts and insights you present to the dataset. It does not need to be very accurate, but it must be able to express the theme you want to present so that your imaginary readers understand. The graph/chart should be drawn in the drawing area and must include a title and graphic elements. After drawing, briefly describe the content of the chart you draw in the story area. We have prepared these tools for you to use freely."

The order of the three tasks is randomly assigned. The participants can mark, calculate, or draw on the dataset. The title must be written in the drawing area, but the position is not limited; the description of the story area is limited to 300 words. The observer conducted semi-structured interviews after the three tasks were completed in order to supplement the participants' insufficient description in the story area. The observer cannot comment on the participants' charts, but they can ask objectively what they want to express.

In addition, the semi-structured interview for Group A contained the questions below:

1. Which Online interactive chart chooser do you like most?
2. What do you think are the pros and cons of the chooser you just selected?
3. Please arrange the six choosers in order of preference.
4. Do you think such choosers will limit the creativity of designers?
5. Do you think choosers can help you create data visualization? Why?

The interview question for Group B replaced the second question and changed it to "Do you think that if you are allowed to use the online interactive chart choosers from the beginning, can they help you draw the chart? Why?" In the final stage, 10 participants completed the SUS usability assessment scale for six online interactive chart choosers.

4   Results

We collected the results from ten participants. Five of Group A referred to OICC in the drawing process, and five of Group B did not refer to OICC. The drawing area contains the chart they hand-drawn and contains the title; the story area contains the text description of the chart. We summarized the types of charts drawn by the participants and mapped them to data relationships and titles. Also, each participant's preferences for the six groups of OICC, SUS (System Usability Scale), and opinions were collected.

4.1 Chart Types and Data Relationship

The observer did not ask the participants to set a target audient for the chart in the description. However, after the task was over, participants were asked who the target audient of the first subject-referendum result was, and they all answered, "the public". The second question, Netflix original series, some people set it as Netflix senior executives, while others want to recommend to audients. The third question is also aimed at the general public.

When the ten participants got the data set, they would first survey the data set and choose which sets of data to use to present the topic in their minds. Group A then referred to the OICC with the highest preference, then conceived the chart and started drawing. Group B, on the other hand, conceived the diagram and drew it directly. When Group A referred to the selected OICC, although they clicked one or two charts to see the explanation, most of the time, it will return to and stay on the first page where all the chart icons can be viewed. The five participants showed that OICC could inspire them but did not choose the specific chart type based on the data relationship corresponding to the topic envisaged in their mind.

All ten participants completed the chart and wrote the title. Group A uses a total of 10 chart types, while Group B uses seven chart types. Three of Group A used different chart types in all three topics, and only one of Group B did not use the chart type repeatedly, but two of Group B continued to use bar charts in the three topics. From Fig. 5 we can see that the data relationships presented in the visual chart are Magnitude and Part-to-Whole as the most, and the bar chart and pie chart are the most on the choice of the chart types.

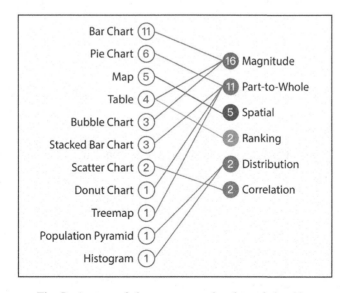

Fig. 5. Amount of chart types mapping data relationships

4.2 Preference for Six OICCs

In the ranking of preferences, participants ranked from favorite to least liked, with six being the favorite and one being the least. The results of the average score, Top 1 is CC02 (4.4 points), Top 2 is CC01 (4.1 points), Top 3 is CC05 (4 points), CC03, and CC04 are both 2.9 points, and CC06 is the lowest with 2.7 points. Among them, four participants chose CC02 as Top 1, another four chose CC05 as Top 1, another one chose CC01, and the other one chose CC06. They describe the advantages of the selected Top 1, which are plentiful, comprehensive, classified, prompted, examples of common mistakes, big pictures, precise information, beautiful graph, proper color matching, good contrast, attractive, clear icons, simple, commentary, and examples. There is a total of fifteen reasons, and there are 11 terms related to practicality and four related to aesthetics. Among them, "classification" is the advantage most people put forward, and it was mentioned five times in total, followed by "clear icons," four times, and "good colors" three times. The shortcomings of CC01 are the weak interaction of web links; CC02 is "improperly typeset (refer to the name of the figure next to the icon)," "no drawing function," "fewer examples," "fewer applications," "not presented data relationship (because it's in the lower half of the page)." In CC05, two people pointed out "no classification," "can't know the usage at a glance," "too many pictures, I don't know what to use for a while." CC06 is "the charts are too small."

4.3 Usability Evaluation of Six OICCs

Ten participants completed the SUS usability assessment scale at the end of the experiment. Whether it is Group A or Group B, the scale is completed while using six OICCs. We use acceptability (Bangor et al. 2008) to describe the SUS score. The unacceptable score is 0 to 51.6 points, and the marginal representative 51.7–71 is an unacceptable range, and the acceptable value is about 71.1 points. Table 3 shows the heat table with three colors of acceptability, as defined in Fig. 6.

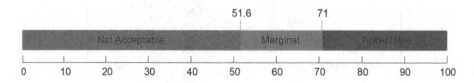

Fig. 6. Acceptability and original SUS score

Table 3. SUS score heat table

Participant ID	CC01	CC02	CC03	CC04	CC05	CC06
01T	42.5	47.5	87.5	65	87.5	72.5
05T	80	55	85	80	92.5	92.5
08T	77.5	67.5	57.5	37.5	70	35
09T	82.5	80	65	52.5	62.5	65
10T	70	90	92.5	45	90	60
02N	50	72.5	65	62.5	77.5	45
03N	35	55	57.5	55	70	40
04N	37.5	37.5	75	62.5	77.5	75
06N	75	80	87.5	40	67.5	75
07N	70	82.5	85	67.5	77.5	62.5
Amount of Acceptable	4	5	6	1	6	4

From the table above, we can see that the total number of "acceptable" that can be obtained for each OICC is in order from CC03, CC05, CC02, CC01, CC06, and CC04. That is to say, CC03 and CC05 are both 60% acceptable. Moreover, an excellent auxiliary tool should make users want to use it often. If we take the average score of the first question, "I think I will be willing to use this website frequently," CC05 average 4.7 is the highest, which is what participants think they would frequently use (see Table 4).

Table 4. SUS Q1 average score

Question	CC01	CC02	CC03	CC04	CC05	CC06
I think that I would like to use this system frequently	3.5	3.6	3.9	2.7	4.7	2.4

During the interview, we asked Group A participants, "Will OICC limit the creativity of charting?" All five answered, "No." "Can OICC assist in drawing?" All five thought they could assist them in drawing charts. Also asked Group B, "If using OICC from the beginning can help them draw three tasks? Four of them thought they could help them, and only one answered," No, because too much style interferes with thinking about the data."

5 Discussion

Among the three sets of data sets, the most common ones are Part-to-Whole, Ranking, and Magnitude. Of the ten participants, only two Group B participants repeated the bar chart three times in three tasks. The remaining eight can draw different types of charts. Bar charts and pie charts are the charts that participants usually see most of the time. Of the chart types drawn by ten participants, these two types also have the most significant number. It also shows that the data types they use are Magnitude and Part-to-Whole. Even if OICCs assisted participants, most of them still chose familiar charts. 01T and 09T stated in the interview that "if there is time, I can refer to CC01" and " "The reason I chose to reference CC06 was because I did not have enough time, and I was familiar with the charts." If more time is given, will participants be able to make full use of those OICCs and carefully refer to the data relationship and chart recommendations? In the future, there can be more in-depth research. Nevertheless, even so, there are still three more chart types in Group A than Group B, and nine out of ten participants also said that OICCs could help them draw charts.

The novice designer's preference for OICC requires more practicality than aesthetics. Because of their aesthetic training, designers have a certain level of requirements for the visual design of the interface. However, under the pressure of time constraints, to complete a task that requires rational thinking and is not familiar with, information and visual clarity are the primary requirements. When OICC has a precise chart classification, it allows users to determine what type to use quickly. Although CC05 is mentioned in terms of "no classification," "cannot know the use at a glance," "too many patterns, and do not know which one to use," these show a common problem, but it is an issue on the operation interface. It categorizes the graphics, and also uses the navigation on the top of the webpage to categorize the graphics in four ways: family, input, function, and shape, and the category will only expand the hidden submenu after clicking the main menu. In twelve minutes, when users first use it, they will ignore the hidden function.

In contrast, CC05 provides a wide variety of charts, even if it has its advantages in visual design. The chart type can be classified according to the different concepts of the user. The idea is good, but the interface is not intuitive. Compared with CC02, CC01, or CC06, the category of the data relationship is directly displayed by the Tab interface component, and the user can directly switch and select.

Preference is a decision made by the participants after a quick review of the OICCs, and the usability evaluations are the results of the participants' evaluation while working through the tasks and taking more time to think. CC01, CC02, CC05 are in the top three rankings for preference and usability. They have some common characteristics, 1) the graphic design and color scheme of the website is planned, and 2) the visual style is consistent. At a glance, the visual experience can attract designers who have received aesthetic training. Although CC03 ranks fourth in preference, the usability evaluation is tied for Top 1 with CC05. CC03, although modest in style, it has the most features in six OICCs. In addition to the chart type description, there are links to actual examples, a list of tools or software that can produce the chart, and a video tutorial introduction. For beginners to visualize charts, it helps a lot.

Based on the evaluation of the participants' preferences and usability evaluations, the difference between the preferences of CC05 and CC02 is only 0.4, and the SUS acceptability is that CC05 is one more than CC02. If we add Peter Morville's [5] "desirable" element (2004) and evaluate it with "I think that I would like to use this system frequently." CC05 will become the OICC that novice designers want to use (Fig. 7).

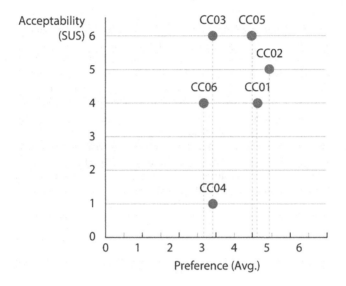

Fig. 7. The SUS acceptability and preference of six OICCs

6 Conclusion and Future Work

Ten participants made 30 charts, using a total of 11 chart types and six data relationships. Participants who refer to OICC can draw more various charts and show their creativity than those who do not. Participants have not seen these six groups of OICC before. CC02, CC01, and CC05 are the top three in evaluating the preferences of OICC, and CC03, CC05, and CC02 are the top three in terms of ease of use. CC05 is not only ranked in the top three in terms of preference and usability, but it is also the reference tool that novice designers want to use frequently in the future.

The practical, beautiful, and clear interface of OICC makes novice designers interested in referencing. At the same time, they also think that by referring to these plentiful materials, they can learn more about data and charts.

Future research work will expand the number of surveys of novice designers, and based on the research results, design a prototype of a visual guide website suitable for novice designers. The design verification of this prototype will be carried out actually to create a visualization guide website for novice designers.

References

Abela, A.: Charts - Extreme Presentation. Accessed 5 Jan 2020. https://extremepresentation.com/design/7-charts/

Bangor, A., Kortum, P.T., Miller, J.T.: An empirical evaluation of the system usability scale. Int. J. Hum.-Comput. Interact. **24**(6), 574–594 (2008). https://doi.org/10.1080/10447310802205776

Few, S.: Visual Business Intelligence – Abela's Folly – A Thought Confuser. Accessed 5 Jan 2020. https://www.perceptualedge.com/blog/?p=2080

Judelman, G.: Aesthetics and inspiration for visualization design: bridging the gap between art and science. In: Proceedings of the International Conference on Information Visualization, vol. 8, pp. 245–250 (2004). https://doi.org/10.1109/iv.2004.1320152

Morville, P.: User Experience Design (2004). Accessed 14 Jan 2020. http://semanticstudios.com/user_experience_design/

Nybro, E., Skolnik, L., Makulec, A.: Data Visualization - An Introduction| Global Health eLearning Center (2015). Accessed 5 Jan 2020. https://www.globalhealthlearning.org/course/data-visualization-introduction

Obie, H.O., Chua, C., Avazpour, I., Abdelrazek, M., Grundy, J., Bednarz, T.: A study of the effects of narration on comprehension and memorability of visualisations. J. Comput. Lang. **52**(April), 113–124 (2019). https://doi.org/10.1016/j.cola.2019.04.006

Tong, C., et al.: Storytelling and visualization: an extended survey. Information (Switzerland) **9**(3), 1–42 (2018). https://doi.org/10.3390/info9030065

The Usability Testessen – An Innovative Framework for Usability Testing in Practice

Hannes Feuersenger[1](✉), Hans-Knud Arndt[1], and Kersten A. Riechers[2]

[1] Otto-von-Guericke-Universität, Universitätsplatz 2,
39106 Magdeburg, Germany
hannes.feuersenger@ovgu.de,
hans-knud.arndt@iti.cs.uni-magdeburg.de
[2] quäntchen+glück GmbH & Co. KG, Mainzer Straße 106,
64293 Darmstadt, Germany
kersten.riechers@qundg.de

Abstract. The knowledge and application of usability methods and practices have not yet found widespread adoption in practice. It is still frequently the case that products are launched on the market that have not been tested for usability once and therefore do not meet the demands and requirements of their customers. This fact seems to be surprising, as customers, especially in the last few years, have developed ever higher demands on the user-friendliness of products and services. Therefore, this paper presents a new framework for testing the usability of products and services - the so-called Usability Testessen. This concept is based on the approach of discount usability engineering developed by Nielsen and is an event that provides a creative and at the same time productive space to test products of several companies free of costs by independent third parties using well-known discount usability methods. Due to the reduction of costs and effort for the preparation and execution of usability tests, this concept is a great advantage especially for small and medium-sized companies and startups, as they usually have to struggle with scarce resources and at the same time high market pressure. In this paper, the individual phases of the Usability Testessen and the stakeholders involved are presented in more detail. A short summary of the key results of a qualitative evaluation should also show that the newly developed concept is very well received in practice.

Keywords: Usability testing · Discount usability · Usability engineering

1 Introduction

While the 20th century was dominated by technology, the 21st century has its focus on the people who have to deal with this technology. Instead of the long-standing mindset that a product is good when it has as many functionalities as possible, the aspect of user-friendliness should become the focus of every product development process. While users are placing ever higher demands on the usability of a product, market developments also show that those companies that think user-oriented and include the

A. Marcus and E. Rosenzweig (Eds.): HCII 2020, LNCS 12200, pp. 97–112, 2020.
https://doi.org/10.1007/978-3-030-49713-2_7

needs of their customers in the development of their products achieve a high level of customer satisfaction and are particularly successful [1].

When testing software for functional errors, for example, it is easy to carry out these tests independently and in some cases even automatically, but testing usability requires more effort and the integration of potential users. Only in this way it is possible to avoid the risk of one's own operational blindness and to satisfy the expectations and needs of customers in the best possible way. According to the motto *test early test often* usability tests should be an essential part of every product development process.

In practice, however, this demand has so far received little attention. Various studies, such as [1–5] show that many companies are still not familiar with the concepts of usability. Especially in small and medium-sized enterprises (SME's) this fact has been increasingly observed [1, 6, 7]. Due to lack of financial resources, limited internal knowledge and low staff capacities, such SME's and startups, which have to deal with the same challenges, find it very difficult to apply known usability methods and thus enable the introduction of an integrated usability engineering [6]. This fact is intensified by the complex appearance of most usability methods, which additionally discourages companies [8]. In addition, there is also the great market pressure that has a negative impact on the companies too. The costs and effort for the coordination and implementation of regular usability tests can often not be handled by SME's and startups.

In this context, the challenge of recruiting motivated and suitable test persons is particularly challenging. Since usability tests usually take place under clinical framework conditions and are also very time-consuming for the test subjects, it is difficult to get people excited about this activity. Furthermore, the long duration of the tests means that there is a risk that the test persons will lose their motivation over the course of the test, which can lead to a decline in the quality of the results [9]. For these reasons, in practice a new product is often brought to market without a single test being carried out on its usability.

In order to avoid the above mentioned situation, the discount usability approach of Nielsen was used in the context of this thesis, as it also addresses the mentioned problems. Based on this approach the concept of the Usability Testessen was developed, which is presented in detail in this paper. Hereby existing methods of usability testing are to be embedded in an innovative, informal, creative and at the same time productive overall context. The Usability Testessen represents an event format, where companies can carry out free usability tests with motivated test persons without extensive coordination efforts. In this way it should be possible for SME's and startups in particular to continuously optimise their products through usability tests in the sense of an agile, iterative development.

The next chapter takes a closer look at the current value of usability in practice. Thereafter the paper deals with the discount usability engineering developed by Nielsen. Thereupon the concept of the Usability Testessen is presented in detail. Thereby a subdivision into the individual phases of the Usability Testessen is carried out. The main part of the paper concludes with a summary of the key results of a qualitative evaluation of the concept. Finally, the contents of the paper are summarized and delimited once again. Furthermore, an outlook on future research regarding the Usability Testessen is given.

2   Usability in Practice

As mentioned in the introduction, the importance of taking the user perspective into account is becoming increasingly important [1]. This refers to the so-called *usability* of a product - i.e. the "extent to which a product can be used by certain users in a certain usage context in order to achieve certain goals effectively, efficiently and satisfactorily" [10].

Despite this fact, in practice a very limited knowledge of usability methods and practices can still be observed. Several studies can also prove this. Within the scope of [1] a comprehensive study with German SME's was conducted. Although more than half of the respondents stated that high usability has been perceived as an important aspect of the company's success for a long time, methods for the optimization of usability are rarely integrated into the product development process [1]. According to the results of [2, 11], a large number of the usability methods developed in research are unknown to almost half of the respondents. It should be emphasized that these results occur although in [2] most practitioners feel a great need for knowledge about usability. This is partly due to the fact that some examples from theory and practice impressively demonstrate the positive effects that the consideration of usability in the development of products can have. Examples of this are shown in [11–14].

However, a look at the usability methods developed in the research reveals a fact that can be identified as the cause for the limited knowledge in practice: A multitude of methods often appears very complex [8]. An example of this is mentioned in [15], where a model, which is supposed to serve the better comprehensibility of a user interaction with a computer, is enriched with approaches of fuzzy logic. Such methods can be regarded as positive achievements in research. For practical application, however, they require too much specific knowledge, so that they are rarely used. The time required and the costs incurred are accordingly estimated to be very high. The resulting obstacle often leads to products not being tested for their usability at all [8].

As described in [6, 7], SME's and startups have an even bigger problem when it comes to adapting usability methods into practice. Many methods and practices are not suitable for these companies because they have limited resources. In addition, researchers provide these companies with few alternatives [6]. This fact is surprising, as politicians, at least in Germany, have already noticed this situation a several years ago and are trying to eliminate the existing problems with subsidies [6].

The iterative execution of tests of the usability and the user experience of a product [11] - so-called *usability tests* - thus seems to be difficult for many companies. The connection between product development and so-called usability engineering, which is required in theory, is rarely used in practice. *Usability engineering* is the methodical way to create the property usability, which should enable a systematic consideration of ergonomic perspectives [16]. Only in this way is it possible to effectively use the potential of knowledge about users for product development [17]. The company Braun, for example, shows how usability engineering can be optimally integrated. In addition to the integration into product development, usability has become an essential part of the company philosophy, which can also be seen in their design process [18].

In contrast, there are also some cases in which, despite usability engineering, products have been developed not having a good usability. One example is the software Microsoft Office 2007. Despite numerous prototypes and many experiments that Microsoft undertook, users were not very satisfied by the new product [19, 20]. The fact that large companies also have problems with the usability of their products shows the great challenges. This is caused by the fact that usability engineering cannot follow a structured, rational process, which results in a product with perfect usability. As usability is about focusing on the human being, and the human being does not only take his actions based on rational motives, but also incorporates emotions and his own preferences, these aspects should also be considered in the context of an integrated usability engineering. This means that when considering usability, the aesthetics and design of a product should also be regarded as important success factors [21]. Finally, this fact makes the challenge of integrating usability into the development of products even more difficult.

3   Discount Usability Engineering

Due to the previously described current situation regarding the consideration of usability in practice and the problems associated with it, a closer examination of the discount usability engineering approach developed by Nielsen has been recommended. In short, this approach assumes that: "In usability, the fastest and cheapest methods are often the best" [22]. Hereby, Nielsen addresses the problems identified in this paper, which can also be seen in Fig. 1, where a comparison of these and the proposed solutions from the discount usability engineering is presented. The reason for this correspondence is the even worse situation of the use of usability at that time. Neither did usability methods find their way into practice [23], nor fundamental principles of good usability were known [24].

Identified Problems in Practice	Proposed Solutions based on Discount Usability Engineering
Usability Testing is costly and time-consuming	Use of intuitive and simplified usability methods
Lack of knowledge regarding usability within companies	
Insufficient integration of usability into the product development process	Education and Propaganda
Testers lose their motivation during traditional usability tests	Short and simple tests outside a laboratory situation

Fig. 1. Comparison of identified problems and proposed solutions according to Discount Usability Engineering

To address these problems, Nielsen uses the following principles as the basis of his discount usability engineering:

- Focus on the users of your product right from the start
- Perform regular empirical measurements of the usability of your product
- Create your product within an iterative design and development process [25]

To ensure that these principles are adhered to, Nielsen has developed special solutions based on his approach.

The problem of high costs and a huge amount of time required to apply most usability methods is an invincible barrier for many companies, especially for SME's and startups [8]. Taking into account the existing gaps in usability knowledge in practice [1–5], it is easy to understand why many companies avoid usability tests. However, to overcome this worst case scenario, Nielsen recommends the use of intuitively accessible, if necessary simplified usability methods [25]. The application of such methods should make it easier for companies to learn about usability and prevent the market launch of non-user friendly products. As a result, companies can improve their knowledge about usability incrementally. The time and monetary expenditure is significantly lower than with traditional usability methods, so that especially SME's and startups can benefit.

Within his approach Nielsen recommends the creation of so-called scenarios and the use of the simplified thinking aloud method. *Scenarios* are a kind of prototype that are limited in their complexity and functionality, so that they can be used for short usability tests [25]. Figure 2 illustrates this once again. The *simplified thinking aloud method* is based on the classical thinking aloud method [26] and does not require the complex recording of the test via video or eye tracking software. However, users still have to express all thoughts and feelings they perceive while testing the product, so that they can be documented [25]. In addition to these two methods, there are also other recommended techniques in the context of discount usability, such as heuristic evaluation, card sorting or walkthroughs [27], which are not further considered in this study.

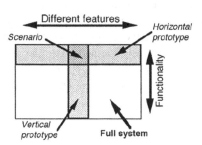

Fig. 2. Creation of a scenario [25]

The integration of usability into the product development process has, as mentioned before, still not taken place in many companies [1, 5]. So far, only a slight increase in knowledge about usability has been noted [4]. In the past, Nielsen already critically noted this fact and therefore recommends considering two aspects in the context of discount usability engineering: All activities to improve usability should have an educational character, so that companies are trained to consider the customer's point of view [28–30]. In addition, these activities should specifically attempt to promote the practical use of usability methods so that attention to this business-critical topic is continuously increasing [31].

Nielsen also recommends a proposed solution to the last problem, i.e. lengthy tests under unattractive laboratory conditions lead to a decrease in the motivation of the test subjects [9]. Discount usability engineering tries to avoid the resulting decrease in the quality of the results by recommending the use of short-term methods. In addition, the tests should be conducted outside of traditional laboratory settings and more in the everyday environments of the test subjects, as these are also closer to the real application of the products [25].

With his discount usability engineering, Nielsen thus follows Voltaire's principle that "the best is the enemy of the good" [32]. Using the best possible methods is useless if they cannot be applied correctly or only with great effort [25]. Companies should therefore prefer to use simpler methods in a first step, which may not yet deliver optimal results, but at least achieve some progress. Based on this, companies can continuously increase their knowledge and consider the use of more complex usability methods, up to the strategic integration of usability into the product development process [25].

4   The Concept of the Usability Testessens

Once the identified problems were countered with the help of Nielsen's discount usability engineering, a transfer into a practically applicable concept of a framework for usability testing was carried out - called the Usability Testessen. In the following section, a distinction will be made between *Usability Testessen in the narrower sense (i.n.S.) and in the broader sense (i.b.S.)*. This only serves to explain the concept in a comprehensible way. Figure 2 is intended to visualize this connection once again.

In a narrower sense, the Usability Testessen is an event that is intended to create a space that is both creative and productive, in order to test the products of several companies using well-known discount usability methods of independent third parties free of costs. In a broader sense, the Usability Testessen also includes the entire organizational process for preparing, evaluating and optimizing the event. As shown in Fig. 3, the concept follows the *Plan-Do-Check-Act (PDCA) cycle* according to Deming and thus aims at continuous improvement [33]. The Usability Testessen i.n.S. represents the execution phase.

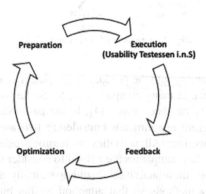

Fig. 3. Usability Testessen in the broader sense (i.b.S.)

The concept of the Usability Testessen is offered voluntarily to all interested parties. The planning, testing and optimization are not carried out centrally by a super-ordinate unit, but decentralized, as there is an independent organizational team for each city in which the event takes place. If several people from one city have decided to establish the concept, they will be given access to the workspace of the Usability Testessen community. This community is an association of people who voluntarily want to help establishing methods and practices of usability in practice. The workspace is divided into a cloud-based repository system for all necessary documents for the preparation, implementation and optimization of the Usability Testessen, a project management tool for communication within the individual organizational teams and between the entire community and a content management system for the maintenance of the shared website. In the following, the Usability Testessen procedure for a particular city is described following the individual phases.

4.1 Preparation

In order to ensure the successful execution of each Usability Testessen, it requires a multitude of preparations, which are carried out by the organization team of the respective city. Figure 4 summarizes the individual steps of this preparation phase graphically.

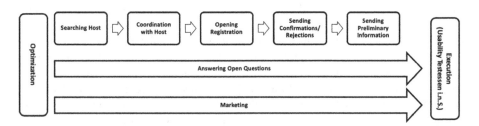

Fig. 4. Procedure for preparing the Usability Testessen

Usually, a Usability Testessen takes place every two months. However, this time frame varies from city to city as the capacities of some organizational teams are limited. Since the Usability Testessen is called a *travelling circus*, which means that each event takes place in a different location, the first activity is to find a suitable host. The host can be any conceivable organization. Ideally, contact to potential hosts can be established during a Testessen. Otherwise, the search is carried out via e-mail enquiries to potential candidates.

Each host's task is to provide innovative rooms in which the Usability Testessen can take place. Usually this is the office of the company or a room belonging to the organization. Together with the organization team it is checked whether the location meets certain requirements, such as the existence of a wifi connection and sufficient space for a minimum number of participants. Following the motto *if there's a problem make a party out of it*, the choice of location explicitly avoids laboratory conditions, as Nielsen recommends with his discount usability engineering [25]. Rather, the varied and innovative locations should increase the creativity, productivity and motivation of all participants. It is also hoped that this variety will reduce the test providers' operational blindness. Furthermore, an increase in the quality of usability tests should be achieved by having the test persons check the products in realistic environments [13, 25]. In addition, the fear that during the usability tests the performance of the test subjects and not the product is tested should be removed.

Besides the location, the host also has to take care of the procurement of catering, i.e. cold drinks and pizza, and provide these to all participants during the Usability Testessen free of charge. The organization team will assist by providing an estimate of the costs based on previous experience. Pizza as food was deliberately chosen, as its diversity means that there is something for every taste and it can also be eaten during the short breaks between the usability tests. The goal behind the provision of free catering is to increase the motivation of all participants while maintaining productivity.

In order to encourage the host to assume the above-mentioned obligations, incentives have also been created for him. On the one hand, he can raise awareness and promote his organization with his innovative facilities and his willingness to voluntarily support other companies in usability testing. He can also continue this in personal contact with the participants during the Usability Testessen. On the other hand, up to three test stations are reserved for the host, where he can test his own products for usability.

After all arrangements with the host have been made successfully, the registration is opened for the test providers and test persons. Thus, anyone who has something to test or would like to test something can register. It does not matter whether the products or services are digital or analogue. Approximately two to three weeks prior to the Usability Testessen, the registration form is deactivated and the selection of the participants takes place. With regard to the test stations, an attempt is made to exhaust the maximum number given by the location. If more test providers than possible have applied, the selection will be based on the quality of their tests. In contrast, the test persons are selected at random. Here, care is taken to ensure that not always the same test persons are selected, so that as many persons as possible can be granted access to the Usability Testessen. The random selection of test persons provides the test stations with feedback from many different perspectives. Target group-specific feedback is deliberately avoided, as the recruitment of target groups would be much more time-consuming. Furthermore, there is also a large number of overlaps in the observation by a heterogeneous user group. Most usability problems relate to the basic handling of certain products by people, which is why the target group is not needed for the Usability Testessen [34]. Thus the principle "the best idea can come from everyone" is valid for the Usability Testessen [18].

Those who have registered will then receive a confirmation or rejection. All the necessary preliminary information is also part of the confirmation. For example, the test providers receive a checklist to help them prepare their test case. With the help of these documents, organizations and test persons who have little knowledge about usability so far are also given the opportunity to participate at the Usability Testessen. The barrier of entrance should thus be lowered and the principle of education fulfilled [28–30]. This fact is particularly desirable with regard to SME's and startups.

As a final step, the organization team prepares all necessary materials for the Usability Testessen. These include name tags, signs for the location or even flow charts so that the test persons know which test stations they have to go to at what time. With the help of these documents, the Usability Testessen is to be structured in such a way that the participants can unleash their creativity without having to deal with comprehension questions.

In addition to these preparation activities, the organization team is also continuously available as contact person for the host, potential test providers and test persons. Open questions can be addressed to the organization team via various communication channels. Next to an optimal coordination of the event, the basic ideas of education and propaganda [28–31] should be passed on through this activity. During the coordination with the stakeholders, common misunderstandings about usability methods and practices can be quickly eliminated. Additionally, the marketing of the Usability Testessen is carried out by the organization team. Especially social media are used, but also classical media, such as magazines, are used so that as many people as possible can be addressed. Participants of the Usability Testessen are also asked to share their impressions and the concept, so that the principle of propaganda [31] can also be followed here.

4.2 Execution - The Usability Testessen i.n.S.

After all the preparatory steps have been successfully completed, the Usability Testessen i.n.S. can be carried out. The process of the Usability Testessen i.n.S. can be described very well by the standardized schedule, which is shown in Fig. 5.

06:00 p.m. – 07:00 p.m.	Onsite Preparation
07:00 p.m. – 07:45 p.m.	Introduction
07:45 p.m. – 07:57 p.m.	Test Round 1
08:00 p.m. – 08:12 p.m.	Test Round 2
08:15 p.m. – 08:27 p.m.	Test Round 3
08:30 p.m. – 08:45 p.m.	Break
08:45 p.m. – 08:57 p.m.	Test Round 4
09:00 p.m. – 09:12 p.m.	Test Round 5
09:15 p.m. – 09:27 p.m.	Test Round 6
09:30 p.m. – 10:00 p.m.	Summary
10:00 p.m. – 11:00 p.m.	Networking

Fig. 5. Procedure of the Usability Testessen i.n.S.

Prior to the official start of the event, some preliminary work has to be done. The organization team will take care of the registration and briefing of the test persons and test providers. They will also set up the location and prepare the technical equipment so that the event runs as efficiently as possible. The test providers must already set up their test stations so that testing can begin immediately after the introduction.

The Usability Testessen then begins with a short welcoming from the host and a presentation by the organization team. In this presentation, the basic idea and history of the Usability Testessen are briefly explained and the advantages of the event for all participants are highlighted. Also part of the introduction is the explanation of the methods used in the tests using an example scenario. Following the basic idea of education [28–30], all participants should also receive a further increase in knowledge. Furthermore, this explanation should guarantee a well organized event. After the end of the introduction, the participants will have the opportunity to eat pizza, to get cold drinks and to talk to each other, so that the motivation increases.

Thereupon the usability tests start. In six test rounds with a duration of twelve minutes each, the test providers are given the opportunity to check their products for their usability. After each round, the test persons change so that each test provider has six different test persons. The number of test subjects was referred to [35], which shows the relationship between costs and benefits in relation to the number of different test subjects. Although it is mentioned in this paper that the best possible cost-benefit ratio is achieved with five test subjects, the sixth test subject is intended to provide a kind of buffer in case a test does not run as expected [35]. Even with six subjects, the benefits are still 100 times higher than the costs. This fact is even more pronounced in the context of Usability Testessen, since the test providers have almost no costs, except for the preparation of their tests. The idea of short-term tests is based on Nielsen's basic assumption that the motivation of the test subjects and thus the quality of the results remain at a high level [25]. The exact duration of twelve minutes, however, crystallized through the continuous improvement process of the usability test eating.

Due to the short duration of the tests, the test stations are asked to create scenarios [25] of their products in order to meet the time schedule. In addition, the Usability Testessen advocates the simplified thinking aloud method, as it can be carried out without additional technology and also allows as much qualitative feedback as possible during the short tests [25]. If the test providers would like to use a different usability method, they have to explain it to the test person independently. In order to maintain motivation during the course of the event, there is a break after three tests, during which all participants can enjoy a snack once again.

After all tests have been carried out, the participants come together and the test providers summarize their findings gained from the event, under the moderation of the organization team. In this way, the test persons indirectly receive feedback that their efforts have been appreciated and represent an added value for the test providers. By ensuring that all participants leave the Testessen with a positive feeling, the effect of the education is increased and the likelihood that the participants will promote the event and especially the establishment of usability within companies is increased too [28–31].

Following this summary, all participants can stay at the location and discuss with each other in a relaxed networking atmosphere. This makes it possible, for example, for test providers to agree on further, more detailed usability tests with test persons who have given positive feedback. It is hoped that open discussions about usability will improve the participants' understanding.

4.3   Feedback and Optimization

The last two phases of the Usability Testessen i.b.S. - the gathering of feedback and the optimization of the concept based on it - are bundled and described in this section. At

The Usability Testessen – An Innovative Framework   107

the end of each Usability Testessen, the participants are asked by the organization team to give feedback on the Testessen, both personally and via e-mail. The aim of this is to continuously optimize the concept.

In order to provide feedback, the participants answer a questionnaire, which is summarized in Fig. 6. The questionnaire is voluntarily and anonymously designed. This is to ensure that negative aspects are also noted and that the feedback is of high quality. When creating the questionnaire, care was taken to keep it as simple as possible so that the barrier to answering is minimal.

Were you present at the last usability test dinner as provider or test person?
How did you hear about the Usability Testessen?
What did you like?
What can we do better next time?
Anything else you want to tell us?
Other event specific questions

Fig. 6. Questionnaire for the optimization of the Usability Testessen

At the beginning of the questionnaire, a distinction is made between test providers and test persons in order to observe whether the individual stakeholders have different needs and concerns. With the help of the second question, it is to be found out through which marketing channels the idea of the Usability Testessen can be spread best. The following two questions serve to identify aspects that are particularly positive or negative. The last question is for other remarks. In addition, the individual organizational teams have the opportunity to add further questions to the questionnaire after each Testessen. For example, the evaluation of a new usability method can be carried out or the quality of the pizza can be queried.

The information obtained is then consolidated by the organization team. Positive aspects can be used for marketing purposes. At the same time, care should be taken to ensure that they continue to leave a positive impression at future Testessen. The negative criticisms must be given the greatest attention. After prioritizing all comments, an agenda for eliminating the negative aspects must be created. The evaluation carried out by the respective city is then made available to the entire Usability Testessen community so that synergy effects can be exploited.

To ensure that the Usability Testessen i.b.S. succeeds, it requires the support of the four stakeholder groups: organization team, host, test providers and test persons. Their tasks and advantages with regard to the Usability Testessen are summarized in Fig. 7 for better comprehensibility.

Stakeholder	Responsibilities	Advantages
Organization Team	• Finding and Supporting Host • Website Maintenance • Coordinate Registrations • Onsite Support • Moderation • Feedback Consolidation • Continuous Improvement	• Free Pizza and Drinks • Networking
Host	• Provide Pizza and Drinks • Provide Location • Greeting	• Marketing and Employer Branding • Free Test Stations • Networking
Test Provider	• Prepare Tests • Run Tests • Consolidate Test Results	• Free Pizza and Drinks • Cheap Usability Tests • Networking
Test Person	• Test Products	• Free Pizza and Drinks • Testing Innovative Products • Networking

Fig. 7. Summary of the tasks and benefits of each stakeholder

5   Evaluation of the Usability Testessen Concept

Since the start of the Usability Testessen in 2013, several qualitative surveys have already been conducted. In this paper only a short overview of the most important results of this evaluation will be given, as a complete report will be published in form of a further paper.

While the Usability Testessen, according to the prototyping approach [36], still started with an untested concept, the event could be continuously optimized thanks to the continuous feedback of all participants. This becomes clear, for example, in the time schedule of the usability tests: In the beginning, they were not limited to a given duration, but varied from test provider to test provider. In addition, test persons were allowed to change their test station on their own. As a result, the tests were disrupted by testers who were already changing. Additionally, the number of test rounds therefore varied. Thanks to the feedback, the duration of the test rounds was limited. Over time, it became clear that twelve minutes is the optimum time to work through a scenario. By standardizing the tests, it was therefore possible to achieve a better comparability between the tests.

Besides the optimization, the evaluation results also confirm the existing lack of knowledge about usability in practice. Both test providers and test persons are regularly testing novices and carry out their first usability tests during the Usability Testessen. This shows that the demand for education and propaganda [28–31] is not unjustified and that the Usability Testessen even complies with it. Especially the marketing of the Usability Testessen is to be emphasized in this context. As can be seen from the press releases and recommendations by the participating persons [37], the principle that one should test as early as possible and as much as possible is becoming increasingly widespread.

Furthermore, the evaluation quickly shows that the concept has met with great acceptance in practice. On the one hand, the continuous expansion of the Usability Testessen community should be mentioned in this context. Meanwhile there are already

29 cities, mainly in Germany but also internationally, which have hosted the Usability Testessen, with an organization team of 143 people. On the other hand, it should be noted that the format is not only accepted by startups and SME's, which usually do not have the necessary resources for larger usability tests. Meanwhile even ten of the DAX companies have taken part in the Usability Testessen, either as hosts, test providers or test persons. Some companies have even integrated regular participation at the Usability Testessen into their product development process and take part at every Testessen in their city.

Finally, the evaluation showed that the test persons are not only participating because of the free catering, but are mainly interested in testing products that are not yet available on the market. The free catering is only a positive side aspect, which, as hoped, leads to additional motivation on the part of the test persons. This shows that the recruitment of test persons is apparently not as difficult as expected. It can therefore be assumed that companies often promote their usability tests unattractively.

6   Conclusion, Limitations and Future Work

In this paper the concept of the Usability Testessen was introduced. It is designed to help eliminate the problems identified in practice regarding the consideration of usability. The developed concept is based on the discount usability engineering, which provides appropriate solutions for the problems found. Thus, the Usability Testessen represents a realization of these solution proposals, which is illustrated in Fig. 8.

Identified Problems in Practice	Proposed Solutions based on Discount Usability Engineering	Usability Testessen Realization
Usability Testing is costly and time-consuming	Use of intuitive and simplified usability methods	• Allocation of costs and effort to different stakeholders • Use of scenarios and simplified thinking aloud
Lack of knowledge regarding usability within companies		
Insufficient integration of usability into the product development process	Education and Propaganda	• Take fear regarding the added value generated by usability tests • Elimination of misbelief
Testers lose their motivation during traditional usability tests	Short and simple tests outside a laboratory situation	• Free pizza and drinks • Continuously changing innovative and informal locations

Fig. 8. Comparison of identified problems, corresponding proposed solutions according to discount usability engineering and realizations within the framework of the Usability Testessen

The use of methods, which can be applied with common sense, should not only reduce costs and time, but also take away the fear that the cost-benefit ratio in usability testing is not worth the effort [38]. This aspect is especially important for SME's and startups. Rather, the Usability Testessen should motivate all participants to continuously expand their knowledge about existing usability methods and practices [25]. Of course, the informal atmosphere should also be helpful in order to promote both the teaching aspect and the idea of marketing usability concepts [28–31].

The Usability Testessen should therefore not only motivate test persons to provide high-quality feedback, but also encourage companies to consider usability as part of their product development. In summary, it can be said that the Usability Testessen is one way getting usability engineering in your organization.

The key results of the evaluation summarized in this paper show that the theoretically developed concept is also positively accepted in practice. One reason for this is that the principle of continuous improvement is pursued and that this allows the needs of the participants to be incorporated into the concept. Based on the results, it can be assumed that the Usability Testessen addresses existing knowledge gaps and has already been able to close them to a certain extent. However, it rather sensitizes companies to think about the integration of their product development process with usability engineering. As mentioned before, a more extensive discussion of the evaluation results was deliberately omitted in this paper due to space problems. For this reason, another paper is already planned, which will deal with a comprehensive evaluation of the concept of the Usability Testessen.

Furthermore it should be mentioned that the Usability Testessen has to be distinguished from other approaches of usability testing. The methods used in the context of the Usability Testessen can only be of a qualitative nature, as the concept is based on just six tests with a duration of twelve minutes each. At the same time, the concept does not claim to replace formal tests under laboratory conditions, although these are critically examined in the context of this paper. Quantitative surveys as well as laboratory studies are very important among the usability methods, but pursue different goals than the methods used in the Usability Testessen. In this context, the deliberate avoidance of target group specific test persons [34] is to be added, which would not be meaningful in another context, but is appropriate in the context of the methods used for the Usability Testessen.

The discount usability engineering approach developed by Nielsen has been partially critically examined in research. Studies such as [39] were considered in the development of the Usability Testessen, but are not discussed this paper, also due to space problems.

During the description of the consideration of usability in practice, the initial situation of SME's and startups was especially emphasized. Due to the insufficient resources available there, the Usability Testessen represents a great added value especially for these companies. Despite this distinction, the concept of the Usability Testessen is not to be considered explicitly in the context of SME's and startups. Although these companies are very satisfied with the event, there are also a multitude of large companies, as already shown in the evaluation, which also attend the Usability Testessen.

Within the scope of future research, it could be considered, in addition to the aspects mentioned above, whether there are other approaches besides discount usability engineering, whose consideration creates an added value for the Usability Testessen. So far, only the use of scenarios and the simplified thinking aloud method are recommended. If companies would like to use other usability methods, they have to consider independently how to implement them in the context of the Usability Testessen. Future research can provide support and determine which (discount) usability methods are additionally suitable for the Usability Testessen.

References

1. Woywode, M., Mädche, A., Wallach, D., Plach, M.: Gebrauchstauglichkeit von Anwendungssoftware als Wettbewerbsfaktor für kleine und mittlere Unternehmen (KMU). Universität Mannheim, Abschlussbericht des Forschungsprojekts (2012)
2. Burmester, M., Laib, M., Benke, I., Minge, M.: Vom ersten Schritt bis zum Dauerlauf. Wie bringt man Usability und User Experience (UUX) ins Unternehmen? In: Mensch und Computer 2019 – Workshopband, pp. 265–268. Gesellschaft für Informatik e.V., Bonn (2019)
3. Laib, M., et al.: User Experience bei Softwareanbietern. In: Mensch und Computer 2015 Tagungsband, pp. 93–102. Oldenbourg Wissenschaftsverlag, Stuttgart (2015)
4. Scoreberlin: Usability Awareness – Umfrage zum Usability Bewusstsein (2002). https://www.scoreberlin.de/usability-artikel/usability-umfrage/. Accessed 31 Jan 2020
5. Shorrock, S.T., Williams, C.A.: Human factors and ergonomics methods in practice: three fundamental constraints. In: Theoretical Issues in Ergonomics Science, vol. 17, pp. 468–482. Taylor & Francis (2016)
6. Hastreiter, I., Heckner, M., Wilhelm, T., Wolff, C.: Software und usability engineering und user experience in kleinen und mittleren Unternehmen. In: Mensch und Computer 2017 – Workshopband, pp. 473–477. Gesellschaft für Informatik e.V., Regensburg (2017)
7. de Lima Salgado, A., Amaral, L.A., Pimenta Freire, A., Fortes, R.P.M.: Usability and UX practices in small enterprises: lessons from a survey of the Brazilian context. In: Proceedings of the 34th ACM International Conference on the Design of Communication (SIGDOC 2016), pp. 1–9. Association for Computing Machinery, New York (2016)
8. Bellotti, V.: Implications of current design practice for the use of HCI techniques. In: Proceedings of the Fourth Conference of the British Computer Society on People and computers IV, pp. 13–34. Cambridge University Press (1988)
9. Nielsen, J.: How many test users in a usability study? (2012). https://www.nngroup.com/articles/how-many-test-users/. Accessed 31 Jan 2020
10. Deutsches Normungsinstitut e.V. (Hrsg.): Ergonomische Anforderungen für Bürotätigkeiten mit Bildschirmgeräten, Teil 11: Anforderungen an die Gebrauchstauglichkeit—Leitsätze, (ISO 9241-11: 1998) Deutsche Fassung EN ISO 9241-11: 1998, S. 4. Beuth Verlag, Berlin/Wien/Zürich, Januar 1999
11. Böttcher, B., Nüttgens, M.: Überprüfung der Gebrauchstauglichkeit von Anwendungssoftware. HMD Praxis der Wirtschaftsinformatik 50, 16–25 (2013). https://doi.org/10.1007/BF03342065
12. Landauer, T.K.: The Trouble With Computers: Usefulness, Usability, and Productivity. Bradford Books. MIT Press, Cambridge (1996)
13. Bossert, J.L.: Quality Function Deployment: A Practitioner's Approach. Quality and Reliability, vol. 21. ASQC Quality Press, Milwaukee (1991)
14. Zerfaß, A., Zimmermann, H.: Erfolgsfaktor Usability. In: Zerfaß, A., Zimmermann, H. (eds.) Usability von Internet-Angeboten – Stuttgarter Beiträge zur Medienwirtschaft, Nr. 10, pp. 5–8 (2004)
15. Karwowski, W., Kosiba, E., Benabdallah, S., Salvendy, G.: Fuzzy data and communication in human-computer interaction: for bad or for good. In: Salvendy, G., Smith, M.J. (eds.) Designing and Using Human-Computer Interfaces and Knowledge Based Systems, pp. 402–409. Elsevier Science Publishers, Amsterdam (1989)
16. Sardonick, F., Brau, H.: Methoden der Usability Evaluation: Wissenschaftliche Grundlagen und praktische Anwendungen, 3rd edn. Verlag Hofgrebe, Bern (2016)

17. Löffler, J., Polkehn, K., Hüttner, J.: Erfolgreiche Usability & UX in Unternehmen Thesen und Erfolgsfaktoren zu Usability/UX-Prozessen, -Strategie und Change. In: Brau, H., Lehmann, A., Petrovic, K., Schroeder, M.C. (eds.) Tagungsband UP13, pp. 22–25. German UPA e.V., Stuttgart (2013)
18. Braun GmbH (eds.): Design for what matters, Kronberg (2018)
19. WinFuture: Office 2007: Der lange Weg zur neuen Oberfläche. https://winfuture.de/news,38052.html4. Accessed 12 Mar 2008
20. Hülsbömer, S., Dirscherl, H.-C.: Die Geschichte von Microsoft Office: Word, Excel, Access (2019). https://www.pcwelt.de/ratgeber/Microsoft-Office-Mit-einer-Maus-fing-alles-an-6091613.html. Accessed 31 Jan 2020
21. Wilhelm, T.: Visuelle Designer sind Künstler und Handwerker. https://www.nutzerbrille.de/visuelles-design/. Accessed 31 Jan 2020
22. Nielsen, J.: Fast, Cheap, and Good: Yes, You Can Have It All (2007). https://www.nngroup.com/articles/fast-cheap-and-good-methods/. Accessed 31 Jan 2020
23. Milsted, U., Varnild, A., Jørgensen, A.H.: Assuring the quality of user interfaces in system development (in Danish). In: Proceedings NordDATA 1989 Joint Scandinavian Computer Conference, pp. 479–484 (1989)
24. Gould, J.D., Lewis, C.H.: Designing for usability: key principles and what designers think. Commun. ACM **28**, 300–311 (1985)
25. Nielsen, J.: Guerrilla HCI: using discount usability engineering to penetrate the intimidation barrier. In: Cost-Justifying Usability, pp. 245–272. Academic Press, Inc. (1994)
26. Ericsson, K.A., Simon, H.A.: Protocol Analysis: Verbal Reports as Data. The MIT Press, Cambridge (1984)
27. Maurer, F., Ghanam, Y.: Discount Usability Testing (2008)
28. Perlman, G.: Teaching user interface development to software engineers. In: Proceedings Human Factors Society 32nd Annual Meeting, pp. 391–394 (1988)
29. Perlman, G.: Teaching user-interface development. IEEE Softw. **7**, 85–86 (1990)
30. Nielsen, J., Molich, R.: Teaching user interface design based on usability engineering. ACM SIGCHI Bull. **21**, 45–48 (1989)
31. Nielsen, J.: Big paybacks from 'discount' usability engineering. IEEE Softw. **7**, 107–108 (1990)
32. Voltaire, F.M.A.: Dictionnaire Philosophique (1764)
33. Deming, W.E.: Out of the Crisis: Quality, Productivity and Competitive Position. University Press, Cambridge (1986)
34. Nielsen, J.: Why You Only Need to Test with 5 Users (2000). https://www.nngroup.com/articles/why-you-only-need-to-test-with-5-users/. Accessed 31 Jan 2020
35. Nielsen, J., Landauer, T.K.: A mathematical model of the finding of usability problems. In: Proceedings of the INTERACT 1993 and CHI 1993 Conference on Human Factors in Computing Systems (CHI 1993), pp. 206–213. Association for Computing Machinery, New York (1993)
36. Richter, M., Flückiger, M.D.: Usability und UX kompakt – Produkte für Menschen, 4th edn. Springer, Heidelberg (2016). https://doi.org/10.1007/978-3-662-49828-6
37. Pressebereich Usability Testessen. https://usability-testessen.org/presse/. Accessed 31 Jan 2020
38. Nielsen, J.: Return on Investment for Usability (2003). https://www.nngroup.com/articles/return-on-investment-for-usability/. Accessed 31 Jan 2020
39. Faulkner, L.: Beyond the five-user assumption: benefits of increased sample sizes in usability testing. Behav. Res. Methods Instrum. Comput. **35**, 379–383 (2003)

Rich Media 2.0: A Methodology to Enhance Media Information Construction for Creating a Better User Experience

Jie Hao[1]([✉]), Chengxing Pan[2], and Enxin Zhang[2]

[1] Beijing Institute of Fashion Technology, No. 2 East Yinghua Street,
Chaoyang District, Beijing, China
jhaohj@126.com
[2] Wukolab, No. A9-1, GeeDee International Innovation Center,
798 Art Zone, Chaoyang District, Beijing, China

Abstract. With the development of technology, there are more and more emerging new definitions in circulation. For instance, a definition of Rich Media has been created, one which does not take a specific form for internet communication media. Rich Media refers to the methods of information transmission through animation, sound, video, and interactive mediums. Such a social phenomenon reveals people's reactions and the way they explore between technology and information transmission. This, in turn, reflects the combination of information transmission and technology required to create a better user experience. Based on this phenomenon and our current situation, the current definition of Rich Media has its limitations. Such limitations often lead to the over-acceptance of new technologies. Whenever the new technology appears, people try to apply it to every object without considering whether it is suitable or not. It is important therefore to pay attention to the new technology. The methodology proposed here can help build up information construction to verify whether a better user experience is achieved. This paper explores argues for this efficient methodology – Rich Media 2.0, a methodology to enhance Media information construction to create a better user experience.

Keywords: Information construction · User experience · Service design · Design process

1 Introduction

With the advent of the 5G era, information has skyrocketed, and the diversified development of communication channels has been promoted. Information transmission can no longer be limited to the dissemination of information to designated objects, but rather it achieves multiple types of interactive information transmission through multiple media. In this context, the designer acts as a bridge for information conversion and tries diversified communication paths to form sufficient media information to achieve a positive user experience. The diversification of information has enabled the design to evolve from problem-solving to constructing a sound service system before the problem emerges. Any nascent problems that have emerged have been resolved from

© Springer Nature Switzerland AG 2020
A. Marcus and E. Rosenzweig (Eds.): HCII 2020, LNCS 12200, pp. 113–129, 2020.
https://doi.org/10.1007/978-3-030-49713-2_8

the perspective of the overall service system. From information design to interaction design, the design approaches the users step by step. The combination of a variety of technologies also helps to efficiently screen, refine, and summarize within the context of an enormous amount of information.

Designers have continued to explore application scenarios in various industries under the development of new technologies. Various types of technology and equipment continue to intervene in real life and widely assume service roles in our society. As new definitions of smart cities, smart manufacturing and smart agriculture continue to emerge, designers have gradually perfected various design projects to ensure positive user experience and feedback. Design is more and more valued for its unique value, and the continuous improvement along with the development of design make the boundaries of design continue to widen. Will the focus of different aspects of the design process have an impact on user experience? A complete project has undergone different cycles from zero to completion, such as technical limitations, even staffing changes, and so on, so it may result that the completed project is in line with the initial expectation: as M. Eigen states,

"It is important to understand that this structure is iterative in its approach. This means that at every stage of a service design process, it might be necessary to take a step back or even start again from scratch. The single but very important difference being in ensuring that you learn from the mistakes of the previous iteration" [1].

However, time cannot stagnate, so how to ensure the accuracy of previous information over time, moreover, whether that information has undergone predictable and unpredictable changes. The methodology that tests the value of current information is increasingly needed.

At the same time, with the rapid development of science and technology, more and more cultures and education industries have adopted emerging technologies in order to solve problems. China has a population of 1.3 billion and embraces an extremely complicated user situation. Adopting traditional design and evaluation methods will make the culture and education industries involved in complex social issues and issues relating to human nature. In the standard design and evaluation phases, methods such as user interviews and behavior observations are often utilized. The process is usually costly and have a long cycle. The changeability of the interviewees may cause a bottleneck in the rapid and effective evaluation of service systems. Studying and evaluating the user's operation time, cognitive modes, behavioral habits, error rate, amenability, and degree of satisfaction will help designers observe user experience, products, environment and service details, and further, obtain much information in the process.

Challenges facing designers:

1: How to create an extensible evaluation system for stakeholders?
2: How to ensure that the service content is sufficient under the premise of meeting the feasibility and the needs of customers?
3: How to effectively deal with participants' feedback during the design process, and turn the information into a productive design force in a timely and accurate manner?
4: How to strengthen the construction of media information to update the design to obtain a better user experience?

2 Purpose

In This paper is based on an in-depth interview and discussion from the perspective of the designer. This paper abstracts the critical elements of the whole design process from multiple design projects. Furthermore, it constructs the nodes of the design process as the methodology of Rich Media 2.0 basic structure.

We were inspired by the hypercycle structure of Manfred Eigen, which functions as follows: "If we ask for a physical mechanism that guarantees the continuous evolution of a translation apparatus, hypercyclic organization is a minimum requirement. It is not sufficient - though necessary - that the information carries involved are of a self-replicative nature. If we analyze the conditions of hypercyclic organization we immediately see their equivalence to the prerequisites of Darwinian selection. The latter is based on self-reproduction which is a kind of linear autocatalysis. The hypercycle is the next higher [sic] level in a hierarchy of autocatalytic systems. It is made up of autocatalysts or reproduction cycles which are linked by cyclic catalysis, i.e. by another superimposed auto-catalysis. Hence a hypercycle is based on non-linear (e.g. second or higher order) autocatalysis." [2] On the one hand, the design process is made up of many different elements and links. While performing its duties, each should take into account the overall process. Moreover, on this basis, design is evolved. On the other hand, the individual information of each link needs to achieve "autocatalysis." [2] That is, "autocatalysis", as a real-time information monitoring tool, can determine the positivity or negativity of feedback information through visualization of the audience's emotions and can enable all the design links to have pure feedback - without interfering factors - thus establishing an improved direction. In this way, in-depth research and creation of effective tools will enable not only the design process to be a virtuous circle, but also all the designed links can capture and update information in real-time.

3 Rich Media 2.0

Rich Media 2.0 is a methodology to strengthen the construction of media information and hence to create a good user experience. This methodology is used to test the real feedback of users. It is a hypercycle model that collects information. We can understand the users' emotional changes, get feedback, and optimize the design through the induction device in order to ensure the effectiveness of the service content. We turn the uncontrollable perceptual service into the information data through the observation of psychological and emotional changes according to user behavior. From social phenomena to life trends, from art installations to cultural and educational design, various languages from different industries are trying to define the concept of human-centred design, which is called Rich Media 2.0. The cases we have carried out below reflect the current attempts of designers to develop this concept.

Case 1: A Intangible Cultural Heritage in China

This intangible cultural heritage in China is a palace architecture built in period of the Ming Dynasty. Now it is a museum of classics, calligraphy and painting. Since 2008, the museum began to display numerous exhibits of calligraphy and painting of national treasure in batches, some of which were not displayed due to site restrictions. For example, if a scroll painting of more than 10 m is rolled up, it is easy to store, but its display space is required to be exigent. When initiating this project, the problem to be solved was to use art technology to make an open-exhibition of painting and calligraphy in a proper way and in a limited space. As a museum of calligraphy and painting, the first task was to make art and cultural education more accessible; to design a new way of exhibiting in order to eliminate the gap between visitors and exhibits.

Based on the above background, we found out that the main problem faced, as in an initial survey, was that the exhibition's rationale regarding the collected works was relatively simple, such as there being a requirement to exhibit according to the classification of dynasties. The main goal of the museum was to become a visitor-oriented cultural organization. Its aim was to focus on the visitors, and improve the content category and way of visiting after understanding the real experience of visitors through researching their visiting routes.

Furthermore, through design scenarios and service roleplay, we could understand the users' behavior from their own perspective and gain a full picture of their mindset. Therefore, visitors were classified according to their purposes: experts, students and tourists. Moreover, we sorted out the relationships of stakeholders, and asked: what can we do for them? How could they give us feedback? We were able to test the impact on service quality through various factors. The museum necessitates the provision of a relatively dark window environment for the protection of ancient calligraphy and paintings, and to display them by stages and by categories. At the same time, we collected information and sorted the key information from research through visitor interviews and questionnaires. For example, Expert A offered a piece of information about the scene light being dark, the exhibits' window being far away, and the viewing capability not being very good; Student B wanted to have an extraordinary explanation of the painting and calligraphy; Tourist C needed more cultural information.

Overall, designers made the reconstruction based on diversified media information in an iterative way to provide an updated solution. We redesigned the service blueprint and visitors' emotional visiting map, creating an independent and neutral methodology. We redesigned the museum through the following three points. First, as shown on the left side of Fig. 1, the digital analysis guide function was provided, which can zoom to three times of the original painting to help visitors to see the original painting more closely and clearly. Second, as shown on the right side of Fig. 1, the methodology allowed a high degree of freedom and expansibility. It could reasonably arrange the different needs of visitors within the visiting service so that visitors could draw virtual paintings themselves and transfer them to mobile phones based on the principle of Chinese traditional painting. Third, digital analysis is provided. Visitors who enjoy this kind of service can have a deeper analysis of the content, including the translation of ancient characters, the background context of the time of the works' creation, the explanation of the composition of the painting and the making process of the painting. Through the above three points, the iterative updating of information was improved. On the whole, we were able to strengthen the human-computer interaction experience, expand the direction of the new service, and make the interactive users' map, which is how we make users become designers too. Moreover, we were able to improve participation in flexible ways.

Fig. 1. (left) The process of translating ancient Chinese characters by touch screen. (right) A self-coloring process to create ancient paintings anew.

However, user requirements will change with time, and the change of information level caused by time is worthy of attention, an issue that will be the core for improving the next step of design. The requirements of the users for the first experience will be different from those for the second or further experiences. However, the content of experience for the user who has experienced visiting many times is not updated in time, and our design should consider this information transformation. This shows the importance of this Rich Media 2.0 methodology. Through Rich Media 2.0, users' emotions can be monitored in real time and essential information can be found to make a redesign.

Case 2: Regeneration Plan of Old Town in Beijing

Located in Xicheng District, Beijing, the old town covers an area of about 37 hectares. Its history can be traced back to the Yuan Dynasty, and it lasted through the Ming and Qing Dynasties. It is mainly composed of the former residences of celebrities, with a temple at the core. The whole cultural area of the old town in Beijing was without protection or promotion. After understanding the background, we underwent a process of research through contextual interviews and storyboards to collect user in-formation and understand the expectation of tourists here. We prioritized these expectations and built "a day in the life", and then used that as the basis for the creation of a blueprint for tourists.

As a consequence of this research, the central axis of this service gradually appeared: we needed to provide users with a quick guide to discover the profound historical background and rich cultural features of the region. We provided services through APP to gain the maximum contact point with tourists, as shown in Fig. 2. We provided a digital guide of services that users may need during their journey, including ancient buildings, former residence of celebrities, traditional food. We also established a scoring system rating places to visit. In the ancient building area, the AR function of the APP could be used to combine the virtual digital image with the actual scene, making the explanation and guide service more intuitive. For example, the ancient building photographed by AR will virtually restore what was happening at that time.

Fig. 2. Finding popular locations through the application's AR capabilities

After the APP had been used, we conducted a follow-up visit for users, and discovered that the knowledge of history and culture was boring for tourists. As an opportunity for improvement, we provided a platform that allowed the residents to tell the story in the APP. With the advancement of time and the increase of visitor flow, the difficulty of auditing and the cost of human resources was getting higher and higher. After reassessment, we cancelled this service. In order to find out what motivated people to use the APP and then combine it with the current entertainment experience, once again, we focused on tourists. How to integrate tourists with the service itself - how to find common ground? To increase attention and relevance, we attempted to mark the scenes that had been filmed in the region in the APP, and then users could find matching scenes.

Overall, we are considering what services we can provide to customers at the functional level. Is it usually difficult to motivate visitors while providing customer service? How to stimulate users to use our services first when they have many alternatives? We need to think about all these questions. As time goes on, media information is presented in a more and more diversified way. It is particularly important to pay attention to the fact that information of such historical and cultural areas changes in real time. The protection of the area does not mean that it is divorced from the surroundings, but protecting it does mean finding a combination of new design products and regional planning.

Case 3: Cocoa Bean Experience Day
In 2017, Shanghai University of Science and Technology held a three-day cocoa themed activity experience day to cultivate the learning interest of 8–10-year-old pupils. What needs to be highlighted is how to teach students to learn the content of extra-curricular learning materials through new media, and how to cultivate students' interest in learning. According to the research, the form of exhibition, explanation and teaching cannot stimulate students' interest. We focused on improving the activity service itself, aiming to combine the interests of children, expand the possibility of teaching methods, and improve the learning efficiency. We used contextual interviews and storyboards to collect insights from teachers, parents, and children. We found that children now prefer to use mobile phones or iPads to experience digital services after class, and that more interaction and animation feedback can attract their attention. Moreover, parent-child interaction to complete the learning task together can improve

the learning experience of children. We tried to visualize the key points of knowledge in the textbook and show them dynamically, and connect the teaching knowledge points through games.

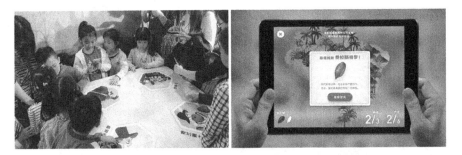

Fig. 3. Learning about cocoa beans through interactive games

The user interface with touch control may generate information exchange as shown in Fig. 3. Diversified presentation is a way that students today accept at an earlier stage. The changes in our times create the distinct characteristics of students. Their focus, daily life style and hobbies are also different. We need to continually reflect and grasp the trend of the times and update the service contact points to meet the current needs and achieve the service goals. It is obvious that the methodology is crucial: one which can monitor users' emotions in real time to feedback information in order to determine design work at a higher stage.

Case 4: APP of the Traditional Culture Museum

In early 2013, the museum launched the APP project in order to popularize the knowledge of cultural relics. The historical data was presented digitally. Although there are essential differences between digital presentation and cultural relics, the former offer easier means of preserving relics and disseminate them.

Based on the above background, the museum can receive 15 million tourists every year. Through the app display, the cultural treasures of the museum will be presented to more Chinese more efficiently. How to choose cultural relics to display and promote? How to explain them in the app? These are the first things we needed to consider. We used the Shadowing Plan to observe visitors to the museum. The Plan, combined with the situational interview, revealed that many visitors had deep feelings for the auspicious beasts on the building and at the gate of the palace. Although many did not know what they were, they still took photos of them. We tried to use auspicious animals to find a clue through the history of cultural relics. We found that our ancestors had used auspicious animals as decorative patterns since ancient times, including flying in the sky, climbing on land and swimming in the sea. We connected these mythical animals and used them as an opportunity to display cultural relics, guiding users to understand cultural knowledge. Through written text and text decoration, we drew a set of auspicious animals by hand, and explained them according to relevant cultural relics stories, and combined these with the actual location of the museum's icon to attract tourists to find auspicious animals on the spot.

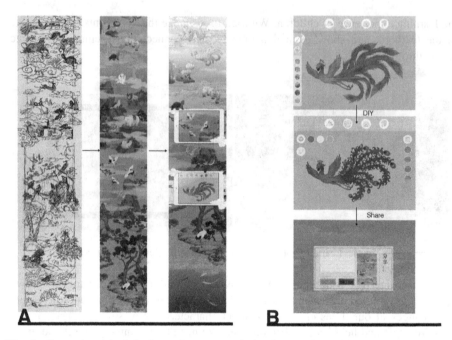

Fig. 4. Group A on the left shows the connected visual map of auspicious animals. And the relationship between buildings and cultural relics. Group B on the right shows the interaction application.

As soon as the APP was launched, the majority of users liked it, and they also asked for derivative products. We took this opportunity to contact the relevant government sector, to launch a series of derivative products, and provided DIY functions to create auspicious animal models, including replaceable parts such as eyes, horns, scales, feathers, head crowns, etc., which were drawn according to the real data shown in Fig. 4. Each detailed part had a prototype, allowing the visitors to customize their own auspicious animal cultural relics. On reflection, we were able to provide expandable services and maintain individual autonomy, so that users could decide the time and intensity of experience according to their actual needs.

Case 5: Digital Marketing Construction of a Jewelry Brand in Beijing International Trade Mall

China International Trade Yintai jewelry concept store is a pioneering practice in China's new retail era. This brand focuses on the new concept of "jewelry personalization": providing each customer with the most suitable jewelry products. The main obstacle to the initial growth of the brand lies in the experience of the service path. There are deficiencies in customer value identification, integration and the practicability of the brand.

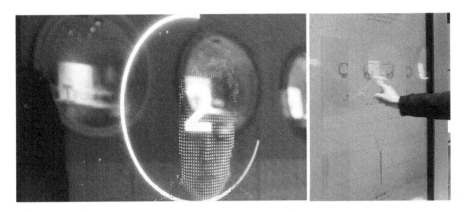

Fig. 5. (left) Facial recognition. (right) Jewelry recommended according to the face shape according to the DATA of Facial recognition.

Based on the above research, we decided to improve the user experience. How to provide customers with the most suitable jewelry products? We focused on how users chose their jewelry and extracted a series of keywords through interviews and insights, including matching temperament, light convenience, etc. Then we put forward the concept of a face jewelry service shown in Fig. 5. The establishment of face jewelry is not just to develop a product, but also to carry out marketing and sales work, in the anticipation that designers become a part of the business and solutions are found together with customers. Starting from the key points of users' attention, we recommended appropriate headwear through the camera to identify users' face shape, hairstyle, and expected weight size so that users could realize that each piece of jewelry should have a unique emotion and become the wearer's self-expression and spiritual strength. We tried to create a product recommendation that could match the user's look and facial features in real time, which, in turn, would expand the Rich Media 2.0 framework.

4   Characteristics of Rich Media 2.0

In addition to all the strategies above, the design process itself proved a way of finding the critical points of redesign after the design was completed. We were then able to integrate the redesign into the methodology, namely, Rich Media 2.0., as shown in Fig. 6.

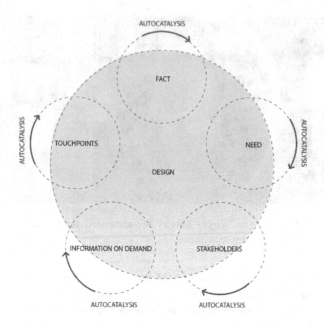

Fig. 6. The construction model of Rich Media 2.0.

4.1   Fact

According to Cambridge dictionary the meaning of fact is 'something that is known to have happened or to exist, especially something for which proof exists, or about which there is information' [3].

The design process is built by facts such as atmosphere, time, events, common sense, space and factors.

4.2   Need

During design project the need influenced by all participants such as provider, user and designer related to function, purpose and service.

4.3   Stakeholders

Stakeholders refers to all associates of a complete project. Status, relevance, balance and value were used to analyze the interaction among different stakeholders.

4.4   Touchpoints

Touchpoints mean the connection between user and service, which happens consciously and unconsciously, and a number of ways to communicate between them.

4.5   Information on Demand

The strategy of information on demand allows the audience to determine the timing, type, and intensity of the media service they participant in.

4.6 Autocatalysis

An essential part of Rich Media 2.0. is a real-time information-monitoring tool. It can judge the positivity or negativity of feedback information through the visual visualization of the visitor's emotions, meaning the design link produces feedback to establish improvement in future directions. That is, in the design process chain, each link can carry out information value tests and strengthen the authenticity of user feedback, in order to promote the higher cycle of the design chain that, in turn, can improve the design and user experience.

Secondly, emotion [4], self-expression produced in the process of human contact and interaction with things, is a feeling state of cognition and behavior that is inspired and integrated by neural circuits, response systems. With the development of technology and computer technology, emotion recognition based on image recognition and physiological signal analysis has gradually evolved into a mature field of emotion research. In the model of Rich Media 2.0 methodology, we propose that users' emotional feedback can be used to assist the design work in every link, that is, through the results of feedback, it can help designers improve the service design in the process. This self-cycling program not only emphasizes the visualization process of emotion but also, more importantly, links the positive and negative aspects of user emotion with changes in time. Emotion is a kind of internal subjective experience, but when emotion occurs, it is always accompanied by some external performance. This kind of external performance reveals some behavior characteristics that can be observed. People's facial expression shows various emotional states through the changes of eye muscles, facial muscles and mouth muscles. People's eyes are best at communicating. Different eye movements can express people's different emotions and feelings. The change of mouth muscles is also an important clue to express emotions, for example, when hateful, "gnashing teeth" and when nervous, "with open mouth" [5]. This way also makes it possible to judge the emotional state of a person by observing the changes.

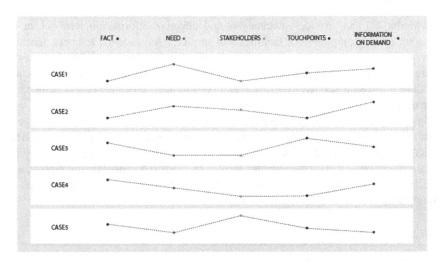

Fig. 7. Evaluation of the Listed Cases by Rich Media 2.0 Mode

Based on the above cycle, autocatalysis is the driving force of the higher cycle. The construction of the framework improves the construction of media information in the design process. Autocatalysis, as the core link, promotes the whole design process chain to find problems and catalyze them so they become a more advanced infinite cycle. It monitors emotions in real time to gain real feedback information that can improve the design. By extracting the features of Rich Media 2.0 and applying it to grounded theory, the following picture shows the framework of its construction mode, and provides a visual analytical method for people, as shown in Fig. 7. As can be seen from the above picture, in the design process, the information fluctuation is presented, which shows the degree of deviation from the original information reality in each design link. The selected cases all present a wavy line, and all need to have the methodology to build the construction of media information. Furthermore, the auto-catalytic effect of autocatalysis is used to show that the prototype of the ideal model may achieve a more stable and balanced route in the future.

5 Constructing Rich Media 2.0

Where should Rich Media 2.0 usefully be applied? First of all, the information will change as time goes on, and autocatalysis will be triggered by re-examining the real feedback of information in each link of the design process. Autocatalysis is used to monitor various emotional states of people. We have a fundamental emotional classification. Most studies tend to agree that there are at least six basic emotions: happiness, anger, fear, sadness, disgust and surprise [6]. It makes the design process carry on effective information reconstruction and recirculation. Conscious or unconscious emotions can give real feedback to the interactive links, which can be widely used in the expansion of the service field. Some are listed as follows:

5.1 Offline Interactive Facilities and Services

Rich Media 2.0 can provide autocatalysis and effective information feedback at the beginning of the completion of facilities and services. As students, teachers, teaching materials, experience methods and social systems change with the service time, just as in case 3, only providing functional solutions is the bottom line to meet the needs, and providing a pleasant service experience can help us gain confidence, and helps us to know ourselves. As the carrier of information and the kind of service are changing with the times, we need to find ways to match the development of the times and the age of users, and to marry these with the content of the experience, such as in the Cocoa Bean project, mining the case of active experiences of 10–13-year-old children, and applying it to teaching contexts to achieve better service purpose. The out-standing significance of Rich Media 2.0 is to excavate a good cycle of evaluation and guidance services for testing offline interactive facilities and services.

5.2   Virtual Information Construction

Digital devices have become an important part of the current social information dissemination process. The convenience of information transmission and the information overload require efficiency and convenience of information construction and screening. Rich Media 2.0 is used to evaluate the location and rationality of on-demand information in the information service chain, therefore re-evaluating the user service experience. For example, in the case 4, it is observed that tourists are interested in auspicious beasts at this stage. We take this as the starting point for service design to meet the trend of the times and users' expectations. No matter what medium or method is used, the service provider determines what consumers can see and how to see it. We need to provide a complete user-initiated content production method to let users begin to intervene in content production. In this way, there is a move from the provider fully leading to the consumer also being involved in production; a move that lets users decide the time and intensity of experience according to their actual needs.

5.3   Digital Exhibition

How to present the information elements appropriately? The application of the digital exhibition maximises the service expectation of users. Rich Media 2.0. has brought about a new role for the value chain, and a redefining of the role and relationship of participants from all sides, so that the presentation mode is not divorced from reality and can be applied to new digitalization. For example, in the case of jewelry brand – the digital marketing construction of Beijing International Trade mall in case 5 - we let customers become members of the design link so they could jointly realize brand value, monitoring and analysis of user behavior in real time and thus accurately feedback their needs.

5.4   Three-Dimensional Urban Structure

Urban public life involves many participants, such as those in engineering, economy, environment, transportation, communication, education, medical treatment, etc. The service field is complex; the changing needs of users and the actual use environment will affect the service journey. By re-examining the relationship between knowledge and concepts in various fields, it is easy to highlight the breakthrough of the project and obtain new ideas to optimize the current situation. For example, in the regeneration plan of old town in Beijing case 2, providing a channel for users to communicate with each other helps to activate the whole regional service experience. With the continuous promotion of services, users' demands for services will change through the process of experience. It is possible to use Rich Media 2.0 to pay attention to this change and explore the multi-level of urban structure.

6 Testing Model

Thanks to the rapid development of the Internet, Internet companies have launched digital services such as virtual products. To ensure the maturity of such virtual products, they will be tested, or their trial versions will be launched. As with online members, there will be trial versions at the initial stage to provide customers with short-term exclusive services. The advantage is that this allows members to enjoy specific offers or exclusive products. This kind of virtual membership product is conducive to industry standardization and clarity of copyright.

Fig. 8. The Interface of Iqiyi.

Recently, the novel adaptation of the ancient costume drama "Celebrating the Rest Year" was popular on iqiyi.com, and was sought after by many people. Iqiyi website launched VVIP service [7]. 'VVIP' means advanced on-demand, that is, based on a VIP watching six episodes first, members were able to watch six more episodes if they paid another 50 CNY as shown in Fig. 8. Therefore, when members realized there was an additional payment, it caused public outcry on the Internet. More than 4 W pirated links increased. The official media of the People's Daily said that this kind of service was an infringement of the rights and interests of consumers. Even as a trial version of the service, it harmed the brand on the network. For the interpretation of user sentiment, we used a combination of discrete model and dimensional model [8]. Six basic emotional states [9] were expressed in a dimensionalized way as shown in Fig. 9.

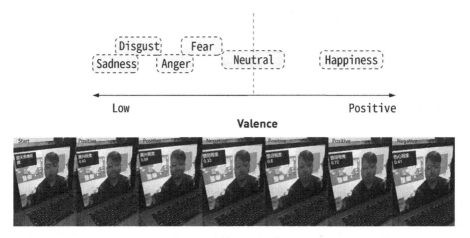

Fig. 9. (up) Construction of autocatalysis analysis model and (down) test

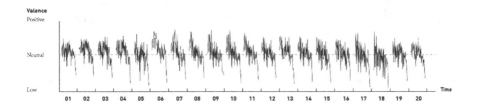

Fig. 10. Evaluation of the 20 participants by autocatalysis analysis model

For this situation, we tried to test with Rich Media 2.0 as shown in Fig. 10. On the one hand, real-time monitoring tools were used to check the problems. On the other hand, we were also able to deduce the solution according to the curve of emotional fluctuation. We chose people from different backgrounds who had not watched the film to participate in the experience. They watched with a VIP account until the last episode of the permission was available. The pop-up recommendation window of VVIP service would then pop up. According to the records, all 20 participants had fluctuating emotions at this time. Nine of them chose to close the page within five seconds. Every time the users interact with the information, they will have emotional fluctuations because of the pictures, words and other information in the service. This kind of emotion is the psychological feedback of customers' contact with products and services. The relationship between emotional fluctuation and time can form valuable information feedback of the user experience. Receiving emotional information from several different periods of the program will further help research and create an accurate and efficient database. According to the mood fluctuation chart, the problem-solving direction is not limited to the following two directions: firstly, a reasonable range of VVIP costs, and secondly, the role and permission assignments.

Ultimately, Iqiyi launched VVIP virtual products to enhance user experience. However, in the early stage of the trial version, Rich Media 2.0 was used as the testing methodology, reducing social impact. Through this, we were able to understand the user's emotions and psychology, and improve the project redesign.

7 Conclusion

This paper proposes a methodology for objectively evaluating user experience, which could be considered as a testing tool for information deviation caused by time evolution during the construction of media information. It is called Rich Media 2.0. Based on the designer research and the concept analysis of related cases, six elements of the design process are extended: need, fact, touchpoint, stakeholders, information on demand, autocatalysis. In addition, the applicable industries of four fields are expanded, such as offline interactive facilities and services, virtual information construction, digital exhibition, and three-dimensional urban construction. The accuracy of Rich Media 2.0 makes autocatalysis able to present the fluctuation of emotion directly during the process of emotion visualization, and hence, to explore customer psychology. The real-time nature of Rich Media 2.0 means its information feedback is not limited by time, but it rather can be used as a process of real-time emotional feedback. Its expansibility makes it possible to develop a wide range of industries. With the development of wearable devices, 5G technology and deep learning, the accuracy of emotion recognition will be improved. With the new technology and recognition dimension, the information of emotional feedback will be more accurate. Customers can also feedback more information, including age, gender, face value, face quality information and types.

By recognizing the value of Rich Media 2.0, we enhance media information construction and thereby create a better user experience. This methodology helps us to filter subjective information during the service process, and expand the scope sufficiently, as well as the dimension of the screening. Overall, this evaluation method can more accurately deliver feedback about the value in the service journey, hence providing a solid basis for redesign.

References

1. Stickdorn M., Schneider J., et al.: This Is Service Design Thinking_Basics, Tools, Cases, p. 210 (2011). ISBN 978-90-6369-279-7
2. Eigen, M., Schuster, P.: The Hypercycle, A Principle of Natural Self-Organization, p. 7. Springer, Heidelberg (1979). https://doi.org/10.1007/978-3-642-67247-7
3. Cambridge Dictionary. http://dictionary.cambridge.org/us/dictionary/english/fact. Accessed 21 Dec 2019
4. Izard, C.E.: The many meaning/aspects of emotion: definitions, functions, activation, and regulation. Emot. Rev. 2(4), 363–370 (2010). https://doi.org/10.1177/1754073910374661
5. Michell, N., Shiota, J., Kalat, W.: Emotion, 2nd edn. Cengage Learning, Boston (2007)
6. van den Broek, E.L.: Ubiquitous emotion-aware computing. Pers. Ubiquit. Comput. 17(1), 53–67 (2013). https://doi.org/10.1007/s00779-011-0479-9

7. Iqiyi. https://www.iqiyi.com/. Accessed 21 Dec 2019
8. Mauss, I.B., Robinson, M.D.: Measures of emotion: a review. Cogn. Emot. **23**(2), 209–237 (2009). https://doi.org/10.1080/02699930802204677
9. Hamann, S.: Mapping discrete and dimensional emotions onto the brain: controversies and consensus. Trends Cogn. Sci. **16**(9), 458–466 (2012). https://doi.org/10.1016/j.tics.2012.07.006

User Experience: How to Drive Innovation on the Fuzzy Front End

Jingran He, Ting Han[⊠], Dian Zhu, Boyang Fan, Chufan Jin, and Zishan Song

Shanghai Jiao Tong University, Shanghai 200240, China
{hojer0204,hanting}@sjtu.edu.cn, 18901626266@189.cn,
boyangfan@163.com, songzishan1996@163.com,
470193648@qq.com

Abstract. The future market and demands of users are unpredictable during the fuzzy front-end of product development. In order to save time and economic cost, user experience may be replaced directly by empathic design and empathy model for experimental and chaotic nature of the front-end. Meanwhile, with acceleration of product innovation and growth of brand, innovation has become an indispensable part of the development of enterprises. Enterprises could survive for a long time only by continuously providing innovative products to the market. Although role-playing and empathic design still has a great impact on designers, they cannot fully meet the needs of fundamental innovation due to their limitations. In recent years, more and more enterprises begin to pay attention to the end users, and explore the user demands, economic and social benefits. Designers also gradually began to study the typical emotional changes of users and their social world in order to seek new breakthroughs. This paper will start with the research of fuzzy front-end and discuss how user experience will bring innovation to fuzzy front-end. Because of the interaction with the environment, there will inevitably emerge social factors and social networks. The participation of users will not only create economic value, but also create emotional and social value, so that innovation can reach a new level.

Keywords: Fuzzy Front-end · User experience · Innovation

1 Introduction

New product development refers to the process of product development, testing and iteration from the research of market trends and insight into design opportunities to the final market. Fuzziness, confusion and complexity is the main reason for the formation of FFE (Fuzzy Front-end). Confusion leads to uncertainty. Dr. Cooper [1] once pointed out that, even if 3000 schemes were produced in the fuzzy front-end, only 14 schemes would enter the product development stage, and finally one successful scheme would win when put onto the market. These statistics also showed that successful products have an inseparable relationship with the creativity of fuzzy front-end. Innovation can bring competitiveness and sustainable value creation for enterprises. Sowrey [2] once explained the innovation of enterprises as follows: enterprises that understand innovation can survive in the market for a long time. It can also be explained that innovation can bring a steady stream of vitality, so that enterprises and teams can reduce the constraints of the existing framework and maintain high enthusiasm during the fuzzy front-end of product development.

However, "If you stay with innovators long enough, you will find that they are all using the old methods to create new things" [3]. After interviewing 100 chief technology and chief innovation officers, Arthur D. Little drew five conclusions of innovation through his research on 'The New Face of Innovation'. "User Based Innovation" is ranked first among them. In the process of exploring future, customers are important sources of open innovation outside the enterprise. Deep and meaningful cooperation and research with users will help enterprises understand users' emotional needs and social networks.

In recent years, more and more enterprises have begun to focus on user experience, but most of them preferred to place UX in the product development and testing stage rather than FFE. And mostly, few of them start from the perspective of users actually. For example, some studies have found that [4] most of the research on users was conducted among enterprises, rather than real users. Designers or developers use empathic design to put themselves into the real user context to define products. Although this is a very popular method, its limitations are gradually highlighted. Therefore, on the basis of literature review, this paper will explore and study the relationship between users and innovation in the front end of product development through model combing and a cooperation with an enterprise.

2 Study Review and Model Extension

2.1 Review of the Important Development of Fuzzy Front-End

The concept of fuzzy front-end originated from the research of new product development (NPD). The "entry" stage is also called pre-development stage [5], 0 stage [6]. In the 1980s, Cooper standardized it and formed Stage-Gate System (see Fig. 1.) [7]. Through Idea, Preliminary Assessment, Detailed Investigation, Development, Testing & Validation, Full Production & Market Launch, these five stages were carried out linearly. The first three stages formed the fuzzy pre-stage of the product.

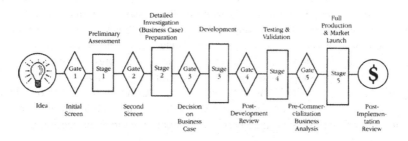

Fig. 1. Stage-Gate System [7]

Moenaert [8] formally put forward the concept of "fuzzy front-end" in 1995. He pointed out that fuzzy front-end is a stage evaluating whether a product concept is worth investing and developing. Fuzzy front-end plays a key role in the process of new product development, which largely determines the success or failure of a product development. Khurana et al. [9] integrated the research of previous literature, put forward the fuzzy front-end model of new product development and pointed out that the fuzzy front-end plays an important role in screening the product concept, strategy and other basic elements of the product (see Fig. 2.). From then the importance of fuzzy front-end was recognized by more and more scholars and enterprises, and most of them believed that the fuzzy front-end should implement the whole process of new product development.

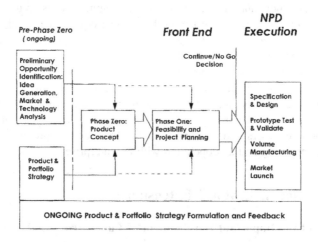

Fig. 2. Stylized model of the FFE [9]

In 2001, Koen et al. [10] proposed New Concept Development (NCD), focusing its model on the early stage of product development, rather than the whole process of Stage-Gate System. At the same time, they also designated the Fuzzy Front-end as the Front-end of Innovation (FEI), aiming to clarify the important work of the FFE–the statement of Fuzzy Front-end over focused on the word "fuzzy" and confused the important tasks of the front end. It implied the significant impact on unpredictable and uncontrollable on the front end instead and couldn't accurately define the leading role in this period, and this would lead to consuming the resources continuously. Actually, innovation is an important factor that really dominates the front-end. Therefore, the combination of innovation into the front-end made clear the tasks that should be concentrated. At the same time, Koen et al. connected the previous linear front-end processes to form the shape of the wheel. "Opportunity Identification", "Opportunity Analysis", "Idea Generation", "Idea Selection" and "Concept & Technology Development" are the five stages that could appear randomly, and they could influence and promote each other to make it the engine of product development (see Fig. 3.).

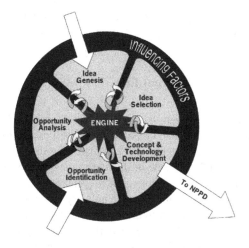

Fig. 3. Front-end of Innovation (FEI) by Koen et al. [10]

The exploration of fuzzy front-end has always been in the process of continuous updating and exploration. Some researchers have carried out the process paradigm, while others have advocated that the fuzzy front-end should be flexible. Although innovation plays a very important role in FFE and the entire life cycle of the product, how to identify innovation as well as the mechanism of innovation has been in a neglected state [11, 12], which is worth further discussion.

2.2 Innovation in Fuzzy Front-End

Most FFE models start from "idea" or "opportunity identification". From another perspective, the development of new products always starts from the continuous innovation of the front end [13], and researches also show that 50% of the innovation time of R & D should come from FFE [14]. It is precisely because of the support of a large number of innovation ideas that constitute the real sense of FFE, and through the continuous selection of ideas to reduce the uncertainty and ambiguity of the front-end.

In 20th century, enterprises regarded R & D as a confidential stage, so innovation has always been spread in the enterprise as a highly confidential information, forming a creative funnel and any ideas must go through the linear process of identification screening to enter the next step. This form is called Internal Innovation. Now it still exists in the government, national defense and other confidential enterprises. However, it is no longer applicable to most enterprises in the market. The competition between enterprises is intensifying, and the internal innovation of enterprises cannot meet the higher requirements from users and market. Therefore, von Hippel [15] put forward the concept of open innovation in 1993, pointing out that the development and innovation of enterprises must draw from the broader external environment (users, universities, etc.), and later more and more researchers confirmed his conclusion.

The process of seeking such innovation can be called Innovation Search. Kieran O'Brien et al. [16] had a deep discussion on internal and external innovation, pointing out that a large number of innovation ideas were very important to product innovation. During the interaction between external and internal innovation, enterprises could achieve more excellent results.

2.3   User Experience in Fuzzy Front-End

Adding User Experience. Through the review of fuzzy front-end and innovation, no matter how the model was updated and iterated, it was still crucial to maintain the high-intensity inflow of external innovation [17], which was directly or indirectly from users. From a certain point of view, one of the major uncertainties of fuzzy front-end is the user's demand, and uncertainty brings amazing innovation ideas.

With the rapid development of the Internet industry in the past decade, companies needed to solve two problems in order to have a place in the fierce market: the attractive content and the changing demands of user experience. "Agile" was exactly created to respond to these problems faced by developers. Agile method could speed up the development efficiency and time-to-market, which were also the goals of all developers. Dr. Cooper pointed out that [18], the previous Stage-Gate was mainly for the project planning at the macro level, while agile is the project regulation method at the micro level (see Fig. 4.). So he thought that the next step of Stage-Gate System of product development is Agile-Stage-Gate.

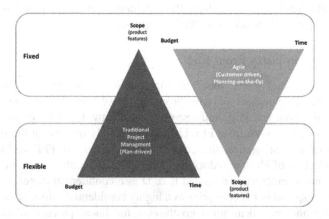

Fig. 4. Traditional project management and Agile [18].

He also took LEGO toys as an example (see Fig. 5.) [19], pointing out that the hybrid model of Agile-Stage-Gate had a positive role in promoting the development of enterprises. Also, it could promote the product release faster, respond better to the user experience and demands, and make the team get a better communication environment.

Fig. 5. The first behavior is traditional product development process, only engineers and designers participate in it, which cannot understand users' needs well; the second behavior is the application of the agile stage gate hybrid model, which adds the consideration of user experience, and can better respond to users' needs [19].

Marc Pallot et al. [20, 21] also began to re-examine the user factor. They integrated the user experience into the fuzzy front-end model directly to form a new model called "UX-FFE" (see Fig. 6.). The six aspects of the original FEI correspond to three macro stages: Strategy, Ideation and Validation. There are two steps of cooperation and exploration in each macro stage of UX-FFE model. It is not hard to see that this new model aims to let developers introduce human and social factors in the front end, so that "social and human values" can be created in each early innovation stage [21].

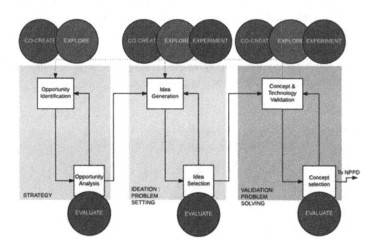

Fig. 6. The UX-FFE model [21].

User Attributes and Empathy Design. FFE model is constantly updating and iter-ating, and innovation is crucial from the stage of idea collection to innovation enhancement and user experience. No matter researchers or enterprises, more and more attention has been paid to the important position of users in the front-end of innovation.

Jesper L. Jensen et al. [22] divided the value of user experience into three dimensions: tangible dimension, use dimension and deep dimension. It can also be understood as functionality, usability and pleasure. Users are the actual creators of experience value. Therefore, in order to create a successful product, designers should not only consider the functional modeling and use value of the product, but also consider more human related factors, which is so-called human centered design or user experience.

But there seems to be no agreement between developers and researchers on what the user experience is. Many people think that the user experience is subjective and dynamic, which is formed according to the context [23]. This opinion implies that the user experience is different from person to person, and is a synthesis of multiple dimensions. ISO [24] has made the following interpretation on user experience: "User experience is a consequence of brand image, presentation, functionality, system performance, interactive behavior, and assistive capabilities of a system, product or service. It also results from the users' internal and physical state resulting from prior experiences, attitudes, skills, abilities and personality; and from the context of use." According to the interpretation by ISO, besides functionality and usability, there also exist user attributes, which can be understood as the "context" mentioned earlier.

Sigma Research Instrument, a German consulting company, summarized this "context" as social environment (Sigma Milieus) [25], pointing out that besides the consideration of user's ethnographic characteristics, users' external environmental characteristics should also be considered. They tried to interpret the automobile market through the social environment method, and subdivide the market by dividing consumers into two dimensions, social stratum (education, income and position) and life attitude/value orientation (lifestyle, life goal, consumption mode, family, health, ideal life mode, interest, achievement, etc.). They also believed that one's life orientation and values tend to be stable, and the individual environment changes with the change of social modernization.

They used Sigma Milieus® to introduce users' living environment, values and attitudes to seek the connection among variables. Their goal was to find innovation and breakthrough points between them (see Fig. 7.).

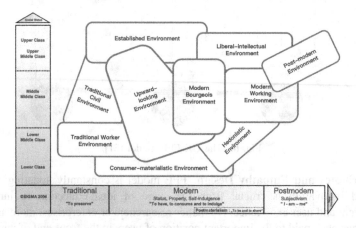

Fig. 7. Sigma Milieus® [25]

With users and market segmentation, in order to better understand users in the complex market, the next step is empathic design. In many cases, getting the user's empathy is the central task of design. Early in the 1970s, Jones et al. [26] realized that with the development of industry, the gap between designers and users as well as manufacturers was growing, and there were even faults between products and users. Designers needed to connect with people and stand in the perspective of users to grasp the needs of users. In 1985, Pat Moore, a 26-year-old designer [27], in order to experience the life of the elderly, dressed herself as an elderly woman in three different forms: rich, middle-income and poor to better understand the needs of the product audience and explore the details that were not found by others. Moore pioneered the model of empathic design, and later some people continued to improve it. They believed that empathic design should not only be reflected in products, but also throughout the whole development life cycle of products. After decades of development, empathy has gradually been widely recognized, known as "one of the most powerful tools for designers" [28], or even as "empathy economy" [29]. It taps design opportunity points for innovation and stimulate potential business value through user experience.

Generally speaking, empathic design is usually divided into three parts: (1) Empathy understanding: Designers put themselves into the identity of a real user and simulate the user's life; (2) Situational map: Designers make the user journey map based on the results of role-playing and find the pain points and design opportunities; (3) User verification: Designers seek the real user to verify the journey map and make modifications.

Even though empathic design has a long history as a means to achieve innovation, Heylighen et al. [30] found that designers often miss two steps while using empathy design: empathy of users and consideration of the user emotions or environment. From our daily design practice, it is not difficult to find that empathy sometimes became the world that the designer imagined, not fully considering the user's spiritual environment and material world, or only using empathy design as the only means to penetrate the user. Under these circumstances, it will greatly reduce the value of design.

2.4 Model Extension

As a positive source of external innovation, user experience is becoming more and more important. But we found that most of the models are still at the macro management level or at the economic level. If they are used by a non-designer or developer, they may still not understand the essence of the user experience, which naturally leads to the "conjecture". For designers, there is also such suspicion. There is no specific bridge to connect the user experience with early development. Therefore, we try to highlight "User Scenario" in FFE model, and use it to guide designers and developers to better innovate. We also divide FFE into three stages: research stage, creative stage and concept stage (see Fig. 8.).

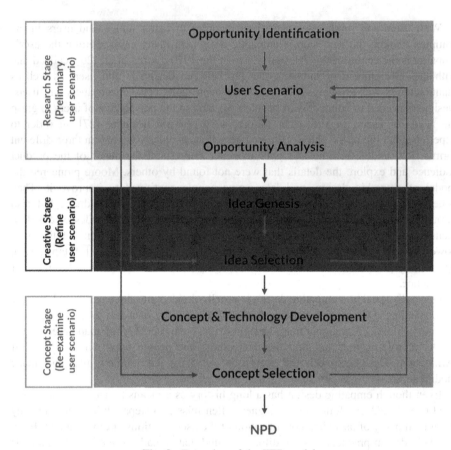

Fig. 8. Extension of the FFE model

(1) Research stage (Preliminary user experience map): Research stage is divided into two steps: opportunity identification and opportunity analysis. In this article, we think that user scenario should be introduced after opportunity identification. Through the analysis of the living conditions of users such as social level, ethnographic level and value orientation level, we can model users and master their behavior habits, and use this as a verification item to verify whether the current identified opportunity is feasible and innovative. After preliminary screening, we can turn into creative generation.

(2) Creative stage (Refine user experience map): Creative stage is divided into two steps: idea genesis and idea selection. According to the summarized user charac-teristics and opportunities, we discuss the interaction between tasks and related people, fields and objects, as well as their psychological perception, emotion and preference changes. Through direct or indirect research on user behavior, we can get further and more detailed innovation points, refine user experience map, and import the results into the user experience map again to verify the effectiveness of the idea in solving problems.

(3) Concept stage (Re-examination of user experience map): Through integration and optimization ideas, the design concepts are introduced into the user context mapping again for final test to explore whether they really meet the design points, or solve the problems.

We think that user experience map is one of the important task processes in the early stage of product development. It should be used as an archive tool for user experience design methods. User experience can be used as an effective control tool to ensure that product development is always on the track of normal development. It is just like the gate in Stage-Gate Model. However, this limitation is a kind of benign control. It can also be said that the users' demand triggered by experience is a standard, which always guides the development direction of the product.

Therefore, we also put forward a hypothesis that user experience should run through the whole process of fuzzy front-end. As a control means, participation of users in the early development process will produce more innovative ideas than simply through the empathic design of the internal innovation, and have a positive innovation effect on the fuzzy front-end innovation.

3   Research Process

Due to the increasingly fierce market competition, the traditional work flow of vehicle enterprises has been unable to meet the increasingly diversified society and competitors. Facing rigid methods and engineering thinking, the transformation and development of enterprises is imminent. We discussed the innovation of user experience by a one-day workshop with five departments in a company, which is one of the world's top 500 automobile enterprises. On the one hand, we tried to let participants know the advantages of user experience. On the other hand, we wanted to explore the innovation brought by user experience in the early stage of fuzziness. The workshop was divided into three stages.

3.1   Research Stage

Before the start of the workshop, we firstly conducted a preliminary survey of 64 employees involved in the workshop, including the design department, vehicle integration department, operation & engineering planning department, AE & Program management department and chassis & powertrain integration department (see Fig. 9.). These employees included technicians, department managers and general managers. Previous survey results showed that 93% of the people supported the idea that user experience can bring design innovation, but only 22% of them thought that user experience had a great impact on product innovation (very absolute attitude), and 8% still thought that the impact was not significant. At the same time, they (88%) thought that most of tasks of the internal enterprise was to repeat mechanized and rigid work. The company believed that it was a suitable time to carry out the reform from top to bottom.

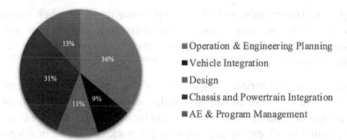

Fig. 9. Composition of participants

We divided all the staff into six groups. In order to ensure the balance of the department information from each group member, each group had the members of the above five departments. At the beginning of the workshop, each member drew the group portrait on his right-hand side to warm up. After that the theme of the workshop was announced. The parent theme was related to car travel service. Each group was invited to introduce their willingness and the goal of the design.

The theme of the workshop was jointly formulated by the enterprise and us. Therefore, according to the theme direction, we recruited 12 typical car users [4] before the workshop, who had profound opinions on the car experience and service. They would have more voice in the workshop process and could quickly integrate into the exchanges and discussions of other participants.

The course was divided into four rounds, which mainly introduced brainstorming & mind mapping, persona, user experience map and concept design. Each part continued for 40 min. Among the four main courses, there were also some widely used design methods such as KANO model, body storming, user interview, etc.

3.2 Creative Stage

The first part of the creative stage was mainly guided by our staff in collaboration. We provided them with methodological guidance rather than intervention of the workshop theme content. The main tasks are: brainstorm and mind map; persona; the stages of using the product; behaviors; contact points; emotional changes; pain points and design opportunities (see Fig. 10.). We set a time limit of two hours. After the first part, we invited each group to report their design requirements and ideas and let our staff recorded their results.

In the second part, the 12 users who previously recruited were arranged into 6 groups on average. Their duties were to answer the questions the staffs found and to make the staffs deepen their questions. We also asked users to give suggestions and opinions so that participants could adjust and modify the solutions carried out in the first part. The second part also continued for two hours (Fig. 11).

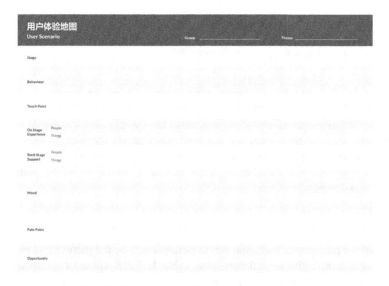

Fig. 10. The user scenario (user experience map)

Fig. 11. Members in the workshop

3.3   Concept Stage

After the study of typical users, the participants synthesized their design concepts by exploring, co-creating, testing, and evaluating, and then we guided them to return to the user experience map to verify whether their methods really solved the problems. They could also use KANO model and other methods to explore the relationship between the design quality and user experience, whether the innovation could effectively solve problems or attract consumers.

At the end of the workshop, we asked all groups to prepare a three-minute drama, which was used to convey their conceptual design. It was aimed to convey their concepts and let them simulate the real scene of users by body storming. In this way, they can understand that empathic design should not only be imagined in the brain, but also be combined with the real physiological characteristics and living environment.

4 Results

4.1 Social Environment in the Subconscious

In the early stage of the workshop, we found an interesting phenomenon. Most of the participants didn't have a good foundation in drawing. When they were asked to draw the characteristics of the members in the group, they would not only draw the facial appearance, but also the industrial departments, family relations and social relations. Most of them were subconscious, and our goal was to make them pay attention to this aspect. As mentioned above, user characteristics are not limited to personal factors such as occupation and age, family relations and social environment are all the contents that should be considered.

4.2 Innovation and Users

We counted the pain points and opportunity points found by the participants before and after the users joined (the second part) (see Table 1, 2.). Because of the focus on the creative ideas rather than content and quality, we did not screen out those ideas that were similar among groups. It could be found that from the macro level, no matter whether pain points or opportunity points, the number increased after the users joined, indicating that the users had a promoting effect on the innovation. But it did not happen in each group, such as the second group, the number of one group did not change. Later we learned from the participants that two ideas they provided were queried by users and deleted after negotiation, and then added new ideas inspired by users. In fact, in our later questionnaire survey, we learned that this was not a case in point. Almost each group encountered such situations. Sometimes users could not understand the ideas proposed by internal personnel, the results would be changed under the mediation of both parties, deletion and addition were common phenomenon. The content in the second part did not have an inclusive relationship with the content in the first part, but more was an intersection relationship. To some extent, it showed that users and enterprises were in a state of mutual balance. Through the "gate" of user experience, we can effectively and reasonably provide and select innovation to make the final results more suitable for users.

Table 1. Number of pain points

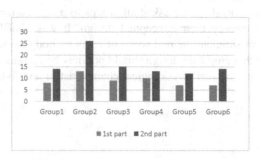

Table 2. Number of opportunity points

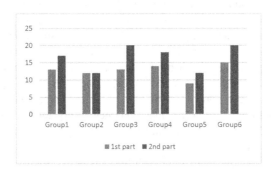

4.3   Innovation Brought by Users

We divided the ideas collected from each group into 13 categories as shown in the figure. After statistics, we found that the ideas in the first part are mostly concentrated in the car interior, driving and other professional aspects, including the car interior (32), safe driving (16), maintenance (3), parking questions (12), taxi (1), travel (1), accounting for 64% of the total (See Table 3.). We think the main reason for this was that they were professionals. In the process of providing creative ideas, they have taken their own professionalism into consideration, and hoped to provide more professional services for users with the same approach.

Table 3. Classification of opportunity points

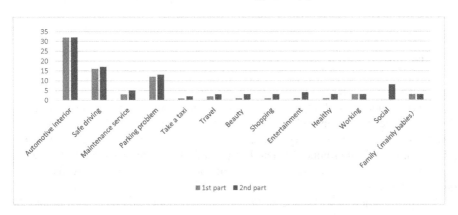

With typical users participating, there was a relatively significant increase in beauty (3), entertainment (4) and social (8). Although the internal personnel had brainstormed through their empathic design in the first part and seemed to be effective, it was still not enough. Even if they had deep empathy with it, they would still have scruples because of their professionalism. They would consider the feasibility of technology, economic costs and other factors, while users would not worry too much about the above factors, they would not provide solutions related to technology, but solutions related to services. Like "what if... ", "I hope it can be like..." were potential design opportunities. In the previous literature [4], users' ideas are negatively related to their technical knowledge–technical knowledge will limit their creativity generation, which was also the case among enterprise personnel.

The users' sense of communication with the outside world also made the social a part that the internal staff did not involve too much. This kind of "super mainstream" consciousness, which is different from the "mainstream consciousness" of the internal personnel, will not be too constrained by the current situation, and will generate more demands through their own connection with the society. The user participation in the whole process helps to control the overall development direction of the product.

4.4   The Result of the Workshop

The staff showed unimaginable enthusiasm and amazing creativity in the one-day workshop. The questionnaire survey after the workshop also showed that 89% of the participants thought that the content introduced in the workshop was very useful for improving innovation awareness, and 96% of them had a positive attitude towards the workshop. When asked about their achievements, we received the most answers as: "They (users) think of things we didn't think of", "It turns out that car companies can connect with so many aspects". The core needs of users can be determined through the interaction between users and enterprises in the early front-end and can be used as a tool for engineers to create sustainable innovation value.

5   Discussion and Future Work

The results of this workshop verified our hypothesis that users, especially typical users, will generate more radical ideas in the front end than through internal innovation alone. Because of the interaction with the environment, social factors will inevitably occur. Besides strong social ties between human to human, weak social connections between people, things and environment can still be part of ongoing research. Additionally, the continuous interaction between users and enterprises also makes the creativity continuously optimized.

The introduction of users' social, life orientation, values and other factors into the fuzzy front-end plays an important role in guiding product development to a large extent. The emergence of social interaction urges designers to consider more emotional and social factors on the basis of people-oriented design. Therefore, to create social and economic value, this design mode will also create more emotional value, so as to bring the innovation to a new level to form the radical innovation. The innovation we observed in this workshop about the employees can be attributed to the gradual innovation, and most of the ideas they provided were about the technical function, such as automatic door, door baffle and umbrella collection. Of course, there are also relatively new innovative ideas such as car body deformation and parking solution.

There are still some shortcomings in this study, such as the problem of time. It was very time consuming to compress the heavy workload task into one day. Our research was mainly carried out in automobile enterprise, and the invited users were all selected and representative. Therefore, there were limited executive questions in the sample number, although they were enough to answer our questions. We need to explore more about the industry in the future.

Acknowledgement. The research is supported by Science Foundation of Ministry of Education of China (Grant No. 17YJAZH029).

References

1. Cooper, R.G., Kleinschmidt, E.J.: Screening new products for potential winners. Long Range Plan. **26**(6), 74–81 (1993)
2. Sowrey, T.: Idea generation: identifying the most useful techniques. Eur. J. Mark. **24**(5), 20–29 (1990)
3. Fischer, B.: Innovation: What's New? (2011). https://www.forbes.com/sites/billfischer/2011/10/17/innovation-whats-new/#39ee8da7344d
4. Magnusson, P.R.: Exploring the contributions of involving ordinary users in ideation of technology-based services*. J. Prod. Innov. Manag. **26**(5), 578–593 (2009)
5. Cooper, R.G., Kleinschmidt, E.J.: New products: what separates winners from losers? J. Prod. Innov. Manag. **4**(3), 169–184 (1987)
6. Khurana, A., Rosenthal, S.R.: Integrating the fuzzy front end of new product development. MIT Sloan Manag. Rev. **38**(4), 103–120 (1997)
7. Cooper, R.: Stage-gate systems: a new tool for managing new products. Bus. Horiz. **33**, 44–54 (1990)
8. Moenaert, R., et al.: R&D-marketing communications during the fuzzy front end. IEEE Trans. Eng. Manag. **42**, 243–258 (1995)
9. Khurana, A., Rosenthal, S.: Towards holistic "Front Ends" in new product development. J. Prod. Innov. Manag. **15**, 57–74 (1998)
10. Koen, P., et al.: Providing clarity and a common language to the "Fuzzy Front End". Res.-Technol. Manag. **44**(2), 46–55 (2001)
11. Frishammar, J., et al.: The front end of radical innovation: a case study of idea and concept development at prime group. Creat. Innov. Manag. **25**(2), 179–198 (2016)
12. Gurtner, S., Reinhardt, R.: Ambidextrous idea generation-antecedents and outcomes*. J. Prod. Innov. Manag. **33**, 34–54 (2016)
13. Boeddrich, H.J.: Ideas in the workplace: a new approach towards organizing the fuzzy front end of the innovation process. Creat. Innov. Manag. **13**(4), 274–285 (2004)
14. Jensen, A.R.V.: Front End Innovation: navigating situated spaces of actors and models (2017)
15. Bhargava, M., Hippel, E.: The sources of innovation. J. Mark. Res. **30**, 528 (1993)
16. O'Brien, K.: Innovation types and the search for new ideas at the fuzzy front end: where to look and how often? J. Bus. Res. **107**, 13–24 (2020)

17. Gilson, L.L., Litchfield, R.C.: Idea collections: a link between creativity and innovation. Innov. Manag. Policy Pract. **19**(1), 80–85 (2017)
18. Cooper, R.G.: Agile-stage-gate hybrids. Res.-Technol. Manag. **59**(1), 21–29 (2016)
19. Cooper, R.G., Sommer, A.F.: Agile-Stage-Gate: new idea-to-launch method for manufactured new products is faster, more responsive. Ind. Mark. Manag. **59**, 167–180 (2016)
20. Lecossier, A., et al.: Application of the UX-FFE model for optimizing the performance of the upstream innovation process. IEEE (2018)
21. Lecossier, A., Pallot, M.: UX-FFE model: an experimentation of a new innovation process dedicated to a mature industrial company. IEEE (2017)
22. Jensen, J.L.: Designing for profound experiences. Des. Issues **30**(3), 39–52 (2014)
23. Law, E.L., et al.: Understanding, scoping and defining user experience, pp. 719–728 (2009)
24. ISO 9241-11 (2018): Ergonomics of human-system interaction. Part 11: 9241-11 (2018)
25. Ascheberg, C.: The SIGMA Milieus® Global Early Warning System for Product Positioning and Trends (2013)
26. Bamber, D.J., Jones, J.C.: Design methods: seeds of human futures. J. Oper. Res. Soc. **32**(12), 1158 (1981)
27. Moore, P., Conn, C.: Disguised: A True Story. Word Books, Waco (1985)
28. Cooper, A., et al.: About Face: The Essentials of Interaction Design. Wiley, Hoboken (2014)
29. McDonagh, D., Woodcock, A., Iqbal, S.: Experience + Experience + Experience = Empathy (2018)
30. Heylighen, A., Dong, A.: To empathise or not to empathise? Empathy and its limits in design. Des. Stud. **65**, 107–124 (2019)

Research on User Experience Classification Based on Phenomenological Method

Jingpeng Jia$^{(\boxtimes)}$ and Xueyan Dong

The College of Special Education, Beijing Union University,
Beijing 100075, China
tjtjingpeng@buu.edu.cn

Abstract. An important issue in the construction of the basic theory on user experience is that user experience classification has not yet received a satisfactory answer. This makes it difficult for user experience researchers and designers to practice without clear recognition on research objects. This article points out the existing classification methods are inadequate to explain an independent and clear experience phenomenon. The key challenge lies in the current research methods are not suitable for the user experience task. To overcome it, we utilize a phenomenological method of inductive reasoning method to construct a new framework including 20 experience classification. In the qualitative research based on phenomenological methods, researcher's own knowledge background tends to have an important impact on the quality and effectiveness of the research. The aim of this research is not trying to provide a once and for all solution, but make the applicability of phenomenological research methods applicable. The proposed framework can provide a possible platform for the discussion of experience classification issues.

Keywords: User experience classification · Phenomenological research method · Experience pattern

1 Introduction

Today, experience factors are increasingly dominating people's consumption decisions [1]. For any innovative product research and development project, it is no longer necessary to repeat how important it is to achieve effective experience innovation. The UX concept has received increasing attention in the business, academic, and education communities over the past decade. However, compared to traditional knowledge areas such as physics, sociology, philosophy, UX is a young discipline. So far, its basic theoretical construction is still in its infancy. Therefore, with many difficult problems encountered in experience research and design practice, no systematic theoretical resources can give guidance. According to the statistics till the end of 2016 from the US innovation management expert Stephen Werwick, throughout the global only one percent of three hundred of all product innovation projects are truly profitable. This reflects the difficulty of experiencing innovative practices. It also indirectly implies the demand to construct the systematic theory framework of UX. This study focuses on a basic theory problem by thinking and questioning: what exactly is UX?

© Springer Nature Switzerland AG 2020
A. Marcus and E. Rosenzweig (Eds.): HCII 2020, LNCS 12200, pp. 147–159, 2020.
https://doi.org/10.1007/978-3-030-49713-2_10

The International Organization for Standardization defines UX as: "a person's perceptions and responses that result from the use or anticipated use of a product, system or service." [2] On the one hand, according to the research of Dr. Effie Law of Leicester University, the definition basically reflects the dominant content of the mainstream view of defining UX concept in industry and academia. On the other hand, for the practical phenomenon of cognition and understanding of user experience research and design, the above definition seems to clearly define the object of practice.

However, once starting specific experience research and design practice, you will find that the above definition does not provide an exact practice object. Primally because it only clarifies the extension of the UX concept, but does not point out the core of the UX concept, that is, it does not point out what specific experience elements the user experience contains. To solve the problem, it is necessary to establish an effective user experience classification system. Specifically, the classification system is supposed to include all experience factors and explain all experience phenomena, and it must allow each experience type in the system to refer to a clear and specific experience category. Although some researchers have realized the importance of the experience classification problem and started to make important efforts to establish the classification system, so far, they have not been able to obtain a comprehensive solution. This makes it impossible for user experience research and design practitioners to obtain sufficiently clear research and design objects. Furthermore, as it lacks clear working boundary, it is difficult to review the existing experience issues of products and plan long-term production experience strategies in an appropriate manner.

For this reason, in addition to summarizing the achievements by the existing experience classification research, this paper makes in-depth reflection on the applicability of the research methods used in the existing studies. For the applicable research methods, a new user experience classification system was established. It should be noted that we do not attempt to give a once and for all solution to the problem of experience classification, but based on the values of the previous research to explore a new research path and carry out our research along the path. In this way, it provides a more effective basic platform for experience classification.

2   Related Work

Through literature review on the three platforms of "ACM Digital Library", "Google Scholar Search", and "Research Gate", there are two kinds of studies on the "Experience Classification".

2.1   Research Work by Marcos

In the paper entitled Typology of the Experiences, the authors Marcos and Stephania [3] adopted pleasant design theory, emotional design theory and experience marketing theory as their research entry point. Relying on deductive reasoning, they developed six experience types found in the user experience phenomenon. First, experience related to the senses. These experiences are directly related to the body's sensory organs, they are produced faster, and they are derived from instinct, so the cognitive expenditure is lower. The visual stimulus of appearance, and the tactile stimulus of touch all trigger such experience. For example: the smell of a brand-new car, the beautiful appearance of a product, or a comfortable surface to touch. In addition, the experience is related to sex. Second, the sensory experience in using the product, which means the emotional response when using the product. This kind of experience is very subjective and varies from person to person. And it even can be related to history experience. For example, when using a product, the customer will think of someone special. Third, social experience. Social experience occurs between individuals and is mediated by products. These experiences can vary greatly depending on the individuals involved, the technology used, and the environment in which the experience is produced. In this category, reactions occur because of the behavior of other participants and are also related to the product itself. For example, a mobile phone that can send text messages, pictures, videos and call relatives and friends. Fourth, cognitive experience. It is related to the user's understanding of things. Product features that affect users' understanding can be aesthetic, semantic, or symbolic. Fifth, use experience. The experience is related to the ease of use and functionality of the product. This experience has been studied in many fields, such as ergonomics, and human-computer interaction in recent years. Its subjectivity is far less than other experience categories. Such as, an easy-to-use car jack. Sixth, motivation experience. The experience type is derived from the experience behavior model in Schmitt's experience marketing theory. That is, the value of a product lies in satisfying a specific behavior of the user. For instance, the significance of a bicycle product is to motivate users to exercise.

For example, the classification of phenomena is the basic method of human perception of the world, and it is also the only way to go. Therefore, in the sense of helping people understand the phenomenon of experience, the Marcos' research results obviously make a useful effort to this end, and provide a useful explanatory for the phenomenon of experience. However, for guiding specific experience research and design practice, the classification system has several shortcomings: First, all of the above experience classifications fail to refer to a sufficiently clear experience category, and thus fail to present clear research and design objects. Second, there is a misunderstanding in the classification operation. According to the results of aesthetic research, aesthetic experience is significantly different from ordinary physiological sensory experience in the experience mechanism. However, the paper classifies aesthetic experience with other physiological and sensory experiences into the experience category "sensory-related experience". Third, it does not explain how the classification system can cover all experience types in the experience phenomenon. Based on our analysis, it is hard to believe that the proposed deductive inference method and the three inference foundations can help answer the questions above.

2.2 Research Work by Pieter

The paper entitled *Framework of Product Experience* authored by Pieter and Paul distinguishes three types of experience through observation and analysis of product experience phenomena [4]. First, aesthetic experience. It is the pleasant experience obtained through form perception. For example, seeing good-looking designs, hearing beautiful music, feeling good and comfortable, or smelling good staff. Second, meaning experience. That is to say, participating the cognitive activities, such as interpretation, memory, reflection, association, to experience the metaphorical meaning behind the product. For example, luxury goods are a metaphor for wealthy living conditions. Third, emotional experience. Experiential activities related to daily life and emotional phenomena discussed in psychology. For example, love, disgust, empty fear, expectation, pride, disappointment, and so on.

To be sure, the classification framework is also helpful to understand the phenomenon of experience. For the guiding significance of experience research and design practice, on the one hand, aesthetic experience and meaning experience in the framework refer to an experience category based on a clear and unique experience mechanism, to provide the exact objects of practice for design activities. On the other hand, the classification system still has one disadvantage: the category of experience referred to as emotional experience is ambiguous. The reason is that any experience tends to be generated by the four phrases: (1) through the stimulus of things, (2) reflection of sensations to form awareness and perspective, (3) specific emotion caused by reflection, and (4) short-term emotions converted to. In the process, different sense-reflection processes may all lead to the same emotion. However, the psychological mechanism of different sense-reflection processes may be quite different. Therefore, even in the face of a certain type of emotion, it is impossible to anchor an exact experience mechanism as the basis for experience research and design. For instance, from feel to reflection phrase (feel-reflection) in aesthetics obtained by appreciating beautiful car shapes and feel-reflection in symbolic meaning obtained by holding luxury products, both result in the generation of pleasant emotion. But the psychological operation mechanism of them is different. We do not deny that the two kinds of feel-reflection triggered by the sense of pleasure may be slightly different. This bring a problem that even if the research object of experience research is determined, it is impossible to discuss how to conduct user research along a clear experience mechanism.

2.3   Implications for Follow-up Research

Although the existing research results have the above-mentioned shortcomings, they give the following important inspirations for subsequent research. First, according to the analysis in Pieter's research, in order to establish an effective experience classification system, each type of experience must refer to an experience based on a clear and unique experience mechanism. Only in this way can we provide the exact object of practice for researchers and designers. So how can we get such experience classification? Based on an examination of the research methods in the above two research works, it is found that the existing theoretical frameworks that have some logical connection with user experience, such as pleasant design theory, emotional design theory, and experience marketing theory. They can explain the experience phenomenon from a basic perspective. Because of this, many researchers can construct their theoretical frameworks in a top-down manner, and use it to structure the thick lines of experience phenomena.

However, there is no logic showing how to use them to obtain a detailed experiment classification. It seems quite hard to include all experience phenomena.

In contrast, based on observations, feelings, and analysis of various experience phenomena, it is more likely to adopt the bottom-up approach to inductively discover the various experience mechanisms behind the phenomenon. We assume the deductive based methods adopted in existing study are not suitable for experience classification problem. Alternatively, qualitative research based on empirical investigations can be one option. From the perspective of qualitative research methodology, the induction method uses the bottom-up way is more specialized in studying experiential phenomena, which is called Interpretative Phenomenological Analysis method. The method use the case study to focus on special cases so that it analyze the phenomenological experience to obtain the meaning behind. This method is a qualitative research that has flourished in the past two decades. It originated in the field of psychology and is dedicated to interpreting how people understand their own life experience through the perspective of researchers, which is a process of dual hermeneutics. At the same time, it adheres to the special research method and focuses its research interest on the uniqueness of the case. By using the method to analyze the experience phenomenon, we can obtain an explanation of the meaning of the experience activity. This research conclusion is given to interpret the corresponding phenomenon [5].

Secondly, the definition of each type of experience is supposed to be made by providing examples of appropriate experience phenomena to explain the concept of the type. This can help to explain the concept of each experience type more clearly, and make it easier for follow-up researchers to make intuitive judgments on their own.

Finally, although some experience classifications in existing research results show ambiguity, all these classification concepts are likely to provide important clues for discovering new and more specific experience types in subsequent studies.

3 Research Design

Based on the analysis and the thinking of the existing experience classification research, we adopted the qualitative research based on phenomenological interpretation analysis. Our research was conducted following the key principles of empirical research. The purpose is to get enough detailed experience classification system. Ensure each experience concept in the system can refer to a clear experience category based on a unique experience mechanism.

3.1 Research Object

In the experiment, 10 graduate students majoring in psychology at Beijing Normal University were selected as participants of this experiment. We have three reasons for this. First, we assume all experience types exist in various product consumption behaviors and service consumption behaviors in our daily lives. Therefore, it is necessary to select those candidates who are fully and deeply involved in daily consumption activities as research objects. As a result, the full picture of the user experience classification system can be outlined. The selected candidates have fully developed their material and spiritual consumption needs because they are supported by their family's economic background and its own knowledge and cultural background. Moreover, they are also participating in various consumption practices and projects. Secondly, our experiment requires participants themselves being able to fully understand academic concepts, such as, experience types. More importantly, they can describe their consumer experience clearly and precisely. Based on this requirement, the selected subjects tend to have a good logical understanding ability and analysis ability, we believe they are competent. Third, the candidates have different backgrounds including literature, psychology, medicine, Korean linguistics, finance, computer science, and design. They are more likely to be representatives with personalized interests and generating various consumer needs. This can ensure that this experiment covers much consumption behavior.

In addition, we also listed the first author himself as a research object for the following considerations. Compared with the 10 graduate students, he has a similar research background, and is also a comprehensive and in-depth participant of consumer practice. At the same time, he is the one who knows the research objectives, theoretical application, and research design of this research best. Therefore, our research can let the author himself use introspection to generate the type of user experience found in his life. Especially at the beginning, the author can help better understand related concepts through setting up examples for student candidates.

3.2 Research Process

This experiment was divided into three steps:

Step 1: Propose experience types that the author himself has explored. In the process, he uses two methods to try to discover as many types of experiences as possible. First, in the process of reviewing past consumer experiences, use the introspection method to distinguish the types of experiences. Second, reading various types of advertising copyright and product reviews to analyze the types of experience involved.

Step 2: Discover new types of experiences through one-on-one interviews with student candidates. During each interview, the interviewees is first told the research intent and look at three typical types of experiences the author has distinguished. Then, a semi-structured interview method is used to encourage them to recollect consumption experiences in the past and to define new experience types, and give a case for each new experience type.

Step 3: Analysis of experimental results. In the process, the author summarizes all the experience types he proposed with other experience types collected from other participants to form a table as the result. The table is divided into five columns which are categories from left to right are: serial number, experience type, experience mechanism, typical case, and number of times mentioned by participants.

4 Results

We analyzed the feedback and reports from candidates and summarized 20 categories of experience classification which are shown in the tables (Table 1, 2, 3 and 4).

Table 1. 20 types of experience classification (from 1 to 5)

No.	Experience type	Experience mechanism	Typical case	Times mentioned
1	Utility experience	By using a product or service, a practical purpose is achieved, which make users feel satisfied [6]	With a nail gun, it is possible to make a hole in the wall that meets user expectations	11
2	Usability experience	In the process of using a certain product or service to achieve the intended goal, due to the intimate design of the product and service, users feel relaxed, convenient and cheerful in the operation behavior [6]	The nail gun is designed with the feature of light in weight, the handle is easy to hold, and the recoil force is small when shooting nails into the wall	11
3	Aesthetic experience	Have pleasant and non-utilitarian feelings through the perception of form [7]	Looking at nice designs; listening to wonderful music; feeling comfortable to the touch of purse; smelling a perfume	11
4	Symbol experience	Through the use of a product or service (signifier), let people around understand the meaning (referent) behind the product or service [8]	By using luxury goods, show one's financial identity and superior living conditions	11
5	Novelty experience	When existing desires and needs are met, people will always hold new desires and needs. This desire is associated with a new and fresh demand. Thus, the feeling of the new attribute of a new product is a novel experience	The BMW 5 Series introduced the 2019 year's new model, it shows slight changes in headlights, taillights, and round shape. Customers can still feel new satisfaction from the small changes	9

Table 2. 20 types of experience classification (from 6 to 10)

No.	Experience type	Experience mechanism	Typical case	Times mentioned
6	Fashion experience	Because a product or service refers to a certain popular culture, atmosphere, or value that has only recently been recognized in the society, users will have a fashion experience or use symbolic ways to gain self-confirmation of your fashion identity [9]	Almost every year there is a popular trend, then if you buy a product meeting the pop value, you will feel yourself very fashion	9
7	Taste experience	By using a product and service, you can get a good experience on aspects such as taste, levels, sentiment, etc. The key is to show this taste to others around you	Someone purchases a Jaguar car, he believes it can express his personal taste in terms of sportiness. Another example is show your taste in dress by buying and wearing the same brand of clothing for a long time	7
8	Culture experience	Because the successful product or service often contains some culture elements. When people use the product, they would identify the culture and express themselves	Culture experience can be obtained by wearing clothing that belongs to a particular culture, such as a sarong in Bali	8
9	Kindness experience	Product purchase does not happen at a specific time but a period of time, so any kind and sweet design and service can make customers feel the same kindness so as to be satisfied	If using a online shopping app, when comes to pay online stage, the app pops up the estimated arrival time. Provide contact information when needed, express sincere thanks. All of these would make customers feel good	3
10	Reflection experience	Through understanding and using products or service, thinking about the values, and discover new meanings to establish new rules of life	By having clothes from MUJI brand, to recognize the importance of the theory of subtracting for life	2

Table 3. 20 types of experience classification (from 11 to 15)

No.	Experience type	Experience mechanism	Typical case	Times mentioned
11	Motivation experience	Based on the design of a business activity, users can feel the incentives similar to those obtained in games	As a result of a number of flights this year, someone won the Platinum Membership of Star Alliance and began to enjoy the corresponding upgrade services	3
12	Cognition experience	Only through the sensory perception of the surface (such as watching product advertisements, touching the surface of the product, or smelling the smell of the product), a judgment of the actual functional value of a product or service is made, and the experience is achieved in the imagination process	After seeing the promotion videos of the brand new BMW 8 Series, customers begin to judge the acceleration performance of the car, and fantasize that he was driving the car	1
13	Living condition experience	By using products or service, feel that life status has been switched	After buying a Mercedes-Benz car, my study and work changes a lot so as to lead a living lift with good condition	7
14	Region experience	The use of a product or service let customers remind of known region environment and the specific experience and culture happened in that region	Dining at an authentic Thai restaurant to remind the local environment and human experience in Bangkok	6
15	Challenge experience	Through a period of learning and practice, one can overcome the challenge and feel happy	After learning the car operation system for a long period of time, feel like being professional	2

Table 4. 20 types of experience classification (from 16 to 20)

No.	Experience type	Experience mechanism	Typical case	Times mentioned
16	Physical experience	Products can stimulate customers' physical body, and customers have some feedback to perception	Such as the smell in the car, the touch of on the steering wheel	8
17	Option experience	When buying a product, there are more than one option to choose. Customer would like to enjoy the rights of selection to decide on buy one of them. That is, many choices give customers more active rights and this make them happy	Although you only like one pair of shoes in the store, but if the store only have the one style, you may also feel disappointed. Therefore, a wise way is to provide many alternative choices. By doing this, customers will feel satisfied by having some kind of control	3
18	Self-achievement experience	By purchasing and using a certain product or service, user achieves self-identification in some field	By purchasing a Mercedes-Benz sedan, users feel that they have entered the elite level	9
19	Emotion experience	Get a specific and temporary emotional experience by buying or using a product or service [10]	Create a temporary cheerful emotion by enjoying a birthday cake	4
20	Mood experience	By purchasing or using a product or service, you can obtain a specific emotional experience over a long period of time	Keep yourself in a certain mood by continuing to use a perfume	8

In summary, this research presents a new user experience classification system consisting of the following 20 experience types: utility experience, usability experience, aesthetic experience, symbol experience, novelty experience, fashion experience, taste experience, culture experience, kindness experience, reflection experience, motivation experience, cognition experience, living condition experience, region experience, challenge experience, physical experience, option experience, self-achievement experience, emotion experience, mood experience. Among them, each type of experience can refer to an independent and precise experience category based on a unique and clear experience mechanism.

5 Discussion

Our research utilizes a qualitative research method based on phenomenological interpretation and analysis to obtain 20 different experience mechanisms in user experience phenomena. Based on them, 20 categories of user experience are formed. For the results, there are several issues worth noting.

Firstly, compared with the previous research, this study presents more types of experience in the quantity, but each type of experience can refer to a unique and clear experience category.

Secondly, a total of 11 subjects were studied in this study. They are 10 graduate students, and the first author himself. Therefore, the highest number of times that each experience type concept can be mentioned is 11. By examine the results, it is not hard to find that some experience was mentioned frequently but some was only once. According to the results of the above research, it includes both the concept of being mentioned a lot and the concept of being mentioned a few times, even being mentioned only once. Then, compared with the categories mentioned less frequently, does that mean they are more important? the answer is negative. The reason is simple. Once one candidate is clearly aware of the existence of a type of experience, then this is good evidence to prove its existence. The small number of mentions only indicates that not many people are aware of this type of experience, but not the experience type is less important. Therefore, if directly using quantitative method, it will be unreasonable to do the statistical analysis without analyzing the reason of a small number of data.

Furthermore, some experience type concepts are mentioned less often because of two possibilities. The first possibility is following the Maslow's hierarchy of needs theory and the theory of superior needs, only a few candidates can feel their own needs for high-level needs or unpopular value. And this situation has become the superior demand in their consciousness. The second possibility is because the candidates have some limitations in language expression, abstract thinking and the ability of retrospection, they feel hard to form a clear understanding on some experiences. On the other hand, those experience type that are mentioned less often are more inspiring for finding new opportunities and discovering new market.

Moreover, we admit our experience classification shows the same weakness as the one discussion in related work. We make a statement first. The 20 types of experience classification can give a comprehensive answer to how to conduct specific user experience practice, but it still cannot cover all possible experience.

Finally, there is a big difference between quantitative study and qualitative research, which is the researcher himself can be the candidate involved in the experiment in qualitative research. This means the quality of the research results of qualitative research is related to the subjective ability of the researcher in terms of background experience and academic ability. In terms of this study, we find that the results are restricted by the ability of the researchers. First, the researchers himself can find out how many practical experience types is the key to the research. Secondly, in 10 interviews, to what extent does the researcher guide the interviewees to review the richest past consumption experience as possible, and help the interviewees to discover and extract the experience mechanism behind the consumption experience? Based on the findings, the significance of this study is not to provide a once and for all solution to the problem of experience classification, but to make the applicability of phenomenological research methods present.

6   Conclusion

This research takes the reflection on research methods as the starting point for research. First, we point out the unsuitability of research methods in previous studies. Then, by analyzing the important tasks of user experience classification research, we give a conclusion that user experience classification research can be carried out using qualitative research ideas based on phenomenological interpretation analysis. The research results show that, with the help of qualitative research methods centered on phenomenological interpretation and analysis. Thus, we can utilize the advantages of the bottom-up induction method to discover the rich and different types of experiences and obtain the experience phenomena mechanism behind. In summary, the main contribution of this research lies in two points. First, the applicability of the qualitative research method using phenomenological interpretation and analysis to the study of experience classification is presented. And to provide a more effective platform for the discussion of experience classification issues. Second, the 20 experience types found in this study show correspondingly clear experience research and design objects for user experience research and design practices. In theory, this can play a useful role in guiding relevant practical activities. Why dare to say theoretically? It is related to the characteristics of the interpretive phenomenological analysis research. The quality of the research is closely related to the subjective ability of the researcher. As Fan Menan pointed out in Research on Life Experience [5], at the birthplace of Explanatory Phenomenology, Dutch scholars are committed to the traditional study of phenomenology. Their work is either perfect or terrible, and it is by no means trivial. So, the significance of the results of this research also needs to be tested and judged in practical applications in the future.

Acknowledgments. This research was supported by the 2019 Science and Technology Plan of Beijing Municipal Education Commission (Grant No. KM201911417005) and the Premium Funding Project for Academic Human Resources Development in Beijing Union University (Grant No. 12210611609-039).

References

1. Gothelf, J., Seiden, J.: Lean UX. O'Reilly Media, Newton (2016)
2. Hassenzahl, M., Tractinsky, N.: User experience - a research agenda. Behav. Inf. Technol. **25**(2), 91–97 (2006)
3. Buccini, M., Padovani, S.: Typology of the experiences. In: Proceedings of the 2007 Conference on Designing Pleasurable Products and Interfaces, pp. 495–504 (2007)
4. Desmet, P., Hekkert, P.: Framework of product experience. Int. J. Des. **1**(1), 57–66 (2007)
5. van Manen, M.: Researching Lived Experience: Human Science for an Action Sensitive Pedagogy. Routledge, Abingdon (2016)

6. Nielsen, J.: Usefulness, Utility, Usability: Why They Matter (2012). https://www.nngroup.com/videos/usefulness-utility-usability
7. Kant, I.: Critique of Judgment. Hackett Publishing, Indianapolis (1987)
8. Klenk, V.: Understanding Symbolic Logic, 5th edn. Pearson, New Delhi (2007)
9. Svendsen, L.: Fashion: A Philosophy. Reaktion Books, London (2006)
10. Norman, D.: Emotional Design: Why We Love (or Hate) Everyday Things. Basic Books, New York (2005)

A Product/Process Model Approach to Formalize Collaborative User Experience Design

Daniel Kerpen[1]([⊠]) [iD], Jan Conrad[1], and Dieter Wallach[1,2]

[1] HCI2B Group, Faculty of Computer Science and Micro Systems Technology,
Hochschule Kaiserslautern – University of Applied Sciences,
Zweibruecken, Germany
{daniel.kerpen,jan.conrad,dieter.wallach}@hs-kl.de
[2] Ergosign GmbH, Saarbruecken, Germany

Abstract. This contribution presents a concept that paves the ground for a formalization of collaborative user experience design (CUXD). CUXD is rooted in Design Thinking and Lean UX and represents an agile, hypothesis-based approach. The CUXD model divides the development process into the three phases of "Understanding", "Exploration", and "Realization", each consisting of different workshops with suggested methods. The value of CUXD is illustrated by examples drawn from the development of a large-scale predictive maintenance platform. Furthermore, we combine CUXD with the product development methodology CPM/PDD to utilize the advantages and findings of DTM within the context of user-centered design. For this purpose, each phase of CUXD is considered separately and compared with the contents of the CPM product model and the process steps of PDD. In sum, we identify relevant touch points of the two CUXD and CPM/PDD approaches. This points out on how CPM/PDD can serve as a basis for the formalization of CUXD.

Keywords: User experience · Collaborative design · User-centered design · Characteristics-Properties Modelling · Property-Driven Development

1 Introduction

If one is concerned with the topics of product and service development, questions such as the following questions arise almost inevitably in the context of digitalization: How does the practice of product development change, how do production cycles change due to digitalization? And, particularly, how can innovation-oriented design and development approaches help to explore creative problem-solving options that can lead to improvements in product and service development?

These are core questions in an interdisciplinary project[1] joining forces of different research institutions and transfer partners. Their common goal is to develop a culture of

---

[1] Project "Offene Digitalisierungsallianz Pfalz" (German for: "Open Digitalization Alliance Palatinate"; grant titles 03IHS075A&B). See acknowledgments for further information.

© Springer Nature Switzerland AG 2020
A. Marcus and E. Rosenzweig (Eds.): HCII 2020, LNCS 12200, pp. 160–175, 2020.
https://doi.org/10.1007/978-3-030-49713-2_11

transfer-orientation in different innovation fields of digitization. This project has started from the premise of an evident need to pool digitization competencies in the engineering and design professions: Such an endeavor is mandatory to support the transformation of traditional products and services towards networked/smart products and innovative interactive services. In the project, we acknowledge the interdependent and recursive relationship between engineering, innovations and their respective environments (e.g. social and economic aspects of innovation contexts) in "integrated", digitized engineering lifecycles [1, 2].

1.1 Problem Statement

The above issues point towards the bigger picture of digital products becoming increasingly complex; at the same time, they must be designed and implemented in ever shorter time [3]. Hence, when a company develops a new interactive product/service, the responsible executives often have to deal with massive time pressure and must efficiently manage staff from different company departments, as well as various interdisciplinary and professional backgrounds ("cross-functional teams" [4]). Agile mindsets [5, 6] and associated agile development methods, e.g. [7, 8], aim to meet this challenge. The activities of the aforementioned cross-functional teams working together over a certain period of time need coordination, i.e. a way of controlling this cooperation without curtailing its agile potential.

In order to achieve this kind of organizationally-embedded processual "knowledge spiral" [9], i.e. to activate, share, transform, integrate, and reinterpret organizational knowledge [10], agile process models such as Scrum recommend a series of workshops and meetings such as "Sprint Planning", "Daily Scrum", "Sprint Review" and "Sprint Retrospective" [11]. This conception, however, reveals the following issue of concern: Such scrum workshops refer to the implementation of the product – the "Product Delivery" – and not to its conception – the "Product Discovery" [11]. The phase of product conception is in fact often also characterized by a combination of time pressure and complexity.

On the one hand, this calls for design methods in product/service development that demonstrate their innovative potential in being flexible enough to tackle complex and open-ended problems. As Dorst [12] states, individuals associated with finding possible solutions to such problems need "to figure out 'what' to create, while there is no known or chosen 'working principle' that we can trust to lead to the aspired value" ([12], p. 524). With reference to Schön's [13] idea of professional "reflective practice" to understand complex organizational/social problems as well as drawing on Whitbeck's [14] idea of a responsible, ethics-based conduct of engineering, Dorst [12] proposes a concept of "design reasoning" in form of "productive" or "open" reasoning ([12], p. 524f.). His discussion points at open questions of the approach when calling out for the need to articulate these design practices in greater detail (see [12], p. 531).

On the other hand, we consider that design practices need to demonstrate their organizational impact in relation to an entrepreneurial point of view. This then calls out for design approaches that need to be standardizable and quantifiable [15]. From a business and management point of view, such 'measurable' design approaches/methods allow to make a significant contribution to operational and strategical success when compared to traditional methods of product development [15–17].

1.2   Scope of this Contribution

Hence, we propose a concept on how to approach Collaborative User Experience Design (CUXD) projects in an iterative and standardizable manner by refering to Characteristics-Properties Modelling/Property-Driven Development (CPM/PDD). This contribution is, first and foremost, a conceptual combination of the two frameworks CUXD and CPM/PDD. Nevertheless, it promotes a valid basis for discussing real-life projects that combine digitized engineering and design methods.

In order to do so, we start with emphasizing a human-centered perspective by exemplifying how to take user experience (UX) into account in collaborative ways and how to make UX quantifiable by metrics (Sect. 2). By doing so, we pave the way for describing the CUXD process (Sect. 3). Herein, we discuss CUXD in context of engineering project groups which increasingly include experts from various professional/interdisciplinary backgrounds. We do so by drawing on the example of the development of a large-scale predictive maintenance platform.

After this, we shortly review the development of (interactive) products and services from a mechanical engineering and engineering design viewpoint. We highlight the field of design theory and methodology (DTM, Sect. 4.1) as an important reservoir for efforts striving to develop integrated frameworks. Such a perspective is described by CPM/PDD (Sect. 4.2). It helps us to finally map the central characteristics and domains of both concepts, CUXD and CPM/PDD (Sect. 4.3) in order to highlight core overlaps and contact points. In this sense—while not being without limitations—the joined CUXD–CPM/PDD process model supports the continuing task of establishing a common set of design approaches (Sect. 5) with which we conclude.

2   CUXD Foundations – Users, Tasks, and Environments Revisited: Stakeholders' Requirements, Design Thinking, and Agile Development

Collaborative User Experience Design (CUXD) is a process model for UX design proposed by Steimle and Wallach [4]. CUXD is targeted at the design of products with a clear focus on defining the entire interaction of a user with a product or service. CUXD is a collaborative approach, i.e. products or services are developed by a cross-functional team. It is rooted in Design Thinking and Lean UX and represents an agile, hypothesis-based approach.

Conrad et al. [18] illustrate how methods from user-centered design (UCD) contribute to making concrete relations by the identification and evaluation of suitable user requirements. There, the referenced ISO 9241-210 [19] serves as the basis for many UCD methods aiming at products and services being usable, manageable, efficient and effective by realizing relevant user requirements.

Based upon an explicit understanding of users, tasks, and environments to go through during systems' design, the ISO 9241-210 proposes four phases, i.e.:

1. understanding and specifying the context of use,
2. specifying the user requirements,
3. producing design solutions, and
4. evaluating the design.

By emphasizing these phases, design solutions are expected to result that comprehensively address the total of a user's experience and which have a strong notion of commitment to and refinery by user-centered evaluation.

Despite UCDs appropriateness in many use cases and application areas, we prefer to use the term human-centered in the remainder of this contribution: in successful development projects, the sometimes-contradictory requirements of the various stakeholders involved must be carefully balanced against each other. An exclusive focus on user needs without appropriate consideration of technical framework conditions or (justified) business goals of managerial addresses might hinder a sustainable product success. In this context, we refer to a development process as *human-centered* if it is based on iterative validations of a product concept with continuous involvement of users, and where the results are shared and discussed by various stakeholders within a development team [4]. Or to put it short: human-centeredness focuses on the needs of the people in the context of "feasibility", "desirability" and "viability" [16].

Luedeke et al. [16] pinpoint design thinking (DT) as another central approach focusing on user needs; following five iterative modes, DT strives to:

1. empathize insights by focusing on human behavior and everyday life by using (scientifically sound) methods including observations and interviews,
2. derive requirements based on a comprehensive understanding of user needs
3. ideate the exploration of a wide variety of possible solutions using iterative ideation methods,
4. prototype idealized solutions by tangible artifacts, and
5. test (refined) solutions while continually improving the design [16, 20].

In sum, the term Design Thinking refers to an innovation-oriented design and development approach that, based on identified user needs, explores creative problem-solving options and balances, prototypes and evaluates them in the light of technical and economic conditions.

Having briefly summarized human-centeredness and DT, we need to consider time as an important constraint—and flexibility as an answer to tackle this constraint. This consideration leads to agile methods that enable organizations to react more flexibly to the changing requirements in development domains, such as software development [4]: Human-Centeredness, incorporating people's needs into new methods of product development, generally compatible with agile project management methods: Human needs can be incorporated into agile processes as requirements and subsequently worked out in incremental development steps. In order to successfully manage large, i.e. extensive and demanding, projects, agile development uses the simple trick to divide a large project into several small projects (sprints), lasting only a few weeks, i.e. between two and four weeks typically. In each sprint, a "piece" (increment) of the development project (typically: software) is fully implemented so that it is available in executable form. Examples of agile methods comprise besides the already mentioned Scrum for instance also "Extreme Programming" or "Crystal" [21].

UX metrics provide crucial directions for designing interactive systems. Metrics for measuring user experience comprise criteria that refer to actual usage situations like the effectiveness or efficiency of a system. Such metrics, as results of measurements, are quantitative by nature: for instance, completion rates or error rates can be used to operationalize the effectiveness of a system, while time on task (i.e. defined as the time resources used in relation to the results) is an example for a quantification of the efficiency criterion. Efficiency is without doubt one of the most important metrics when judging the performance of an interactive system [15].

By having summarized human-centeredness, DT, and agile methods, we have established a common ground to conclude the related work in order to have a closer look at Collaborative User Experience Design (CUXD).

3   CUXD Outline and Process Description

The CUXD approach divides the development process into the three phases of "Understanding", "Exploration", and "Realization", each consisting of different workshops using appropriate methods (see Fig. 1). The three phases are iteratively linked.

As mentioned in the introduction, conception and development of software increasingly take place in cross-disciplinary teams [4]. Individual members of such a team contribute and bring expertise in various areas—product management, marketing, UX design, implementation, testing, and operation—to the table. By working together over a longer period of time, interdisciplinary teams conceive and design a product/service in joint workshops that build on each other. These workshops refer to the following individual core issues: scoping, synthesis, ideation, conceptualization, prototyping, validation, and MVP-planning. Workshops are useful formats because they allow clear guidance of the process steps and offer the possibility of flexible project planning depending on the availability of team members.

CUXD formed the basis of complex project recently conducted by a leading provider of maintenance, repair and overhaul (MRO) services. The aim of the project[2] was to create a cloud-based platform in order to make data optimally usable for fleet optimization and predictive maintenance scenarios. In addition, CUXD was also used to actively support the MRO's workflow towards Lean UX.

---

[2] Project information publicly available: https://www.aviatar.com, last accessed 2020/2/28, and https://www.ergosign.de/de/work/case-studies/aviatar.html, last accessed 2020/2/28.

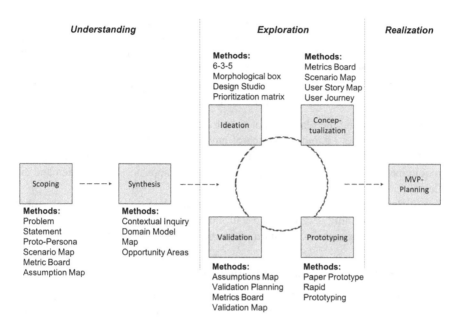

Fig. 1. Collaborative UX Design process and methods ([22] based on [4])

3.1 CUXD Process Phase 1: "Understanding" the Issue, Context(s), and Assumptions

The Scoping workshop format follows the goal to get a design project up-and-running. By drawing on problem statements or scenario maps, a team sharpens the project's mission and objectives, e.g. the core goal of a project. Team members work out the status quo of market companions' products and characterize their peculiarities, advantages, and disadvantages. An essential goal of scoping workshops is to uncover the—often implicit—assumptions behind project missions, for example, to substantiate existing hypotheses about the (prospective) users of an application. In sum, critical assumptions are identified and research measures are selected for verification within the scoping workshop, after which the defined research measures are tackled.

In the Synthesis workshop, members of a team evaluate the results of research activities. For this purpose, descriptions of existing workflows are created and product opportunities for their optimization are identified. Such analyses allow the verification of assumptions about users and support the formulation of empirically founded Personas as archetypically modelled user representatives. At this point, a reflection of the previously defined project goal is important: is it still compatible with the new state of knowledge or do corrections have to be made?

The two workshops outlined so far—Scoping and Synthesis—are primarily concerned with gaining a comprehensive understanding of the problem/issue, its context(s), and underlying assumptions: hypotheses are formed, data collected and hypotheses validated. This serves as a solid starting point to explore possible solutions in subsequent workshops.

The vision for the aviation MRO project was set by the management: developing a platform optimizing the entire aircraft operation. The implementation was largely under the responsibility of the autonomous teams, consisting of product owner, developers, and designers. Each team wasself-contained and fully capable of acting, i.e. each one determined its own objectives and working methods independently. Using various creative methods, initial ideas were generated, including:

1. Neutrality: building the platform not only for the own fleet, but as a service for all airlines worldwide, i.e. independence of any OEM or MRO provider;
2. modularity and user-centric approach: configuration according to customer-specific requirements, i.e. it can be compiled on the basis of apps according to demand and fleet;
3. fast implementation, requiring little effort on client-side: i.e. cloud-based application with a self-explaining user interface with no prior training necessary;
4. platform encourages the co-creation of predictive maintenance functionalities.

3.2   CUXD Process Phase 2: "Exploration" of Possible Solutions

During the Ideation workshop, the team rallies to search for solution ideas to identified product opportunities. In the workshop, different creativity methods are used for the mutual inspiration of the team members (e.g. group-structured brainwriting using the 6-3-5 method): the aim of the workshop is to generate as many ideas as possible. The result of the Ideation workshop is a prioritized idea catalogue for product design.

In the Conceptualization workshop, the previously developed idea catalogue is formed into a coherent solution. Hereby, team members develop a vision of possible usage scenarios and—on this basis—derive a picture of future functionalities of a solution: in this workshop, a first and abstract (high-level) view of the future user interface of a product is created. The abstract concept of the user interface is successively concretized until a concept proposal for the product is finally available. As a result of the workshop, a user journey can be created, illustrating user interactions through a series of visualized screens in order to achieve work goals.

It is important to note that the user journey again conceals assumptions: assumptions about the suitability of certain solution approaches to fulfil user needs. The identification of these assumptions is the subject of a Prototyping workshop, their validation is the focus of the subsequent Validation workshop. For this purpose, a validation plan is derived which describes the type of prototype required to validate the concept. After this, work is targeted at the joint development of a prototype. The aim here is not to specify a solution, but primarily to prepare a concept review. After the Prototyping workshop, developed prototypes are finalized and evaluated. In a formative evaluation session, for example, user interacting with a prototype are observed and their feedback documented.

The results of these observations are evaluated in the Validation workshop. Members of a team compile recorded observations, categorize and weight them. During validation, reference is continuously made to the originally defined assumptions, and it is evaluated whether the developed concept is based on a sufficiently resilient foundation. If this evaluation supports the concept, then its implementation in a first small release and the subsequent evaluation of market feedback should be the obvious choice. Often, a Validation workshop opens up various detailed issues that lead to revisions of a prototype. A fundamental revision of the concept might also become necessary and thus require further ideation workshops. Hence, in this phase, iterations between workshops are just as much a part of a typical project as far-reaching modifications of prototypes.

3.3   CUXD Process Phase 3: "Realization" in a Lean Way

If, on the other hand, a concept proves its worth, the aim of the last workshop—MVP-Planning—is to define a first minimum version of a convincing release, a Minimum Viable Product. For this purpose, the relevant functionalities of a product are prioritized again in the team. Various factors, such as the expected benefit for users and customers, the contribution to business goals or the costs of implementation need to be considered. A roadmap to define future enhancements is defined and concrete quantitative metrics to measure a product's/service's success (or the lack of it) using a metric board [15] are established.

These seven central workshops taken together form CUXD as a process model that is theoretically based on the cornerstones of human-centeredness, design thinking, agile development, and Lean UX. Let us shortly focus on the latter one, Lean UX [7], with its notion of solving time constraints through increased flexibility. Consider the image of an interdisciplinary team with members working together over a certain period of time and sharing a joint (physical) workspace; a team in which, ideally, every stakeholder is involved in each phase. Roles should have as little significance as possible, no matter whether team members are developers, designers or product managers. This consideration points to the advantages of a cross-functional cooperation: the entire know-how of the team is incorporated into the product design. Problems that would otherwise only occur by information—or even only chance—discovered during commissioning of the final product can be disclosed at an early stage. This avoids high revision costs and misinvestments. Furthermore, the effort associated with comprehensive specification documents can be drastically reduced because long specification documents are replaced by descriptive prototypes. Members of the involved team can identify themselves with a product concept, all team members are responsible for the success of the product—an attribute that CUXD inherits from Lean UX.

In a nutshell, at CUXD's core, a defined process is iteratively repeated: the team selects a relevant question, asks users about it, begins to develop an optimized solution concept, visualizes and validates it with users, and, if necessary, quickly adapts and implements it and evaluates the result.

3.4   CUXD Summary

Collaborative User Experience Design (CUXD) is a process model for UX design and is targeted at the design of an interactive system with a clear focus on defining the entire interaction of a user with the interactive system. CUXD is a collaborative approach, i.e. products are developed by a cross-functional team. Individual members of such teams bring expertise in various areas—product management, UX design, implementation, testing, marketing, etc.—to the table.

CUXD is rooted in Design Thinking and Lean UX and represents an agile, hypothesis-based approach. The CUXD model divides the development process into the three phases of "Understanding", "Exploration", and "Realization", each consisting of different workshops with suggested methods. Here, CUXD demonstrates its innovative potential in being flexible enough to tackle complex and open-ended problems. On the other hand, CUXD is conceptualizable in combination with more formalized approaches from design and engineering. We will further expand on this aspect of CUXD formalization in the next section.

4   CUXD Formalization with CPM/PDD

4.1   Foundations of CUXD Formalization: Design Theory and Methodology (DTM)

Weber [23] presents a comprehensive overview of Design Theory and Methodology (DTM). Refering to this overview Conrad et al. [18] point at DTM's objective, which is to determine how much designing can be systemized and automated on the one hand, as well as to develop concepts that make the activity teachable and trainable on the other hand.

DTM combines a large number of different approaches, with some of them—not surprisingly—being incompatible with each other. In the variety of approaches available, some have emerged as particularly popular during the last decades since their formulation in the 1980s/1990s [18]: For instance, John Gero's [24] "function behavior structure model" as an approach from the research field of artificial intelligence (AI), whereas Suh [25] introduced a model called "Axiomatic Design" that basically describes the design process as a mapping from a functional space to a physical space. Following Conrad et al. [18], the VDI guideline 2221 [26] and the fundamental works of Pahl and Beitz [27] play an essential role as a general framework and summary for design guidelines in Europe and especially in German-speaking countries.

With several models existing in parallel, an integrating framework is considered as being beneficial ([23], p. 328). Such an integrating endeavor is presented by the approach of modelling products and development processes based on product characteristics and properties, called CPM/PDD (Characteristics-Properties Modelling, Property-Driven Development).

4.2   Outline of CPM/PDD

In this section, we briefly explain the Characteristics-Properties Modelling/Property-Driven Development (CPM/PDD) approach by relying on and summing up of previous work by Conrad et al. [18, 28]. We will first highlight our notion of CPM/PDD as an approach incorporating both strands of a more analytical product model domain on one side together with the more synthesis-oriented domain that allows for incremental and iterative changes of features or additions in the product development process. After outlining CPM/PDD subsequently, we will explore how to use this notion of dual analysis/synthesis characteristics for applying CPM/PDD to a procedure and its accompanying methods, finally resulting in a close collaboration- and user experience-oriented, agile approach. The most significant feature of the Characteristics-Properties Modelling/Property-Driven Development (CPM/PDD) approach is the differentiation between characteristics and properties of a product [18]: Characteristics (C) cover all the items of a product that can be directly determined and influenced by a designer. These include, for example, the geometry, structure, shape, spatial configuration and material consistency. Properties (P) describe "a product's behavior" and cannot be directly determined by a designer (e.g. weight, safety, aesthetic properties, usability), but indirectly influenced through modifications of characteristics.

The links between characteristics and properties are represented by relations. These can be read in two directions: in the analysis direction (R), characteristics are known and the product's properties are derived (Fig. 2 left). In the synthesis direction (R^{-1}), properties are known/required and the product's characteristics are established (Fig. 2 right). In addition, Dependencies (D) respect potential constraints on the characteristic side and External Conditions (EC) represent the context in which such relational statements are valid.

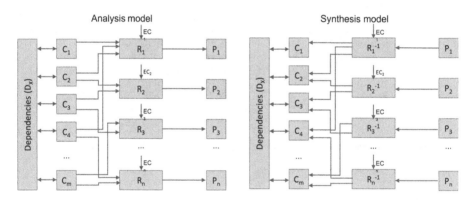

Fig. 2. Differentiation between analysis and synthesis model ([22] based on [18, 28, 29])

The modelling of both, the product and the process is a major advantage of the CPM/PDD compared to models mostly focusing on the process model. Among other things, this simplifies the development of products, where requirements are usually not directly realizable (if users are particularly addressed, see below). Especially, CPM/PDD provides a clear framework for evaluation and process control due to its strong focus on analytical rigor: "based on known/given characteristics (structural parameters, design parameters) of a product, its properties are determined (and therefore, its behavior), or—if the product does not yet exist—predicted" ([23], p. 332). With a focus tending more to synthesis, the task of a development engineer/designer is to find appropriate solutions, i.e. putting together an appropriate set of characteristics that meet a (prospective) users' requirements satisfactorily.

We have highlighted the notion of CPM/PDD as an approach incorporating both strands of a more analytical product model domain on one side together with the more synthesis-oriented domain allowing for incremental and iterative changes of features or additions in the product development process. The modelling of both, the product and the process, is a major advantage of the CPM/PDD compared to models focusing solely on the process model. Among other things, CPM/PDD simplifies the development of products and, especially, it provides a clear framework for evaluation and process control due to its strong focus on analytical rigor.

4.3   CUXD and CPM/PDD Synthesis

The first phase "Understanding" with its workshops Scoping and Synthesis are preparatory steps that are not directly addressed in the CPM/PDD model. Nevertheless, fundamental and necessary components of the model are created and defined here.

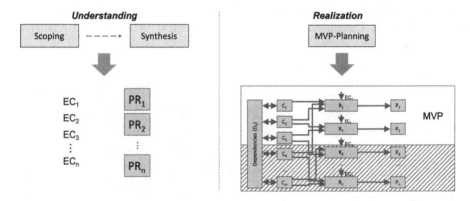

Fig. 3. Formalizing the "Understanding"- (left) and "Realization"-phase (right) ([22] based on [18, 28, 29])

In particular, a result of these workshops is a quantity of the product's required properties (PR). Through the way of determination (e.g. through Problem Statements, Proto-Personas or Journey Maps), these are determined in a user-centered manner to promise a good matching with the "real" user requirements (see Sect. 2). An important side effect of this phase is the determination of External Conditions (EC), i.e. the framework conditions under which the later relations (R or R^{-1}) are valid. The left side of Fig. 3 summarizes the outcomes of the first phase.

Refering to the CUXD process description above, we keep in mind that the "Understanding"-phase is followed by the "Exploration"-phase. This phase is an iterative sequence of ideation, conceptualization, prototyping, and validation (see Fig. 4).

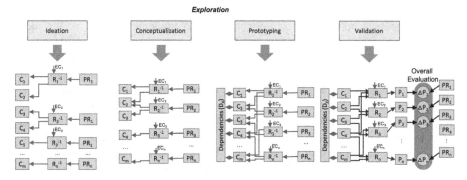

Fig. 4. Formalizing the "Exploration"-phase ([22] based on [18, 28, 29])

First, Ideation is supposed to generate as many ideas as possible for the identified user requirements. The user requirements are mostly considered individually and translated into features. The synthesis methods used (see Fig. 2) are rather informal and strongly influenced by intuition and creativity. The evaluation of the developed solutions is also largely based on common sense. For CPM/PDD, this means that there is a multitude of different CPM product models based on individual required properties (PR). The synthesis relations (R^{-1}) are not formalized but largely based on the abilities of the people involved.

Followed with the Conceptualization step, the results of previous activities are more formalized and fewer different solutions are considered. In order to obtain results that completely fulfil the problem, the user requirements are more strongly integrated. For the considerations in CPM/PDD, this means that there are fewer different CPM product models, but these fulfil already several required properties PR. The formalization of synthesis relations is also increasing.

Afterwards, Prototyping produces the first tangible results. It focuses on one or very few variants that already integrate many of the user requirements. The range of these prototypes extends from low- to high-fidelity. Typical techniques for low-fidelity prototypes are paper prototypes or pencil scribbles. This is particularly useful in the early phases of prototyping so that these can be discarded easily and without emotional reference. In later iterations, the prototypes become more and more sophisticated, e.g. clickable user interfaces or 3D printing. For the CPM model, this implies that (almost) all PR are considered in the analysis step. For sophisticated prototypes, the synthesis relations become increasingly complex and might require the creation of CAD models or writing source code.

Finally, the Validation workshops determine the fulfilment of the user requirements by the prototype. Not only the fulfilment of individual requirements is relevant for the development process, but also the consideration of an overall evaluation. For CPM/PDD the analysis of the submitted solution is in focus: the individual properties are evaluated with regard to their target fulfilment. The overall evaluation of the solution is particularly interesting as it determines the next steps. If the overall evaluation is sufficient for the problem statement, the next phase can begin.

In the "Realization"-phase, a product is—partially—reified. In the sense of the MVP and the lean approach, it is only intended to implement a part of the most important requirements. This fact can be delineated very clearly in the CPM model since it becomes visible which characteristics are necessary for the implementation of the MVP (see Fig. 3 on the right side); however, the possibilities and limitations of MVPs in mechanical engineering is a particular topic that should be considered separately in research and practice. Without the possibility of going into more detail at this point, at least a brief remark should be made here: Although it is invented to assess the market fit at a very early stage, a MVP needs to fully address a need or solve a problem for the user in order to be useful. This implies that for technically demanding projects the transition between prototype, MVP, pilot project and finished product can be fluid.

5 Conclusion

In this contribution, we have shown that it is possible to formalize the lean and agile CUXD process approach (abbreviated for Collaborative User Experience Design) through a combination with Characteristics-Properties Modelling/Property-Driven Development (CPM/PDD). CUXD is a cross-disciplinary, human-centered development model focusing on collaboration in teams. CPM/PDD is a methodology to describe a product as well as the product development process based on the clear distinction of characteristics and properties. We identified relevant touch points of the two approaches and pointed out on how CPM/PDD can serve as a basis for the formalization of CUXD. Thus, this contribution is, first and foremost, a conceptual combination of the two frameworks CUXD and CPM/PDD.

The proposed formalization is necessary to make the approach of developing (interactive) products and services quantifiable and trainable/teachable. This is especially important in context of engineering project groups which increasingly include experts with various professional/educational backgrounds. Refering to the description of the CUXD process model and its foundations, we have to keep the following success factors of CUXD in mind: the inclusion of all relevant (prospective) stakeholders when putting together interdisciplinary teams, the use of adequate methods for a reliable identification of relevant features of the problem space and (potentially conflicting) constraints for finding solutions, the critical (empirical) testing of assumptions, the illustration and formative optimization of solution approaches through prototypes, the definition of (quantitative) metrics for the evaluation of solutions, as well as a controlled execution of all activities in time-boxed workshop formats.

In this sense, the joined CUXD–CPM/PDD process model supports the continuing task of establishing a common set of design approaches.

We suggest that the CUXD and CPM/PDD combination can be particularly helpful for at least:

1. the determination of the maturity level of a current development process,
2. supporting the internal organizational communication and co-operation, especially when considering development through cross-functional teams, and
3. being compatible to the inclusion of digital tools which are important means of support in everyday work life.

We are well aware that from a practitioner's perspective, e.g. from an industry application perspective, conceptual approaches cannot be seen without limitations. Therefore, future work needs to illustrate the value of the contribution by using case studies from the engineering lifecycle to present the broad applicability of the concept. For instance, and with regard to the points 1–3 listed above, we plan to support and to evaluate the development process by using digital tools for recording the product features and properties in the individual steps of the CUXD. On this basis, synthesis and analysis relations can be accompanied digitally; furthermore, collaboration can be realized by distributed teams working jointly together via remote collaboration tools in different research/design labs.

Acknowledgments. We gratefully acknowledge funding for the project [30] by the German Federal Ministry of Education and Research (under grant titles 03IHS075A&B). Additional funding was provided by the German Federal Ministry for Economic Affairs and Energy (under grant title 01MF1170113D). This contribution is a revised and extended version of [22], accepted for publication in "Proceedings of the Design Society Proceedings: DESIGN conference" by Cambridge University Press, for which copyright (including, without limitation, the right to publish the work in whole or in part in any and all forms and media, now or hereafter known) is retained by the authors.

References

1. Tafvizi Zavareh, M., Sadaune, S., Siedler, C., Aurich, J.C., Zink, K.J., Eigner, M.: A study on the socio-technical aspects of digitization technologies for future integrated engineering work systems. In: Ekstroemer, P., Schuette, S., Oelvander, J. (eds.) Proceedings NordDesign 2018 (no pagination). The Design Society, Glasgow (2018). ISBN 978-91-7685-185-2
2. Eigner, M., Dickopf, T., Huwig, C.: An interdisciplinary model-based design approach for developing cybertronic systems. In: Marjanović, D., Štorga, M., Pavković, N., Bojčetić, N., Škec, S. (eds.) Proceedings of the Design 2016/14th International Design Conference, pp. 1647–1656. The Design Society, Glasgow (2016). ISSN 1847-9073
3. PwC (PricewaterhouseCoopers): Digital Product Development 2025. Agile, Collaborative, AI Driven and Customer Centric. https://www.pwc.de/de/digitale-transformation/pwc-studie-digital-product-development-2025.pdf. Accessed 20 Dec 2019
4. Steimle, T., Wallach, D.: Collaborative UX design. dpunkt, New York (2018). ISBN 978-3-86490-532-2
5. Kotter, J., von Ameln, F.: Agility, hierarchy and lessons for the future. John Kotter on the legacy and future of change management. Gr. Interakt. Org. **50**, 111–114 (2019). https://doi.org/10.1007/s11612-019-00461-5
6. Senge, P., von Ameln, F.: We are not in control—embrace uncertainty and trust in what emerges. Peter Senge on the legacy and future of change management. Gr. Interakt. Org. **50**, 123–127 (2019). https://doi.org/10.1007/s11612-019-00460-6
7. Gothelf, J., Seiden, J.: Lean UX: Designing Great Products with Agile Teams, 2nd edn. O'Reilly, Beijing (2016). ISBN 978-1-49195-360-0
8. Ries, E.: The Lean Startup: How Constant Innovation Creates Radically Successful Businesses. Portfolio Penguin, London (2011). ISBN 978-0-67092-160-7
9. Nonaka, I.: A dynamic theory of organizational knowledge creation. Organ. Sci. **5**(1), 14–37 (1994). https://doi.org/10.1287/orsc.5.1.14

10. Grant, R.M.: Nonaka's 'dynamic theory of knowledge creation' (1994): reflections and an exploration of the 'ontological dimension'. In: von Krogh, G., Takeuchi, H., Kase, K., Cantón, C.G. (eds.) Towards Organizational Knowledge. NOSKI, pp. 77–95. Palgrave Macmillan, London (2013). https://doi.org/10.1057/9781137024961_5

11. Steimle, T., Wallach, D.: Collaborative UX design. https://upload-magazin.de/25535-collaborative-ux-design/. Accessed 20 Dec 2019

12. Dorst, K.: The core of 'design thinking' and its application. Des. Stud. **32**(6), 521–532 (2011). https://doi.org/10.1016/j.destud.2011.07.006

13. Schön, D.A.: The Reflective Practitioner: How Professionals Think in Action. Temple Smith, London (1983). ISBN 978-0-46506-878-4

14. Whitbeck, C.: Ethics in Engineering Practice and Research, 2nd edn. Cambridge University Press, Cambridge (1998). ISBN 978-0-52172-398-5

15. Wallach, D., Conrad, J., Steimle, T.: The UX metrics table: a missing artifact. In: Marcus, A., Wang, W. (eds.) DUXU 2017. LNCS, vol. 10288, pp. 507–517. Springer, Cham (2017). https://doi.org/10.1007/978-3-319-58634-2_37

16. Luedeke, T.F., et al.: CPM/PDD as an integrated product and process model for a design-thinking based, agile product development process. In: Marjanović, D., Štorga, M., Škec, S., Bojčetić, N., Pavković, N. (eds.) Proceedings of the Design 2018/15th International Design Conference, pp. 2063–2074. The Design Society, Glasgow (2018). https://doi.org/10.21278/idc.2018.0311

17. Tullis, T., Albert, B.: Measuring the User Experience. Collecting, Analyzing, and Presenting Usability Metrics, 2nd edn. Morgan Kaufman/Elsevier, Waltham/MA (2013). ISBN 978-0-12415-781-1

18. Conrad, J., Koehler, C., Wallach, D., Luedeke, T.: Design theory and methodology in HCI: applying CPM/PDD to UCD. In: Marcus, A., Wang, W. (eds.) DUXU 2018. LNCS, vol. 10918, pp. 27–39. Springer, Cham (2018). https://doi.org/10.1007/978-3-319-91797-9_3

19. ISO 9241-210: Ergonomics of Human-System Interaction. Part 210: Human-Centered Design Process for Interactive Systems. ISO, Geneva (2018)

20. d.school bootcamp bootleg. https://dschool.stanford.edu/resources/the-bootcamp-bootleg. Accessed 14 Dec 2018

21. Haberfellner, R., Fricke, E., de Weck, O., Voessner, S.: Systems Engineering, 14th edn. Orell Füssli, Zurich (2018). ISBN 978-3-28004-179-6

22. Kerpen, D., Conrad, C., Wallach, D.: A formalization approach for collaborative user experience design. In: Proceedings of the Design 2020/16th International Design Conference (forthcoming)

23. Weber, C.: Modelling products and product development based on characteristics and properties. In: Chakrabarti, A., Blessing, L.T.M. (eds.) An Anthology of Theories and Models of Design, pp. 327–352. Springer, London (2014). https://doi.org/10.1007/978-1-4471-6338-1_16

24. Gero, J.S.: Design prototypes – a knowledge representation schema for design. AI Mag. **11** (4), 26–36 (1990). https://doi.org/10.1609/aimag.v11i4.854

25. Suh, N.P.: The Principles of Design. Oxford University Press, New York (1990). ISBN 978-0-19504-345-7

26. VDI-Guideline 2221: Systematic approach to the design of technical systems and products. VDI, Duesseldorf (1987)

27. Pahl, G., Beitz, W., Feldhusen, J., Grote, K.H.: Engineering Design. A Systematic Approach, 3rd edn. Springer, London (2007). https://doi.org/10.1007/978-1-84628-319-2

28. Conrad, J., Koehler, C., Wanke, S., Weber, C.: What is design knowledge from the viewpoint of CPM/PDD? In: Marjanović, D., Štorga, M., Pavković, N., Bojčetić, N. (eds.)

Proceedings of the Design 2008/10th International Design Conference, pp. 745–752. The Design Society, Glasgow (2008)

29. Weber, C.: CPM/PDD – an extended theoretical approach to modelling products and product development processes. In: Proceedings of the 2nd German-Israeli Symposium on Advances in Methods and Systems for Development of Products and Processes, pp. 159–179. Fraunhofer-IRB, Stuttgart (2005)

30. Joint project "Offene Digitalisierungsallianz Pfalz" (Open Digitalization Alliance Palatinate) of the Hochschule Kaiserslautern – University of Applied Sciences, TU Kaiserslautern, and the Fraunhofer Institute for Industrial Mathematics ITWM. https://www.offenedigitalisierungsallianzpfalz.de. Accessed 20 Dec 2019

Should We Measure UX Differently?

Apala Lahiri Chavan[1($\boxtimes$)] and Girish Prabhu[2]

[1] Manipal Academy of Higher Education, Manipal, India
apala@humanfactors.com
[2] Design and Innovation, Human Factors International, Mumbai, India

Abstract. The design of User Experience today is built upon a choice architecture that is meant to acquire and retain customers and hence increase revenue on the one hand and save cost for businesses through efficiency and speed, on the other. The impact of this can be seen in the form of an ever expanding, instant gratification led experience economy that constantly fuels consumerism. Since there is no plan(et) B, if we are to survive as the human race, this planet has to be saved by switching to a less consumerist and more sustainable lifestyle. Just as User Experience design is contributing to the increasing consumerism today, a change in the evaluation criteria and definition of what is 'good' and 'successful' UX can transform the impact of User Experience design by ensuring that the goal of UX Design is a balance between what is good for the human race and what is good for commerce.

Keywords: UX design index · Sustainable UX design · Future of UX

1 Introduction

The field of User Experience has increasingly been in the spotlight as technology infiltrates and disrupts our lives at an exponential pace. Making the technology 'experience' easy, intuitive, efficient and persuasive is the focus of mainstream User Experience. User Experience Design is being looked at as a business differentiator that will lead to an increase in sales and delighted customers and allow a brand to stay ahead of its competition. The 'user' seems to play a marginal role in the entire process. The fact that she plays any role at all is simply because even a little understanding of the user would help create an experience that would help increase sales of the product/service. UX therefore is really a sales/marketing activity using a profit centred design philosophy that is a key contributor to our current consumerist lifestyles and pushing the world closer to an unsustainable future.

However, as Management thinker Peter Drucker is often quoted as saying that "you can't manage what you can't measure." Drucker means that you can't know whether or not you are successful unless success is defined and tracked. Hence, one of the critical aspects to review is what gets measured and tracked as good and successful UX design today. Are those criteria suitable for envisioning alternate modes of practicing User Experience or do they need to change?

Most leading practitioners/practices and their methods, used in the field of User Experience today, (cf. Norman, Cooper, Ideo, HFI) define and design User Experience

A. Marcus and E. Rosenzweig (Eds.): HCII 2020, LNCS 12200, pp. 176–187, 2020.
https://doi.org/10.1007/978-3-030-49713-2_12

in terms of what the business wants the 'system' to be, how the 'user's' needs can be aligned to best suit what the business wants and finally how to make the design as familiar and easy to use by integrating elements from the user's context, as far as possible.

In recent years, User Experience has also focused on understanding the emotional state of the user and building trust based on emotions. This has meant a tighter alignment with marketing objectives such as conversion (to buy something or renew current subscriptions/usage etc.). None of these methods and practices take into consideration whether what the business needs to be designed has a negative impact on the ecosystem of the very 'users' who are being targeted as the consumers of the designed experience (E.g. will the current design method lead to wastage of resources and hasten the destruction of the planet?). The primary focus on business needs as drivers of design also leads to specific sections of the population (lower income groups) being excluded because the 'return on investment' for including them as potential users is not attractive.

The challenge for alternate approaches to the way UX is practiced now, has been, the fact that the predominant underlying economic structure of our lives, that of capitalism and its recent avatar, neo liberalism, makes it impossible to model the creation of 'experiences' without following the diktat of the 'market'. And, the market is always focused on maximizing profit rather than on issues of social impact, marginalized/excluded 'users' and alternative futures. It has, therefore, largely been a theoretical exercise to reimagine UX and create an alternate model of practice so far. However, at this point in time, the winds of economic change are blowing.

Several authors like Jeremy Rifkin (2014) and Paul Mason (2015) contend that information technology is making a shift inevitable and this shift could completely reshape our familiar notions of work, production and value; and destroy market and private ownership based economic structures. They points out that we do actually have the 'chance to create a more socially just and sustainable global economy'.

Hence at this point in time, it is a very appropriate moment, to re-examine the potential contribution of UX to advancing alternate economies. The new economic system that is being ushered in by these new trends such as parallel currencies, the sharing economy, peer to peer lending, Big Data, Internet of Things, 3D printing and characterized by collaborative commons, abundance (rather than scarcity as the underlying economic philosophy) and prosumers (producers cum consumers) demands exploration of a different UX 'ideology' that will help reframe UX practice from what is currently mainstream.

2 Measurement of Impact – How Does User Experience Measure Itself Today?

In mainstream UX practice today, when it comes to measurement criteria for good User Experience, the priority is to measure, at the granular level of 'tasks' (a 'task' for example, would be whether the user is able to book a ticket on an airlines site) how fast and efficiently the user is able to achieve success. The most commonly used metrics are (and have been for the last 3 decades) success rate (whether users can perform the task at all), time a task requires, error rate, users' subjective satisfaction, efficiency and learnability.

There have been some attempts to broaden the scope of what is important to measure differently for User Experience versus Usability/HCI (Pavliscak 2014). In this categorisation of UX metrics (and others such as Google's HEART framework (Rodden 2012) largely marketing oriented measures have been added under 'engagement' and 'conversion', thereby viewing the difference between User Experience and Usability/HCI as simply that of integrating the business/sales perspective to user centered design. An example would be, measuring not just time spent on a task on a website but also the attention paid by the user to the brand's content on the site. This is measured by tracking how long a user stays on the website and also time spent on various sections of the site. And, finally, how the design helped the user take steps towards buying a product or signing up for a newsletter, etc.

A review of current design indices and design awards further clarifies the focus of user centred experience design today and what is defined as 'good' or 'successful' UX. The focus is clearly on an ever expanding, instant gratification led experience economy that constantly fuels consumerism.

2.1   Design Indices

The best known design indices are the McKinsey Design Index and the DMI Design Value Index. Both take similar routes to measure value of Design and that is by evaluating the financial performance of organisations who have 'invested' in design. The conclusion both arrive at is also similar and hence reinforces the message that investing in design leads to better market performance (Figs. 1, 2 and 3).

Fig. 1. McKinsey Design Index

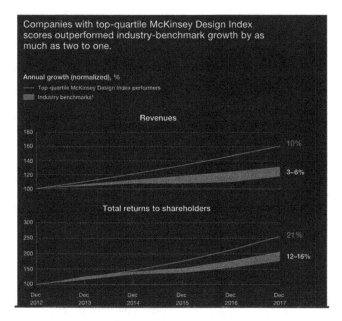

Fig. 2. McKinsey Design Index

The dmi:Design Value Index

DMI and Motiv Strategies, funded by Microsoft, began analyzing the performance of US companies committed to design as an integral part of their business strategy. Completed in 2013 the dmi:Design Value Index tracked the value of publicly held companies that met specific design management criteria, and monitored the impact of their investments in design on stock value over a ten-year period, relative to the overall S&P Index.

2015 results show that over the last 10 years design-led companies have maintained significant stock market advantage, outperforming the S&P by an extraordinary 211%.

Fig. 3. DMI Design Index

The Mckinsey Design Index consists of four themes – Analytical Leadership, Cross Functional Talent, Continuous Iteration and User Experience, themes that seek to create a robust business driven process that incorporates components of the mainstream UX design process to ensure that the products, services and customer touchpoints are in synch with business and user goals (Fig. 4).

The DMI Design Value Index differs from the McKinsey Index in terms of its entire focus being on evaluating how robustly the investment in design, integration of design within the entire organisational structure and leadership commitment to design can be demonstrated over time, by an organisation (Fig. 5).

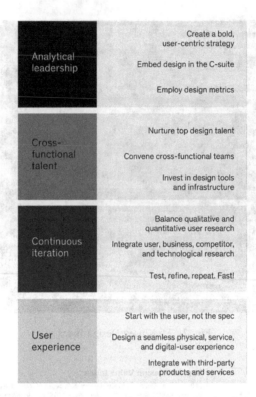

Fig. 4. What Constitutes the McKinsey Design Index

Design Value Index Selection Criteria

What constitutes good design can be viewed as highly subjective; therefore the selection criteria developed for inclusion in our index focus on the following:

1) The organization must be publicly traded in the US for 10+ years.
Only public companies were eligible for selection to ensure access to financial data surrounding share prices and stock performance. The 10-year time-frame was established to select for companies that have maintained a consistent, long-term focus on design.

2) The scale of the design organization and deployment is an integrated function.
The strategic use of design is employed in the organization, both within business units and as a centrally managed function with a high degree of influence with its senior leadership team. The use of design can have outsized influences on a company's bottom line that multiply as it is assimilated into the organization and its culture.

3) Growth in design-related investments and influence have increased overtime.
Design has been well resourced through talent acquisition, appropriate facilities, competitive technologies, and the application of design research as a tool, among other investments. Design cannot be expected to thrive when proper resourcing is neglected.

4) Design is embedded within the organizational structure.
It is well understood where and how design fits within the organization. While there are several precedents set for successful operating models that can be used, the common theme is that design is clearly built into the structure and processes of the organization.

5) Design leadership is present at senior and divisional levels.
Design is given a seat at the table with an experienced executive or executive-level head of design who can interface with senior leadership. Typically, this head of design has 15 to 20 years of experience managing design-related functions that drive the company forward with design goals.

6) There is a senior-level commitment to design's use as an innovation resource and integrative force.
An organization's commitment to design shows up in many ways, including the level of interaction the design executives and function have with other parts of the organization, and in how the CEO and other leadership team members represent the importance of design in their day-to-day work and public relations efforts.

Fig. 5. What Constitutes the DMI Design Value Index

Hence both these indices look at design as a value add for business and apply relevant criteria to measure that value addition and demonstrate the correlation in terms of focus on design leading to better market performance and return to shareholders.

2.2 Design Awards

A look at three popular design awards yielded an interesting dichotomy between what is stated as the objective of the awards and the actual criteria based on which designs gets evaluated. Take the Webby awards, for example, which states on their site (for 2017 - https://www.monkeysfightingrobots.co/the-2017-webby-awards-vote-for-the-best-of-the-internet/), that *'In a year marked by so much discord and divisiveness, the Webby Awards is honored to recognized the work and efforts of our nominees as they explore new ways to use the internet to inform our world and bring people together.'* However, an examination of the actual criteria for the web design category, reveals a much narrower focus, as described in the paragraph after next.

The UX design award instituted by the International Design Centre, Berlin (http://www.ux-design-awards.com/en/awards/about/) describes its purpose and the criteria for evaluation as follows: *'The UX Design Awards are a singular competition for user experience – a key added value in connected life and work. The Awards communicate opportunities: How accomplished experience design and innovative technologies add value and make a positive impact in peoples's lives. The UX Design Awards recognize excellent experience qualities in products, services, environments and future-oriented concepts in all areas of life'*. But, once again, between the description of the award and the actual criteria used for evaluation, falls a shadow.

A Sampling of the Stated Reward Criteria for the Above Mentioned Awards

- Navigation is around speed and ease of use: *where you want to go quickly and offers easy access to the breadth and depth of the site's content, thereby, learning time should be minimal, errors must be easy to correct*
- Optimizing the use of technology through design: *is the use of technology on the site. Good functionality means the site works well. It loads quickly, has live links, and any new technology used is functional and relevant for the intended audience, Does the technology work? Does the innovation alter the way technology is developed and utilized in the future?*
- Improving bottom line through customer retention: *is effective experience design enabling brands to develop propositions that add human value, driving their market success, one has probably had a good overall experience if (s)he comes back regularly, places a bookmark, signs up for a newsletter, participates, emails the site to a friend, or is intrigued enough to stay for a while*
- Providing aesthetically engaging experience: *is communicating a visual experience that may even take one's breath away*
- Using the award as a marker of success to attract more customers in the global marketplace *A distinction for excellent user experience enhances the recognition of skills, products and services on the global market*

Yet another well-known design award – the Red Dot Design Award also states the following as the evaluation criteria https://www.red-dot.org/pd/about/ (Fig. 6).

The **Red Dot Award**: Product **Design awards** the best products of the year.

...

The judging criteria include amongst others:

- Degree of innovation.
- Functionality.
- Formal quality.
- Ergonomics.
- Durability.
- Symbolic and emotional content.
- Product periphery.
- Self-explanatory quality.

Fig. 6. Award Criteria for Red Dot Design Awards

If the criteria for determining UX design that is worth rewarding (via indices and awards) is still only about speed, efficiency, learnability, market success, customer acquisition and retention on one hand and aesthetic delight on the other, then the processes leading to successful UX design will also focus on designing based only on these criteria. The cycle of market led design will then continue instead of evaluating a more holistic set of criteria that could help shift the desired outcome of UX design from just being about creating convenience and wealth to also playing a role in enhancing capabilities of its human users and thereby empowering users to make more informed decisions about their lives, the experiences they chose and have clarity about the impact those decisions will have on the future of the world.

But is there another set of criteria with which to evaluate UX? Let us for a moment look at an entirely different area, that of measuring human development and welfare in development economics, for parallels to our search for more holistic measurement criteria.

3 Is There an Alternative Way to Evaluate UX Holistically?

This journey of measuring humanity's progress 'only' in terms of financial and growth numbers instead of 'also' in terms of growth numbers till a reform movement of sorts shifts the narrative to a more humane perspective has been seen in the field of development economics. Just as in mainstream UX design today, there was a time not long ago when GDP was the celebrity measure for tracking the progress of the human race in development/welfare economics.

"We are stealing the future, selling it in the present, and calling it GDP."—Paul Hawke

4   The Transformation in Measuring Human Development

The concept and measurement of human welfare has undergone a massive change, from the origins of economic "utility" theory to Amartya Sen's human capabilities approach. Present measures of social welfare used in the fields of economics and development, include not just national income but a variety of composite measures such as the Human Development Index, Better Life Index, Happiness Index, etc.

In 1990, the United Nations Development Program (UNDP) transformed the landscape of development theory, measurement, and policy with the publication of its first annual Human Development Report (HDR) and the introduction of the Human Development Index. HDR 1990 presented the concept of "human development" as progress towards greater human well-being and provided country-level data for a wide range of well-being indicators. The UNDP's establishment of the HDR expanded both the availability of measurement and comparison tools used by governments, NGOs, and researchers, and our common understanding of development itself.

The Humanist Revolution in economics was ushered in by Amartya Sen and Martha Nussbaum, who are together credited with the origination of the "capabilities" approach to human well-being based on Rawlsian philosophy (Pattanaik 1994). Sen and Nussbaum, like Aristotle privileged the 'being' and 'doing' of human beings, instead of what they 'have'. Moving the discussion away from utility and towards "capabilities" allowed Sen and Nussbaum to distinguish means (like money) from ends (like well-being or freedom) (Crocker 1992; Sen 1979; Sen 1999; Nussbaum 2001).

Sen searched for measures to adequately represent people's well-being and deprivation and found that neither income and command over commodities, nor happiness and fulfillment of desires constituted good enough indicators of human well-being or lack of it. Sen's argument in terms of analysing quality of life/poverty was that true well-being resulted from the power and control people have over what they can be and do. Hence he posited that focusing on human functionings and capabilities would provide a construct for assessing in a more reasonable manner (than just what he/she possesses materially) to assess an individual's advantages and disadvantages.

4.1   New Measures of Well Being

Amartya Sen's capabilities approach offers this broad based perspective of development where everything revolves around people's well-being. This humanist approach to measuring welfare led to several new/alternative (to the popular GNP, GDP measures) emerging that reflected a broader conception of wellbeing (Fig. 7).

Alternative national indicators of welfare and well-being		
Indicator	Explanation	Coverage
Index of Sustainable Economic Welfare (ISEW) & Genuine Progress Indicator (GPI) Type: GDP modification Unit: dollar	Personal consumption expenditures weighted by income distribution, with volunteer and household work added and environmental and social costs subtracted.	• 17 countries, several states and regions • 1950 - various years
Genuine savings Type: Income accounts modification Unit: dollar	Level of saving after depreciation of produced capital, investments in human capital, depletion of minerals, energy, and forests, and damages from local and global air pollutants are accounted for.	• 140 countries • 1970 - 2008
Inclusive Wealth Index Type: Capital accounts modification Unit: dollar	Asset wealth including built, human, and natural resources.	• 20 countries • 1990-2008
Australian Unity Well-Being Index Type: Survey based index Unit: Index	Annual survey of various aspects of well-being and quality of life.	• Australia • 2001-present
Gallup-Healthways Well-Being Index Type: Survey based index Unit: Index	Annual survey in taking into account five elements: purpose (employment, etc), social, financial, community and physical (health).	• 50 states of the USA, expanded to 135 countries in 2013. • 2008-present
Gross National Happiness Type: Survey based index Unit: Index	Detailed in-person survey around nine domains: psychological well-being, standard of living, governance, health, education, community vitality, cultural diversity, time use, and ecological diversity.	• Bhutan • 2010
Human Development Index Type: Composite index Unit: Index	Index of GDP per person, spending on health and education, and life expectancy.	• 177 countries • 1980 - present
Happy Planet Index Type: Composite index Unit: Index	A calculation based on subjective well being multimplied by life expectancy divided by ecological footprint.	• 153 countries • 3 years
OECD Better Life Index Type: Composite index Unit: Index	Includes housing, income, jobs, community education, environment, civic engagement, health, life satisfaction, saftey, and work-life balance.	• 36 OECD countries • 1 year

theconversation.com   Source: Author

Fig. 7. Popular Indices Measuring Welfare and Well Being

4.2 Have New Indices Brought New Insights?

It is important to note that with the use of new measures of well-being, it has come to light that not all countries that have high economic output have high level of well-being (examples – USA and UK). On the other hand, countries that score high on economic output AND creativity AND innovation also score high on happiness and subjective well-being (example – Nordic countries).

Does an environment that harbors emancipative values lead to more creativity and innovation? According to a World Values Survey report (http://www.worldvaluessurvey.org/wvs/articles/folder_published/article_base_54), the critical cultural components that constitute the process of human empowerment are the presence of emancipative values. Once this process is in place, people are empowered to exercise their freedoms through their action.

Human empowerment built on a foundation of emancipative values builds social capital, leads to increased self-expression and revitalises civil society. Emancipative values also lead to an overall rise in the level of subjective well-being that society experiences by shifting people's narrow focus on a strategy of survival to one of increased human agency.

5   An Alternative Approach to Measuring UX – A Holistic Design Index

Just as the move away from GDP as the only way to measure progress and well-being of the human race has led to new ways of looking at the connections between economic prosperity and various categories of wellbeing and hence given rise to new policies and programs, constructing a new holistic design index that reimagines the potential impact that the design of experience can have on people would throw new light on alternative ways UX can be practiced.

Perhaps a more meaningful approach to measuring (and hence defining) how an 'experience' can make fundamental enhancements to the user's core capability to function with agency is urgently needed.

Based on Amartya Sen and Martha Nussbaum's capability theory, a list of parameters that evaluate whether capabilities of users interacting with digital products and services were enhanced as a result of using those products and services could form the basis of this new design index. Since the success criteria of 'good' User Experience would now have measures around capability enhancement in addition to some of the current measures like speed, efficiency, increased conversion, etc., the very definition and process of UX design would have to transform so that successful and award winning User Experience could incorporate a balance between profit centred design and capability centred design.

5.1   Design Led Empowerment Index

What could a more holistic design index look like? Having reviewed indices that measure human wellbeing in a more holistic manner than simply looking at GDP, per capita income, etc. (Human Development Index, Better Life Index (OECD 2013), Happy Planet Index, World Happiness Index, Gross National Happiness, Global Creativity Index (Florida 2011), etc.) as part of the first author's ongoing PhD research, the following dimensions have been identified as key factors contributing to overall happiness and wellbeing.

- Material living standards (income, consumption and wealth);
- Health;
- Education;
- Personal activities including work

- Social connections and relationships;
- Environment (present and future conditions);
- Insecurity, of an economic as well as a physical nature.
- Generosity
- Freedom

All these dimensions shape people's well-being, and yet conventional income measures miss many of these. Taking inspiration from these dimensions, we present here a list of parameters that could form the basis of a more holistic design index.

These parameters could be used to evaluate whether a UX design concept/prototype/fully working product does the following for its users? The design could be scored based on how it fares on each of the items below.

1. Improves Personal Capabilities to think, feel, imagine, reason
2. Connects people and enables community building
3. Enhances Life Satisfaction
4. Provides a sense of flow and delight
5. Reduces Effort and Facilitates Convenience
6. Helps Save or Make Money
7. Enhances Personal and Family Health and safety
8. Enhances Feeling of Purpose
9. Facilitates/enhances ways to live a more sustainable and socially responsible life
10. Is designed to be inclusive

Using an index with parameters such as the list includes would go a long way in shifting the current mainstream UX narrative of designing ONLY for increased efficiency, speed and revenue to ALSO designing for these. Including the additional parameters (from the list given above) as part of an index that measures 'good' UX design will also mean that current design frameworks and processes will need to transform to meet the new definition of what is 'good' UX. As the Nobel Prize winning economist Joseph E. Stiglitz (2010) said, "What you measure affects what you do. If we have the wrong metrics, we will strive for the wrong things."

With an alternative design index that focuses on holistic empowerment of the design's users, the journey to reframe how we practice UX Design will get a head start and we will pay attention to what is needed for design to contribute towards a sustainable and inclusive world.

6 Conclusion

At this point in time, when technology is creating a major fork in the road between what could be a better world for all versus a more divided, automated and unequal world, designers can and should play a critical role in making the choice for humanity. And for that to happen, the measurement and process of design must take a more humanitarian turn just like it did in economics.

Note. This paper presents ongoing doctoral research work by the 1st author that is part of an unpublished thesis.

References

Stiglitz, J., Sen, A., Fitoussi, J.: Report by the Commission on the Measurement of Economic Performance and Social Progress (2010)

Florida, R.: Creativity and Prosperity: The Global Creativity Index, Martin Prosperity Institute (2011)

OECD: OECD Guidelines on Measuring Subjective Well-being. OECD Publishing, Paris (2013)

Sen, A.: Equality of What? The Tanner Lecture on Human Values. Stanford University, Stanford (1979)

Ura, K., ALkire, S., Zangmo, T., Karma, W.: A Short Guide to Gross National Happiness Index. https://opendocs.ids.ac.uk/opendocs/handle/123456789/11807. Accessed 20 Oct 2018

Pavliscak, P.: Choosing the Right Metrics for User Experience. http://www.uxmatters.com/mt/archives/2014/06/choosing-the-right-metrics-for-user-experience.php. Accessed 07 Mar 2016

Rifkin, J.: The Zero Marginal Cost Society: The Internet of Things, the Collaborative Commons and the Eclipse of Capitalism. St. Martin's Press, New York (2014)

Rodden, K.: How to choose the right UX metrics for your product. https://www.gv.com/lib/how-to-choose-the-right-ux-metrics-for-your-product Accessed 15 Apr 2015

Mason, P.: Post Capitalism: A Guide to Our Future. Penguin Books, New York (2015)

Nussbaum, M.: Women and Human Development: The Capabilities Approach. Cambridge University Press, Cambridge (2001)

Sen, A.: Development as Freedom. Oxford University Press, Oxford (1999)

McKinsey Design Index. https://www.mckinsey.com/business-functions/mckinsey-design/our-insights/the-business-value-of-design. Accessed 07 Dec 2019

DMI Design Value Index. https://www.dmi.org/page/DesignValue/The-Value-of-Design-.htm. Accessed 04 Dec 2019

Crocker, D.: Functioning and Capability: The Foundations of Sen's and Nussbaum's Development Ethic. Sage Journals, Thousand Oaks (1992)

Pattanaik, P., Suzumura, K.: Rights, Welfarism, and Social Choice. American Economic Review (1994)

How Do Designers Make User-Experience Design Decisions?

Yu-Tzu Lin$^{(\boxtimes)}$ and Morten Hertzum

University of Copenhagen, Copenhagen, Denmark
linyutzu@hum.ku.dk

Abstract. As they go about their work, user experience (UX) designers make numerous decisions. This study investigates how UX designers make use of recognition-primed decision (RPD) mechanisms as well as mental models and information seeking in making design decisions. Based on field observation and interviews in two design teams, we find that the RPD mechanisms of pattern recognition and mental simulation are common in three UX design layers: scope, structure, and skeleton. Mental models tend to be common in the design layers where RPD is not common. The mental models involve causal relationships, empathy, and simple statements. Information seeking is common in all design layers, except the scope layer, and often consists of seeking information to justify decisions the designers have already more or less made. We discuss two implications of our findings for systems to support designers' decision-making.

Keywords: Decision-making · Information seeking · Mental models · UX design

1 Introduction

Design options abound in user experience (UX) design. Thus, UX designers constantly face decisions about whether to do things in one way or another. These decisions concern the design product as well as the work process, and they ultimately determine whether the designs succeed or fail. While many studies have examined how designers collaborate [18, 23], generate ideas [7, 25], and acquire information [9, 19], we focus on how they make decisions.

While models of decision-making conventionally depict it as a rational process of defining the problem, identifying decision criteria, developing alternatives, and selecting the best alternative, this process is rare in practice [26]. In practice, professionals often make decisions on the basis of intuition, experience, analogy, and the like [2, 10, 12, 13, 30]. Klein's [13] recognition-primed decision (RPD) model has become a prominent conception of how experienced professionals make decisions. We take the RPD model as our starting point and add a focus on mental models, which have long been an important notion in design [17, 22]. In addition, we heed Allen's [2] advice to study decision-making together with information seeking.

This study investigates, based on observation and interviews, *how UX designers use the mechanisms of RPD, information seeking, and mental models in making UX*

© Springer Nature Switzerland AG 2020
A. Marcus and E. Rosenzweig (Eds.): HCII 2020, LNCS 12200, pp. 188–198, 2020.
https://doi.org/10.1007/978-3-030-49713-2_13

design decisions. Furthermore, we identify the UX design layers in which these mechanisms are used. The study contributes insights about how UX designers arrive at their decisions and, on that basis, discusses implications for decision-support systems for designers.

2   Related Work

Klein [13] developed the RPD model on the basis of studies of command-and-control (C2) staff, such as fire fighters. C2 staff must be able to react rapidly and flexibly in dynamic, high-stake situations. Rational decision-making is ineffective under such conditions because it is too slow. Instead, Klein [13] found that C2 staff mainly makes decisions through pattern recognition and mental simulation. Pattern recognition is the ability to recognize analogies between the current situation and previously experienced situations, without explicitly stating these analogies beforehand. It turns experience into an action-oriented ability. Mental simulation is the process of consciously enacting a sequence of events [16]. It enables the actor to mentally try out an explanation or idea to learn how well, or poorly, it matches the current situation.

While UX designers' decision-making has not received much research attention, several researchers have investigated decision-making in other design fields, including engineering design [1, 4, 8] and software design [3, 30]. Designers often make tentative decisions during design processes [4, 8]. It is not until criteria emerge and consequences are clarified to a satisfactory level that designers would make final decisions [8]. This way, decisions remain tentative until the designers have gained confidence in the decision-making process that forms the basis for the decisions [4, 8]. In addition, researchers have extended and refined the RPD model. For example, Ahmed et al. [1] found that experienced designers rely on intuition and pattern recognition by referring to past designs. Dwarakanath and Wallace [4] found that designers use the RPD model by evaluating an alternative as soon as it is generated. Furthermore, it is only in the early design phases that they generate different alternatives and compare them with criteria; during detailed design their decision-making process becomes more implicit [4]. Zannier et al. [30] found that in addition to mental simulation, designers also turn to mental models when they face complex questions. In the naturalistic decision-making community, mental models are defined as "a person's beliefs about causal relationships" [14, p. 167]. Nielsen [21] similarly states that mental models are based on belief rather than fact.

Multiple researches have investigated the role of information seeking in decision-making [12, 20, 27]. One noteworthy finding is that C2 staff often seeks information to justify their decisions, rather than to make them. For example, Mishra et al. [20] found that emergency-response commanders tend to look for information that provides post hoc justification for their decisions. This behavior accords with Allen's [2] information-behavior modes and extends Wilson's [29] problem-solving model of information seeking. Outside of C2 settings, people also seek information to justify their decisions. For example, Soelberg [27] found that people often look for justification for their decisions, rather than for information to help them arrive at their decisions in the first place. In Soelberg's [27] study the decision makers spent weeks on justification before they were ready to act on their decision (about which job to choose); in the study by Mishra et al. [20] the more experienced emergency-response commanders acted near immediately and often did not seek justification until they were retrospectively asked for it. Regarding designers, Girod et al. [6] identified that the designers who used informal decision-making methods sought more external information. Informal decision-making methods emphasize subjective assessment over evaluation matrices and numerical scales. Although these methods appear similar to naturalistic decision-making, informal decision-making is not, at least not necessarily, based on the expertise that comes from years of experience. The use of informal decision-making and external information often resulted in less effective decision-making because the designers spent less time on defining criteria than seeking information [6].

Dwarakanath and Wallace's [4] finding that designers' decision-making changes from early to detailed design creates a need for a categorization of the elements in the design process. Based on analyses of website design, Garrett [5] categorizes UX elements into five layers. Ordered from abstract to concrete, these layers are strategy, scope, structure, skeleton, and surface. The layers are interdependent. For example, strategy design frames scope design, but scope design also has an influence back on strategy design. Table 1 gives the definitions of the five UX layers.

Table 1. The definitions of the UX layers [5]

Layer	Definition
Strategy	Product direction, for example the product objectives, user needs, and market positioning
Scope	The scope of the content and functionality, for example the function specification and content requirements
Structure	The organization of the overall information in a product, for example the information architecture
Skeleton	The organization of the information in an interface, for example the wireframe and user-interface design
Surface	The product's appearance, for example its graphic design

3 Method

We conducted 113 h of field observation and five interviews in two digital product teams in a logistics company in Denmark. The first team was designing a decision-support system for company-internal trade managers, and the second team was designing a cargo-monitoring and information-sharing platform for the company's customers. Both teams were agile teams and used a Kanban board – an agile project-management tool. The Kanban boards showed all tasks as user stories. A sample task title was "As a user, I want to do… so I can…" Each task description specified criteria that the team members needed to achieve when designing the product.

In the teams, we observed product owners (PO1 and PO2), UX designers (UX1 and UX2), and a user researcher (UR2). We collectively refer to these team members as designers. The product owners were included as designers because they often made UX design decisions. During the field observation we sat in on team meetings and also observed the designers' informal discussions with each other and with other people on site. As part of the field observation we occasionally asked designers for explanations of their decisions. After the field observation we interviewed PO1, PO2, UX1, UX2, and UR2 about how they arrived at their decisions. Each interview lasted about an hour. Prior to the field observation and interviews, the company and the designers gave their informed consent to participate in the study.

Table 2. The decision-making mechanisms

	Definition	Example
RPD	Mental simulation: Designers consciously enact a sequence of events	PO1 pointed at a wireframe in her notebook and said that if users use one filter to search, then the other filters won't work
	Pattern recognition: Designers see analogies with previous situations and experiences	PO2 said that in lots of services, such as proto.io, users can scale the payment up and down as they please
Information seeking	Designers look for information from information sources such as documents or people	UX2 looked through the page to find UR2's comment and showed it to a designer. After they had read it, UX2 said that he thought hovering is a good solution
Mental model	Designers' beliefs, including their beliefs about causal relationships	PO2 showed the team his design of the interface. UX2 asked him a question and he replied that "at least for me as a user, I want to click on something and see..."

The field observation was documented in written notes, the interviews were audio-recorded and transcribed. In analyzing the data we first identified the decision points, using Klein et al.'s [15] definition of decision points. Four cues were used in identifying the decision points:

- Explicit verbal cues, such as "I had to decide..."
- A designer considered multiple alternatives and then proceeded according to one of them
- A designer made a judgement that affected the outcome of the design process
- A designer proceeded in one way in a situation where another team member might have proceeded in another way.

As the second step of the analysis, we identified which UX design layer each of the decision points was about. We used Garret's [5] five layers, see Table 1. For example, when a designer decided to include certain information on the interface to make it available to the users at that point in the dialogue, the designer was making a decision about the structure layer. Third, we analyzed how designers reached their decisions by distinguishing among three mechanisms: RPD, information seeking, and mental models. We identified RPD by its two main components: mental simulation and pattern recognition [13]. For mental models we applied the definitions of Klein [14] and Nielsen [21]. Table 2 gives the definitions of these decision-making mechanisms along with an example. Fourth, we used open coding to analyze in more detail how the designers used information seeking and mental models to make decisions.

4   Results

After excluding 31 decision points for which we could not determine the decision-making mechanism, we had 48 decision points for analysis. At only two of these 48 decision points (both in the strategy layer) did the designers generate multiple alter-natives before making a decision. Thus, the widely touted process of rational decision-making was rare.

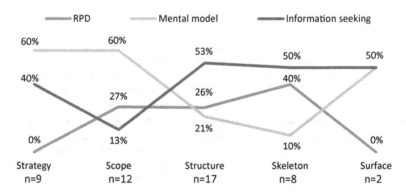

Fig. 1. Percentage of RPD, information seeking, and mental models in decision-making at the five UX design layers. Because the designers used two mechanisms at eight of the decision points, the total number of mechanism instances was 56.

4.1   RPD

The designers used RPD consistently from scope to skeleton design, see Fig. 1. Overall, 23% of the mechanism instances were RPD. During scope design the designers mainly used pattern recognition; during structure and skeleton design they mainly used mental simulation.

The designers pattern recognized on the basis of personal experiences, not on the basis of information they learned from other sources. They for example did not pattern recognize on the basis of user behavior because they, apart from UR2, seldom personally observed user behavior during user-research sessions. Instead, they recognized and made use of analogies with Gmail, Proto.io, and other systems they often used themselves. As an example, one of the designers decided to provide their customers with both old and revised system versions because other companies did so: *"Like google, for example. They allow you to switch between the new beta inbox design or, if you want, the old Gmail design."* The reason why the designer used Google as an analogy was its product quality and large user base. She also pointed out that it is important to show other team members the results of user research in order to convince them that a decision is right.

Regarding mental simulation, the designers used it in two ways: to simulate user-computer interactions and to simulate the consequences of modifying user-interface elements. The designers tended to do the former based on their experience of interacting with similar systems and the later through technical considerations. For example, in a meeting, PO1 immediately simulated how users would use filters for searching by using a wireframe UX1 had designed: *"PO1 pointed at the wireframe UX1 had drawn on her notebook and said that if users use a filter to search, then the other filters won't work."* PO1 later described the simulation of user-computer interactions by saying that *"you know just as much as other users from experiences that make sense [...] It's a lot easier to empathize with your users than it is to have a technical understanding of how the back-end infrastructure should work."* This example shows that PO1 thought that simulating user-computer interactions is easier than simulating technological solutions because he can empathize with users but does not possess engineering knowledge.

With respect to simulating the consequences of modifying user-interface elements, we observed an instance in which UX2 decided that a certain element should be larger. When we later interviewed UX2, he explained that the interface element had to be enlarged to account for the possibility that the interface language was switched to a language in which the text occupied more space: *"When looking at those tiles, you immediately switch to development perception [...] Some languages require more space than others to express whatever it is you're trying to express. What will happen if you switch to another language?"* In general, we observed fewer instances of the second type of simulation than of the first type.

4.2 Information Seeking

Information seeking was a frequent decision-making mechanism. A total of 39% of the mechanism instances were information seeking, distributed across all five layers (Fig. 1). The designers sought information the most during structure design. Their Kanban policy stated that they had to conduct user research after user-interface design and for that reason they conducted user-feedback sessions during structure design. Starting from structure design, they also sought information, such as design criteria, in documents:

> "UR2 told UX2 that PO2 thought there were too many call-to-action buttons, but UX2 explained and showed UR2 the user story with design criteria. He read a user need aloud and pointed at the screen."

In looking for design inspiration we observed that designers sometimes tried out design features on websites that appeared not to be directly related to the design they were doing. Furthermore, they sometimes shared inspiring examples with their team via an internal communication tool.

The company culture created frequent opportunities for the designers to acquire information from other designers. For example, the weekly UX meetings provided opportunities for the designers to share their designs and get feedback. None of the 48 decisions changed as a result of these UX meetings. However, in one instance we noticed that two designers had different mental models for the same decision. The meeting improved both designers' understanding of the decision point:

> "In weekly UX meetings, designers show and talk about what they are working on. UX2 shows the UX team his interaction design [...] UX1 asks why UX2 has chosen to use the users' name, rather than their email, for login. 'I think it was to create something', UX2 replies. UR2 joins the discussion and says 'no'; it is more about users who do not want their emails to be given to the company."

In almost half of the information-seeking instances the designers sought information to justify their decisions. That is, they already had a decision in mind when they asked other team members for their opinion. There were two reasons for this behavior: to bolster their personal confidence in the decision and to create team ownership of the decision by talking about it. UX1 stated that receiving opinions from her colleagues made her feel more confident: *"You either get validation – they agree that it is a good idea – or they question you and make you question whether it is a good direction [...] That makes you feel a little bit more comfortable about the direction you are going"*. We did observe instances where designers changed their decisions on the basis of feedback. In all these instances the feedback came from users, not from other designers. However, the majority of the feedback confirmed ideas and decisions rather than suggested new designs.

4.3   Mental Models

Mental models were frequent during strategy, scope, and surface design (Fig. 1). A total of 38% of the mechanism instances were mental models. We identified three kinds of mental models: (1) causal relationships, (2) empathy, and (3) simple statements.

The causal-relationship mental models were similar to Klein's [9] definition of mental models. For example, PO1 decided to create a new user-authentication system because it would enable users to find all the information they were allowed to access in one place. In another instance, PO2 decided not to establish a traditional partnership because it would be too much effort. He had previously had his own business and knew from that experience that: *"Traditional partnerships require a lot of time and energy, and you have to do the same things again and again."*

Like causal relationships, empathy was also a frequent kind of mental model, particularly during strategy and scope design. The designers imagined themselves as users and made decisions that would improve their own user experience. For example, in one instance PO2 decided that the product should be the users' best friend. He said: *"if I put myself in their shoes, what I would really want is to have this really knowledgeable guy helping me, being friendly, and making my workdays easier."*

Lastly, simple statements were the least frequent kind of mental model. Some of these mental models were expressed as knowledge about principles for good design.

For example, a designer chose a sans-serif font because *"serif is not good on the screen."* Most simple-statement mental models were however expressions of information derived from the designers' personal experience. As an example, UX2 and UR2 were designing a notification feature and needed to decide whether to add a pop-up screen to explain to the users why they received the link contained in the notification. UX2 reasoned (using mental simulation) that they should add the pop-up: *"If a sender just pastes the link instead of providing additional information, then the user will not have the context."* UR2 countered this reasoning with a simple statement derived from his user research, namely that he had *"the impression from our customers that users would be provided with a context."*

5 Discussion

The UX designers use a mix of pattern recognition, mental simulation, information seeking, and mental models in their decision-making. While pattern recognition and mental simulation are restricted to the three middle UX design layers, mental models are primarily used in the most abstract and most concrete layers. The absence of mental simulation during strategy design is understandable because this layer does not have clear user-interaction goals, thereby making it difficult for the designers to match the outcome of mental simulations against desired goals. Hence, when asking for a colleague's opinion, a designer received confirmation for her decision but also the feedback: *"You have to come up a decision and figure it out [whether it is a good decision]."* The designers' preference for mental models in the abstract design layers indicates, we surmise, that strategy and scope decisions are more readily made using causal relationships and empathy. The frequent use of causal relationships also suggests that the designers may lack the experience base necessary for pattern recognition [1, 24]. The importance of empathy in UX design decisions extends previous RPD research [13–15]. Consistent with RPD research the UX designers rarely generate multiple alternatives before making decisions, and they only do it during strategy design.

Information seeking is spread across decisions in all five UX design layers. It is about evenly divided between information seeking to reach a decision and information seeking to justify a decision that has already been reached. The high incidence of information seeking for justification is consistent with previous research [2, 20, 27]. In fact, the experienced emergency responders studied by Mishra et al. [20] appear to have an even higher incidence of information seeking for justification. Justification serves to increase the designers' confidence in their decisions but has little impact on the quality of their decisions. The high incidence of justification is also similar to Weick's [28] description of sensemaking as a retrospective process. Weick asserts that actors make sense of an event by looking back at it to see what they have experienced. This way, sensemaking may inform future decisions, but it lags behind the decision-making process that produced the current event. Like other designers [9, 19], the UX designers often seek information from colleagues, rather than in documents. Consulting other people is a straightforward way of acquiring feedback on designs and ideas, either as informed opinion or as impetus for creative discourse.

We see two implications of our results for decision-support systems. The first is a shift of decision support away from the documentation of the unfolding decision-making process. To support UX designers in pattern recognition they must experience a rich variety of examples. Klein [14] proposes decision games as a vehicle for C2 staff to play out decisions and experience their consequences in dynamically evolving situations. However, UX design does not possess situational dynamics similar to those of C2 work. We contend that UX designers are more in need of experiencing a curated collection of design features that exemplify good solutions to different design problems. A decision-support system built around such a collection will both sensitize designers to problems they should consider and to alternative ways in which these problems may be solved depending on the context. The system may be used for training as well as for real design projects. The key idea is to shift the focus of decision support from documentation to creative input into the decision-making process.

The second implication is that decision-support systems should approach UX design decisions as teamwork rather than individual work. We observed information exchanges among designers and also instances in which two designers used different criteria for the same decision point. Thus, a system that juxtaposes multiple designers' considerations will support and align with current UX design practices. The system may also support activities such as timeouts, in which the designers briefly suspend their individual activities to meet and collaboratively discuss the design issues each of them are currently facing [10]. If such a system succeeds in strengthening the incentives to collaborate then it will increase the number of design criteria considered before turning to justification.

6 Limitations

Three limitations should be remembered in interpreting the results of this study. First, the two studied design teams are from the same company. Conventions, practices, and so forth may be different in other settings, such as design consultancies. Second, we acknowledge that much of decision-making is only indirectly accessible to observation. However, by observing meetings and informal conversations, we got data where the designers reasoned about their designs and design decisions [11]. Furthermore, we occasionally asked questions during the field observation and supplemented it with interviews. Third, we did not follow the two teams for the whole product development process. Observing the teams earlier or later in the process might influence the distribution of the decision-making mechanisms across the UX design layers.

7 Conclusion

This study makes three contributions. First, it shows how UX designers make decisions in practice. In addition to mental simulation and pattern recognition, UX designers also make decisions by seeking information and by using mental models. The designers' use of these mechanisms is unevenly distributed across the different UX design layers. Second, UX designers seek information to justify their decisions as well as to reach them. In almost half of the information-seeking instances the studied designers sought information to justify decisions they had already more or less made. Third, UX designers' mental models extend beyond their beliefs about causal relationships to also include other kinds of beliefs. The studied designers' mental models consisted of causal relationships, empathy, and simple statements. In terms of implications, we propose that future work on decision-support systems for UX designers should focus on creative input rather than documentation and on teamwork rather than individual work.

Acknowledgement. The authors would like to thank the Ministry of Education, Taiwan, for its sponsorship of the first author's Ph.D. scholarship. Special thanks are due to the designers who participated in this study.

References

1. Ahmed, S., Wallace, K.M., Blessing, L.T.: Understanding the differences between how novice and experienced designers approach design tasks. Res. Eng. Des. **14**(1), 1–11 (2003)
2. Allen, D.: Information behavior and decision making in time-constrained practice: a dual-processing perspective. J. Am. Soc. Inform. Sci. Technol. **62**(11), 2165–2181 (2011)
3. Christiaans, H., Almendra, R.A.: Accessing decision-making in software design. Des. Stud. **31**(6), 641–662 (2010)
4. Dwarakanath, S., Wallace, K.M.: Decision-making in engineering design: observations from design experiments. J. Eng. Des. **6**(3), 191–206 (1995)
5. Garrett, J.J.: The Elements of User Experience: User-Centered Design for the Web and Beyond, 2nd edn. New Riders, Thousand Oaks (2011)
6. Girod, M., Elliott, A.C., Burns, N.D., Wright, I.C.: Decision making in conceptual engineering design: an empirical investigation. Proc. Inst. Mech. Eng. Part B: J. Eng. Manuf. **217**(9), 1215–1228 (2003)
7. Gonçalves, M., Cardoso, C., Badke-Schaub, P.: What inspires designers? Preferences on inspirational approaches during idea generation. Des. Stud. **35**(1), 29–53 (2014)
8. Hansen, C.T., Andreasen, M.M.: A mapping of design decision-making. In: DS 32: Proceedings of Design 2004, the 8th International Design Conference, Dubrovnik, Croatia, pp. 1409–1418 (2004)
9. Hertzum, M.: People as carriers of experience and sources of commitment: information seeking in a software design project. New Rev. Inf. Behav. Res. **1**, 135–149 (2000)
10. Hertzum, M., Simonsen, J.: How is professionals' information seeking shaped by workplace procedures? A study of healthcare clinicians. Inf. Process. Manag. **56**(3), 624–636 (2019)
11. Hyldegård, J., Hertzum, M., Hansen, P.: Studying collaborative information seeking: experiences with three methods. In: Hansen, P., Shah, C., Klas, C.-P. (eds.) Collaborative Information Seeking. CSCW, pp. 17–35. Springer, Cham (2015). https://doi.org/10.1007/978-3-319-18988-8_2
12. Kahneman, D.: Thinking, Fast and Slow. Farrar, Straus and Giroux, New York (2013)
13. Klein, G.A.: Sources of Power, How People Make Decisions. MIT Press, Cambridge (1998)
14. Klein, G.A.: A naturalistic decision making perspective on studying intuitive decision making. J. Appl. Res. Mem. Cogn. **4**(3), 164–168 (2015)
15. Klein, G.A., Calderwood, R., MacGregor, D.: Critical decision method for eliciting knowledge. IEEE Trans. Syst. Man Cybern. **19**(3), 462–472 (1989)
16. Klein, G.A., Crandall, B.W.: The role of mental simulation in problem solving and decision making. In: Hancock, P., Flach, J., Caird, J., Vicente, K. (eds.) Local Applications of the

Ecological Approach to Human-Machine Systems, vol. 2, pp. 324–358. Erlbaum, Hillsdale (1995)

17. Kolko, J.: Exposing the Magic of Design: A Practitioner's Guide to the Methods and Theory of Synthesis. Oxford University Press, Oxford (2010)

18. Lauche, K.: Collaboration among designers: analysing an activity for system development. Comput. Support. Coop. Work (CSCW) **14**(3), 253–282 (2005). https://doi.org/10.1007/s10606-005-5413-0

19. Lin, Y.-T., Hertzum, M.: Service designers' information seeking: consulting peers versus documenting designs. In: Stephanidis, C. (ed.) HCII 2019. CCIS, vol. 1032, pp. 41–48. Springer, Cham (2019). https://doi.org/10.1007/978-3-030-23522-2_6

20. Mishra, J., Allen, D., Pearman, A.: Information seeking, use, and decision making. J. Assoc. Inf. Sci. Technol. **66**(4), 662–673 (2015)

21. Nielsen, J.: Mental models and user experience design. Nielsen Norman Group (2010). https://www.nngroup.com/articles/mental-models/. Accessed 16 Jan 2019

22. Norman, D.A.: The Design of Everyday Things. Basic Books, New York (2013)

23. Olson, G., Olson, J., Carter, M., Storrosten, M.: Small group design meetings: an analysis of collaboration. Hum.-Comput. Interact. **7**(4), 347–374 (1992)

24. Rasmussen, J.: Skills, rules, and knowledge; signals, signs, and symbols, and other distinctions in human performance models. IEEE Trans. Syst. Man Cybern. **SMC-13**(3), 257–266 (1983)

25. Shroyer, K., Lovins, T., Turns, J., Cardella, M.E., Atman, C.J.: Timescales and ideaspace: an examination of idea generation in design practice. Des. Stud. **57**, 9–36 (2018)

26. Simon, H.A.: Rational decision making in business organizations. Am. Econ. Rev. **69**(4), 493–513 (1979)

27. Soelberg, P.: Unprogrammed decision making. Ind. Manag. Rev. **8**(2), 19–29 (1967)

28. Weick, K.E.: Making Sense of the Organization. Wiley, Blackwell, Malden (2000)

29. Wilson, T.D.: Models in information behaviour research. J. Doc. **55**(3), 249–270 (1999)

30. Zannier, C., Chiasson, M., Maurer, F.: A model of design decision making based on empirical results of interviews with software designers. Inf. Softw. Technol. **49**(6), 637–653 (2007)

NeuroDesign: Making Decisions and Solving Problems Through Understanding of the Human Brain

Wei Liu[✉], Yanjie Jin, Binbin Li, Zhengfang Lyu, Wenjie Pan, Nan Wang, and Xin Zhao

Faculty of Psychology, Beijing Normal University, Beijing, China
wei.liu@bnu.edu.cn

Abstract. This paper introduces an emerging research field called NeuroDesign, which combines psychology, neuroscience, computer science, and design. It applies the cutting-edge cross-domain research methods to collect the designer's physiological data and psychological data, which has essential experimental support significance for this research field. Studies on NeuroDesign are based on neuroscience and use psychology methods and computer models to study design-related activities. The combination of neuroscience and design is an emerging field, and researching in this field has considerable significance.

Keywords: NeuroDesign · Design thinking · Neuroscience · Problem-solving · Decision-making · Psychology

1 Introduction

NeuroDesign, as an emerging discipline with research from psychology and neuroscience, is complemented by computer science models that apply to understand our design process and how to respond to designs. Neuroscience allows us to ignore the physiological mechanisms behind the perception of beauty in the process of understanding art and design. Cavanagh [2] studies how artists use it by examining the wrong light and shadows in paintings and other unrealistic depictions. The characteristics of the brain convey information economically. Hofel [9] showed that the stimuli of beauty and non-beauty showed significant differences 400 ms after the stimulus presentation. Both beautiful paintings and intricate artworks significantly activate the human cortex's frontal cortex. The beautiful object activates the bottom-up default system of the human brain in 360–1225 ms [5, 9].

Psychologists [10] explain people's perceptions of design and beauty from the perspectives of developmental psychology and psychoanalysis. Infants have the ability to perceive beautiful things in two to three months, and children have developed an aesthetic appreciation in primary school. In adolescence, individuals gradually develope an aesthetic evaluation with autonomy due to the formation of self-awareness. Psychologists [7, 10] also used projection techniques and pictures to compile famous projection tests, such as the Rorschach ink test and the theme test, from the perspective

A. Marcus and E. Rosenzweig (Eds.): HCII 2020, LNCS 12200, pp. 199–208, 2020.
https://doi.org/10.1007/978-3-030-49713-2_14

of psychoanalysis and applied them to treatment and evaluation. There are also a large number of case studies that prove that painting is an excellent way to deal with emotional conflicts, trauma, loss, and etc. when used in psychotherapy.

Theoretical models of computer science provides a theoretical framework. For example, the computational framework used by Munakata [14] provides a mechanical approach to understanding meme differences at a conceptual level, so that the results can be used for category learning, infants, amnesia, and developmental forgetting, as well as the development of flexible behavior. Goucher-Lambert and McComb [7] used hidden Markov models to discover brain activation patterns in the fMRI datasets associated with design.

The applied art of design includes industrial design, graphic design, fashion design, and decorative art that traditionally includes crafts. Gero [5] classify the research content of design activities: design process, cognitive behavior, and interaction, while the future direction of design creativity research includes design process, cognitive behavior, social interaction, and cognitive neuroscience measurement. Cognitive neuroscience is designed to be creative and is an open field of research that will study brain activity when the brain performs design tasks. It is one of the foremost research directions for NeuroDesign in the future.

The cross-disciplines are more relevant in these disciplines, including user experience, cognitive neuroscience, and computer aesthetics, which are also important subject areas and sources. The interdisciplinary user experience covers three parts: neuroscience, psychology, and design. According to Garrett [4], user experience includes user's experience of brand identity, information availability, functionality, content, and etc. Norman [15] extends user experience to all aspects of users and products. The application of the EEG and other brain measurement methods to the user's measurement of the first impression of the interface also allow us to open up new research ideas in the context of such disciplines and NeuroDesign [11]. Research results can, in turn, be applied to user experience domains.

Cognitive neuroscience is developed on the basis of brain neuroscience and cognitive science. Zeki [23] believes that 'art is also abstracted, and thus the way of working inside the brain is embodied'. Zeki officially proposed a new field of research, neuro-esthetics, to study the neural basis of artistic creation and aesthetics. Researchers use their brain function imaging analysis of brain neural activity to obtain substantial evidence about the brain mechanism of cognitive activity, making the research results more scientific and reliable [17].

Computer aesthetics is the most widely used in today's user interface design and interface design. The translators developed by Chen [3] extract visual features in UI images and encode the spatial layout of these features. Interface design involves a wide range of projects, from computer systems to automotive and commercial aircraft. Researchers [16] also incorporate user-centric design concepts into their own wearable EEG headset development projects.

2 Significance of This Research

By exploring the relationship between design and brain nerves, researchers are able to discover principles behind design guidelines to validate the design guidelines. Researches that based on neuroscience have found some new design guidelines. In the past few years, people have unconsciously used some effective means to modify people's perceptions, preferences, and choices about products. But if there is no guidance from neuroscience, they won't know how to make choices in so many categories of products and choose more potential products. For example, research has found that people don't like products that have images pointing to them or pointing downwards [1, 22]. Another study found that people prefer products or packaging that seem to smile at them. These are design criteria that have been discovered through neuroscience-supported methods [18]. In addition, neuroscience-supported methods are more widely used to design labels and logos. Neuroscience insights have also begun to provide a guide to the design of the business. In some cases, these insights will affect the design of the typeface in the near future [21].

In the process of designer designing activities, exploring the brain activities of designers, discovering some brain rules of design activities, and making the rules as designing a basis make design activities more able to promote cooperation and stimulate creativity. In previous studies, when studying designers' activities, the degree of activation of the brain, and various activities during the design were explored. For example, there are three different design tasks for designers and engineers, and then some instrument is used to detect their brain activity and discover the neural mechanism of the designer when they work independently [19].

The field of neuroscience and the field of design are both highly developed, but the study of the combination of the two is relatively rare, especially the research of designers' collaboration. It is a blank field. By studying the brain mechanism of the collaboration, this blank field could be filled. It is an interdisciplinary discipline with higher relevance extended from these disciplines. In this emerging discipline, the study of designer collaborative design is a blank field and a part of the later research that needs to be focused on neural design. Focusing on the brain activities of designers in the design process and exploring the brain mechanism behind the design guidelines, designers design a product that is people-centered. In this emerging discipline, the study of designer collaborative design is a blank field and a part of the later research that needs to be focused on NeuroDesign.

3 Methodology

NeuroDesign is able to draw on existing research methods and combine these research methods. It incorporates research methods in psychology and research methods in the interdisciplinary fields of neuroscience and other disciplines to study its own fields. See Fig. 1 for an impression.

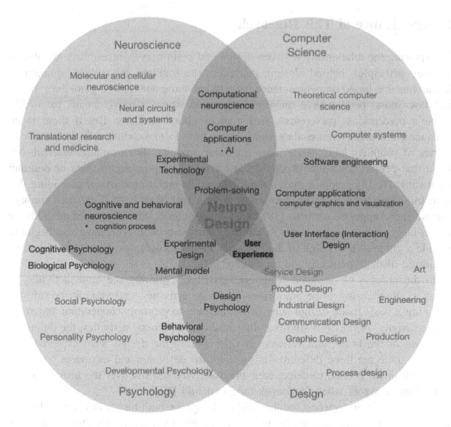

Fig. 1. The interdisciplinary research fields for NeuroDesign

Psychology research methods study the designer's behavior and brain activities, which is of great significance to this research field. The reaction time is one of the most commonly used reaction variables in psychology. It refers to the time required after the stimulation rather than when the reaction is performed. It is applied to the organism to the beginning of the obvious reaction, that is, the time interval of the stimulus-reaction. Any mental activity takes some time. Therefore, almost all psychological studies apply the principles and methods of reaction. Through this method, design behaviors can be initially studied and analyzed. The method is used to initially study and analyze the designer's design behavior, such as the reaction time of symbols or graphics are compared with non-designers, whether the analysis is significantly different. Functional near-infrared spectroscopy (fNIRS) uses the main components of blood to achieve good scattering of 600–900 nm near-infrared light, and obtain changes in oxyhemoglobin and deoxyhemoglobin during brain activity, so that calculate the amount of blood oxygen and blood volume changes in the region and monitor the functional activities of the cerebral cortex. This method is used to detect the degree of activity of the designer in the brain area of the design activity. DC-stimulated tDCS is directly stimulated by weak currents, causing temporary resilience of brain function excitation or inhibition, or long-term regulation of cortical plasticity. Through this excitement or inhibition, researchers understand which brain areas are excited or inhibited when the designer completes the task.

In addition, NeuroDesign is a cross-disciplinary field of neuroscience and design. The research team refers to neuroscience and other research methods to select some suitable research methods. In recent years, neuromarketing has had a series of research and development. The discipline uses neurological methods to determine the driving force behind consumer choice. Similarly, NeuroDesign also uses neurological research methods to study the brain changes of designers to reveal the meaning behind their behavior in the design process. Functional magnetic resonance fMRI achieves brain function imaging by examining changes in the magnetic field of blood flow into brain cells, which gives a more precise structural and functional relationship and calculates whether these brain activities are related to attention, emotion, and memory processes, identity, and decision-making, etc. The technology's good spatial resolution detects which parts of the brain are activated by the designer when completing individual tasks and collaborative tasks. EEG is a safe and harmless brain scanning technique that measures voltage fluctuations from ion currents in neurons in the brain and has a very high temporal resolution compared to fMRI. By analyzing the EEG of a specific brain region, real-time changes in brain activity such as attention, emotion, memory process, and identity in the design process are obtained. Eye-tracking is a technique for tracking eyesight. During the experiment, the eye movement instrument will emit invisible infrared rays. By recording the surface reflection of the eyeball, the eyeball activity can be analyzed and accurately positioned, and the brain activity is speculated. The position of the gaze accurately reflects the position of people's attention. Through eye tracking, researchers analyze which elements the designer pays the most attention to when completing the design task. GSR is a technique for measuring the degree of skin electrical conductivity (often used as a polygraph) and is very sensitive to sympathetic activation and emotional excitement. This technique is used in conjunction with EEG to measure the excitement of a designer's work. The surface EMG signal is a one-dimensional time series signal from the muscle surface guided and recorded by the muscles of the neuromuscular system. The changes are related to the number of participating sports units, the movement unit activity pattern, and the metabolic status. Reflecting muscle activity status and functional status in real-time, accurate, and non-injury conditions, researchers find the difficulty by calculating the emotional changes in the design process by measuring the designer's changes in myoelectricity.

4   Research Settings

This article explores a variety of design methods, design principles, design theories, and applies them to all areas of the world as a high-level neurological activity. However, the neural mechanisms and psychological processes behind it are still not understood well. It is also unclear how many different levels of physiological mechanisms, cultural backgrounds, cognitive models, and subconscious minds that affect the design. Now, based on the nerves, using psychological methods and computer science models as an aid, design research has been greatly assisted. Studying the neural mechanisms in the design process, general principles of NeuroDesign to practice will be found, exploring the brain mechanisms behind the design criteria, the specific design could be evaluated through neural research. The neural mechanism in user experience process makes the designer designing a more human-centered product. The brain mechanisms behind the design guidelines also provide theoretical support for the designer's design. Future research direction will focus on the brain activities of designers in the design process, especially the brain activities of designers in collaboration, or the similarities and differences between collaborative design and individual design in cognitive neural level. That is the further exploration of the relationship between neuroscience and design.

5   Possible Research Domains and Discussion

NeuroDesign is a combination of cognitive neuroscience and design. On the one hand, design researchers use the technology and research results of cognitive neuroscience to improve the development of this discipline, so as to make design, a discipline in the field of humanities and arts, more scientific, so as to eliminate and verify the existing differences and opposition between various theories. On the other hand, the field of design also provides cognitive neuroscientists with a new research direction and ideas, prompting more cognitive neuroscientists to engage in the field of design research. The integration of cognitive neuroscience into the design process is achieved through three parallel and continuous levels of analysis. The first is to analyze user experience or the neural mechanism in the process of product design. The second is to analyze the neural mechanism of designers in the process of design at the cognitive level. The third is to explore the brain mechanism behind the design criteria from the existing design criteria. This paper analyzes the research direction of NeuroDesign from the second angle. See Fig. 2 for an impression.

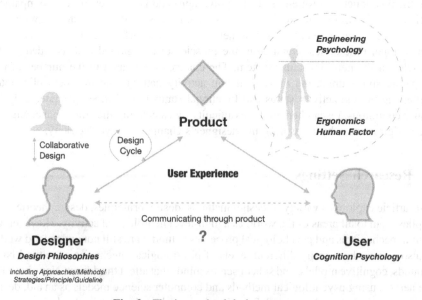

Fig. 2. The intertwined design process

The second research orientation of NeuroDesign is elaborated from two aspects, such as the research topic and the research object. First, as for the research topic, classic cognitive psychology research paradigms such as decision-making, problem-solving, and creativity are hot topics in the field of NeuroDesign. In terms of the research object, the design process is actually a process consisting of a series of unique events [6], from characteristic of design activity, independence and parallel, the design can be seen as a series of independent activities, therefore, from the perspective of the individual, the designer alone to carry on the design activity of neural activity. Concerning the integrity, cooperation and continuity of the design process, the relationship between human neural activities in the process of collaborative design is studied from the perspective of collaborative design. As far as the design process is concerned, its essence is the process of discovering problems, proposing solutions, choosing solutions, and designing outputs, which is analyzed from the cognitive level, including multiple cognitive processes, mainly including creativity, problem-solving, and decision-making. Both individual design and collaborative design are necessary to carry out the above cognitive process. Therefore, starting from the specific cognitive process and relying on the existing cognitive neuroscience research practice will be helpful to explore the research field of NeuroDesign.

5.1   Individual Design

Decision-making is a cognitive process, after which an individual decides on actions or opinions to be expressed in various choices according to individual beliefs or reasoning combined with various factors [8]. Every decision-making process aims to produce the final decision and select the final choice, which takes the form of an action or an opinion. Decision-makers are often faced with different options and choices, and some degree of uncertainty about the consequences of their decisions. The decision-maker needs to balance the advantages and disadvantages as well as risks of various choices in order to reach the optimal decision result.

Problem-solving is usually defined as a series of purpose-oriented cognitive operation processes, which is the most general form of thinking and the basic way for human beings to adapt to the environment and solve various problems in survival and development. The essence of problem-solving is a cognitive problem, and the process is described with the idea of information processing, and the influence of existing knowledge on this process can also be discussed with the idea of knowledge structure, and even the acquisition of knowledge in problem-solving.

Most psychologists now believe that creativity has two key elements, namely 'novelty' and 'applicability', which define creativity as the ability of an individual to produce new and unique ideas or products of practical value [20]. In a narrow sense, any thinking with novel and unique meaning to a specific thinking subject is called creative thinking. Over the past 10 years, many cognitive neuroscientists have used brain imaging technology with high spatial resolution and electroencephalography technology with a high temporal resolution to study and analyze the above three cognitive processes in different aspects, and achieved fruitful results, such as stages of processing in face perception: a MEG study [13].

5.2   Collaborative Design

For many people, designing behavior is an act involving others. For most people, the design process includes other members of their profession and members of other professions. At the appropriate time, each participant contributes what they can to a different area of expertise. The participants work together because each participant has specific expertise that contributes to the solution process. Therefore, the study on the cognitive neural process of each participant in the process of collaborative design provides practical and effective suggestions for the improvement of the efficiency of existing collaborative design and group design [12].

Collective decision-making studies how a group makes a joint action decision. The so-called joint action choice may be a process in which all parties participate in the same action for the common interests, just as a group of designers participates in the same design concept, or it may be a process in which all parties participate in the same action for different interests, such as the collaborative design process of designers, from different companies. Not only in the field of collaborative design, but also in other situations of collective decision-making, scholars at home and abroad have little exploration on the neural mechanism of group decision-making. On the one hand, the study of process organization involves many subjects such as decision science, psychology, mathematics, communication science, and sociology. On the other hand, people do not pay enough attention to it. In fact, a large number of collective decision-making questions need to be answered by the study of process organization.

Collective problem-solving, strictly speaking, and problem-solving in the psychology of originally refers to the cognitive and thinking activity. Still this kind of problem-solving thinking determines the behavior to solve the problem, researchers study the cognitive activities of problem-solving as individuals on the basis of the individual and collective, thinking, and behavior, research on the exploration to the collective problem-solving in the process of collaborative design as the research subject to explore and research. NeuroDesign is an emerging interdisciplinary research field combining cognitive neuroscience and design, aiming to provide more data support for the cognitive neuroscience of design, so that this field of humanities and arts are scientifically analyzed and interpreted. The current research focuses on decision-making and problem-solving in the individual design process or the collaborative design process. The field is growing fast, and there is plenty of room for growth. In the future, the research idea of integrating and separating research and combining bottom-up and top-down research will be helpful to establish a unified research paradigm in the field of NeuroDesign. The related research of NeuroDesign is of great significance to promote the scientization of design science and broaden the research dimension of cognitive neuroscience. Through analysis and discussion, researchers see that each research direction has its own advantages and disadvantages, which are applicable to different situations and purposes. Our article only discusses part of the research content and research methods, all of which have their own limitations. Therefore, both researchers and practitioners need to choose a more appropriate direction for specific research based on the understanding of various research models, according to their own research problems and research situations, and further enrich and improve in specific research practice.

6   Conclusion

NeuroDesign is a new research field of the fusion of psychology, neuroscience, computer science, and design. It is interdisciplinary. This emerging interdisciplinary research field aims to provide cognitive neuroscience data supporting design science to enable scientific analysis and interpretation of this humanities art field. Current research focuses on areas, such as decision-making and problem-solving, in both the individual design process and collaborative design process. This field is growing rapidly, and there is a wide space for its development.

Acknowledgments. We would like to thank the Leifer NeuroDesign Research Program at the Center for Design Research (CDR) at the School of Engineering at Stanford University. This research is supported and funded by the Master of Applied Psychology (MAP) Program at the Faculty of Psychology at Beijing Normal University and the Fulbright Research Scholar 2019-2020 Program (ID: PS00284539).

References

1. Ariely, D., Berns, G.: Neuromarketing: the hope and hype of neuroimaging in business. Nat. Rev. Neurosci. **11**, 284–292 (2010)
2. Cavanagh, P.: The artist as neuroscientist. Nature **434**(7031), 301–307 (2005)
3. Chen, C., Su, T., Meng, G.: From UI design image to GUI skeleton: a neural machine translator to bootstrap mobile GUI implementation. In: Proceedings of the 40th International Conference on Software Engineering, pp. 665–676. ACM (2018)
4. Garrett, J.: The Elements of User Experience: User-Centered Design for the Web and Beyond. Pearson Education, London (2010)
5. Gero, J.: Future directions for design creativity research. In: Taura, T., Nagai, Y. (eds.) Design Creativity 2010, pp. 15–22. Springer, London (2011). https://doi.org/10.1007/978-0-85729-224-7_3
6. Gero, J., Neill, T.: An approach to the analysis of design protocols. Des. Stud. **19**(1), 21–61 (1998)
7. Goucher-Lambert, K., McComb, C.: Using hidden markov models to uncover underlying states in neuroimaging data for a design ideation task. In: Proceedings of the Design Society: International Conference on Engineering Design, vol. 1, pp. 1873–1882 (2019)
8. Greeno, J.: Nature of problem-solving abilities. In: Estes, W.K.(ed.) Human Information Processing. Lawrence Erlbaum Associates, Hillsdale (1978)
9. Höfel, L., Jacobsen, T.: Electrophysiological indices of processing aesthetics: spontaneous or intentional processes? Int. J. Psychophysiol. **65**(1), 20–31 (2007)
10. Kail, R.: Developmental Psychology (1998)
11. Kim, N., Koo, B., Yoon, J.: Understanding the formation of user's first impression on an interface design from a neurophysiological perspective-EEG pilot study. In: Proceedings of HCI Korea, pp. 139–145. Hanbit Media, Inc. (2016)
12. Kvan, T.: Collaborative design: what is it? Autom. Constr. **9**(4), 409–415 (2000)
13. Liu, J., Harris, A., Kanwisher, N.: Stages of processing in face perception: an MEG study. Nat. Neurosci. **5**(9), 910–916 (2002)
14. Munakata, Y.: Computational cognitive neuroscience of early memory development. Dev. Rev. **24**(1), 133–153 (2004)

15. Norman, D.: The invisible computer (2005)
16. Perego, P., Sironi, R., Lavezzari, R.: User-centered design for wearable neuro-rehabilitation system. In: Proceedings of the 2015 Workshop on Wearable Systems and Applications, pp. 57–58. ACM (2015)
17. Poldrack, R.: The role of fMRI in cognitive neuroscience: where do we stand? Curr. Opin. Neurobiol. 2(2), 223–227 (2008)
18. Shen, X., Wan, X., Mu, B., Spence, C.: Searching for triangles: an extension to food & packaging. Food Qual. Prefer. 44, 26–35 (2015)
19. Spence, C.: Neuroscience-inspired design: From academic neuromarketing to commercially relevant research. Organ. Res. Methods 22(1), 275–298 (2019)
20. Sternberg, R.: Handbook of Creativity. Cambridge University Press, Cambridge (1998)
21. Velasco, C., Woods, A., Hyndman, S., Spence, C.: The taste of typeface. i-Perception 6(4), 1–10 (2015)
22. Velasco, C., Woods, A., Spence, C.: Evaluating the orientation of design elements in product packaging using an online orientation task. Food Qual. Prefer. 46, 151–159 (2015)
23. Zeki, S.: Neural concept formation and art: Dante, Michelangelo, Wagner. 9(3), 53–76 (2002)

Strateegia.digital: A Platform that Assumes Design as a Strategic Tool

André Neves[1]([⊠]), Silvio Meira[2], Leonardo Medeiros[2],
Milena Ferraz[2], Clarissa Soter[2], Sergio Cavalcanti[2],
Pedro Cavalcanti[2], and Virginia Heimann[2]

[1] Federal University of Pernambuco, Recife, Brazil
andremneves@gmail.com
[2] The Digital Strategy Company, Recife, Brazil

Abstract. Our challenge is addressing the time, scale, and space of strategies for creating, adapting, evolving, changing, transforming, and undertaking a business, product, or service to the platform economy in a detailed, comprehensive, deep, sophisticated in a simple, elegant, effective and efficient way. It is in this sense that we present the strateegia.digital platform, the result of years of experience in creating, evolving and transforming business from design as a strategic approach in Brazil.

Keywords: Digital transformation · Platform economy · Design thinking · Strategy · Business design

1 Introduction

No transformation is trivial. Especially a transformation that requires the rethinking of the foundations of business, a leap from analog to digital platforms, the new and little known substrate to compete in contemporary markets. It is no different when it comes to the transformation of successful organizations, where past history and past learning, governed by rules that took time - decades, perhaps - to be established, ensure performance everyone is proud of. It is in this context that strateegia.digital is presented as a platform that assumes design as a strategic tool.

Why transforming? It is the obvious question in such a context. And the answer is, because markets – all of them - are undergoing an adaptation, an incremental shift in the fundamentals of supporting the creation and delivery processes, at the same time capturing value across all types of organizations, with the analogue or digitized analog bases being swapped for interconnected digital platforms that redefine the vast majority of markets. Those who do not take - now - the step forward from analog to digital will risk no longer being able to - soon - make a managed transition between the two states of the organization. All businesses - large and consolidated, or small and growing - need to adapt to the platform economy.

Adapting to these digital platforms means being prepared for continuous and (most frequently) rapid changes. The digital, unlike the analog, is fluid and goes through uninterrupted evolution; here, nothing is definitely as ready: everything is set to change

© Springer Nature Switzerland AG 2020
A. Marcus and E. Rosenzweig (Eds.): HCII 2020, LNCS 12200, pp. 209–223, 2020.
https://doi.org/10.1007/978-3-030-49713-2_15

in response to the context. The digital around us is mutable, programmable and is being programmed; therefore, it is changing all the time. All businesses, big and small, need models (framework) and tools (platforms) in order to move from the past (analogical) to the future (digital).

Understanding design as a tool to create and build futures is critical to discovering the suitable models and designing the tools required for this journey. In strateegia. digital, we adopt design as our own way of intervening that observes people and organizations, besides exploiting technologies to infer viable business opportunities in order to transform the environment in which they operate. From this perspective, design not only adds value to a product, service, or business; design is value, and, for our context, value is strategy. It is through this strategic thinking that strateegia.digital leads individuals, teams and organizations to imagine and create digital futures.

Our main challenge is addressing the time, scale, and space of strategies for creating, adapting, evolving, changing, transforming, and undertaking a business, product, or service to the platform economy in a detailed, comprehensive, deep, sophisticated yet in a simple, elegant, effective and efficient way.

It is in this sense that we present the strateegia.digital platform, the result of years of experience in creating, evolving and transforming business in Brazil. The platform is an online web system which has modules that represent the components of the framework strateegia for digital transformation. The strateegia.digital platform moves away from linear processes that promise a directed transformation to an evolutionary adaptational movement. Our platform encourages a conversational environment that leads to actions which uses design methods, business models and digital systems for an emergent strategy.

2   Time to Transform

Everything is – or will be – networked and interconnected.

One of the most striking features of digital platforms is that all of its facets are – and are defined by - interconnected through a digital network.

People's working methods within business are connected; if this is not the case – when there are no degrees of freedom of decision making and action -, the efficiency and effectiveness of articulations within the business will not be able to create - and will not keep up with - the network effects on the market.

Business systems - at least those that want to survive - are interconnected. They use the network to cooperate and at the same time are inputs to network competition. They enable the largest and most competitive yet collaborative set of agents (to compete and collaborate) that will define their markets.

The same is true of (business) models, which have always been networked in one form or another. They are now in real-time digital networks, thus enabling agents who can fully and individually address each member of their network, whether it's a supplier, consumer, partner, or collaborator, while creates multifaceted, transparent, networked forms for creation, delivery, and capturing value: digital value, inside a digital network.

Historically, one of the biggest challenge when it comes to changing processes is that the process itself and its outcomes are evaluated by indicators of the past – and perhaps even the present - rather than the future of the business itself. One of the advantages of digital (business) space over analog is that the digital is - should be - nearly real time, just like its performance indicators.

A networked business is, therefore, connected, based on methods, systems, models and indicators which are connected, digital and real-time operated.

2.1   From Analog to Digital

The digital (almost present) future demands great capacity for business adaptation. Likewise, digital demands a set of evolutions in the thinking of ...

Technology and tools for people and cultures;
Immediate changes for continuous adaptation;
Radical changes for evolutionary changes;
Rigid structures for flexibility;
Analyze indefinitely to act strategically;
Competition and exclusion for collaboration and inclusion; and,
Certainty for curiosity!

strateegia.digital was designed to support this adaptive evolution, while being flexible, adaptable and going through constant evolution.

From the main triad people - technology - business, strateegia promotes organizational adaptation and evolution as the basis for a dynamic, measurable and sustainable transformation in the business.

2.2   Layers of Transformation

The transition from analogue to digital brings a series of challenges, including assuming that this is a process of people and technologies, and mainly of how we integrate these two layers of the business in a well-balanced system (Fig. 1).

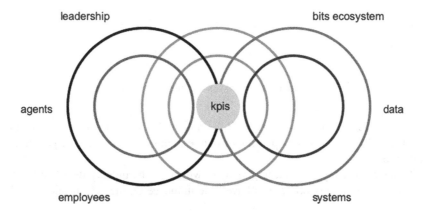

Fig. 1. A balanced flux in strateegia.digital.

First of all, when it comes to people, it is necessary to engage employees based on a leadership that can truly motivate, which realizes the relevance and urgency for the transition from analogue to digital, and activates innovation agents.

Secondly, through the technology perspective, the challenge redesigning databases and structures for new or legacy systems to interact with the increasingly connected bit ecosystem of the platform economy.

Our proposal in strateegia is to always act with both perspectives (people and technology), focusing on business performance.

2.3   Peripheral Opportunities

The first challenge digital transformation [or adaptation] process faces is mapping opportunities. If we metaphorically compare market segments to planets, it is possible to see that different layers have greater or lesser potential for innovation.

For instance, looking for opportunities – in most of segments - in order to initiate a digital transformation from the hard core of the organization is very difficult, risky, and may implode the whole process (Fig. 2).

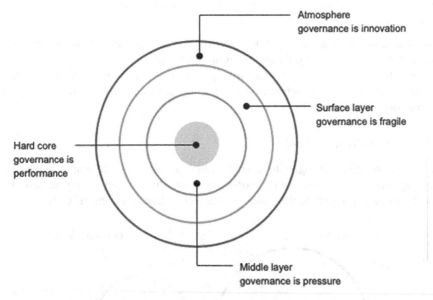

Fig. 2. Innovation atmosphere in strateegia.digital.

The upper core – used to working all the time under internal and external pressure - is not the place to look for opportunities either, considered the risk of jamming the organization.

The lower core represents a fragile layer, which can be quickly detached from the organization, so these opportunities have little influence on the organization itself.

However, there are critical (peripheral) opportunities that circulate the market in a kind of atmosphere that once handled digitally, represent great potential of being incorporated by the organization and promoting innovation to the marketplace in which it is inserted.

2.4   Organic Innovation

In strateegia, understanding that innovation happens from people, to people, and to people, all the time, is critical.

Innovation for consistent digital transformation (or adaptation) must come from experiences that spread organically and systemically across the business, contaminating all internal and external agents.

Innovation in strateegia does not represent changes that are solely the result of technology bases. These are technological changes as well, but they are essentially changes in people attitude in order to gain scale and long-term digital sustainability in the organization's culture.

In the context of the platform economy, innovation is sustainable from the combination of executing it with responsibility and respecting people all the time.

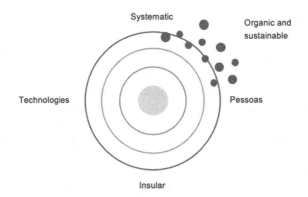

Fig. 3. Innovating organically and systemically in strateegia.digital.

We are then talking about systemic innovation, embedded in the organization, increasingly centered on people, organic, and, therefore, sustainable (Fig. 3).

2.5   Evolutionary Adaptation

During the journey from analog to digital in strateegia, we move away from linear processes that promise a guided transformation. Instead, we promote an evolutionary adaptative movement.

Taking natural ecosystems as references, we divided the process into phases that complement each other as in the formation of a DNA chain.

The first stage (the adaptation phase) aims to identify opportunities for innovation.

Once the opportunities are well defined and mapped, we move on to an evolutionary phase that aims to prototype, validate and disseminate solutions in order to meet these previously identified opportunities.

The third and final phase (Transformation) aims to support the development of the business based on the experiences lived throughout the cycle (Fig. 4).

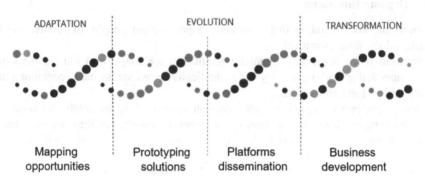

Fig. 4. Evolutionary adaptation in strateegia.digital

2.6   Incremental and Iterative

The transformation (or adaptation) from analogue to digital cannot be dragged down by rational excuses that lead to analysis paralysis, nor to stick to fears and emotional reactions, which ultimately prevent us from doing what is known to be right.

In strateegia, we work on the digital transformation (or adaptation) process from a continuous spiral, in which the creation, development and dissemination of digital platforms takes place in evolutionary redesign and refinery cycles.

Strateegia encourages a short design effort [little design up front] that leads to agile development based on rapid prototyping [lean development] in addition to dissemination mechanisms that use permanent monitoring and analysis of performance data [big data analytics] for the [re] design and the adequate adjustments in time of use [redesign loop].

It is this approach that enables us to incrementally and iteratively produce innovative solutions.

3   Design as a Strategic Approach

All businesses [big and small] need models [framework] and tools [platform] to move from the past [analog] to the future [digital]. Understanding design as an approach to creating and building futures is critical to discovering the models and designing the tools needed for this journey.

In building strateegia.digital, we adopt design as our own way of intervening, people-watching and exploring technologies to infer business opportunities that transform the environment in which we operate.

From this perspective, design not only adds value to a product, service, or business; design is value and, for our context, value is strategy. It is through this thinking that strateegia.digital leads individuals, teams and organizations to imagine and create digital futures.

3.1   Strateegia Toolbox

Metaphorically, strateegia is a set of toolboxes, in which its modules represent the components of a framework for digital transformation (or adaptation).

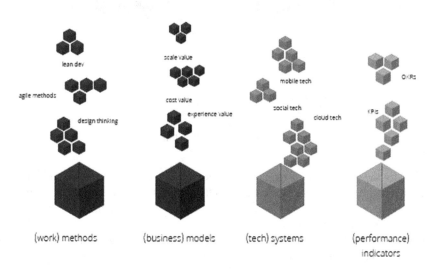

Fig. 5. Modular and flexible toolboxes

Currently, strateegia is composed of four toolboxes (Fig. 5): (work) method box, (business) models box, (tech) systems box, and lastly a (performance) indicators box.

The [work] methods box is made of modules that were brought mainly from design thinking, agile methodologies and lean development techniques.

The [business] model box contains models that are part of the business essence of the platform economy.

The [technology] systems box is where we point out the main software solutions to be applied in the creation, development and operation of digital solutions.

The [performance] indicator box is where the KPIs and OKRs that assist in monitoring results are located.

3.2   Modular over Time

Each strateegia project is unique and therefore follows different paths between the modules (Fig. 6) of the tool boxes.

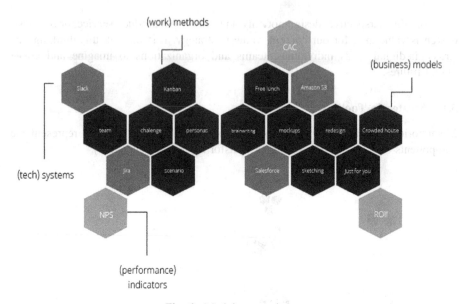

Fig. 6. Modular over time

In order to simplify the visualization of these paths, we use a modular map in time where the modules of the boxes are added as the projects advance in time. Each project has a modular map in its own time that represents the creation, development and implementation of the business.

Unlike the methodologies adopted in the analogical paradigm for product development, we understand that the choice of methods is part of the dialogic experience of digital culture. In other words, strateegia is a digital framework for those going digital.

3.3   Modular and Minimalist

In general, frameworks for digital transformation usually put a paradoxical situation for those who apply them: sometimes they restrict the number of techniques and thereby limit the scope of the transformation, whereas sometimes they expand the techniques and limit the audience capable of dealing with the diversity of maps, graphics, canvas and other structures that each technique requires.

In strateegia we adapt the application of (work) methods, (business) models, [technology] systems and [performance] indicators to a unique technique, based on the formulation of essential questions corresponding to each module of the toolboxes.

The essential questions of each module are defined based on a filter that reduces syntactic, semantic and pragmatic aspects to the central points of each technique.

The use of any module in the strateegia toolbox enables individuals to apply the other modules, thus reducing the learning curve of the framework and simplifying its application in multidisciplinary teams.

3.4   Modular in Practice

In strateegia, all the hexagons that compose the modular map in time lead to a new layer of hexagons superimposed.

The overlapping layer displays information about the definition, the objectives, a set of key questions, dynamics suggested for application and references about the [work] method, the [business] model, the [technology] system or the [performance] indicator related to each hexagon of the modular map over time (Fig. 7).

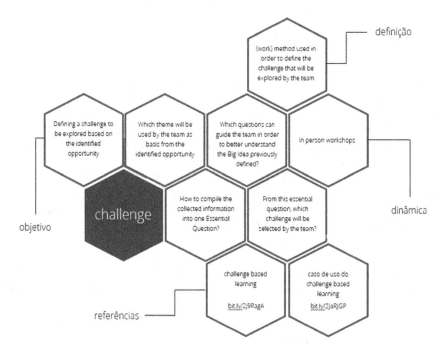

Fig. 7. Modular in practice

This standardization in the way of dealing with the diversity of toolbox modules simplifies the application of strateegia by reducing cognitive effort to a single procedure for all modules.

In practice, applying any module of the strateegia toolboxes means answering some fundamental questions predetermined by our team of specialists who filtered the essential questions of each technique [work] method, [business] model, [technology] system or framework [performance] indicator.

3.5   Work Methods Toolbox

From rigid structures to flexible working methods
In strateegia, all the hexagons that compose the modular map in time lead to a new layer of hexagons superimposed. From rigid structures to flexible working methods.

Digital culture carries a series of relevant changes in the behavior of individuals and organizations. Among many, the emergence of agile, flexible and dynamic methods, which stimulate digital behaviors in the creation, development and deployment of digital platforms.

In the strateegia framework, we adopt a methodological approach that involves an association between contemporary and flexible design thinking methods and the dynamic and rapid techniques of agile methodologies, with lean experimental practicality and the active multiplicity of omnichannel strategies.

It is based on this perspecive that we build a strateegia (work) method toolbox.

3.6   Technology Systems Toolbox

From airtight systems to open data environments
In strateegia, all the hexagons that compose the modular map in time lead to a new layer of hexagons superimposed. From rigid structures to flexible working methods from airtight systems to open data environments.

The [technology] systems box was built according to the main technology that each system utilizes and the impact of these very same technologies on businesses based on the economy of digital platforms.

[1] systems that use social networking technologies for relationships between people and organizations; [2] systems that exploit mobile technologies as part of the digital platform; [3] systems that use data analysis technologies to measure impacts; [4] systems that use cloud computing technologies for shared digital platforms; [5] systems that use IoT technologies to connect objects with objects and people; and, [6] legacy technological systems of organizations that are not discarded at first.

As new systems are launched/available in the digital scenario, they are added to the strateegia framework, in a continuous movement of learning and adaptation to the state of the art in digital technologies.

3.7   Business Models Toolbox

From commercial departments to user-centered teams
The digital paradigm brought a series of important changes to business, including the way to convert and retain customers, and, more importantly, the way to monetize from these customers.

In strateegia, we work with business models that explore different acquisition, retention and monetization paths, which are typical of the digital scenario.

Business models in the digital world are classified in our [business] model box into three groups: [1] cost value; [2] experience value; and [3] scale value.

As they experience more complex digital experiences in strateegia, individuals and organizations experience innovative digital business models.

3.8   Performance Indicators Toolbox

From intuition to data-based intelligence

In strateegia we propose the use of performance indicators as a way to monitor the strategic evolution of the digital experiences.

Performance indicators are formed by an association between strategic and tactical objectives [OKRs] and digital performance indexes [KPIs] that use data and not assumptions as a source for measuring results.

Some of these KPIs can be found next: NPS [Net Promoter Score] CSAT [Customer Satisfaction Index] ESI [Employee Satisfaction Index] ROII [Return On Innovation Investment] API [Application Program Interface] CES [Customer Effort Score] FCR [First Contact Rate] ETR [Employee Turnover Rate] MRR [Monthly Recurring Revenue] CAC [Customer Acquisition Cost] LVT [Lifetime Value] MQL [Marketing Qualified Leads] CTR [Click Through Rate] WTS [Web Traffic Sources]...

3.9   Experimentation and Performance

strateegia has as its main foundation the acculturation around the digital through stages of maturity with innovative digital experiences that lead from an analog culture to a digital culture path.

In order to implement the process of acculturation through strateegia, we propose experimentation and performance laboratories. These are structures that mix the physical and the virtual, and aim to provoke divergence cycles, contacts with new methods [of work], systems [of technology], models [of business] and [performance] and convergence indicators, while building innovative businesses based on the platform economy.

These cycles of divergence and convergence are repeated in an iterative and continuous way, where those involved with strateegia experience the creation, development and dissemination of innovative and sustainable businesses in a set of articulated co-creation movements.

4   strateegia as an Online Plataform

Following the construction of the strateegia framework, we designed an online platform in order to integrate the different agents of the global innovation ecosystem. The platform was designed based on the premise that the digital future will be based on a platform economy (Fig. 8), in which global class businesses integrate the largest organizations in the world on digital business platforms.

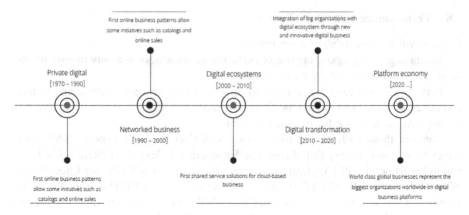

Fig. 8. Digital future

4.1 Contextualized Conversations

The practical application of the framework occurs through strateegia.digital: an online platform where conversations between people are built in the context of previously explained methods [of work], systems [of technology], models [of business] and indicators [performance].

The strateegia.digital platform was designed and developed in order to expand access to the strateegia framework, in practice, by people looking for a simple, yet efficient, flexible and iterative way to build digital futures. strateegia.digital promotes dialogical interaction (Fig. 9) between people on the team and between these people and external experts who support the development of innovative businesses.

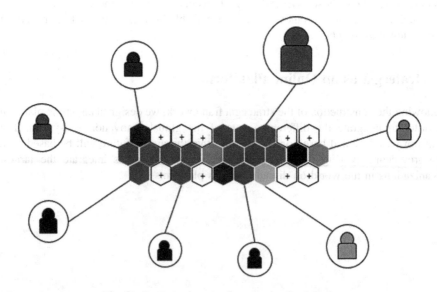

Fig. 9. Conversations in the context of strateegia

Finally, strateegia.digital is an environment for exchanging experiences revolving the creation, development and dissemination of business in [and for] the digital future.

4.2 Dialogic Interface

The strateegia.digital interface was intentionally designed from references of text messaging systems.

Basically, we replaced the conversation lists with projects and text messages with modules from the strategy toolboxes.

The proposal of the analogy to messaging systems has on one hand, a practical connotation: people already know how to use tools with this type of interface; and, on the other hand, a conceptual reference: the construction of conversations in the context as a fundamental mechanism for designing emerging strategies.

The strateegia.digital interface is therefore an explicit invitation to dialogue between the various agents involved in building digital futures (Fig. 10).

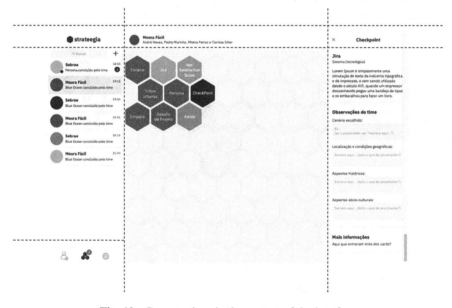

Fig. 10. Conversations in the context of the interface

4.3 Measurable Dialogues

As people progress on the modular time strateegia map, they also evolve their skills and abilities as part of the process of switching from an analog culture to the digital paradigm.

In order to measure the degree of maturity of people and businesses around digital, we created a digital proficiency strateegia index, which is a numerical value that represents the understanding and engagement with methods [of work], systems [of technology], models [of business] and typical [performance] indicators of the [digital] platform economy.

The strateegia proficiency index helps to identify different profiles and their potential when considering forming teams [networks of people] that complement each other in order to create and operate innovative digital businesses.

4.4   Proficiency Index in strateegia

In order to measure the evolution of the degree of maturity of people and businesses around digital culture, we assign a value to each unit of the strateegia toolboxes.

The values are defined according to the degree of complexity and proximity to the economy of [digital] platforms.

The scale of values ranges from 1 to 20 to account for the diversity of methods [of work], systems [of technology], models [of business] and indicators [of performance] of strateegia.

Based on the values assigned to the strateegia toolbox modules, we monitor the performance of people and businesses to measure their digital proficiency indexes (Fig. 11).

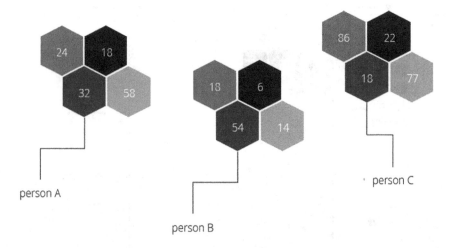

Fig. 11. Proficiency index with strateegia

We use a scoring system that assesses how much each person involved in the business develops skills in methods [of work], systems [of technology], models [of business] and indicators [of performance] of strateegia.

We understand that as the business evolves on its path from analogue to digital, people mature, while absorbing skills and developing new abilities which are typical of digital culture.

It is obvious to expect that people with different backgrounds and pace will share, develop and evolve different aspects of the digital culture. This movement of exchange and maturation is the basis of the proposal for acculturation of strateegia.

5   Conclusion

strateegia.digital is a platform created to instantiate the modular and flexible logic that was described earlier: creating a digital environment in which projects and methods are easily visualized and organized in a single language and quickly understood.

The user experience on the platform was designed for multidisciplinary teams to interact, make strategic choices and manage the progress of their projects, while interconnected and at any time.

The platform, therefore, serves so that the strategic decisions designed can be visualized, with agility, in an environment based on the iterative dialogue that promotes continuous innovation.

It would be a contradiction to claim that the strateegia.digital platform, and consequently its framework has been finalized, since its flexibility and adaptability for different markets and projects is, in itself, its differential.

This article presented the conceptual framework to the development of the platform.

References

1. Digital transformation market expected to be worth US$ 462 Billion By 2023. MarketWatch, 13 August 2018. https://www.marketwatch.com/press-release/digital-transformation-market-expected-to-be-worth-us-462-billion-by-2023-2018-08-13. Accessed 18 July 2019
2. $665 Bn digital transformation market by technology, deployment type, business function, vertical, region - global forecast to 2023 - ResearchAndMarkets.com. AP NEWS, 17 April 2019. https://www.apnews.com/8b3e5a8a74914c4f989941c79e93e944. Accessed 18 July 2019
3. Tabrizi, B., Lam, E., Girard, K., Irvin, V.: Digital transformation is not about technology. Harv. Bus. Rev. 13 March 2019. https://hbr.org/2019/03/digital-transformation-is-not-about-technology. Accessed 19 July 2019
4. Rogers, B.: Why 84% of companies fail at digital transformation. Forbes, 07 January 2016. https://www.forbes.com/sites/brucerogers/2016/01/07/why-84-of-companies-fail-at-digital-transformation/#b5809a3397bd. Accessed 19 July 2019
5. Lockwood, T., Walton, T.: Building Design Strategy: Using Design to Achieve Key Business Objectives. Skyhorse Publishing Inc., New York (2010)
6. de Mozota, B.B.: Design Management: Using Design to Build Brand Value and Corporate Innovation. Allworth Press, New York (2008)
7. Buchanan, R.: Wicked problems in design thinking. Design Issues, 8(2), 5–21 (1992). www.jstor.org/stable/1511637
8. Brown, T., Katz, B.: Change by Design: How Design Thinking Transforms Organizations and Inspires Innovation. Harper Business, New York (2019)
9. Osterwalder, A., Pigneur, Y.: Business Model Generation: A Handbook for Visionaries, Game Changers, and Challengers. Alexander Osterwalder & Yves Pigneur, Amsterdam (2010)
10. Neves, A.: Design Doctoral Conference 2016: TRANSversality Proceedings of the DDC 3rd Conference. IADE – Creative University/EDIÇÕES IADE, 2016, pp. 50–57 (2016). https://www.dropbox.com/s/9v26duq5ee919gj/Proceedings-e-Book_DDC.pdf?dl=0

Why (not) Adopt Storytelling in Design?

Identifying Opportunities to Enhance Students' Acceptance of Storytelling

Qiong Peng[✉] and Jean-Bernard Martens

Eindhoven University of Technology, Eindhoven, The Netherlands
{q.peng,J.B.O.S.Martens}@tue.nl

Abstract. Several methods and tools have been developed to support story-telling used in design. While the benefits of storytelling have been argued extensively in literature, the willingness to adopt it in actual practice, especially in students' design projects, has however been slow. The lack of empirical studies on actual adoption of storytelling calls for a deeper understanding of the considerations that influence design practitioners, especially design students, to adopt or reject storytelling in design. This paper presents an exploratory study that aimed to identify the main obstacles that design students raise against using storytelling in their design process, and to explore ways to address such obstacles. The results imply that the main underlying reasons for poor adoption are the lack of perceived usefulness and the lack of tools to support. Based on the experimental observations, an opportunity for enhancing students' acceptance of storytelling is identified.

Keywords: Storytelling · Acceptance · Tools · Design pitching · Design

1 Introduction

The suggestion to incorporate storytelling into the design process is not new, and has even inspired new design methods. StoryPly [1] is an example of a recent method that has been developed by our research group. It is a method in support of designers to envision and discuss user experience through crafting and visualizing stories. The current paper is inspired by the observed discrepancy between the positive attitudes towards the method in a number of workshops (with both design students and design professionals) and the resistance of design students to actually adopt the method in their design projects.

In an early study, we assumed that the ability to create storyboards was the main bottleneck influencing the adoption of storytelling in design, leading us to conduct a study into the requirements for tools that can support storyboarding [2]. While design students did participate in this study, they were at the same time observed to show relatively little interest in storytelling, despite being encouraged by their tutors and being introduced to the potential benefits in favor of storytelling as defined in literature. Specifically, students were confronted with the lack of argumentation for the relevance of their design concepts and how storytelling could potentially help them to take

A. Marcus and E. Rosenzweig (Eds.): HCII 2020, LNCS 12200, pp. 224–239, 2020.
https://doi.org/10.1007/978-3-030-49713-2_16

aspects of the context and the user better into account when arguing the value of their design concepts. Despite such arguments, students at large argue that "It's useful, but I don't want to use storytelling in my design."

Existing literature provides several arguments for the statement that designers are storytellers [3]. Advocates of incorporating storytelling into design have highlighted its value as an important design thinking tool [4], as an inquiry [5] to collect user stories, and as a method for communication [6] to share design ideas, convey information, etc. The benefits would enhance, seem to be apparent, but a closer inspection of literature has not revealed any empirical studies that lend support to such theoretical considerations. In order to understand the conflict between theoretic claims and the observed reluctance in our design students to adopt the method in their own practice, we decided to undertake such a study by ourselves. We aim to collect design students' opinions on storytelling in design, defined here as any approach adopting story-crafting and/or storytelling in any form applied in design practice. Storytelling is related to narratives, personas as well as scenarios and stories are often visualized and shared in the form of storyboard [7].

More specifically, we aim to collect more detailed information on the following three main research questions:

Q1: Do design students use storytelling in their design practice?
Q2: If using/not using storytelling, what are the reasons?
Q3: What are the problems that they encountered and do they have suggestions to deal with such problems?

The paper is structured in three sections. We started with a literature review on storytelling within the context of design. Next, we discuss an empirical study conducted with the help of a focus group, a questionnaire and a field study. We conclude by identifying the main insights obtained and by proposing an alternative opportunity to incorporating storytelling into design.

2 Related Work

Utilizing stories and storytelling in design has become popular in HCI, as evidenced by a substantial body of literature. On the one hand, the similarities shared by design and storytelling such as context-dependence, and organization of chaotic information, etc. [8] support the pervasiveness of storytelling in design. On the other hand, as the focus of Industrial design shifts from creating artefacts towards design for experience [9], experimental aspects like emotions, motivation, desire, needs etc. become vital. While these aspects are usually too abstract to be interpreted easily, stories are concrete accounts with vivid characters, rich description of the context, human activities, and told based on a coherent and casual plot [10]. As a "common language" [7] storytelling hence is a promising way to support designers to discuss human-related aspects in design practice. Recent edition of the CHI conference also demonstrate the increased interest in "design stories", "design futures" and "design fiction" [11], which all rely on storytelling as a way to inspire design.

Literature of storytelling in design could be summarized into three main directions: D1-highlighting values or benefits of storytelling in design; D2-combining storytelling into design practice; D3-designing for storytelling.

In the first direction, values and benefits of storytelling have been stressed by many researchers. Early in 1996, Erick advocated that storytelling with strong power as communication catalyst can be introduced throughout the design process as an element to initiate a dialogue between designers and users [12]. Peter Llyod et al. identified the role of storytelling in developing a common language within design teams [13] and in development of design expertise [14]. As an essential part of design thinking [15], storytelling is viewed as a "critical success factor for design processes and outcomes" [16] to inform and inspire design [17], to share design perspectives [18], to trigger empathy [19] and humanize the design [8].

In the second direction, storytelling is incorporated into different domains of design in various ways. It is important in interactive design [10, 19] and CSCW design [6], and broadly applied in user experience design [20, 21] to represent the subjective aspects of experience [23], and to improve the quality of concepts [22]. Storytelling is also an efficient tool in service design [24] to design better service experience [25].

Different types of stories can be distinguished, for instance, fictional stories and customer stories [26], as well as original stories, concept stories and usage stories [27]. In the third direction there are some representative studies about designing for storytelling by developing method and tools. For instance, StoryPly [9] is a method for constructing concept stories that allow to explain and discuss the user experience and the end-user value of a design concept. The fictional inquiry method [28], instant card technique [29] as well as Storytelling Group [30] have also been developed to evoke ideas from users for future practice [31]. The UserX story template related to usability requirement is a tool for usage stories [32].

To sum up, most literature prefers the rationale of using storytelling and designing with storytelling. Apparently, literature is empirically weak with regard to the practitioners' practice of storytelling. The challenges and problems seem to be underestimated. For design students who are conventionally skilled in the visual thinking, they are neither trained nor experienced in looking into design from the perspective of storytelling. It is a big challenge for them to craft and tell a compelling story about their design. It demands a more in-depth understanding of students' practice of storytelling in order to comprehend the underlying problems and the reasons for (not) adopting the method in their design.

3 Methodology

We specially focused on our study on design students as they seem to be reluctant adopters of storytelling in design, and were also easily available. An exploratory research was set up including three separate studies: a focus group study, a questionnaire survey and a field study. A focus group was first conducted with the aim to collect students' thoughts on storytelling in the design practice. Ten participants got involved in the focus group, and the first author acted as a moderator for the discussion which was based on the pre-prepared questions. The whole process of the focus group lasted for 2 h and was audio-recorded.

The results of the focus group implied a general problem in the acceptance of storytelling. We then made other two studies to deeply understand these two aspects and explore the possible solutions. A questionnaire survey was conducted as the second study to see students' attitudes to the values of storytelling claimed by literature, and what values were/were not most recognized by students. 130 claims were collected from the literature from 1996 to 2018. To match the design context, these claims were categorized into 5 groups according to the main phases of the design process: user study—design analysis—ideation—prototyping—presentation/pitch. As some claims in the same category share the same meaning, 21 claims were finally selected for the questionnaire. They were the most representative ones in each category proposed by established researchers in the field, such Thomas. Erickson, Dan Gruen, and Tim Brown, etc. They were scored on a seven-point Likert scale ranging from 1 "Totally disagree" to 7 "Totally agree". The questionnaire was delivered to the students within our industrial design department. 31 effective questionnaires were collected back for analysis. These claims were ranked and three most agreed claims were identified and then discussed in regarding to the opportunities of seeing the practical usefulness of storytelling.

In the third study, a field study was conducted to understand acceptance-related aspects. We traced and observed the students' design practice in a design squad within our department for one semester. A primary prototype was developed and introduced to the students at the beginning of the design projects as a stimulus to promote the involvement of storytelling in their design practice. It was five-page templates with the titles of Beginning—Development—Climax—Solution—Ending on each page based on the Freytag's five-act structure curve [33] to provide a basic framework for storytelling. Each page was consisted of the title, explanations and a blank area (shown in attachment 1) that students could fill in with text and images for storytelling. The students were encouraged to tell stories about their design projects rather than been forced to use these templates. A USE questionnaire with 20 questions (Usefulness—7 questions: Q1—Q7, Satisfaction—6 questions: Q8—Q13, and Ease of use—7 questions: Q14—Q20) was filled in by the students to collect their viewpoints on the templates. In the USE questionnaire, statements had to be scored on a seven-point Likert scale ranging from 1 "Strongly disagree" to 7 "Strongly agree". Several sessions of interview were conducted with students. Questions were asked firstly about explanation of the answers to the questions in the questionnaire, and then about their opinions on the templates, and suggestions for improvements. All the interviews were audio recorded.

4 Results

4.1 The Results of Study 1

10 students, 60% male and 40% female, including 40% undergraduate students, 40% master students and 20% PhD students participated in the focus group. They were

recruited within our design department from 4 different countries, 4 Dutch, 4 Chinese, 1 Spanish and 1 Indian. The data collected from the audio records was firstly transcribed verbatim and individual quotes were extracted and labelled. The data analysis was followed a thematic approach [34] which allowed the themes to develop based on the prepared questions (examples shown in Table 1) that were asked during the focus group. To avoid the potential personal bias on interpretation and guarantee the consistency of the coding process, 2 researchers were involved in this analysis.

Table 1. Examples of the topics in the focus group.

No.	Examples
1	What is your definition of storytelling in the context of design?
2	Did you ever adopt storytelling in your design practice?
3	If yes, when, why and how?
4	If not, what are the reasons that you don't adopt storytelling?
5	What problems did you ever encounter when adopting storytelling in design?
6	Suggestions to promote practice of storytelling in design

We finally identified 5 main categories for the collected 120 quotes in total. Except for one first-year student who had ever used storytelling in his previous design work, all the students clarified their past experience in storytelling either orally or using storyboards. However, 60% of the participants told us they actually didn't like storytelling for different reasons. 30% participants liked storytelling and 10% participants showed a neutral attitude. Table 2 shows the identified categories and some example quotes.

Table 2. Categories and examples of the quotes in study 1

Main categories	Sub-categories	Quote no.	Examples
Definition	What storytelling it is	10	"Storytelling means to first to build a story and then tell it to introduce your design concept to others. Designers can orally tell the story or use storyboards" "For me, storytelling in design is to make storyboards to show how your product will be used by users"
Current status of storytelling adoption	Use and why	9	"Yes, storytelling/storyboard helps to explain how my design concept works, how people interact with it" "Yes, I often make storyboard when interpret my concept. It's easy to show the using scenarios"

(continued)

Table 2. (*continued*)

Main categories	Sub-categories	Quote no.	Examples
	Not use and why	1	"I never used storytelling in my design project, because I think the sketches and prototypes are clear enough to show my design concepts. I don't think I need it"
	When and how	20	"When we make presentation to introduce our design concept, storyboard is often used, and we also orally told stories based on it"
Preference	Like storytelling	3	"Yes. Storytelling is easy to show how user will use the product" "Yes. I make storyboard to tell stories when introducing my design concept to others"
	Neutral attitudes	1	"My attitude is neutral because I know it's helpful, but it is not my first choice"
	Not like storytelling	6	"I don't think so. I know it's quite useful, but it takes much time and effort when storyboarding" "No, I prefer use sketch and prototype directly to explain my design ideas" "No. I know it is useful, but I actually don't like to use it"
Reasons of not adopting storytelling	Not easy To use	20	"It takes time and effort to draw a storyboard" "It is complex to tell a story. First, you need to build a story and then decide how to tell it. If prepare for a video story, good preparation is necessary" "I am actually not sure how to craft and tell a good story. Every time I made a storyboard to show my idea, but I don't know whether people understand it based on the storyboard. There is no feedback"
	Other choices	10	"I never only orally tell stories because the audience must depend on their imagination of the story. Instead, I prefer using the sketches or prototypes to show my ideas because they are direct visuals. People can easily and quickly understand my ideas"
	Other reasons	15	"We just tell stories in our own style. There is no training or guideline that can support us. We don't know when should storytelling, and whether we tell the right story in the right way"

(*continued*)

Table 2. (*continued*)

Main categories	Sub-categories	Quote no.	Examples
Suggestions	Possible Solutions and suggestions	25	"I believe that concrete guidelines or instructions for building a good story is in demand because I always do it in my own style and I don't know whether it is right or not. There seems no criteria or standards "Appropriate tools or templates are definitely helpful"

4.2 The Results of Study 2

The questionnaires were answered by 31 design students. The participant division was 54.8% male and 45.2% female, including 38.7% undergraduate students, 38.7% master students and 22.6% PhD students. The median scores with 95% confidence intervals for the responses to the 21 claims are shown in Fig. 1(a), showing a median response that is significantly above the neutral score of 4 for all claims, except claim C9 —"Storytelling is a critical success factor in design processes and outcomes". A more meaningful analysis is however to look at effect size. More specifically, in Fig. 1(b) we show the estimated probability (with confidence interval) that subjects agree with the claim, which corresponds to a score of 5 or higher. The three claims with the highest probability of agreement were related to the ability to convince others about the value of the proposed design: C20—"Storytelling during a presentation is an excellent way to sell design ideas"; C12—"Storytelling can deliver understanding when used in a design pitch"; and C16—"Storytelling approach can be applied as user experience tool to collect insights about the underlying motivation and needs". The three claims with the lowest probability of agreement referred to the positive role of storytelling in the design process itself: C9—"Storytelling is a critical success factor in design processes and outcomes", C5—"Stories can be valuable at every stage of the product life-cycle" and C10—"Stories convince people of the value of a proposed product in a real-world domain, and by analogy that it would be valuable in their own settings."

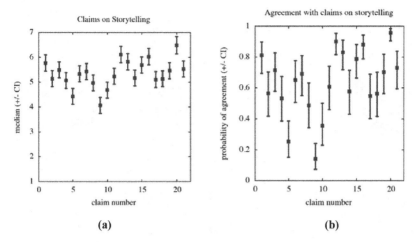

Fig. 1. Medians and effect sizes for the 21 claims about the positive role of storytelling in design

4.3   The Results of Study

Results of observation

We involved 30 students doing design projects in the field study. They were divided into 8 different project groups consisting of either bachelor or master students. The participant-observation showed that 5 groups with 20 students used our proposed prototype for storytelling, while the other 3 groups with 10 students neither used the templates nor used storytelling. For these 5 groups, storytelling occurred in different phases, as illustrated in Fig. 2. For instance, all of them both told stories orally and visually with storyboards in their mid-term and final presentations. Three groups applied storytelling with the help of the templates to explore alternative solutions in early ideation phases. However, they tried it only once, in the sense of completing the story sheets in text or simple sketches. One group made storyboards based on the framework provided by the templates for the sake of feedback from peers (other students), while another group did it for the sake of internal reflection upon their design concept at the end of ideation phase.

They primarily used storyboards containing sketches or images as the way to present (or pitch) their design concept. The stories in these storyboards showed the influence of using the template, as they paid explicit attention to story elements such as people, scenarios, products, interaction, etc. They are however better characterized as flat narratives rather than true stories, as an obvious story plot or dramatic conflict was not apparent.

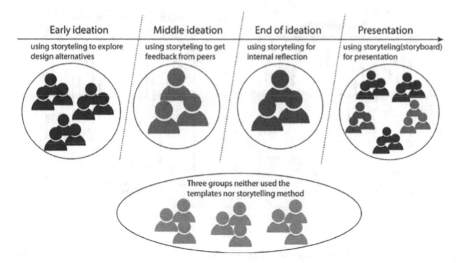

Fig. 2. Students used storytelling during the design process.

Results of the USE Questionnaire

We The USE questionnaire was only filled in by the 20 students from the 5 groups that actually used the storytelling templates. They were 11 male and 9 female participants, divided over 14 bachelor and 6 master students. We separately analyzed data for three categories of questions: Usefulness (Q1—Q7), Satisfaction (Q8—Q13), and Ease of Use (Q14—Q20). For many of the questions, the participants held views which were relatively close to a neutral attitude, corresponding to a median score close to the median of 4.

In median scores for the 7 questions on perceived usefulness of the storytelling templates are shown in Fig. 3(a), showing a significant positive average score for Q3—useful and a significant negative average score for Q5—save time. This is also reflected in the effect size shown in Fig. 3(b) which is defined here as the estimated probability (with confidence interval) that subjects have a positive attitude to the usefulness attribute being questioned, which corresponds to a score of 4 or higher. The message conveyed by this analysis is that the provided templates for storytelling were considered useful but that they were not convinced that using them saved time in their design process.

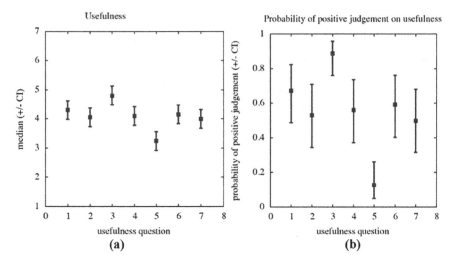

Fig. 3. Medians and effect sizes for the 7 questions about perceived usefulness

In median scores for the 6 questions on satisfaction of the storytelling templates are shown in Fig. 4(a), while the corresponding effect sizes are reported in Fig. 4(b). A significant (positive) effect was only observed for Q13-I feel that I need it, while Q11-It's wonder was obviously least appreciated (marginally significant negative effect). The students were obviously divided in their judgements and their stance was mostly neutral.

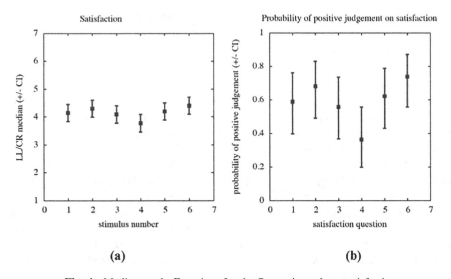

Fig. 4. Medians and effect sizes for the 7 questions about satisfaction

In median scores for the 7 questions on perceived ease of use of the storytelling templates are shown in Fig. 5(a), while the corresponding effect sizes are reported in Fig. 5(b). In the section perceived ease of use, participants held positive attitudes to all the questions, expect Q18-effortless, while the most positive effect was observed for the first 4 questions. This indicated that the templates were generally easy to use, but did require an effort when actually using them (which is not surprising, as building a story is a non-trivial creative exercise).

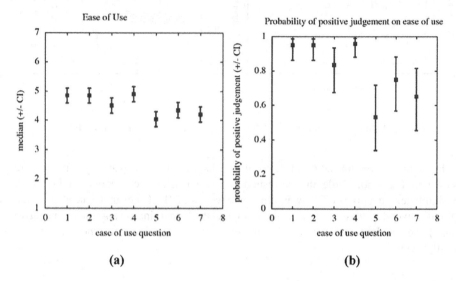

Fig. 5. Medians and effect sizes for the 7 questions about perceived ease of use

Results of Observation

The data of the interviews was analyzed and clustered into four main categories. Category 1 contained 16 quotes from the interviews with the three student groups who decided not to include storytelling into their design process. Students in one of those three groups believed that "We don't need storytelling because we are working on prototyping. Once people try the prototype, they can understand what it is and how it works. It's not possible to only imagine it in a story."

The other three categories contained the quotes from the interviews with the students in the other 5 groups who did apply storytelling in their process;121 quotes related to both positive and negative aspects were collected.

Category 2—the positive aspects (54 quotes) addressed benefits and strengths of storytelling templates. For instance, "The templates enhanced our awareness of storytelling as we actually didn't care about it before, and they helped us to build a story." And "The templates provide a basic structure for storytelling and promote us to think about a background story for our design concepts."

Category 3—the negative aspects (67 quotes) provided more details about the problems and concerns that the students encountered when they used the templates.

These quotes revealed four sub-categories of concerns: (1) about the usefulness of the time and effort invested (19 quotes), for example: "It took both time and efforts. We used about one hour to use these templates to build a story." (2) about the effort of creating stories (16 quotes) for example: "Storytelling is not simple. The templates helped to build a story, but also required much effort to do it." (3) about satisfaction with the outcome (17 quotes), examples are: "I am not sure whether I need to use storytelling or not. It depends on the design project." (4) other concerns (15 quotes), for instance, "I am not good at either storytelling or storyboarding. This is why storytelling is not my first choice."

The 60 quotes which were put into category 4 contained suggestions for improvement of the story templates and the storytelling practice. 15% of quotes identified the need to develop appropriate tools to support and promote storytelling in the design practice. Another direction, supported by 25% of the collected quotes, was to target storytelling more to specific design phases. For instance, "If storytelling is used for a specific purpose in a specific time, for example in presentation, it could be easier to apply. And the tools should support this purpose." "We mostly use storytelling when introducing or presenting our design to others. But we actually don't know how to do it better. Support is necessary." Another main direction, supported by 28.3% of the collected quotes, refers to improving the existing templates (and give them a more professional look and feel). "It needs better graphic design." "to make the templates more professional with details, instructions and good visual design." The remaining 21.7% quotes contained opinions of participants shared for how to improve the storytelling method. For instance, "It should be simple to start with and easy to use." "Provide guidelines or instructions for users to follow." "I think an appropriate storytelling tool should have two main functionalities: to tell us when we need storytelling, and it can support for that specific purpose."

5   Discussion

5.1   The Reasons that Students Don't Adopt Storytelling

The study reported in this paper provided more detailed insight into the current status of the practices of storytelling by design students. It should be acknowledged that storytelling might be particularly suitable for some design domains such as user experience design, service design, etc. The multiple benefits make the storytelling approach worthy being applied broadly and frequently in such kind of design. However, the reasons for poor adoption of storytelling by design students seemed related to acceptance. As the theory of acceptance stated with perceived usefulness and perceived ease of use [35], we discuss the reasons from these two aspects:

On one hand, the perceived usefulness of storytelling is an important premise for acceptance. In the discipline of design, storytelling is believed valuable at all stages of the design process and the product life cycle [22, 36] in informing product functionalities, exploring and communicating design ideas, conveying values and emotions, provoking comments and reactions, promoting innovation, etc. [5, 10, 37]. However, only emphasizing the theoretical arguments in favor of the usefulness of storytelling is clearly not sufficient, as many students remain skeptical. The results of study 1 indicated that students often preferred other options such as sketches, prototypes, etc. over storytelling as the unique and practical usefulness of storytelling was (insufficiently) perceived. While unmatched values of storytelling, such as expressing emotions, demonstrating values, triggering empathy, managing information, etc., have been hypothesized, such arguments do not easily carry over to the design practice, and students do not easily comprehend when and how such values are essential in their design process. In study 2, the most agreed claims for values of storytelling indicated that the value of storytelling was obviously recognized in case of design pitching/presenting. In study 3, the 5 (out of 8) student groups who did apply the storytelling templates in their design practice provided useful directions for improving the storytelling method that we provided to them.

On the other hand, ease of use also influences the acceptance. The results of study 1 implied that the definition of storytelling influence the practice. As storytelling was often perceived by students as being equivalent to storyboarding, the limited sketching (or photoshop) abilities of many students was perceived as a major obstacle [2]. Storyboarding hence tends to be viewed as a time-consuming and effort-requiring process by many (but not all) students. The results of study 1 also confirmed that a lack of dedicated support for storytelling such as appropriate tools, guidelines, and instructions, etc. affected the perception of ease of use. In both study 1 and 3, a demand for better support for storytelling was subscribed to by many students. In study 3, the positive feedback on our templates, and the arguments in support of the positively valued Q13-I feel I need it, demonstrated the necessity to develop methods or tools that better support storytelling.

5.2   A Proposition to Develop Tools that Support Pitching Design Concepts in the Form of Stories

Based on the insights obtained from our empirical studies, we propose to develop a dedicated tool in support of one specific phase of the design process, i.e., design pitching. Three distinct considerations underlie this choice:

Firstly, to enhance students' acceptance of storytelling, we identified a design pitch as a good opportunity to show the practical values of storytelling. In study 2, two of the top three claims of storytelling's values that most students agreed on were related to design presentation and design pitch. In study 3, all student teams adopted storytelling for their design presentation. Therefore, the unique and practical usefulness of storytelling seems to be most easily recognized when storytelling is used for a design presentation or a design pitch. We particularly focused on the design pitch rather than presentation because it is more condensed and structured than a general design presentation. Good pitches always use storytelling. Storytelling triggers empathy, promotes understanding, and invites feedback. Empathy occurs when the audience watches or listens to the storytelling pitch and can make a connection to their own context or person. The feedback from the audience on such pitches can in turn help students to better appreciate the usefulness of storytelling.

Secondly, to avoid the influence of personal differences in a design pitch, we further propose to focus on preparing a design pitch using established methods from storytelling. Storytelling is analysis-oriented [5, 14], and preparing a design pitch with storytelling thus could help students to reflect upon, analyze and discuss the design concepts. It could enable students to view storytelling holistically by understanding its usefulness in information management, not only limited in knowing its usefulness in communication.

Thirdly, to enhance students' acceptance of storytelling, we proposed to develop tools for storytelling with a higher professional standard (in terms of look-and-feel but also support) so that students may be more inclined to use them when preparing a design pitch. Storytelling is often too generic to be utilized in practice, and appropriate tools could help. Tools are instruments which can extend the ability of people, facilitate design practice, and guide us toward solutions [38] The studies demonstrated a need for supporting storytelling, and concrete suggestions for improving the existing (research) tool were collected.

5.3 Limitation

There are three obvious limitations in the empirical study reported in this paper. First, we based our insights on the observation of the storytelling practice of industrial design students in our own design department, which is part of a Dutch university of technology. The students from art colleges were not involved in the study, and neither were students from other cultures. The argument in favor of or choice, next to convenience because of the easy access to participants, were that our students are very critical and used to conveying their criticism. Second, as we could extract more than 100 claims of storytelling's values in literature, it was impossible to collect participants' attitudes on all these claims. The selection of the claims for the questionnaire in study 2 was based on the researcher's own standards. Third, we only proposed a general direction for an approach to enhance the acceptance of storytelling as a tool for pitching, and developing and testing this proposal in more detail is the topic of future research.

6 Conclusion

In this paper, we discussed an investigation into the current adoption of storytelling practice by design students. It was aimed at understanding the acceptance of storytelling in design as there seems to be a lack of related studies in literature. The results helped us to reflect upon students' practice of storytelling and identify opportunities to enhance their acceptance by focusing on a specific of storytelling in design pitching where the advantages would be most easy to perceive. Our future work will be to further explore this direction by developing a professionally looking and supported tool that can be distributed online.

Acknowledgements. The authors would like to thank all the participants involved in the study.

References

1. Atasoy, B., Martens, J.-B.: STORYPLY: designing for user experiences using storycraft. In: Markopoulos, P., Martens, J.B., Malins, J., Coninx, K., Liapis, A. (eds.) Collaboration in Creative Design, pp. 181–210. Springer, Heidelberg (2016). https://doi.org/10.1007/978-3-319-29155-0_9
2. Peng, Q., Martens, J.-B.: Requirements gathering for tools in support of storyboarding in user experience design. In: Proceedings of the 32nd International BCS Human Computer Interaction Conference, Swindon, UK, 2018, pp. 1–10 (2018)
3. Bertolotti, E., Daam, H., Piredda, F., Tassinari, V.: The Pearl Diver. The Designer as Storyteller. DESIS Philosophy Talks-Dipartimento di Design, Politecnico di Milano (2016)
4. Brown, T., Katz, B.: Change by design. J. Prod. Innov. Manag. 28(3), 381–383 (2011)
5. Parrish, P.: Design as storytelling. TechTrends 50(4), 72–82 (2006). https://doi.org/10.1007/s11528-006-0072-7
6. Gruen, D.: Beyond scenarios: the role of storytelling in CSCW design. In: CSCW 2000 (2000)
7. Lotus Research: Storyboarding for design: an overview of the process, 3(11), 10 (2000)
8. Danko, S.: Humanizing design through narrative inquiry. J. Inter. Des. 31(2), 10–28 (2006)
9. Atasoy, B., Martens, J.-B.: STORIFY: a tool to assist design teams in envisioning and discussing user experience. In: CHI 2011 Extended Abstracts on Human Factors in Computing Systems, pp. 2263–2268 (2011)
10. Gruen, D.: Stories and storytelling in the design of interactive systems. In: 3rd Conference on Designing Interactive Systems: Processes, Practices, Methods, and Techniques, pp. 446–447 (2000)
11. Tanenbaum, J.: Design fictional interactions: why HCI should care about stories. Interactions 21(5), 22–23 (2014)
12. Erickson, T.: Design as storytelling. Interactions 3(4), 30–35 (1996)
13. Lloyd, P.: Storytelling and the development of discourse in the engineering design process. Des. Stud. 21(4), 357–373 (2000)
14. Lloyd, P., Oak, A.: Cracking open co-creation: categories, stories, and value tension in a collaborative design process. Des. Stud. 57, 93–111 (2018)
15. Liedtka, J., Ogilvie, T.: Ten tools for design thinking (2010)
16. DeLarge, C.A.: Storytelling as a critical success factor in design processes and outcomes. Des. Manag. Rev. 15(3), 76–81 (2010)
17. Beckman, S., Barry, M.: Design and innovation through storytelling. Int. J. Innov. Sci. 1(4), 151–160 (2009)
18. Garcia, A.C.B., Carretti, C.E., Ferraz, I.N., Bente, C.: Sharing design perspectives through storytelling. AI EDAM 16(3), 229–241 (2002)
19. Fritsch, J., Judice, A., Soini, K., Tretten, P.: Storytelling and repetitive narratives for design empathy: case Suomenlinna. Nordes, (2) (2009)
20. Strom, G.: Stories with emotions and conflicts drive development of better interactions in industrial software projects. In: Proceedings of the 19th Australasian conference on Computer-Human Interaction: Entertaining User Interfaces 2007, pp. 115–121 (2007)
21. Michailidou, I., von Saucken, C., Lindemann, U.: How to create a user experience story. In: Marcus, A. (ed.) DUXU 2013. LNCS, vol. 8012, pp. 554–563. Springer, Heidelberg (2013). https://doi.org/10.1007/978-3-642-39229-0_59
22. Quesenbery, W., Brooks, K.: Storytelling for User Experience: Crafting Stories for Better Design. Rosenfeld Media, Brooklyn (2010)

23. Forlizzi, J., Ford, S.: The building blocks of experience: an early framework for interaction designers. In: Proceedings of the 3rd Conference on Designing Interactive Systems: Processes, Practices, Methods, and Techniques 2000, pp. 419–423 (2000)
24. Stickdorn, M., Schneider, J., Andrews, K., Lawrence, A.: This is Service Design Thinking: Basics, Tools, Cases, vol. 1. Wiley, Hoboken (2011)
25. Gausepohl, K.A., Winchester, W.W., Smith-Jackson, T.L., Kleiner, B.M., Arthur, J.D.: A conceptual model for the role of storytelling in design: leveraging narrative inquiry in user-centered design (UCD). Health Technol. **6**(2), 125–136 (2016). https://doi.org/10.1007/s12553-015-0123-1
26. Gruen, D., Rauch, T., Redpath, S., Ruettinger, S.: The use of stories in user experience design. Int. J. Hum.-Comput. Interact. **14**(3–4), 503–534 (2002)
27. Lichaw, D.: The User's Journey: Storymapping Products that People Love. Rosenfeld Media, Brooklyn (2016)
28. Dindler, C., Iversen, O.S.: Fictional inquiry—design collaboration in a shared narrative space. CoDesign **3**(4), 213–234 (2007)
29. Beck, E., Obrist, M., Bernhaupt, R., Tscheligi, M.: Instant card technique: how and why to apply in user-centered design. In: Proceedings of the 10th Anniversary Conference on Participatory Design, pp. 162–165 (2008)
30. Kankainen, A., Vaajakallio, K., Kantola, V., Mattelmäki, T.: "Storytelling group–a co-design method for service design. Behav. Inf. Technol. **31**(3), 221–230 (2012)
31. Buskermolen, D.O., Terken, J.: Co-constructing stories: a participatory design technique to elicit in-depth user feedback and suggestions about design concepts. In: Proceedings of the 12th Participatory Design Conference: Exploratory Papers, Workshop Descriptions, Industry Cases, vol. 2, pp. 33–36 (2012)
32. Choma, J., Zaina, L.A.M., Beraldo, D.: UserX story: incorporating UX aspects into user stories elaboration. In: Kurosu, M. (ed.) HCI 2016. LNCS, vol. 9731, pp. 131–140. Springer, Cham (2016). https://doi.org/10.1007/978-3-319-39510-4_13
33. Harmon, R., Holman, J.: A Handbook to English Literature, London (1996)
34. Braun, V., Clarke, V.: Using thematic analysis in psychology. Qual. Res. Psychol. **3**(2), 77–101 (2006)
35. Davis, F.D.: Perceived usefulness, perceived ease of use, and user acceptance of information technology. MIS Q. **13**(3), 319–340 (1989)
36. Ogaick, T.: Once upon a design - storytelling and interactive fiction in the design process. Doctoral dissertation. Carleton University (2014)
37. Pucillo, F., Michailidou, I., Cascini, G., Lindemann, U.: Storytelling and a narrative analysis-based method for extracting users' motives in UX design processes. In: DS 81: Proceedings of NordDesign 2014, Espoo, Finland 27–29th August 2014, pp. 396–405 (2014)
38. Dalsgaard, P.: Instruments of inquiry: understanding the nature and role of tools in design. Int. J. Des. **11**(1) (2017)

Visually Impaired Accessibility Heuristics Proposal for e-Commerce Mobile Applications

Kevin Pereda[✉], Braulio Murillo, and Freddy Paz

Pontificia Universidad Católica del Perú, San Miguel, Lima 32, Peru
{kevin.pereda,fpaz}@pucp.pe,
bmurillov@pucp.edu.pe

Abstract. E-Commerce has been reaching considerably amount of sales around the globe, being a key factor mobile devices. However, not all enjoy its characteristics as is the case of visually impaired people. This study follows the methodology proposed by Quiñones to elaborate heuristics centered in a specific user experience aspect as is accessibility, in order to understand needs and help develop better mobile apps.

Keywords: Human-computer interaction · Accessibility · Heuristics · Visually impaired · e-Commerce · Mobile applications

1 Introduction

E-Commerce is well-known for providing a better product understanding, superior availability compared to physical stores, global access, privacy, and, in general, lower prices [11].

According to eMarketer [13], in 2017, e-Commerce sales reached 2,304 billion dollars, being mobile devices a key factor with 58.9% respect to total sales.

Despite e-Commerce's growth and impact, not all people enjoy all its characteristics as is the case of visually impaired people [30].

In fact, according to the World Health Organization (WHO) [9], in 2015 around 189 million people had mild visually impairment and 217 million were moderately or severely visually impaired. Even though WHO is in charge of developing action plans such as the Universal eye health: a global action plan 2014–2019, the growth and change in age structure of world's populations is causing a substantial increase in the number of people with vision impairment, which appears to be accelerating [9].

Additionally to a higher presence of visually impaired people, legislation and accessibility initiatives for the disabled are being reaffirmed, in which businesses must anticipate or remove any disadvantage presented. Examples of these are European Accessibility Act [14], the Equality Act [2] and ADA Regulation [1]. Furthermore, litigation events related to accessibility have been reported [19,27].

A. Marcus and E. Rosenzweig (Eds.): HCII 2020, LNCS 12200, pp. 240–252, 2020.
https://doi.org/10.1007/978-3-030-49713-2_17

In the smartphone level, people with visual impairment have disadvantages when using them. Consider for instance, difficulty in text entry [32], layout proximity [20], screen size that hinders the location of interface components [32] and correct feedback on the current state of the system through alternative means such as vibrations or sounds [10].

While at the level of e-commerce web applications, some of the problems identified are due to complex navigation menus owning many elements [8]; the large number of results shown when performing a search; and images shown that do not have alternative text [34], which could confuse people with visual impairment when browsing pages with many images and content; and long product names and no established standard.

When considering both areas, we can show that there are difficulties for people with visual impairment on e-Commerce either on websites or mobile applications in general. This relationship can not be ignored since one key factor, according to estimates, is that by 2021 mobile e-Commerce would represent 72.9% of total electronic commerce [13] and people with visual impairment are part of that market.

The World Wide Web Consortium (W3C) is an internationally accepted community whose mission is to develop protocols and guidelines that guarantee the growth of the web. Among these guidelines is WCAG 2.0 (Web Content Accessibility Guidelines) [31], which can be adapted to a mobile environment. Although the guidelines proposed in WCAG 2.0 cover relevant aspects of accessibility in mobile applications, for the specific domain in question, some were not identified. For instance the feedback through sounds or vibrations or adjustable screen readers [10].

Thus, when considering the problems faced by people with visual impairment, the projected growth of the sale by electronic commerce on mobile devices, the increase of people with vision problems and the reaffirmation of accessibility laws, it is necessary to establish guidelines that can assess the accessibility of said mobile e-commerce applications, in such a way that they facilitate the inclusion of people with visual impairment, alleviate the main inconveniences they have, in addition to preventing future legislative conflicts in the case of companies linked to retail sales.

2   Background and Related Works

2.1   Accessibility

According to ISO/IEC Guide 71 [18], an accessible design is one focused on principles of extending standard design to people with some type of performance limitation to maximize the number of potential customers who can readily use a product, building or service. Meanwhile, for W3C web accessibility means that websites, tools, and technologies are designed and developed so that people with disabilities can use them. In other words, accessibility is about inclusion and not discrimination to people with some sort of impairment, being mild or severe, in the use of products infrastructure or services.

2.2 Web Content Accessibility Guidelines

The Web Content Accessibility Guidelines [4] developed by W3C consists of four principles:

- Perceivable - Information and user interface components must be presentable to users in ways they can perceive
- Operable - Users can navigate and use the interface components
- Understandable - Information and the operation of user interface must be understandable
- Robust - Content must be robust enough to be interpreted by a variety of users, current and future technologies.

2.3 Vision Impairment

Vision impairment is related to the clarity or sharpness of the vision. Usually, this concept is exemplified by the term "20/20" which would represent a normal state of visual acuity. These numbers are interpreted as follows: a person can appreciate everything that is 20 feet away, which is considered a usual scenario. However, "20/100", will indicate that, to see what a person with normal vision sees at 100 feet, one would have to approach up to 20 feet to really appreciate it. Having a vision of "20/100" does not imply just approaching to be able to see correctly, other factors must be considered, such as peripheral vision, eye coordination, depth perception, ability to concentrate on certain objects and perception of the color [7].

The International Classification of Diseases [3] categorizes visual impairment through vision acuity (Table 1).

The main causes of visual impairment, according to the World Health Organization [16] are:

- **Uncorrected refractive errors**, which occur when the shape of the eye prevents light from reaching the retina. The retina converts light rays into messages that are sent through the optic nerve to the brain and it interprets the images we see. The result of these errors is blurred vision, which when reaching a severe degree causes visual impairment [21]. Among the different types of refractive errors are [33]:
  - Myopia, difficulty seeing distant objects clearly
  - Far-sightedness, difficulty seeing nearby objects clearly
  - Astigmatism, distorted vision due to an irregularly curved cornea
  - Presbyopia, gradual loss of ability to focus on nearby objects due to aging
- **Cataracts**, given by the cloudiness of the lens (the lens) that affects vision. The lens is the part of the eye that helps focus on light or images. They are present more frequently in adults older than 80 years [22].
- **Age-related macular degeneration**, a condition that causes the center of vision to be blurred while the sides are not affected. This is because the macula is the central part in the retina, the inner layer at the back of the eye responsible for detailed central vision [24] (Figs. 1 and 2).

Table 1. Visual impairment including blindness (binocular or monocular)

Category	Worse than:	Same or better than:
Mild or no visual impairment		6/18 3/10 (0.3) 20/70
Moderate	6/18 3/10 (0.3) 20/70	6/60 1/10 (0.1) 20/200
Severe	6/60 1/10 (0.1) 20/200	3/60 1/20 (0.05) 20/400
Blindness	3/60 1/20 (0.05) 20/400	1/60 1/50 (0.02) 5/300 (20/1200)
Blindness	1/60 1/50 (0.02) 5/300 (20/1200)	Light perception
Blindness	No light perception	No light perception

- **Glaucoma**, a disease in which the optic nerve is damaged by accumulation of fluid in the front of the eye. Without treatment, people with glaucoma slowly lose their peripheral vision (on the sides) [6] (Fig. 3).
- **Diabetic retinopathy**, a complication of diabetes that occurs when small blood vessels in the retina are damaged [23]. Blood vessels damaged by diabetic retinopathy can cause a vision problem in two ways:
  - Proliferative retinopathy, which consists of the development of abnormal blood vessels that can drip blood in the center of the eye, obscuring vision.
  - Macular edema, through fluid that drips into the macula, causing it to swell, clouding the vision (Fig. 4).

2.4   Related Works

Several studies were taken into consideration in order to find out which guidelines or recommendations could be adapted from a general mobile environment to the specifics, among these:

In Damaceno et al. [10], a systematic review is carried out whose purpose is to identify the most frequent problems that affect people with visual impairment in mobile devices. These have been assigned to seven different categories: buttons, input of information,gesture-based interaction, screen readers, screen size, feedback to the user and voice commands. Guidelines for all these categories are proposed.

Fig. 1. Vision of a person with cataract [23]

Fig. 2. Vision of a person with macular degeneration [15]

Fig. 3. Vision of a person with glaucoma [25]

Fig. 4. Vision of a person with diabetic retinopathy [26]

In Acosta-Vargas et al. [5] they propose a heuristic method for the evaluation of accessibility in mobile air quality applications. They are based on the guidelines proposed by WCAG 2.0, and their method consists of 7 phases, select applications to evaluate, select target users, identify common scenarios, evaluate the application through the barrier walkthrough, record the results, analyze the results and propose improvements.

Ghidini et al. [17] sought to answer what kind of interaction makes it easier to use mobile applications for people with visual impairment. For this purpose, an investigation is carried out in the literature, a survey of people with visual impairment in which various problems are identified, such as not being informed of the current status of the operations carried out or that applications with voice commands do not request confirmation of messages. Subsequently, the authors propose a prototype of a calendar application in which they incorporate all the aspects collected, to finally conduct another survey with the people initially questioned, and thus conclude that the guidelines applied improved the application in aspects of accessibility.

In Díaz-Bossini et al. [12], surveys are carried out to older adults in order to evaluate proposed accessibility guidelines for mobile devices. Participants were able to quantify which guidelines seemed most appropriate after having used mobile applications to perform basic tasks. Among them are: providing an understandable language, frequent screen scrolling is not convenient, iconography must be understandable, background colors should not be invasive and complementing certain tasks with audio is beneficial.

Additionally, studies related to e-Commerce websites accessibility for the visually impaired were also considered.

In Yang et al. [34] certain usability and accessibility problems for e-commerce websites are described, among which are: excessive classification options, lack of detailed description for product photos, very long product names. Subsequently, a prototype evaluated by 10 students with visual impairment is developed in which certain guidelines were provided to follow as: show confirmation messages after selecting certain products, brevity in the titles but developed description, the products must be displayed in order of ratings, in addition to being able to take into account the comments of the other buyers.

In Sohaib et al. [30] an identification of the main accessibility problems in Australian e-commerce websites was made. The choice of this population is due to the fact that 75 % of Australians have made overseas purchases, according to a study carried out in 2015. Results are alarming because none of the 30 portals chosen met the minimum stipulated by WCAG 2.0, so recommendations are proposed for each of the disabilities described above, such as that product images should be displayed denoting their purpose and not appearance or to avoid low contrast design.

3   Defining Visually Impaired Accessibility Heuristics for e-Commerce Mobile Applications

In order to define the accessibility heuristics, the methodology proposed by Quiñones et al. [29] was followed. The methodology fits the needs to focus especially on the accessibility dimension of the user experience. The eight stages proposed in the methodology were covered as follows.

Step 1 - Exploratory Stage: we performed a systematic review about heuristics related to the specific domain, researched about guidelines and standards.

A systematic review was performed in order to find out if there were available heuristics related to the specific domain.

After the systematic review performed, we found out that there were standards well-referred such as WCAG 2.0, Section 508, and from companies as Google, Apple and BBC, which are mentioned in Section 508. Also, many studies proposed guidelines to assess accessibility in a mobile environment or e-Commerce websites for the visually impaired.

For the standards, we proposed the following question: Which of these guidelines proposed by the standards minimize the difficulties faced by people with visual impairment within an e-commerce flow?

In order to approach the answer, we established a nexus criteria between WCAG 2.0, Section 508, Google Accessibility Guidelines, Apple Accessibility Guide for iOS using the accessibility principles by W3C in order to find similarities among them.

The same procedure was applied for the guidelines found on literature.

Step 2 - Experimental Stage: we performed user testing with five impaired people in which we could identify specific needs and problems related to current interfaces.

The guidelines, both from standards and literature were summed up, and associated to questions referenced in user testing.

The experiment was carried out with five impaired people whom had glaucoma, astigmatism and myopia. All of them had used e-Commerce even once before the experiment. The mean age was 35 years old, and they all had around 4 inch screen smartphone.

Users were put into a scenario in which they had to navigate through the interface of two e-Commerce mobile applications: Falabella and Amazon app and at the end answer the questions related to the guidelines.

As results of the user testing, we could identify that some of the guidelines were covered in the apps, mostly Amazon, such as being concise in titles, not using images as titles, associate buttons to purchase functionalities, or the ones related to support the operating system features.

However, there were also guidelines that were not identified by the users such as the availability of voice commands, listening feedback from the products, zoom support, adequate contrast ratio, provide tutorials or text size increasing options. Plus, there were additional problems, among these: iconography could not be perceived correctly due to its contrast and small size, some products had large titles and were cumbersome to read using screen readers, not all the users had a keyboard with voice commands as an option, users could not change the contrast of the mobile interface since some of them were accustomed to low light contrast apps, some promotions or products were inside images that could not be zoomed in.

Step 3 - Descriptive Stage: we identified specific domain characteristics that were validated through expert judgement, specified that the user experience aspect mainly considered was accessibility, also the Nielsen heuristics were taken as a basis for defining related heuristics.

According to the methodology proposed by Quiñones et al. [28], the information regarding to the application should be prioritized. In this case, all the definitions shown in Sect. 2 (Background) were given a value of 3, since they were all important and relevant to this proposal.

Among the accessibility features for mobile applications for people with visual impairment, both general and specific characteristics (for e-Commerce) were considered, which are shown in Tables 2 and 3.

Table 2. General features regarding accessibility aspects

General features	Given value
Feedback	3 (priority)
Visibility of content	3 (priority)
Ease of navigation	3 (priority)
Quick access	3 (priority)
User help	3 (priority)

The specific characteristics were elaborated based on the systematic review performed and was validated through expert judgement, in which the experts concluded they were adequate terms for the specific study.

The user experience attributes prioritized for this study were evaluated taking into consideration that it is mainly centered in accessibility, however, there are

Table 3. Selected features of the specific application domain

Specific features	Given value
Audio and vibration feedback	3 (priority)
Simple purchase flow	3 (priority)
Simplified characteristics of products	3 (priority)
Visual help to the user	3 (priority)
Touch gesture systems	3 (priority)
Alternative input methods	3 (priority)
Support for operating system features	3 (priority)

Table 4. Prioritization of attributes individually

	Value	Attribute	Author of the proposal	Justification
UX	2	Useful	Morville	Four of the seven factors proposed by Morville are considered. However, due to the assigned score, accessibility will be the main focus to consider
	2	Usable		
	2	Desirable		
	1	Findable		
	1	Credible		
	3	Accessible		
	1	Valuable		
Usability	2	Learnability	Jakob Nielsen	While heuristics will be focused on accessibility, some of their attributes overlap with usability, of which four out of five proposed by Nielsen have been considered
	2	Efficiency		
	2	Memorability		
	2	Errors		
	2	Satisfaction		

aspects in the purchase flow for the visually impaired that also need a degree of usability attributes. The following chart (Table 4) shows the authors considered for the selection of the attributes and the corresponding justification.

Since there is no evidence of similar heuristics, we considered the guidelines applicable to the specifics and the problems found on user testing. Nielsen heuristics were also considered since they help cover attributes related to the usability as described above. The value for each was assigned based on the users perspective, therefore not all guidelines were assigned a value of three.

Step 4 - Correlation Stage: The specific domain characteristics were correlated with the guidelines, identified problems for the users and the Nielsen heuristics which could not cover all the user and domain needs since it is mainly accessibility.

In first place, the specific domain characteristics were associated with the user experience attributes. As a second step, the guidelines were associated to the specific domain characteristics and user experience attributes as a whole. Third, the same association criteria was applied to the list of identified problems. Finally, Nielsen's heuristics are linked to the correlated element.

Since the main focus of the proposal is accessibility, some Nielsen heuristics did not cover all the correlated elements. This outcome, according to the methodology followed, is a good indicator for the need of developing new heuristics to cover all the correlated elements.

Step 5 - Selection Stage: initially, four heuristics were created and four modified from Nielsen's.

Step 6 - Specification Stage: the heuristics were formally defined according to the template proposed in the methodology.

Step 7 - Validation Stage: we performed the validation through user testing and heuristic evaluation, both results were compared since there were no control heuristics as is the case with usability.

Step 8 - Refinement Stage: the heuristics were refined through the results obtained in the validation stage and experts feedback.

The mentioned process had two iterations, the first throughout the cycle, while the second iteration was mainly focused on refining heuristic definitions.

4   Results

The heuristics were defined for a specific domain, mobile e-commerce applications for people with visual impairment; domain-specific characteristics were taken into account, which were validated by experts; and everything collected in the literature, standards and tests with users was considered as input. The heuristics proposed are defined as follows:

(MH1) Feedback on the Purchase Process Through Audio-Description and Vibration: The system must keep users informed of everything that is happening in the purchase process, through feedback within reasonable times with audio-description or vibrations.

(MH2) Adaptation to Readable Contrasts: The system must have the option of changing the contrast to an appropriate ratio, as stipulated by WCAG 2.0.

(MH3) Correct Application of the Accessibility Tools of the Operating System to the Application: The accessibility tools of the operating system in relation to people with visual impairment must be able to maintain their value and not be interrupted within the application.

(MH4) Minimization of Steps in the Purchase Process: Accelerators - not seen by the novice user - should expedite the buying process for the expert user so that the system can serve both inexperienced and expert users.

(MH5) Simplified Characteristics of the Products in Navigation: Each additional element not focused on highlighting the product interferes with the perception that can be had in the first interaction.

(MH6) Magnification Support in all the Graphic Components of the Application: The application must allow the magnification of the platform components in such a way that the perception of users is improved.

(MH7) Encourage Voice Input Methods: The system must provide voice input methods.

(MH8) Standardization of Tactile Gestures Between e-commerce Applications: The system must have cross gestures in the other mobile e-commerce applications for common actions.

(MH9) Help and Documentation: Even if it is better that the system can be used without documentation, help and documentation should be provided. Any information about tactile gestures, input methods, contrast change should be easy to search, focused on the user's task, listing concrete steps to be carried out and not very long.

The heuristics were validated through two experiments, according to the methodology used. It was noted that, in fact, the problems identified by experts are consistent with those experienced by users. Additionally, there were heuristics that needed to be refined, because, although the experts understood the heuristics once they were explained with examples, at the time of performing the heuristic evaluation the definition of these was ambiguous.

5   Conclusions

The conclusions obtained from the development of this research were:

- The relevance of focusing on other aspects of the user experience, such as accessibility in specific and emerging domains, such as e-Commerce applications and their interaction from the perspective of people with visual impairment.
- There are internationally accepted accessibility guidelines, such as WCAG 2.0; however, they turn out to be general, so experimenting with users and obtaining their perspective for the domain in question contributes to obtaining relevant and specific aspects when evaluating the accessibility of the domain.
- The methodology used for the project turned out to be useful and clear in its majority of stages, since in the validation stage some considerations were taken because these were centered in comparison with heuristics of usability control, which the present project did not have.
  Although the project objective has been achieved, which is to propose a set of heuristics to evaluate the accessibility of mobile e-commerce applications. As future work, elements are proposed to improve the results of the project:
- Increase population for user tests. Although these were performed with five people, mostly with astigmatism, myopia and one with glaucoma, considering more diseases could contribute more to the detection of problems.
- Iterate the validation process again taking into account the refinements made, the iteration could occur again with heuristic evaluation with different experts.

References

1. 2010 ADA regulations. https://www.ada.gov/2010_regs.htm
2. Equality Act 2010: guidance - GOV.UK. https://www.gov.uk/guidance/equality-act-2010-guidance
3. ICD-10   Version:2016.   http://apps.who.int/classifications/icd10/browse/2016/en#/H54
4. Web Content Accessibility Guidelines (WCAG) 2.1 (2018). https://www.w3.org/TR/WCAG21/
5. Acosta-Vargas, P., Salvador-Ullauri, L., Pérez-Medina, J.L., Zalakeviciute, R., Hernandez, W.: Heuristic method of evaluating accessibility of mobile in selected applications for air quality monitoring. In: Nunes, I.L. (ed.) AHFE 2019. AISC, vol. 959, pp. 485–495. Springer, Cham (2020). https://doi.org/10.1007/978-3-030-20040-4_44
6. American Academy of Ophthalmology:¿Qué es el glaucoma? (2018). https://www.aao.org/salud-ocular/enfermedades/que-es-la-glaucoma
7. AOA: Presbyopia.   https://www.aoa.org/patients-and-public/eye-and-vision-problems/glossary-of-eye-and-vision-conditions/presbyopia
8. Bose, R., Jürgensen, H.: Accessibility of E-Commerce Websites for Vision-Impaired Persons, pp. 121–128. Springer, Cham (2014). https://doi.org/10.1007/978-3-319-08596-8_18
9. Bourne, R., et al.: Magnitude, temporal trends, and projections of the global prevalence of blindness and distance and near vision impairment: a systematic review and meta-analysis. Lancet Global Health 5(9), e888–e897 (2017)
10. Damaceno, R.J.P., Braga, J.C., Mena-Chalco, J.P.: Mobile device accessibility for the visually impaired: problems mapping and recommendations. Univ. Access Inf. Soc. 1–15 (2017). https://doi.org/10.1007/s10209-017-0540-1
11. DeLone, W.H., McLean, E.R.: Measuring e-Commerce success: applying the DeLone & McLean information systems success model. Int. J. Electron. Commerce 9(1), 31–47 (2004). https://doi.org/10.1080/10864415.2004.11044317
12. Díaz-Bossini, J.-M., Moreno, L., Martínez, P.: Towards mobile accessibility for older people: a user centered evaluation. In: Stephanidis, C., Antona, M. (eds.) UAHCI 2014. LNCS, vol. 8515, pp. 58–68. Springer, Cham (2014). https://doi.org/10.1007/978-3-319-07446-7_6
13. EMarketer: Worldwide Retail and Ecommerce Sales: eMarketer's Updated Forecast and New Mcommerce Estimates for 2016–2021 - eMarketer. https://www.emarketer.com/Report/Worldwide-Retail-Ecommerce-Sales-eMarketers-Updated-Forecast-New-Mcommerce-Estimates-20162021/2002182
14. European Commission: European Accessibility Act - Employment, Social Affairs & Inclusion. http://ec.europa.eu/social/main.jsp?catId=1202
15. EyeDOCS: Age-Related   Macular   Degeneration   (AMD).   http://www.eyedocsottawa.com/services-special-vision/special-vision-concerns/age-related-macular-degeneration-amd/
16. Flaxman, S.R., et al.: Global causes of blindness and distance vision impairment 1990–2020: a systematic review and meta-analysis. Lancet Global Health 5(12), e1221–e1234 (2017). http://www.ncbi.nlm.nih.gov/pubmed/29032195
17. Ghidini, E., Almeida, W.D., Manssour, I.H., Silveira, M.S.: Developing apps for visually impaired people: Lessons learned from practice. In: Proceedings of the Annual Hawaii International Conference on System Sciences, vol. 2016-March, pp. 5691–5700 (2016)

18. International Organization for Standardization: ISO/IEC Guide 71:2014 - Guide for addressing accessibility in standards (2014). https://www.iso.org/standard/57385.html
19. Law Office of Lainey Feingold: Big Win for Blind Shopper in First U.S. ADA Web Accessibility Trial. https://www.lflegal.com/2017/06/winn-dixie/
20. Mi, N., Cavuoto, L.A., Benson, K., Smith-Jackson, T., Nussbaum, M.A.: A heuristic checklist for an accessible smartphone interface design. Univ. Access Inf. Soc. 13(4), 351–365 (2014). https://doi.org/10.1007/s10209-013-0321-4
21. National Eye Institute: Facts About Refractive Errors (2010). https://nei.nih.gov/health/errors/errors
22. National Eye Institute: Facts About Age-Related Macular Degeneration (2015). https://nei.nih.gov/health/maculardegen/armd_facts
23. National Eye Institute: Facts About Cataract (2015). https://nei.nih.gov/health/cataract/cataract_facts
24. National Eye Institute: Facts About Diabetic Eye Disease (2015). https://nei.nih.gov/health/diabetic/retinopathy
25. National Eye Institute: Facts About Glaucoma (2015). https://nei.nih.gov/health/glaucoma/glaucoma_facts
26. National Eye Institute: La Retinopatía Diabética Lo que usted debe saber (2016). https://nei.nih.gov/health/espanol/retinopatia
27. Pennsylvania Record: Blind woman sues Toys "R" Us, alleging violation of federal disabilities act. https://pennrecord.com/stories/510637970-blind-woman-sues-toys-r-us-alleging-violation-of-federal-disabilities-act
28. Quiñones, D., Rusu, C.: Applying a methodology to develop user eXperience heuristics. Comput. Standards Interfaces 66, 103345 (2019)
29. Quiñones, D., Rusu, C., Rusu, V.: A methodology to develop usability/user experience heuristics. Comput. Standards Interfaces 59, 109–129 (2018). https://www.sciencedirect.com/science/article/abs/pii/S0920548917303860
30. Sohaib, O., Kang, K.: E-commerce web accessibility for people with disabilities. In: Gołuchowski, J., Pańkowska, M., Linger, H., Barry, C., Lang, M., Schneider, C. (eds.) Complexity in Information Systems Development. LNISO, vol. 22, pp. 87–100. Springer, Cham (2017). https://doi.org/10.1007/978-3-319-52593-8_6
31. W3C: Mobile Accessibility: How WCAG 2.0 and Other W3C/WAI Guidelines Apply to Mobile (2015). https://www.w3.org/TR/mobile-accessibility-mapping/
32. Watanabe, T., Yamaguchi, T., Minatani, K.: Advantages and drawbacks of smartphones and tablets for visually impaired people - analysis of ICT user survey results. IEICE Trans. Inf. Syst. E98.D(4), 922–929 (2015). https://www.jstage.jst.go.jp/article/transinf/E98.D/4/E98.D_2014EDP7317/_article
33. World Health Organization: What is a refractive error? (2013). http://www.who.int/features/qa/45/en/
34. Yang, H., Peng, Q., Gao, Q., Patrick Rau, P.-L.: Design of a clothing shopping guide website for visually impaired people. In: Rau, P.L.P. (ed.) CCD 2015. LNCS, vol. 9180, pp. 253–261. Springer, Cham (2015). https://doi.org/10.1007/978-3-319-20907-4_23

A Systematic Review of User-Centered Design Techniques

Elizabeth Salinas$^{(\boxtimes)}$, Rony Cueva , and Freddy Paz

Pontificia Universidad Católica del Perú, San Miguel, Lima 32, Peru
{e.salinas, cueva.r, fpaz}@pucp.pe

Abstract. There are many systems that do not have an adequate level of usability, even though this is one of the most relevant quality attributes in software products. Therefore, it chooses to redesign these systems through techniques that provide favorable results in usability evaluations. Several authors have proposed the User-Centered Design framework as the right one to obtain optimal results with respect to metrics of this attribute, since it aims to design understandable software products, considering the needs and interests of end-users. Because of that, this article presents a systematic review to identify the techniques and tools that have been used to make redesigns of graphical user interfaces of software products following the User-Centered Design approach and that have been successful in usability measurements. It also shows the most reported usability evaluation methods in these cases, and the reasons why this process took place. A total of 146 studies were identified, of which 19 were selected as relevant to this review. According to the analysis, the most used technique to perform redesigns is prototyping and the usability evaluation method more employed is testing with users.

Keywords: Usability · Redesign · User-centered design · Usability evaluation · Systematic review

1 Introduction

Nowadays, both usability and user experience (UX) are considered key factors for the success of a software product [1]. The current competitive market has forced companies to concern not only in the functionality, but also in the user experience. Graphical user interfaces of a software product must be understandable and easy-to-use enough, to allow end users to achieve their goals with effectiveness, efficiency and satisfaction [2]. Moreover, the concept of usability has evolved, and the main interest nowadays is related to ensure a positive perception and responses that result from the use or anticipated use of a product, system or service [3]. Usability as well as positive user experience can be achieved if a user-centered design (UCD) process is followed during the software development [4]. However, there is not still a consensus about the methods that must be used in each phase of the UCD framework.

The user-centered design process, described in the ISO 13407 standard, establishes four activities that cover, from the conception of considering the user's opinion for the development of the software products, until the evaluation of obtained results. Likewise,

A. Marcus and E. Rosenzweig (Eds.): HCII 2020, LNCS 12200, pp. 253–267, 2020.
https://doi.org/10.1007/978-3-030-49713-2_18

the iterative nature of these activities is instituted. User-centered design involves iterating until the goals are achieved, and the ISO 13407 establishes the basic principles and guidelines without defining the methods. In this work, we present a systematic literature review to determine the methods and tools that can be used in each activity of UCD. This proposal is based on the review of success stories reported on redesigns of software products. This study is intended for developers and designers to be used and serve as a guide for decision making in the development and improvement of software systems.

2   Background

2.1   Usability

According to the ISO 9241-220 standard, usability is the "extent to which a system, product or service can be used by specified users to achieve specified goals with effectiveness, efficiency and satisfaction in a specified context of use" [5].

Jakob Nielsen defines usability as "a quality attribute that assesses how easy user interfaces are to use" [6]. This author also mentions that usability "refers to methods for improving ease-of-use during the design process" [6] and it is defined by five quality components:

- **Learnability:** How easy it is for users to accomplish basic tasks the first time they encounter the design.
- **Efficiency:** Once users have learned the design, how quickly they can perform tasks.
- **Memorability:** When users return to the design after a period of not using it, how easily they can reestablish proficiency.
- **Errors:** Number of errors made by users, the severity of these errors and how easily users can recover from the errors.
- **Satisfaction:** How pleasant it is to use the design.

2.2   User-Centered Design (UCD)

User-Centered Design (UCD) is defined as "a software design methodology for developers and designers. Essentially, it helps them make applications that meet the needs of their users" [7].

Another definition of UCD is given by the ISO 9241-210 standard, which defines it as an "approach to systems design and development that aims to make interactive systems more usable by focusing on the use of the system and applying human factors/ergonomics and usability knowledge and techniques" [8].

Likewise, according to the ISO 13407 standard [9], UCD is composed of four activities, which are:

(1) To understand and specify the context of use
(2) To specify the user and organizational requirements
(3) To produce design solutions
(4) To evaluate designs against requirements

2.3 Usability Evaluation Methods

According to Fernandez *et al.*, [10], the usability evaluation methods are defined as procedures which are "composed of a set of well-defined activities for collecting usage data related to end-user interaction with a software product and/or how the specific properties of this software product contribute to achieving a certain degree of usability".

Because of the importance of usability "in the context of the software development process" [11], several methods have been proposed to evaluate it. These methods can be classified into three categories: Inspection, Testing and Inquiry [12]. The objectives of inspection methods are to identify usability issues and improve "the usability of an interface design by checking it against established standards" [13]. On the other hand, the testing category is composed of a set of methods that involve the participation of the end users of the software product to be evaluated. The purpose of this is to obtain information about how the users use the system and the problems they have when performing some tasks with the graphical interfaces [13]. Finally, the aim of inquiry methods is to evaluate the usability of a software product by obtaining information about the experiences of the end users with the system. This is done through interviews, observations while users are using the software product or through surveys [14].

3 Conducting the Systematic Review

A systematic literature review is "a means of identifying, evaluating and interpreting all available research relevant to a particular research question, or topic area, or phenomenon of interest" [15].

The present work was performed following the methodology defined by Kitchenham and Charters [15] in order to carry out an objective search. Four research questions were formulated to guide this review and a search string based on the PICOC criteria (Population, Intervention, Comparison, Output, Context) was developed. The databases used for the primary search were Scopus, IEEE Xplore and ACM Digital Library.

3.1 Research Questions

The purpose of this systematic review was to identify the techniques and tools that have been employed in order to make redesigns of graphical user interfaces of software products following the User-Centered Design (UCD) approach and that have been successful in usability measurements. Additionally, it shows the most reported usability evaluation methods in these cases, and the reasons why this process took place. In this way, the following research questions were formulated:

RQ1: What techniques have been used for the redesign of graphical user interfaces of software products following the User-Centered Design framework and that have shown successful results in usability evaluations?

RQ2: What have been the most reported software tools in the literature that have been used for the redesign of graphical user interfaces of software products following the User-Centered Design framework?

RQ3:   What methods are the most reported in the literature to evaluate the usability of software products within the UCD framework?

RQ4:   What are the reasons for redesigning the graphical user interfaces of a software product following the User-Centered Design methodology?

In order to structure the research questions and the information search to perform this systematic review the general concepts based in PICOC were defined. These concepts are Population, Intervention, Comparison, Output and Context. The "Comparison" criterion was not taken into consideration because this research is not intended to compare interventions (Table 1).

Table 1. PICOC criteria defined for systematic review

Criterion	Description
Population	Software Products
Intervention	User-Centered Design methodology to redesign interfaces
Comparison	It does not apply
Output	Case studies where User-Centered Design techniques have been applied for the redesign of software product interfaces
Context	Academic and industrial context

3.2   Source Selection

Three recognized databases were selected to perform the search process because they are the most relevant in the area of computer engineering. For this work, grey literature was not considered since it is not peer-reviewed. The selected databases were the following:

- Scopus
- IEEE Xplore
- ACM Digital Library

3.3   Search String

Definition of Search Terms. For the elaboration of the search string, five general concepts were proposed taking into consideration the Population and Intervention criteria previously defined. Different terms were established for each general concept (Table 2).

Table 2. Defined terms for the search string

General concepts	Terms
GC1 – Redesign	Redesign
GC2 – User Interface	User interface/User interfaces/GUI/Graphical user interface/UI
GC3 – Software	Software/System/Systems/Application/Applications/App/Apps
GC4 – User-Centered Design	User centered design/UCD/User-centered design/User Experience/UX/Usability
GC5 – Methodology	Methodology/Methodologies/Method/Methods/Technique/Techniques

Definition of the Search String. After establishing the search terms, the following basic search strings were defined:

CG1: "redesign"
CG2: "user interface*" OR "GUI" OR "graphical user interface" OR "interface" OR "UI"
CG3: "software" OR "system*" OR "application*" OR "app*"
CG4: "user centered design" OR "user-centered design" OR "UCD" OR "user experience" OR "UX" OR "usability"
CG5: "methodolog*" OR "method*" OR "technique*"

Then, the final search string was the following:
("redesign") **AND** ("user interface*" **OR** "GUI" **OR** "graphical user interface" **OR** "interface" **OR** "UI" **OR** "software" **OR** "system*" **OR** "application*" **OR** "app*") **AND** (("user centered design" **OR** "user-centered design" **OR** "UCD") **OR** (("user experience" **OR** "UX" **OR** "usability") **AND** ("methodolog*" **OR** "method*" **OR** "technique*"))).

Finally, the search strings adapted to the syntax used by the search engine of each database were established:

SCOPUS: TITLE-ABS(("redesign") AND ("user interface*" OR "GUI" OR "graphical user interface" OR "interface" OR "UI" OR "software" OR "system*" OR "application*" OR "app*") AND (("user centered design" OR "user-centered design" OR "UCD") OR (("user experience" OR "UX" OR "usability") AND ("methodolog*" OR "method*" OR "technique*")))).

IEEE Xplore: ("redesign") AND ("user interface*" OR "GUI" OR "graphical user interface" OR "interface" OR "UI" OR "software" OR "system" OR "systems" OR "application" OR "applications" OR "app" OR "apps") AND (("user centered design" OR "user-centered design" OR "UCD") OR (("user experience" OR "UX" OR "usability") AND ("methodolog*" OR "method*" OR "technique*"))).

ACM Digital Library: ("redesign") AND ("user interface*" OR "GUI" OR "graphical user interface" OR "interface" OR "UI" OR "software" OR "system*" OR "application*" OR "app*") AND (("user centered design" OR "user-centered design" OR "UCD") OR (("user experience" OR "UX" OR "usability") AND ("methodolog*" OR "method*" OR "technique*"))).

In order to obtain updated results and analyze the current state of the art, only relevant studies whose publication date was since 2015 were considered for this review.

3.4   Inclusion and Exclusion Criteria

Each article obtained as a result of the search string was principally examined through its title and abstract in order to determine its inclusion in the present systematic review. Likewise, inclusion and exclusion criteria were defined to carry out this process.

The inclusion criteria were the following:

1. The article is written in English.
2. The article presents a case study of redesign of graphical user interfaces of a software product following the User-Centered Design framework and has been successful in usability evaluations.
3. The article presents the use of methods, tools or techniques for the design of graphical interfaces or for the usability evaluation of software products whose interfaces have been redesigned.

On the other hand, to determinate which studies will not be considered, the following exclusion criteria were established:

1. Articles not related to usability studies of software products.
2. Studies about redesign or usability evaluation of software products for people with disabilities.
3. Articles related to usability studies of virtual reality or 3D virtual environments software products.

3.5   Data Collection

The automated search for this systematic review was performed on September 17th, 2019 in the Scopus database and on September 19th, 2019 in IEEE Xplore and ACM Digital Library. A total of 146 results were obtained from the three consulted databases. After the inclusion and exclusion criteria were applied, 19 articles were selected as relevant for this review process.

Table 3 shows the number of articles that were found during the search process, and Table 4 shows more details about the selected articles.

Table 3. Summary of search results

Database name	Search results	Duplicated papers	Relevant papers
Scopus	109	0	12
IEEE Xplore	11	5	3
ACM Digital Library	26	7	3
Total	**146**	**12**	**18**

Table 4. Details of selected articles

ID	Database	Year of publication	Author(s)	Paper title
A01	Scopus	2019	Shabrina G., Lestari L.A., Iqbal B.M., Syaifullah D. H.,	Redesign of User Interface Zakat Mobile Smartphone Application with User Experience Approach
A02	Scopus	2019	Moquillaza A., Falconi F., Paz F.,	Redesigning a Main Menu ATM Interface Using a User-Centered Design Approach Aligned to Design Thinking: A Case Study
A03	Scopus	2019	Cong J.-C., Chen C.-H., Liu C., Meng Y., Zheng Z.-Y.,	Enhancing the Usability of Long-Term Rental Applications in Chinese Market: An Interaction Design Approach
A04	Scopus	2019	Olney C.M., Vos-Draper T., Egginton J., Ferguson J., Goldish G., Eddy B., Hansen A.H., Carroll K., Morrow M.,	Development of a comprehensive mobile assessment of pressure (CMAP) system for pressure injury prevention for veterans with spinal cord injury
A05	Scopus	2018	Adinda P.P., Suzianti A.,	Redesign of user interface for E-government application using usability testing method
A06	Scopus	2018	Michel C., Touré C., Marty J.-C.,	Adapting enterprise social media for informal learning in the workplace: Using incremental and iterative design methods to favor sustainable uses
A07	Scopus	2017	Forte J., Darin T.,	User experience evaluation for user interface redesign: A case study on a bike sharing application
A08	Scopus	2017	Lin W.-J., Chiu M.-C.,	Design a personalized brain-computer interface of legorobot assisted by data analysis method
A09	Scopus	2016	Suarez-Torrente M.D.C., Conde-Clemente P., Martínez A.B., Juan A.A.,	Improving web user satisfaction by ensuring usability criteria

(continued)

Table 4. (*continued*)

ID	Database	Year of publication	Author(s)	Paper title
				compliance: The case of an economically depressed region of Europe
A10	Scopus	2016	Schachner M.B., Recondo F.J., González Z. A., Sommer J.A., Stanziola E., Gassino F. D., Simón M., López G. E., Benítez S.E.,	User-centered design practices to redesign a nursing e-chart in line with the nursing process
A11	Scopus	2015	Melton B.L., Zillich A.J., Russell S.A., Weiner M., McManus M.S., Spina J. R., Russ A.L.,	Reducing prescribing errors through creatinine clearance alert redesign
A12	Scopus	2015	Russ A.L., Chen S., Melton B.L., Johnson E. G., Spina J.R., Weiner M., Zillich A.J.,	A novel design for drug-drug interaction alerts improves prescribing efficiency
A13	IEEE Xplore	2018	Ira Puspitasari, Dwi Indah Cahyani, Taufik	A User-Centered Design for Redesigning E-Government Website in Public Health Sector
A14	IEEE Xplore	2017	Nannapas Banluesombatkul, Prapansak Kaewlamul, Prapaporn Rattanatamrong, Nadya Williams, Shava Smallen	PRAGMA Cloud Scheduler: Improving Usability of the PRAGMA Cloud Testbed
A15	IEEE Xplore	2017	Hannah Thinyane, Ingrid Sieborger, Edward Reynell	Evaluating a mobile visualization system for service delivery problems in developing countries
A16	ACM Digital Library	2018	Adam Roegiest, Winter Wei	Redesigning a Document Viewer for Legal Documents
A17	ACM Digital Library	2017	Emily Manwaring, J. Noelle Carter, Keith Maynard	Redesigning Educational Dashboards for Shifting User Contexts
A18	ACM Digital Library	2016	José Miguel Toribio-Guzmán, Alicia García-Holgado, Felipe Soto Pérez, Francisco J. García-Peñalvo, Manuel A. Franco Martín	Heuristic evaluation of socialnet, the private social network for psychiatric patients and their relatives

4 Report and Analysis of Results

4.1 Techniques Used for the Redesign of Graphical User Interfaces of Software Products Following the User-Centered Design Framework

Results Report

In order to determine the techniques used to redesign graphical user interfaces, the number of relevant articles in which each technique was reported was identified. The results are summarized in Table 5.

Analysis of Results

According to the results obtained from the systematic review, a large number of techniques used to work following the UCD methodology were identified and the most reported were prototyping, usability evaluation of the original graphical user interfaces, identification of stakeholders/end users, interviews and focus group.

Prototyping is a technique that aims to design the initial or "draft" version of a system, which allows the designers to explore their ideas and show them to end users before investing resources into development [16]. This has been the most reported technique in the selected articles (a total of twelve papers), since according to many authors "the prototypes are primarily used for the communication, exploration, refinement, and evaluation of design ideas" [17].

The second most reported technique was the usability evaluation of the original graphical user interfaces. In nine of the selected articles, a usability evaluation method was applied to these interfaces in order to identify the problems they had and correct them in the redesign.

The third most used technique was the identification of stakeholders/end users, which was reported in six articles. The fourth most employed technique was the interview, which was used in A17 in order to identify the needs of the users [18] and in A13 to determine the requirements from the perspective of the interviewees [19]. This technique is relevant since according to the UCD methodology it is important to know the needs and perspectives of the users to develop a good design.

Focus group was another of the main techniques employed. It consists of bringing together a group of users to discuss a specific topic through their personal experience. The application of this technique in A03 aimed to know the needs and suggestions that users had regarding perceived usability when they used existing rental applications [20].

Table 5. UCD techniques reported in the systematic review

ID	Technique	Number of articles in which the technique was reported	Articles
T01	Prototyping	12	A01, A02, A03, A06, A07, A08, A10, A11, A12, A13, A17, A18
T02	Usability evaluation of the original graphical user interfaces	9	A01, A05, A07, A09, A10, A13, A14, A16, A18
T03	Identification of stakeholders/end users	6	A02, A06, A13, A14, A17, A18
T04	Interviews	5	A08, A10, A13, A16, A17
T05	Focus group	4	A03, A04, A06, A10
T06	Brainstorming	3	A02, A10, A17
T07	Meetings/Face-to-face meetings	3	A02, A06, A10
T08	Usability heuristics of Jakob Nielsen/heuristics of Pierotti	3	A05, A08, A18
T09	User tasks analysis	3	A08, A10, A13
T10	Storyboarding	2	A02, A13
T11	Personas	2	A16, A17
T12	User profiles	2	A02, A07
T13	Competitor analysis	2	A02, A07
T14	Requirements Specification/Establishment of Requirements	2	A13, A15
T15	Surveys/Questionnaires	2	A03, A08
T16	Human factors principles	2	A11, A12
T17	Card sorting	2	A01, A02
T18	Literature review/study	2	A10, A13
T19	Tag cloud	1	A02
T20	Data analysis	1	A02
T21	Visual thinking	1	A02
T22	Non-participatory observations	1	A03
T23	Empathy maps	1	A17
T24	User stories	1	A16
T25	Use case diagrams	1	A13
T26	Sequence diagrams	1	A13
T27	Principles of human computer interaction	1	A14
T28	TRIZ method	1	A01
T29	Layout design	1	A13
T30	Interaction Design Principles	1	A03

4.2 Software Tools Used for the Redesign of Graphical User Interfaces of Software Products Following the User-Centered Design Framework

Report and Analysis of Results

Many of the articles obtained from the systematic review did not report the software tools that were used for the redesign of the graphical interfaces, because of that, it was only possible to identify three tools for the prototyping and four that were used during the usability evaluations.

With respect to prototyping tools, one of them is Drupal, a content management system (CMS). In A06 Drupal was used for the elaboration of the prototype skeleton and its importance is that it allowed the design team to "accelerate the development and modifications of the prototype according to the users' feedback" obtained during the focus group [21]. Another tool reported was POP 2.0, this was used in A07 to design high fidelity prototypes [17]. The last tool reported was Balsamiq Mockups, which allows the creation of wireframes or low-fidelity prototypes [22]. This tool was employed in A10.

As for the software tools used during usability evaluation, one of them is Prometheus, which was used in A09. Prometheus is a web tool developed to detect usability issues in different types of web pages. It provides "a percentage score to determine the level of usability achieved on the website and a list of failed criteria sorted by priority" [23]. During the systematic review process, support tools for usability evaluations were also identified, such as: OBS Studio and AZ screen Recorder (which were used in A07); and Morae (used in A10, A11 y A12). The last one has been the most reported (in a total of three articles) and it is used to capture "video of the computer screen actions" [24].

4.3 Methods to Evaluate the Usability of Software Products Within the UCD Framework

In this section, the most reported usability evaluation methods are detailed. The results are summarized in Table 6.

Table 6. Usability evaluation methods reported in the systematic review

ID	Usability evaluation method	Number of articles in which the evaluation method was reported	Articles
E01	User testing	9	A02, A03, A07, A08, A10, A12, A14, A15, A16
E02	Surveys/Questionnaires	9	A01, A03, A04, A05, A07, A08, A09, A10, A15
E03	Interviews	6	A04, A06, A07, A10, A11, A12
E04	Usability metrics/Performance metrics	6	A01, A05, A08, A11, A12, A14
E05	Heuristic evaluation	4	A02, A09, A13, A18
E06	Thinking aloud	2	A11, A12
E07	Focus group	1	A04
E08	Prototype evaluation	1	A17
E09	Qualitative evaluation	1	A06
E10	Field study	1	A07
E11	Assessment meeting	1	A02

Results Report

Analysis of Results

Through the systematic review, twelve methods used for usability evaluation could be found. The five most reported were:

1. **User testing:** It consists in selecting a representative amount of end users to perform a set of pre-defined tasks in a software product. The aim of this method is to identify usability issues in the system evaluated. Normally, this evaluation is applied in a usability laboratory [11].
2. **Surveys/Questionnaires:** "It is a list of questionnaire items that representative users have to answer according to a Likert scale" [11]. The objective of each element is to measure an usability aspect of the system or a dimension of the user satisfaction [11].
3. **Interviews:** In this method, both end users and usability specialists "participate in a discussion session about the usability of a software application" [11].
4. **Usability metrics:** The objective of this evaluation method is "to establish quantitative measurements" [11]. In order to quantify the usability of a software product regarding effectiveness, efficiency and satisfaction; usability metrics are used. In this method "the participation of a representative number of users is required to generalize the obtained results" [11].
5. **Heuristic evaluation:** The heuristic evaluation consists in evaluating the graphical user interfaces of a software product according to certain rules. The purpose of this evaluation is to detect usability problems in a system [25].

According to the results obtained, one of the most reported usability evaluation method was user testing, this is because it provides direct information about the problems that users could have with the interfaces they are testing. That is why, according to Nielsen, it is considered as "the most fundamental usability method and is in some sense irreplaceable" [25].

4.4   Reasons for Redesigning the Graphical User Interfaces of a Software Product Following the User-Centered Design Methodology

Report and Analysis of Results

According to the articles resulting from the systematic review, there are different reasons for redesigning the graphical user interfaces of a software product following the User-Centered Design methodology. These reasons may vary depending on the use of the software. These include adapting the software product to the needs and requirements of the users (articles A06 and A13) [19, 21], improving user participation in the effective use of software (A06) [21] and improving the quality of information dissemination (A13) [19].

In addition, two reasons were identified as the most reported. One of them was to improve the usability of the software product (reported in nine articles) and the other was to improve the quality of the user experience (five articles). With this, it can be concluded that UCD is a framework that helps to design software products with good usability and an adequate user experience, since the articles selected for the systematic review have been reported as successful case studies in usability evaluations. Likewise, it is important to remember that UCD is a methodology based on the interests and needs of end users and that is why its use results in a software product that is usable, understandable and has a good user experience [5].

5   Conclusions and Future Works

From the systematic review of the literature we can conclude that the User-Centered Design methodology is one of the most suitable for designing graphical user interfaces (GUI) of software products that show good results in usability evaluations.

Following a predefined protocol, 146 studies were identified, from which 18 were selected. This work allowed to determine that: (1) prototyping, (2) usability evaluation of the original graphical user interfaces, (3) identification of stakeholders/end users, (4) interviews and (5) focus group are the most reported techniques for redesigning graphical interfaces according to the literature. Moreover, in this study we have identified that one of the most used usability evaluation method is User Testing, since it provides very useful information to detect the problems that users have with the GUI of a system. In addition, according to the systematic review, we have determined that the main reasons for redesigning the graphical user interfaces of a software product following the UCD framework are to improve the usability and user experience with respect to the original interfaces.

As future work, each reported technique could be analyzed more deeply and a list of criteria that take into account the characteristics of the software projects and the stakeholders could be established; this in order to identify which technique would be the most appropriate to apply in each phase of the UCD methodology according to the defined criteria.

Acknowledgement. This study is highly supported by the Section of Informatics Engineering of the Pontifical Catholic University of Peru (PUCP) – Peru, and the "HCI, Design, User Experience, Accessibility & Innovation Technologies" Research Group (HCI-DUXAIT). HCI-DUXAIT is a research group of PUCP.

References

1. Quiñones, D., Rusu, C.: Applying a methodology to develop user eXperience heuristics. Comput. Stand. Interfaces **66**, 103345 (2019). https://doi.org/10.1016/j.csi.2019.04.004
2. Paz, F., Paz, F.A., Pow-Sang, J.A.: Experimental case study of new usability heuristics. In: Marcus, A. (ed.) DUXU 2015. LNCS, vol. 9186, pp. 212–223. Springer, Cham (2015). https://doi.org/10.1007/978-3-319-20886-2_21
3. Rusu, C., Rusu, V., Roncagliolo, S., González, C.: Usability and user experience: what should we care about? Int. J. Inf. Technol. Syst. Approach (IJITSA). **8**, 1–12 (2015). https://doi.org/10.4018/IJITSA.2015070101
4. Aguirre, J., Moquillaza, A., Paz, F.: A user-centered framework for the design of usable ATM interfaces. In: Marcus, A., Wang, W. (eds.) HCII 2019. LNCS, vol. 11583, pp. 163–178. Springer, Cham (2019). https://doi.org/10.1007/978-3-030-23570-3_13
5. ISO: ISO 9241-220:2019, Ergonomics of human-system interaction—Part 220: Processes for enabling, executing and assessing human-centred design within organizations. International Organization for Standardization, Geneva, Switzerland (2019)
6. Nielsen, J.: Usability 101: Introduction to Usability. https://www.nngroup.com/articles/usability-101-introduction-to-usability/. Accessed 23 Dec 2019
7. Lowdermilk, T.: User-Centered Design. O'Reilly Media, Sebastopol (2013)
8. ISO: ISO 9241-210:2019, Ergonomics of human-system interaction—Part 210: Human-centred design for interactive systems. International Organization for Standardization, Geneva, Switzerland (2019)
9. ISO: ISO 13407:1999, Human-centred design processes for interactive systems. International Organization for Standardization, Geneva, Switzerland (1999)
10. Fernandez, A., Insfran, E., Abrahão, S.: Usability evaluation methods for the web: a systematic mapping study. Inf. Softw. Technol. **53**, 789–817 (2011). https://doi.org/10.1016/j.infsof.2011.02.007
11. Paz, F., Pow-Sang, J.A.: A systematic mapping review of usability evaluation methods for software development process. Int. J. Softw. Eng. Appl. **10**, 165–178 (2016). https://doi.org/10.14257/ijseia.2016.10.1.16
12. Gulati, A., Dubey, S.: Critical analysis on usability evaluation techniques. Int. J. Eng. Sci. Technol. **4**, 990–997 (2012)
13. Holzinger, A.: Usability engineering methods for software developers. Commun. ACM **48**, 71–74 (2005). https://doi.org/10.1145/1039539.1039541
14. Şengel, E., Öncü, S.: Conducting preliminary steps to usability testing: investigating the website of Uludağ University. Procedia – Soc. Behav. Sci. **2**, 890–894 (2010). https://doi.org/10.1016/j.sbspro.2010.03.122

15. Kitchenham, B., Charters, S.: Guidelines for performing systematic literature reviews in software engineering. Keele University and Durham University Joint Report, Technical report (2007)
16. Affairs, A.S. for P.: Prototyping. https://www.usability.gov/how-to-and-tools/methods/prototyping.html. Accessed 21 Dec 2019
17. Forte, J., Darin, T.: User experience evaluation for user interface redesign: a case study on a bike sharing application. In: Marcus, A., Wang, W. (eds.) DUXU 2017. LNCS, vol. 10290, pp. 614–631. Springer, Cham (2017). https://doi.org/10.1007/978-3-319-58640-3_44
18. Manwaring, E., Carter, J.N., Maynard, K.: Redesigning educational dashboards for shifting user contexts. In: Proceedings of the 35th ACM International Conference on the Design of Communication, pp. 27:1–27:7. ACM, New York (2017). https://doi.org/10.1145/3121113.3121210
19. Puspitasari, I., Cahyani, D.I., Taufik: A user-centered design for redesigning e-government website in public health sector. In: 2018 International Seminar on Application for Technology of Information and Communication, pp. 219–224 (2018). https://doi.org/10.1109/ISEMANTIC.2018.8549726
20. Cong, J.-c., Chen, C.-H., Liu, C., Meng, Y., Zheng, Z.-y.: Enhancing the usability of long-term rental applications in chinese market: an interaction design approach. In: Marcus, A., Wang, W. (eds.) HCII 2019. LNCS, vol. 11586, pp. 431–441. Springer, Cham (2019). https://doi.org/10.1007/978-3-030-23535-2_32
21. Michel, C., Touré, C., Marty, J.-C.: Adapting enterprise social media for informal learning in the workplace: using incremental and iterative design methods to favor sustainable uses. In: Escudeiro, P., Costagliola, G., Zvacek, S., Uhomoibhi, J., McLaren, B.M. (eds.) CSEDU 2017. CCIS, vol. 865, pp. 457–476. Springer, Cham (2018). https://doi.org/10.1007/978-3-319-94640-5_22
22. Balsamiq: Balsamiq Mockups 3 Application Overview - Balsamiq for Desktop Documentation| Balsamiq, https://balsamiq.com/wireframes/desktop/docs/overview/. Accessed 22 Dec 2019
23. Suarez-Torrente, M.D.C., Conde-Clemente, P., Martínez, A.B., Juan, A.A.: Improving web user satisfaction by ensuring usability criteria compliance: the case of an economically depressed region of Europe. Online Inf. Rev. **40**, 187–203 (2016). https://doi.org/10.1108/OIR-04-2015-0134
24. Melton, B.L., et al.: Reducing prescribing errors through creatinine clearance alert redesign. Am. J. Med. **128**, 1117–1125 (2015). https://doi.org/10.1016/j.amjmed.2015.05.033
25. Nielsen, J.: Chapter 6 - Usability testing. In: Nielsen, J. (ed.) Usability Engineering, pp. 165–206. Morgan Kaufmann, San Diego (1993). https://doi.org/10.1016/B978-0-08-052029-2.50009-7

A Reusable Approach to Software Support for Adaptive Navigation

Yonglei Tao[(✉)]

School of Computing and Information Systems, Grand Valley State University,
Allendale, MI, USA
taoy@gvsu.edu

Abstract. Adaptive navigation intends to guide users to their specific objectives within the application by altering the normal way the application allows to navigate, aiming to provide better experience for users with diverse needs and in different context conditions. Knowledge about activities that the user performs at runtime is crucial for adaptation decision making. It not only serves as a basis for evaluating relevance of the available information (such as user status, usage patterns, and context of use), but also facilitates reasoning about user needs. However, implementation of the user activity tracking capability often relies on intimate knowledge of the target application, which makes it difficult to develop loosely coupled modules to address separate concerns. In this paper, we describe a reusable approach to the development of the user activity tracking capability with the intent to support adaptive navigation. We use aspect-oriented instrumentation to capture user interface events and conduct model-based analysis to identify tasks that the user performs. A proof-of-concept experiment shows that our approach makes it possible to develop adaptation code that is reusable when the user interface and its adaptation logic evolve.

Keywords: Adaptive user interface · Reusable software design · User activity tracking

1 Introduction

Interactive applications evolve along one or more dimensions during its lifetime, including functionality, implementation, and user interface. Changes in one dimension often affect, interact, and impact others [1]. It is a great challenge to develop a reusable design to accommodate anticipated changes.

Adaptive user interfaces have the ability to identify circumstances that necessitate adaptation, and accordingly, enable appropriate adaptation strategies. As such, they promise to provide better usability for users with diverse needs and in different context conditions [6].

Navigation defines possible paths that users can take through an application to access certain information or functionality. It is a key area of user interface design. Studies show that ineffective navigation is a main cause of end-user frustration [8]. While one-size-fits-all user interfaces cause certain users to have a less efficient or

© Springer Nature Switzerland AG 2020
A. Marcus and E. Rosenzweig (Eds.): HCII 2020, LNCS 12200, pp. 268–277, 2020.
https://doi.org/10.1007/978-3-030-49713-2_19

substantially different experience compared to their peers [5], adaptive navigation offers an effective way to improve user experience.

Adaptive navigation guides users to their specific objectives by altering the normal way an application allows to navigate [3]. As such, information that underlies the adaptation decision making process, such as user status, usage patterns, and context conditions, must be made available by the adaptation code in the target application. In particular, it is crucial to have the capability of automatically identifying activities that the user performs during an interaction session. Knowledge of user activities at runtime not only serves as a basis for evaluating relevance of the available information [1], but also facilitates reasoning about user needs in order to determine appropriate adaptation strategies. However, implementation of the user activity tracking capability often relies on intimate knowledge of the target application, making it difficult to develop loosely coupled modules to address separate concerns.

In this paper, we describe a reusable approach to the development of the user activity tracking capability with the intent to support adaptive navigation. Roughly, we use aspect-oriented instrumentation to capture user interface events that occur when the user interacts with the application via its user interface and then conduct model-based analysis on event traces to identify user activities. Aspect-oriented instrumentation and model-based analysis make it possible to develop adaptation code that is reusable when the user interface and its adaptation logic evolve.

The rest of this paper is organized as follows. Section 2 covers related work. Section 3 describes design issues on adaptive navigation and Sect. 4 reusable support for adaptive navigation. Section 5 explains how to track user activities in a non-intrusive and application-independent way, which is the key to make the reusable support for adaptive navigation possible. Section 6 discusses a proof-of-concept experiment to investigate the feasibility of our approach. Finally, Sect. 6 concludes this paper.

2 Related Work

"Strive for consistency" has long been viewed as one of the golden rules for user interface design [18]. If applied appropriately, it allows developers to create a user interface that exhibits predictable behavior and therefore is easy to learn and to use. However, this rule often inadvertently leads to the focus shifting from user tasks and work context to common visual characteristics that can accommodate diverse users [5]. In many cases, the one-size-fits-all user interfaces become a source of unintended, but systematic discrimination causing some user groups to be less likely than others to take advantage of the available functionality, or causing them to have a less efficient or substantially different experience compared to their peers [19]. As software applications continue to grow in complexity, accessibility, and applicability, it becomes increasingly important to develop user interfaces for diversity in both end-users and context of use [9, 12].

User interface adaptations often take place in three areas of an interactive application: the selection of content to be displayed, the visual characteristics of information presentation, and navigation that defines the possible paths users can take through an application in order to access certain information or functionality [20]. Due to their high complexity, adaptive user interfaces are difficult to specify, design, verify, and validate. Moreover, the current lack of reusable design considerations that can be leveraged from one adaptive application to another further intensifies the problem [12].

A large number of proposals on the development of adaptive user interfaces can be found in the literature [14]. Notably, to reduce the development effort, reusability is an important consideration and there are several approaches to maximizing reusability in user interfaces development.

Model-based user interface development is a well-established approach. Its basic idea is to generate an actual user interface automatically from an abstract model that describes all relevant aspects of the user interface, including desired interaction means, target users, tasks, and screen elements [10, 11]. But the resulting user interface is often not of as high quality as one that a developer can create. Graphical user interfaces have immense complexity; it is difficult to represent them in their entirety via abstract models [6].

On the other hand, design pattern-based development separates the adaptive logic from the functional logic in order to facilitate reusable design [12, 13]. Adaptation-oriented design patterns provide proven solutions for specific interaction contexts, end user characteristics, and contextual requirements. Also, they are associated with software components that can be modified and composed into an application. Adaptability is achieved by combining design patterns that suit for specific users and context conditions. But adaptation-oriented design patterns vary in granularity and level of abstraction; the lack of consensus among researchers limits their potential uses for a broad range of applications.

Unlike the two major approaches in this area as mentioned above, our proposal treats the key capabilities in support of automatic adaptation as a separate module and allows it to be integrated into the target application in a loosely coupled manner. Since the original developer is responsible for user interface development, the quality of the user interface won't be compromised. While both of the major approaches aim at a comprehensive solution for adaptive user interface development, our proposal has a limited scope; it only addresses certain architectural issues with respect to the development of adaptive applications.

3   Design Issues on Adaptive Navigation

We have chosen a course schedule application as the basis to investigate issues on adaptive navigation. A course schedule application is intended to assist users, include students, professors, and staff members, to search for information about a university's course schedule. It is crucial to design its navigation structure for diversity in end-users and context of use. Figure 1 shows part of a navigation diagram for the course schedule application.

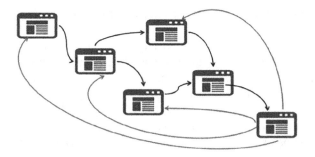

Fig. 1. A navigation diagram for the course schedule application

In Fig. 1, a rectangle depicts a screen and an arrow a path from one screen to the next. We omitted screen contents in order to focus on user navigation among those screens. Figure 1 shows possible paths that a user may follow through the application in order to find one or more courses for certain purposes. Here, the black arrows show how a user can navigate from the initial screen (on the upper left corner) to the final screen (on the lower right corner) to complete the "search for a course" task.

A user often performs the "search for a course" task multiple times to achieve one's objectives, for example, a freshman who wants to register for courses in the coming semester. A design issue in such a case is to which screen the user should be allowed to navigate from the final screen after a successful completion of the "search for a course" task each time. When taking all scenarios into consideration, we can identify four desirable ways for all users to continue a search as shown by the red arrows in Fig. 1; which one is the most optimal depends on what the user needs. In the traditional "one-size-fits-all" approach, we would choose a common denominator (for example, the initial screen) to accommodate all the scenarios, meaning that users, regardless of their needs, would perform search in the same sequence and manner. Obviously, it would cause certain user groups to have a less efficient experience than others.

Adaptive navigation guides users through different navigation paths on the basis of their needs and therefore can improve user experience in such a case. Here, the question is what information is needed for the adaptation code to make such a decision. In the course schedule application, knowledge about the user status is useful in the adaptation decision making process. Such information is available prior to user interaction with an application and remains static throughout an interaction session. In many cases, however, static information alone is not sufficient. It is also necessary to take into consideration information available at runtime, especially activities that the user performs, in order to better understand the user's overall objectives. Obviously, the capability to monitor user's activities is essential to support adaptive navigation. Knowledge of user activities not only serves as a basis for selecting relevant facts and also helping infer user needs in order to make appropriate adaptation decisions.

Hence, the user activity tracking capability is indispensable in support of adaptive navigation in particular and for adaptive user interface in general.

4   Reusable Support for Software Development

Changes in user interface design occur frequently in both development and operational phases. Application developers have to design user interfaces for diversity in end-users and context of use. As applications become more and more complex, it is often difficult to know at development time all the conditions in which applications will be used [16]. Hence, it is crucial to develop a reusable design to cope with potential changes in adaptive user interface and its adaptation logic.

An ad hoc solution to user activity tracking is quite simple; for example, identifying the task that the user performs on the basis of screen elements that the user selects from a user interface. However, when adaptation code is embedded into the target application, issues of extensibility, flexibility and reusability would arise [15].

As shown in Fig. 2, we view the adaptation code as an additional unit to an application with a static user interface. It is responsible for monitoring application state and context of use, detecting conditions warranting adaptation, choosing adaptation strategies, and notifying the static user interface to alter its navigation path. Buhagiar et al. propose a similar architecture for the development of adaptive user interfaces with different objectives in [7].

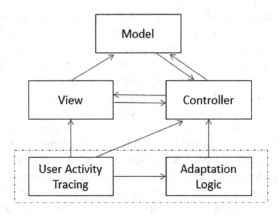

Fig. 2. Structure of adaptive application

Here, the structure of an adaptive application reflects a loosely coupled design; the adaption code interacts with the target application, but not vice versa. If its implementation does not depend on specific details of the application code as we describe in the section below, the coupling between them is minimal; in other words, changes in one would not affect the other to a great extent. A loosely coupled design increases flexibility and reusability, allowing the user interface and its adaptation logic to evolve with minimum impact on the target application.

Moreover, our current work is focused on adaptive navigation, but we believe that the proposed design is also applicable to reusable support for adaptive user interfaces in general.

5 Our Approach

Modern window-based applications are event-driven. User interface events result from user actions such as clicking a toolbar button and pressing a key, as well as system responses, such as updating the screen display and bringing up a message box. Whereas the former are observable actions that users perform, the latter correspond to their cognitive actions because users have to perceive the state change of the application in order to proceed. Hence, event traces reflect action sequences that users perform for task completion.

Event traces, as they unfold during program execution, provide insight into user behavior with respect to the user interface [2]. Because they are extremely voluminous and rich in detail, user interface events must be captured in an automatic manner. As discussed in the section above, it is very important to provide a reusable solution to extracting relevant events and analyzing them in order to understand user behavior. Partially based on our previous work [4], we describe below a reusable approach to accomplishing these objectives.

5.1 Aspect-Oriented Instrumentation

Instrumentation is a common technique for event tracing. It requires the developer to insert code at specific locations in an application in order to capture useful information at runtime. Instrumentation code tends to be distributed throughout the application and intimate knowledge about the application's implementation is required to create the code. Obviously, it is not appropriate when reusability is a desirable design consideration.

AspectJ is an aspect-oriented extension to the Java programming language [21]. It provides a construct, called aspects, to modularize processing elements that would otherwise span multiple modules. One can define an aspect to describe when it should act and what it should do; for example, reporting what is going on when certain method calls are made. Aspect-oriented techniques provide an effective way to modularize instrumentation code that would otherwise be scattered over an application, allowing to capture user interface events in a non-intrusive manner [17].

Window-based applications are often structured according to the Model-View-Controller (MVC) architecture. Components in the application must notify each other about what the user does in order to collaborate and achieve the overall functionality. Notification events as such correspond to steps that the user takes for task completion. We use aspects to trace events that occur across boundaries of the MVC architecture. Ignoring low-level events, such as those that appear between the application and its run-time environment, effectively reduces the amount of analytical effort without loss of relevant information.

Furthermore, aspects that are intended to capture notification events are application independent. In a Java GUI program, for example, a user action triggers an event, which in turn notifies its listener that implements a built-in interface. In other words, notification events can be recognized through calls to methods that standard Java interfaces define without having to rely on specific details of the application code. Since aspects are defined to capture notification events, they won't be affected by changes with respect to the event sources in the user interface and therefore are reusable when the user interface or its adaptation logic evolves.

5.2 Model-Based Analysis

While allowing to identify individual user actions and system responses, the information carried within user interface events themselves is inadequate to allow their meanings to be appropriately interpreted due to the lack of contextual information [2]. Contextual information plays a crucial role in analyzing event traces. Since contextual information spreads across multiple events, it is necessary to analyze event traces at a higher level of abstraction, that is, the level of user tasks.

Interactive application development is model driven. In the development process, task models, such as the Hierarchical Task Analysis (HTA) model, are created to specify user activities that are to be supported by an application and hence, they are considered as a critical component in user interface design. HTA task models are also used to understand an existing user interface for redesign and evaluation purposes. Since user interface design originates from a task model, event traces can be analyzed at the abstract level that the task model defines; that is, the task model provides necessary information for analyzing event traces in context.

User actions with respect to an application's user interface are grammatical in nature. Grammars can be used to analyze the syntactic structure of event traces and subsequently to identify user tasks. Note that BNF (Backus-Naur Form) grammars can be derived from HTA task models in a systematic manner. Using BNF grammars offers a number of significant benefits for task identification. BNF grammars give a precise, yet easy to understand syntactic description for event traces. Also, they allow an efficient parser to be constructed automatically. Such a parser makes it possible to map event traces to user tasks.

Although a task model is application-specific, it is taken as input in the event-analysis process, allowing the adaptation code to be built independently.

6 Feasibility Evaluation

We built a prototype for the course schedule application to investigate the feasibility of our approach. In our proof-of-concept experiment, the focus was on its ability to choose appropriate paths through the "search for course" task when the user interacts with the application. In order to evaluate the reusability of the proposed solution, we conducted this experiment in an incremental manner.

We created a prototype of the course schedule application at first. Its adaptability for the user interface is based on user status. Information such as user status is known prior to interaction and remain static throughout an interaction session. Adaptation decisions about which navigation path to be enabled are made as soon as an interaction session begins. Subsequently, we integrated adaptation code with the user activity tracking capability into the prototype, allowing the user interface to adjust its navigation path according to user needs. Here, attention was given to the nature of changes that need to be made in the prototype as a result of the integration. It is desirable that the developer can make necessary changes without having to know much about specific details of the application code.

Incremental development allows us to discover how much effort is necessary to integrate adaptation code into the target application. If modifications that have to be made in the target application are simple and minimal, then the proposed solution can be considered as reusable.

Our experiment was largely satisfactory. Even though the scope of our experiment was limited, it has demonstrated that aspect-oriented instrumentation and model-based analysis are an effective way to provide reusable support for the development of adaptive user interfaces.

In addition, there are applications in which usage patterns of the user interface by different users are available. It would be helpful to provide such an application with the ability to monitor user activities at runtime and manipulate its navigational structure according to the known usage patterns. Our approach offers a reusable solution in such a situation as well.

7 Conclusion

Software support for adaptive navigation provides the ability for a user interface to adapt its navigation structure to a variety of objectives at runtime. It is intended to offer better usability for users with different characteristics and in different contexts of use. We have illustrated through a use case for the course schedule application that adaptive navigation is an effective alternative to the traditional one-size-fits-all approach in user interface design.

Our intention is to provide reusable support for adaptive navigation at the task level. User interface development is model driven; task models are created and then used as the basis for design and development activities. Additionally, users often perform a sequence of tasks to achieve their objectives when they interact with an application. Hence, tasks offer a proper granularity to understand user behavior and determine adaptation strategies.

Adaptation logic depends on knowledge about user characteristics and context of use in order to make appropriate adaptation decisions. As we illustrated with the above-mentioned use case, it is also necessary to discover activities that the user performs to achieve one's objectives at runtime. As such, the user activity tracking capability is essential in support of an adaptive user interface.

We proposed a reusable solution to the development of adaptation code for a window-based application. In our approach, aspect-oriented instrumentation captures user interface events that cross the architectural boundaries of the target application. It is non-intrusive, allowing the instrumentation code to be modularized and developed independently. Furthermore, model-based analysis takes as input the HTA task model in the form of a BNF grammar to analyze event traces and identify user tasks. Event traces are analyzed by a parser that is automatically constructed from the underlying task model. As such, it can accommodate changes in the user interface as well as in its adaptation logic.

As described above, aspect-oriented instrumentation and model-based analysis makes it possible to develop adaptation code that is largely application-independent and therefore offers a great potential for reuse. We conducted a proof-of-concept experiment for the course schedule application to evaluate its feasibility.

Our approach has been successfully applied to a prototype for a realistic application. Although the experimental results were largely satisfactory, there are still a few issues to be addressed and more comprehensive evaluation needs to be conducted, which will be the focus of our research effort in the near future.

References

1. Tao, Y.: Toward computer-aided usability evaluation for evolving interactive software. In: Proceedings of the International Workshop on Reflection, AOP and Meta-Data for Software Evolution, 21st European Conference on Object-Oriented Programming (ECOOP 2007), Berlin, Germany (2007)
2. Hilbert, D.M., Redmiles, D.F.: Extracting usability information from user interface events. Comput. Surv. **32**(4), 384–421 (2000)
3. Brusilovsky, P.: Adaptive navigation support. In: Brusilovsky, P., Kobsa, A., Nejdl, W. (eds.) The Adaptive Web. LNCS, vol. 4321, pp. 263–290. Springer, Heidelberg (2007). https://doi.org/10.1007/978-3-540-72079-9_8
4. Tao, Y.: Grammatical analysis of user interface events for task identification. In: Marcus, A. (ed.) DUXU 2014. LNCS, vol. 8517, pp. 197–205. Springer, Cham (2014). https://doi.org/10.1007/978-3-319-07668-3_20
5. Grudin, J.: The case against user interface consistency. Commun. ACM **32**, 1164–1173 (1989)
6. Gullà, F., Ceccacci, S., Germani, M., Cavalieri, L.: Design adaptable and adaptive user interfaces: a method to manage the information. In: Andò, B., Siciliano, P., Marletta, V., Monteriù, A. (eds.) Ambient Assisted Living. BB, vol. 11, pp. 47–58. Springer, Cham (2015). https://doi.org/10.1007/978-3-319-18374-9_5
7. Buhagiar, A.J., Pace, G.J., Eberjer, J.: Engineering adaptive user interface using monitoring-oriented programming. In: IEEE QRS-C, pp. 200–207, 25–29 July 2017
8. Ceaparu, I., Lazar, J., Bessiere, K., Robinson, J., Shneidenman, B.: Determining causes and severity of end-user frustration. Int. J. Hum.-Comput. Interact. **17**, 333–356 (2004)
9. Castillejo, E., Almeida, A., López-de-Ipiña, D.: User, context and device modeling for adaptive user interface systems. In: Urzaiz, G., Ochoa, S.F., Bravo, J., Chen, L.L., Oliveira, J. (eds.) UCAmI 2013. LNCS, vol. 8276, pp. 94–101. Springer, Cham (2013). https://doi.org/10.1007/978-3-319-03176-7_13
10. Quade, M.: Model-based evaluation of adaptive user interfaces. In: Wichert, R., Van Laerhoven, K., Gelissen, J. (eds.) AmI 2011. CCIS, vol. 277, pp. 318–322. Springer, Heidelberg (2012). https://doi.org/10.1007/978-3-642-31479-7_54
11. Blumendorf, M., Lehmann, G., Albayrak, S.: Bridging models and systems at runtime to build adaptive user interfaces. In: EICS, pp. 9–18. ACM (2011)
12. Ramirez, A.J., Cheng, B.: Design patterns for developing dynamically adaptive systems. In: SEAMS, pp. 49–58. ACM (2010)
13. Nilsson, E.G., Floch, J., Hallsteinsen, S., Stav, E.: Using a patterns-based modelling language and a model-based adaptation architecture to facilitate adaptive user interfaces. In: Doherty, G., Blandford, A. (eds.) DSV-IS 2006. LNCS, vol. 4323, pp. 234–247. Springer, Heidelberg (2007). https://doi.org/10.1007/978-3-540-69554-7_19

14. Jason, B., Calitz, A., Greyling, J.: The evaluation of an adaptive user interface model. In: SAICSIT, pp. 132–143. ACM (2010)
15. Akiki, P.A., Bandara, A.K., Yu, Y.: Adaptive model-driven user interface development systems. ACM Comput. Surv. **47**(1), 9:1–9:33 (2014)
16. David, P.-C., Ledoux, T.: An aspect-oriented approach for developing self-adaptive fractal components. In: Löwe, W., Südholt, M. (eds.) SC 2006. LNCS, vol. 4089, pp. 82–97. Springer, Heidelberg (2006). https://doi.org/10.1007/11821946_6
17. Shekh, S., Tyerman, S.: An aspect-oriented framework for event capture and usability evaluation. In: Maciaszek, L.A., González-Pérez, C., Jablonski, S. (eds.) ENASE 2008. CCIS, vol. 69, pp. 107–119. Springer, Heidelberg (2010). https://doi.org/10.1007/978-3-642-14819-4_8
18. Shneiderman, B.: Designing the User Interfaces, pp. 74–76. Addison Wesley, Boston (2005)
19. Gajos, K.: Making the web more inclusive with adaptive user interfaces. In: Engineering Interactive Computing Systems (EICS). ACM (2014)
20. Brusilovsky, P., Maybury, M.T.: From adaptive hypermedia to the adaptive web. Commun. ACM **45**(5), 31–33 (2002)
21. Kiczales, G., et al.: Aspect-oriented programming. In: Akşit, M., Matsuoka, S. (eds.) ECOOP 1997. LNCS, vol. 1241, pp. 220–242. Springer, Heidelberg (1997). https://doi.org/10.1007/bfb0053381

How Effectively Do Experts Predict Elderly Target-Users of Assistive Devices? Importance of Expert Knowledge in Device Development

Makiko Watanabe[1] , Takuya Washio[2] , Masashi Iwasaki[2],
Takeshi Arai[3], Miki Saijo[2] , and Takumi Ohashi[2(✉)]

[1] Knowledge Mobility Based System Inst., Minato-ku, Tokyo 108-0023, Japan
[2] Tokyo Institute of Technology, Meguro-ku, Tokyo 152-8550, Japan
ohashi.t.af@m.titech.ac.jp
[3] Tokyo University of Science, Noda, Chiba 278-8510, Japan

Abstract. Many assistive devices have been developed to assist in the activities of daily life (ADLs) of frail elderly people. However, one of the significant barriers to device development is to conduct multiple user tests due to burdensome to the elderly. Therefore, the potential need for devices must be determined efficiently with some limited opportunities. In this study, we examined whether it is possible to identify target users who can adapt to, and continuously use the device, by utilizing the knowledge of experts who are familiar with the mental and physical conditions of the elderly. As a case study, we analyzed a two-month user test of 57 elderly people with the use of a four-wheel electrically assisted cycle. As a result, the accuracy rate of the expert's prediction of continuous/discontinuous use over the whole study period was 66.7% before use, but it was improved to 87.7% when the prediction was made again after two rides by elderly people. We also attempted to model this identification rule by multiple regression analysis, and found that experts could predict whether users would use the device long-term by evaluating the following three factors: 1) subjects' willingness to exercise, 2) their anxiety and dissatisfaction associated with the product, and 3) the ease with which they became fatigued. It is thus proposed that target users can be identified by having a small number of elderly people use the equipment several times, and obtaining expert predictions regarding whether users will continue to use or stop using the device.

Keywords: Target user · User-test · Expert knowledge · Elderly people · Assistive device development

1 Introduction

The global human population is rapidly aging; that is, becoming increasingly biased towards older age classes. In particular, the 65 years-plus age class is occupying an increasing proportion of the total population. The population of Japan was 126.93 million as of October 1, 2016. Those aged 65 years-plus numbered 34.59 million, accounting for 27.3% of the total population (Cabinet Office Japan 2017). According to

© Springer Nature Switzerland AG 2020
A. Marcus and E. Rosenzweig (Eds.): HCII 2020, LNCS 12200, pp. 278–293, 2020.
https://doi.org/10.1007/978-3-030-49713-2_20

the World Health Organization (WHO), Japan is the only country in which the proportion of people aged 60 years and over exceeded 30% in 2015. However, by the middle of this century, it is predicted that the elderly population proportions of many countries will be the same as that of Japan. Therefore, the "super-aged" society will present challenges not only for Japan but for the whole world (WHO 2015). Global attention is now focused on meeting these challenges.

In recent years, welfare assistive devices have attracted attention from the viewpoint of assisting caregivers and assisting and/or suppressing cognitive and physical decline in frail elderly people (WHO 2015; Schulz et al. 2014). Focusing on the latter point of view, physical activity (such as moderate exercise) is known to reduce various types of health risk (Laurin et al. 2001) and devices that assist the activities of frail elderly people are desirable. However, the symptoms and disorders of the elderly are diverse and it is not possible to discuss them collectively. In order to develop new technologies and tools and utilize them in supportive applications, it is essential to ensure their safety and to define which people are suited to using them. In this study, we aim to identify target users, defined as users who can adapt to a given tool and are likely to use it continuously. Estimation of target user characteristics will aid in the development of assistive devices; likewise, identifying frail elderly people who cannot become target users will help to identify problems in current devices and overcome them (Fig. 1).

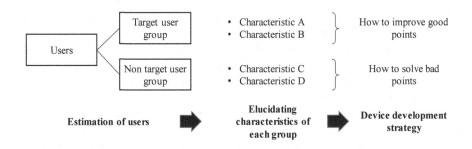

Fig. 1. Device development process based on the identification of target users.

Identification of target users requires user-testing of assistive devices by frail elderly people; however, this has certain problems. For example, it would be necessary to conduct user tests with frail elderly people with the cooperation of experts. However, only 5.3% of nursing homes have experience in cooperating in the development of technology, as most are too busy (MHLW 2014). Therefore, a simple method for conducting demonstration tests is urgently needed. However, it is not always easy to carry out demonstration experiments with elderly people whose mental and physical functions are low, as it may be difficult to secure examinees and organize multiple experimental sessions with them.

Because of such constraints, in the past, target user characteristics had to be estimated from the results of a small number of experiments conducted on a small number of subjects under slightly different conditions. However, the various health issues of the elderly can complicate such processes.

In this study, we propose a method for estimating the characteristics of target users of a new device based on a limited number of experiments. This involves utilizing the knowledge of experts who are experienced in elderly care and rehabilitation services and understand the mental and physical conditions of the elderly. As a case study, we conducted a test at a rehabilitation hospital in Kakegawa City, Shizuoka, Japan, in which a four-wheel electric-power-assisted cycle was used by elderly patients (end users) for an average of two months. We also examined the predictions made by expert physical therapists (PTs) regarding user uptake of the device. This was then used to establish a methodology by which experts may accurately predict end user utilization of assistive devices.

2   Target User Identification Rules and Expert Knowledge

What information should an expert have in order to identify target users, during a behavioral change study, in which elderly potential target users receive training in the use of a new device and have the option to continue using it?

According to the health belief model (HBM), health-related action depends on persistent susceptibility, sustained severity, sustained benefits, sustained barriers, incentives to behave, and self-efficacy (Rosenstock et al. 1988). In this study, we focus on persistent benefits and barriers, and analyze the causes of elderly behavior in terms of both positive and negative aspects.

According to the transtheoretical model, when a person changes their behavior, the process involves the stages of precontemplation, contemplation, preparation, action, and maintenance. This cycle may be terminated (discontinuation of action) or repeated (Prochaska et al. 1997, 2008, 2015).

In this study, therefore, we defined the outcomes according to whether or not behavioral change (in this case, using a new device) continued or was interrupted, and examined whether this can be predicted by experts, namely, PTs. Also, to understand how the PTs predict the outcome, we attempted to elucidate their identification rules; we defined the identification rules as specific rules formed based on his/her expertise, in order to predict whether or not the user will use the device.

2.1   Definition of Outcomes

In this section, we organize the process of behavioral change as follows. Assume that the intention of the user to utilize a device at time t is M_t, and that the activity is scheduled when the intention to use M_t exceeds a certain threshold L. Intention to use (M_t) varies depending on various factors during usage, therefore:

The user's involvement is suspended if $M_t < L$; and
The user will use the device when $M_t \geq L$.
Even if it is intended to be used, the actual act of using the device requires supporters and an assessment of the situation at the time, therefore:

The user performs behavior A (using the device) with probability p.

Thus, at the end of the experimental period, users with $M_t > L$ are considered to be suitable for using the device.

On the other hand, since M_t cannot be directly observed, the usage rate U_m for each user is obtained by dividing the number of observable behaviors A by the number of visits to the rehabilitation hospital, which is the number of available opportunities, and this is discussed as an outcome.

2.2 Definition of Identification Rules Based on Expert Knowledge

Although M_t is not observable because it is a user's internal thought process, it is assumed that the PT may predict it from a set of information X_t obtained from the user's behavior at some point T. The information set X_t is assumed to contain the usage results up to the time point $(t - 1)$, including data on the actions of the users. At some point T, the PT performs his/her prediction P_t of user's device usage continuation/discontinuation by his/her identification rule F_t, formed by the information set X_t from the user m and the expert knowledge. We attempted to formalize this identification rule F_t as a part of this study.

2.3 Objective of This Study

In this study, through the case study shown in Chapter 3, we attempted 1) a comparison between the actual usage rate U_m and expert's predictions P_0 and P_2, and 2) modeling of the identification rules F_0 and F_2, before use ($t = 0$) and at the second use ($t = 2$). The purpose of this study is to elucidate the processes of establishing a target user identification methodology using expert knowledge.

3 Case Study: User-Testing of a Four-Wheel Electrically Assisted Cycle for Frail Elderly People

3.1 Methodology

A case study was conducted based on user testing of the Life Walker (LW; Fig. 2), which was developed by the Yamaha Motor Engineering Co., Ltd. (YEC; Saijo et al. 2014; Ohashi et al. 2017). The LW is an electrically-assisted pedal-powered device designed to assist in the mobility of the frail elderly. It is easy to pedal due to having an electrical assistance function and is equipped with an automatic brake pedal. It is approved by the Japanese Industrial Standard (JIS) so that it can travel on footpaths in the same way as a wheelchair. It was developed to help elderly and sick people expand their range of activity, improve physical fitness, and recover motor function, but is not yet available on the market. After receiving guidance and advice from YEC on how to ride the LW, it was lent to Kakegawa Kita Hospital for experimental use.

Fig. 2. Photograph of the life walker mobility device.

Table 1. Summary of research scenario.

Location	Kakegawa Kita Hospital, Shizuoka, Japan
Dates	December 2, 2014 to February 6, 2015
Users	57 elderly patients
Number of LWs	Three
PT team	3 physical therapists with 8-, 2-, and 1-years' experience and 3 rehabilitation assistants with 8-, 1-, and 1-years' experience
Methods (Details in Fig. 3)	• Interviews with PT team before and after lending the device • Interviews with users • Questionnaire surveys and test rides by PT team • Test drive recordings with mini video camera

An outline of the survey is shown in Table 1. The study was conducted at Kakegawa Kita Hospital twice, in fiscal year 2014-2015. Test rides of the LW were recommended to all visitors who were judged by the PT team, including three PTs and three rehabilitation assistants, to be free from serious mental and physical issues, were able to communicate, and were able to use the LW. At the time of the recommendation, all the PT team members and other users were shown the vehicle and asked if they would like to ride it. Although elderly patients were asked if they would like to use the LW, some chose not to. Out of 138 elderly patients using the rehabilitation hospital to restore their physical function, 10 people were not recommended to try the device by

PT team, 71 people did not use the device even when the PT team recommended, and 57 people used the device according to the recommendation. For the investigation, a PT team consisting mainly of physical therapists (PTs) was set up at Kakegawa Kita Hospital and the LWs were used as part of the usual rehabilitation program. Before use, instruction on how to ride the LW was given to the PT team, and surveys and questionnaires prepared by researchers were given to the users.

Each time the users arrived at the hospital, the PT team checked whether they 1) were using the LW, 2) intended to continue using it for that day, and 3) predicted they would continue use until the end of the experimental period. This was checked before the first use and after the second use, and the reasons noted.

3.2   Data Collection

As shown in Fig. 3, the survey in this study was conducted via interviews with PT team. Test ride experiments were conducted by the PT team in accordance with the study methods. The 1st study period (Saijo et al. 2014) was conducted in fiscal year 2012–2013. The 2nd study period (fiscal year 2014–2015) is described here. Approximately half of the users (30 users) participated in both study periods.

A questionnaire-based survey (basic attributes, basic checklist; MHLW 2012) was conducted before the first and third uses of the LW. During LW use, the person in charge of the PT team accompanied and assisted the user. After the first and second uses, a test ride performance evaluation was conducted, together with collecting feedback from users.

The PT team predicted twice whether each user would continue use of the LW: once before the first use, and then again after the second use. In the 1st study period, it was difficult to determine whether the user would continue with the device, as pre-use PT team forecasts were mainly based upon nursing care level, or the answers to a basic checklist. Since it was recognized that the physical conditions of the elderly users were different, in the 2nd study period, the predictions were described in terms of mental and physical aspects of users.

Usage predictions were made by the PTs based on a variety of information, including the patient's motivation, daily behavior, and reactions during use. These observations were shared in daily reports and at end-of-day meetings.

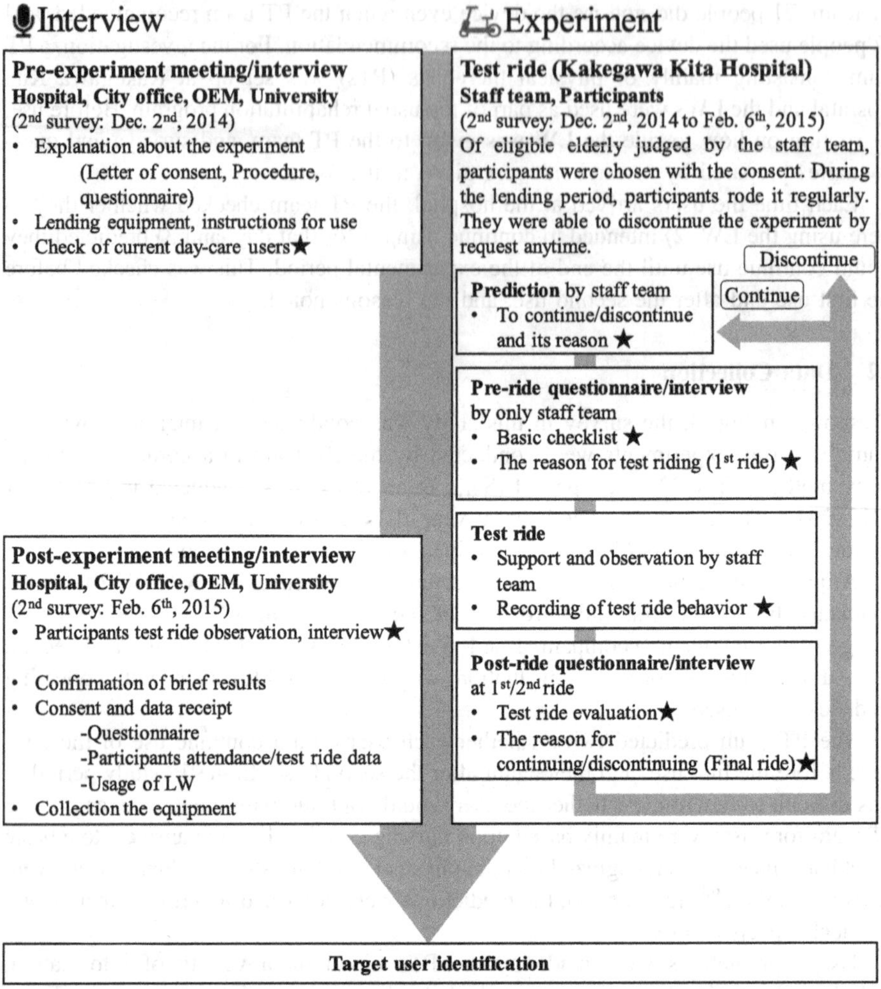

🎤Interview   🦽Experiment

Pre-experiment meeting/interview	Test ride (Kakegawa Kita Hospital)

Pre-experiment meeting/interview
Hospital, City office, OEM, University
(2nd survey: Dec. 2nd, 2014)
- Explanation about the experiment
  (Letter of consent, Procedure,
  questionnaire)
- Lending equipment, instructions for use
- Check of current day-care users★

Test ride (Kakegawa Kita Hospital)
Staff team, Participants
(2nd survey: Dec. 2nd, 2014 to Feb. 6th, 2015)
Of eligible elderly judged by the staff team, participants were chosen with the consent. During the lending period, participants rode it regularly. They were able to discontinue the experiment by request anytime.

Discontinue

Prediction by staff team   Continue
- To continue/discontinue
  and its reason ★

Pre-ride questionnaire/interview
by only staff team
- Basic checklist ★
- The reason for test riding (1st ride) ★

Post-experiment meeting/interview
Hospital, City office, OEM, University
(2nd survey: Feb. 6th, 2015)
- Participants test ride observation, interview★

- Confirmation of brief results
- Consent and data receipt
  -Questionnaire
  -Participants attendance/test ride data
  -Usage of LW
- Collection the equipment

Test ride
- Support and observation by staff team
- Recording of test ride behavior ★

Post-ride questionnaire/interview
at 1st/2nd ride
- Test ride evaluation★
- The reason for continuing/discontinuing (Final ride)★

Target user identification

Fig. 3. Experiment and data flowchart (★ indicates data used in this study).

3.3   Results of the Experiment

Test Ride Results. Of the 57 users, 30 (52.6%) continued to test ride the LW until the end of the experiment (Fig. 4). Among the users, there were 27 males and 30 females, 18 people aged 65–74 years and 36 people aged over 75 years old (mean age = 78.7 years, standard deviation = 7.3). Their needs for nursing care varied but this did not significantly affect their continuation/discontinuation of LW use.

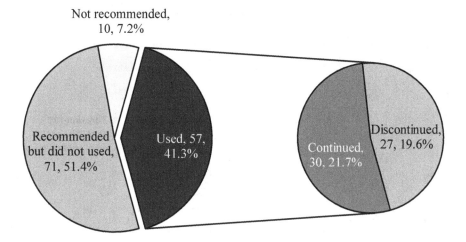

Fig. 4. Percentages of elderly patients using day-care facilities (left) and the mobility device (right).

In both the 1st and 2nd study periods, a PT gave advice regarding getting on, driving, and getting off the device. Although many elderly people had difficulty walking on their own, they often used the LW during the 1st study period (70 test riders, mean uses = 7.4; Saijo et al. 2014). The situation was similar in the 2nd study period (mean uses = 8.7 times). The continuation/discontinuation threshold was the same as in the 1st study period, with a maximum cumulative use of 40% at the end of the experiment (Fig. 5). Here, the usage rate for each user is obtained by dividing the number of test rides by the number of visits to the hospital. The maximum cumulative usage rate is defined as the usage rate at the end of 2nd study period. The thin red and blue lines indicate each user's usage according to whether they continued or discontinued usage, respectively. The bold red and blue lines indicate the maximum and minimum usage rates of the users on each day of the experiment, respectively.

Therefore, in this study, the continuation/discontinuation threshold was set at 40%, which was the maximum cumulative discontinuation rate at the end of the experiment. Moreover, the correlation between the usage rate and number of days visited was 0.013, indicating that even if there were many opportunities, the LW was not always used.

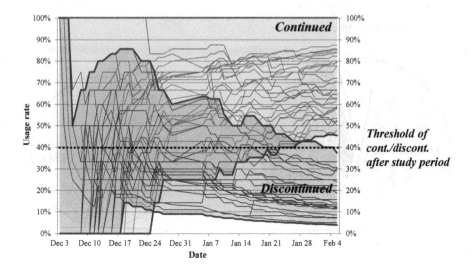

Fig. 5. Variation in individual usage rates over time. (Color figure online)

Comparison Between Test Ride Results and PT Team Predictions. The users were all elderly persons who were judged as able to use the LW. Since all of the users made positive comments at the beginning of the trial, the initial behavior of all users was recorded as "using". However, their behavioral status could change to "stop using" or "continue to use" after repeated usage. The users' behavioral decisions were made at each visit, and the experts predicted whether each user would continue to use the device.

The PT team made correct predictions 66.7% of the time at P_0 (before usage) and 87.7% of the time at P_2 (after the second use) regarding whether users would continue or discontinue use of the device (Table 2). Predictive factors for continued use were the user's functioning in daily life, their willingness to use the device, and whether they used the device a second time. The survey also found that 26.4% of predictions were revised based on how the users utilized the device and their comments on their use, indicating that the timing of the prediction is important for improving the accuracy of the judgments.

Table 2. Percentages of users continuing usage: predictions and results.

Result	Initial Prediction P_0		Result	Second Prediction P_2	
	Continuation	Discontinuation		Continuation	Discontinuation
Cont.	**30 (52.6%)**	0 (0.0%)	Cont.	**28 (49.1%)**	2 (3.5%)
Discont.	19 (33.3%)	**8 (14.0%)**	Discont.	5 (8.8%)	**22 (38.6%)**
Result: P_0		**66.7%**	Result: P_2		**87.7%**

4   Modeling the Identification Rules of the Experts (PTs)

As shown in Table 2, experts found that they could correctly predict continued use of the LW in 66.7% of cases. Furthermore, after two instances of observing device usage, the judgement accuracy improved significantly. This suggests that experts can use their tacit knowledge as an identification rule, and further refine it based on observation of users' behavior while using the device. So, how can implicit identification rules be expressed in an accurate model? In this chapter, we aim to model identification rules based on the results of questionnaires, interviews with users, and the reasons for PT team predictions.

4.1   Modeling by Questionnaire Results

Gender, age, required care level, and test ride evaluation, which were the basic attributes obtained from the questionnaires. These were examined as explanatory variables of the objective variable *usage rate*. Multiple regression analysis was conducted with *usage rate* as the objective variable, but no statistically significant explanatory variables were found.

4.2   Modeling by Users' Reasons for Using and Continuing/Discontinuing to Use the Device

Users' reasons for starting to use the LW (at time = 0) and for continuing/discontinuing its use at the end of the experiment (time k) were obtained from interviews with users and categorized as qualitative data. They were used as dummy variables to estimate the reasons for continuing/discontinuing use.

The main reason for starting use was that none of the users saw the device in a negative way, suggesting that, at the beginning, they did not intend to stop using it. In addition, as a result of factor analysis using reasons as dummy variables, three main reasons for starting use of the device were identified: "ambitiousness", "to accept the recommendation" and "due to interest in the device". However, in the multiple regression analysis of *usage rate*, these variables were not statistically significant. From this, it can be said that at the start of the program, it was impossible to predict whether a user would continue or stop use of the device.

At the end of the program (time k), more than five users mentioned reasons for continuing/discontinuing use of the LW: "it provides exercise (X_{k1})," "it allows me to go out (X_{k2})," "I get tired easily (X_{k3})," "its speed is slow (X_{k4})," and "it is troublesome (X_{k5})". As a result of the multiple regression analysis using these explanatory variables and *usage rate* U_m as an objective variable, three explanatory variables were found: "it provides exercise (X_{k1})," "it allows me to go out (X_{k2})," and "its speed is slow (X_{k4})."

$$U_m = 0.274 + 0.302x_{mk1} + 0.407x_{mk2} - 0.217x_{mk4} \qquad (1)$$

Although the adjusted coefficient of determination is only 0.411, the regression equation is statistically significant (Table 3) and all explanatory variables are also statistically significant (Table 4). Therefore, we conclude that these variables have explanatory power, indicating that it is possible to identify potential users based on the main reasons for continuing/discontinuing use mentioned by the users themselves.

Table 3. Analysis of variance.

Variation	Sum of squares	Degrees of freedom	Unbiased estimate of population variance	Variance ratio	P-value	Judgment
Overall variation	4.57	56				
Variation due to regression	2.02	3	0.67	14.02	0.000	[**]
Residual variation from regression	2.55	53	0.05			

Table 4. Multiple regression equation

Variable	Number of samples	Partial regression	Standardized partial regression coefficient	F-value	P-value	Judgment	Standard error	VIF
It provides exercise	28	0.302	0.534	24.1	0.000	[**]	0.062	1.12
It allows me to go out	5	0.407	0.406	13.9	0.000	[**]	0.109	1.13
It is troublesome	8	−0.217	−0.266	6.5	0.014	[*]	0.085	1.04
Constant term		0.274		32.4	0.000	[**]	0.048	

4.3   Modeling by Underlying Rationale of Expert Predictions

Table 5 shows the reasons given for the initial prediction P_0 and second prediction P_2. It can be seen that the reasons given for the second prediction P_2 are more specific than those given for the initial prediction P_0. It can also be seen that some variables have different numbers of responses while others do not when comparing P_0 and P_2. For example, many gave the psychological reason of "Interest in the device" for predicting P_0, which seemed to be divided into two reasons for predicting P_2: "It is like a bicycle" and "It is troublesome," indicating that the users' behaviors changed depending on their user experience. From this, it can be inferred that the factors determining initial use and continuous use were different. Focusing on the physical aspect of the reasons used for prediction, paralysis and functional impairment may be positive factors when the symptoms are mild, or negative when they are severe. This is because the LW can be used even if one foot is paralyzed and falls off the pedal, since it can be fixed with a strap or other device. Therefore, it is inferred that the identification of continuation/discontinuation is unclear when the degree of physical disability is mild to severe.

In this study, we categorized the reasons used for the initial prediction P_0 and second prediction P_2 as dummy variables, and performed multiple regression analysis with *usage rate* as the objective variable to analyze whether these factors can be used for identification.

Table 5. Reasons used for prediction of use (psychological and physical aspects) and numbers of responses. ± indicate positive/negative reasons.

	Reasons (psychological)	P_0	P_2		Reasons (physical)	P_0	P_2
+	Have the will to exercise	18	13	+	Independent in daily life	11	9
+	Have the will to rehabilitate	14	10	+	Movement is self-sustaining	7	6
+	Like bicycles	1	3	+	Walk independently	7	4
+	High ambition to walk	2	2	+	Walk with a cane	1	1
+	Interest in the device	9	2	+	Dysfunction is mild	1	1
-	Anxiety and complaints about device	0	11	+	Paralysis is mild	3	3
-	Decreased physical mobility	3	2	-	Dysfunction is severe	2	2
-	Sensitive person	2	1	-	Old	1	1
-	Anxiety about the lower back	0	1	-	Severe hemiplegia	1	1
-	Frequent knee pain	0	1	-	Lower back pain	1	2
				-	Prone to fatigue	1	7
				-	Slow movement	1	1
				-	Motor paralysis	2	1
				-	Sitting position is unstable	0	3

Explanation by Reasons of Initial Prediction P_0. In order to clarify the factors determining continued use from the reasons considered in prediction P_0, a correlation analysis was carried out. The reasons could be used in multiple regression analysis using *usage rate* as an objective variable. However, no significant explanatory variables were obtained. From this fact, it can be said that the first prediction instance has no explanatory power for the identification of continuation/discontinuation.

Explanation of Reasons in Second Prediction Instance P_2. As shown in Table 5, in the second-prediction instance (P_2), the reasons for continuation/discontinuation became more specific than in the initial-prediction instance. Also, the number of negative factors increased, which is considered to be because 15 users (26.3%) who were predicted to continue at P_0 were then predicted to discontinue at P_2. As a result of selecting variables by factor analysis, three factors were obtained as explanatory variables: "Has the will to exercise (X_1)," "Anxiety and complaints about device (X_7)," and "Fatigues easily (X_{17})". Then, a multiple regression equation of *usage rate* was obtained as below:

$$U_m = 0.471 + 0.184x_{m2 \cdot 1} - 0.235x_{m2 \cdot 7} - 0.327x_{m2 \cdot 17} \qquad (2)$$

Though the adjusted coefficient of determination is 0.370, the regression equation is statistically significant (Table 6) and all explanatory variables are also statistically significant (Table 7). Therefore, we conclude that variables with explanatory power were selected.

Table 6. Analysis of variance table.

Variation	Sum of squares	Degrees of freedom	Unbiased estimate of population variance	Variance ratio	P-value	Judgment
Overall variation	4.574	56				
Variation due to regression	1.844	3	0.615	11.94	0.000	[**]
Residual variation from regression	2.729	53	0.051			

Table 7. Multiple regression equation.

	Simple correlation	Partial regression	Standardized partial regression coefficient	F-value	P-value	Judgment	Standard error
Has the will to exercise	0.416	0.184	0.273	5.841	0.019	[*]	0.076
Anxiety and complaints about device	−0.366	−0.235	−0.328	8.778	0.005	[**]	0.079
Fatigues easily	−0.439	−0.327	−0.379	12.063	0.001	[**]	0.094
Constant term	−0.275	0.471		119.874	0.000	[**]	0.043

4.4 Validation of the Obtained Model

The validity of the factors used in Eq. (2) (in which the rationale for PT predictions after the second usage were used as explanatory variables) is examined by comparison with the factors used in Eq. (1) (in which the reasons given by users for continuation/discontinuation of the experiment were used as the explanatory variables).

There were three main reasons given for the re-prediction in Eq. (2): "has the will to exercise," "anxiety and complaints about device," and "fatigues easily,". There were also three reasons for continuation/discontinuation of the experiment given by users: "It is exercise," "It allows me to go out," and "It is slow." The same factors were elucidated for "exercise motivation" and "anxiety and dissatisfaction with the product." Although "It allows me to go out" and "fatigues easily" may seem different at first glance, it was inferred that the users who want to go out are physically able to drive outdoors (in this case, the hospital parking lot) and were not people who were easily tired or had difficulty in going outdoors. Therefore, Eqs. (1) and (2) use almost the same factors, and the factors clarified by the analysis are highly valid.

In this chapter, we have attempted to model the identification rules implicitly used by experts. As a result, a valid model of an identification rule was derived after the second usage instance, at which time the continuation/discontinuation predictions were 88.6% correct. In addition, it was suggested that the experts were able to identify users who were highly compatible with the LW with high accuracy through only two experiments that focused on three factors: 1) motivation to exercise, 2) anxiety and dissatisfaction with the product, and 3) ease of fatigue.

5   Conclusions

In order to implement the use of assistive devices for the elderly, it is necessary to know what kind of elderly people are the target users, which is not easy. In this study, we considered elderly people who continued to use the device to be typical target users. We proposed an experimental and analytical method that combines the results of a small number of experiments conducted on a small number of users with a discriminant model obtained from experts who are familiar with the mental and physical conditions of the elderly.

This method was applied to the case of a four-wheel electrically-assisted pedal mobility device for facilitating mobility and rehabilitation. Initially, it was difficult to know whether users would use the device long-term. However, this could be predicted by evaluating the following three factors: 1) willingness to exercise, 2) anxiety and dissatisfaction with the product, and 3) ease of fatigue. At the same time, it was found that factors suggestive of utilization prior to use (e.g. ambitiousness) were not able to predict usage patterns consistently, suggesting that in order to promote the use of assistive devices, experiments must be conducted on elderly people.

Our results suggest that even if it is difficult to conduct a large number of experiments on a large number of users under the same conditions (or a long-term study), target users can be identified by 1) having a small number of elderly people use the equipment several times, and 2) obtaining expert predictions regarding whether users will continue to use or stop using the device. This method allows the time required for prediction to be greatly shortened.

In order to disseminate the method proposed in this study (using comprehensive judgment based on expert knowledge), it is necessary to further investigate and analyze its applicability to other devices. The present study was conducted by a team that included rehabilitation assistants who were not highly experienced. Thus, we believe there is a possibility that the approach can be widely used to develop devices with teams that include not only PTs with similar expertise but also medical professionals who can explain and understand the reasons for usage continuation/discontinuation.

Acknowledgements. This study was partly supported by the JSPS Grants-in-aid for Scientific Research ("Kakenhi," JP23300260). We are sincerely grateful to Kakegawa City Hall, Medical Corporation Ryouwakai Kakegawa Kita Hospital, and Yamaha Motor Engineering Co., Ltd., for their generous cooperation and support, and to all the research participants who have cooperated with our research.

Ethics Permission. This study was approved by the Tokyo Institute of Technology Ethics Review Committee:

1st study period: Approval Number 2012021 (approved in October 11, 2012).

2nd study period: Approval Number 2014066 (approved in November 10, 2014).

References

Cabinet Office Japan: Annual report on the aging society FY2017 (2017). https://www8.cao.go.jp/kourei/english/annualreport/2017/pdf/c1-1.pdf. Accessed 30 Sept 2019

Laurin, D., Verreault, R., Lindsay, J., MacPherson, K., Rockwood, K.: Physical activity and risk of cognitive impairment and dementia in elderly persons. Arch. Neurol. **58**(3), 498–504 (2001)

Ohashi, T., Watanabe, M., Saijo, M.: An interaction analysis of user-testing to extract salient user experience with the robotic assistive device Life-Walker. In: ICRA 2017 Workshop on Advances and Challenges on the Development, Testing and Assessment of Assistive and Rehabilitation Robots: Experiences from Engineering and Human Science Research, vol. 1, p. 57 (2017)

Prochaska, J.O., Velicer, W.F.: The transtheoretical model of health behavior change. Am. J. Health Promot. **12**(1), 3848 (1997)

Prochaska, J.O., et al.: Initial efficacy of MI, TTM tailoring, and HRI's in multiple behaviors for employee health promotion. Prev. Med. **46**, 226–231 (2008)

Prochaska, J.O., Redding, C.A., Evers, K.E.: The transtheoretical model and stages of change. In: Health Behavior: Theory, Research, and Practice, pp. 125–148 (2015)

Rosenstock, I.M., Strecher, V.J., Becker, M.H.: Social learning theory and the health belief model. Health Educ. Q. **15**(2), 175–183 (1988)

Saijo, M., Watanabe, M., Aoshima, S., Oda, N., Matsumoto, S., Kawamoto, S.: Knowledge creation in technology evaluation of 4-wheel electric power assisted bicycle for frail elderly persons: a case study of a salutogenic device in healthcare facilities in Japan. In: Proceedings of the International Conference on Knowledge Management and Information Sharing, KMIS-2014, pp. 87–97 (2014)

Schulz, R., Wahl, H.W., Matthews, J.T., De Vito Dabbs, A., Beach, S.R., Czaja, S.J.: Advancing the aging and technology agenda in gerontology. Gerontologist **55**(5), 724–734 (2014)

The Japanese Ministry of Health, Labour and Welfare (MHLW): Guidelines for long-term care prevention (2012). https://www.mhlw.go.jp/topics/2009/05/dl/tp0501-1_1.pdf. Accessed 9 Oct 2019. (in Japanese)

The Japanese Ministry of Health, Labour and Welfare (MHLW): Guidelines for development of welfare equipment and nursing care robots (2014). http://www.techno-aids.or.jp/research/robotebiki_mhlw_140922.pdf. Accessed 9 Oct 2019. (in Japanese)

World Health Organization: World report on aging and health (2015). http://apps.who.int/iris/bitstream/10665/186463/1/9789240694811_eng.pdf. Accessed 30 Sept 2019

Usability Heuristic Evaluation for the Hearing Impaired Language Training Mobile App

Wei Xiong[1], Tian Yao[1], Qiong Pan[2(✉)], and Zhen Liu[1]

[1] School of Design, South China University of Technology, Guangzhou 510006, People's Republic of China
[2] Department of Art and Design, Guangdong Industry Polytechnic, Guangzhou 510300, People's Republic of China
6788036@qq.com

Abstract. Usability heuristics are an effective method widely used in usability research. Sometimes it's necessary to build unique usability heuristics to address usability in specific domains. This paper develops a heuristic evaluation for the hearing impaired language training mobile application by collecting and analyzing previous studies. A comprehensive set of 19 heuristics and detailed explanations are presented in this study for the hearing impaired language training app. The new heuristics for the hearing impaired language training app were validated through surveys and case studies with the help of users and usability experts. Based on our findings, those results can be used as the reference to design or evaluate language training apps for the hearing impaired.

Keywords: Human-computer interaction · Usability evaluation · Hearing-loss · Language rehabilitation

1 Introduction

The usability of a software product, which refers to the ease that a system can be learned and used, greatly influences the user experience. Usability is a quality attribute that assesses how easy user interfaces are to use. The word "usability" also refers to methods for improving ease-of-use during the design process. Usability is defined by five quality components: Learnability, Efficiency, Memorability, Errors and Satisfaction [1].

There are different methods, techniques and tools related to the interaction between a user and the software product. There are several methods for evaluating usability, which vary according to the time/benefit-cost, rigor, number of users, number of evaluators and the knowledge they possess. Usability inspection (usability problem identification techniques that do not involve testing with potential users) is the generic name for a set of cost-effective ways of evaluating user interfaces to find usability problems. They are fairly informal methods and easy to use. Usability inspection methods include Heuristic evaluation, Cognitive walkthroughs, Formal usability inspections, Pluralistic walkthroughs, Feature inspection, Consistency inspection and Standards inspection [2]. Heuristic evaluation can work very well [3].

© Springer Nature Switzerland AG 2020
A. Marcus and E. Rosenzweig (Eds.): HCII 2020, LNCS 12200, pp. 294–307, 2020.
https://doi.org/10.1007/978-3-030-49713-2_21

Heuristic evaluation [4] is a method for finding usability problems in a user interface design by having a small set of evaluators to examine the interface and judge its compliance with recognized usability principles. Independent research has found heuristic evaluation to be extremely cost-efficient, confirming its value in circumstances where limited time or budgetary resources are available.

Nielsen proposed the ten usability heuristics for the design of user interfaces. Other authors designed specific heuristics for some types of software [5–7]. In a previous study, from the literature some usability heuristics were gathered for deaf web user experience [8] and assistive courseware for the hearing impaired [9], but there is no research focused on the language rehabilitation for the hearing loss.

The aim of this work is to formalize the development process of a proposal of usability heuristics for the hearing impaired language training app. This article is structured as follow: In Sect. 2, the methodology we used to formalize the heuristics is presented, then in Sect. 3, literature reviews and basic surveys are done in order to get the first version of the set of heuristics. The set of heuristics is listed in Sect. 4. After that in Sect. 5, we validate the preliminary set of heuristics through case studies of the pronunciation training part in Voibook app and Angel Sound app (a listening training app for the hearing impaired), and finally the final version of heuristics set is introduced formally.

2 Methodology

A methodology created by Daniela Quiñones [10] was used to formalize the development of the heuristics proposal for the hearing impaired language training mobile app. This methodology is a formal methodology aimed at developing usability heuristics in specific application domains and it has 8 steps: Exploratory stage, Experimental stage, Descriptive stage, Correlational stage, Selection stage, Specification stage, Validation stage and Refinement stage.

The exploratory stage is to perform a literature review to collect information about the specific application domain. The experimental stage is to gain some additional information that hasn't been identified in previous stages through experiments such as usability tests, interviews and surveys. This next step is optional. The descriptive stage highlights the most important topics of the previously collected information while the correlational stage is matching the characteristics of the specific domain with existing heuristics. Then classified heuristics can be formed through keeping, adapting, creating and eliminating in the selection stage. The specification stage is using a standard template to specify the set of heuristics formally. Finally, the proposed set of heuristics should be validated through user testing or expert judgment in the validation stage. Finally, the set of proposed heuristics based on the feedback from the validation stage should be refined in the refinement stage.

3 Defining Usability Heuristics for the Hearing Impaired Language Training Mobile App

3.1 Exploratory Stage

Actually, the amount of information on usability tests and usability heuristic for people with hearing impairments is scarce and there are even fewer language training applications for the hearing impaired. Except for researching the existing heuristics for the hearing impaired language training application and features of those applications, the systematic review was also addressed domains such as E-learning, the user experience of deaf people (include children). Therefore, we listed the relevant articles in Table 1 and selected heuristics from those articles in Table 2.

Table 1. Selected studies

ID	Authors	Year	Title
S1	Debevc, Stjepanovič et al. [11]	2007	Accessible and adaptive e-learning materials: considerations for design and development
S2	Yeratziotis and Zaphiris [8]	2018	A Heuristic Evaluation for Deaf Web User Experience (HE4DWUX)
S3	Siebra, Gouveia et al. [12]	2017	Toward accessibility with usability: understanding the requirements of impaired uses in the mobile context
S4	Alroobaea [13]	2017	Developing Specific Usability Heuristics for Evaluating the Android Applications
S5	Leporini and Buzzi [14]	2007	Learning by e-learning: breaking down barriers and creating opportunities for the visually-impaired
S6	AlShammari, Alsumait et al. [15]	2018	Building an Interactive E-Learning Tool for Deaf Children: Interaction Design Process Framework
S7	Alsumait and Al-Osaimi [5]	2009	Usability heuristics evaluation for child e-learning applications
S8	Schefer, Areão et al. [16]	2018	Guidelines for Developing Social Networking Mobile Apps to Deaf Audience: a Proposal Based on User experience and Technical Issues
S9	Di Mascio, Gennari et al. [17]	2013	Designing games for deaf children: first guidelines
S10	Yeratziotis [18]	2012	Guidelines for the Design of a Mobile Phone Application for Deaf People
S11	Mutalib and Maarof [9]	2010	Guidelines of assistive courseware (AC) for hearing impaired students
S12	Namatame, Kitajima et al. [19]	2004	A preparatory study for designing web-based educational materials for the hearing-impaired
S13	Mohid and Zin [20]	2010	Courseware accessibility for hearing impaired
S14	Nathan, Hussain et al. [21]	2016	Deaf mobile application accessibility requirements
S15	Mohid and Zin [22]	2011	Accessible courseware for kids with hearing impaired ('MudahKiu'): A preliminary analysis

Table 2. Selected heuristics (extract)

ID	Heuristics
S1	Provide alternative ways to all sonorous content of applications, such as caption or transcriptions in Sign Language (preferential)
	Video subtitles
	Captions
	Prepare captions in all multimedia presentations
	Interactive, motivating, use of captions
	Provide equivalent alternatives to auditory and visual content
	Attach the synchronized caption for hearing-impaired people in the case of audio material, video material, and multimedia material
	Provide captions with all multimedia presentations support the Windows Show Sounds feature that allows a user to assign a visual signal and caption for each audio event
S2	Visibility of status and actions
	Match between website and the deaf world
	User control and freedom
	Consistency and standards
	Flexibility and efficiency of use
	Aesthetic and minimalist design
	Deaf skills
	Pleasurable and respectful interaction
	Privacy
	Sign language video content
	Captions

3.2   Experimental Stage

A survey about the usage of language training app for the hearing loss was sent and 135 responses were obtained. The survey was about problems the hearing impaired found when they were using the language training app. Also, we did an interview with 5 users who keeps doing listening and voice training through mobile apps. The interview was about how they use the app to help them do the training and the usability issues they found.

Through the survey and interview, we knew that not many people know language training apps designed for the hearing impaired and it is usually very hard for the hearing impaired to insist training since those apps are not very well designed. Some popular apps for the hearing impaired training are Angel Sound, Voibook and Learn Putonghua. With the obtained feedback and ideas, we can know that there is a lot of room for improvement. Those usability problems are concluded and listed as follows:

– They hope they can have training like English tests to improve the training efficiency.
– Keep practicing is kind boring.
– They think some apps just did simple follow-up training.

- They don't know how to improve their pronunciation after the voice training.
- They don't know how they pronounce when they were doing the training.
- There is no pinyin in some apps (pinyin is the romanization of the Chinese characters based on their pronunciation.).
- They hope they can repeat listening if they want.

3.3 Descriptive Stage

We analyzed, grouped and classified the information collected from previous studies. Problems or heuristics related to totally deaf people were discarded because deaf people can't receive audible feedback, then it means it's almost impossible for them to learn how to listen and speak. That's also the reason sign language exist. Therefore, our main focus are on the people who can get audible feedback whatever through the hearing aid or the cochlear implant surgery. Finally, a total of 21 heuristics were obtained. In Table 3 is listed those heuristics

Table 3. Heuristics identified in similar domains

No.	Heuristics
1	Prepare all audio information in visual form (images, text or sign language)
2	Provide linear and intuitive navigation
3	Easy reading content and minimalist design
4	Provide vibration alerts to applications notifications
5	Provide assistance to find content and guide users through the system
6	Inform the hearing impaired of the success or failure of an operation immediately
7	Provide coverage of uses errors and suggestions about their corrections
8	Provide users with control over the training (pause, skip, repeat)
9	Provide training status guide to track users' progress
10	Explorable interfaces
11	Avoid limits of time control to users' reading or interaction
12	Encouragement
13	Users should learn all the status
14	Exit signs are visible
15	Flexibility to customize the app as per user needs
16	The program is designed to speed up interactions for the expert hearing-impaired, but also to cater to the needs of the inexperienced hearing impaired.
17	Training objectives should be balanced with multiple ways to train
18	The program provides the instructor with the evaluation and tracking reports
19	The application is paced to apply pressure but not frustrate the hearing impaired
20	The user-driven content management system (such as edit/delete, or liked/marked content) should facilitate the user
21	All the training materials should be added pinyin (for text) or captions (for video)

3.4   Correlational Stage

In this stage, those problems identified from the survey and interview are matched to the heuristics we concluded. In Table 4, we can see the specific heuristics that address certain problems.

Table 4. Matches among identified problems and the existing heuristics

No.	Problem	Heuristics
1	They hope they can have training like English tests to improve the training efficiency.	Training objectives should be balanced with multiple ways to train
6	Keep practicing is kind boring	Multimedia representations assist the training process. (game, video, text, pictures, sign language)
2	They think some apps just did simple follow-up training	
3	They don't know how to improve their pronunciation after following the voice training	Provide users suggestions for improvement
4	They don't know how they pronounce when they were doing the training.	Users can record their pronunciation and listen
5	There is no pinyin in some apps	All the training materials should be added pinyin (for text) or captions (for video)
7	They hope they can repeat listening if they want	Provide the hearing impaired with control over the operations (pause, skip, repeat)

3.5   Selection Stage

Then the heuristics set with reference to Nielsen's 10 usability heuristics were started to create. According to the user tests, "Exit signs are visible" was deleted and "Users can record their pronunciation and listen", "Provide users right and wrong answers to compare and learn", "Provide users suggestions for improvement" were added to the heuristics set.

4   A Set of Usability Heuristics for the Hearing Impaired Language Training Mobile App

As a result, the first version of heuristics for the hearing impaired training app was concluded. The heuristics was named HHITA due to its acronyms "Heuristics for the Hearing Impaired Training APP". We described each proposed heuristics in a formal way in Table 5:

Table 5. The first version of heuristics for the hearing impaired training app

ID	Heuristics	Definition
HHITA01	Prepare all audio information in visual form	Audio content should be replaced with images, text or sign language where relevant to suit mobile space in the system
HHITA02	Minimalist design	The system should provide linear and intuitive navigation, easy reading content and contrast color
HHITA03	Provide vibration alerts to applications notifications	Notifications in the system should be issued in vibration
HHITA04	Provide assistance to guide users through the system	The system should help users to find contents they want
HHITA05	Tolerance for error	The system should provide coverage of use's errors and suggestions about corrections
HHITA06	User control and freedom	The system should provide users with control over the training, such as pausing, skipping and repeating. Users can also edit/delete or liked/marked content if they want
HHITA07	Provide training record	The system should provide training record to track users' progress. The training record is also for instructor to evaluate users
HHITA08	Multiple training ways	Training objectives should be balanced with multiple ways to train to encourage the explorative training process
HHITA09	No time limit training	The system should avoid limits of time control to users' reading or interaction
HHITA10	Encouragement	The system should provide games, punch card system or social media to encourage users insist training
HHITA11	Visibility of system status	Users should learn all status, the system can provide a double-high status bar to show the condition if it's necessary
HHITA12	Flexibility	Flexibility to customize the app as per user needs. The system is designed to speed up interactions for the expert hearing-impaired, but also cater to the needs of the inexperienced hearing impaired
HHITA13	Suitable Content	The system is paced to apply pressure but not frustrate the hearing impaired
HHITA14	Provide pinyin captions	All the training materials should be added pinyin (for text) or captions (for video)
HHITA15	Provide immediate feedback	The system should inform the hearing impaired of the success or failure of an operation immediately
HHITA16	Users can record their pronunciation	Users can record their pronunciation first, then listen and compare with the standard pronunciation in the system
HHITA17	Answer analysis	The system should provide users right and wrong answers to make users compare in order to learn it efficiently
HHITA18	Provide users suggestions for improvement	The system should provide users how they did the training and give users suggestions for improvement

5 Usability Heuristics for the Hearing Impaired Language Training Mobile App: Validation

5.1 Validation Stage

Six experts were recruited to evaluate the two selected apps using heuristics from the specification stage and the Nielsen's heuristics. One of the experts is the product manager of an app designed for hearing impaired and he is also a hearing impaired. Therefore, he is an expert in hearing-impaired products and usability problems. Four of the evaluators were master's degree holders in HCI who are familiar with heuristics evaluation. The other is a speech therapist who did a lot of rehabilitation training for the hearing impaired.

Language rehabilitation for the hearing impaired is mainly consisted of listening and speaking training, so we chose Angel Sound and Voibook as our evaluated applications. Angel Sound (see Fig. 1) is a PC-based interactive listening rehabilitation program developed by TigerSpeech Technology and freely distributed by a non-profit organization. It also has a mobile version and it's mainly focused on listening training for the hearing impaired. Voibook (see Fig. 2) is a barrier-free communication app designed for people with hearing disorders (hearing loss/deaf). One of the modules of Voibook applies for speaking training.

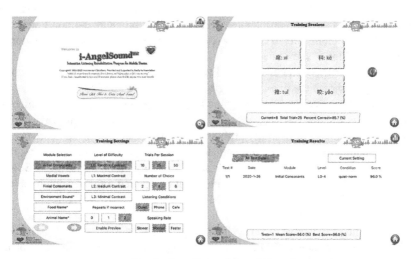

Fig. 1. Interfaces of Angel Sound

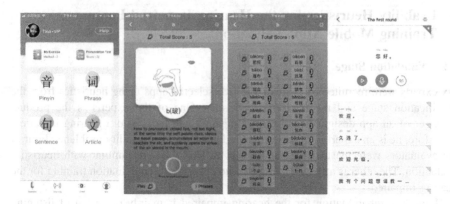

Fig. 2. Interfaces of Voibook

The experiment was carried out by two separate groups of evaluators, and there are three experts in each group. One group used the set of heuristics for the hearing impaired training app concluded from the specification stage, while the other group used Nielsen's heuristics.

Evaluators are asked to inspect the Angel Sound and Voibook's interface using the heuristics. The mismatch will be recorded if those evaluators felt there is a usability problem. Evaluators are also asked to give each problem a severity rating using a 5-point rating scale: 1-Cosmetic problem, 2-Minor usability problem, 3-I don't agree, 4-Major usability problem and 5-Usability catastrophe. We asked each evaluator to explain his/her ratings at the same time.

Table 6 presents the number of usability problems identified by each group of evaluators. It also shows the average severity of the usability problems.

We calculated the total number of problems found in the two apps using different heuristics and tracked the severity of each problem. Evaluators found 13 usability problems in Voibook and 12 usability problems in Angel Sound by using heuristics for the hearing impaired training app. For evaluators who use the Nielsen's heuristics, they only found 3 usability problems in Voibook and 7 usability problems in Angel Sound. Therefore, we can know the heuristics for the hearing impaired training app are able to identify more usability problems than the Nielsen's heuristics.

Moreover, the average severity for the heuristics for the hearing impaired training app is 4.37, while the average severity for the Nielsen's heuristics is 4.17. Hence it seems the usability problems identified by the group who used the heuristics for the hearing impaired training app were qualified as more severe.

Table 6. Usability problems identified in Voibook and Angel Sound

Group1: Using heuristics for the hearing impaired training app			Group2: Using Nielsen's heuristics		
ID	Number of problems	Average severity	ID	Number of problems	Average severity
HHITA1	1	3.83	H1	3	4
HHITA2	1	3.67	H2	0	4.17
HHITA3	2	4	H3	1	4.67
HHITA4	2	4.17	H4	1	4.33
HHITA5	1	4.33	H5	2	4.5
HHITA6	5	4	H6	0	3.83
HHITA7	1	4.5	H7	0	3.83
HHITA8	2	4.5	H8	1	3.16
HHITA9	1	4	H9	1	4.67
HHITA10	2	4.17	H10	1	4.5
HHITA11	1	3.67			
HHITA12	1	4.5			
HHITA13	0	4.83			
HHITA14	1	5			
HHITA15	0	4.67			
HHITA16	1	4.83			
HHITA17	1	5			
HHITA18	2	5			
Total	25		Total	10	
Average severity		4.370555556	Average severity		4.166

5.2 Refinement Stage

Finally, we gathered the usability problems (see Table 7) through the heuristics evaluation and proceeded to analyze them. According to opinions of experts and based on Nielsen's heuristics, the heuristics for the hearing impaired training app were developed.

For HHITA02, the meaning can be richen, such as the movement of elements on the interface should be suitable, the content on the interface shouldn't be too crowded and the notification should be noticeable. For HHITA09, the system should avoid limits of time control to users' reading or interaction in daily training, but for a test or a game, the system can set time limit to raise users' interest. For HHITA11, A double-high status bar might be unnecessary. For HHITA12, the system can provide users training contents according to their level in a smarter way. We can add HHITA19: Provide users enough time to understand the feedback.

Table 7. Usability problems in Voibook and Angel Sound

Voibook	Angel Sound
There is no vibration notification	There is no visual notification when playing the sounds
There is no button that can help users find what they want	The notification on the bottom is too small to see when they system is comparing the right and false answer
On the registration interface, the default of phone number is American number rather than Chinese phone number	There is no vibration notification
In the pinyin training part, users can't mark what they want to practice later	There is no assistance when training
There is no training record	Users can't go back to previous questions
The following-up training is kind boring	Users can't speed up training
There is time limit when testing the pronunciation	Users can't mark the question and practice later
There is no encouragement system	Multiple choices only
The training is not intelligent enough	There is no encouragement system
The article training part has no pinyin captions	There is no status shown
Users can't record their pronunciation	There is no suggestions for improvement
There is no training analysis	Time is not enough for users to learn the feedback provided by the system
There is no suggestions for improvement	The exit button is not clear
The feedback between pinyin part and other parts is different	

6 Formal Specification of the Usability Heuristics for the Hearing Impaired Language Training Mobile App

- HHITA01: Prepare all audio information in visual form
  Audio content should be replaced with images, text or sign language where relevant to suit mobile space in the system.
- HHITA02: Minimalist design
  The system should provide linear and intuitive navigation, easy reading content and contrast color. The movement of elements on the interface should be suitable. The content on the interface shouldn't be too crowded. The notification should be noticeable.
- HHITA03: Provide vibration alerts to applications notifications
  Notifications in the system should be issued in vibration.
- HHITA04: Provide assistance to guide users through the system
  The system should help users to find contents they want.
- HHITA05: Tolerance for error

The system should provide coverage of use's errors and suggestions about corrections.

- HHITA06: User control and freedom
  The system should provide users with control over the training, such as pausing, skipping and repeating. Users can also edit/delete or liked/marked content if they want.
- HHITA07: Provide training record
  The system should provide training record to track users' progress. The training record is also for instructor to evaluate users.
- HHITA08: Multiple training ways
  Training objectives should be balanced with multiple ways to train to encourage the explorative training process.
- HHITA09: No time limit training
  The system should avoid limits of time control to users' reading or interaction in daily training, but for a test or a game, the system can set time limit to raise users' interest.
- HHITA10: Encouragement
  The system should provide games, punch card system or social media to encourage users insist training.
- HHITA11: Visibility of system status
  Users should learn all the status.
- HHITA12: Flexibility
  Flexibility to customize the app as per user needs. The system is designed to speed up interactions for the expert hearing-impaired, but also cater to the needs of the inexperienced hearing impaired.
- HHITA13: Suitable Content
  The system is paced to apply pressure but not frustrate the hearing impaired.
- HHITA14: Provide pinyin captions
  All the training materials should be added pinyin (for text) or captions (for video).
- HHITA15: Provide immediate feedback
  The system should inform the hearing impaired of the success or failure of an operation immediately.
- HHITA16: Users can record their pronunciation
  Users can record their pronunciation first, then listen and compare with the standard pronunciation in the system.
- HHITA17: Training analysis
  The system should provide users right and wrong answers to make users compare in order to learn it efficiently.
- HHITA18: Provide users suggestions for improvement
  The system should provide users how they did the training and give users suggestions for improvement.
- HHITA19: Provide users enough time to understand the feedback.
  The system should provide users suitable feedback and give them time to understand.

7 Conclusions and Future Works

Mobile apps are very useful tools to help the hearing impaired do language training. Since the hearing-impaired interaction style is different from hearing people and the current use of guidelines for the hearing-impaired is seriously limited. Therefore, it's necessary to develop a set of specific usability heuristics.

In this study, a proposed set of 19 heuristics which cover the usability of language training apps designed for the hearing impaired are presented. Those heuristics can be used to evaluate the existed language training app and find usability problems. What's more, when designing language training apps for the hearing impaired, those heuristics can be used as guidelines.

The future direction of this research is to design a listening and speaking training app for the hearing impaired that covered the proposed heuristics. In addition, a user-centered usability test will be carried out to implement the heuristics.

Acknowledgments. The author would like to thank all the participants in the experiments such as the surveys, interviews and the case study.

References

1. Nielsen Norman Group. https://www.nngroup.com/articles/usability-101-introduction-to-usability. Accessed 03 Jan 2012
2. Nielsen, J.: Usability inspection methods. In: Conference Companion on Human Factors in Computing Systems, pp. 413–414. ACM, Boston (1994)
3. Nielsen, J.: Finding usability problems through heuristic evaluation. In: Proceedings of the SIGCHI Conference on Human Factors in Computing Systems, pp. 373–380. ACM, Monterey (1992)
4. Nielsen, J., Molich, R.: Heuristic evaluation of user interfaces. In: Proceedings of the SIGCHI Conference on Human Factors in Computing Systems, pp. 249–256. ACM, Seattle (1990)
5. Alsumait, A., Al-Osaimi, A.: Usability heuristics evaluation for child e-learning applications. In: Proceedings of the 11th International Conference on Information Integration and Web-Based Applications & Services, pp. 425–430. ACM, Kuala Lumpur (2009)
6. Desurvire, H., Wiberg, C.: Game usability heuristics (PLAY) for evaluating and designing better games: the next iteration. In: Ozok, A.A., Zaphiris, P. (eds.) OCSC 2009. LNCS, vol. 5621, pp. 557–566. Springer, Heidelberg (2009). https://doi.org/10.1007/978-3-642-02774-1_60
7. Inostroza, R., Rusu, C., Roncagliolo, S., Jimenez, C., Rusu, V.: Usability heuristics for touchscreen-based mobile devices. In: 2012 Ninth International Conference on Information Technology-New Generations, pp. 662–667. IEEE, Las Vegas (2012)
8. Yeratziotis, A., Zaphiris, P.: A heuristic evaluation for deaf web user experience (HE4DWUX). Int. J. Hum.-Comput. Interact. **34**(3), 195–217 (2018)
9. Mutalib, A.A., Maarof, F.: Guidelines of assistive courseware (AC) for hearing impaired students. In: KMICe 2010: Proceedings of the 5th Knowledge Management, pp. 186–191. Universiti Utara Malaysia, Kedah (2010)
10. Quiñones, D., Rusu, C.: How to develop usability heuristics: a systematic literature review. Comput. Stand. Interfaces **53**, 89–122 (2017)

11. Debevc, M., Stjepanovič, Z., Povalej, P., Verlič, M., Kokol, P.: Accessible and adaptive e-learning materials: considerations for design and development. In: Stephanidis, C. (ed.) UAHCI 2007. LNCS, vol. 4556, pp. 549–558. Springer, Heidelberg (2007). https://doi.org/10.1007/978-3-540-73283-9_61
12. Siebra, C., et al.: Toward accessibility with usability: understanding the requirements of impaired uses in the mobile context. In: Proceedings of the 11th International Conference on Ubiquitous Information Management and Communication, p. 6. ACM, Beppu (2017)
13. Alroobaea, R.: Developing specific usability heuristics for evaluating the android applications. In: Kim, K.J., Joukov, N. (eds.) ICMWT 2017. LNEE, vol. 425, pp. 139–147. Springer, Singapore (2018). https://doi.org/10.1007/978-981-10-5281-1_15
14. Leporini, B., Buzzi, M.: Learning by e-learning: breaking down barriers and creating opportunities for the visually-impaired. In: Stephanidis, C. (ed.) UAHCI 2007. LNCS, vol. 4556, pp. 687–696. Springer, Heidelberg (2007). https://doi.org/10.1007/978-3-540-73283-9_75
15. AlShammari, A., Alsumait, A., Faisal, M.: Building an interactive e-learning tool for deaf children: interaction design process framework. In: 2018 IEEE Conference on e-Learning, e-Management and e-Services (IC3e), pp. 85-90. IEEE, Langkawi Island (2018)
16. Schefer, R.P., Areão, A.S., Zaina, L.A.M.: Guidelines for developing social networking mobile apps to deaf audience: a proposal based on user experience and technical issues. In: Proceedings of the 17th Brazilian Symposium on Human Factors in Computing Systems, p. 26. ACM, Belém (2018)
17. Di Mascio, T., Gennari, R., Melonio, A., Vittorini, P.: Designing games for deaf children: first guidelines. Int. J. Technol. Enhanc. Learn. 5(3/4), 223–239 (2013)
18. Yeratziotis, G.: Guidelines for the Design of a Mobile Phone Application for Deaf People. Nelson Mandela Metropolitan University (2012)
19. Namatame, M., Kitajima, M., Nishioka, T., Fukamauchi, F.: A preparatory study for designing web-based educational materials for the hearing-impaired. In: Miesenberger, K., Klaus, J., Zagler, W.L., Burger, D. (eds.) ICCHP 2004. LNCS, vol. 3118, pp. 1144–1151. Springer, Heidelberg (2004). https://doi.org/10.1007/978-3-540-27817-7_168
20. Mohid, S.Z., Zin, N.A.M.: Courseware accessibility for hearing impaired. In: 2010 International Symposium on Information Technology, pp. 1–5. IEEE, Kuala Lumpur (2010)
21. Nathan, S.S., Hussain, A., Hashim, N.L.: Deaf mobile application accessibility requirements. In: AIP Conference Proceedings, vol. 1, p. 020098. AIP Publishing, Kedah (2016)
22. Mohid, S.Z., Zin, N.A.M.: Accessible courseware for kids with hearing impaired ('MudahKiu'): a preliminary analysis. In: 2011 International Conference on Pattern Analysis and Intelligence Robotics, pp. 197–202. IEEE, Putrajaya (2011)

Interaction Design and Information Visualization

Lifestyle as the Object of Design: Elements Exploration from Experience Perspective

Wa An[1(✉)], Xiangyang Xin[2], Xiong Ding[1], and Yi Liu[1]

[1] Guangzhou Academy of Fine Arts, Guangzhou 510006, China
anwa_design@163.com
[2] XXY Innovation, Wuxi 214000, China

Abstract. A good lifestyle has a close relationship with people's health and well-being. Research on lifestyle is always playing an important in philosophy, sociology, economics and other subjects. As people entering into the age of information, many products and services that change people's lifestyle have emerged. If people's lifestyle can be guided and changed, then what elements should lifestyle have as design's objective? This research taking design thinking as a tool and from the perspective of experience, have concluded four elements of lifestyle through qualitative research, which are: behavior (motivation, behaviors' changing and behavior's habits); rhythm (intensity, repetitiveness and duration); relationship (strong and weak relationship, role relationship); and meaning (intentional meaning and accidental meaning). Dealing with lifestyle as an object of design could begin with these four elements.

Keywords: Lifestyle · Experience · Behavior · Design

1 Lifestyle to Be the Object of Design

For a long time, lifestyle has been an important research object in philosophy, sociology, economics and other fields, demonstrating the importance of life style research to social development. In the German ideology, Marx and Engels considered the establishment of free life as the development goal of human society, and proposed that the development process of human society is "the production process of life" [1]. In addition to viewing lifestyle as a manifestation of social development, there are also a number of studies linking lifestyle to human health. The world health organization (WHO) has noted that "the greatest threat to humanity in the 21st century is lifestyle disease." In 1948, the world health organization proposed the definition of health as: "Health is not only the absence of disease and infirmity, but also the maintenance of physical, psychological and social adaptation in all its aspects" [2]. In fact, social adaptation refers to people's ability and coping methods to deal with various complicated things in life, including how to deal with interpersonal relations, how to face difficulties and challenges, and how to change bad living habits, reflected in the exploration of life experience and life quality.

The rapid development of information technology, big data computing and artificial intelligence has brought new experiences and unlimited imagination to lifestyle. Under such a technological background, how to use information technology to create a better way of lifestyle has become a problem that many enterprises are discussing in recent years. The appearance of iPhone has not only changed the interaction between people and mobile phones, but also redefined the concept of "mobile phone". Mobile phone has changed from a product with communication function to a comprehensive life service terminal satisfying people's social life, shopping life, entertainment experience and other behavioral activities.

WeChat, emerged in 2011, has become the largest and most comprehensive platform to communicate, socialize and find life-assisting tools in China. Intelligent household life also provides users with a new lifestyle. The user can control appliances by various sensors (e.g., TV, refrigerator, air conditioning, lights, curtains, etc.). These products even can teach themselves to learn users' habits and provide a better user experience at the right time and context.

It is easy to say that the content of design has expanded from meeting personalized needs to social ones, from single service to comprehensive ones. The designed objects deal with non-material things which are much more complicated and comprehensive and relating to life, including emotion, behavior, relationship, experience and meaning. As the emergence of products and services change people's lifestyle, then whether lifestyle could be the object of design?

Herbert Simon, a famous social scientist made a clear definition in The Science of the Artificial: "Design is when people spare no effort in changing the current situation into their expectation" [3]. He realized that people are always walking from the current situation to a much satisfied future, and he also admitted that design is the way for people to achieve that goal. Richard Buchanan has proposed a 'Four orders of design' [4], and he believed that design has transformed from product design, graphic design and environment design to another dimension, including symbols, things, behaviors and meaning. The aim of design is shown in how to embed meaning into technology in the modern society, resulting in a reasonable lifestyle and value. Carnegie Mellon University has mentioned Transition Design since 2014, which claimed that design should focus on the changes of life and a more sustainable development of society. Design could affect lifestyle and guide it. In other words, lifestyle has already become an object of design.

2   The Research of Different Disciplines on Lifestyle

Scholars in sociology, economics, literature, drama, rhetoric and other disciplines have all made different comments on lifestyle from different perspectives (see Fig. 1), such as the interaction between individuals and society, class and status, lifestyle and consumption behavior, human experience, life happiness and so on.

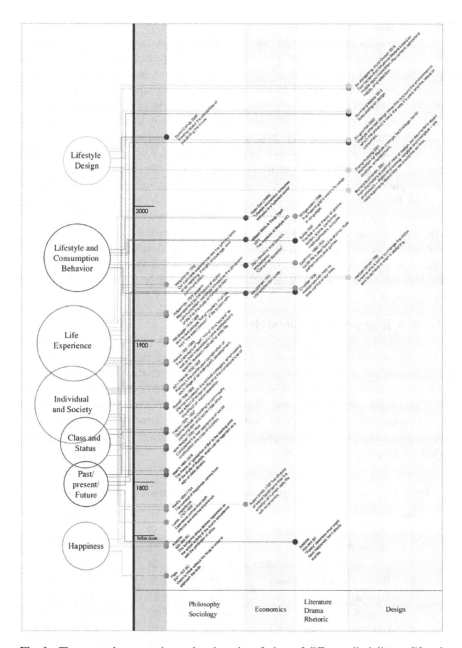

Fig. 1. The research perspective and main point of view of different discipline to lifestyle.

Plato [5] and Aristotle [6] used to propose the philosophic thinking related to lifestyle and happiness. The sociologists in the early times considered lifestyle as a measurement of class and status. "Lifestyle"- this word was firstly created by Max Weber, a famous Germany sociologist and philosopher. Weber mentioned the idea of lifestyle in Class, Status, and Power and he thought lifestyle can help people distinguish a certain class of people from others [7]. Philosophers such as Dewey [8], Mead [9] mentioned that people's experience and meaning appeared during the interaction between people and society. People's lifestyle is not alone, and it will be affected by social environment. When people establish the society, they are building their own life. Schutz, Habermas [10] and other people took the perspective of behavior, admitting the fact that individual's behaviors will affect society, and they thought people's actions and social environment are closely related to and reinforced each other.

Western economists always study lifestyle and the way of consumption together. Weber and Veblen studied lifestyle from the perspective of consumption. Economists study lifestyle on three aspects: 1. Classify the market through lifestyle; 2. How lifestyle affect behaviors of consumers; and 3. the research on certain group of people's lifestyle.

Although sociology and economics focused on lifestyle for a long time, most of them consider lifestyle as an influencing factor of social development and consuming behaviors, or study in the context of lifestyle. There is few design method or theory which consider lifestyle as the object of design in its subject.

3   Design Research on Lifestyle

The research on lifestyle design started from 1980s, and the number of researches became to increase after 21st century and have achieved certain results gradually. The number of researching institutions on lifestyle amounted to 572 units between 2003 and 2007. Table 1 has presented the top 10 researching institutions. What's more, developed countries and those with well welfare focus much more on the research on lifestyle. The first Chinese researching institution on lifestyle is The Hong Kong Polytechnic University, ranking 60.

Table 1. Distribution of lifestyle design research institutions from 1991 to 2017.

No.	Institution	Country	Number	Percentage
1	University of Amsterdam	Holland	33	2.277
2	Maastricht University	Holland	32	2.208
3	University of South Carolina	United States	28	1.932
4	University of Queensland	Australia	25	1.725
5	Karolinska Institute	Sweden	22	1.518
6	Monash University	Australia	22	1.518
7	University of Sydney	Australia	22	1.518
8	University of Melbourne	Australia	20	1.380
9	Newcastle University	United Kingdom	20	1.380
10	Lander University	Sweden	19	1.311

In design study, there has no powerful theoretical studying system, method and model been formed on this object. In China, the author searched "lifestyle and design" in journals, doctoral dissertation, master's thesis, Chinese conferences, international conferences, newspaper and yearbook from CNKI, 4162 articles related to "lifestyle" and "design" are found. Most of these researches consider lifestyle as the context of design or conduct researches on targeted people. The researches on lifestyle mostly concentrate in healthcare, social development, economic development, city construction and other areas, which regards lifestyle as the object of design is few.

4 The Exploration of Elements of Lifestyle

Scholars from different disciplines have proposed the elements of lifestyle from their own perspectives. A western scholar Mead thought people's life is the meaning system composed by people's intention, social interactivity, environment and behaviors these four elements [9]. David Popenoe has mentioned in Sociology that social life comprises non-individual factors and individualized factors [11]. Non-individual factors including physical environment, culture, society, economy, technology, population and others. Physical environment refers to natural one and artificial one. Individual factors refer to people's physiology, psychology and educational background.

4.1 Research Perspective

Lifestyle research, it is difficult to summarize the general law through big data because of the diversity and complexity of life itself. The motivations, decisions, emotions and experiences of people in different life situations are all affected by complex internal and external factors, and the answer cannot be obtained through conventional calculation formulas. As behavioral economist Richard H. Thaler has realized that the economic behavior of people are not always rational, he combined the human psychology and economics research, pay close attention to a lot of real life cases in people's daily life, from man's behavior, emotions, and even some "wrong" behavior of people's consumption behaviors to find out Law of consumption behavior [12], the study won the 2017 Nobel Prize in economics. The author believes that lifestyle-oriented research, like Richard thaler's economic research, the research and design should focus on life itself and the different behaviors and experiences of people in life situations. Therefore, this scientific research method is different from the quantitative research based on big data.

This research takes the perspective from "Experience" and explore the elements of lifestyle through "Inquiry" (questionnaire and in-dept interviews). Inquiry is a process to research on something that is vaguely-targeted, lacking clear meaning and influence. Words such as 'uncertain, unsolved, confused' are usually used to describe these things [13]. Inquiry means reclassifying things which are unclear and complicated (through finding the linkages among different things), then concluding a new package of perspective to view and understand things.

Dewey has mentioned in Art as Experience that human experience emerges from the interconnection between people's mindset and physical things, or subjective and objective things [8]. Experience transferred the focus from the way of designing life to the meaning of designing the life. Professor Xiangyang Xin mentioned in his speech titled "from UX to EX" that "Experience not just as principles, but also as pathways that guide choices and purposes of our lives" [14]. Experience is not only a principle, but also a way to guide people's choices and goals of life. In his speech, he also talked about "Experience shifts attention from designing means for living to designing meanings of lives" [14]. During the interaction between people and the world, the "experience" and "meaning" appeared. Experience is a social interaction, affecting our attitudes and behaviors towards things, and influence the cognitive meaning of things. People constantly change their relationship between themselves and society during the experiences, and creating their own meaning at the same time.

4.2 Research Analysis

Through online questionnaire, we get ideas of people's recognition, attitude, perspective and expectation towards lifestyle, then analyzing the reasons and influencing factors and forming system of users' lifestyle. Questionnaire mainly focus on two core problems: 1. The elements of lifestyle; 2. The influencing factors of lifestyle's formation. This research has received 179 effective questionnaires. Among the interviewees, 44.5% of them are male, and 55.5% of them are female. In terms of age, 33% of them were born after 1980, 50.4% of them were born after 1990. As for educational background, 60.5% of them are bachelors, 26.1% of them are masters, and 6.7% of them are doctors or acquire much higher degree. From the perspective of job, 21.2% of them are government officials, public servants, and business managers. 16.1% of them are professionals, such as doctor and teacher. 27.9% of them are white-or blue-collars. 28% of them are students. In terms of income, 36.1% of them earn less than 5000, 27.7% of them ear between 5000 and 10000, 23.5% of them ear between 10000 and 20000, only 6.5% of them ear more than 30000. From the result of these date, it can be concluded that the participants of questionnaire cover all age groups, and the average degree is bachelor or higher, and most of them are middle-incomers.

The research has acquired nearly 800 pieces of vocabulary from questionnaire, including noun, verb, adjective; words describing the status quo and expectation. Through classification, only 237 pieces are left after combing words which have similar or the same meaning. Getting rid of the vocabulary which are different in meaning and appeared only once, the left vocabulary appeared between 2 to 5 times. Putting these vocabularies into two dimensions (see Fig. 2): individual's internal side and social environment; long-term stability and short-term updates, analyze unique features and patterns in different quadrants.

Fig. 2. Word frequency analyze of lifestyle description.

4.3 Four Elements of Lifestyle

With questionnaire and interviews into consideration, through classification and relevance analysis, we concluded the elements of lifestyle as (see Fig. 3): 1. Behaviors, including motivation, changes of behaviors and habits of behaviors. 2. rhythm, including intensity, repetition and duration. 3. relationship, including strong and weak relationship as well as roles. 4. Meaning, including intentional meaning and accidental meaning. These four elements can be considered as objects of design and can function as influencing factors of lifestyle.

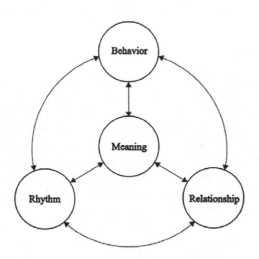

Fig. 3. The four elements of lifestyle.

First Element: Behavior. Lifestyle refers to behaviors transformed from an unstable condition to a long-term and stable one and back to unstable one again. It is a cycling process. When a short-term behavior has developed into a long-term one, we can regard it has formed a lifestyle. The exploration on behaviors is always highly connected with people's recognition, attitude, willingness, ability and other abilities. Behaviors can be considered as the direct response to all kinds of things when people stay in certain environment. Thus, the research on lifestyle is a research on people's behavioral pattern.

The author concluded three sub-elements of lifestyle: motivation, changes of behaviors and habits of behaviors. The following Table 2 gives an explanation of these three sub-elements. Motivation is the early stage when we do everything. Motivation included internal and external ones. If a motivation did not persist, it may be a condition at that moment. The changes of behaviors base on the motivation, and it is a process to find an alternative behavior for a habitual one. The form of habits of behavior requires motivation and changes of behaviors. Attitudes and determination are the main reasons to form habits.

Table 2. Sub-elements of behaviors and explanation.

Sub-element		Explanation
Motivation	Internal motivation	The choices of behaviors are totally motivated by self-determination
	External motivation	The trigger of behaviors is accompanied by the motivation of pressure, such as encouragement, and stimulus factors
Change of behaviors	Habitual behaviors	Previous habits of behaviors
	Alternative behaviors	A new behavior to replace the previous one
Habits	Attitude	The reason why people can have certain behaviors is that this behavior has already become a normal idea
	Determination	It is the internal motivation to transform the short-term behavior to a long-term one

Second Element: Rhythm. Everyone has their own pace of life. Something happens once but has a far-reaching influence (a trip to Disney, for example, can be unforgettable); Something happens every day (such as eating, sleeping, etc.) but their presence seems can't be felt. The study of rhythm often combined with "emotion" and "experience", just as time passes quickly in happy moments while slowly in rough patch. In Having an Experience, John Dewey described the emotional, continuity, purpose, completeness and ideological characteristics of experience [8]. The elements of experience has mentioned in Making Meaning, they are duration, intensity, breadth, interaction, triggers and significance.

We combined the elements related to time and rhythm proposed by Michelle Berryman, the design director from THINK Interactive-a U.S. company, with the observation on interviews, Table 3 has concluded the sub-elements of life rhythm into: intensity, duration and repetition.

Table 3. Sub-elements of rhythm and explanation.

Sub-element	Explanation
Intensity	Refers to the effect of a thing on people, including emotion, ability, value and other aspects
Duration	Refers to how long a behavior has continued, or how long it has lasted, and the influence of this experience on people
Repetition	Refers to the repetitive appearance of one behavior. From the perspective of motivation, repetition can be divided into self-repetition and external-inferred repetition

Third Element: Relationship. The interaction of human society is a process of adjusting oneself to the external environment. People can not avoid having relationship with different people, things and item to some extent. The sociologist Liz Spencer and Ray Pahl used "strong and weak relationship" to present the level of interpersonal relationship [15]. We always believe that people or things that are in strong relationship may affect our life dramatically, and strong relationship can bring more results that meet our expectations and interests. However, weak relationship also plays an important role in life. In 1973, The Strength of Weak Ties, a paper published by Dr. Mark Granovetter of Harvard University, proposed that Weak Ties have great potential in connecting communities and creating trust and connection between strangers [16]. One respondent mentioned that "Go to watch the movie or not, it decided on the comments on my WeChat moments. If three of my friends think it is good, I will go to the cinema". It proves that people can gain more knowledge, expand social network, and obtain the reference for decision-making, etc. Weak relationship can much more easily and usually bring the experience and surprises out of expectation.

Table 4. Sub-elements of relationship and explanation.

Sub-element		Explanation
Strong & weak relationship	Strong relationship	Refers to people or things that are highly related to one's life
	Weak relationship	Refers to people who are seldom connected or things which are hardly used. In terms of emotion or the frequency, they are not so close as in strong relationship.
Role's relationship		People have to define their own role in the interaction of human society

In our daily life, we can figure out the relationship not only from strong or weak relationship but also from individuals and society. Dewey once said: "People are not born to be human, but through social life. People can only define their roles from the interaction with society. In this way, the process that people establish their own life-style is the one that identify the relationship with other people." Table 4 concludes "strong and weak relationship" as well as "role relationship" as sub-elements of relationship.

Forth Element: Meaning. Meaning is the original motivation of behavior, the belief for people to insist on one thing and the reason to live. Meaning guides the direction and methods of life. Dewey has proposed in Experience and Nature that meaning is the aim, and it is a thing that people want to achieve.

The meaning of life has the same meaning in rhetoric, both can be generated in the specific circumstances of life. In rhetoric, it is believed that the material world is meaningless but people use rhetorical "language" to give meaning. Wittgenstein, an Austrian philosopher, put forward the theory of "use determines meaning" from the perspective of language in his "language game". His famous definition "the meaning of a word is its use in language" [17]. Meaning in specific context, is located in the form of life, is the meaning of interaction gives people's life. For example, a chair itself doesn't make sense, but if it's the chair you sat on when you met your boyfriend first time, it has a special meaning for you. Therefore, the meaning of the same product is not the same all the time, but will change with different situations (such as who uses it, how to use it, and the experience of using it).

In design, we always say we need to satisfy users' demand, which are the source of meaning. Meaning refers to everything that people think are valuable in their life and in line with their value as well as interest. Not all meanings meet the expectation of people. The emergence of some meaning may be accidently and out of expectation. Thus, Table 5 concludes the sub-elements of meaning into intentional meaning and accidental meaning.

Table 5. Sub-elements of meaning and explanation.

Sub-element	Explanation
Intentional meaning	Users' demand or aim, referring to meaning that meet people's original expectation and dreams. It has a close relationship with people's past history and value
Accidental meaning	Meaning which are accidental and out of expectation

Evaluate the Four Elements. The case study method is widely used in sociology, anthropology, management and other fields, especially in constructing new theories or verifying existing theories [18]. Typical case study is one of the commonly used methods in modern design research [19]. In case studies, many scholars advocate "typical case studies" as the center to carry out detailed exploration, description and explanation of the case [20].

In the survey, respondents believed that software have the greatest impact on life-style, such as WeChat, Alipay, takeaway software and Taobao. Some respondents mentioned that physical products, such as smartphones and high-speed trains had also brought important changes to lifestyle.

Richard Buchanan has mentioned in Philosophy and Rhetoric that is a product can successfully lead us to form a certain lifestyle, it proves that the designer of this product has stroke a balance among usefulness, possibility of using and willingness to use [21].

This research take "WeChat" as a classic example by using literature researching method, interviews and questionnaire to explore the specific design methods of WeChat on four elements of lifestyle. The research has interviewed 25 WeChat users. The content is considered from the following three aspects: What problems does WeChat as a tool solve in daily life and how to solve them? How WeChat as a creative product affect lifestyle through good design and user experience? What changes does WeChat bring to its users? Author has concluded all 25 pieces of questionnaire and classified and analyzed them centering on four core problems: the motivation to use WeChat, the reason for continued use, the changes of lifestyle because of WeChat and the meaning brought by it. Finally, we concluded the influence of WeChat on lifestyle as following part (see Fig. 4): 1. It changes behaviors such as socialize, work and payment through combining all sorts of services. 2. helps it users to establish and develop a new social network and becomes an important tool to maintain daily rela-tionship. 3. It changes the rhythm of life and has effects on life efficiency and emotion. 4. Users have gained a new life meaning through using WeChat.

It is easy to see this research has proved the four elements of lifestyle by WeChat through studying people's specific behaviors and situations for using WeChat. WeChat, through providing integrated life services has changed people's behaviors and life pace. Thus, it can help people to build new relationship between people and people as well as people and business, also bring new meaning to people.

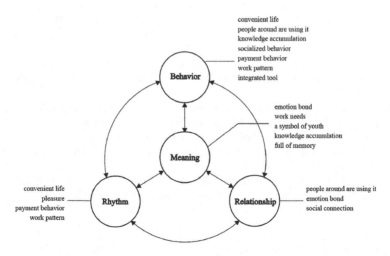

Fig. 4. The conclusion of elements for participants to use WeChat.

5 Conclusion

The age of experience economy brings many changes to people's life, and it also raises some new requirement to designers. This thesis studies at the lifestyle, using questionnaire and interviews, rearranging the elements of lifestyle: motivation, rhythm, relationship and meaning. Meaning is the core of all elements, and no natter behaviors, relationship or rhythm are motivated and guided by meaning. The changes of behaviors are always accompanied by the changes of relationship and rhythm. The changes of relationship will affect people's behaviors and rhythm. And the changes of rhythm are coupled with changes in behaviors, relationship and meaning. In a nutshell, behaviors, rhythm, relationship and meaning can be influencing factors of the formation and changes of lifestyle, at the same time, they can be the objects of design.

Acknowledgements. This research is supported by the National Social Science Fund of China (18CG201), Innovation Talents Project of Guangdong Ordinary University "Young Innovation Talents Project" (2016WQNCX072), and University-level Project of Guangzhou Academy of Fine Arts (18XJA021).

References

1. Sun, Y.L.: The discovery of life and the formation of historical materialism-the study of German ideology. Fudan University Press, Shanghai (2011)
2. WHO.: Constitution of the world health organization. WHO, Geneva (1948)
3. Simon, H.A.: The sciences of the artificial, 3rd edn. MIT Press, Cambridge (1996)
4. Buchanan, R.: Branzi's dilemma: design in contemporary culture. Des. Issues **14**(1), 3–20 (1998)
5. Plato: Plato Complete Works. People's Publishing House, Beijing (2002)
6. Aristotle: Poetics. The Commercial Press, Beijing (1999)
7. Sobel, M.E.: Lifestyle and Social Structure. Academic Press Inc., New York (1981)
8. Dewey, J.: Art as Experience. Capricorn Books, New York (1939)
9. Mead, G.H.: Mind Self and Society. University of Chicago, Chicago (1992)
10. Habermas, J.: The theory of communication action. In: System and Lifeworld: A Critique of Functionalist Reason, vol. 2, p. 126. Beacon Press, Boston (1987)
11. David, P.: Sociology, 10th edn. Beijing Renmin University of China Press, Beijing (1999)
12. Thaler, R.H.: Misbehaving: The Making of Behavioral Economic. China CITIC Press, Beijing (2017)
13. Dewey, J.: Logic: The Theory of Inquiry. Saerchinger Press, New York (2008)
14. Xin, X.Y.: From UX to EX. China Interaction design conference speech record. http://shijue.me/show_text/53ccda95e744f946c4038014. Accessed 22 Aug 2018
15. Adams, P.: Grouped: How Small Groups of Friends Are the Key to Influence on the Social Web. New Riders, Berkeley (2011)
16. Granovetter, M.S.: The strength of weak ties. Am. J. Sociol. **78**(6), 1360–1380 (1973)
17. Wittgenstein: Philosophical Studies. Sanlian Bookstore, Beijing (1988)

18. Eisenhardt, K.M.: Building theories from case study research. Acad. Manag. Rev. **14**(4), 532–550 (1989)
19. Wang, J.H.: Case studies and their relevant academic specifications. J. Tongji Univ.: Soc. Sci. Ed. **18**(3), 87 (2007)
20. Ouyang, P.B.: Case study of business administration. Manag. Rev. **7**(2), 100–105 (2004)
21. Buchanan, R.: Design and the new rhetoric: productive arts in the philosophy of culture. Philos. Rhetoric **34**(3), 183–206 (2001)

Embodied Cognition and Tactile Interaction: A Review on How Multi-sensorimotor Experiences Assisted by 3D Printing Can Shape the General Perception of Daily Activities

Vinicius Castilho[1], Diogo Henriques[2(✉)], Walter Correia[2], Lucas de Melo Souza[1], and Silvio de Barros Melo[2]

[1] Laca2i, Department of Design, UFPE, Recife, Brazil
{vckp,lms12}@cin.ufpe.br
[2] CORE, Center of Informatics, UFPE, Recife, Brazil
{dbbh,sbm}@cin.ufpe.br, ergnonomia@me.com

Abstract. Embodied cognition is a theory that grounds the idea that the many aspects of human cognition are influenced by the combination of experiences in the physical world, including tactile interaction with daily use products and physical interfaces, and the direct influence of the sensorimotor system over the mind itself.

As 3D printing is known as a strategic tool by allowing the creation of customizable user/activity oriented objects which are shown to be more emotional (and experience) directed rather than just utilitary or operational, showing a crescent demand of a user-driven approach of design methodologies.

Improvements in 3D Printing manufacturing and material science allow the development of novel breakthrough designs and surfaces that show emergent potential use in exploratory learning through new tactile perceptions, thus providing more complex user experiences (UX) for human-object interaction. This article reviews how the many 3D Printing applications over the last decade can be responsible for recreating daily interactions and experiences revealing new design opportunities in a parallel with human cognition and perception during the use of 3D printed objects.

Keywords: Embodied cognition · 3D printing · UX

1 Introduction

An analysis of each feature implementation during the whole product design workflow can show a major concern of the designers on how multiple aspects such as shape, grasp, material and texture can directly influence the user's decision process and experience during the use of a determined product. The ergonomics

© Springer Nature Switzerland AG 2020
A. Marcus and E. Rosenzweig (Eds.): HCII 2020, LNCS 12200, pp. 324–338, 2020.
https://doi.org/10.1007/978-3-030-49713-2_23

science provides several valuable data that can assist those designers to develop artifacts that friendly meet the user's expectations and needs by optimizing the user-product interface. Obtaining more realistic interactions between user and prototypes can be crucial in the product development chain by showing if there are any issues that escaped the conceptual and evaluation phases to be corrected before giving continuity to the production chain.

In the current state of the industry, the development of rapid prototyping technologies such as Additive Manufacturing is ever more allowing the manufacturing of parts with a high level of detail with lower manufacturing time and cost. This advance is possible thanks to scanning technologies, parametric modelling software, and more sophisticated 3D printers. Nowadays, the 3D printing machinery is not only built to prototype simple objects, but there is a concern in being ready-to-use by producing parts with high-fidelity and optimal mechanical resistance such as assemble-ready industrial pieces and reproductions of human body parts that are used for recovery surgeries and organ replacing.

By allowing the possibility of generating such complex artifacts, the additive manufacturing technologies show great potential in being used as a tool to instigate the human sensory system due to volumetric representations that can simulate tactile interactions in the most diverse cases of application such as artifact representations for visually impaired users or new forms of customizing daily use objects such as a spoon, for example. Following to attend these necessities, 3D printing machines must be able to reproduce different kinds of materials, textures and even physical and structural behavior that can be applied to the variety of activities users can perform in their daily routine.

Knowing about the relevance that the interaction with daily objects can perform through user experience, it is primal to gather an understanding about the concepts of sensorial patterns that impose different stimulus on their cognitive system shaping the perception of these types of activities. For cognition scholars the perception consists in an action guided by cognitive structures which emerge from sensorimotor patterns in the body-ambient relation. Such structures are not represented, but embedded in an action that derives from an incorporation of the user's body structure to the ambient, which originates informational properties (affordances) and opportunities for possible future actions. Being so, the way things are perceived is shaped by how people can really act upon them through a manipulation interaction.

Embodied Cognition (EC) is a study of the intelligent behavior through the analysis of the user's body interaction linked with the ambient or artifact in a two-way manner (reciprocity). The main premise of the idea is based on the fact that the brain, part of a body, is able to perceive a variety of sensations through the many sensorial agents such as sensory epithelial cells receipts, sensory organs and others.

This type of approach can be perceived in daily activities where users can learn through their personal experiences how to create criteria that will direct them on their actions on determined ambients or tasks where the body has the major relevance despite of mental representations. Experiments under

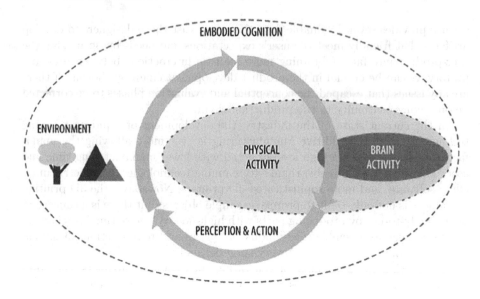

Fig. 1. A model for embodied cognition [7].

embodied cognition no longer evaluate simply input and output data as parameters to achieve an optimal experience while interacting with interfaces. Modern technology has taken a significant shift towards becoming more immersive, wearable gestural and collaborative and so the science must follow these advances. Under this category, user experience should be considered encompassing freehands movement and gestures, eye tracking, wearables, physical conduits operating in six degrees of freedom and interactive environments (Fig. 1).

This paper approaches tangible interfaces and cognitive science to frame a review on how embodied cognition relates to the use of 3D printed objects during different types of activities. The sections of this survey gather scientific publications that maintain a correlation between 3D Printing and cognition, tactile interaction, instruction (learning), customization and accessibility.

2   Cognition and 3D Printing

Many 3D printing related experiments are focused on understanding the decision process while manipulating innovative artifacts or virtual ones. This emphasizes a major concern with the perception of their characteristics through the user affordance background, which demands a study of perception and cognition.

2.1   Cognitive Workload Demands Using 2D and 3D Spatial Engineering Information Formats

[4] This experiment was conducted to evaluate how the information can be processed to the user depending on the way it is presented. The experiment consists

of assembling a structure where the user has a model of the structure. The test used three models: A 2D drawing, a 3D computer model, and a 3D printed part, where each subject needed to assembly in different sequence. The experiment measured six factors based in National Aeronautics and Space Administration raw task load index (NASA-rTLX), as following: Mental demand, Physical demand, temporal demand, Performance, Effort and Frustration.

By hypothesis test and ANOVA matrix, the results manifest that 3D printing provides a better conceptual building, reducing mental demand load, and overall workload cognition needed. However, the learning curve was not affected by the model used, and it means that regardless of the model presented to the subject, the assembly task performed several times, the final result it is the same.

2.2 "Like Popcorn": Crossmodal Correspondences Between Scents, 3D Shapes and Emotions in Children

[14] The authors perform an investigation on how multisensory experiences interact with each other and how this impacts user experiences. With an exeperimental case study with children aged 10 through 17, the authors gathered results that support a pre-existing mapping between cornered shapes and lemon scent with arousing emotion and rounded shapes and vanilla scent with calming emotions (Fig. 2).

Fig. 2. 3D printed models used as tangible stimuli [14].

During the study. The participants were tasked with associating scent stimuli with 3D shapes in sessions of 30 min. They also discuss design of richer and more engaging multisensory experiences supporting inclusive interactions between children.

2.3 Understanding Physical Activity Through 3D Printed Material Artifacts

[9] In this paper, the authors explore representing physical activity in the form of material artifacts. Their aim is to understand how these artifacts might reflect

upon the users' physical activity. The research was based on the application of a system called SweatAtoms that transforms the physical activity data based on heart rate into 3D printed material artifacts. A study was conducted by deploying the system in six households where participants experienced five different material representations of their physical activity for a period of two weeks each. They found that the material artifacts made participants more conscious about their involvement in physical activity and illustrated different levels of engagement with the artifacts.

This work provides a conceptual understanding of the relationship between material representations and physical activity. With the deployment of the system SweatAtoms through a case study, it was possible to explore how participants' physical activity can be affected through design. The authors encourage design researchers to consider and incorporate digital fabrication in their HCI design practice, not only trying to print models of physical objects, but consider printing artefacts constructed from data, such as heart rate.

2.4 Roma: Interactive Fabrication with Augmented Reality and a Robotic 3D Printer

[15] The authors propose an interactive fabrication system with a real time modeling experience where the users' actions within an AR CAD editor are replicated by a 3D printing robotic arm which shares the same design volume with the CAD editor. The authors claim the partially printed physical model serves as a tangible reference for the designer as new elements are added to the design. The system is equipped with a handshake mechanism to allow for the designer to quickly interrupt printing or to let the robot to take control of the printing process and finish it on its own (Fig. 3).

The designer can rotate the platform and integrate real-world constraints into a design rapidly and intuitively and allows the designer to directly design and print on and around a physical object.

3 Tactile Interaction

Tactility is an example of an interaction that results in a tangible feedback that can be perceived through physical/perceptual interaction with objects and textures. This type of feedback is retrieved by the human peripheral nervous system and conducted to the central nervous system until it finally reaches the brain. The tactile perception is exclusively dependant of cutaneous stimulus and demands that the individual stays in static, otherwise, kinesthetic senses would be recruited. Other manner of tactual perception remains in the haptic form of tactility which involves both tactile and kinesthetic perception.

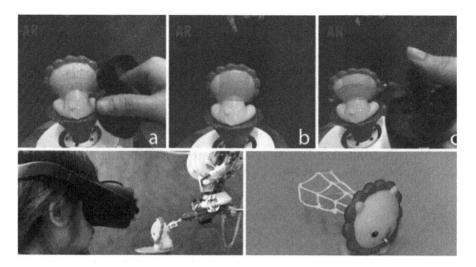

Fig. 3. AR controller used to manipulate a robotic arm [15].

3.1 Surface Roughness of 3D Printed Materials: Comparing Physical Measurements and Human Perception

[6] This paper proposes a comparative study of differences between 3D printed part surface roughness perception by optical equipment and human tactile perception. By a one-factor-a-time experiment based on an initial 3D printing setup, the factorial chart showed different behaviour to each parameter influence.

The data obtained revealed that smaller rugosity differences are still perceptible by the human sensory system, but did not account the correct value, due to limitations regarding hand adhesion groove during the inspection, consequently missing peak values in the part roughness profile. It makes clear that the mathematical parameters (Ra and Rq) cannot capture differences between surface models, given that different surface profiles can have the same value of Ra or Rq.

3.2 Museum Visitor Preference for the Physical Properties of 3D Printed Replicas

[20] Here has an exciting approach that used 3D printing to evaluate what are the most crucial beauty characteristics captured by human senses. The work consisted of creating 3D printed replicate of museum parts using different materials and processes. Then it sorted the samples in a preference order by a group of visitors and used the data for correlative analysis with the following adjectives: good quality – bad quality, unclear – clear, cheap – expensive, soft – hard, light – heavy, weak – strong, brittle – durable, rough – smooth, glossy – matte, unrealistic – realistic, undetailed – detailed, and boring – interesting.

However, the data did not present normal behavior. Nevertheless, other statistical parameters worked well, and some interesting pieces of information were obtained regarding the 3D printed objects: the most object notable characteristics are part detailing, the verisimilitude which embraces visual/tactile clarity.

Some issues were reported due to difference of opinion to each age range. For younger visitors, characteristics relative to robustness, clarity and color presented more correlation than other adjectives.

3.3   The Development of 3D Food Printer for Printing Fibrous Meat Materials(Conference Paper)

[12] This work developed a new 3D printing food process, using fibrous meat with emphasis on improving the chewing experience for the elderly which may suffer from poor teeth and tasting conditions. The nutritional components are set up before printing in a manner with is appropriate for individuals with a lack of protein. The material consisted of a mix of gelatine powder, water, meat fibrous and optional proteins.

Nevertheless, the process has some problems with flow control, such as overflow, retraction problem, printing accuracy and odd behaviour in the 3D printed material.

3.4   Towards User Empowerment in Product Design: A Mixed Reality Tool for Interactive Virtual Prototyping

[1] In this case, 3D printing assisted in creating devices to improve the communication between users and designers in the prototype process. The issue consists of finding a way to collect data about the product requirements to the user. In [1], mixed reality interface was proposed, utilizing the tangible user interface artifacts 3D printed to capture user experience, reproducing modifications in product representations.

It improves the user presence during the product conception and also immersion because the interface works in function of the human sense. That definition was used by [18]. That process is based on Kansei Engineering, a methodology which consists in creating a product by subjective impression, emotions or affect expressed by the user.

3.5   3D Printing and Immersive Visualization for Improved Perception of Ancient Artifacts

[5] In this paper, [5] got different conclusions from previous papers. The research consisted of testing three different designs of present ancient artifacts to museum visitors, evaluating how the public can detect some aspects: color, size, texture, and usefulness. The methods used are Powerall, using a stereoscope, Look, using a display case, and 3D printing by a replicate 3D printed.

The results obtained show that 3D printing is not useful as the other methods in analyzing color and weight, also causing misunderstanding during the study.

The author proposed a different environment to be applied to the museum, where the subject first examines 3D printed parts and after that, goes to a novel environment with 3D digital images, increasing a lot the experience and cognitive activity, and teaching the public about ancient cultures.

3.6   Environment-Scale Fabrication: Replicating Outdoor Climbing Experiences

[19] WHITING et al. (2017) propose a study on replicating the sensorimotor experience of an outdoor activity - rock climbing - through 3D printing fabrication. The hold grasps of the climbing holds were prototyped so their use could enable in an indoor gym. The major challenges during the research were fabricate accurate and durable replicas keeping the same configurations of the original outdoor site such as the geometry of the holds, its graspability and friction characteristics.

A main differential of this work was focusing not only on how to manufacture feasible structures, but also on analyzing how users interact with them by comparing the original outdoor route with the new indoor one made with 3D printed structures and using pose references extracted from videos of users practicing the activity.

Although the study proposed an exclusive use of FDM technology, it could not be accurate enough to produce the granular sensation that the original piece would have in an outdoor practice, so the piece was made by a mold to cast a final piece in resin that was based on the original ABS printed part that had an addition of sand in its surface to replicate the granularity. Also, an alternative piece made with foam was made using a CNC router aiming to bring improved friction.

As a result, the majority of climbers (seven out of nine) agreed the foam holds felt more realistic (higher fidelity to the original rock). One preferred foam for a more pleasant climbing experience but did not have an opinion about realism. The last user had no stated preference. Zero users preferred the 3D printed holds.

4   Instruction and Learning

In the age of Experience, UX presents itself as fundamental for the instructional and learning experience. Designers focused on such types of applications must consider several important issues such as what knowledge does the learner requires, how can the learner be aided to accomplish the learning objectives and how to keep the learner motivated. Designing the experience based on these issues will assist in creating the proper learning objectives, lessons, activities and keeping the learning experience challenging enough to keep the user motivated while avoiding frustration.

4.1 3D Printing in Preschool Music Education: Opportunities and Challenges

[2] This work is based on TUI and demonstrates how 3D printing can be a powerful resource in children's preschool music learning. The authors proposed a case study based on music parameters such as pitch, time, and timbre associating with geometrical parameters.

Using a paper sheet, a musical chart with two axes (horizontal to time, and vertical to pitch) and blocks 3D printed. The case study used length linked to time, color with timbre, and block positions put on the paper sheet. Thus, the children would train music, and also space notion while fostering his creativity (Fig. 4).

Fig. 4. A musical scale represented by 3D printed blocks [2].

The most important opportunity is to create their instruments, based on some modifications in already-existent musical instruments by low-budget projects.

4.2 Three-Dimensional Physical Modeling: Applications and Experience at Mayo Clinic

[13] On the medicine field, 3D printing has helped a lot. In this report from [13], who described effects in creating a hospital-based three-dimensional printing laboratory. The used workflow consisted of capturing 2D image data and importing by Mimics to get an STL file, which in turn was sent to the 3D printer.

The organ generated is useful to the surgeon, to preoperative planning, reducing risks and waste of time during the procedure. This application afforded a better understanding experience through an easy visual/haptic 3D model. After this implementation, the demand for surgeons has raised substantially, what is an evidence of 3D printing helping on cognitive activities in medical procedures.

4.3   Exploring Material Representations of Physical Activity

[8] Ashok (2014) developed a system to prototype a physical representation of physical activities, aiming to raise consciousness and engagement for the purpose of living a healthy life. The workflow consisted of taking heart rate data and prototyping an interactive fluid made of energy drinks, being an edible artefact.

Some works which supported this paper theoretical basis: Vande Moere (2008) argued that material representations about work encourage people to reflect regarding their behaviors, yielding more and improving the educational experience. Golstejin (2012) concluded that material artefacts serve to create memories triggers, creating a memory landscape.

The results found that the material artefacts made participants more conscious and involved in physical activities, and that methodology can be used in several gyms and similar sites.

4.4   Brain 3M - A New Approach to Learning About Brain, Behavior, and Cognition

[10] Li et al. (2015) discuss recent findings in embodied learning experiments in the education of children at school age and college ones revealing gaps in the education of brain sciences. By using a behavioral approach to develop learning tools along with innovative education techniques, a test was proposed for finding disruptive ways to teach about anatomy, function and evolutionary history of brains. An experimental phase was firstly inserted where students could manipulate and assemble virtual and physical replicas of different types of brains so the researchers could compare the efficiency of a technology-based form of learning with traditional ones. Brain 3M is a method of combining interfaces of mobile apps, web based tools, magnetic resonance images and 3D printed models.

5   Customization and Accessibility

The many demands in the 3D printing industry grow along with the plural user necessities that require specific strategies for developing usability adaptations. For example, users with physical disabilities need different approaches to solve daily routine activities, thus, a concern with accessibility issues are a crescent when dealing with the application of new forms of interface.

Adaptations and optimizations in the way users approach the manipulation of interfaces may be needed to achieve a better completion of the optimal product to be delivered.

5.1 Braille3D: Using Haptic and Voice Feedback for Braille Recognition and 3D Printing for the Blind (Conference Paper)

[17] This study related a smartphone application developed to improve the yield Braille alphabet learning, using TalkBack resource, that becomes a useful tool to read and explain each content in the screen, varying the gender voice, the language and also the speech rate and accent, being assisted by 3D printing.

The interface created consists in working as a course divided into four modules, where the first three levels focused in the alphabet (A–Z), and the last in the numbers (0–9). To feel the dots, when the student hovers the finger above a raised dot, he or she feels a vibration stimulus, and after this step, there are some questions to test the student learning. When the TalkBack reads the question, and the student slide his fingertip above the screen to find the correct answer, simultaneously the TalkBack reads the alternative selected.

During the learning, some words work as examples to help in understanding. The platform also uses 3D printing resources to create 3D models to explicit the word meaning, which increases the student's engagement. This app presented 100% yield to blind students, and over one half of the partially blind students presented a good score. It happened because the blind students were already familiar with the Braille language.

5.2 Reprise: A Design Tool for Specifying, Generating, and Customizing 3D Printable Adaptations on Everyday Objects

[3] In this paper the authors discuss how adaptations on everyday objects such as faucets or pliers can be made accessible through the use of low-cost 3D printing. However, users with limited modeling skills may find impractical to perform these adaptations themselves. For this effect, the users propose a methodology for performing such adaptations dubbed Reprise. The major workflow of reprise can be divided into four major steps: firstly, the actions to be performed on the object are defined; then the adaptations occur, which comprises the intended modifications of the model; next, the adjustments happen, which will ensure a better fit between the model and the proposed adaptations; and lastly, the attachment, where adaptations are made attachable to the objects by means of fasteners.

Among possible actions, the authors mention grasping and holding, pushing and pulling, rotating, clutching, and joining, where the objects move towards or away from each other (such as a key and a lock).

The authors claim their method empowers users to rapidly explore different adaptations and variations of a given design simplifying the design experience for 3D printed adaptations of models based on everyday objects.

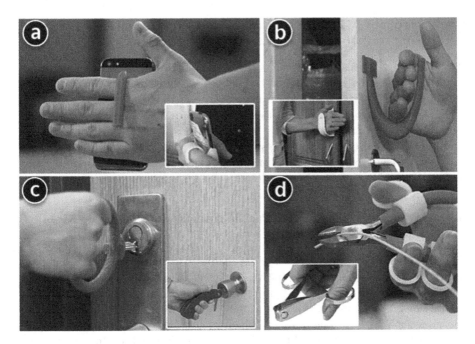

Fig. 5. 3D printed handle adaptations [3].

5.3 User Experience Design Methodology for Optimizing Kids' Toy Customization Platform Architecture: A Case Study

[11] This work presents a case study for a kid's toy internet customization platform. During the case study, the authors analyzed basic characteristics of children in order to propose a user experience based on interfaces, contact points, process organization and service design.

The authors present an association of the children's age with their developmental stage, phenomena and toys based on cognitive-developmental theory. From there they build on a method which exposes the mental space of children's behaviour before, during and after toy customization. This is mapped onto a customer journey map relating both the child's and the parents actions with their thoughts and emotions across different stages of the consumer relation.

Finally, the authors present a blueprint and an overall architecture for a service format based on "customization-design-manufacture-logistics-social" which serves as a reference for the development and promotion of personalized customization and intelligent manufacturing (Fig. 5).

5.4   RetroFab: A Design Tool for Retrofitting Physical Interfaces Using Actuators, Sensors and 3D Printing

[16] Adjusting physical interfaces may present a challenge because of their rigidity. To address this issue. An end-to-end design and fabrication environment allowing for non-experts to retrofit physical interfaces is presented in this work.

As home automation and smart objects becomes increasingly popular, users will desire additional functionality from their existing objects. The proposed framework is able to augment the physical interfaces of these objects using a simple workflow. Retrofitting could enable users with disabilities to operate interfaces they would otherwise be unable to.

5.5   Interactiles: 3D Printed Tactile Interfaces to Enhance Mobile Touchscreen Accessibility

[21] The authors investigate mobile accessibility for users with visual impairments by means of 3D-printed tactile interface. The study first explores challenges and impediments faced by users with visual impairments in touchscreens interactions. A significant factor claimed by the authors is the lack if tactile cues such as keys and buttons which creates a barrier for certain users. Increasing tactile feedback and tangible interaction on touchscreens can improve accessibility.

As part of their study, the authors present a 3D-printed hardware and software customization to enhance tactile interaction on Android touchscreen mobile devices which helps address an important gap in adding tangible interaction to mobile phones.

The approach proposed is cross-app compatible instead of a static overly that has limited functionality for a single screen configuration. During their study, the authors performed a technical validation with Android's top 50 apps. Another important factor pointed out is the low-cost production of the hardware composed of readily available materials and built through 3D-printing process.

6   Conclusion

This work has reviewed a total of 18 different studies related to user experience and embodied cognition. The works were classified according to their adherence to one of these major areas: cognition and 3D printing; tactile interaction; instruction and learning; customization and accessibility.

During our research the importance of UX and design experience is demonstrated to be more relevant than ever considering modern users and consumers are in search of the provided experience. Among the research collected in this survey, the necessity for UX has become a requirement for fields such as learning, accessibility, 3D printing and tactile interaction.

References

1. Arrighi, P.-A., Mougenot, C.: Towards user empowerment in product design: a mixed reality tool for interactive virtual prototyping. J. Intell. Manuf. **30**(2), 743–754 (2016). https://doi.org/10.1007/s10845-016-1276-0
2. Avanzini, F., Baratè, A., Ludovico, L.A.: 3D printing in preschool music education: opportunities and challenges. Qwerty-Open Interdisc. J. Technol. Culture Educ. **14**(1), 71–92 (2019)
3. Chen, X.A., Kim, J., Mankoff, J., Grossman, T., Coros, S., Hudson, S.E.: Reprise: a design tool for specifying, generating, and customizing 3D printable adaptations on everyday objects. In Proceedings of the 29th Annual Symposium on User Interface Software and Technology, pp. 29–39 (2016)
4. Dadi, G.B., Goodrum, P.M., Taylor, T.R., Carswell, C.M.: Cognitive workload demands using 2D and 3D spatial engineering information formats. J. Constr. Eng. Manage. **140**(5), 04014001 (2014)
5. Di Franco, P.D.G., Camporesi, C., Galeazzi, F., Kallmann, M.: 3D printing and immersive visualization for improved perception of ancient artifacts. Presence: Teleoperators Virtual Environ. **24**(3), 243–264 (2015)
6. Hartcher-O'Brien, J., Evers, J., Tempelman, E.: Surface roughness of 3D printed materials: comparing physical measurements and human perception. Mater. Today Commun. **19**, 300–305 (2019)
7. Hinton, A.: Understanding Context: Environment, Language, and Information Architecture. O'Reilly Media Inc., Sebastopol (2014)
8. Khot, R.A.: Exploring material representations of physical activity. In: Proceedings of the 2014 Companion publication on Designing Interactive Systems, pp. 177–180 (2014)
9. Khot, R.A., Hjorth, L., Mueller, F.F.: Understanding physical activity through 3D printed material artifacts. In: Proceedings of the SIGCHI Conference on Human Factors in Computing Systems, pp. 3835–3844 (2014)
10. Li, P., Chaby, L.E., Legault, J., Braithwaite, V.A.: Brain 3M-a new approach to learning about brain, behavior, and cognition. In: International Association for Development of the Information Society (2015)
11. Li, X., Song, X.: User experience design methodology for optimizing kids' toy customization platform architecture: a case study. In: Stephanidis, C. (ed.) HCII 2019. CCIS, vol. 1032, pp. 355–362. Springer, Cham (2019). https://doi.org/10.1007/978-3-030-23522-2_46
12. Liu, C., Ho, C., Wang, J.: The development of 3D food printer for printing fibrous meat materials. In IOP Conference Series: Materials Science and Engineering, vol. 284, p. 012019. IOP Publishing (2018)
13. Matsumoto, J.S., et al.: Three-dimensional physical modeling: applications and experience at mayo clinic. Radiographics **35**(7), 1989–2006 (2015)
14. Metatla, O., Maggioni, E., Cullen, C., Obrist, M.: "Like Popcorn" crossmodal correspondences between scents, 3D shapes and emotions in children. In: Proceedings of the 2019 CHI Conference on Human Factors in Computing Systems, pp. 1–13 (2019)
15. Peng, H., et al.: Roma: interactive fabrication with augmented reality and a robotic 3D printer. In: Proceedings of the 2018 CHI Conference on Human Factors in Computing Systems, pp. 1–12 (2018)

16. Ramakers, R., Anderson, F., Grossman, T., Fitzmaurice, G.: Retrofab: a design tool for retrofitting physical interfaces using actuators, sensors and 3D printing. In Proceedings of the 2016 CHI Conference on Human Factors in Computing Systems, pp. 409–419 (2016)
17. Samonte, M.J., Laurente, E.D., Magno, K.M., Perez, C.: Braille3D: using haptic and voice feedback for braille recognition and 3D printing for the blind. In: IOP Conference Series: Materials Science and Engineering, vol. 482, p. 012027. IOP Publishing (2019)
18. Slater, M., Linakis, V., Usoh, M., Kooper, R.: Immersion, presence and performance in virtual environments: An experiment with tri-dimensional chess. In: Proceedings of the ACM Symposium on Virtual Reality Software and Technology, pp. 163–172 (1996)
19. Whiting, E., Ouf, N., Makatura, L., Mousas, C., Shu, Z., Kavan, L.: Environment-scale fabrication: Replicating outdoor climbing experiences. In: Proceedings of the 2017 CHI Conference on Human Factors in Computing Systems, pp. 1794–1804 (2017)
20. Wilson, P.F., et al.: Museum visitor preference for the physical properties of 3D printed replicas. J. Cult. Herit. **32**, 176–185 (2018)
21. Zhang, X., et al.: 3D printed tactile interfaces to enhance mobile touchscreen accessibility. In: Proceedings of the 20th International ACM SIGACCESS Conference on Computers and Accessibility, pp. 131–142 (2018)

Transforming Diagrams' Semantics to Text for Visually Impaired

Charlie Cross, Deniz Cetinkaya$^{(\boxtimes)}$ (iD), and Huseyin Dogan (iD)

Department of Computing and Informatics, Bournemouth University,
BH12 5BB Poole, UK
{i7432987,dcetinkaya,hdogan}@bournemouth.ac.uk
http://hci.bournemouth.ac.uk/

Abstract. Using models and diagrams is a very useful and effective tool for representing information and systems in a graphical form to communicate and understand them better. On the other hand, graphical representations bring extra cognitive load and the process for understanding the diagrams is long and tedious in most cases for the visually impaired. To solve this problem, semantics of the diagrams should be converted to a different format that is both human and machine readable as well as communicable for the visually impaired. Most existing diagramming tools are not easily usable for the visually impaired as a tool for creating and using diagrams. In this paper, we propose an online system for defining specific diagrams and converting their semantics to text which can have a speech output for the visually impaired. We present analysis and design of this online system as well as a proof of concept prototype implementation. The prototype system provides create, save, load and transform features and tested with participants to recreate the diagrams using the automatically generated text output. Our case study showed that the results are very promising and the proposed solution can provide a way to correctly and accurately represent the information in diagrams textually.

Keywords: Assistive technology · Modelling for visually impaired · Diagrams to text

1 Introduction

Visual impairment and sight loss are affecting millions of people's lives in the world. In the UK, there are around 2 million people living with sight loss whereas around 360,000 are registered as blind or partially sighted [13]. Recent technological improvements and research in assistive technologies can help to support these people. For example, there are a number of ways to support reading and writing such as braille, text-to-speech, making text much larger, etc.

One of the challenging tasks for the visually impaired, especially in education and business life, is working with diagrams or graphical representations.

© Springer Nature Switzerland AG 2020
A. Marcus and E. Rosenzweig (Eds.): HCII 2020, LNCS 12200, pp. 339–350, 2020.
https://doi.org/10.1007/978-3-030-49713-2_24

Using models and diagrams is a very useful and effective tool for representing information and systems in a graphical form to communicate and understand them better. Diagrams are commonly used in most presentations and often make understanding a system or technology easier. Especially while teaching a new subject or introducing a new concept, diagrams, models or graphical representations are frequently used. However, visually impaired do not get the same benefits from the use of diagrams as the normal sighted do. Through research and interviews we identified that little to no solutions exist for supporting conversion of diagrams to a readable format for the visually impaired [2,4]. Related work in the literature does not provide a practical and implemented solution so understanding the diagrams is still a difficult process for visually impaired people. So, the aim of this research is to provide the visually impaired with a system that will not only support them to easily understand diagrams but also provide a platform that is efficient and easy to use.

During our interviews, we explored that the current process is as follows: first a tactile version of the diagram is printed and then the labels are separated from the objects. Then, labels are printed out in braille as well as a separate diagram that has braille labels in the objects. This whole process is lengthy and other alternatives lack context when revealing information about the diagram.

A common tool used by the visually impaired is text-to-speech tools. There are various text-to-speech programs for example a program called NVDA [16], which allows blind people to access and interact with the Windows operating system and some other third-party applications provides such a feature. On the other hand, text-to-speech software can only read out what is available in the text and actually they cannot explain diagrams, pictures, etc. unless text is there to describe them.

To solve this issue of there being no easy way for the visually impaired to understand diagrams, we propose the idea of having an online system that converts a diagram's semantics into text. When the system converts the diagram into text, the text will be formatted in a way that explains the diagram's semantics and what it means sentence by sentence. As a quick example, for a given flowchart the text will be generated something like "This diagram is a flow chart. Object number one is labelled as 'start' and leads onto object number two".

The goal is to make the automatically generated text being as natural as possible for the user so they can fully understand each part of the diagram and they do not need to use other methods like printing out tactile versions of the diagrams. The system will be an accessible web application to create diagrams, save them in a predefined format that can be easily read by the system and converted into a text format for the visually impaired.

In this paper, we present an online system for defining specific diagrams and converting their semantics to text which can be read out for visually impaired people. We explain analysis and design of this online system as well as demonstrate a proof of concept prototype implementation. The prototype system provides create, save, load and transform features and tested with participants to recreate the diagrams using the automatically created text output. This research will have both academic and social impact. Having a tool that can be used with little effort while working with graphical representations and diagrams would greatly help with saving time and effort of the visually impaired especially students at different levels.

The rest of the paper is organised as follows: next section provides the background information; Sect. 3 explains the requirements analysis and design of the system; Sect. 4 presents the implementation details and testing; finally Sect. 5 discusses the evaluation of the study, concludes the paper and draws the future agenda.

2   Background Information

When designing and building a program with a heavy focus on user experience, it's always important to consider how we can make the application as usable and accessible as possible. Hence, during software design and development, we prioritised the usability and accessibility of the software [12].

Usability can be broken down into five different components as learnability, efficiency, memorability, errors and satisfaction [5,15]. Using these five different components gives a clear focus on how to build a usable system. To build a successful system there are three main principles described by Nielsen: firstly having an early focus on users, then conducting empirical usability studies and finally using an iterative design process [14].

Therefore, we analysed different technologies used by the visually impaired to understand the available methods and tools as well as to identify the areas for potential improvement. During the interviews with the visually impaired, it has been recognized that one of the most common technologies used by visually impaired is text to speech tools.

Text to speech is an incredibly powerful tool that is constantly growing in terms of usability and accessibility. NVDA [16] is an application for the visually impaired to help them access and navigate their computer. On top of software that reads out everything that is on a desktop, there are now libraries such as Google's Text-to-Speech API [7] that can be integrated into websites to help read out information for users in mostly any language and in an accent, which is nearly natural.

Another commonly used technology by the visually impaired is tactile diagrams, this is done by with a heat fuser machine that uses heat to raise swell paper to add texture [8]. Hughes [9] showcases the technology and describes the main difference for visually impaired when reading diagrams through tactile is that they have to first look at all the details of the diagram to build an understanding of it.

There are many software for creating diagrams such as Microsoft Visio, Powerpoint, Lucidchart, draw.io, SimpleDiagrams, etc. Most of this software supports different types of diagramming techniques and modelling languages. Besides, they generally provide functionality to save the diagrams in different formats including text or XML. However, none of these programs are easily usable for the visually impaired as a tool for creating diagrams, that's where programs like PlantText may help [17]. PlantText allows users to create diagrams using a strict word language, this way the visually impaired only need to write to be able to create diagrams. Figure 1 shows an example screenshot of PlantText.

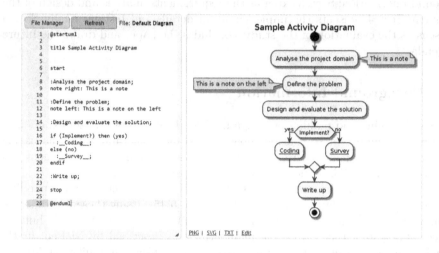

Fig. 1. PlantText example online edited [17].

In addition, refreshable braille displays are an extremely useful tool that can convert text from a digital format to braille on a mechanical output. This has been mentioned as a helpful method to easily check what has been written during the interviews.

Our research focuses on transforming diagrams' semantics to text for visually impaired people. We present an online system for defining specific diagrams and converting their semantics to text which can be read out for visually impaired people. Although related work exists in the literature, to the best of our knowledge there is no practical solution for this problem yet. Some early attempts are evident e.g. the TeDUB project to give the visually impaired a way to access diagrams [10,19]. TeDUB was a European Union-funded project running from 2001 to 2005. It was intended to deliver a way for blind people to access technical diagrams and drawings. In addition, recent studies proposed methods to convert abstract meaning representation graphs to text [18] and raised some interesting points about how converting AMR nodes to text phrases can be far from literal due to the information in the graph and this can make generating clear sentences difficult.

3   System Analysis and Design

During the analysis of the functional requirements interview and walkthrough review methods are used [1]. We made interviews with a severely visually impaired student from our department to analyse the problem domain. During the walkthrough reviews we made preplanned weekly meetings during the design and development stage to review the work done so far and reach a consensus [3]. MoSCoW method is used to prioritise the requirements. An agile methodology with regular meetings and an incremental software development approach was used during implementation.

3.1 Requirements

The requirements are gathered at the early stages and minor amendments are done in later stages. A prototyping method is utilised for requirements validation. The intended end users for the system are the visually impaired as well as anyone who wants to define models and/or transform them into text format with diagram's semantics. Major functional requirements are listed as follows:

- System must provide an editor to create specific type of diagrams.
- System must have a Save function to save created diagrams.
- System must have a Load function to load and edit saved diagrams.
- System must have a Generate function to generate textual output describing the diagram by converting diagrams' semantics into text.
- System must have a Save Output function to save textual output that describes the diagram.
- System must have a Check function to check if the file has the correct format.
- System must have a Save As function to convert diagrams into different formats such as XML, JSON or CSV.
- System could have integrated text-to-speech software.

  Non-functional requirements are considered as well.

- System must be reliable and error free.
- System must be accessible and can be used on popular browsers.
- System must be efficient and respond quickly to actions.
- System must have a responsive design for different devices.
- System must be easy to use and navigate.
- System should conform to accessibility guidelines focusing primarily on visually impaired.

3.2 Design

Use case diagrams are used to give an understanding of the complete sequence of events from a user perspective [6]. An important consideration for the page layout is that it must accommodate the visually impaired, this means that navigation must be simplistic and easy to navigate through, avoiding elements like dropdowns, burger menus, etc. There was careful consideration when planning to avoid additional features like logins that would add extra complexity to the system with little reward for the purpose of the visually impaired. Each page was iteratively designed using whiteboard wireframes to quickly be able develop

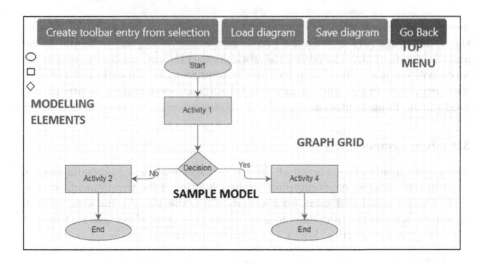

Fig. 2. Design for creating a diagram.

a design for the whole system that could then be implemented. When designing these pages, minimal inputs were placed so that the visually impaired can easily tab between controls in the proper order. Figure 2 shows the user interface design for creating diagrams functionality.

The designs have gone through a few iterations as new features were added and some features were moved to popup modals to make the page simpler lookout.

4   Online System for Converting Diagrams into Text

We developed an online system as a prototype with JavaScript and PHP. We used Bootstrap as CSS framework. We used an open source library MxGraph which is a client side JavaScript library for 2D diagrams [11]. Other well-known libraries are: Rappid, statejs, Draw2D, GoJS, etc. Most of these libraries have a well-developed set of tools creating, loading and saving diagrams to meet the user's needs.

We chose MXGraph because it supports most popular browsers, it is open source, it does not require any third-party plug-ins and it provides custom diagram layout. It is also easy to implement due its large range of examples provided in the download package and detailed documentation of its features. Figure 3 shows the overall system design and main file structure.

To implement the diagram container the main required libraries are called for the use of necessary functions. Changing the layout and user interface can be done through the JavaScript code by changing the styling of certain objects or through changing the linked images that are in the images folder. As seen in Figure 4, containers are defined first before the graph is initialised into one of the defined containers.

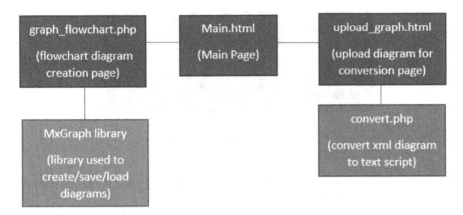

Fig. 3. System design overview.

```
// Creates the model and the graph inside the container
// using the fastest rendering available on the browser
var model = new mxGraphModel();
graph = new mxGraph(container, model);
graph.dropEnabled = true;
```

Fig. 4. Graph initialisation.

MxGraph has an impressive number of features that can be added and cus-
tomised to a user's specific diagram, so when it came to select what features
to add, only the ones that would be essential for helping create diagrams and
increase ease of use were included.

Essential features included:

– Naming cells
– Deleting cells
– Creating connector lines
– Snap connectors
– Scrolling the page

Ease of use features included:

– Copying a cell
– 90° connector lines
– Creating custom toolbar entries
– Tool tips

There are many other features that increase the ease of use and are essential
for diagram creation, however they are included with the base graph e.g. resizing
cells and selecting groups of cells. Most features that were added were completed

```
// Enables new connections in the graph
graph.setConnectable(true);
graph.setMultigraph(false);
// Enables tooltips and panning
graph.setPanning(true);
graph.setTooltips(true);
```

Fig. 5. Enabling available features.

by simply enabling them as can be seen in Figure 5. However, other features required custom code which was specific to its function.

The diagrams are saved into an XML format, which is completed by using multiple function calls that encode the data and then gets the XML from the encoded information. This information is then set as a JavaScript element which will be downloaded to the user's local storage. Generate function takes the XML file and converts it to the designed text format. The screenshot of the main page is shown in Figure 6.

Diagram to text

Select an option to start using the app!

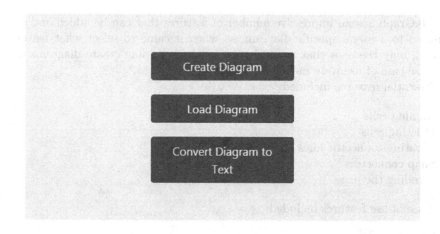

Fig. 6. Main page screenshot of the prototype.

Generating the output relies on natural flow through the diagram. This is challenging as the diagrams' semantics should be known and the algorithm should figure out the flow of the diagram. We implemented and added Flow Chart diagrams as an example. Other diagramming techniques can be added into the system but the generate function should be defined for each technique.

For Flow Charts, the start of a flow and end of a flow can be identified easily as the beginning cell does not have line targeting it and the ending cell does not have a line coming from it. Activity cells lead onto one cell and never any more, so they can be identified easily. The difficult part however is decision cells because a decision cell can split the main flow into many paths. Each new path must properly be labelled so that no confusion happens when the text is converted into speech. Figure 7 and Figure 8 show a diagram example and associated text output respectively.

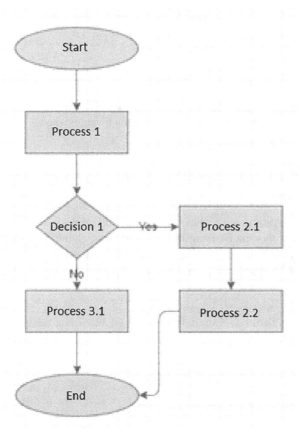

Fig. 7. A diagram example.

The information for the cells is stored in an array in the correct path order, and hence the algorithm iterates through the array and prints the related information with added custom text depending on the element type.

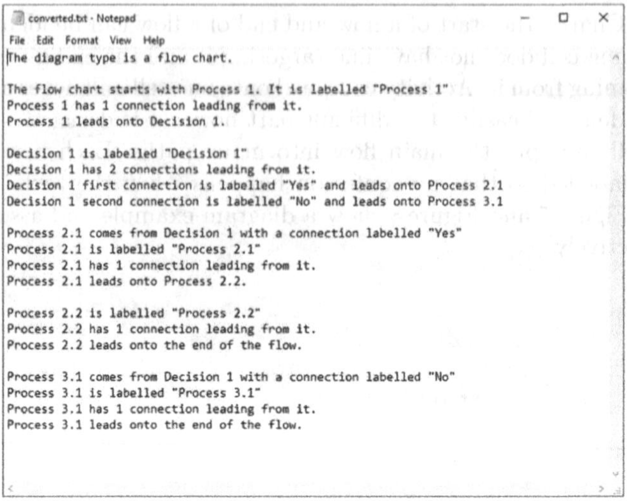
converted.txt - Notepad
File Edit Format View Help

The diagram type is a flow chart.

The flow chart starts with Process 1. It is labelled "Process 1"
Process 1 has 1 connection leading from it.
Process 1 leads onto Decision 1.

Decision 1 is labelled "Decision 1"
Decision 1 has 2 connections leading from it.
Decision 1 first connection is labelled "Yes" and leads onto Process 2.1
Decision 1 second connection is labelled "No" and leads onto Process 3.1

Process 2.1 comes from Decision 1 with a connection labelled "Yes"
Process 2.1 is labelled "Process 2.1"
Process 2.1 has 1 connection leading from it.
Process 2.1 leads onto Process 2.2.

Process 2.2 is labelled "Process 2.2"
Process 2.2 has 1 connection leading from it.
Process 2.2 leads onto the end of the flow.

Process 3.1 comes from Decision 1 with a connection labelled "No"
Process 3.1 is labelled "Process 3.1"
Process 3.1 has 1 connection leading from it.
Process 3.1 leads onto the end of the flow.

Fig. 8. Text output for the given example.

5 Discussion

5.1 Evaluation

We tested the system with various models and measured the accuracy of the outputs. Simple models had around 10 modelling elements while more complex ones had around 30 elements. The results of the tests are given in Table 1 and they show that the application is fault free, whereas the failed tests were marked, corrected and retested.

Table 1. System test results for black box testing.

Test result	Number of tests	Percentage
Passed	32	97%
Failed	1	3%

To evaluate the study, we designed acceptance tests and run them by five participants who are students at our university. Participants had basic information about flow chart diagrams. Participants did not see the diagrams but they are only provided the text output generated by the prototype system and this was read to the participants. The participants are then asked to recreate the diagram. Each participant attempted to recreate the same diagram separately. The test is repeated for three different diagrams with different complexity.

An average of the diagram's accuracy was calculated by comparing the participants created diagrams to the original one. For each cell or information that was not in the diagram or wrongly placed, a percentage was taken away. For instance, if there were ten cells and the participant missed one cell, then the percentage accuracy would be 90%.

Table 2. Acceptance test results.

Diagram tested	Accuracy
Diagram 1	100%
Diagram 2	96,4%
Diagram 3	96%

Results were promising as all results were over 95% as shown in Table 2. The more complex the diagrams the less accurate the participants were when recreating the diagrams. Having a percentage loss of only 4% on the most complex diagram shows good promise for the system as the most complex diagram is not realistic and purposely complex in design.

The survey with the participants showed that they were only confused by multiple decision subpaths, however the overall feedback was very positive. Participants said that the information given for describing a diagram helped them to easily visualise the diagram.

5.2   Conclusion and Future Work

This paper presented a research study to transform diagrams' semantics to text for visually impaired people. An online system was created to define diagrams and then to convert them automatically into text as a way for the visually impaired to understand the diagrams better. This system was built as a prototype for the purpose of analysing whether a system like this could be effective and useful for the visually impaired.

The background study and literature review showed that there is work going on in other domains to help the visually impaired understand pictures, graphs, etc. However, little work has been done to give the visually impaired a way to understand domain specific diagrams like UML and flow charts.

As a future work, we would like to extend our work with adding other diagramming techniques. Currently, we are using manual integration to text-to-speech software. A fully integrated solution will increase the impact and usage of the prototype. Future development of this web application would likely find great value in supporting formats for braille and having tactile versions of diagrams, as this seems to be a popular method for the visually impaired to understand diagrams.

Acknowledgments. We would like to thank the participants and interviewees for their valuable input and comments.

References

1. Alvarez, R., Urla, J.: Tell me a good story: using narrative analysis to examine information requirements interviews during an ERP implementation. SIGMIS Database **33**(1), 38–52 (2002). https://doi.org/10.1145/504350.504357
2. Cohen, R.F., Meacham, A., Skaff, J.: Teaching graphs to visually impaired students using an active auditory interface. SIGCSE Bull. **38**(1), 279–282 (2006). https://doi.org/10.1145/1124706.1121428
3. Cross, C.: Online system for creating and converting diagrams to text. Final Year Project Dissertation, Bournemouth University (2019)
4. Doherty, H., Cheng, B.: UML modeling for visually-impaired persons. In: International Proceedings on HuFaMo@MoDELS (International Workshop on Human Factors in Modeling Co-located with 18th International Conference on Model Driven Engineering Languages and Systems (MoDELS 2015)), pp. 4–10. ACM/IEEE (2015)
5. Ferré, X., Juristo, N., Windl, H., Constantine, L.: Usability basics for software developers. Softw. IEEE **18**, 22–29 (2001). https://doi.org/10.1109/52.903160
6. Gemino, A., Parker, D.: Use case diagrams in support of use case modeling: deriving understanding from the picture. J. Database Manage. **20**, 1–24 (2009)
7. Google-API: Cloud text-to-speech. https://cloud.google.com/text-to-speech/. Accessed 30 Jan 2020
8. Gupta, R., Balakrishnan, M., Rao, P.V.M.: Tactile diagrams for the visually impaired. IEEE Potentials **36**(1), 14–18 (2017). https://doi.org/10.1109/MPOT.2016.2614754
9. Hughes, S.: How to create tactile graphics (2017). Royal Blind Learning Hub. https://learninghub.royalblind.org/mod/page/view.php?id=370
10. King, A., Blenkhorn, P., Crombie, D., Dijkstra, S., Evans, G., Wood, J.: Presenting UML software engineering diagrams to blind people. In: Miesenberger, K., Klaus, J., Zagler, W.L., Burger, D. (eds.) Computers Helping People with Special Needs, pp. 522–529. Springer, Heidelberg (2004). https://doi.org/10.1007/978-3-540-27817-7_76
11. MxGraph: mxgraph 4.0.0. website and tutorial. https://jgraph.github.io/mxgraph/. Accessed 2 Jan 2020
12. Nganji, J., Nggada, S.: Disability-aware software engineering for improved system accessibility and usability. Int. J. Softw. Eng. Appl. **5**, 47–62 (2011)
13. NHS: Blindness and vision loss. Retrieved from NHS Website. https://www.nhs.uk/conditions/vision-loss/. Accessed 2 Jan 2020
14. Nielsen, J.: 25 Years in Usability. Nielsen Norman Group, Fremont (2008)
15. Nielsen, J.: Usability 101: Introduction to usability. Nielsen Norman Group, Fremont (2012)
16. NV-Access: Homepage. Retrieved from nvaccess. https://www.nvaccess.org/. Accessed 2 Jan 2020
17. PlantText: Uml editor - an online tool that generates images from text. https://www.planttext.com/. Accessed 2 Jan 2020
18. Song, L., Zhang, Y., Wang, Z., Gildea, D.: A graph-to-sequence model for AMR-to-text generation. In: Proceedings of the 56th Annual Meeting of the Association for Computational Linguistics, pp. 1616–1626, January 2018. https://doi.org/10.18653/v1/P18-1150
19. TeDUB-project: Technical drawings understanding for the blind. https://cordis.europa.eu/project/rcn/60750/factsheet/en. Accessed 30 Jan 2020

Usability Heuristics Evaluation in Search Engine

Ana Carolina dos Santos Pergentino[1(✉)], Edna Dias Canedo[1(✉)], Fernanda Lima[2(✉)], and Fábio Lúcio Lopes de Mendonça[1,2(✉)]

[1] Computer Science Department,
University of Brasília (UnB), Brasília, DF 70910-900, Brazil
`anacpergentino@gmail.com`, {`ednacanedo,ferlima`}`@unb.br`,
`fabio.mendonca@redes.unb.br`
[2] National Science and Technology Institute on Cyber Security,
Electrical Engineering Department, University of Brasília (UnB), Brasília, Brazil
`http://www.cic.unb.br`

Abstract. Network growth through recent years reveals our continuous search for information. With the urge of consuming information, search engine popularity rises, becoming our browser's primary function when typing in the navigation bar. The increasing information volume amplifies the demands of search refining with emphasizes on the concern about presenting data correctly and delivering answers to the users successfully. This paper presents a usability evaluation in the Brazilian Federal Court of Accounts (Tribunal de Contas da União - TCU) search engine for official documents. The need to update and centralize the search engines arised with the increasing technology quality in recent years. Despite good functionalities already implemented, the outdated interfaces with no common standards would no longer fit in today's use. The urge to create a pattern in TCU systems brought the idea of centralizing different types of documents in only one search engine. Applying the inspection method proposed by Nielsen's [1], it was possible to gather issues that were neglected in the development process. The results were outstanding: 49 issues found in a product that had already been released. Expecting user's feedback to correct a software product is far from ideal, making necessary to apply inspection methods in evaluating the system's usability. Severity ratings were applied in the inspection method, in order to categorize the issues and sort their solutions priorities. By summarizing their frequency, impact and persistence to rates, it was possible to combine those rates in a single severity rate, assigned to each issue. The work reported in this paper made possible the correction of several usability errors occurring in the system. Being a wide project, the amount of issues found, though seemed a large number, are proportionally not so huge: approximately one issue per screen is an acceptable result. The limitations of the studies were related to the amount of specialists involved, although the results indicate that a small group of evaluators is sufficient, specially when the projects, despite having many screens, has a lot of replicated components, where screens are not the same, but reuses interfaces modules. The contribution is primarily internal, by assisting

A. Marcus and E. Rosenzweig (Eds.): HCII 2020, LNCS 12200, pp. 351–369, 2020.
https://doi.org/10.1007/978-3-030-49713-2_25

in the deliver of a better product. But the study and reporting used in this paper allowed the authors to summarize the benefits of the heuristic inspection method, presenting the results in a real context, with explicit numbers and categorizing.

Keywords: Search engines · Usability · Usability heuristics · Heuristic evaluation · Usability factors

1   Introduction

Search engines are so generally used in the world wide web that became our main feature when navigating through the internet. Today, only two steps are necessary to find anything, since our browser bar is already shortcutted to search for terms inserted in a simple enter command. Network growth leads to information volume increase, amplifying the needs of search refining and making relevant the concern about results presentation to the user.

The algorithms behind search engines are strongly studied, but the need for evaluating their interfaces should not be neglected. Studies to capture the interaction between humans and computers are primordial in the development of a successful application [2]. The means to display information are an essential aspect of interactive systems. Technology field goes through frequent changes, and therefore the usability applied can become obsolete, although some principles and techniques used remain efficient over the years [3].

A system's navigation flow must reflect users' understanding. The system's goal should always be evaluated to reach the real context, analyzing which optimizations should be applied to result in comfort and time saving to the user. Navigation design is about the mental process and the steps to define navigation flow, regardless of the website kind, team size and their general goals in building a website [4].

Usability is the capacity of using a product easily, centering the systems perception from the users point of view, focusing in human factor. According to ISO 9241-11 [5] usability is the "extent to which a system, product or service can be used by specified users to achieve specified goals with effectiveness, efficiency and satisfaction in a specified context of use" [6]. It is also inserted in ISO 9241-11 usability definition, the particularities of "combination of users, goals and context of use for which usability is being considerate", and that usability "is also used as a qualifier to refer to the design knowledge, competencies, activities ans design attributes that contribute to usability, such as usability expertise, usability professional, usability engineering, usability methods, usability evaluation, usability heuristic" [6].

It is noticeable, according to Nielsen in Usability Engineering [1], that the need to a prior evaluation on product use satisfaction allows saving and agility. Many systems do not reach their goals because they have non intuitive interfaces, were erroneously planned, fail to consider major use implications, that may damage the dialogue, which means the communication between system and human applied in this context.

To define possible usability flaws, the heuristic evaluation created by Nielsen [1] propose a set of requisites that a usable system must contain. This list has become a main method of usability inspection, besides, it assists in the implementation of user-centric systems.

Heuristic evaluation is majorly performed by specialists, but it can also be executed by developers or common people. The plurality of views is important when gathering reports to enumerate all possible usability problems recognized. Different visions will find different errors, that combined generates a wider inspection.

This paper's goal is to evaluate a search engine based on Nielsen's set of usability heuristics [1], but also based on collecting knowledge from papers containing systematic reviews [7,8] and applied evaluation. Finding usability problems specifically in search engines brings the discussion of how usability is applied in a different context. We also evaluate the severity of problems found in the system, leading to achieving a better product by fixing issues found during development.

This paper is organized as follows. Section 2 shows the theoretical foundation for the understading of this work. Section 3 presents the research questions selected and Sect. 4 results obtained for those questions. Section 5 contains our conclusions about the evaluation conducted.

2   Background

2.1   Usability

According to Jakob Nielsen [1], the term usability itself can not be explained by a simple abstraction. It is composed by 5 attributes that will better consolidate what is really necessary to consider a project Usable, which includes: **Learnability**, **Efficiency**, **Memorability**, Low **Errors** Rate and **Satisfaction**. Learnability is how we search a way to make it easy for a user to learn how to navigate through the system and reach for his goal. Efficiency is about how many tasks can a user complete after learning how to use the system, that means how efficient the system has become to the user. Memorability means that the system should be easily remembered, as when an user tries after some time to access the system find it easy to complete tasks wanted. Errors are supposed to be prevented, which would cause a low errors rate and that is a project goal. Finally, satisfaction is how it deliveries what stakeholders asked in a way that users can simply navigate and get all the functionality they need [1,8,9].

Intending to reduce the amount of rules in usability guidelines, Nielsen [1] resumed use evaluation down to 10 heuristics. These 10 principles are all that is necessary to explain most of design interface problems. Though, to apply these principles correctly in all cases it is necessary a amount of experience, however this metrics can help non-experts finding errors. An interesting approach is to ask different people to evaluate, because different people can find different problems. These usability heuristics defined in Usability Engineering [1,9] are:

UH1 - Aesthetic and minimalist design: for the system to be accessible, only essential information should be kept so that the information transmission to the user is efficient. Each secondary unity of information interferes in information that are, in fact, important and decreases, relativity, it's visibility.

UH2 - Compatibility between system and user: the system should be comprehensive to the user, use the same language that the user does, through concepts and words that already belong to the environment that it is inserted.

UH3 - Minimize user memory load: it is better to offer patterns to the users, so they will not need to memorize new information while using the system.

UH4 - Consistency and patternization: there must be consistency between screens inside the application. User should not wonder if there are different meanings to words, actions or situations.

UH5 - Status visibility: it is fundamental that the interface allow users to find themselves inside the system, so they know where they were, where they are, and in which other environments they can be. This is possible through feedback inside reasonable time.

UH6 - Clearly marked exits: an "emergency exit" must be available for the case of users commit errors. System should allow the users to, for example, undo actions that might had made by mistake.

UH7 - Shortcuts to efficiency and flexibility of use: it is interesting that the interface can be accessible even to non-users, as to the experienced users. Accelerators can maximize interaction between system and specialist user, however, without ignoring inexperienced users needs.

UH8 - Assistance for users to recognize, diagnose, and recover from errors: assist users to repair mistakes they commit. Messages informing error should be in simple language, indicate explicitly the problem and suggest a solution.

UH9 - Error prevention: occasionally the user intended to perform an action, but happens to perform an different action. The user can also commit a mistake because of the misunderstanding of some information. Ideal would be to have a system developed in a way to avoid those mistakes to happen. Dialog boxes that question actions selected by users are an approach to prevent this kinds of errors.

UH10 - Help and documentation: the most indicated is an interface that is so user friendly that no documentation or user instruction is needed, although it is important to offer documentation in case the user requires help, being able to solve doubts and, in this way, being more independent.

2.2 Interface Evaluation - Severity Ratings

Usability errors may not be fast and inexpensive to fix. Severity classifications are created in order to prioritize the correction of such issues. Multiple specialists evaluations combined allows a wide vision of corrections that should be done. Severity assessments provide guidance to evaluators, though there are other factors that may influence in how the evaluator categorize the severity. In order to define an effective severity rating, there is a need to comprehend the competing factors to determine evalutor's response to usability evaluations [10].

Nielsen propose a set of severity evaluation measures. One of those are a single rating scale: [1]

0 = this is not a usability problem at all;

1 = cosmetic problem only - only fixed if there is available extra time on project;

2 = minor usability problem - low resolution priority;

3 = major usability problem - important to fix, high resolution priority;

4 = usability catastrophe - must be fixed before releasing the product.

Another scale that is also defended in [1] is the combination of two usability problems dimension: how many users may find this issue and how the issue can harm their goals in using the system. Table 1 illustrates this frequency x impact scale. Also known as Problem Severity Classification (PSC) rate, and used by IBM, this classification might contain an intermediate impact level.

Table 1. Usability issues severity rates based in frequency and impact

		Frequency	
		Few	Many
Impact	Minor	Low severity	Medium severity
	Major	Medium severity	High severity

Additionally, the severity evaluation can be improved by attaching a new category: persistence. That means, if the issue persistently causes an inconvenience to the user rarely, commonly or always.

2.3   Measurement of System and Software Product Quality

Product quality must be evaluated from defined parameters, in order to create a standard, ISO/IEC 25023 [11] includes usability measures to complement the software quality analysis [5].

The International Organization for Standardization (ISO) is an independent, non-governmental entity that produces the standardization and normalization standards for 164 countries [12]. The standards are defined by international groups composed of representative experts from various national standards organizations. The International Electrotechnical Commission (IEC) is an international organization similar to ISO, but commited with standardization of electric, electronic and related technologies. Together, ISO/IEC deal with particular fields of technical activity through technical committees, established by the respective organization [12].

In this paper, we define an use established between Nielsen's heuristics and the attributes defined by ISO/IEC 25023, as presented in Table 2. This set of measurements is based on "dialogue principles" in ISO 9241-11 [5].

Table 2. Correlation between ISO/IEC 25023 attributes and Nielsen's heuristics.

ISO/IEC 25023 Attributes		Heuristics
Appropriateness recognizability	Description completeness	UH10
	Demonstration coverage	UH10
	Entry point self-descriptiveness	UH3
Learnability	User guidance completeness	UH10
	Entry fields defaults	UH4, UH7
	Error message understandability	UH8, UH2
	Self-explanatory user interface	UH3, UH2
Operability	Operational consistency	UH4
	Message clarity	UH1
	Functional customizability	UH7
	User interface customizability	UH2
	Monitoring capability	UH5
	Undo capability	UH8
	Understandable categorization of information	UH3, UH4
	Appearance consistency	UH4
	Input device support	UH9, UH6
User error protection	Avoidance of user operation error	UH9
	User entry error correction	UH8
	User error recoverability	UH8
User interface aesthetics	Appearance aesthetics of user interfaces	UH1
Accessibility	Accessibility for users with disability	UH2
	Supported languages adequacy	UH2

Table 2 was created in order to demonstrate that than heuristic evaluation covers majorly the demands proposed by the conventional professional standards.

2.4   The System: TCU Official Documents Search Engine

The system evaluated is the search engine *Pesquisa textual/Federal Court of Accounts (TCU - Brazil)* for official documents in the Brazilian Court of Audit

(TCU), a government organization that has the same purpose as U.S. General Accounting Office. It is responsible for executing the "accounting, financial, budgetary, operational and patrimonial inspection of the Union and direct and indirect administration" [13].

Everyday TCU produces official documents regarding these data, and stores for later acess. The search engine evaluated here contains these documents. It is a public system with restrictions, which means all citizens can use it, but not all documents or all research bases can be accessed by anyone. The system needs to please majorly the product owners: TCU ministers, auditors, and administrators. But it is also mandatory to be accessible to all citizens with the purpose to demonstrate large transparency about the Union's account [13].

The system is a propose of renewing the search bases in TCU, by improving usability and providing a modern appearance. The need to update and centralize the search engines arised among technology quality in recent years. Despite good functionalities already implemented, the outdated interfaces with no common standards would no longer fit in today's use. The urge to create a pattern in TCU systems brought the idea of centralizing different types of documents in only one search engine.

The system construction started in 2018, and the development was gradual as the conversion from the old search engines. Instead of creating all services and interfaces as a complete product, we started by a base (being base a type of document), releasing it for internal use in a development environment server and providing the access only to TCU staff, asking professionals in sectors involved with the released base to use it. Using a payed framework (hotjar) the screens were captured keeping a heat map and the recording of interactions made, for further analysis.

The system is composed by 18 search bases, 12 of them are enabled to public access, and 6 are restricted. The restriction corresponds to each role in the staff. Each base correspond to a type of formal document, and each base has 3 correspondent screens: a search form, the search results with a list of abbreviated documents, and the detailed description of the chosen document within the results. Besides, it contains also a initial dashboard composed by an integrated search and shortcut buttons to each base. The result of the integrated search presents the amount of documents in each base that matches the search term (Figs. 1, 2, 3, 4, 5, 6, 7 and 8).

The restricted section presents, to the user with porprer permition, which bases are accessible to their roles, and contains a favorite's section for documents and search. You can either put a research form in favorites, or a selected document.

The research forms are adapted to each base promoting shortcuts to provide user efficiency, each base has their own inputs studied as more relevant during design. The results contain options to order the results: by date relevance, filters by type and other variables according to each base, document exportation of each document and of the results table, besides the main term input, and

Fig. 1. Specific search form example.

Fig. 2. Results page with summarized documents example.

Fig. 3. Detailed document example (1/2).

Fig. 4. Detailed document example (2/2).

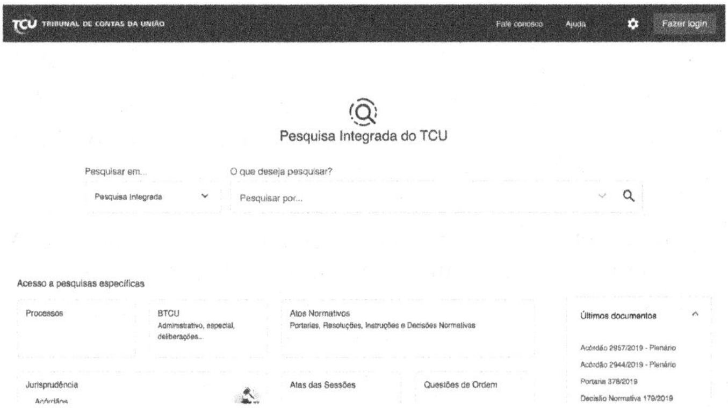

Fig. 5. Integrated search dashboard (1/2).

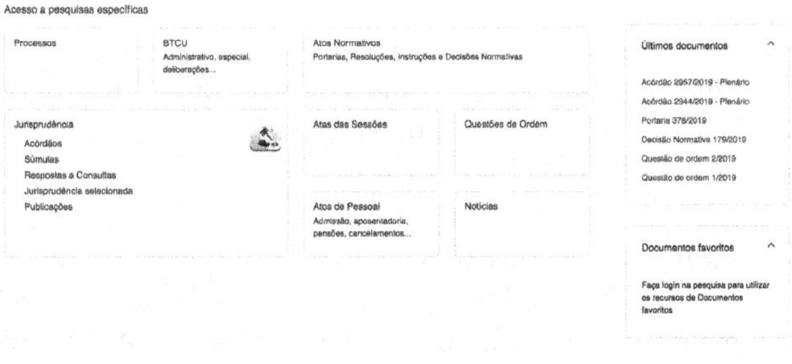

Fig. 6. Integrated search dashboard (2/2).

Fig. 7. Favorites search form page.

Fig. 8. Favorite document. Information has been removed for privacy reasons.

navigation bar and menus. The detailed result presents the most relevant information, that generally matches all form inputs but in some cases incorporate even more details.

3   Study Settings

3.1   Research Goal

The paper goal is to perform an heuristic evaluation in a real context system's interface. The system was designed using Agile and Design Thinking methodologies, in a human-centered approach, including planning, prototyping, interviews, among other tools to assist a high usability system's development.

Following usability engineering it becomes noticeable that no project is issue-free. A main goal in performing the evaluating is to find and categorize issues to optimize and prioritize corrections, in order to deliver an effective, efficient and satisfactory product.

The system's main goal is to deliver relevant information in official documents search. The system has public access with some restrict search bases and documents, so the presentation should be accessible to all possible users. As this is an internal initiative, it is easier to understand the expectations towards the system from the TCU staff point of view. In order to facilitate the use of the system to TCU parts that deal directly with these documents, the information relevance presented in results, so as the form organizations, were directly influenced by TCU members.

3.2   The Evaluation

The heuristic evaluation was performed by a TCU team, represented by an user experience designer, an user interface designer and two front-end developers as presented in Table 3. It consisted in a detailed navigation inspection, where each evaluator performed tasks to each search base analyzing thoroughly to verify the existence of any inconsistency or flaw.

Table 3. Evaluator's profile

Role	Degree	Experience
User Experience Designer	Specialist	8 years
User Interface Designer	Graduate	5 years
Front-End Developer	Graduate	3 years
Front-End Developer	Graduate	3 years

A generic guide, based in da Costa et al. [7], was set to support the evaluation process, composed by basic features that should be tested and components that should be observed in each search base.

All results were organized in an shared spreadsheet, that contains:

- An identification number to each issue found;
- Where the issue was found, in this case, which screen and page;
- A description of the problem;
- The heuristic associate to the issue;
- The severity factors composed by frequency, impact and persistence;
- The resulting severity factor composed by the average of factors evolved;
- And the description of the solution proposed to the issue correction.

In order to avoid computing multiple errors, we associated the frequency rating to how many evaluators had found the flaw, applying 0 to a problem that only one evaluator had noticed, and 3 a problem noticed by all members in team. It was also perceptible that most of the errors present on the system were found by the specialist in user experience.

3.2.1   Severity Ratings

In order to analyze severity in each issue, we defined rates to each attribute used in order to find a unique measure. The attributes and their measures are:

- **Frequency**: Estimated according to the number of evaluators that noticed the problem.

0 = The problem is only identified by one evaluator;
1 = Two evaluators identified the problem;
2 = Three evaluators noticed the problem;
3 = The problem is experienced by all evaluators.
- **Impact**: Does the problem affect users to accomplish their tasks?
    0 = The problem does not cause difficulty for users;
    1 = The problem causes simple difficulties to get around;
    2 = The problem causes difficulty in performing the action;
    3 = The problem makes the action impossible.
- **Persistence**: Is it a recurring problem?
    0 = The problem is not noticed by users;
    1 = The problem is disregarded by users;
    2 = The problem is frequently experienced by users;
    3 = The problem occurs in all cases.

In our evaluation model we established part of Nielsen's single rating scale [1], as being defined by the average of frequency, impact and persistence, as presented below

0 = cosmetic problem only - only fixed if there is available extra time on project
    1 = minor usability problem - low resolution priority
    2 = major usability problem - important to fix, high resolution priority
    3 = usability catastrophe - must be fixed before releasing the product

3.3   Research Questions

The paper aims to perform an heuristic evaluation to improve the evaluated system, validate the proposed heuristic set in its current version, and present results to contribute to the academic field. To achieve the goal, the research questions presented in Table 4 were defined.

Table 4. Research Questions (RQ) and motivation for each RQ

Research Question (RQ)	Motivation
RQ.1. Which are the possible usability issues in a system designed using design thinking principles and developed in agile methodology?	Identify possible usability problems in a human-centred designed system
RQ.2. Which are the severity of the issues found?	Notice if problems found block users
RQ.3. Are the issues found correctable?	Estimate correction difficulties in issues found

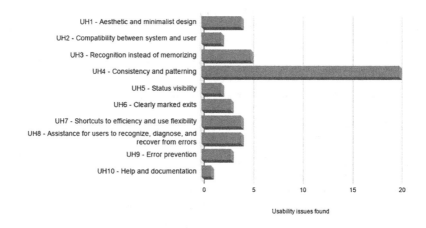

Fig. 9. Number of issues encountered by usability heuristic.

4   Study Results

4.1   RQ.1. Which are the Possible Usability Issues in a System Designed Using Design Thinking Principles and Developed in Agile Methodology?

The system here evaluated was designed and planned with agile methodology and applying Design Thinking techniques. Prototyping, testing and interviewing are some of the tools applied by the UX and UI designers in the project. Results obtained with the evaluation conducted as presented in Fig. 9.

The system contains 59 screens and the amount of usability errors found is 49, therefore, the system presents an error rate proportional to its size, less than 1 error per screen.

A great amount of flaws refer to a rupture in the usability heuristic UH4 - Consistency and Patterning, representing 41,7% of total flaws. Although, those issues concentrate in the low severity rate, which means that even being a big amount of errors, consistency and patterning tend to have a lower impact in user experience. Both catastrophic flaws found represent the usability heuristic UH8 - Assistance for users to recognize, diagnose, and recover from errors. That means that, when an error is categorized by the rupture of an UH8 heuristic, usually the error has a significant impact in the user's execution of a determined task.

In the evaluation performed in this paper, errors were described by their location and functionality. The Table 5 is obtained by grouping the amount of errors per screen.

Table 5. Errors per pages

Tela (Screen)	Errors
Ajuda (Help)	1
Documentos e pesquisas favoritas (Favorites: Documents and Search)	1
Documentos favoritos (Favorites: Documents)	1
Download arquivo Atas das Sessões (Files Download in "Acts of the Sessions")	1
Fale conosco (Contact Us)	1
Favoritar pesquisas (Mark search as favorite)	1
Formulário Acórdãos (Form: "Judgments")	2
Formulário Atas das Sessões (Form: "Acts of the Sessions")	1
Formulário Atos de Pessoal (Form: "Staff Acts")	1
Formulário Atos Normativos (Form: "Atos Normativos")	3
Formulário Jurisprudência Selecionada (Form: "Selected Jurisprudence")	2
Formulário Respostas a Consultas (Form: "Replies to Law Consultations")	2
Formulário Súmulas (Form: "Súmulas")	1
Formulários pesquisas especéficas (Form: specific search each base)	2
Label dos campos de pesquisa livre (Label in search field)	1
Limpar formulário (Clear form)	1
Pesquisa Atos de Pessoal (Search: "Staff Acts")	1
Pesquisa integrada (Search: integrated)	1
Pesquisa integrada (campo de busca) (Search: integrated - search field)	1
Pesquisa integrada (home) (Search: integrated - home)	6
Pesquisa integrada (resultados) (Search: integrated - results)	7
Pesquisa Processos (Formulário Administrativos) (Search: "Processos" - Form: "Administrative")	1
Pesquisa publicações (resultados) (Search: "Publications" - results)	1
Questões de ordem (documento detalhado) ("Questions of Order" - detailed document)	1
Resultado pesquisa CNPJ (Search results: "Taxpayers' Registry")	2
Resultado pesquisa CPF (Search results: "Individual Taxpayers' Registry")	1
Resultados das pesquisas (Search results: general)	2
Tela com resultados de pesquisas especéficas (Search results: general)	1
Tela pesquisas favoritas (Favorites: Searches)	1
URL	1
Total de Erros Encontrados (Total errors found)	**49**

4.2   RQ.2. Which are the Severity of the Issues Found?

In study settings it was established the single scale used to categorize severity, based in the attributes frequency, impact and persistence.

In this evaluation the frequency rate was adapted to reflect the amount of evaluators that perceived each issue, and the results show that 29 out of 49 issues where noticed at least by two evaluators, and only one issue was noticed by only one of the evaluator, as presented in Fig. 10 reinforcing the concept that the heuristic evaluation must be made by a team, but also reflecting that a 4 four people team, given the evaluated system case, was a reasonable choice.

The impact rate is the severity factor that defines if an issue found inhibits a user from accomplishing a task. The study presents that despite the fact that errors harms user's usability, the issues found are not an obstacle in most cases. As seen in Fig. 11, errors may cause difficulties to user, but most issues found cause no difficulties at all, or simple difficulties, easy to get a around.

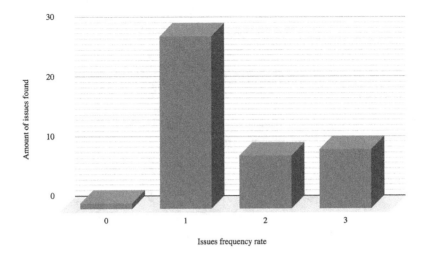

Fig. 10. Amount of issues by frequency rate.

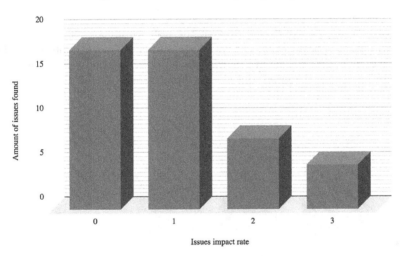

Fig. 11. Amount of issues found by impact rate.

We can conclude that having an user-centered design for development facilitates the applicability of an user-friendly interface, where issues exist, but rarely influence badly the conclusion of a task.

Observing persistence, the greater range belongs to issues that are frequently experienced by the user, in this paper's case, by the evaluators. The persistence rate reflects how an issue presents itself, if it occur most times that the task is performed, as shown in Fig. 12.

Combining those three factors in one single severity rate, the chart Fig. 13 presents how many issues were found matching this single rate.

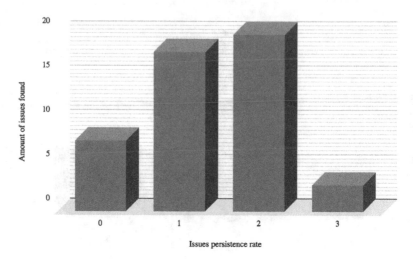

Fig. 12. Amount of issues found by persistence rate.

The catastrophes encountered prevent the user from completing an evident action. Errors found that configure a catastrophe are both corresponding to UH8, where a system's error occurred but was not reported to the user, not allowing the user to recognize, diagnose and recover from errors.

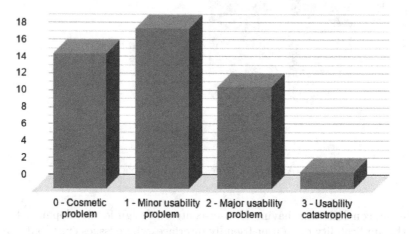

Fig. 13. Amount of issues found by severity rate.

4.3 RQ.3 Are the Issues Found Correctable?

The study highlights a well-known concept in software quality: an issue-free product does not exist. The whole intention of performing the inspection was to improve software quality, and by categorizing the issues found, facilitates the resolution planning.

The evaluation leads us to correct catastrophic mistakes in urgent priority. In one week both catastrophic issues were already fixed. In two weeks, 9 issues were already repaired. Until the release of this paper's extended abstract, 40 days after the end of the evaluation, 43 issues, from the 49 found, were already resolved. Two months after the evaluation, all errors were corrected. Now, it should be considerate a new evaluation, since the project has grown and new errors may appear.

It is noticeable that even though there were many high priority issues, a low priority can be easier to fix, which results in having minor usability problems fixed earlier than major issues.

4.4   Discussion of Results of Heuristic Evaluation

The obtained results highlight that a system designed with human-centered approach has errors, but the amount of errors reflect a low rate when taking account the system's size.

The Consistency and Patterning flaws (UH4) are the most present in the system, but are minor impact flaws, present a closer relation to aesthetics then to functionality itself.

The catastrophic flaws are associated to UH8 - Assistance for users to recognize, diagnose, and recover from errors, showing that this heuristic is fundamental in the system use. The lack of correct application of this heuristic may compromise the use in a way that the user can not conclude a task.

The severity rates found concentrate in cosmetic and minor usability problems, pointing that most errors do not impact user's performance. That indicates the correct use of human-centred development, where the methodology applied in the project's design was focused in usability performance.

In the error's correction, catastrophic flaws were prioritize. Following, we prioritized major usability errors, but in parallel minor errors and cosmetic flaws were also being corrected, and it was observed that minor issues were faster resolved than major issues.

The evaluation conducted in this study had the goal of flaws correction, and for that purpose succeed. All corrections were already implemented two months after the evaluation. It is now noticeable the need for a new evaluation, since the system continues to grow and be developed. Today, new search bases were already implemented, while others were optimized. An example of a new base implemented is the BTCU search, responsible for official newsletter containing all daily information about official documents. It was sliced in three different searches: internal processes, external processes, and processes' pieces.

4.5   Threats to Validity

In future works, the set of heuristics and severity rates established in this paper should be approved by other specialists. It is also necessary to conduct the methodology used in other search engines, to validate the correctness of the study settings.

The evaluation performed in this work had as limitation the staff and time. The amount of specialists involved was low, as well as the deadline was urgent, because the system was already in production environment, available to internal and external use, and flaws should be corrected as soon as possible.

5   Conclusion

Usability evaluation is the key to find issues that passed unnoticed through developers. The system used was already released and being used when the evaluations were performed, but still contained mistakes that were not reported and would only be noticed by user's feedback. It is important to notice that the system is focused on legal documents, majorly composed by law related information, and not commonly used by the developers.

When testing your own product, if you do not have a full understanding about the area in which it is applied, you will not deal with errors that are encountered by users who are immersed in the specific context of the product, such as internal information from professionals in a given area of knowledge. An heuristic evaluation allows the team to navigate with another perspective, having a script composed by usual tasks performed in the system, combined with the guidelines provided by the heuristics, it becomes possible to notice flaws that in developing process were neglected.

The size of the evaluated system justifies the number of errors encountered, even though the system's design was created applying Design Thinking principles, there is no impeccable product, and a User Experience designer is not able to find all these issues by himself, it exists a need to gather a team of specialists. Most issues can be rapidly repairable, and performing this evaluation allowed the team to deliver continuously a better product.

For future work, the set of heuristic applied in this study should be validated by other specialists, as well as the severity ratings. It is also important to apply the methods here defined in other search engines to ensure the correctness of methodology.

Acknowledgements. This research work has the support of the Research Support Foundation of the Federal District (FAPDF) research grant 05/2018.

References

1. Nielsen, J.: Usability Engineering. Morgan Kaufmann Publishers Inc., San Francisco (1993)
2. Barbosa, S.D.J., da Silva, B.S.:Design da interaÇÃo humano-computador com molic. In: Companion Proceedings of the 13th Brazilian Symposium on Human Factors in Computing Systems. IHC 2014, Porto Alegre, Brazil, Brazil, Sociedade Brasileira de Computação, pp. 79–80 (2014)

3. Hearst, M.A.: Search User Interfaces, 1st edn. Cambridge University Press, New York (2009)
4. Kalbach, J.: Designing Web Navigation. O'Reilly Media, Sebastopol (2007)
5. Bevan, N., Carter, J., Earthy, J., Geis, T., Harker, S.: New ISO standards for usability, usability reports and usability measures. In: Kurosu, M. (ed.) HCI 2016. LNCS, vol. 9731, pp. 268–278. Springer, Cham (2016). https://doi.org/10.1007/978-3-319-39510-4_25
6. Standardization, I.O.F.: ISO 9241–11: Ergonomic Requirements for Office Work with Visual Display Terminals (VDTs): Part 11: Guidance on Usability. ISO (1998)
7. da Costa, R.P., Canedo, E.D., de Sousa Júnior, R.T., de Oliveira Albuquerque, R., García-Villalba, L.J.: Set of usability heuristics for quality assessment of mobile applications on smartphones. IEEE Access **7**, 116145–116161 (2019)
8. Dourado, M.A.D., Canedo, E.D.: Usability heuristics for mobile applications - a systematic review. In: Proceedings of the 20th International Conference on Enterprise Information Systems, ICEIS 2018, Funchal, Madeira, Portugal, 21–24 March 2018, vol. 2, pp. 483–494 (2018)
9. Hix, D., Hartson, H.R., Nielson, J.: A taxonomic model for developing high impact formative usability evaluation methods. In: CHI Conference Companion, pp. 464–465. ACM (1994)
10. Hertzum, M.: Problem prioritization in usability evaluation: from severity assessments toward impact on design. Int. J. Hum. Comput. Interact. **21**, 125–146 (2006)
11. Nakai, H., Tsuda, N., Honda, K., Washizaki, H., Fukazawa, Y.: Initial framework for software quality evaluation based on ISO/IEC 25022 and ISO/IEC 25023. In: 2016 IEEE International Conference on Software Quality, Reliability and Security Companion (QRS-C), pp. 410–411. IEEE (2016)
12. Heires, M.: The international organization for standardization (ISO). New Polit. Econ. **13**(3), 357–367 (2008)
13. Federal Court of Accounts. https://portal.tcu.gov.br/english/. Accessed 30 Sept 2019

Managing Information in the Case of Opinion Spamming

Liping Ge[1(✉)] and Stefan Voß[2(✉)]

[1] Leuphana University of Lüneburg,
Universitätsallee 1, 21335 Lüneburg, Germany
liping.ge@leuphana.de
[2] Institute of Information Systems, University of Hamburg,
Von-Melle-Park 5, 20146 Hamburg, Germany
stefan.voss@uni-hamburg.de

Abstract. The rapid innovation of information and communication technology (ICT) within the last decades has come along with the development of new opportunities and challenges, new business models, new systems, etc. Companies like Amazon, Google or Alibaba shape business functions and percolate our daily life. Business operations go hand in hand with new types of user experiences when buying goes different than just traditional ways. Often it is not only the buying behavior but also the way recommendations are perceived as they may be readily available. This relates to opinion mining and, unfortunately, opinion spamming. We survey the issue of opinion spamming and fake review detection and focus on both sides of fake review groups, i.e., how to detect such groups but also how to set up a group that might be undetected with current methods. As both directions go hand in hand we elaborate on learning in both directions with the aim to improve related methods.

Keywords: Opinion spamming · Digital innovation · Information management · Digital transformation

1 Introduction

Product reviews have become an important part of decision making especially for individuals but also for organizations and companies when making buying decisions. This also relates to reviews on services and alike. One of the major problems faced in this context refers to *opinion spamming* which includes especially the notion of writing fake reviews to promote (or demote) certain products. Opinion spamming can go along the lines of individuals trying to work as influencing bodies. Even more so, fake review groups have become a popular means of enhanced opinion spamming. That is, here we are concerned about spam detection in a collaborative setting as well as the question on how to discover fake review groups.

A. Marcus and E. Rosenzweig (Eds.): HCII 2020, LNCS 12200, pp. 370–384, 2020.
https://doi.org/10.1007/978-3-030-49713-2_26

Opinion spamming and opinion mining are closely related to the field of sentiment analysis. Sentiment analysis refers to extracting opinions and/or emotions from documents or just simple pieces of text. While sentiment analysis can be used to investigate diverse media such as audio, video or images, we are mainly focused on extracting sentiments from written texts.

To be more specific, recent challenges arising while conducting sentiment analysis incorporate those occurring within the area of detecting fake reviews and spam. Social media, online vendor websites and other websites generally contain fake entries, comments and reviews [38]. Although responsible companies advertise that they follow their responsibility by deleting purchased reviews, agencies such as the Fivestar Marketing AG continue to offer fake review services which they present as allegedly legal methods [16,29]. This phenomenon is known in academia and even to the public; see, e.g., [2,28]. Also word-of-mouth tells us that there are a wealth of fake review groups all around the world without yet being detected.

To act against such distortions of public opinion, there are different measures that can be applied. For instance, the author's reputation could be checked and duplicates should be identified [39]. In [20], we see a wealth of data types that can be used in detection techniques. Moreover, these authors provide a review in the area of detection of spam reviews as well as related spam detection methods and techniques.

In this paper, we survey – again – the issue of opinion spamming and especially fake review groups. Several questions are considered.

- One of the questions is related to languages, i.e., to which extent are websites under different language regimes revealing a different approach; see, e.g., [47] for the Chinese market.
- How much value is in a report?
- Are reviews authentic? [40]
- Another research question, may be not necessarily an opportune one, relates to how a fake review group has to be set up so that detection with existing algorithms is difficult. This question should not necessarily increase the number of fake reviews but allow researchers to investigate new algorithms and methods to account for these settings.
- If opinion spamming refers to providing wrong or false information in reviews to misguide consumers and influence product sales, we might not necessarily have a comprehensive view on the subject. This is due to the fact that information in fake reviews may even be correct. How to deal with correct reviews from fake reviewers? (This would even open up the issue of having mystery shoppers included in the ball game.)

Elaborating on the above questions and the methods at hand (see the above or below references), after some more comprehensive but yet selective literature review, we start by using some frequent item set mining method to find a set of candidate groups. Behavioral models may investigate possible collusion among fake reviewers. Though, if we define groups based on different settings and relationships we end up in something that may just be related to reviewed products.[1] In literature attempts are seen that successfully label fake review groups. Therefore, in our research we investigate both sides. On one hand we describe different approaches and models to set up fake review groups. On the other hand we apply available methods to see to which extent these groups may be discovered. This includes the extension of item sets as well as the specific "training" of related methods to find or not find what we have set. We conclude with managerial implications for both sides, i.e., the way of setting up those groups as well as the definition of methods aimed at detecting them. We end up – on a meta-level – with some critical reflection upon such research efforts, food for thought.

2   Opinion Spamming Issues and Literature Review

Generally, information may be viewed as purpose-oriented knowledge, demonstrating their use under various conditions and developments in reality to let decision makers take some actions; action-determined knowledge might be a similar focus. We define *information management* as purpose-oriented provision, processing, and distribution of the resource information for decision support as well as the provision of respective infrastructure [45]. That is, information management is understood, among others, as an instrument for making information distribution operable for an enterprise as well as for decision makers. In that respect it becomes an enabler for efficient business operations. Though, information management also has to enable decision makers to distinguish between different types of information when taking decisions: objective information (that would be needed), subjective information (a decision maker might think is needed), available information (including misleading or wrong information like fake information). Moreover, one might distinguish regarding the ease or difficulty of being able to reach some information. With that opinion spamming might be seen as part of information management.

In the spirit as mentioned in the introduction, papers stressing the reasoning for the advent of fake reviews seem to be a dime a dozen. Often, we also see connections to different words having the same or slightly different meaning, like deception theory, in the sense that reviews influence in the same way as information management tells us, e.g., that 'one cannot not communicate,' among others; see, e.g., [45] and some references therein. But, no matter where we consult the topic, fake reviews and opinion spamming are meant to increase the popularity (and at the end the revenues of related companies) of products, services, etc. Online reviews, influencers and alike are becoming more and more popular. Companies often use that kind of attention to post (or let others do so) reviews in favor of their own products and services or against those of other companies.

Spamming can be done by individuals [28] or by groups, where a coordination effort can be undertaken or not, i.e., individuals are possibly working together

---

[1] Just consider a fictitious person in some country setting up a fake review company using classmates abroad with diverse groups of friends and relations.

without explicitly knowing. Individuals can be on hire or just sellers of one or more products promoting themselves and their products or services. In case of groups there may be coordinated efforts regarding people spamming while they have a homogenous or even a diverse background.

Next, we provide pointers to survey papers in the area, refer to the discussion of related issues on a meta-level and also mention some legal issues. Moreover, we provide references specifically dealing with fake review groups.

2.1 Survey Papers

Opinion spamming can be seen as a subfield of sentiment analysis. In sentiment analysis one studies phenomena along the extraction of opinions and/or emotions from documents like text, among others. Surveys on sentiment analysis seem to be a dime a dozen; for some recent examples see, e.g., [19,25,27,39,51]. Reviews/surveys focusing on opinion spamming and the detection of fake reviews include [8,20,23,40].

An interesting observation, even if we might over-exaggerate a little, is that this area seems to have a larger proportion of surveys and reviews over original research papers than other areas (see also [27]).

An example for a recent and more or less comprehensive survey is [23]. They boil their search down to some 76 relevant papers or studies within a dozen years from 2007–2018 written in English. While we do not doubt the good intentions of the authors in finding some good references and conclusions, a considerable number of papers cited in our paper is not cited in theirs', though their search string should have found them. Moreover, if we understood their settings correctly, even their own paper would not have been found assuming the time horizon was extended to 2019. This could happen, e.g., if the searched databases for the study and the publication outlet for the study are not coinciding.

2.2 Meta-Level and the Value of Reviews

Opinion spamming is also observed on a meta-level. This means that we are not necessarily interested in individual reviews and their impact but more on generic issues regarding reviewing or evaluating in general. Among others, this relates to the knowledge of the public to which extent reviews could be manipulated. While even newspapers and magazines report about this in an ongoing manner [16,28,29], the comprehension still seems quite different in different settings. For instance, in [2] it is argued whether it pays for a company to inform the public about the (possible) existence of fake reviews. For a well-established brand this may be beneficial while new kids on the block might be better off to let independent sources (like the mentioned newspapers) report on this. Using more or less bad prejudice, our interpretation of that and related studies is that have-nots are get-nots ('if you are born poor you will stay poor').

From an academic standpoint discussions on the meta-level can often be found in marketing as well as information systems outlets. As an example see the journal where papers like [2] have appeared.

Different social media platforms are building the foundation of reviews and opinion mining. This does not only concern the internet but also media like Twitter or Instagram. Especially on the latter platforms, we see some means of influencer marketing involving endorsements and product placement from people and/or organizations who have a purported level of social influence in their field. An influencer may provide testimonial advertising or play the role of a potential user or buyer. Their actions and behavior may be more subtle than that of professionals like journalists, academics or industry analysts.

Let us first exemplify regarding the use of Twitter and alike for opinion mining. Subjective user opinions of mobility networks can be used to judge upon the satisfaction level of users of mass transit systems, especially in the case of disturbances [18, 26]. Based on these social media platforms it is possible to design a system architecture allowing to automatically capture the user comprehension and perspective based on sentiment analysis of the user-generated content. Being aware of data security issues, users or customers may be used or exploited as sensors of mobility dynamics (in a sense contributing towards the building of heatmaps), indicating where and how disturbances are observed within the public transport network. Nowcasting or microblogging from messages posted on Twitter provides real-time sensing of traffic-related information.

[35] study the motivations behind incentivized consumer reviews generated via influencer marketing campaigns.

Some of the issues related to opinion mining and opinion spamming concern the implications that reviews may have not only towards other users or potential customers but also as a feedback mechanism towards the company itself. Once analyzed in detail, reviews, whether they are fake reviews or real ones, may help to improve or advance services and products. That is, suggestions, tips and advice, which are often explicitly sought and needed by both brand owners and consumers may be seen as suggestions and the related task of mining suggestions from opinionated text on social media may be termed *suggestion mining* [32]. Once interpreted in a slightly different way, this may also be viewed as crowd-sourcing; see, e.g., [30]. This connection to crowdsourcing and the possibility of disintermediation between customers and companies is also exemplified in [44].

Let us take a different domain as an example: Writing nice book reviews can be an art and still they may be fake reviews. Consider, e.g., the phrase "This book has a solid cover; so far for its advantages." Actually this need not be a fake review and even the issue whether the sentiment can be discovered as negative might not be clear in all cases. Based on this, let us turn towards the following question: How much value is in a report?

Considering book reviews, we may consult [7] as they refer to the characteristic of a product or a service being hedonic, including books (while our example in the Appendix, Fig. 1, might not be what they mean). Hedonic aspects of products are even more difficult to evaluate than technical ones. In this case, opinion leaders, such as critics, may serve as key informants to consumers (later we may also come to the case of mystery shoppers who are somewhat different). The study of [7] considers the different roles and incentives of literary critics and how they influence the success of books. Similar issues actually also hold for movies. Both involve multisensory, fantasy, emotive aspects and relate to symbolic motives. Moreover, the diffusion patterns of these products are also different than technical ones. Nevertheless, fake reviews may be an issue, too. Extending the above-mentioned issues, [42] provide elasticities as standardized measures for the relationships between the success of different types of products like movies or video games and critics' volume, average, positive and negative valence, and the variation in critics' appeal; like other issues in this paper, food for thought.

Without going too much into detail, language might have a major impact regarding opinion spamming as there may be native speakers publishing in their own language, non-native speakers publishing in other languages than their mother tongue. While most of the companies that we may look at, are using multiple language environments, this need not be true in general. An interesting issue is to which extent this influences the behavior of opinion spammers and their possible detection.

For examples considering the issues in different languages see, e.g., [36] (Russian) and [47] (Chinese).

2.3   Legal Issues

Fake reviews may be judged differently throughout the world according to different legal policies and laws. That is, often spamming may become a legal issue and the question arises to which extent lawmakers have done a good job to set up an environment where lawbreakers may be prosecuted; see, e.g., [22] for an Australian investigation. A comprehensive consideration with a focus on US law is given by [44]. The overall question, though, refers to the fact that lawmakers still seem to have considerable difficulties to set the pace on an international transboundary level.

Recently, to give some specific example, the German Bundesgerichtshof decided a specific case (regarding Yelp) such that reputation software may be used to filter reviews [4]. The problem that seems inherent is that the quality of the software and its algorithms is nontransparent.

Touching the information management issue is done in [34].

2.4   Literature on Fake Review Groups

When opinion mining aims to summarize the amount of appreciation and criticism in a given text, this may be done favorably also or especially in a collaborative effort, i.e., using fake review groups. Fake review groups relate to opinion spamming in a collaborative effort. There are quite a few sources available studying spam detection in this setting including [6,31,48,49].

Considering fake review groups means forming (eventually artificial) communities that are working together to increase the possible influence of their opinions. Analyzing community structures built through abnormal non-random positive interactions is done, e.g., by [6]. On the one hand one has fake reviewers who eventually post spam reviews and/or support comments of others, especially fellow group members. Through extensive experimental analysis, [6] show the impact of a community-based approach in terms of accuracy and reliability. They show that their approach can successfully identify spam reviews without relying on review content, while achieving the same level of accuracy as state-of-the-art pure content-based classifiers. Once calling the same or similar issues as coming from deception theory we may refer to, e.g., [50].

We should note that the issue of fake reviews may be different in different settings (while we have not yet put any evidence on related commonalities and differences). Table 1 in the appendix provides examples with comments and references regarding various related events observed over time.

3   Methods

Various algorithms are available, mostly coming from areas such as machine learning, statistics and operations research. Besides describing the methods themselves, one also needs to think about possible datasets.

3.1   A Sketch of Available Methods

The above mentioned survey papers also include a comprehensive list of references regarding available methods. In the sequel, we first summarize a few pointers and then sketch a limited number of available methods.

- Binomial regression: [41]
- Latent Dirichlet Allocation (LDA): [11]

An example for a comparative implementation of different supervised techniques such as Support Vector Machine (SVM), Multinomial Naive Bayes (MNB), and Multilayer Perceptron can be found in [21]. The presented results indicate that all the mentioned supervised techniques can successfully detect fake reviews with more than 86% accuracy.

In [11] an unsupervised topic-sentiment joint probabilistic model based on an LDA model is proposed. To be more specific, the automatic identification of topics to describe the distribution of words within a considered cluster is related to LDA. LDA is a generative probabilistic model proposed by [3], which has been successfully used to identify latent topics within corpora. In a nutshell, LDA assumes that documents in a corpus are represented as random mixtures over latent topics and, in turn, each topic is characterized by a distribution over a set of words. For each document in a corpus, the generative process of the words included in that document works as follows: (i) Select a topic from a multinomial distribution, and (ii) select a word from that topic. Thus, LDA is about estimating two probability matrices, i.e., a document-topic matrix, giving the probability that a certain document contains a latent topic, and a topic-word matrix, modeling the probability that a latent topic uses a certain word. For an in-depth presentation of LDA, along with its application to topic modeling, document classification, and collaborative filtering we direct the interested reader to [3].

Further references include the following. In [52], an interesting approach is followed regarding spam detection. While this is not the same as fake review detection, the approach itself is worth being considered. Actually, as a starting point, the authors use a wrapper-based feature selection method to extract crucial features. Second, a decision tree is chosen as the classifier model with a well-known training approach. Actually, particle swarm optimization (PSO) is used to solve the related problem. In [10] the geolocation features of shops are included.

3.2   Datasets

The survey of [23] lists a table with some ten references with various datasets used by the cited authors, including those from Amazon, Datatang, Resellerratings and TripAdvisor. The number of reviewers goes from a couple of hundreds towards a bit more than a million where multiple reviews by the reviewers have been performed in some up to many cases.

Datasets used in [21] are mimicking cases from Amazon and TripAdvisor. Amazon Mechanical Turk can also be used to generate datasets; see [33] for an example to do so.

4   Conclusions

In this paper we have looked at opinion spamming based on selected literatures. Implicitly an information management approach gave us a slightly different edge over existing reviews. In passing, we have seen quite a few issues that are worth being explored further. In that sense we can see the value of this paper as one initializing further research. Let us distinguish between some food for thought and some explicit future research directions.

4.1   Lessons Learned and Food for Thought

One of the questions not comprehensively answered in current research relates to what a fake review is or can be and who is responsible for it. Let us provide a recent example from a platform like Ebay or Amazon. Let us assume that we bought some item (say, a face mask) from some vendor for a certain price and we provided a good review (say good value for money given the paid price). Based on the current situation (early 2020 with the spread of the corona virus) the price was multiplied by a factor of, say, about five to six or even more. Now our review is still in the system but the basic notion of good value for money has turned and we would have dared to give any star if we would have known or paid the current price. That is, the vendor made our review and those of fellow reviewers a fake review. How is this detected?

In the area of public transport where we are dealing with the provision of services as a product, we have seen the use of Twitter etc. for traffic-related comments (see Sect. 2.2). These are reviews, too; they are or may be opinionate and one might learn how to set up an environment where fake reviews are not so frequent.

Academic papers are supposed to be 'peer-'reviewed, too. Though, also that system may be flawed and one might have to think on how to cope with that [9,13].

4.2   Future Research

Future research should enhance different views on fake reviews. Interesting observations could be done by mystery shoppers. Mystery shopping is a form of participant observation, which uses especially trained persons to perform the tasks of buyers to let personnel believe that they are serving real customers or real potential customers. For an entry point to mystery shoppers we refer to, e.g., [24,46]. For specific applications in the above mentioned public transport context see, e.g., [15,43].

While a mystery shopper might not have the same computing capability standing behind an automatic evaluation of reviews, he/she might be able to judge upon statements and judgements based on real experience. Based on that experience mirrored with automatic evaluations, a different kind of training approach might be observed worth being explored as future research. If this is seen in the light of algorithm development, we might actually see advanced methods for fake review detection.

Appendix

In this appendix we provide a hands-on set of arguments why fake reviews might be an issue; see, e.g., [12,17]. Moreover, we survey quite a few companies and settings in which fake reviews may have some major impact; see Table 1.

Let us exemplify possible reasons for fake reviews. First of all, there are many advisors trying to support businesses in selling on online platforms. And, secondly, there is their advise. As a producer one provides detailed product descriptions, high-quality images and videos, competitive pricing and possibly some customer service. Once this has been set up and one tries to be sold through an e-commerce or online platform, there are eventually recommendations of the system, rankings and alike. If one does not make it to the 'first' page, one might be overseen. Customers might use some sorting and check for one or two pages, not more, do they? Therefore, an online seller might have to understand how a product ranking works (and of course the specificity of the request might do the job, too). There are actually two types to consider.

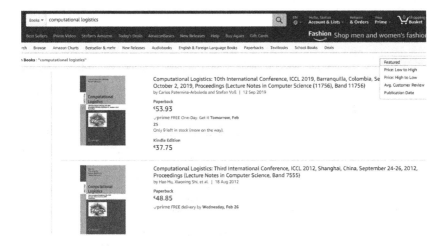

Fig. 1. Searching on Amazon; example

- Traditional Search Rank. This is where your product appears when someone does a search for a related keyword; this is related to common search engines.
- The Buy Box. This is where Amazon differs from many others. The buy box is a box that can be found on the product page that customers click on to an item to their shopping cart (see especially the upper part and the right hand upper corner of Fig. 1). When multiple sellers offer the same item, one has to compete to appear there.

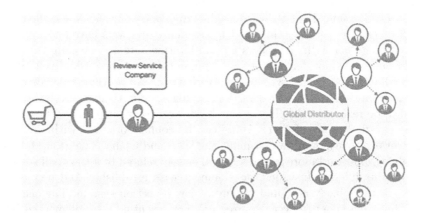

Fig. 2. Settings of fake review groups.

Advise goes on in claiming that sellers should price their items competitively, maintain a positive selling history, increase sales and provide thorough

Table 1. Companies and webpages, study objects

Company/webpage	Area specifications	Comments	(Selected) references
Alibaba.com	E-commerce platform (main focus on business-to-business)	Alexpress.com as an online shopping company belongs to Alibaba	[5]
Amazon.com	Technology company focusing on e-commerce, cloud computing etc.	Listed on Nasdaq. Many data sets for further study and comparison can be found on the web	[1], for data sets see, e.g., [6]
Booking.com	Lodging	Companies like Booking.com have decreased the possibilities for fake reviews by allowing only actual users of their reservation system who have booked and stayed in a particular hotel to write a review about it	
Google.com	Web search engine	The company also includes Google Play and many others	[37]
Taobao.com	E-commerce platform (main focus on consumer-to-consumer)		
TripAdvisor.com	Transportation, lodging, travel experiences, and restaurants	Listed on the Nasdaq, includes Expedia etc.	[14,22]
Yelp.com	Business directory service and crowdsourced review forum	Traded at NYSE. Occasionally, journalists say "to yelp" when they mean "to write an online review"	[4]

product information. Actually, maintaining a positive selling history includes as a tip to actively seek (positive) reviews. Moreover, it is claimed that buying fake reviews is an offence, but the way it is done, it makes the issue an interesting one in any dimension. That is, based on the importance of reviews and the traditional literature review defecting model, now many reviewers have become more advanced. Together with the sellers and an intermediate service company, they possibly build up (more or less large) communication groups using well-known social media like Facebook, Whats'app, Wechat etc. and continue to involve new members to anti-fake reviewer defection, trying to hide themselves deeply and pretend to be real reviewers. If one searches for review groups on Facebook, one actually can find many of them. Units can be country-oriented with the most prominent examples found in Germany, the USA and China. The group focuses on involving more and more new reviewers, closely related to a snowball system. Based on the different historical development with established and new users, reviews are more likely accepted by any review detection system. The classical idea is that each fake reviewer gets free products eventually supplemented by a commission (say, within 5–30 US$, depending on the value of the product and the urgency of reviews needed). Moreover, the commission fee may be different depending on whether, e.g., photos or videos are included. In a sense, fake reviewer groups have developed a 3-layer distribution system (see Fig. 2).

References

1. Ata-Ur-Rehman, et al.: Intelligent interface for fake product review monitoring and removal. In: 16th International Conference on Electrical Engineering, Computing Science and Automatic Control (CCE), pp. 1–6 (2019). https://doi.org/10.1109/ICEEE.2019.8884529
2. Bambauer-Sachse, S., Mangold, S.: Do consumers still believe what is said in online product reviews? A persuasion knowledge approach. J. Retail. Consum. Serv. **20**(4), 373–381 (2013). https://doi.org/10.1016/j.jretconser.2013.03.004
3. Blei, D., Ng, A., Jordan, M.: Latent Dirichlet allocation. J. Mach. Learn. Res. **3**, 993–1022 (2003). http://www.jmlr.org/papers/v3/blei03a. Accessed 24 Feb 2020
4. Bundesgerichtshof: Zur Zulässigkeit der Bewertungsdarstellung von Unternehmen auf einem Internet-Bewertungsportal (www.yelp.de) (2020). https://www.bundesgerichtshof.de/SharedDocs/Pressemitteilungen/DE/2020/2020007.html. Accessed 24 Feb 2020
5. Chengzhang, J., Kang, D.: Detecting spamming stores by analyzing their suspicious behaviors. In: 17th International Conference on Advanced Communication Technology (ICACT), pp. 502–507 (2015). https://doi.org/10.1109/ICACT.2015.7224845
6. Choo, E., Yu, T., Chi, M.: Detecting opinion spammer groups through community discovery and sentiment analysis. In: Samarati, P. (ed.) DBSec 2015. LNCS, vol. 9149, pp. 170–187. Springer, Cham (2015). https://doi.org/10.1007/978-3-319-20810-7_11
7. Clement, M., Proppe, D., Rott, A.: Do critics make bestsellers? Opinion leaders and the success of books. J. Med. Econ. **20**(2), 77–105 (2007). https://doi.org/10.1080/08997760701193720
8. Crawford, M., Khoshgoftaar, T.M., Prusa, J.D., Richter, A.N., Najada, H.A.: Survey of review spam detection using machine learning techniques. J. Big Data **2** (2015). Article no 23. https://doi.org/10.1186/s40537-015-0029-9
9. Cyranoski, D.: China cracks down on fake peer reviews. Nature **546**(7659) (2017). https://doi.org/10.1038/546464a
10. Deng, R., et al.: SpamTracer: manual fake review detection for O2O commercial platforms by using geolocation features. In: Guo, F., Huang, X., Yung, M. (eds.) Inscrypt 2018. LNCS, vol. 11449, pp. 384–403. Springer, Cham (2019). https://doi.org/10.1007/978-3-030-14234-6_21
11. Dong, L.Y., et al.: An unsupervised topic-sentiment joint probabilistic model for detecting deceptive reviews. Expert Syst. Appl. **114**, 210–223 (2018). https://doi.org/10.1016/j.eswa.2018.07.005
12. Dunne, C.: 5 ways to help you generate genuine Amazon reviews (2020). https://www.feedbackexpress.com/the-how-tos-for-amazon-reviews/. Accessed 24 Feb 2020
13. Faria, J., Goel, R.: Returns to networking in Academia. Netnomics **11**, 103–117 (2010). https://doi.org/10.1007/s11066-010-9048-z
14. Fenton, S.: TripAdvisor denies rating system is flawed, after fake restaurant tops rankings in Italy. The Independent (2015). https://www.independent.co.uk/life-style/gadgets-and-tech/news/tripadvisor-denies-rating-system-is-flawed-after-fake-restaurant-tops-rankings-in-italy-10354818.html. Accessed 24 Feb 2020
15. Georgiadis, G., Xenidis, Y., Toskas, I., Papaioannou, P.: A performance measurement system for public transport services in Thessaloniki, Greece. In: Transport Research Arena (TRA) 5th Conference: Transport Solutions from Research to Deployment, Paris (2014)

16. Gierow, H.: Amazon löscht eine halbe Million gekaufter Bewertungen (2016). https://www.golem.de/news/online-shopping-amazon-loescht-eine-halbe-million-gekaufter-bewertungen-1611-124718.html
17. Grosman, L.: Five tips to improve your ranking on Amazon (2017). https://www.forbes.com/sites/forbescommunicationscouncil/2017/02/28/five-tips-to-improve-your-ranking-on-amazon/#33f6707e9fed. Accessed 24 Feb 2020
18. Haghighi, N., Liu, X., Wei, R., Li, W., Shao, H.: Using Twitter data for transit performance assessment: a framework for evaluating transit riders' opinions about quality of service. Public Transp. **10**, 363–377 (2018). https://doi.org/10.1007/s12469-018-0184-4
19. Hemmatian, F., Sohrabi, M.: A survey on classification techniques for opinion mining and sentiment analysis. Artif. Intell. Rev. **52**(3), 1495–1545 (2019). https://doi.org/10.1007/s10462-017-9599-6
20. Heydari, A., Tavakoli, M., Salim, N., Heydari, Z.: Detection of review spam: a survey. Expert Syst. Appl. **42**(7), 3634–3642 (2015). https://doi.org/10.1016/j.eswa.2014.12.029
21. Hossain, M.F.: Fake review detection using data mining, Master thesis, Missouri State University (2019)
22. Hunt, K.M.: Gaming the system: fake online reviews v. consumer law. Comput. Law Secur. Rev. **31**(1), 3–25 (2015). https://doi.org/10.1016/j.clsr.2014.11.003
23. Hussain, N., Turab Mirza, H., Rasool, G., Hussain, I., Kaleem, M.: Spam review detection techniques: a systematic literature review. Appl. Sci. **9**(987), 1–26 (2019). https://doi.org/10.3390/app9050987
24. Jacob, S., Schiffino, N., Biard, B.: The mystery shopper: a tool to measure public service delivery? Int. Rev. Adm. Sci. **84**(1), 164–184 (2018). https://doi.org/10.1177/0020852315618018
25. Kaur, H., Mangat, V., Nidhi: a survey of sentiment analysis techniques. In: 2017 International Conference on I-SMAC (IoT in Social, Mobile, Analytics and Cloud), pp. 921–925. IEEE (2017). https://doi.org/10.1109/I-SMAC.2017.8058315
26. Kokkinogenis, Z., Filguieras, J., Carvalho, S., Sarmento, L., Rossetti, R.J.: Mobility network evaluation in the user perspective: real-time sensing of traffic information in Twitter messages. In: Rossetti, R.J., Liu, R. (eds.) Advances in Artificial Transportation Systems and Simulation, pp. 219–234. Academic Press, Boston (2015). https://doi.org/10.1016/B978-0-12-397041-1.00012-1
27. Körner, T., Voß, S.: State-of-the-art and scientific contribution in the field of sentiment analysis. Technical report, IWI, University of Hamburg (2019)
28. Kühn, A.: Wie Schüler mit frisierten Bewertungen bei Amazon Geld verdienen und Käufer in die Irre führen. Spiegel 42/2019, 83 (2019)
29. Kwidzinski, R.: Diese Firma verkauft gute Bewertungen. Allgemeine Hotel- und Gastronomie-Zeitung, 7 August (2017). https://www.ahgz.de/news/online-marketing-diese-firma-verkauft-bewertungen,200012241347.html
30. Martin, N., Lessmann, S., Voß, S.: Crowdsourcing: Systematisierung praktischer Ausprägungen und verwandter Konzepte. In: Bichler, M., et al. (eds.) Multikonferenz Wirtschaftsinformatik 2008, pp. 1251–1263. Gito, Berlin (2008)
31. Mukherjee, A., Liu, B., Glance, N.: Spotting fake reviewer groups in consumer reviews. In: Proceedings of the 21st International Conference on World Wide Web, WWW 2012, pp. 191–200. ACM, New York (2012). https://doi.org/10.1145/2187836.2187863
32. Negi, S., Buitelaar, P.: Suggestion mining from opinionated text. In: Pozzi, F., Fersini, E., Messina, E., Liu, B. (eds.) Sentiment Analysis in Social Networks, pp.

129–139. Morgan Kaufmann, Boston (2017). https://doi.org/10.1016/B978-0-12-804412-4.00008-5

33. Ott, M., Cardie, C., Hancock, J.: Estimating the prevalence of deception in online review communities. In: Proceedings of the 21st International Conference on World Wide Web, pp. 201–210. ACM, New York (2012). https://doi.org/10.1145/2187836.2187864

34. Patterson, M.R.: Antitrust Law in the New Economy: Google, Yelp, LIBOR, and the Control of Information. Harvard University Press, Cambridge (2017)

35. Petrescu, M., O'Leary, K., Goldring, D., Ben Mrad, S.: Incentivized reviews: promising the moon for a few stars. J. Retail. Consum. Serv. **41**, 288–295 (2018). https://doi.org/10.1016/j.jretconser.2017.04.005

36. Pisarevskaya, D., Litvinova, T., Litvinova, O.: Deception detection for the Russian language: lexical and syntactic parameters. In: Proceedings of Natural Language Processing and Information Retrieval Workshop, pp. 1–10, Varna, Bulgaria (2017). https://doi.org/10.26615/978-954-452-038-0_001

37. Rahman, M., Rahman, M., Carbunar, B., Chau, D.H.: Search rank fraud and malware detection in Google Play. IEEE Trans. Knowl. Data Eng. **29**(6), 1329–1342 (2017). https://doi.org/10.1109/TKDE.2017.2667658

38. Rahmath, H.: Opinion mining and sentiment analysis - challenges and applications. Int. J. Appl. Innov. Eng. Manag. **3**(5), 401–403 (2014). http://www.ijaiem.org/volume3issue5/IJAIEM-2014-05-31-124.pdf

39. Rajalakshmi, S., Asha, S., Pazhaniraja, N.: A comprehensive survey on sentiment analysis. In: Fourth International Conference on Signal Processing, Communication and Networking (ICSCN), pp. 1–5. IEEE (2017). https://doi.org/10.1109/ICSCN.2017.8085673

40. Rastogi, A., Mehrotra, M.: Opinion spam detection in online reviews. J. Inf. Knowl. Manag. **16**(04, article #1750036) (2017). https://doi.org/10.1142/S0219649217500368

41. Savage, D., Zhang, X., Yu, X., Chou, P., Wang, Q.: Detection of opinion spam based on anomalous rating deviation. Expert Syst. Appl. **42**(22), 8650–8657 (2015). https://doi.org/10.1016/j.eswa.2015.07.019

42. Schulz, P., Hofmann, J., Clement, M., Burmester, A.B.: The role of professional critics in product success - a meta-analysis. Technical report, University of Hamburg, Hamburg Business School (2019)

43. Sidorchuk, R., Efimova, D., Lopatinskaya, I., Kaderova, V.: Parametric approach to the assessment of service quality attributes of municipal passenger transport in Moscow. Mod. Appl. Sci. **9**(4), 303–311 (2015). https://doi.org/10.5539/mas.v9n4p303

44. Tessuto, G., Bhatia, V.K., Garzone, G., Salvi, R., Williams, C. (eds.): Constructing Legal Discourses and Social Practices: Issues and Perspectives. Cambridge Scholars, Newcastle upon Tyne (2018)

45. Voß, S., Gutenschwager, K.: Informationsmanagement.. Springer, Berlin (2001). https://doi.org/10.1007/978-3-642-56878-7

46. Wilson, A.M.: Mystery shopping: using deception to measure service performance. Psychol. Market. **18**(7), 721–734 (2001). https://doi.org/10.1002/mar.1027

47. Xu, C., Zhang, J., Chang, K., Long, C.: Uncovering collusive spammers in Chinese review websites. In: Proceedings of the 22nd ACM International Conference on Information & Knowledge Management, pp. 979–988. ACM, New York (2013). https://doi.org/10.1145/2505515.2505700

48. Xu, G., Hu, M., Ma, C., Daneshmand, M.: GSCPM: CPM-based group spamming detection in online product reviews. In: IEEE International Conference on Communications (ICC), pp. 1–6 (2019). https://doi.org/10.1109/ICC.2019.8761650

49. Ye, J., Akoglu, L.: Discovering opinion spammer groups by network footprints. In: Appice, A., Rodrigues, P.P., Santos Costa, V., Soares, C., Gama, J., Jorge, A. (eds.) ECML PKDD 2015. LNCS (LNAI), vol. 9284, pp. 267–282. Springer, Cham (2015). https://doi.org/10.1007/978-3-319-23528-8_17

50. Yoo, K.H., Gretzel, U.: Comparison of deceptive and truthful travel reviews. In: Information and Communication Technologies in Tourism, pp. 37–47, Vienna (2009). https://doi.org/10.1007/978-3-211-93971-0_4

51. Yousif, A., Niu, Z., Tarus, J., Ahmad, A.: A survey on sentiment analysis of scientific citations. Artif. Intell. Rev. **52**(3), 1805–1838 (2019). https://doi.org/10.1007/s10462-017-9597-8

52. Zhang, Y., Wang, S., Phillips, P., Ji, G.: Binary PSO with mutation operator for feature selection using decision tree applied to spam detection. Knowl.-Based Syst. **64**, 22–31 (2014), https://doi.org/10.1016/j.knosys.2014.03.015

Make Me Care: Ethical Visualization
for Impact in the Sciences and Data Sciences

Katherine J. Hepworth$^{(\boxtimes)}$ (iD)

University of Nevada, Reno, NV 89509, USA
khepworth@unr.edu

Abstract. Scientists and data scientists have long aspired to eliminate bias from their visualizations. This paper argues that eliminating bias from visualizations is impossible, efforts to do so have negative real-world consequences for people, and that strategically emphasizing bias in visualizations is not only desirable, but also ethical. The growing public mistrust in science has not been helped by efforts to produce visualizations devoid of bias. This paper further argues that ethical visualization can only be achieved by acknowledging and embracing the treacherous nature of data visualization as a medium, committing to an ethics of care in visualization, investigating the potential for both benefit and harm when visualizing specific data, and then employing strategies to mitigate the harm involved in creating, using, and sharing visualizations. These strategies center around consciously crafting a visual frame (ie bias) for communicating data to a given audience. This paper offers 1) a critical lens on the rhetorical nature of visualizations, 2) the Hippocratic oath as a means of committing to maximizing the benefit, and mitigating the harm, done by visualizations, 3) ethical visualization for impact as a practical strategy for taming treacherous visualizations, and 4) compassionate visualizations as the end goal of following ethical visualization practices.

Keywords: Visualization · Care ethics · Science communication · Compassion

1 Introduction

Visualizations amplify the biases, constraints, and ideological perspectives of the people, organizations, and cultures they originate from. They do this in the form of arguments that are particularly persuasive firstly because they are processed largely unconsciously, and secondly because they present their bias in the guise of impartial, scientific truths. These arguments are usually constructed unconsciously, too, and herein lies the potential for harm. Whether they display big data or small data, whether they are online and interactive or printed and static, whether their intended purposes are scientific, artistic, or somewhere in between, visualizations without consciously crafted arguments always persuade, in the sense of projecting "a set of beliefs about the way the world should be, and present[ing] this construction as truth" [6]. At best, unconsciously constructed arguments in visualizations have a counterproductive effect on what the visualizer is trying to show; at worst they perpetuate harmful, counterfactual public narratives that increase mistrust in science and societal division [14].

© Springer Nature Switzerland AG 2020
A. Marcus and E. Rosenzweig (Eds.): HCII 2020, LNCS 12200, pp. 385–404, 2020.
https://doi.org/10.1007/978-3-030-49713-2_27

386   K. J. Hepworth

Visualizations can be made more ethical—that is less harmful and more effective—by applying reflexivity and critical thinking to the process of constructing them. Ethical Visualization for Impact, the main subject of this paper, is in part a call for scientists and data scientists to pay attention to, and harness, the amplification effect and bias inherent in visualization as a medium.

For example, the NOAA Interactive Sea Level Rise Viewer is a publicly available, online interactive geographic visualization created by the US National Oceanic and Atmospheric Administration (NOAA) to try to educate people about the risks to their communities and homes from climate-driven sea level rise [30]. Several governments and organizations around the world have created similar tools. This one contains lots of data from atmospheric physicists, biologists, oceanographers, and social scientists about the relationships between climate change, sea level rise, and population.

To demonstrate how it works, I'll use the example of the city Norfolk, Virginia in the United States. In terms of population, it's about the same size as Copenhagen, the host city for HCII 2020. Like Copenhagen, it's near the sea, and built around a river. Using the viewer to assess the risk to Norfolk of sea level rise involves navigating a lot of options in the viewer (see Fig. 1). The options are grouped in six key categories that relate to data collected from various research disciplines. The user can move the slider on the left up and down, and the map shows which parts of the city would be under water if the sea level rose. Navigating the variables, it becomes evident in a short amount of time that major areas of downtown Norfolk would be underwater in many scenarios. In fact, Norfolk is one of the most vulnerable cities in the Americas to sea level rise. There's a lot of the city shown as underwater in the view in Fig. 1. Seeing this, I would be tempted to move away, or at least look for a place to live on higher ground. To an impartial viewer, this seems obvious, right?

Technical communication researchers Sonia Stephens and Dan Richards wanted to test this seemingly obvious conclusion, so they conducted usability studies on a sea level rise viewer with people in Norfolk. They found that people consistently made decisions that were less in their interest, and less based on scientifically accurate information, after interacting with a sea level rise viewer [31, 34]. Although their research involves only a small number of participants, the implications of it are huge. A lot of time and money have perhaps been wasted on sea level rise viewers that not only don't do what is intended, but they also put people in greater harm and lead to greater misunderstanding. So, how did this happen?

Richards and Stephens work highlights a present-day, real-world risk of the common assumption, especially when it comes to visualization of data science and scientific findings, that "numbers speak for themselves" [15]. This assumption, rife in computational and scientific research, is based on other assumptions: 1) that what is obvious to researchers will be obvious to their audiences; and 2) that the medium—data visualizations themselves—are objective, something like a blank page on which data can be placed in order to be understood. A growing body of literature demonstrates how untrue this series of assumptions is.

Fig. 1. NOAA Interactive Sea Level Rise Viewer, 2017, 5 feet scenario, zoomed in on Norfolk, Virginia, United States. Visual frame: Sea level rise is too complex and abstract to worry about.

2   Treachery in Visualizations and How to Transmute It

For over a century, scholars working with visualizations have regularly acknowledged that data visualization—here loosely defined as data-informed charts, diagrams, maps, models, and tables with a considered use of visual composition for the goal of impactful communication—is fraught with pitfalls. Visualizations contribute to, reinforce, and thereby amplify, cultural assumptions and stereotypes. For as long as there has been explicit instruction on how to create data visualizations, there have been warnings about the perils of the medium. In his *Graphic Methods for Presenting Facts*, widely recognized as the first instructional manual on data visualization, Engineer Willard Brinton, describes in detail how data visualizations have the potential to mislead [2].

Various subdisciplines are now devoted to critiquing the biases inherent in visualizations in multiple fields, including: critical infovis in computer science [10], critical cartography [7, 27–29] and critical GIS [8, 24] in geography, feminist data visualization [11, 12], and ethical data visualization [5, 21, 23]. While some of this literature makes distinctions between visualizations with various levels of haptic engagement, interactivity, or physicality, [7] the definition used here is intentionally expansive enough to include a wide variety of visual representations of data, as *visual means and the goal of having an impact are the key qualities of visualization addressed in this paper*. The following subsections supplement these understandings with a detailed breakdown of the mechanics of argumentation in some key visualization forms, content types, and design elements, demonstrating how these individual elements influence attitudes individually, leading to a greater understanding of how they can reinforce one another to present a cohesive and powerful argument when they are all working in concert.

2.1 Argumentation Through Form

All visualization forms contain the historical and contemporary cultural associations of their invention and prior uses [16, 28, 34]. The shadows of the arguments that were contained within early and common examples of the visualization form linger, to some degree, in present-day uses, even when they contain very different data or are presented in a different context. When used unconsciously, for example, by unquestioningly accepting the "suggested" visualization form after inputting raw data into a partially automated (black box) visualization software, argumentation can be introduced into the new visualization that contradicts the visualizer's goals. However, when prior associations are considered, they can be harnessed to emphasize and amplify goals.

For example, consider Dmitri Mendeleev's periodic table of elements in an early form, the present-day version by the Royal Society of Chemists [31], and Marisa Bate's Periodic Table of Feminism (see Fig. 2). The original periodic table of elements functioned as a convincing argument, or frame, about groups (or periods) of physio-chemical properties of atoms being able to be predicted by atomic weight and valence. Since its first introduction, the periodic table of elements been expanded, the visual composition has been formalized, and it has become widely celebrated and used as an instructional tool. It has taken on a broader positivist cultural meaning and argument through these changes [3].

The Royal Society of Chemists' version is an example of a contemporary periodic table, with inclusion of later discoveries (such as inert or noble gases), some reorganization of individual elements (now organized by atomic number), further categorization of elements into groups and blocks, and color coding and visual organization to emphasize the relationships between elements and categories. It supplements these understandings with extensive interactive effects, including the ability to learn about each element through element-specific podcasts, videos, and scientific discovery narratives. This well-known, widely used contemporary periodic table conveys the visual frame that the building blocks of matter are fundamental, orderly, mastered by science, and intelligible to all to seek to know them. Bates' Periodic Table of Feminism leverages this association, applying the same positivist logic to her subject: the history of feminism. Her periodic table, by utilizing the visualization form of the better known periodic table, combined with her compositional and categorization choices, makes a visual argument, or visual frame, that feminists thinkers are fundamental to society—as fundamental as matter is to science, and that they too, are orderly, and intelligible to all who seek to know them.

2.2 Argumentation Through Content

At a more minute level, individual pieces of content and design decisions used within each visualization also contain argumentative qualities and associations that further the overall argument contained within a visualization. Content types and design elements that are explicit about their argumentation are titles, captions, annotations and emphases. Implicitly argumentative content types and design elements include data breaks, categorizations, scale, priming, nudges, priming, sizing, and proportional ink.

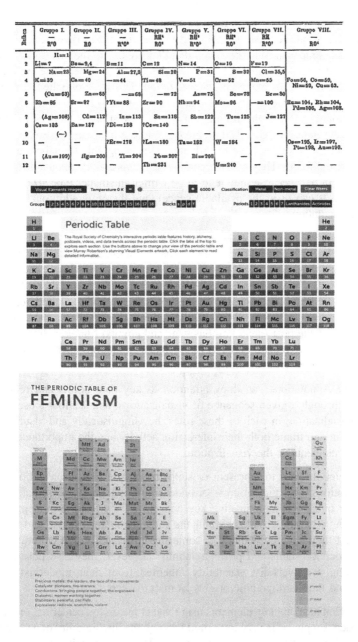

Fig. 2. Periodic tables. Figure 2a (top) Mendeleev's periodic table of elements, 1871. Visual frame: groupings of physiochemical properties (periods) of atoms are able to be predicted by atomic weight and valence. Figure 2b (middle) Periodic table of elements, 2019. Visual frame: the building blocks of matter are fundamental, orderly, mastered by science, and intelligible to all to seek to know them. Figure 2c (bottom) Periodic table of feminists, 2019. Visual frame: feminist thinkers—and by extension, feminism—are as fundamental to society as matter is to science, and they too are intelligible to all who seek to know them.

Titles. Titles and subtitles are the most explicit use of rhetoric in visualizations found in visualizations, both because we are used to reading text as rhetorical, and because titles are usually emphasized to the extent that they are one of the first things people see when looking at a visualization [12]. For example, in Fig. 2a, Mendeleev references his argument in the title of his pioneering visualization. This is despite the term "periodic" not being in common use to describe matter at the time – the naming of his visualization contributed to both the framing of his visualization as well as future understandings of the nature of chemical elements. While a title can make reference to an intended argument, subtitles have the advantage of being able to elaborate upon, and reinforce, a visual frame. They provide additional details and are often able to be longer than captions (in part because they tend to be written in smaller type size, so a greater number of words can fit in the available space), and therefore additional capacity for explicit argumentation.

Captions. Captions are nearly as explicitly argumentative as titles. A caption functions as a linguistic frame for the entire visualization, highlighting what is important to the visualizer, what they want the user/viewer to notice in the visualization [24]. For example, in Fig. 2, I have included each visualization example's author, title, and year —they are the elements I want readers of this paper to contrast and compare, in order to strengthen my own argument. When visualizations are shared on social media, the textual content of the post (including hashtags and emojis) functions the same way as captions. In this context, the number of likes, shares and replies operate to reinforce the argumentative power of the caption content.

Annotations. Annotations can draw attention to key data points and relationships, guide a user through a given sequence of visualizations, and scaffold a user's journey through a visualization; in each of these roles they linguistically and visually direct a user's attention and frame both their interaction activity and the importance they place on annotated elements of the visualization.

Symbols. Symbols used to represent or supplement data in a visualization—such as icons, illustrations, and pictograms—provide simplified visual cues that serve as a shorthand for quickly communicating key concepts. They foster argument by clearly communicating what the visualizer wants the audience to know most, and through the priming effect they have on audiences, conjuring up related visual cultural references and their associated status and power relations. However, they also pose the risk of communicating a universalist sensibility inherited from their modernist origins as pictograms and their cartographic origins as map markers [1, 16].

Emphases. Emphasizing key elements using visual hierarchy, centering, ordering, and negative space. Emphasis is very important for both the intelligibility of a visualization, and for the efficacy of the argument it presents. However, uncritical use of emphasis comes with the risk of fostering "inward-directed worldviews, each with its separate cult centre safely buffered within territories populated only by true believers" [13]. In saying this, art historian Samuel Edgerton was referring to cartography, although his observation applies to visualization generally.

Visual hierarchy draws attention to elements in a specific order, offering a subtler argumentative effect in with a similar effect to annotations. It is the coordinating design technique that combines the following strategies into a cohesive and intelligible whole. Centering, or determining what is positioned at the center of a visualization upon initial or default view, can be used as a way of declaring what is of most value, and studying what is centered can reveal the biases and world view of the visualization creators and sponsors [16].

Ordering data representations within a visualization includes a vast array of techniques encompassing map projections, data bins and polygons, and arranging data within one or more structured lists. These choices are typically made for pragmatic, logistical purposes in the moment, but nevertheless, like centering, they reinforce social norms of the time and culture in which they are created and commonly used, as in the much-cited case of the Mercator Projection [29]. Ordering information also determines what will be read first and last in a series of data, and therefore what will be given importance by viewers and users subconsciously, by harnessing serial position effects. For example, ordering information in a bar chart alphabetically will compositionally emphasize items with labels starting and ending at the ends of the alphabet.

Areas of a visualization that do not contain data or ornamentation, known in communication design and photography as negative space (or the more problematic, white space) and in critical geography as "silences", convey argument and emphasis through omission [16]. In communication design practice, the use of negative space is commonly understood as a functional technique of emphasis that fosters efficacy; the more space without design elements in a given visualization, the more attention is drawn to those that are present. However, decisions about what is most important to visualize are also decisions about what doesn't matter enough to be communicated. Omissions and negative space communicate a hierarchy of power that perpetuates and amplifies discrimination and cultural biases endemic to the cultures, institutions, and visualizers they are produced by.

Implicit Argumentation. Although the subtler forms of argumentation are seldom obvious, they are nevertheless imbued with meaning, persuading audiences of arguments they are barely aware of in nuances of representation such as data breaks, categorizations, nudges, scale and sizing, and priming. For example, data breaks, or the places where the individual portions of a scale range are cut off, are subtly perceived as significant, whether or not they are carefully considered by the research team. Where data breaks use solid colors to delineate individual data groupings, the data groupings are perceived as more discrete, or separate, than when the visualization uses a gradient color ramp with data breaks. Categorizations also contain subtle argumentation; which categories are chosen to visualize form a visual frame of what is important in the visualization, and the language found in labels used to describe categories reinforce this frame. Nudges, or interaction effects that provide a sort of animated motion-based visual annotation, are implicitly argumentative in that they cajole the user into certain behaviors within the navigation of the visualization, while dissuading others [33]. Scale and sizing of individual elements and the visualization itself both impact audience perceptions about what is significant in the visualization, and how the other elements in the visualization can be, or should be read. Priming, the effect of conjuring up past emotional and visual associations with design elements that reference other cultural and visual associations, is perhaps one of the most pernicious implicit forms of argumentation in visualizations. For this reason, some scholars rail against use of ornamentation in visualizations [26].

2.3 Committing to Doing No Harm

Each of the elements described above, and their associated argumentative capacities, can be harnessed to present a powerfully coordinated argument. With such power, comes great potential for harm, so much so that some visualization scholars advocate taking a *"do no harm" approach to visualization practice* [4, 18]. If we are to follow a Hippocratic oath approach to doing no harm in visualization, this means both not hurting people, and helping people, when they are in three types of relationships with visualizations. Firstly, *audiences of users of visualizations; doing no harm to these people includes not misleading them,* while helping them includes cultivating their empathy for represented subjects, and using the smallest feasible amount of their cognitive load to communicate effectively (and therefore, not making visualizations harder to navigate than is absolutely necessary). Secondly, *subjects whose data is represented in visualizations; doing no harm to these people includes not harming the flesh and blood humans behind the data,* as well as communicating their personhood, effectively representing their humanity. Thirdly, *people who are significantly impacted by the represented data*; these are people who have a close connection to the represented data, for example, descendants of people whose data is depicted in a given visualization. Doing no harm to these people means *treating the data with a culturally-appropriate sensibility and effectively communicating the humanity of all represented subjects.*

3 Ethical Visualization for Impact

While tactics for avoiding egregious manipulation in visualizations have been suggested by visualization scholars and practitioners, and general principles have been established, few strategies have been offered that can integrate ethical tactics and principles into the day-to-day, practical task of visualizing data. In 2018, with my collaborator Christopher Church, I argued that the ethical visualization workflow could be used by digital humanities scholars as one such strategy [21]. Since the 2018 publication of "Racism in the Machine: Ethical Visualization in the Digital Humanities," this workflow has been iteratively adjusted and developed to be a workable process for fields beyond the digital humanities, and particularly, for scientists and data scientists. The work informing this adjustment has involved review of allied literature, research in historical archives of scientific visualization and information design, and discussions with data scientists, designers, and scientists who rely on visualization in their work. While this research is ongoing and will be further developed to take into account new discoveries in the burgeoning fields of visualization practice and visualization ethics, the Ethical Visualization for Impact process described below represents the current state of this work. It is intended to be of use to people visualizing data in scientific research and the data sciences [19].

The stages of Ethical Visualization for Impact take a complete communication context and whole data pipeline approach to mitigating harm in visualizations, in acknowledgement that decisions made throughout the process of planning, collecting and cleaning data all contribute to shaping the visual frame and resulting argumentation contained within a visualization.

3.1   Discover the Data

The process of sense-making about, or gaining insight into, data in a raw, or minimally processed form, within a research team (defined as an individual or group of people with intimate knowledge of the data, including details such as collection, sources, modeling structure, and processing). This discovery typically occurs immediately after, or in conjunction with, a data collection event (loosely defined as an experiment, data harvest such as a web scrape, or compilation of items such as survey data). Sometimes referred to as 'visualization for analysis,' this stage utilizes visual means to reduce the cognitive load demanded by a given dataset to a degree that is acceptable for the people who are intimately engaged with it, and therefore highly motivated to understand it [20, 22]. In this stage, understanding among the research team is fostered by visual identification of potential correlations, patterns, relationships, and trends. Activity in this step is guided by the question:

What can you find in this data?

The process of discovery in data is typically undertaken using one of two main avenues: 1) a reason-dominant approach, emphasizing investigation for seeking knowledge about the content of the raw data, or *2) an emotion-dominant approach,* emphasizing exploration, to get a felt sense for the meaning that might be made of the data [15]. Both approaches incorporate quick renderings of a range of visualization forms produced iteratively, with very rough visualizations produced quickly initially, typically progressing to more and more detailed versions of a visualization form that make sense of the data for the research team. Sense-making in this stage includes identifying potential correlations, patterns, trends, and outlying data points that could be significant to the research team.

For ethical visualization that has impact, a balance between investigation using reason-driven approaches and exploration using emotion-driven approaches is recommended in this stage. By shifting between analytical and playful modes of sense-making, the research team can gain an understanding of the scope of insights that may be relevant or valuable to their desired audience, as well as to themselves. It is worth noting that although these visualizations make sense to the research team, bringing understanding to a small group of people, this does not mean they will bring understanding to people with less intimate knowledge of the data. To have impact outside of the research team, the final visualizations presented to other people need to pass through many stages of iteration and contextualization in the steps below.

3.2 Scope the Impact

Determine the overall bounds of the visualization activity by identifying what the research team finds most important to the visualize, how important they find it, who they want to visualize data for, and which impact type is going to be most efficacious for reaching that audience.

Assess Stakes. Determining what is at stake in people understanding what the research team is has to share. This will motivate a research team to go through the additional stages required to communicate data effectively to an external (ie outside of the research team) audience.

What is at stake in this visualization effort?

Identify what might be lost or gained if this visualization effort is effective, ineffective, or outright misleading. This can be measured on a matrix of high, medium, or low stakes on various levels of impact: on global, societal, organizational, and personal levels. After determining the stakes, it is possible to make a realistic determination about what an appropriate allocation of resources, time, and effort to this visualization effort might be. In my experience, data scientists and scientists overestimate their available resources for data discovery and dramatically underestimate the time required to visualize findings effectively. A realistic look at the research team's available time, effort, and skills, combined with the stakes of the visualization's efficacy at this stage, will provide the research team with the opportunity to shift resources to the visualization effort. *Ethical visualization demands allocation of an appropriate proportion of the total available resources to visualization for impact.*

Establish Purpose. Noting the reason for visualizing data through this particular visualization. This is a short statement (approximately one sentence) of the research team's motivation for sharing data and intended impact in the research team's own words. It should reference the stakes identified above.

What is your motivation for sharing what you found in this data?

In this step it can also be helpful to identify counter purposes, ie what is the opposite of what the research team intended in sharing this data? Answers to both of these questions provide guides for activity in future steps and benchmarks to use in the last two stages. They are useful in the final stages *to measure the proximity between the impact intended by the research team, and the impact felt by their audience.*

Identify and Learn About Audiences. Determining who the research team wants to have impact on with this visualization is important early on. This can be as simple as identifying one group of people the research team wants to communicate to, or it can include more groups. In professional communication disciplines (such as communication design, marketing, and technical communication) it is common to identify primary, secondary, and even tertiary audiences, and the same can be done in this step.

Who do you want your visualization to reach the most?

Irrespective of how many audiences are identified, it is important to note that most visualizations are seen by many more people, and types of people, than are initially intended. For example, a visualization produced in a thesis may be intended for the eyes of a research student's supervisor only. However, that thesis will likely end up in a publicly available data repository, will be viewed and used by other researchers, and if the findings are significant, people in professions where the findings have value. Therefore, *identifying unintended audiences of a visualization is also helpful, and potentially important for mitigating harmful uses.*

After identifying audiences in order to effectively communicate with them, it is important to develop an empathetic understanding of those audiences. Identifying details about the audience can be done in three ways: interpersonally (by meeting and asking them questions), through profiling (by using a combination of available data on the audience and thinking tools), and through identifying distance from researchers. The first two approaches are professional skills that some professions take years to develop. Interpersonal approaches originate in anthropology and design research, and commonly rely on ethnographic interviewing. Profiling approaches originate in advertising and strategic communication, and commonly rely on building an audience profile that is synthesized from demographic and psychographic insights.

While working with people from these professions would be ideal in the case of large visualization projects with high stakes of global significance, and large budgets, a simpler third option is presented here for lower stakes visualization for impact. *If the research team can identify the distance between themselves and their audiences,* in terms of geography, language, discipline, age, expertise, cultural background, and prior familiarity with the subject, *they will gain good enough insight into the difference between the context in which they operate and the context in which their visualization is likely to be received.*

Determine Impact Type. *Five ways visualization can have an impact on audiences are: management, dissemination, entertainment, decoration, and expression.* Visualization for management has impact by aiding decision making. It is generally performed by people motivated to surveil and understand something. One micro level example is people wishing to surveil themselves (in the case of the quantified self movement), a medium level example is policy makers (using data dashboards to inform policy decisions), and a macro level example is found in military personnel studying security threats within and to a national population (in the case of human dynamics) [9, 18].

Visualization for dissemination has impact by fostering understanding of something the research team has found with people outside of the research team. For example, visualizations contained in research reports, research presentations, flyers, brochures, and promotional materials for research initiatives are all types of visualization for dissemination. Visualization for entertainment has impact by telling stories about the research team's data. Examples of visualization for entertainment include science-informed fictional movies, data journalism, and science education for children. Visualization for decoration has impact by crafting pleasurable experiences for people. Examples include when data-informed reactive artworks are put in public spaces, and when items such as fashion or soft furnishings (pillows, blankets, curtains etc.)

incorporate data visualization into the design of their surfaces or functionality. Visualization for expression has impact by demonstrating virtuosity in a given medium, or making fine artworks, and sometimes both. An example of this kind of impact is found in data visualization being increasingly used in fine art and contemporary art practice using a broad range of media.

Which impact type will be most effective for your audiences?

The first two impact types, management and dissemination, deliver impact primarily through information; relying primarily on reason, and using felt sense and aesthetic experience as secondary sources of information retention. The remaining types of impact – entertainment, decoration, and expression – deliver impact primarily through impression (felt sense and experience of aesthetics); they rely on experiential factors as the primary mode of communication and use reason as a secondary support. While ethical visualization will demand utilization of both information and impression, identifying the most effective mode for your audience, purpose, and stakes will guide the development of future stages. *Each of these impact types can be used either ethically or unethically. Following these stages of Ethical Visualization for Impact is recommended to prevent the unethical use of any impact type.*

3.3   Develop the Frame

Critically assessing the reason for data exploration and visualization, and forming both a verbal and visual sense of the appropriate expression of the frame. The frame is a persuasive statement (argument or explicitly stated bias) communicated through coordinated use of visual, textual, and experiential design elements that is believable and relevant to the audience. It integrates the discovered data and the intended impact of the research team with the needs and goals of the audience. The result of this stage is a persuasive summary statement or sketches that are research informed and intentionally persuasive, in order to harness the inherent biases in visualization that can amplify an ethically derived message.

Empathize with Audiences. Understanding of the intended and unintended audiences gained in the previous stage is expanded here into empathizing with your audiences, and summarizing their motivations and needs.

What are your audiences' greatest needs?

For each identified audience, immediate and existential needs can be identified by interviewing, observing, profiling, and surveying. The extensiveness of such audience research will be determined by stakes, and the resultant resources allocated to the visualization effort. Immediate needs are situational and usually reason-based, as in the case of someone who is running late for a meeting but needs to use a building map to find the meeting room. Existential needs are more abstract, emotionally mediated, and demand reassurance to enforce primal feelings of security and avoid primal feelings of abandonment. For example, members of a given audience might need to feel justified in a particular course of action, which can be thought of as a need for security. A person making a high-level policy decision may need a data dashboard to reassure them a course of action is appropriate. On a more personal level, a person who is trying to give up smoking may need a visualization within a behavior change app to reassure them they are making positive progress.

Utilization of existential needs in crafting visual frames is very effective, and should be used with great caution. Much harm can be done by using this approach (in terms of fueling extreme emotional reactions about visualized subjects), and best practices in this particular area are yet to be established.

Formulate Goal. Stating the goal for a visualization incorporates insights gained in previous steps, combining the data, the research team's intended impact and the audiences' needs. It expands upon the purpose identified earlier in the process in a somewhat formulaic manner.

What is the goal for the visualization?

This answer can be formulated as follows: *[impact type] of [data content] for [impact purpose] to/for [intended audience] about [audience need] so that [purpose].* Contra-goals can also be identified in this stage using the same process, to identify worst case scenarios of what might happen if the visualization was used by the unintended audiences developed earlier in the process. *Ethical visualization is goal-driven, as well as contra-goal-driven, meaning that it considers both the potential for benefit and for harm engendered in the design of a visualization.*

Create Frame. Using the goal as the basis for creating a frame (a persuasive argument that is believable and relevant to the audience) around data. Sub-frames can also be developed in this process, to give further nuance to achieving the goal outlined in the previous step.

Which frame best achieves this goal?

Wherever possible, for example in cases where there is a short distance between the research team and the audience, and in cases where there is a large amount of resources available, the frame should be tested with the intended audiences to determine believability and relevance. Where testing is possible, the frame can be refined to increase its relevance to the desired audience. The end result of this process will be a frame in either the form of a persuasive statement or a sketched visualization form detailing key persuasive elements (such as title, caption, or data emphasis). The sketches produced in this step differ from those produced in 3.1 in that the focus of the visualization is now on communicating data outside of the research team.

Review Literature about Frame. Searching for, identifying, and reviewing available literature about the created frame. Various fields, including communication studies, health communication, and science communication offer detailed testing and analysis of common frames for specific audiences and contexts, as well as hypotheses about lesser known frames. Familiarizing themselves with this literature can provide the research team with valuable insight into what kind of framing that is similar has worked in the past.

What does the literature say on this frame?

The results of this interdisciplinary literature review inform the following steps, thereby allowing the research team "to compensate for the data set's shortcomings by seeking out and including new information, or to limit the scope of the visual argument to be produced with said data" [21].

3.4 Prepare the Dataset

Creating a custom dataset specifically for the visualization for impact from available, reputable sources. This a custom dataset, created for each visualization for impact both ensures the data is relevant to the created frame and minimizes the risk of perpetuating unwanted biases from other researchers, institutions and organizations by using their unaltered datasets. This custom dataset includes, but is not limited to, the data in the initial data collection event. Depending on the frame decided upon, the data from the original data collection event may be deemed far too extensive and in need of pruning. It will also likely need supplementing from other sources in order to be impactful.

Combine Sources. Creating a preliminary, visualization-specific aggregated dataset, by 1) identifying the data from the original data collection event that is most valuable for communicating the frame, 2) transferring that data into a new set, and 3) identifying reputable datasets and data sources to supplement the original data collection, and 4) adding as much potentially valuable data to the new, aggregated set as is feasible.

What sources will you draw from?

The search for reputable datasets and addition of data to the new, aggregated dataset is guided by the frame and goal identified in the previous stage.

Improve Veracity. Using computational methods to increase the accuracy of the aggregated dataset. This action is guided in this stage by the question:

Will the data hold up under scrutiny?

Computational methods are used to clean, normalize, and refine the aggregated dataset, and manual oversight of the results of these processes can identify accuracy and anomalies. The key to impactful normalization in the context of the visualization-specific aggregated dataset is supplementing existing data with *normalizing data that is meaningful to the intended audiences* [31]. The appropriateness and authenticity of data is also checked in this stage, and questionable data points are pruned.

Structure Data. Creating a working dataset by adding necessary descriptions and context in the form of metadata, as well as appropriate structuring for the required visual frame. For example, if the chosen visual frame includes a network chart, the data will likely need significant structural adjustment to make this possible.

Is the dataset intelligible and navigable?

Additional organization, supplementation, and categorization can be added in this step through processes such as topic modeling.

Refine Frame. Adjusting the frame based on the content of the visualization-specific dataset. The process of improving veracity and structuring data presents opportunities for different framing, and sometimes makes the original frame not possible to claim in an unaltered form. The research team explores the refined, custom dataset for the objective of answering the following question:

How does the frame need to be adjusted?

The chosen visual frame may need to be adjusted, given the available data. In some cases, the activities of this stage may have provided additional insights that strengthen the original conception of the visual frame. In others, the visual frame may need to be made more modest in its claims, when less supporting data has made it through the rigorous preparation process than would be needed to support the original frame.

3.5   Visualize the Frame

Identifying the most appropriate context, media, and medium for presenting the frame within the final visualization.

Review Literature About Ethics. Finding and reviewing the latest literature relevant to ethical visualization (in the range of allied fields discussed earlier). This enables the research team to learn about current best practices.

What are the latest ethical recommendations?

By completing this review as the first step of visualization, the research team can ensure they have up-to-date methods and are applying recommended best practices.

Determine Context. Considering contextual factors including the type of media most appropriate for presenting the visualization in, and the level of interactivity that will best support the created visual frame. Printed documents such as posters and reports can be much more directed in terms of who sees the visualization and may therefore be more appropriate for very sensitive or highly controversial visual frames. Online publication has both greater potential for impact and greater potential for harm, although neither is a given. Online publication is the hardest media in which to control audience reception. Higher levels of interactivity can come foster engagement and a greater sense of agency in audiences. However, as seen in the case of sea level rise viewers, this is not a given, and more interactivity can also lead to more erroneous conclusions.

What is the most appropriate media context for your frame?

Another contextual factor to consider is which data to visualize for the purpose of normalizing representations of the data. For example, including census data on the total population in a given place, alongside data about number of murders by firearms in the same place, is a normalized data representation. It is as important that visualizations be normalized as it is that data be normalized; *people make sense of the key findings presented in data visualizations by comparing them with associated data that is meaningful in the context of their day-to-day lives.*

An audience-related contextual factor is the design elements and media formats that are relevant, familiar, and engaging for your audiences. "The persuasive and culturally bound associations those audiences necessarily have with design elements, explanatory text, headers, legends and interaction experiences need to be considered. The choice of colors and color ramps, as well as graphic or cartographic elements like political boundaries, invariably influence the argument produced by the visualization, as do map default views at certain screen widths, and zoom options" [21].

Design Visualization. Designing and testing rapidly iterated visualizations and restructuring the dataset as necessary for creating more refined visualizations. This process starts by "creating test visualizations (these are more rudimentary than, and distinct from, alpha prototypes)" [21]. These visualizations are intentionally quick and intended to test how effectively the composition, data selection, normalization, and legibility communicate the frame.

What design decisions will visualize the frame effectively?

The extensiveness of testing undertaken in the design process should be determined by the stakes and available resources. After test visualizations, a range of prototypes are designed and tested, moving from alpha prototype level through various stages of refinement to a high fidelity visualization or set of visualizations. Selection of a set of final visualization forms is important in this step, as is selecting design elements (for example, colors, typefaces, grids, interaction affects, and transitions), functionality (for example, annotation, customization, filtering, transition between visualizations, and exporting), and guidance (for example annotations, captions, navigation pathways, and nudges) that communicate the frame developed in stage 3.3.

Test Visualization. Administering a final round of user-testing on the close-to-finalized visualization to determine likely reception and efficacy of the visual frame. The success of this step will be aided by testing in as close an approximation to the media, format, functionality, and context that the finished visualization will have.

Does your visualization communicate the frame?

Completion of a round of pre-release testing provides an opportunity for pre-release correction to improve efficacy, and also offers the opportunity to mitigate any potential unforeseen harms that may be discovered. For data, audiences, and contexts where stakes are particularly high, in this step the visualization can also undergo pre-release testing with unintended audiences who may encounter it in the published format. For example, a visualization published online is available to all internet users with sufficient computational power and internet speeds to view it, and therefore could be tested for unintended effects with a random sampling of people with access to such technology. Feedback on the visualization will allow tweaking of design elements and functionality to ensure the visualization communicates the frame as closely as possible.

3.6   Publish the Visualization

Publishing the visualization is the end goal of a standard visualization process. However, for ethical visualization for impact, the issue of measuring impact remains at this point, along with the issue of highlighting the visualization as particularly ethical.

Release Visualization. Publishing the visualization, and, wherever possible without doing harm, the dataset on which the visualization is based.

Will publishing base data do harm to any intended or unintended audience?

Where there are potentially harmful consequences of publishing the dataset, or where rights to the data are not owned by the research team, extensive citation of where audiences can find the datasets is important for demonstrating veracity and thereby increasing trustworthiness of the visualization.

Report Process. Publicizing the process undertaken to complete this particularly ethical visualization in "show your work" documentation.

How can your ethical process be best demonstrated?

This is important for increasing both the reputation of the research team and disambiguating the visualization from poor science and disreputable creators of similar visualizations [12].

Measure Efficacy. Administering further user-testing after the visualization is published, to measure its actual impact.

What is the felt impact of your published visualization?

Simple measurement at this stage can be in the form of surveys, while detailed testing could take the form of ethnographic observation, eye tracking, think aloud protocols, or qualitative interviews.

Feedback Results. Reflecting on the efficacy of the findings, including measuring the extent to which the published visualization's intended and actual impact are in line with one another. This is important for multiple reasons. It allows highlighting, and therefore correction of any major and potentially harmful experienced impacts from the visualization (such as a data dashboard that encourages users to make decisions against their own interests). It also provides valuable information to the research team about the differences required in their communication amongst themselves and with their audiences. This can be surprising, especially when the audiences seem close to the research team (for example, a colleague in the department) but have very different experiences and understandings of the visualization than the research team intended.

How do the visualization's intended impact and felt impact compare?

Research teams can also supplement their "show your work" documentation with this added information as it becomes available, providing periodic reporting on both the ethical intentions and rigor of the research team's communication efforts and their commitment to having significant broader impacts. When there is an avenue for the updates to visualization documentation, additional information can also be updated, such as details of when new data is added, as in the "data updates" section of the NOAA Sea Rise Level Viewer.

4 Conclusion: Visualizations that Foster Compassion

Visualization is a technology that has impact because of its amplification effect that broadcasts the perceptions of its designers, data scientists, data repositories, institutional affiliations, and funders through visual and haptic means. Similar to the widespread critical commentary regarding artificial intelligence, data visualization can perpetuate negative personal and institutional biases, and, as in the case of sea level rise viewers, can at times appear to add support to inaccurate public assumptions. This is particularly true in cases when the arguments inherent in visualizations are not consciously crafted—when visualizers attempt to "let the data speak for itself." Visualizations have such capacity to be so problematic because they are human-made tools, and we ourselves contain a multitude of biases. However, as well as being riddled with biases, people are also riddled with compassion and empathy, positive qualities that can also permeate our human-made tools – including the visualizations we produce – if we let them.

The time for attempting to remove bias from visualizations is past. As our realities are increasingly shaped by computational processes mediated by visualizations, we need new, radically different approaches to visualization that prioritize ethical visualization practices in the service of producing visualizations that foster compassion. *Visualizations produced using the Ethical Visualization for Impact process exhibit four compassion-fostering qualities: they are humane, effective, trustworthy, and empowering.* In terms of humaneness, ethical visualizations build empathy in audiences and honor human dignity, including the dignity of users, represented subjects, and people particularly effected by the visualization. Ethical visualizations are also humane in the sense of being relatable. They foster understanding of how the data relates to them and their world, by creating a visual frame that gives users a compelling, humane bias as well as contextual information through devices such as normalizing representations.

Ethical visualization is effective in the sense that it meets the goals of the research team as well as the needs of individual users through an appropriate visual frame. Visualizations signal that they are trustworthy when they have a consciously-crafted, coordinated visual frame, when they clearly state both what is known and what is not (through citations, margins of error, and caveats), show their process of visualization development, and clearly state their data sources and affiliations (authorship, funding, etc). Ethical visualizations are empowering when they give users agency to navigate data using appropriate scaffolding, within the confines of the visual frame, and give users a felt sense of agency through a welcoming user experience, that is, one that utilizes minimal cognitive effort and attention to achieve the above. As experts with intimate knowledge of the power of our data, we have a responsibility to communicate its importance to our key audiences ethically, that is, in a way that makes them care.

References

1. Bakker, W.: Pictopolitics: Icograda and the international development of pictogram standards: 1963-1986. In: Frascara, J. (ed.) Information Design as Principled Action, pp. 114–145. Common Ground Publishing, Champaign (2015)
2. Brinton, W.C.: Graphic Methods for Presenting Facts. The Engineering Magazine Company, New York (1914)
3. Brito, A., Rodríguez, M.A., Niaz, M.: A reconstruction of development of the periodic table based on history and philosophy of science and its implications for general chemistry textbooks. J. Res. Sci. Teach. **42**, 84–111 (2005). https://doi.org/10.1002/tea.20044
4. Cairo, A.: Ethical infographics. IRE J. **37**, 25–27 (2014)
5. Cairo, A.: How Charts Lie: Getting Smarter about Visual Information, 1st edn. Norton & Company, New York (2019)
6. Cosgrove, D.E.: Social Formation and Symbolic Landscape. University of Wisconsin Press, Madison (1998)
7. Crampton, J.W.: Maps as social constructions: power, communication and visualization. Prog. Hum. Geogr. **25**, 235–252 (2001). https://doi.org/10.1191/030913201678580494
8. Crampton, J.W.: Mapping: A Critical Introduction to Cartography and GIS. Wiley, Hoboken (2011)
9. Crampton, J.W.: Collect it all: national security, Big Data and governance. GeoJournal **80**, 519–531 (2015). https://doi.org/10.1007/s10708-014-9598-y
10. Dork, M., Feng, P., Collins, C., Carpendale, S.: Critical InfoVis: exploring the politics of visualization. Presented at the CHI 2013. Extended Abstracts. ACM, Paris (2013). https://doi.org/10.1145/2468356.2468739
11. D'Ignazio, C., Klein, L.: Feminist data visualization. Presented at the IEEE VIS Workshop on Visualization for the Digital Humanities. Springer, Heidelberg (2016)
12. D'Ignazio, C., Klein, L.F.: Data Feminism. The MIT Press, Cambridge (2020)
13. Edgerton, D.: From Mental Matrix to Mappamundi to Christian Empire: The Heritage of Ptolemaic Cartography in the Renaissance. Art and Cartography: Six Historical Essays (1987)
14. Hall, P., Heath, C., Coles-Kemp, L.: Critical visualization: a case for rethinking how we visualize risk and security. J. Cyber. Secur. **1**, 93–108 (2015). https://doi.org/10.1093/cybsec/tyv004
15. Hall, P.A.: Bubbles, lines and string: how visualisation shapes society. In: Atzmon, L., Triggs, T. (eds.) The Graphic Design Reader. Bloomsbury Academic, London (2017)
16. Harley, J.B.: Maps, knowledge, and power. In: Cosgrove, D., Daniels, S. (eds.) The Iconography of Landscape: Essays on the Symbolic Representation, Design and Use of Past Environments, pp. 277–312. Cambridge University Press, Cambridge (1988)
17. Hepworth, K.: Governmentality, technologies, & truth effects in communication design. In: Vermaas, P.E., Vial, S. (eds.) Advancements in the Philosophy of Design. DRF, pp. 497–521. Springer, Cham (2018). https://doi.org/10.1007/978-3-319-73302-9_23
18. Hepworth, K.: A panopticon on my wrist: the biopower of big data visualization for wearables. Des. Cult. 1–22 (2019). https://doi.org/10.1080/17547075.2019.1661723
19. Hepworth, K.: Ethical Visualization for Impact. Ethical Visualization for Impact (2020). https://kathep.github.io/ethics/. Accessed 18 Mar 2020
20. TEAM-Based Approach. Dialectic **2**. http://dx.doi.org/10.3998/dialectic.14932326.0002.104
21. Hepworth, K., Church, C.: Racism in the machine: visualization ethics in digital humanities projects. Digital Hum. Q. **012** (2018)

22. Hepworth, K., Ivey, C.E., Canon, C., Holmes, H.A.: Embedding online, design-focused data visualization instruction in an upper-division undergraduate atmospheric science course. J. Geosci. Educ. 1–16 (2019). https://doi.org/10.1080/10899995.2019.1656022

23. Kostelnick, C.: Humanizing Visual Design: The Rhetoric of Human Forms in Practical Communication, 1st edn. Routledge (2019)

24. Leszczynski, A.: Spatial big data and anxieties of control. Environ. Plan. D 33, 965–984 (2015). https://doi.org/10.1177/0263775815595814

25. Lidwell, W., Holden, K., Butler, J.: Universal Principles of Design: 100 Ways to Enhance Usability, Influence Perception, Increase Appeal, Make Better Design Decisions, and Teach Through Design. Rockport, London (2003)

26. Manning, A., Amare, N.: Visual-rhetoric ethics: beyond accuracy and injury. Tech. Commun. 53, 195–211 (2006)

27. Monmonier, M.S.: Maps, distortion, and meaning, Resource paper - Association of American Geographers, Commission on College Geography , vol. 75, no. 4. Association of American Geographers, Washington (1977)

28. Monmonier, M.: How to Lie with Maps. University of Chicago Press, London (1991)

29. Monmonier, M.: Rhumb Lines and Map Wars: A Social History of the Mercator Projection. University of Chicago Press (2010)

30. NOAA: NOAA Interactive Sea Rise Level Viewer (2017)

31. Richards, D.P.: Not a cape, but a life preserver: the importance of designer localization in interactive sea level rise viewers. Commun. Des. Q. Rev. 6, 57–69 (2018). https://doi.org/10.1145/3282665.3282671

32. Royal Society of Chemistry: Periodic Table (WWW Document) (2019). https://www.rsc.org/periodic-table. Accessed 18 Mar 2020

33. Schüll, N.D.: Data for life: wearable technology and the design of self-care. BioSocieties 11, 317–333 (2016). https://doi.org/10.1057/biosoc.2015.47

34. Stephens, S.H., DeLorme, D.E.: A framework for user agency during development of interactive risk visualization tools. Tech. Commun. Q. 28, 391–406 (2019). https://doi.org/10.1080/10572252.2019.1618498

35. Tufte, E.R.: Visual Explanations: Images and Quantities, Evidence and Narrative. Graphics Press, Cheshire (1997)

Involving Users in Sound Design

Frederik Moesgaard, Lasse Hulgaard$^{(\boxtimes)}$, and Mads Bødker

Department of Digitalization, Copenhagen Business School,
Copenhagen, Denmark
{frmo11ab,lahul2ab}@student.cbs.dk

Abstract. Sound plays an important role in our well-being, our experience of the world around us and our understanding of products, services and interactions. Sound affects our sense of place, and it can modulate our feelings, agency and attention. In a world of increasingly ubiquitous digital technologies, sound may prove a valuable resource for sense making as well as experience- and UX design. Yet the possibilities and challenges of user participation in sound design processes are not well understood. This paper reports on a pilot study examining how participants can be involved in different phases of a sound design process. The results and reflections aim to help researchers and designers in an effort to better understand some of the dynamics of moving from a largely expert driven approach to sound design towards a more user-oriented and participatory approaches.

Keywords: Ambience · User experience · Co-creation · Video prototype · Sound design · Sound prototype · Sound sketching · Soundwalks · Participation

1 Introduction

Most of us are surrounded and supported by digital technologies from the moment we wake up until we fall asleep. Moving towards a world where an increasing number of electronic devices will be demanding our attention, it is important for designers to consider and explore new ways of achieving meaningful user experiences that respect human attention and positively contribute to the experience of everyday life. With the abundant and ubiquitous access to computing resources (such as pervasive computing, the proliferation of embedded devices and systems, etc.), designers need to explore the creation of devices and services that allow for peripheral or even 'natural' interactions, where the interface essentially disappears into the environment and allows us to live our lives with less perceived technological friction and distraction (Case 2016). Important and seminal work in this field was carried out by Weiser (1991) and Weiser and Brown (1997) who advocated for ways in which digital technologies should aim to inform discretely, create calm rather than be spectacular, and require the smallest amount of focused attention.

Historically the Graphical User Interface (GUI) paradigms that evolved in the 1970s and onwards have foregrounded the visual aspects of interaction design. Sound seems to be a design material that is somewhat marginalized (Case and Day 2019), and designers tend to forego auditory experiences as critical components of user

A. Marcus and E. Rosenzweig (Eds.): HCII 2020, LNCS 12200, pp. 405–425, 2020.
https://doi.org/10.1007/978-3-030-49713-2_28

experience design. Since we do not merely experience the world by looking at it, designing with audio can help create interactions that respect attention, providing a positive user experience. Without burdening with focal information or demanding a focused engagement, sound can communicate messages, alter moods, taste, behaviours and even help treat certain illnesses (Case and Day 2019). As Case & Day point out, the application of sound in design has been gaining traction, but to truly realise its potential as a central modality that can extend the boundaries of interactive design, we see a need to extend the concepts, methods and principles for collaborative sound design. Within the field of interaction design, designers have access to a wide variety of guidelines, frameworks, processes and terminology. With some notable exceptions that tend to cover functional aspects of sound (e.g. Gaver 1986; Hermann and Hunt 2005; Case and Day 2019) guidelines and frameworks are relatively scarce when it comes to user-centred and collaborative design with sound. A smaller amount of research has been dedicated to the issue of collaborative practices in the field of sonic interaction design (e.g. Barras 1996; Hug 2010; Adams et al. 2008; Ekman and Rinott 2010), and the current paper aims to join this conversation. In this paper, we explore how users can be involved when designing sound, and we set the stage for some preliminary reflections on how to go from a largely *expert driven* approach to more user driven approaches in the field of designing with sound or for sonification. Our pilot study reported in the paper uses a convenience sample of students and recent graduates recruited from Copenhagen-area universities. The intention is to provide aspects of a methodological scaffold for participatory methods in interactive sound design. Our results can help widen the range of possibilities for staging collaborative design processes to better utilise the vast potential of sound in the design of new products and service experiences.

1.1 The Importance of Sound in Interface Design

In 1965, Moore predicted an exponential growth in computing power (Moore 1965). Even if processor speeds are not increasing quite in the way Moore forecasted, computer history has largely confirmed the spirit of these predictions; supercomputers of the 1980s and 90s are now packed into units the size of credit cards and wristwatches. As computing power increases, the size of technological artefacts and surfaces to interact with similarly decreases (Janlert and Stolterman 2015), effectively shrinking the surface area available for visual, screen-based interfaces or interfaces with physical controls like buttons, keys or levers. Moreover, improvements in internet infrastructure have allowed computers to be increasingly and pervasively distributed into products and physical spaces, making them a ubiquitous-yet-invisible backdrop to all aspects of everyday life. As the visual modality for interaction design is thus increasingly in a "tight squeeze", a focus on improving sound design might be able to extend interactive and positive experiential properties of ubiquitous computing. While distributed and ubiquitous systems can enable improved context and depth to the information that can be communicated by computational artefacts, it also challenges most traditional interface design approaches that rely on the tangible or visual availability of information and controls. With increased complexity and the gradual reduction of a focal, recognizable surface area for interaction, and perhaps even no discernable surface at all, designers have to rethink how users might interact with computational things. This, we believe, includes exploring how modalities such as sound can be approached as a design material in collaborative design processes.

1.2   The Need for Developing Collaborative Sound Design Approaches

In the 1970s, as computer artefacts began to broadly impact the work processes in both industrial and knowledge work settings, designers began exploring ways of involving users in the design process. One line of research primarily focused on addressing users as somewhat 'abstract' objects with specified attributes, various (cognitive) capacities for information processing (i.e. a user-centred approach, see Card et al. 1983), whereas others have focused more on the direct involvement of users as active partners in the design process (e.g. participatory design, see Ehn 1988; Sundblad 2010; Sanders and Stappers 2008). Many commonly used design frameworks are arguably influenced by both schools, and frameworks such as the highly influential *Design Thinking* framework (Brown 2008) presents ways of focusing all design efforts on user needs as well as structuring processes around direct involvement and end-users as co-creators. Such approaches are typically useful when designing for a broader set of purposes, meanings, emotions and experiences, rather than discrete products and purely functional specifications (Sandersand and Stappers 2008).

Even though sound holds a huge potential in forming experiences, these frameworks do not include methods specific to sound design, and they do not explicitly account for the challenges associated with designing with sound. The intangible and ambiguous nature of sound would suggest that developing participatory design methods that focus on enhancing the articulation and sharing of experiences with sound are essential. As human beings, we are exposed to many different and seemingly 'meaningless' sounds throughout the day (and night). Sounds affect our mood, emotions, experience and our overall well-being, however we tend to ignore them because visual prompts take up the bulk of our conscious attention (Bødker and Chamberlain 2016; Case and Day 2019). Thus, we find the need to explore methods that are likely to promote a capacity to articulate and discuss 'sound' if we want to involve users in processes of design. To address this, researchers working on 'acoustic ecologies (e.g. Schafer 1977; Truax 2001) have developed approaches to help people better understand and communicate about sound. An example of such a method is 'soundwalking' which is intended to help the listener reactivate a sense of hearing to better communicate ideas and impressions of sound (Westerkamp 1974). Similarly, 'sound sketching', a form of vocal prototyping where designers (in case; designers unskilled in sound design and production rather than users) vocalise sounds in concert with interaction gestures (Ekman and Rinott 2010) and the 'Radio Play' method (Pirhonen et al. 2007) where sounds are inserted into concept scenarios or user stories, have been proposed.

Research on sound design has also resulted in highly specified frameworks to help designing with sound. Case and Day (2019) propose a range of suggestions for different forms of user involvement but do not engage explicitly with models to further users as co-creators in early stages of a design process. Brazil and Fernström (2009) have researched and developed frameworks for designing with sound, but they do not include any specific attention to users in the design process. Given that sounds have profound effects on our everyday experiences (Langeveld et al. 2013), we believe users should be involved and carefully *enabled* to inform the design process. We find that it is fair to suggest that sound design frameworks have not yet evolved to the same level of user participation or even distinct user-centeredness compared to many other design fields, including product-, service-, or visual design.

1.3 Sound Design for Experiences

An experience can be defined as a story emerging from a dialogue between a person and their world (Hassenzahl et al. 2013). Experiences are tied to a level of affectivity that may be positive or negative. Positive experiences are crucial in forming moments of happiness and day-to-day exposure to positive experiences results in a sense of well-being and prolonged happiness (McCarthy and Wright 2004; Hassenzahl et al. 2013). Experiences are described by the author, B. Joseph Pine II, as something that *"uses goods as props and services as the stage to engage each individual in an inherently personal way, to create a memory — the hallmark of experiences."* (Rossman and Duerden 2019: 1). Designers have the ability to impact the lives of people as well as drive value for businesses. From a business perspective, the intentional design of experiences is related to the staging of experiences that result in positive affective states in the users, in order to create bonds between the user and the offering, creating lasting memories of the experience delivered (Rossman and Duerden 2019). However, it is essential for any business to understand the psychological and experiential needs of their stakeholder as the fulfilment of these are the prerequisite of the creation of positive experiences (Hassenzahl et al. 2013). Moreover, the technologies available and their communicative and interactive properties such as sound, as a distinct design material, must also be understood in order to stage the experiences that positively resonate with people's expectations or needs.

1.4 How Sounds Affect Experiences

How then can we describe how sound influences or modulates our awareness and how does it modulate experiential and affective states? In their book on the intersection between architecture and sound, Blesser and Salter (2007) point towards a functional model of auditory awareness that can help us understand how sound affects the user. Firstly, sound is received by our ears and the raw stimuli are perceived, a process which requires no cognitive effort and can be described as a biological property of human hearing. Secondly, the sound is perceived affectively and cognitively. We are able to decode sounds as either speech, music or sirens. Thirdly, we generate emotions and moods based on the sounds. Sounds become meaningful. However, not all sounds are necessarily given value. According to Westerkamp, we have become used to filtering out sounds we perceive as irrelevant. Our ears are accustomed to tuning in and out (2002). Thus, the sounds we encounter can be either overt or subliminal in their capacity to create affective states, resulting in strong emotional experience or subtle arousals, mood changes, or subtle modulations of awareness, depending on the person listening (Blesser and Salter 2007). This is further described by Katherine Norman, who suggests that *"As listeners [...] we may return to real life disturbed, excited and challenged on a spiritual and social plane by a music with hands-on relevance to both our inner and outer lives.* "(1996: 4). However, the perceived quality, associations, or performative and affective impact of sound is always contextualized within an individual's life story or cultural background (Blesser and Salter 2007).

1.5   Designing with Users

In the early 1970's, pioneers envisioned the practice of direct user involvement in design processes as a radical challenge for maintaining the representation of different interests and viewpoints in a *"man-made world"* (Sanders and Stappers 2008). However, it has taken a long time for organisations to embrace the full potential and responsibilities of co-designing with users and applying co-design methods across the entire spectrum of the design process. The requirement of a more engaged and directed understanding of users as valuable stakeholders in the process of building product or services is reflected in recent design approaches such as Design Thinking. The Design Thinking process proposes that a designer should to co-design with the user and other stakeholders early in the design process by applying various facilitation techniques to further the dialogue across the user/designer divide (Brown 2008).

A number of models have been proposed to help understand and structure a Design Thinking process. The Double Diamond (DD) Framework by the Design Council (Design Council 2019) is based on the dynamics of divergent ('discovery' or problem oriented) and converging ('solution' oriented) movements in a design process. The model splits the process into four phases; in the first phase, user behaviour and needs are explored. In the second phase, the problems the design team should address are defined. In the third phase, solutions, which may consist of prototypes, are developed. In the final phase, the developed solution is delivered and tested. Relevant methods for data collection and analysis are applied throughout the process (Design Council 2019) (Fig. 1).

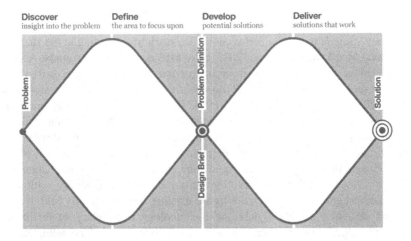

Fig. 1. Double Diamond Framework (Design Council 2019)

While the DD Framework does not explicitly indicate how to involve users, we suggest that the problem discovery and definition phases (as well as the ensuing practices of developing and delivering a solution) are likely to involve user-centred methods as well as stakeholder participation. This includes for examples processes that allow users to indicate needs, aspirations and suggestions as well as the facilitation of articulating, sometimes in material form such as prototypes or sketches, possible alternatives and solutions. The methods applied in the current pilot study include soundwalks, interviews, 'think-aloud', and the use of prototyping techniques. Our approach is informed by the left-hand diamond, which primarily describes the 'fuzzy' parts of a design process where a 'language' and common ground needs to be established to arrive at a productive dialogue about design outcomes and consequences. We exploratively venture into the right side of the model (i.e. the second diamond), using a co-creating workshop for defining sound concepts worth pursuing. Two early prototypes are developed, and their respective potential is assessed with participants.

1.6   Designing with Sound: Establishing a Mutual Language

In the following section, we will discuss how sound design can benefit from improving its capacity to engender participatory processes. We live in a dominantly visual culture (Jay 1996) that tends to marginalize sensory modalities such as touch, taste, the olfactory and auditory senses in design (Jacucci and Wagner 2007) and elsewhere. However, on a daily basis we encounter sounds that play a vital role in forming our experience of the world around us. Some of the more obvious cases are the beeping smartphone notifying us of a new message (and perhaps making us stressed or uncomfortable, see Bødker and Jensen 2017), a service announcement on a train platform (sending us running to reach the train, or making us slump if a delay is announced), the loud alerts from a ticket machine (allowing us to walk on or stopping if an error sound occurs) or when a metro door closes creating a sudden rush of stress. All are examples of intentional sounds that are added to communicate something to the user (Langeveld et al. 2013).

Concurrently, sounds appear all the time as a consequence of actions or surroundings; the sound of footsteps on a concrete floor, people brushing against each other as they struggle to enter a metro car or the metro train arriving at the station in a gust of wind, what Langeveld et al. (2013) refer to as consequential sounds. According to Langeveld et al., *"knowledge from interaction design, psychoacoustics, audio engineering and music perception will form the theoretical basis of the design of these sounds"*. (2013: 70) Where Langeveld et al. focus on specialised and professional forms of knowledge that a designer might want to possess, in the following sections we will outline ways to facilitate dialogues and vocabulary building in the design of both intentional and consequential sounds. Engaging in a productive discussion of sound with participants in a design project requires the emergence of common language that allows for a meaningful communication across different disciplinary, cultural and professional backgrounds. From exploring the existing literature in this field, it appears that sound designers largely ignore the methodological corollary of facilitating a common language, although there seems to be a collective understanding that it is necessary to develop methods that enable people to better talk about sound (see e.g. Supper 2012; Cerwén et al. 2017; Hug 2010).

We have selected two approaches that focus specifically on sound as a possible design material. One way to help participants (or; users) to become attentive to and talk about sound is by performing soundwalks; simple walks in a defined space where the focus is on listening and reflecting on the sonic and acoustic environment (Westerkamp 1974, 2002). Furthermore, we explore sound sketching as an approach to enable co-creation efforts in sound design.

Soundwalks. In order to better understand how sound can be used to improve the experience of a product or service, it is important to train the attention towards existing sounds in the environment (Case and Day 2019). Throughout the 1960's and 70's sound studies and work on 'acoustic ecologies' became increasingly prominent in the humanities and social sciences, inspiring academics and artists such as Schafer (1977), Oliveros (2005), Barry Truax (2001) and Westerkamp (1974) to explore methods such as 'deep listening' and soundwalks that aim to direct attention to the sonorous environment. Westerkamp has proposed that the soundwalk method is *"any excursion whose main purpose is listening to the environment."* (Westerkamp 1974: 1). Soundwalks can be done alone or in any size of group, in a single spot, or across various areas. There are no boundaries to the soundwalk, as long as listening is the highest priority. According to Westerkamp (1974), soundwalks, or perhaps more accurately 'listening walks', have the potential to open a sensory space for noticing and simply paying attention to sounds that otherwise would not have been given any immediate value or meaning. By listening attentively whilst moving through a soundwalk, participants are sensitised to a dynamic sonorous context. Thus, a connection between the listener and the place of the soundwalk is formed (Westerkamp 1974). Blesser and Salter (2007: 15) describes it as *"feeling included in the life of the soundscape"*. The 'sensory connections' that are potentially formed in a soundwalk can be used to facilitate an improved vocabulary and attentiveness to sonic matters. As a method, soundwalks are relatively simple to plan and execute, and they are typically meaningful to participants who have little or no experience with active and attentive listening practices.

Soundwalks Using a Recorder and Headphones In order to make it easier for the user to engage in active listening during the soundwalk, Case and Day (2019) suggest using a stereo digital recorder that can record in high resolution formats, such as .wav or .aiff rather than .mp3 or compressed formats, which potentially introduce unwanted sonic artefacts. Uncompressed formats allow for a better listening experience and a more precise reproduction of a soundscape. According to Westerkamp (2002), using a microphone during the soundwalk alters listening and produces a sense of an enhanced awareness to the soundscape. Walking with a recorder and wearing a pair of headphones, participants are able to amplify existing sounds, which gives them an enhanced sense of direction and ability to localise sounds in the environment while walking through it. Not only is the listening experience intensified, but it often heightens the participant's own curiosity and encourages them to venture into unknown territory (Westerkamp 2002).

Sound Sketching. According to HCI pioneer Bill Buxton[1], sketching is *"the archetypal activity of design"* and should pay a prominent role in exploring innovative concepts in

---

[1] Award-winning Canadian computer scientist, designer, and researcher at Microsoft Research.

UX design (Buxton 2007: 111). Sketching works as a means to quickly externalize and critique concepts, giving designers room to suggest alternatives. It is sufficiently light weight, often only requiring a pen and paper, and easy to apply in participatory design processes, allowing future users to quickly ideate and suggest alternatives. Interrogating the design space of a product, service or experience that relies on sound as a central modality can be done through "sound sketching". According to Langeveld et al. (2013) *"the ultimate goal of sound sketching is to find auditory links that may underlie the selected concept (and the desired experience, directly or indirectly)"* (Langeveld et al. 2013: 60). Similar to paper-based sketching, a sound sketch can be considered as a simple and rapid way to articulate and discuss ideas. Sounds used for sound sketching can be real (e.g. humming, singing, instrumental), synthetic (digital audio clips) or a mix of both (Brazil and Fernström 2009). Synthetic sounds for the sound sketch can be found online (e.g. YouTube, Apple Music, Spotify or Soundcloud), and the sound sketch can be tested by using a portable speaker or headphones.

2   Method and Study Design

To help us better understand this particular phenomenon of including users in the sound design process, we propose a *Co-creation Framework for Sound Design*. Inspired by the Double Diamond Framework, this framework is made up of both divergent ('discovery' oriented) and converging ('solution' oriented) movements in a design process (Fig. 2).

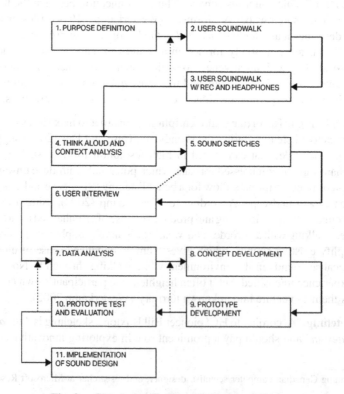

Fig. 2.   Co-creation Framework for Sound Design

The framework relies on insights from both existing sound design methods and more general user-driven design methods that are not developed specifically for sound design, personal observations and the initial analysis of results from our study. Going through the framework in the following sections allow us to elaborate on the various activities that we suggest, providing a sense of how they lead to the kinds of affective outcomes that are reported and discussed in the results and concluding discussion sections.

2.1 Pilot Study in the Copenhagen Metro

The pilot study was conducted in five Copenhagen metro stations (Frederiksberg, Nørrebros Runddel, Nørreport, Marmorkirken, Kongens Nytorv) between 19th – 26th of October 2019. These locations were chosen due to their immediate accessibility, the perceived sonic complexity of the site and the many possibilities for constructing a variety of sonic interventions on the sites. The sites present as an assemblage of loud consequential sounds, such as noise from trains, people talking on their phones, cars above, as well as intentional sounds, such as alarms indicating that the train doors are closing, ticket stands or card readers, and announcements from embedded speakers around the stations.

Our study was carried out with 6 participants (2 women, 4 men), who were all regular users of the Copenhagen metro (min. one trip per week). All participants were aged from 26–31 years. The study used a convenience sample of students and recent graduates recruited from Copenhagen universities, and the intention was to provide an initial methodological scaffold for participatory methods in interactive sound design (Fig. 3).

P1	P2	P3	P4	P5	P6
Male	Male	Male	Female	Male	Female
29	28	30	26	29	31

Fig. 3. Overview of participants

The overall purpose of the sound design was defined loosely as using sound to "explore ways to improve the experience of passengers using the Copenhagen metro". While there are clearly a number of more discrete sound sources and acoustic qualities that could become objects for redesign (e.g. ticketing machines, the harsh acoustics of a metro platform made primarily from concrete and tiles etc.), we chose to explore a more holistic sonification approach (using soundscapes in appropriate locations) that should ideally create an intriguing and pleasant journey experience. This approach allowed us to improvise and to remain open to directions suggested by our participants.

2.2 Soundwalks, Think-Aloud and Sound Sketching

Each participant conducted a quick soundwalk around the metro. The soundwalk started at the entrance of the metro station. The participants were asked to walk around the metro station for approx. 10 min and were asked to carefully listen to the sounds they encountered, in order to put words to their experience afterwards. Immediately after the first soundwalk, each participant was asked to do another soundwalk around the same metro station, but this time carrying a recorder and wearing headphones (Zoom H6 stereo digital recorder and AIAIAI TMA-2 headphones). The participants were able to control the sensitivity of the microphone attached to the recorder during the soundwalk (Fig. 4).

Fig. 4. Soundwalk w/microphone and headphones

After the soundwalk, the participants were debriefed and interviewed in order to describe and analyse how moving through the sonic context of the metro felt. Leading up to an unstructured interview, we conducted a short think-aloud procedure, asking the participants to tell us about their immediate experience of the soundwalk and what immediately stood out as significant for them. Based on the 'think-aloud', interview questions touched on topics such as: How would you describe the experience? What did you feel? How do you think other people feel? What was the difference between the first and second soundwalk? What surprised you? How would you describe the different areas in regard to the sound and noise?

The purpose of the interview was to understand if the two soundwalks were suitable as a method for involving and engaging participants in a design process. The interview provided a means to begin a contextual analysis of the metro space. The participants were able to identify acoustic regions that caused discomfort or unease, thereby assisting the designers in identifying regions better suited for implementation of intentional sounds such as those described by Langeveld et al. (2013) (Fig. 5).

Fig. 5. User interview

A sound sketching activity involving the participant was performed immediately after the soundwalk, think-aloud and interview. In this process, the participants were involved in discussing types of sounds to consider for a prototype and where to implement these sounds. After the initial sound walk, different sounds were chosen by the participant from YouTube and Spotify.

Using a portable speaker, the researcher played these sounds to the participant in various locations of the metro. The researcher and participant then discussed whether the sound felt appropriate and what feelings were invoked by the sounds. One of the purposes of this activity was to involve the participants as early as possible in the sound design process. Furthermore, by sensitising the users through the different activities, they became increasingly aware of the affective dynamics of sound and gradually became more articulate about how sound impacts and affects them.

2.3   Data Analysis and Concept Development

After having carried out the soundwalks and sketching activities, the qualitative data collected in these two steps was analysed by carrying out a thematic analysis of the notes, recordings and images from the previous activities, focussing on developing clusters of meaning from patterns observed in the data (Aronson 1995) (Fig. 6).

Fig. 6. Co-creation workshop

Based on the insights from the data analysis, five sound concepts were developed. This was done in a co-creation workshop (Enninga et al. 2013) using sticky notes (Christensen et al. 2020) involving two participants, who had also taken part in the soundwalks. These five sound concepts were then narrowed down to two using dot-voting where participants take turns prioritizing the different concepts (Turner 2018).

2.4   Sound and Video Prototyping[2]

Based on our findings from the previous steps, sound prototypes were created in collaboration with composer and music producer, Julius Sylvest, using Ableton Live and Logic Pro X Digital Audio software. Multiple iterations were created before the sound prototypes matched the sound concepts suggested by our users (Fig. 7).

Fig. 7. Sound prototype development

To evaluate the design, a video prototype (Mackay 1988) was developed by filming the passengers' journey (in POV perspective) through the metro station. The footage was then edited down to a short narrative using film editing software Adobe Premiere Pro, and relevant sound concepts identified in the previous activities with the users were added to the existing sound environment. The prototypes were tested with three participants (Fig. 8).

Fig. 8. Testing video prototype with participant

---

[2] Prototypes can be accessed here: https://bit.ly/2T7A1t9.

After having exposed the users to the video prototype, a Wizard of Oz prototype was carried out by using a B&O BeoPlay A2 Portable Bluetooth Speaker connected to an iPhone. The Wizard of Oz is a prototyping approach that uses off the shelf tools to emulate (or 'fake') a working system in order to test relevant aspects of the system without spending unnecessary time or other resources (Buxton 2007; Bernsen et al. 2020). In our case, a portable speaker was held above and behind the participants as they walked through the metro station. Multiple sound prototypes were tested with each participant (Fig. 9).

Fig. 9. Testing the Wizard of Oz sound prototype

Immediately after exploring both prototypes, a brief think-aloud activity and user interviews were again used to evaluate the experience and give input to the ongoing design activities.

3   Results and Observations

3.1   Soundwalks and Think-Aloud

While their responses were different, the participants all expressed a general sense of curiosity and surprise at the richness of the sound experience. This was particularly evident in the soundwalk activity. Soundwalks helped participants in terms of 'tuning in' to the sound environment. The soundwalks appeared to be an activity that was somewhat surprising to the participants, and some stated that they had a feeling of being welcomed into a new world of sound. One participant said:

"What surprised me the most was the nuances and stories some the sounds told. I have never paid attention to this in the same degree before. It opened a new world to me."[3] (P5)

This falls in line with the work of Westerkamp (1974), suggesting that soundwalks are effective in 'reactivating' our sense of hearing. Participants generally found the

---

[3] Interviews (P1 – P6): https://bit.ly/2wbmF6i.

addition of a microphone and headphones during the second soundwalk to be helpful as it allowed them to easier focus on particular sounds.

"With the microphone it was easier to hear all the mechanical sounds of the metro, like the metro coming and doors closing." (P4)

Moreover, the soundwalks opened a space for not only noticing and observing sounds as they occurred along the walk, but events happening around the participants. Listening attentively to sounds made small events come to life, and participants were able to use the soundwalks to reflect on the sonic qualities and particularities of the place as well as the overall moods and feelings.

"Being aware of the sounds and noise made me feel like being part of a system. A system on the move." (P6)

"It was kind of sad to see how people didn't look very happy - mostly like zombies" (P5)

"People seem to be in their own little bubbles. Either staring at their phones or listening to music on their headphones or just looking a bit sad." (P6)

The participants suggest that the activity increased a sense of belonging as well as a sense of directing their attention towards 'affective' scenes in the context of the metro. The soundwalks were also valuable in pinpointing locations suitable for sound intervention. The entrance from ground level was perceived to be an interesting area, where the change in environment was obvious on a physical, visual as well as sonic level. Moreover, the escalators where found to be a place of comfort and relative silence and thereby potentially suitable for sound interventions. One participant stated that:

"I think the entrance would be a nice place to implement a nice soundscape. [...] I find it harder to imagine implementing sound down on the platform. Because there's a lot of practical information and sounds that you need to focus on. I find it hard to imagine how there could be room for anything else down there" (P1)

While interviews are often used to follow up on an activity, a think-aloud is normally done while performing an activity, but when working with sound it was found useful to conduct the think-aloud method after performing the soundwalks. This was done in respect of the purpose of the soundwalk, which was to notice and sense the acoustical environment without interruptions, as we felt that the soundwalk in itself was a relatively complex activity that required presence. However, a limitation to this method may be that participants forget important observations during the 5 – 10 min soundwalk. Having participants speak in the microphone/recorder concurrently with the activity might solve this issue, but with the drawback of disturbing the concentration and focus needed for the activity. As it stands, we assume that a 'retrospective' rather than the standard 'concurrent' think-aloud approach (see Nielsen et al. 2002) improves the participant's ability to be attentive when faced with an unusual activity such as a soundwalk.

3.2   Sound Sketching

Sound sketching was found to be an effective way of getting participants to co-design and communicate ideas. Playing sound sketches helped participants articulate their desired outcomes of a sound intervention. This supported the designers in developing sound concepts by better understanding what participants are longing for. Furthermore, the sound sketching activity uncovered how participants had different perceptions of sounds based on their personal experiences, and also confirmed that sounds indeed impact emotions.

> *"The rain made me want to go to the mountains and be out in nature. It makes me long for the same experience that would trigger those same emotions that I'm experiencing. With the bird sounds I actually felt like it would be nice to be out in nature, in Costa Rica for example. So, whenever I hear these sounds it triggers some emotions and then I think about moments where I've had the same emotions and experiences. You long for the same feeling."* (P4)

Participants found it hard to predict what sounds could be interesting to implement before having tried the sound sketch. However, one participant stated that:

> *"It's hard to put sound experiences into words. Especially when you don't have anything to listen to beforehand. But when you start listening to some different sketches or sounds it becomes much more tangible. It's easier to imagine what sounds would work and what sounds are annoying to listen to. [...] After the sound sketch, I also realised that it would be nice to have a dynamic soundscape that changed over time"* (P6)

Furthermore, two participants changed their understanding of where intentional sounds could be implemented after the sound sketch activity, indicating that the sound sketching was a valuable method to support soundwalks. One participant said that:

> *"It was very different from what I expected."* (P2)

Another participant described her experience and how it expanded her attentiveness to sounds in this way:

> *"After having tried the sound sketch, I realised that it was really nice to listen to on the escalator, because that's actually where you often have time to just stand still and wait and enjoy the sound. Whereas most other places you are always on the move."* (P4)

The results indicate that early prototyping, in this case in the form of sound sketching, was a valuable method to aid in communicating ideas, allowing our participants to begin to articulate their feelings on what good or interesting sound design might imply. Using prototypes in the early 'discovery' phases may seem rushed, however the double diamond model and the design thinking process in general, is rarely a linear process (Design Council 2019) and this way of skipping between phases is a significant part of actual design practice.

3.3   Sound Prototyping

Working with a composer proved valuable in developing professional sound designs, but also challenging as the composer/sound designer was not involved directly in the collaboration with the users. Thus, the design team need to make an effort to effectively communicate the desired concepts to the sound designer, who might have his own ideas of what would be exciting or musically expressive. Consequently, there is a risk that the sound prototype developed reflects the artistic vision of the composer/sound designer rather than the visions or needs derived from the interactions with the participants in the design process.

A designer working with sound must find the right balance between theoretical insights (e.g. from acoustics, psychology, anthropology, and sociology), empirical insights (e.g. from the various activities in a design project, such as soundwalks or user interviews) and creative expression (with inspiration from the arts). The challenge of translating insights from empirical work and analysis and the collaborative work with users on sound concepts into sound prototypes represents a considerable challenge for designers working with sound. The fact that participants find it hard to express what types of sound they prefer to listen to, makes this an even bigger challenge for designers to overcome and facilitate.

3.4 Video Prototyping

Video prototyping seemed to work effectively as a method for evaluating sound. The method made it easy to evaluate different prototypes with more participants, without having to physically be in the metro station.

> "I think the film prototype was a really good tool to judge the different sound designs, especially because you could still hear the other existing sounds from the metro station." (P6)

As an evaluation tool, video prototyping was in some cases superior to most other prototypes, because it allowed the designer and participant to manipulate existing sounds in ways that would otherwise not have been possible. An example of this was the alarm sound when the metro doors are closing. By using video prototyping, the existing alarm sound could easily be removed, and new sound prototypes could be added to evaluate their effect. Participants could also adjust the volume levels themselves and determine when the sound design should fade in and out:

> "For some purposes the video prototype worked better than testing it with speakers in a real-life setting. [...] It was really nice that I could adjust the volume levels myself and easily switch between the different sound prototypes. It actually made it more playful." (P6)

3.5 Wizard of Oz Prototype

The Wizard of Oz prototyping session was carried out in a way that was similar to the sound sketching exercise (i.e. with a wireless portable speaker) but by replaying the sound design prototypes created in collaboration with the composer. By using a handheld portable speaker, the researcher was able to adjust volume levels, and easily test the sound prototype in different locations of the metro. As such, this method of prototyping offered a cost-effective way of quickly assessing the appropriateness of the sound and location of the prototype.

> "It felt very real. It could easily have been a speaker system placed in the metro station. It made it feel very real. So, in that sense I don't think any other methods could have been much better than that." (P1)

By using a portable speaker, we were able to fade the sound in and out, adjust volume quickly and test the different sound designs. One participant reported that:

"It was also interesting to experience how the sound faded in and out during the test. It worked very well because it gave you this surprising element. It was more dynamic. Stuff like that is hard to imagine without having tested it in real life with real sounds like we just did." (P6)

Moreover, the prototype was used to evaluate how the sound designs could improve the experience of using the metro. Sounds were only played at the entrance and escalators, as participants had pointed out those regions as being the ones best suited for an intervention. Participants generally expressed a feeling of excitement and curiosity after being exposed to the different sound designs:

"The tracks were fairly similar, and I felt an immediate curiosity. It made me want to stop for a second and just listen. Like a moment of disconnect from the 'real world'" (P5)

"It touched something. Definitely. It had a mysterious vibe to it that got my brain going. It was a bit Sci-fi-ish, and got me thinking of Star Trek, and how crazy it is that we can go to outer space" (P4)

3.6   Users as a Source of Creative Experimental Potential

When exposed to sound and being facilitated in a process of paying attention to soundscapes and acoustics of a location, our participants gave widely divergent accounts of how they perceived and interacted with sounds in the metro. After the various activities, the participants expressed a wide-ranging set of responses, indicating a multiplicity of possible positive affective qualities of sound experience that a design project might wish to pursue:

"I was surprised how the sound of nature certainly triggered something inside of me. It reminded me of my childhood home in the countryside." (P6)

"Wow. I would describe it as entertaining and something that spiked my curiosity. The bird squeaks made me instinctively look up and try to find the birds!" (P5)

"It was actually like being to an exhibition [...] It was really interesting." (P2)

After trying the soundwalking, sketching and both prototyping activities, using different ways of expressing the experience, our participants suggest that sounds trigger a relatively ambiguous sense of positive wonder and excitement. This resonates with McCarthy and Wright's idea of technology as an experience (2004). They argue that in order to design technology for experiences, we must design for 'potential' rather than assuming a direct causal relationship between a design feature and a particular experience. Since we cannot ensure the meaning of an experience for the individual, we should treat people and users of products, services and interactive systems as a source of creative experiential potential. Each user brings with them a rich history of experiences, ideas and memories which affects how they interact with the technology or services. As users of technology, we create our own understanding of what the technology is and can be. Thus, design projects should consider the potential of working with more open and ambiguous designs, allowing users to articulate their own potential meanings as they interact with them (McCarthy and Wright 2004). Techniques such as technology to encourage serendipitous meaning making such as randomness and playful unpredictability (Leong et al. 2006) or "reflective designs" that suggests how technology can work against the grain of the dominant productivity paradigms, introducing a self-reflective stance that includes affective, socio-political and critical orientations (Sengers et al. 2005), may be useful motifs for designers to explore further.

4   Discussion and Conclusion

The purpose of our study was to expand the way interaction designers can work with sound in collaborative design processes, allowing users to attain a clearer voice in interventions into the sonic world of everyday life. Throughout the project, a number of sensitising methods such as soundwalks and sound sketching were used to improve the collaboration between users/participants and designers. We have proposed aspects of a *Co-creation Framework for Sound Design* that, at this time, focuses on vocabulary building and user involvement.

Following Westerkamp (1974), our use of soundwalks to engender dialogue about qualities and affective meanings of sound were found to focus the participants' attention on an otherwise hidden or chaotic materiality of sound. The context for our pilot study was to create a sound intervention to improve the experience of the Copenhagen metro stations. The methods for user involvement explored in this study have therefore been chosen to accommodate this context and situation. However, it is our belief that the proposed framework and methods explored, such as video proto-typing, soundwalking and sound sketching can be beneficially used with many similar kinds of sound design scenarios. This can include the design of sounds for physical products and functional sounds, this is to say, sounds that carry information about a product or an interaction. Further exploration of the proposed methods for user involvement is needed in order to better understand the dynamics of each method when designing for different types of sound scenarios, for different contexts and with different kinds of users.

Expressing experiences with sound can be a challenging task for people who are not working professionally with sound. Most people lack a rich vocabulary with which to talk about and discuss sound in a meaningful way. This language barrier is difficult to address and resolve, and therefore represents an essential challenge when co-creating sound design. In the pilot project, soundwalks were a way to overcome some of the initial challenges in terms of sharing their experience with sound. They allowed participants to spend time on becoming attentive to the sounds in their environment and to reflect on the affective qualities of sounds and the acoustic qualities of the metro station.

Similarly, sound sketching was seen to be an effective method in getting participants to verbalise and discuss different sounds and sound concepts. The desired outcome of sound sketching is similar to the desired outcome of photo elicitation, which is based on the simple idea of inserting photographs into a research interview (Harper 2002). Photo elicitation was first described by researcher and photographer John Collier in 1957. In his research, Collier and his team used photographic surveys to facilitate interviews and found that the photos sharpened participants' memory and reduced areas of misunderstanding. According to Harper *"the parts of the brain that process visual information are evolutionarily older than the parts that process verbal information. Thus, images evoke deeper elements of human consciousness that do words; exchanges based on words alone utilize less of the brain's capacity than do exchanges in which the brain is processing images as well as words."* (2002: 1). Based on the concept of photo elicitation, we suggest further investigating a concept of *audio elicitation*, where designers or researchers use a variety of sounds as triggers during an interview and ask participants to articulate and reflect on the different sounds they encounter and the experiences they prompt.

As the auditory and tactile notifications of our devices and technology around us increasingly demand our attention, designers and companies are realising their responsibility to explore new ways of designing products and services that respect our states of mind rather than disrupt them. One way to do this is by utilising the potential of sound.

Sound affects our well-being and emotions, but it is often a neglected medium in design, and typically relegated to the hands of professional sound designers or practitioners with distinct musical or artistic visions that may or may not resonate with users. This paper has presented a pilot study examining how users can be involved in different phases of the sound design process. By drawing on insights and methods for user participation from other design fields, including product-, service-, or visual design, the study shows how different methods for sound sketching, and prototyping can be helpful tools with which to include participants in a sound design process. To help designers and researchers overcome some of the potential barriers of using a participatory approach to sound design, we have proposed a series of co-creation methods and a first draft of a *Co-creation Framework for Sound Design*. As such, we aim with this pilot study to join the early conversation around moving towards more participatory approaches to sound-oriented interaction design.

References

Adams, M., et al.: Soundwalking as a methodology for understanding soundscapes. In: 2008 Institute of Acoustics Spring Conference, Reading, UK (2008)

Aronson, J.: A pragmatic view of thematic analysis. Qual. Rep. **2**(1), 1–3. (1995). http://nsuworks.nova.edu/tqr/vol2/iss1/3

Barras, S.: Earbenders: using stories about listening to design auditory interfaces. In: Proceedings of the First Asia-Pacific Conference on Human Computer Interaction APCHI'96, Singapore (1996)

Bernsen, N., Dybkjær, H., Dybkjær, L.: Wizard of Oz prototyping: when and how? (2020)

Blesser, B., Salter, L.: Spaces Speak, Are You Listening?. The MIT Press, Cambridge (2007)

Brazil, E., Fernström, M.: Empirically based auditory display design. In: SMC 2009 (2009)

Brown, T.: Design thinking. Harvard Bus. Rev. **86**, 84 (2008)

Bødker, M., Chamberlain, A.: Affect theory and autoethnography in ordinary information systems. In: Twenty-Fourth European Conference on Information Systems (ECIS), Istanbul, Turkey (2016)

Bødker, M., Jensen, T.B.: Sounding out IS? Moods and affective entanglements in experiential computing. In: Twenty-Fifth European Conference on Information Systems (ECIS), Guimarães, Portugal (2017)

Buxton, B.: Sketching User Experiences: Getting the Design Right and the Right Design. Morgan Kaufaman Publishers Inc., San Francisco (2007)

Card, S.K., Moran, T.P., Newell, A.: The Psychology of Human-Computer Interaction. Lawrence Erlbaum, Hillsday (1983)

Case, A.: Calm Technology. O'Reilly Media, Sebastopol (2016)

Case, A., Day, A.: Designing with Sound. O'Reilly Media, Sebastopol (2019)

Cerwén, G., Kreutzfeldt, J., Wingren, C.: Soundscape actions: a tool for noise treatment based on three workshops in landscape architecture. Front. Archit. Res. 6(4), 504–518 (2017)

Christensen, B.T., Halskov, K., Klokmose, C.N.: Sticky Creativity - Post-it Note Cognition, Computers, and Design. Academic Press, London (2020)

Design Council: What Is the Framework for Innovation? Design Council (2019). https://www.designcouncil.org.uk/news-opinion/what-framework-innovation-design-councils-evolved-double-diamond. Accessed 8 Dec 2019

Ehn, P.: Work-oriented Design of Computer Artifacts. Arbetslivscentrum, Falköping, Sweden (1988)

Ekman, I., Rinott, M.: Using vocal sketching for designing sonic interactions. In: Proceedings of the 8th ACM Conference on Designing Interactive Systems (DIS 2010), pp. 123–131 (2010)

Enninga, T., et al.: Service Design, insights from nine case studies. HU University of Applied Sciences Utrecht (2013)

Gaver, W.W.: Auditory icons: using sound in computer interfaces. Hum. Comput. Interact. 2(2), 167–177 (1986)

Harper, D.: Talking about pictures: a case for photo elicitation. Vis. Stud. 17(1), 13–26 (2002)

Hassenzahl, M., Eckoldt, K., Diefenbach, S., Laschke, M., Lenz, E., Kim, J.: Designing moments of meaning and pleasure. Experience design and happiness. Int. J. Des. 7(3), 21–31 (2013)

Hermann, T., Hunt, A.: An introduction to interactive sonification. IEEE Multimedia 12(2), 20–24 (2005). Editorial, Spec. iss. on interactive sonification

Hug, D.: Investigating narrative and performative sound design strategies for interactive commodities. In: Ystad, S., Aramaki, M., Kronland-Martinet, R., Jensen, K. (eds.) CMMR/ICAD -2009. LNCS, vol. 5954, pp. 12–40. Springer, Heidelberg (2010). https://doi.org/10.1007/978-3-642-12439-6_2

Jacucci, G., Wagner, I.: Performative roles of materiality for collective creativity. In: Proceedings of the 6th ACM SIGCHI Conference on Creativity and Cognition - C&C 2007, pp. 73–83. ACM Press, New York (2007)

Janlert, L., Stolterman, E.: Faceless interaction - a conceptual examination of the notion of interface: past, present, and future. Hum.-Comput. Interact. 30(6), 507–539 (2015)

Jay, M.: Vision in context: reflections and refractions. In: Brennan, T., Jay, M. (eds.) Vision in Context: Historical and Contemporary Perspectives on Sight, p. 3. Routledge, New York (1996)

Langeveld, L., van Egmond, R., Jansen, R., Özcan, E.: Product sound design: intentional and consequential sounds. In: Advances in Industrial Design Engineering, pp. 47–73. IntechOpen (2013)

Leong, T.W., Vetere, F., Howard, S.: Randomness as a resource for design. In: DIS 2006. University Park, Pennsylvania, USA (2006)

Mackay, W.E.: Video prototyping: a technique for developing hypermedia systems. In: ACM CHI 1988 Conference Companion Human Factors in Computing Systems. ACM/SIGCHI, Washington, D.C. (1988)

McCarthy, J., Wright, P.: Living with technology. In: Technology as Experience, pp. 1–22. The MIT Press, Cambridge (2004)

Moore, G.E.: Cramming more components onto integrated circuits. Electronics **38**(8), 114–117 (1965)

Nielsen, J., Clemmensen, T., Yssing, C.: Getting access to what goes on in people's heads?: reflections on the think-aloud technique. In: Proceedings of the Second Nordic Conference on Human-Computer Interaction 2002, Aarhus, Denmark, 19–23 October 2002 (2002)

Norman, K.: Real-world music as composed listening. Contemp. Music Rev. **15**(Part 1), 1–27 (1996)

Oliveros, P.: Deep Listening: A Composer's Sound Practice. iUniverse, New York (2005)

Pirhonen, A., Tuuri, K., Mustonen, M.-S., Murphy, E.: Beyond clicks and beeps: in pursuit of an effective sound design methodology. In: Oakley, I., Brewster, S. (eds.) HAID 2007. LNCS, vol. 4813, pp. 133–144. Springer, Heidelberg (2007). https://doi.org/10.1007/978-3-540-76702-2_14

Rossman, J.R., Duerden, M.D.: Designing Experiences. Columbia University Press, New York (2019)

Sanders, E.B., Stappers, P.J.: Co-creation and the new landscapes of design. CoDesign **4**(1), 5–18 (2008)

Schafer, R.M.: The Tuning of the World. Knopf; original: University of Michigan, Michigan (1977)

Sengers, P., Boehner, K., Shay, D., Kaye, J.: Reflective design. In: CC 2005: Proceedings of the 4th Decennial Conference on Critical Computing, pp. 49–58 (2005)

Sundblad, Y.: UTOPIA: participatory design from Scandinavia to the world. In: Impagliazzo, J., Lundin, P., Wangler, B. (eds.) HiNC 2010. IAICT, vol. 350, pp. 176–186. Springer, Heidelberg (2011). https://doi.org/10.1007/978-3-642-23315-9_20

Supper, A.: Lobbying for the Ear: The Public Fascination with and Academic Legitimacy of the Sonification of Scientific Data. Maastricht, The Netherlands (2012)

Truax, B.: Acoustic Communication, 2nd edn. Ablex Publishing, London (2001)

Turner, R.: How to perfect the facilitation tool, "sticky dot voting". Michigan State University (2018). https://www.canr.msu.edu/news/how_to_perfect_the_facilitation_tool_sticky_dot_voting. Accessed 5 Dec 2019

Weiser, M.: The computer for the 21 st century. Sci. Am. **265**(3), 94–105 (1991)

Weiser, M., Brown, J.S.: The coming age of calm technology. In: Denning, P.J., Metcalfe, R.M. (eds.) Beyond Calculation, pp. 75–85. Springer, New York (1997). https://doi.org/10.1007/978-1-4612-0685-9_6

Westerkamp, H.: Soundwalking. Sound Heritage **3**(4), 18–27 (1974)

Westerkamp, H.: Linking soundscape composition and acoustic ecology. Organ. Sound **7**(1), 51–56 (2002)

Visualizing Information in Scientific Figures

What Do You Want Me to Know?

Judith A. Moldenhauer[(✉)]

Wayne State University, Detroit, MI, USA
judith.moldenhauer@wayne.edu

Abstract. Computer software can help scientists develop visual representations of their research, but the key to the effective communication of scientific concepts, data, and processes, is for scientists to approach the presentation of their research from the perspective of those who will be encountering it and who ask, "what do you want me to know?" and then state "show this to me in a way that I can understand it." This paper explores the use of visual variables and of systems of visual organization in revealing the relationship between the intent and visual display of information in scientific figures.

Keywords: Chart and diagram design · Design thinking ·
Information/knowledge design/visualization

1 Introduction

When I am introduced as an information designer to scientists, one of the first questions I receive is, "What is the best software to use for creating figures about my research?" My response is that it is not the software that makes effective visual communication, but rather your decisions about what to say and how to say it visually; the computer software can then help you express your ideas. The effective communication of scientific concepts, data, and processes rests on "transforming information into a visual form for comprehension." [20] To make this transformation possible, scientists must approach the presentation of their research from the perspective of the those who will be encountering it and who ask, "what do you want me to know?" and then state "show this to me in a way that I can understand it." Kress and van Leeuwen in *Reading Images: The Grammar of Visual Design* emphasize that "visual structures point to particular interpretations of experience." [8, p. 2] And as Edward Tufte demonstrates in his book, *Envisioning Information* [10], making sense of information depends on how it is visualized. The shape, size, color, etc., of visual elements and their arrangement provide signals about how we are to interpret and navigate information – what to read and do first, second, etc. And those choices determine whether the information being presented will be meaningful for the individuals who are supposed to use it. Too often scientists cram many components of their research into a single figure with few (and/or conflicting) visual cues to distinguish the components or explain why they are there. The result is a competing set visual "stuff" that gives little direction about how to read and interpret the information– the complexity obscures the communication. This issue

© Springer Nature Switzerland AG 2020
A. Marcus and E. Rosenzweig (Eds.): HCII 2020, LNCS 12200, pp. 426–438, 2020.
https://doi.org/10.1007/978-3-030-49713-2_29

is at the heart of the Cheng, Chen, Larson, and Rolandi study on the re-design of graphical abstracts in scientific papers [3] that were "hard to see and understand." [3, p. 82] By reducing the complexity of the figures through the application of various visual principles – such as size, shape, contrast, and placement – study participants cited the re-designs as being easier to understand and having a better opinion of the information and the papers' authors.

2 The Relationship of Form and Meaning

The relationship between the intent and visual display of information in scientific figures is about the relationship between form and meaning. The appearance of things and the way they are arranged are the formal elements (type, lines, shapes, pictures) that create meaning. How we see and understand things, including scientific information, is rooted in semiotics. Semiotics is the study of signs and addresses the "patterns and functions of language in everyday use" and "the fundamental processes by which meaning is established and maintained" [4, p. 104] and rests on "the idea that language operates on the basis of relationships: first, on the relationship between the signifier and the signi-fied, and then on relationships among the rules of the system by which distinct signs are combined" [4, p. 124]. In visual terms, semiotics is about the relationship of form – what we see (signs) and how we see it (syntax) – to meaning (context).

In the verbal world, signs are made of two parts: 1) the signified – an entity such a thing, idea, place, person, etc. and 2) the signifier – the sound or word conjures up that entity in your mind. Applied to the visual world, the signifier consists of variables such as shape, size, color, placement, etc., that define the entity in a particular way. The meaning of the resulting sign, that is, how we are to interpret it, comes from its relationship to other signs around it (its context). The visual arrangement of signs, known as a composition, provides a system for understanding the meaning of both the signs as a whole and of an individual sign based on its role within the composition. The ordering of the signs – how things are grouped or placed on a page – is based on patterns of visual grammar or syntax. Just as a word can have a different "spin" depending on how it used in a sentence, visual elements in a composition can convey different information depending on their use in a composition.

Scientific data can yield many different kinds of information, each of which will require a different set of visual variables and arrangement of visual elements to con-figure a hierarchy of the information that will tells something specific about the data. The hierarchy of information communicates the focus of the data and the "primary goal of a figure." [17] Change the visual variables and the organization of the information in a scientific figure and it will tell something different about the data.

3 Visual Variables

Visual principles are the foundation of the theory and practice of art and design. They go by a variety of names – such as principles, elements, and variables – and have been discussed and categorized in numerous ways over the centuries by proponents of different schools, theorists, and practitioners of art and design. [8, 15, 21] They are important factors in creating effective user-centered information design, which focuses on people's ability to complete specific tasks. [2, 7, 12] I am using the term visual variables to emphasize their inherent ability to alter our perception of visual form and thus transform the focus of information in scientific figures. (To learn more about the science of perception and its impact on visual form, see Colin Ware's book, *Information Visualization: Perception for Design*.) [13]

This paper addresses the visual variables of size, weight, shape, spacing, color, and placement. Here are brief definitions of those terms:

Size	= height, length
Weight	= thickness, thinness
Shape	= contours, edges; density (if a filled shape)
Spacing	= the distance between things
Color	= hue or graytone
Placement	= location in a composition

What you want to communicate in a scientific figure affects the use of visual variables. Bang Wong, in his Point of View column titled "Design of Data Figures," notes that visual variables encode scientific information and thus they need to be configured so that people can interpret them accurately. [18] The following examples highlight the use of visual variables to alter the visual emphasis – and thus the interpretation and communication objective – of a figure.

Figure 1 is a diagram submitted for a grant proposal submitted by Wayne State University to the NIH BEST (Broadening Experiences in Scientific Training) program. The purpose of the program was to provide guidance for science (primarily biomedical) PhD students who were interested in pursuing a variety of careers that utilized their scientific knowledge. This diagram presents the goal of the program: to provide students with exposure to other disciplines that can lead to a variety of career opportunities.

The colorful shapes surrounding the big circle are the most visually dominant aspect of the diagram; those shapes represent unique career opportunities. Their visual dominance comes from their use of color (hues) and complex contours, their even spacing placement around the big circle, and their relatively large size (amplified by the type next to them). They contrast with the rest of the diagram which is in black-and white and uses simple contours. The shapes are placed the same distance from the edge of the big circle and their accompanying type is placed to not interfere with the visual connection between the shapes and the circle. The even amount of space between the shapes around the circle communicates their equal value as careers. The size and weight of the type in the diagram (even the larger size of the headings) is relatively small and does not compete with the shapes. The same is true of the arrows pointing from the circle to the shapes with the exception of the largest arrow (representing students coming into the program) which points into the circle. The type inside the big circle lists the disciplines that students will explore; each discipline is paired with a small, black basic shape, the shape of which is reflected in the contours of the complex shapes. The small circle represents the traditional option of research in academia and industry; the two graytone shapes around it do not compete with the seven colorful shapes around the big circle. No extra lines are used in the diagram; a box around the diagram, for example, would have taken away attention from the relationship between the shapes and the circles.

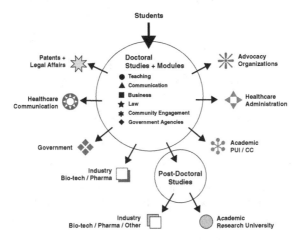

Fig. 1. Diagram of the Wayne State University NIH BEST (Broadening Experiences in Scientific Training) program's goal: to provide students with exposure to other disciplines that can lead to a variety of career opportunities.

Now let's examine two examples that demonstrate how changing one of the visual variables – weight – alters our understanding of the information in the diagram. Colin Ware calls this kind of change the "pop out effect." [14]

In Fig. 2, the weight of the big circle has changed. This thick black line now puts the visual focus on what is inside the circle: the variety of disciplines that students can encounter. The bolder weight of the type inside the big circle amplifies the importance of the content of the circle. The weight of the circle is close to the weight of the arrow (under the word "students," now also in bold) that intersects the circle and visually links students entering the program to what they will encounter in the program.

In Fig. 3, the weight of the arrows has changed (the type reverts back to its former weight). The thick black shafts of the arrows and their larger arrowheads now put the visual focus on the students entering and then exiting the program for a variety of the career opportunities.

Figure 4 is another diagram from the WSU BEST grant proposal. It connects the variety of disciplines to the Phases of the BEST program and to the course study for PhD students. The graytone rectangle surrounding "Doctoral Studies" and the number of years of study is co-dominant with the group of colorful shapes below it. The column is the axis that visually connects 1) the variety of discipline experiences through the modules with 2) how that experience plays out through the different BEST Phases and with 3) resulting career opportunities associated with the BEST program. Next to "Year 5" is "PhD Completion" which is connected to the group of shapes by a solid line. In contrast, the diagram uses dotted lines to indicate Master's Degree "off ramps" and the corresponding BEST benefits for students who opt to leave the PhD program early.

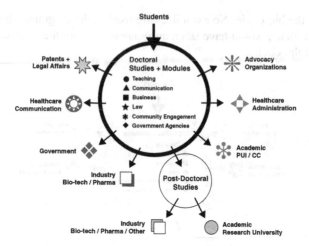

Fig. 2. Diagram of the Wayne State University NIH BEST (Broadening Experiences in Scientific Training) program's goal with an emphasis on the variety of disciplines that students can encounter through the program.

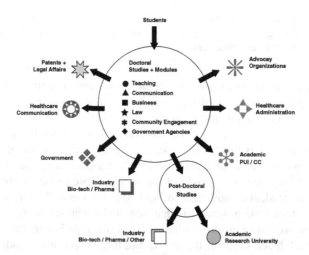

Fig. 3. Diagram of the Wayne State University NIH BEST (Broadening Experiences in Scientific Training) program's goal with a focus on the cohort of students entering and exiting the program for a variety of the career opportunities.

In Fig. 5, the elements of the diagram have been rearranged: here the emphasis is on correlating the five years of doctoral study to career opportunities. The vertical rectangle is now solid black with white type and is the most visually dominating element in the diagram; no other visual element uses black background and white type and the Modules and Phases listed on either side of the black rectangle fade in importance. The words, "PhD Degree Completion," and the colorful shapes are now centered under the black rectangle, emphasizing the time it will take to complete the degree by directly connecting the years of doctoral study to the career opportunities.

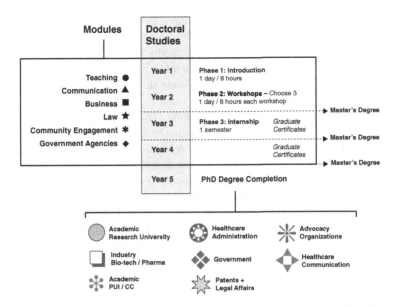

Fig. 4. Diagram of how the Wayne State University NIH BEST (Broadening Experiences in Scientific Training) program connects the variety of disciplines to the Phases of the BEST program and to the course study for PhD students.

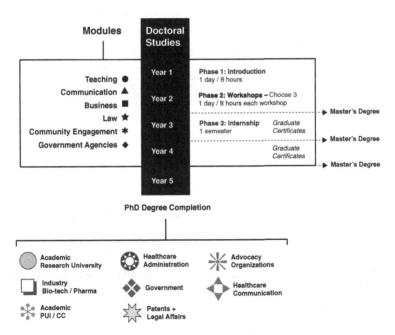

Fig. 5. Diagram of the Wayne State University NIH BEST (Broadening Experiences in Scientific Training) program that emphasizes the time it will take to complete the degree and directly connecting the years of doctoral study to the career opportunities.

Figure 6 shows the elements of the diagram suffering from what Edward Tufte calls chartjunk and a skewed data-to-ink ratio (too much ink for the amount of data presented). [11] The chartjunk here is the repeatedly used stereotypic icon of a rolled diploma secured with a ribbon; it takes attention away from the Master's and PhD completion stages and adds nothing to the understanding of the words "degree completion." The large areas of background colors and multiple diploma icons waste ink and distract from the content of the information. The use of background colors (hues) has no visual logic: colors are arbitrarily applied to different years of study. The darker colors do not translate well when converted to black-and-white (e.g., in a photocopy or FAX). Red is especially problematic because it translates to black making the black type on red or purple background quite difficult to see. Lighter colored backgrounds may contrast sufficiently with black type, but not with the various colors of the career opportunity shapes; the colors lose their effectiveness. The ochre colored background shared by the list of disciplines and the career opportunities may symbolize a connection of content, but that connection is diluted by the contrast problem with the shapes' colors. The result is a diagram that is drowning in poorly applied visual variables that make the information difficult to read and comprehend.

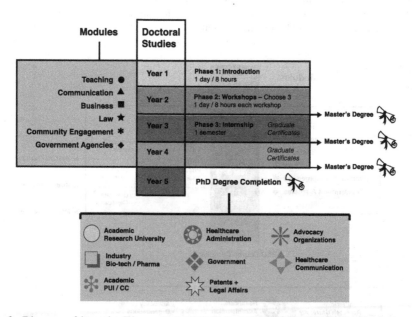

Fig. 6. Diagram of how the Wayne State University NIH BEST (Broadening Experiences in Scientific Training) program that suffers from Tufte's chartjunk and a skewed data-to-ink ratio (too much ink for the data presented).

4   Systems of Visual Organization

In his article, "Hats," the designer Richard Saul Wurman provides a vivid example of organizing hats on a hat rack to illustrate the importance of visual organization. [22] The hats can be sorted and grouped in many different ways such as the time the hats were placed on the hat rack, country where they were made, size, kinds of accessories, color, construction, and many other categories. Each time Wurman changes the way the hats are grouped, he changes the hierarchy of the information about the hats. All the distinct traits about the individual hats still reside in the hats, but his decision to highlight one trait over the others put the communication focus on that individual trait. What he wants to communicate about the hats is made clear by the way he organizes the hats' visual variables. The arrangement of signs (like Wurman's hats) shows us patterns – or systems – that provide the semiotic context for making sense of information; Ware refers to them as "semantic pattern mappings." [14, pp. 62–64] and Meirelles refers to them as "structures." [9] In the same way, what scientists choose to emphasize about their research in a figure influences not only the use of visual variables, but also its organizational structure.

This paper addresses eight systems of visual organization: axial, bilateral, radial, translateral, the golden section, grid, modular, and random. These systems have been used in art and design for centuries. For example, the golden rectangle (or golden ratio) has been used by the Renaissance artists de Vinci, Botticelli, and Michelangelo but also by the 20th century architect Le Corbusier. An extensive discussion of these systems and their application to design can be found in Kimberly Elam's books, *Typographic Systems* [6] and *The Geometry of Design* [7].

Here are brief definitions of those terms.

Axial	= asymmetric, unequal parts on either side of an axis
Bilateral	= symmetric, equal parts on either side of an axis
Radial	= spreading out from a center point
Translateral	= layers
Grid	= intersecting horizontal and vertical lines; intervals are often uneven
Modular	= intersecting horizontal and vertical lines; intervals between lines are consistent
Golden Rectangle	= results in a spiral, the pace of which is based on the mathematical proportions of the golden ratio
Random	= arbitrary

Figure 7 shows the "skeleton" structures of the systems of visual organization. In the following discussion, I will be using the abbreviation SVO to refer to systems of visual organization.

Systems of Visual Organization

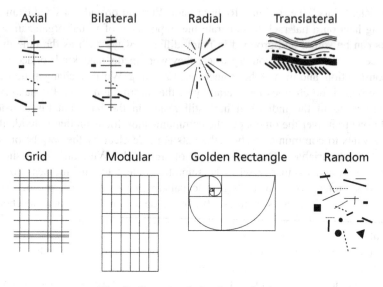

Fig. 7. Systems of visual organization.

5   Using Visual Variables and Systems of Visual Organization Together

The successive four Figures show several examples of visual variables and SVOs (some singly, some in combination) being used to present the data from a hypothetical ornithological research center in southeast Michigan, USA, that documented the species and number of birds visiting one of its feeding stations over six successive 10-min intervals spanning nine days in early February 2020. Instead of cramming all the data together and trying to make multiple points about it in one complex Figure, each example presents a specific communication goal that is revealed through the kind of data displayed and the choice of visual variables and SOV structure. Note that the examples use the elements of type, lines, and shapes and employ "negative space" (also known as whitespace) to "get certain content noticed" [19]; like the needless diploma icon in the BEST grant figures, pictures or drawings would only be chartjunk for the bird feeding station data. Pictorial images are best suited to "procedural schematics" that describe a process. [16] And also note that these examples do not utilize diagrammatic conventions such as bar or line graphs and pie charts that lend themselves to skewed data-to-ink ratios and less imaginative ways of visually connecting data to meaning. (See the "Top Ten Worst Graphs" posted by Karl Broman, professor of Biostatistics and Medical Informatics at the University of Wisconsin – Madison.) [1]

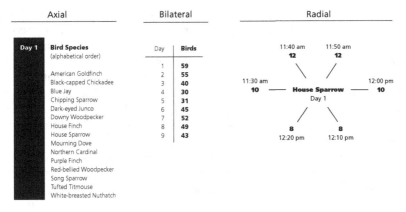

Fig. 8. Examples of data organized using axial, bilateral, radial SVOs.

Figure 8 shows three different arrangements of data about the birds at the feeder. The left one uses the axial SVO to list the species spotted on the first day of the study. The solid black vertical rectangle containing the words "Day 1" is the visual focus and organizing point of the diagram; "Bird Species" heads the column of species names (in lightweight type to the right of the rectangle) and aligns with "Day 1." The center arrangement uses the bilateral SVO to record the number of all birds for each of the nine days of the study. The bold type used in one side puts the visual focus on the bird numbers in contrast to the lightweight type used for the other side to count out the days; the placement of the lightweight horizontal and vertical lines emphasizes the differences between the columns of numbers. The right diagram uses the radial SVO to communicate the number of House Sparrows that appeared within the 10-min intervals of Day 1. The numbers and name of the bird are in the same type size and weight and have the boldest presence; the day and times are in lighter weight type and are thus of secondary importance. The six intervals are evenly spaced around the name of the bird to underscore the even time increments and placement echoes the face of a clock.

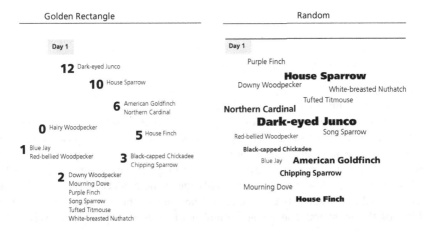

Fig. 9. Examples of data organized using golden rectangle and random SVOs.

Figure 9 shows data about the number of individuals of each species at the feeder on the first day. The left diagram groups the names of all species in the study according to number of sightings; the large number next to each list is the dominant visual element, ordered from most to fewest along the spiral of the golden rectangle SVO. Although there were no sightings of the Hairy Woodpecker on Day 1, it is included here for comparison to days when it did appear. The right diagram correlates the number of sightings to type weight and size: the more the sightings, the larger and darker the type. The use of the random SVO visually highlights the literal and figurative flutter of activity of the birds at the feeder.

Figure 10 uses the grid SVO to organize information about all the birds in the study based on classification: vertical columns list order, family, and common names of the species while the horizontal spacing varies according to number of species. The order and family names are emphasized with bold type, with italic distinguishing the family names. The upper-right diagram shows the addition of the translateral SVO through a 10% graytone horizontal rectangle, creating horizontal layers that shift the focus of the hierarchy of the information to the birds' orders.

Grid			Grid and Translateral		
Bird Species (**Order**)	Bird Species (**Family**)	Bird Species (Common Name)	Bird Species (**Order**)	Bird Species (**Family**)	Bird Species (Common Name)
Columbiformes	*Columbidae*	Mourning Dove	**Columbiformes**	*Columbidae*	Mourning Dove
Paseriformes	*Corvidae*	Blue Jay	**Paseriformes**	*Corvidae*	Blue Jay
	Cardinalidae	Northern Cardinal		*Cardinalidae*	Northern Cardinal
	Emberizidae	Chipping Sparrow Dark-eyed Junco Song Sparrow		*Emberizidae*	Chipping Sparrow Dark-eyed Junco Song Sparrow
	Fringillidae	American Goldfinch House Finch Purple Finch		*Fringillidae*	American Goldfinch House Finch Purple Finch
	Paridae	Tufted Titmouse Black-capped Chickadee		*Paridae*	Tufted Titmouse Black-capped Chickadee
	Passeridae	House Sparrow		*Passeridae*	House Sparrow
	Sittidae	White-breasted Nuthatch		*Sittidae*	White-breasted Nuthatch
Piciformes	*Picidae*	Downy Woodpecker Hairy Woodpecker Red-bellied Woodpecker	**Piciformes**	*Picidae*	Downy Woodpecker Hairy Woodpecker Red-bellied Woodpecker

Fig. 10. Examples of data organized using grid and translateral SVOs.

The four diagrams in Fig. 11 use the modular SVO to display equal amounts of information about the number of House Sparrows during each 10-min interval of the nine days in equally sized spaces. The upper-left diagram uses bold type to emphasizes the totality of the numbers. The upper-right diagram adds the translateral SVO to emphasize the morning count by applying a 10% graytone vertical rectangle over the "AM" numbers. The lower-left diagram adds the random SVO to the grid SVO to communicate the sporadic pattern of the birds' appearance through changes in the type qualities of the numbers. The greatest number of birds to appear was twelve; that

Modular

House Sparrow / Appearances at feeder

	AM			PM		
	11:30	11:40	11:50	12:00	12:10	12:20
Day 1	12	10	8	7	12	10
Day 2	10	10	9	10	12	12
Day 3	8	12	10	10	8	10
Day 4	10	10	10	12	11	10
Day 5	9	10	8	8	9	7
Day 6	12	12	11	10	10	12
Day 7	12	11	10	11	10	12
Day 8	10	11	12	10	8	6
Day 9	11	11	12	8	9	11

Modular and Translateral

House Sparrow / Appearances at feeder

	AM			PM		
	11:30	11:40	11:50	12:00	12:10	12:20
Day 1	12	10	8	7	12	10
Day 2	10	10	9	10	12	12
Day 3	8	12	10	10	8	10
Day 4	10	10	10	12	11	10
Day 5	9	10	8	8	9	7
Day 6	12	12	11	10	10	12
Day 7	12	11	10	11	10	12
Day 8	10	11	12	10	8	6
Day 9	11	11	12	8	9	11

Modular with Random

House Sparrow / Appearances at feeder

	AM			PM		
	11:30	11:40	11:50	12:00	12:10	12:20
Day 1	12	10	8	7	12	10
Day 2	10	10	9	10	12	12
Day 3	8	12	10	10	8	10
Day 4	10	10	10	12	11	10
Day 5	9	10	8	8	9	7
Day 6	12	12	11	10	10	12
Day 7	12	11	10	11	10	12
Day 8	10	11	12	10	8	6
Day 9	11	11	12	8	9	11

Modular with Random and Translateral

House Sparrow / Appearances at feeder

	AM			PM		
	11:30	11:40	11:50	12:00	12:10	12:20
Day 1	12	10	8	7	12	10
Day 2	10	10	9	10	12	12
Day 3	8	12	10	10	8	10
Day 4	10	10	10	12	11	10
Day 5	9	10	8	8	9	7
Day 6	12	12	11	10	10	12
Day 7	12	11	10	11	10	12
Day 8	10	11	12	10	8	6
Day 9	11	11	12	8	9	11

Fig. 11. Examples of data organized using modular, translateral, and random SVOs.

happened thirteen times. To visualize this irregularity, the number 12 "pops out" due to its contrast with the other numbers: bold roman vs. light italic. The lower-right diagram also employs the random SOV, to emphasize the irregular appearances during each of the nine days: the alternate use of 10% graytone bands calls out each day's information.

6 Conclusions

In their eagerness to share their research, scientists often make figures that are far too complicated by explaining too many things at once, making confusing arrangements of data, not clearly defining visual elements, and adding extra visual baggage (chartjunk). While working with an information designer is the best option, scientists themselves can create effective scientific figures by fine-tuning the communication goal of each figure and then matching that goal to appropriate visual variables and systems of visual organization. Ultimately the purpose of the figure is show meaningful relationships in the data by linking form to content, demonstrating semiotics at work. This is accomplished by using the visual variables of size, weight, shape, spacing, color, and placement in conjunction with the axial, bilateral, radial, translateral, the golden section, grid, modular, and random systems of visual organization to produce scientific figures that are clear and easy to comprehend. "Scientists that create accessible, informative and engaging images will reach larger audiences, and therefore catalyze new explorations and discoveries [3, p. 85].

All figures designed by Judith A. Moldenhauer.

References

1. Broman, K.: Top Ten Worst Graphs. https://www.biostat.wisc.edu/~kbroman/topten_worstgraphs/. Accessed 23 Feb 2020
2. Cairo, A.: The Functional Art: An Introduction to Information Graphics and Visualization. New Riders, San Francisco (2013)
3. Cheng, K., Chen, Y., Larson, K., Rolandi, M.: Proving the value of visual design in scientific communication. Inf. Des. J. 23(1), 80–95 (2017)
4. Davis, M.: Graphic Design in Context: Graphic Design Theory. Thames and Hudson, New York (2012)
5. Elam, K.: The Geometry of Design. Princeton Architectural Press, New York (2001)
6. Elam, K.: Typographic Systems. Princeton Architectural Press, New York (2007)
7. Katz, J.: Designing Information: Human Factors and Common Sense in Information Design. Wiley, Hoboken (2012)
8. Kress, G., van Leeuwen, T.: Reading Images: The Grammar of Visual Design, 2nd edn. Routledge, New York (2006)
9. Meirelles, I.: Design for Information. Rockport Publishers, Beverly (2013)
10. Tufte, E.: Envisioning Information. Graphics Press, Cheshire (1991)
11. Tufte, E.: The Visual Display of Quantitative Information. Graphics Press, Cheshire (1983)
12. Visocky O'Grady, J., Visocky O'Grady, K.: The Information Design Handbook. HOW Books, Cincinnati (2008)
13. Ware, C.: Information Visualization: Perception For Design, 3rd edn. Morgan Kaufman, Waltham (2012)
14. Ware, C.: Visual Thinking For Design. Morgan Kaufman, Burlington (2008)
15. White, A.: The Elements of Graphic Design, 2nd edn. Allsworth Press, New York (2011)
16. Wong, B.: Points of view: the overview figure. Nat. Methods 8(5), 365 (2011)
17. Wong, B.: Points of view: simplify to clarify. Nat. Methods 8(8), 611 (2011)
18. Wong, B.: Points of view: design of data figures. Nat. Methods 7(9), 665 (2010)
19. Wong, B.: Points of view: negative space. Nat. Methods 8(1), 1 (2010)
20. Wong, B.: Points of view: visualizing biological data. Nat. Methods 9(12), 1131 (2012)
21. Wong, W.: Principles of Two-Dimensional Design. Van Nostrand Reinhold, New York (1972)
22. Wurman, R.: Hats. Des. Q. 145, 1–32 (1989)

Intermodal Improvement: Nudging Users to Use Keyboard Shortcuts

Niels Erik Raursø⬥, Mikkel Kappel Persson$^{(\boxtimes)}$⬥,
Kristinn Bragi Garðarsson⬥, Daniel Mazáň⬥, Simon Andreasen⬥,
Elizabete Avotiņa⬥, Alex Ventegodt⬥, and Evangelia Triantafyllou⬥

Department of Architecture, Design and Media Technology, Aalborg University,
Copenhagen, Denmark
{nraurs18,mperss18,kgarda18,dmazan18,sban18,
eavoti18,avente18}@student.aau.dk, evt@create.aau.dk

Abstract. Keyboard shortcuts have been proven to be the most efficient method of issuing commands in computer software. Using the mouse in graphical user interfaces provides an intuitive but slow method for executing functions in a software. Many fail to make the transition to faster modalities, such as keyboard shortcuts. This is not just the case for novices, but also users with years of experience. This study examines the research on this behavior, as well as how the concepts of nudging and ambient suggestion can be used to actively encourage and support the usage of keyboard shortcuts. Based on this research, a design is proposed and implemented in a simple word processor application. A user experience evaluation was done, by having participants perform writing and formatting tasks inside the application. Using the Microsoft Reaction Card Method followed by a semi-structured interview, the users elaborated on their experience. In the interviews topics and questions of motivation, distraction, and annoyance were raised. The results showed that most participants found the system convenient and helpful in learning shortcuts without being too obtrusive. There are promising first indications of it having potential in promoting the usage of keyboard shortcuts, however further research is required in order to make any generalizations.

Keywords: User-interface design · Keyboard Shortcuts · Nudging ·
Ambient suggestion · User experience

1 Introduction

KeyBoard Shortcuts (KBSs) have been proven to be the most efficient method of issuing commands in computer software, nevertheless they are remarkably underutilized [17,23]. This is not solely the case for novices, but also for users with years of experience within a given software. While the efficiency gains might appear small in isolation, with regular use of a software the time saved will accumulate considerably over time.

ⓒ Springer Nature Switzerland AG 2020
A. Marcus and E. Rosenzweig (Eds.): HCII 2020, LNCS 12200, pp. 439–451, 2020.
https://doi.org/10.1007/978-3-030-49713-2_30

The behavior of adhering to methods already learned is understandable, as learning a new method requires further effort, and could take away time and focus from the task at hand. As a consequence, users can underestimate the efficiency gains of adopting faster methods [18]. This is a fundamental consequence of Graphical User Interfaces (GUIs). Presenting options in a visually salient manner is useful for novices, but may avert users from adopting expert methods, as users are biased towards incremental interactive actions [11]. If users choose to adopt another modality, e.g. KBSs instead of clicking toolbar icons, a performance dip is likely to occur, further dissuading users [22].

Taking inspiration from existing approaches, this paper attempts to apply mechanisms of nudging [4] and ambient suggestions [8] in order to shift user's inertia. To this end, we have adjusted and tested the GUI of a Word Processing Application (WPA), which aims at nudging users to use KBSs.

2   Background

Software solutions that assist users in learning and using KBSs do exist, but they often require the user to be intrinsically motivated and proactive in learning and utilizing KBSs. Some aid the user by providing overview of an application's KBSs[1,2], but this requires that the user makes an effort to adopt this higher-level strategy, and remembers it in the heat of completing a main goal. A complete overview of all KBSs could present itself as information overload and be slower for the user if the KBSs are not retained.

Other applications apply transient notifications whenever a KBS could have been used[3,4]. They contain basic features such as disabling notifications for certain functions and tracking missed opportunities for using the KBS. The fact that these notifications appear *after* choice and action, mean their preventive power is small. They require that the user takes note and remembers the shortcut for future use.

More forceful approaches have experimented with using obtrusive deterrences such as limiting functionality, adding time buffers, or requiring actions from the user [12,16]. Although they might increase KBS usage, such approaches might not be appropriate in practice due to their obtrusive nature.

Inspired by the approaches above, in this study we investigate a possible middle ground solution that both facilitates KBS usage and proactively dissuades the user from using the mouse.

2.1   User Behavior

While people are usually aware of the benefits and the efficiency gains of using KBSs, few make an effort in trying to switch to this modality [11,23]. The

---

[1] https://www.cheatsheetapp.com/CheatSheet/ last accessed 28th of January 2020.
[2] https://www.ergonis.com/products/keycue/ last accessed 8th of October 2019.
[3] http://www.veodin.com/keyrocket/ last accessed 13th of March 2019.
[4] https://github.com/halirutan/IntelliJ-Key-Promoter-X last accessed 28th of January 2020.

reasoning behind the lack of effort can be described with the term *satisficing*. The term was coined by Herbert A. Simon in 1947 and is a portmanteau of 'suffice' and 'satisfy'. It covers the tendency to accomplish the task at hand to a *sufficient* level, instead of accomplishing it at the most efficient and optimal level.

A reason for this may be as Czerwinski et al.'s [9] study shows, *"that users can mistrust their abilities, leading to underestimates of potential benefit with the new modality"* [8]. Wai-Tat Fu et al. state as well that *"In interactive tasks, people are biased towards the use of general procedures that start with interactive actions. These actions require much less cognitive effort, as each action results in an immediate change to the external display that, in turn, cues the next action"* [11]. It is commonly agreed that recognition is easier than recalling [1]. Therefore one reason why people tend to access commands by using the menus or clicking the icons, is that it is easier cognitively than remembering the exact shortcut for the exact command they wish to use.

Charman et al. [7] states that breaking habits is difficult and takes additional cognitive effort. This coupled with the fact that the aspirational level of the user often is to just invoke a command but not maximize the efficiency of the operation [23], creates an environment with little reason to improve. This motivational paradox as referred to by John M. Carroll et al. [6], can be used to explain why even experienced users cling to less efficient methods.

One way to increase users' motivation is through the use of gamification. McGonigal [21] defines the following four traits of game: A *goal* specifies what the player works for, providing a sense of purpose. *Rules* set up constraints and a system on how to achieve the goal. *Feedback* provides the player with progress. The last trait is *voluntary participation*, which concerns acceptance of the other traits.

2.2 Performance Within a UI

As a new user of a software interface, one must rely on any previous experiences and the visual cues within the interface. Interface designers have the challenge of developing interfaces that support both novice and high-performance expert use. Due to users' tendency to satisfy and the reluctance to explore faster strategies, high-performance functionality often has a low usage rate. Designers must therefore be aware of this, and develop interfaces that support the transition from novice to expert.

Cockburn et al. [8] deconstructs the interaction with interfaces into the **functions**, the commands and capabilities within software, and the various **methods** with which these can be accessed. An example of this is the bold function, available in word processing software by various methods. Each *method* has a *performance characteristic* that include the user's performance within that method, as well as a floor and ceiling of possible performance. Performance has before been estimated using the Keystroke-Level Model [5], which shows show how keystrokes a far faster than aiming with the mouse.

By this deconstruction Cockburn et al. introduce the domain of intermodal performance improvement. It concerns transitioning users to faster modalities such as KBSs. Scarr et al. [22] suggests with the switch, a dip in performance is likely to occur as it requires further cognitive resources and time to become acquainted with the new modality or method. It is therefore of importance that perceived cost of making the switch is minimized, and that the switch is rapidly rewarded. The first step in this transition is making the user aware of the new modality. Once the user is aware of the new modality, whether or not they choose to use it, is dependent on their perception of the potential gain in efficiency.

2.3   Ambient Suggestion

Another domain that Cockburn et al. [8] put forth concerns making the user aware of the unused functionality. Here focus is on using ambient suggestions and recommendations rather than explicit instruction. The presented themes by Cockburn et al. concern how to generate useful recommendations and how to present them best.

Cockburn et al. state that *"Presentation should be dynamically updated to the user's context, should be continuously available to the user, and should be presented in an ambient manner that allows quick access without interrupting task execution"* [8].

Cockburn et al. note the importance of feedback's relevance and the likelihood of disrupting the user for any interface. Citing research by Bødker [3], Cockburn et al. describes the two types of task disruption as *"**Breakdowns** result in severe disruption, forcing the user's attention to a new activity. **Focus-shifts** cause only a brief attention switch and cause less disruption"* [8]. Interface designers needs to balance between being obtrusive and going unnoticed.

Concerning how information is presented and perceived by the user, Cockburn et al. present the following factors: *"the probability that system feedback accurately reflects the user's intention, the ease with which causal relationships between action and effect can be learned, their stability and predictability, the temporal connection between action and response, the user's degree of focus on the work environment, and the potential costs of interruption"* [8].

Matejka et al. [20] argue that in order for a recommendation to be good, it should be both unfamiliar to the user, and useful within the context.

An example of ambient suggestions is Matejka et al.'s Patina [19] which overlays a heat map onto the interface of an application. The heat map highlights interface elements using a color mapping with opacity showing the usage of interface elements, and hue distinguishing if the usage is by the user, other users, or both.

A field in which information likewise must be pushed gently, in a way that does not take focus away from the task at hand, is video games. Dyck et al. [10] describe how 'calm messaging' with the use of transient text, animations crafted to match visibility with importance, serves as a fluid way to deliver information to the user. Attention-aware elements that, for example, modify the transparency based on the users attention. This way elements are still accessible and is a part of the users awareness, but not necessarily occluding their view.

2.4 Nudging

Nudging is the concept of influencing behavior towards a predictable outcome by the way options are presented. In a digital context this has been defined as *"the use of user-interface design elements to guide people's behavior in digital choice environments"* [24].

Nudges have been categorized along two axes, transparency and mode of thinking [4, 13]. The mode of thinking refers to whether the nudge engages mainly our automatic or reflective mind, or respectively system 1 & 2 as put forth by Kahneman and Egan [15]. Automatic thinking is the fast, effortless thinking that guides most of our decision-making. Reflective thinking takes over when slow, rational and effortful thinking is required. Transparency refers to how clear the intentions and working of a nudge is to the user.

In a paper by Caraban, Karapanos, Gonçalves, and Campos [4], 23 nudge mechanisms are found by review of the use of nudging in HCI research. The mechanisms are categorized into categories such as: *facilitate, reinforce, fear,* and *confront*.

Facilitate nudges reduce mental or physical effort, thus making a particular choice easier to choose. They can be designed in a way that aligns with the user's own interests and goals. One way this nudge can be performed is by *suggesting alternatives* that might otherwise not have been considered. This type of nudges is at the transparent and reflective end, as a proposed option is up for the user to reflect upon.

Reinforce nudges attempts to reinforce behavior by situating them/it in the user's mind. This can be done with *just-in-time prompts*, that attempts to highlight behavior at a well timed moment. *Ambient feedback* too attempts to reinforce behavior, but with minimizing disruption of the user's task. A less transparent way such nudges can work, is using *subliminal priming* per the *mere exposure effect*, as exposure could develop a preference based on familiarity.

Fear nudges work by invoking negative feeling such as fear, loss, and uncertainty, in order to dissuade users from certain behaviors.

Confront nudges try to stop an undesired action by causing doubt. *Reminding of the consequences* is also a transparent mechanism that attempts to cause the user to reflect on the consequences of their choice.

Friction nudges are less intrusive, as they do not necessarily demand attention or action. They therefore only offer slight reflection.

Hassenzahl and Laschke [14] has elaborated on this concept with the term *Pleasurable Troublemaker*. Unlike purely automatic nudges, pleasurable troublemakers should ideally create just enough friction at the moment of choice to cause reflection and sustained behavioral change. It should allow sidestepping it, they argue that this adds an ironic element to the object, and that it emphasizes the personal choice, thus becoming more likable. A slightly annoying object

should have expressive character and be understanding and naive in order for it
to create a bond with a person.

3   Methods

To evaluate if nudging and ambient suggestion can be used to support and
actively encourage the use of KBSs, a solution incorporating these elements was
designed. Following qualitative semi-structured interviews on proposed design
ideas, a final design was chosen. The UI is implemented in Java and built on-top
of an existing WPA demo[5], which contains a toolbar with icons for basic text
formatting.

3.1   Design Choices

The proposed prototype features *suggestions*, UI-elements that consist of the
icon and KBS of a function in the WPA as seen in Fig. 1.

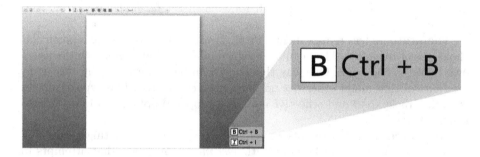

Fig. 1. Illustration of the modified WPA, and a close-up of a *suggestion*.

Whenever a toolbar icon is clicked, a *suggestion* appears in the bottom-right
corner. As more icons are clicked, the added suggestions form a list. A suggestion
does not disappear until its corresponding KBS has been used.

Each suggestion can shake, change transparency and color based on the interaction with the system. The goal of these visual states is to attract no or varying
attention depending on the context. The three main visual states can been seen
in Fig. 2.

By default, focus should be on the task within the application. The suggestion
will therefore be transparent most of the time. Hovering with the cursor over
the suggestions' area makes them all fully opaque.

When a suggestion appears, they fade-in and alert the user for a brief
moment. Whenever the user is likely to apply a function, the system fades into

---

[5] https://github.com/FXMisc/RichTextFX.

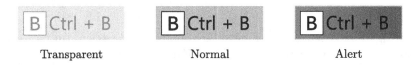

Fig. 2. Illustration of the three different states of a suggestion. (Color figure online)

attention by becoming non-transparent. Moments in the WPA that are indicative of such are whenever text is selected by either mouse or keys.

A behavior the system attempts to proactively dissuade is when the user is going for the toolbar area using the mouse. In this case, suggestions call further gradual attention to themselves. When the cursor gets closer to the toolbar, all suggestions become gradually less transparent. The corresponding suggestion becomes increasingly red as the cursor is moved closer to a specific toolbar icon, and the suggestion shakes as the cursor enters the icons area. This is in an attempt to invoke the feeling of doing something wrong. When a KBS for a suggestion is performed, the suggestion exits with a bouncing animation before exiting on the right. These animations, as seen in Fig. 3, intends to add an expressive element to the suggestions.

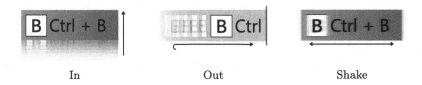

Fig. 3. Illustration of the suggestions' three different animations. (Color figure online)

With this study, we wanted to investigate whether these suggestions could nudge the user into using KBSs by their presence and selective calls to attention.

Their persistent presence makes them different from transient notifications that, by their nature, do not necessarily demand attention or action. The suggestions appear as a consequence of the user's action, and embodies a single alternate choice, when taken, also makes them disappear. Their persistent but actionable nature also set up rules. If the goal of using KBSs is accepted and the user engages, progress and feedback is seen by the suggestions' existence, and possibly performance improvement. It is voluntary to participate, with the only obstacles being calls to attention.

Friction is added with attempts to dissuade the user with animation. This friction does not prevent user action, unless it disrupts by demanding too much attention.

3.2 Evaluation

To investigate to what extend nudging and ambient suggestion can be used to support and actively encourage the use of KBSs, a user experience evaluation was conducted. The evaluation involved two writing tasks, which the participants were asked to perform.

The participants were provided with a printed example for each task. The participants were asked to write new content, but to follow the formatting from the examples. The first tasks required them to describe their favorite things. The second task was a fictional CV with sentences to fill in. Each task required them to use several formatting functions multiple times. The first task was for the participants to become familiar with the WPA, and did not include this papers implementation. For the second task, the implementation was included. The participants were not informed of this change. The interviewer took notes of unexpected occurrences and the strategy the participants took. Following the tasks, the Microsoft Reaction Cards Method (MRCM) [2] was used. The participants were asked to pick five cards with an adjective written on them and elaborate on their selection. The cards were picked from a pile of 30 cards, 12 of which were negative, 13 positive, and 5 neutral. The answers served as a starting point for the semi-structured interviews. In the interviews the participants were asked if they noticed each element of the system, and elements they did not notice were shown to them. During the interview, questions relating to motivation, distraction, and annoyance were posed.

The application was tested on ten university students from different lines of study, seven of which were male and three female. The participants were equal parts Windows and macOS users. The interviews were conducted by two interviewers.

4 Results

All cards chosen in the MRCM, are presented in Fig. 4. Most participants chose positive words over negative when choosing cards.

A common theme throughout the MRCM evaluation was that the users found the system helpful and convenient for learning new shortcuts. Multiple participants mentioned that they could see it being effective for people that use an extensive amount of time working in WPAs, especially while formatting a document.

In terms of motivation, several participants said the system would convince them to use KBSs more and would be a convenient way to learn KBSs, as it was easy to understand and comprehend instantly. One participant noted that it would be especially useful when learning to use a new program, like applications for mathematics or photo manipulation programs. One participant acknowledged that such a system could be helpful for other people, but did not find it useful for himself. The participant could not see the benefit of saving two seconds once in awhile, and did not think he would remember all the KBSs. One participant noticed and acknowledged the intent of the system, but rejected learning and

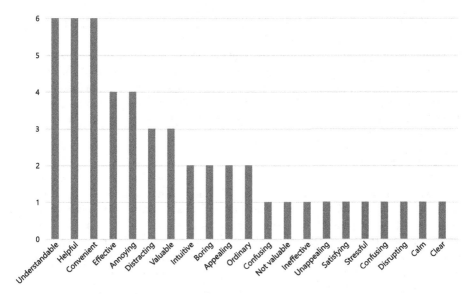

Fig. 4. The MRCM cards and frequency with which they were chosen by the participants.

using these specific shortcuts. The participant knew KBSs relevant for him in WPA, but did not perform formatting of text often enough to use or bother learning all the specific KBSs of the WPA.

Regarding distraction, the vast majority found neither the design of the system to be intrusive nor distracting enough to disrupt their workflow. One participant explicitly mentioned liking that the suggestions faded out whenever not in use and that they would fade in when a toolbar icon was about to be clicked. Several mentioned they found the suggestions helpful and ready at hand without being too obstructive. A little less than half noticed the system right away, a few noticed it, but chose to ignore them afterwards. One participant attempted to select multiple words one at a time, which was not a feature of the WPA. The participant then thought it was not possible to use KBSs, and then chose to ignore the suggestions. Another participant thought the suggestions were notifications from other applications and therefore ignored them, having a habit of ignoring notifications in general. Two participants found either the color changes or shaking animation to be too distracting. When directly asked, a few others said that the animation and color changes could potentially be too distracting. A couple of participants thought the placement of the suggestions were too far from the toolbar, as they were not noticeable when clicking a toolbar icon.

As for annoyance, half of the participants did not find the system annoying. Some noted that they did not find it annoying after a while, or after getting used to it. A couple of participants found the effects like shaking and the color changing to be specifically annoying. Some mentioned it was annoying that a suggestion for rarely used function would stay until the corresponding KBS was used.

One topic raised by several participants concerns customization of the interface, such as placement of KBS suggestions, or the ability to disable the system or parts of it. Some suggested to limit the KBS suggestions to a max of five visible at a time, others that they should be sorted after relevance. It was observed that several participants tried to remove the suggestions by clicking on them.

5   Discussion

Some participants considered both the WPA and suggestions as a single product when choosing MCRM cards, instead of focusing only on the suggestions. Therefore, it is not possible to decide with absolute certainty which parts of the system caused them to pick the cards, as the cards reflect their overall experience. The interviews used them as a starting point for discussing, in order to invite participants to elaborate on their experience. As they were performed by two different interviewers, some variation is expected.

The application was largely successful in making participants more motivated in learning shortcuts. When asked about choosing a word, several participants talked about how the application helped and reminded them to utilize KBSs. It was mentioned that to learn and retain the KBSs, the disappearance of the suggestion was not useful.

The suggestions were less conspicuous than expected, as some participants did not notice the system. They noticed the entrance of the suggestions, but paid no particular attention to them, as they were dismissed as just another notification. Had the suggestions been introduced to the participants this probably wouldn't be the case, but this finding could still indicate that the design is too similar to other pushed information that is easily dismissed.

The fact that some participants were overly focused on the task of writing could be a consequence of the unnatural testing environment. When discussing KBSs usage during the task some participants mentioned that they used KBSs less than normal due to the fact that they were not familiar with the keyboard used during the testing.

Some participants were unwilling to use KBSs which highlights the importance of relevance. They rejected learning the particular KBSs for the WPA, as they would not be of future use of the participant. The suggestions shown should make sense for the user to learn, and be perceived to be of importance. If the suggestions' visual urgency does not match the quality of the recommendation it would be highly disruptive and just a nuisance. Choosing to highlight particular repetitive actions could therefore be considered, as this would more rapidly pay off in performance and perceived relevance. The level of urgency conveyed visually should be tuned to just highlight the option enough for users, but not causing too much disruption making them reject it.

The attempt to invoke a fear of doing something wrong using colors and animation was by some participants recognized to have an affect on their choice by reminding them. The most common comment was that it might be too disruptive and annoying. It was however not consistently noticed or perceived, possibly because the animation occurred outside of their attention on the toolbar icon. Whether these calls for attention could be performed closer to their center of attention, like the toolbar, would be up for further research as to the effect and how disruptive it would be.

As the tasks given to test participants were short and with a considerable amount of formatting required, the suggestions possibly appeared more often than they would under ordinary circumstances. This could have caused the suggestions and their animations to be considered more distracting. Further evaluation in a natural setting would therefore be of importance.

In some cases the system failed to convince the test participants, stating they would not be able to recall the shortcuts and was therefore reluctant to learn them. This is likely underestimating their own ability to remember KBSs if used regularly.

While the solution focuses on its use in WPAs, there could be potential for a system such as this to assist the user to improve intermodal performance in a wide range of applications. However, this raises further challenges concerning prediction of context and relevance, and designing the suggestions to not appear obtrusive. As the dormant gray rectangles were generally considered not to be a distraction, more elaborate designs that both convey urgency at an appropriate level, and facilitate the use of KBSs could be investigated further.

6   Conclusion

Looking at optimizing performance while using a user interface, research has shown there is space of improvement. As described with term *satisficing*, even experienced users within a given software are reluctant to optimize their efficiency. KBSs are considered the fastest method when it comes to productivity, but many people are not using them.

This study aimed at investigating if nudging and ambient suggestions could be used to support and actively encourage the use of KBSs. The proposed prototype featured *suggestions*, UI-elements that appear whenever a toolbar icon has been clicked, and are removed when the corresponding KBS has been used. The suggestions are displayed in an ambient manner by using animations, transparency, and color for selective calls for attention. Furthermore, they attempt to actively dissuade the user from clicking toolbar icons without preventing them from doing so. Participants were asked to perform two writing tasks with and without the prototype activated. The user experience was evaluated by using the MRCM to measure participants' emotions and desirability towards the interface. Following the MRCM, a semi-structured interview was conducted to evaluate if and how the UI, among other things, motivated or distracted the user.

Promising results were found from the user experience evaluation. The majority of the participants found the system helpful, convenient and motivating. Furthermore, most participants did not find the system to disrupt their workflow, or be too obtrusive. There are first indications that nudging and ambient suggestions could be used to facilitate KBSs and proactively remind users to use them. Further research into different elements of the design, as well as testing in a more natural environment is required in order to make any generalizations.

Most software include various methods for functions allowing better performance, so there is a good reason for developers to consider ambient suggestion and nudging to provide a more user friendly experience when the user transitions to expert methods.

References

1. Anderson, J., Bower, G.: Recognition and retrieval processes in free recall. Psychol. Rev. **79**, 97–123 (1972). https://doi.org/10.1037/h0033773
2. Benedek, J., Miner, T.: Measuring desirability: new methods for evaluating desirability in a usability lab setting. In: Proceedings of Usability Professionals Association, vol. 2003, no. 8–12, p. 57 (2002)
3. Bødker, S.: Applying activity theory to video analysis: how to make sense of video data in HCI. In: Nardi, B. (ed.) Context and Consciousness: Activity Theory and Human Computer Interaction, pp. 147–174. MIT Press, Cambridge (1996)
4. Caraban, A., Karapanos, E., Gonçalves, D., Campos, P.: 23 ways to nudge: a review of technology-mediated nudging in human-computer interaction. In: Proceedings of the 2019 CHI Conference on Human Factors in Computing Systems, CHI 2019. ACM, New York (2019). https://doi.org/10.1145/3290605.3300733
5. Card, S.K., Newell, A., Moran, T.P.: The Psychology of Human-Computer Interaction. L. Erlbaum Associates Inc., Hillsdale (1983)
6. Carroll, J., Rosson, M.B.: Paradox of the Active User, pp. 80–111. MIT Press, Bradford (1987)
7. Charman, S.C., Howes, A.: The adaptive user: an investigation into the cognitive and task constraints on the generation of new methods. J. Exp. Psychol. Appl. **9**(4), 236 (2003)
8. Cockburn, A., Gutwin, C., Scarr, J., Malacria, S.: Supporting novice to expert transitions in user interfaces. ACM Comput. Surv. (CSUR) **47**(2), 31 (2015)
9. Czerwinski, M., Horvitz, E., Cutrell, E.: Subjective duration assessment: an implicit probe for software usability. In: Proceedings of IHM-HCI 2001 Conference, vol. 2, pp. 167–170 (2001)
10. Dyck, J., Pinelle, D., Brown, B.A., Gutwin, C.: Learning from games: HCI design innovations in entertainment software. In: Graphics Interface, vol. 2003, pp. 237–246. Citeseer (2003)
11. Fu, W.T., Gray, W.D.: Resolving the paradox of the active user: stable suboptimal performance in interactive tasks. Cogn. Sci. **28**(6), 901–935 (2004)
12. Grossman, T., Dragicevic, P., Balakrishnan, R.: Strategies for accelerating on-line learning of hotkeys. In: Proceedings of the SIGCHI Conference on Human factors in Computing Systems, pp. 1591–1600. ACM (2007)
13. Hansen, P.G., Jespersen, A.M.: Nudge and the manipulation of choice: a framework for the responsible use of the nudge approach to behaviour change in public policy. Eur. J. Risk Regul. **4**(1), 3–28 (2013)
14. Hassenzahl, M., Laschke, M.: Pleasurable Troublemakers, pp. 167–196. MIT Press, Cambridge (2014). http://www.jstor.org/stable/j.ctt1287hcd.13

15. Kahneman, D., Egan, P.: Thinking, Fast and Slow. Farrar, Straus and Giroux, New York (2011)
16. Krisler, B., Alterman, R.: Training towards mastery: overcoming the active user paradox. In: Proceedings of the 5th Nordic Conference on Human-Computer Interaction: Building Bridges, pp. 239–248. ACM (2008)
17. Lane, D.M., Napier, H.A., Peres, S.C., Sandor, A.: Hidden costs of graphical user interfaces: failure to make the transition from menus and icon toolbars to keyboard shortcuts. Int. J. Hum. Comput. Interact. **18**(2), 133–144 (2005)
18. Malacria, S., Scarr, J., Cockburn, A., Gutwin, C., Grossman, T.: Skillometers: reflective widgets that motivate and help users to improve performance. In: Proceedings of the 26th Annual ACM Symposium on User Interface Software and Technology, pp. 321–330. ACM (2013)
19. Matejka, J., Grossman, T., Fitzmaurice, G.: Patina: dynamic heatmaps for visualizing application usage. In: Proceedings of the SIGCHI Conference on Human Factors in Computing Systems, pp. 3227–3236. ACM (2013)
20. Matejka, J., Li, W., Grossman, T., Fitzmaurice, G.: CommunityCommands: command recommendations for software applications. In: Proceedings of the 22nd Annual ACM Symposium on User Interface Software and Technology, pp. 193–202. ACM (2009)
21. McGonigal, J.: Reality is Broken: Why Games Make Us Better and How They Can Change the World. Penguin, New York (2011)
22. Scarr, J., Cockburn, A., Gutwin, C., Quinn, P.: Dips and ceilings: understanding and supporting transitions to expertise in user interfaces. In: Proceedings of the SIGCHI Conference on Human Factors in Computing Systems, CHI 2011, pp. 2741–2750. ACM, New York (2011). https://doi.org/10.1145/1978942.1979348
23. Tak, S., Westendorp, P., Van Rooij, I.: Satisficing and the use of keyboard shortcuts: being good enough is enough? Interact. Comput. **25**(5), 404–416 (2013)
24. Weinmann, M., Schneider, C., vom Brocke, J.: Digital nudging. Bus. Inf. Syst. Eng. **58**(6), 433–436 (2016). https://doi.org/10.1007/s12599-016-0453-1

Identifying Interaction Patterns for Face Recognition Interfaces Through Research, Prototyping and Testing

Flavio Ribeiro$^{(\boxtimes)}$, Guto Kawakami , and Taynah Miyagawa

Sidia Instituto de Ciência e Tecnologia, Manaus, Brazil
flavinho.sr@gmail.com, guto.kawakami@gmail.com,
taynah.araujo@gmail.com

Abstract. Face recognition is a biometric system used by companies and users in order to promote security. This research aims to understand how the graphic interfaces for this type of technology work and which interaction patterns can be used in order to provide a better experience for a local retailer's average consumer while using the available in-store kiosks. To contemplate these goals, Design Thinking was used as methodology and divided into four distinct phases: products with facial recognition available in the market were identified through *desk research* and, for the sake of proposing a better interface solution, *ideation* sessions followed by *prototyping* and *user testing* were performed. As a result, a minimalist interface was created for the product (using only the necessary interface elements in order to avoid information conflicts), along with a specific communication language defined with the help of user feedback. A list of interaction patterns for face recognition interfaces was also defined.

Keywords: Face recognition · User testing · Information design

1 Introduction

Security is a key factor in the corporative world. Currently, companies are using an abundance of biometrics (e.g. fingerprints, voice, iris, palm and face recognition) in order to promote the security of their employees and customers by creating a secure access to contents, payments, and other functionalities.

Among these technologies, face recognition consists in identifying patterns in facial features, such as: mouth shape, face shape and distance between the eyes [1]. This process unfolds in three steps: biometric reading, features extraction and their addition to the database (Fig. 1).

© Springer Nature Switzerland AG 2020
A. Marcus and E. Rosenzweig (Eds.): HCII 2020, LNCS 12200, pp. 452–463, 2020.
https://doi.org/10.1007/978-3-030-49713-2_31

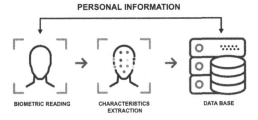

Fig. 1. Face recognition steps

In an interview to IstoÉ[1], James Miranda, a specialized face recognition consultant, stated that it is possible to verify growth for this system in the Brazilian market. He claims that it is possible to foresee a growth of 20% to 30% per year in this market that is also finding expansion opportunities in residential and corporate condominiums in addition to commercial activities.

To exemplify how much this system is being explored as a solution, the American multinational technology company Apple Inc. has designed and developed its own facial recognition system (Face ID) to be used in its devices. Among other features, this system allows biometric authentication for unlocking devices, making payments and accessing sensitive data (Fig. 2).

Fig. 2. Face ID setup

The technology that enables Face ID is in the devices' TrueDepth camera that captures face data by projecting and analyzing over 30,000 invisible dots to create a facial depth map, also capturing an infrared image of the user's face. The system then transforms the captured data into a mathematical representation – each time the user tries to unlock the device, the camera captures data that is matched against the stored mathematical representation to authenticate [2]. The main advantage in this technology is security: only the user will be able to unlock the device, so sensitive data will be kept safe.

---

[1] https://istoe.com.br/sistemas-de-reconhecimento-facial-crescem-no-brasil/.

The current research emerged by focusing in this technology while trying to explore and solve a market demand from a local retailer that decided to use this technology in its in-store kiosks – used for purchases, payments and account-related information – in order to improve not only their customers' experience, but also the amount of time used for interaction. This document consists in describing the design process used for defining and developing this product's interface and identifying interaction patterns in order to meet users' needs and to provide them a great experience.

2   Theoretical Framework

2.1   Information Design

Information is something present in people's everyday lives and it can be presented in several ways, such as: voice, reading, writing, gestures, drawings, and codes. In the context of design, there is a field that has the purpose of studying information and its concepts: Information Design is an area that aims to organize and present data by transforming it into meaningful and valuable information – essentially, an area that studies the process of how information must be presented to a receiver [3].

2.2   Information Architecture

For several years now, the design area has expanded its possibilities and is not only based in producing material objects but also on developing graphic-digital interfaces through which the user interacts in cyberspace [4]. These interfaces are composed of data that is studied by professionals and strategically organized so that receivers can have a good understanding of each product.

In the technology market, big companies like Apple, Google and Microsoft have created their own visual interface standards, thus imposing conventions of information understanding unto receivers, who then come to understand information based on their previous interaction with the components developed through these standards' architecture.

Information Architecture can be understood as four interdependent systems: Organization system (the way content is organized and categorized), labeling system (verbal/visual signs for each informational element), navigation system (ways of moving through the information space) and search system (that determines possible questions and the answers that can come from the database) [5].

This research also focuses on understanding how the organization, labeling and navigation systems should be structured to provide good interactions for the user when using a facial recognition interface.

3 Methodology

3.1 Desk Research

Since it is necessary to understand what competitors have developed in order to increase the range of ideas and obtain a greater knowledge in the project's focus area, products with facial recognition available in the market were identified during desk research. This kind of research is a search for information on the project's theme from various sources (e.g. websites, books, magazines, blogs, articles) [6].

The main focus of this phase was to explore available products, identify trends and understand how information design was used for the creation of this type of graphical interfaces – by analyzing how the user accesses the information it is possible to detect information architecture structures and interface parameters.

3.2 Ideation

Seeing that the study arose from a market demand and understanding the need to involve different kinds of people in the creative process, co-creation workshops were organized.

Co-creation workshops are organized meetings with a series of group activities to stimulate creativity and collaboration, fostering the creation of innovative solutions [6]. One of the biggest advantages of co-creation is that it has the ability to facilitate collaboration as it brings groups together and creates a feeling of ownership for the innovation being created [7].

These workshops were conducted in order to assess the client's current system and define possible new interactions. In this phase, a multidisciplinary team consisting of the project's product designers and the staff of the client company took part in discussing the product and generating ideas. This formation allowed solutions to be immediately verified and validated by the client's own staff (Fig. 3).

Fig. 3. Co-creation session with the client's staff

3.3 Prototyping

Elaborated ideas were then analyzed, filtered and promising solutions were chosen by the product design team to become prototypes. A prototype can vary in terms of tone and complexity, but the common factor is the ability to test proposed solutions in a close to real life scenario [7]. Herein, project prototypes were developed for user testing and feedback collection.

Project prototypes focused on demonstrating interaction flows through main interface screens, which are the connection between the consumer and the in-store kiosk's facial recognition system. These prototypes were developed in high fidelity by the product design team through specialized graphic user interface software and then handed to the development team to be coded.

Prototyping is an evolving feedback mechanism. Furthermore, through the creation of prototypes, it is possible to determine whether to continue with a specific design direction or to explore a different possibility, before moving on to the next phases of the project [8]. Considering these facts, team members opted for testing initial prototypes internally so that it was possible to obtain a first feedback on the prototype, correct minor errors and to investigate the team's opinion. Through these actions, prototypes were refined before being finally used with the product's target users.

3.4   User Testing

User testing is a tool used for obtaining information on product satisfaction and real life applicability. Moreover, the test when applied allows more usability problems that directly affect end users to be identified [9].

Objective. In this research, user testing had two main objectives: (a) to identify opportunities for improvement in the interface/prototype and (b) to detect interaction patterns. To achieve these objectives, tests with real consumers were carried out inside the retail store during business hours, followed by profile-focused interviews.

Participants. A total of 79 consumers served as participants for the study, with ages ranging from 21 to 45 years of age (Fig. 4).

Fig. 4. Participant during a test

Procedures. To carry out the tests, the research team set up a space inside the store to simulate the kiosk. The area had controlled lighting conditions and each individual test process took about 3 min.

The tests were performed through the following procedures: (a) consumer invitation; (b) interview to identify this consumer's profile; (c) carrying out the test and (d) acknowledgments.

In the first procedure, the research team would approach consumers already at the retail store by letting them know about the project and inviting them to be a test participant. Then, consumers who agreed to participate went through an interview that would define their consumer profile by collecting data (i.e.: sex, age, education level, profession, height, store loyalty in years, frequency of purchase and previous experience with the store's kiosks).

After the profile interviews, researchers would guide participants through activities to be performed in the prototype: (1) select the face registration button; (2) enter CPF[2] number and date of birth; (3) go through the tutorial; (4) position face in the defined area; (5) follow interface instructions. During the activities, researchers would take notes focusing on difficulties, behaviors and feedbacks.

Data Collection. Through debriefing, it was possible to obtain a participant data report and also a test activities report.

The first step was to check for incorrect or missing information and verifying the discrepancies contained therein. With the final report fully verified, its analysis revealed issues that were classified as: high, medium and low. This classification is based on frequency and impact factors, chosen according to the severity classifications for usability problems. Correct classification can be used to allocate the maximum resources to correct the most serious problems while also providing a rough estimate of the need for additional usability efforts [10]. Thus, the following definition was used:

- High level – it happens frequently and has a strong impact on the user experience;
- Medium level – it can happen frequently but has no strong impact on the user experience;
- Low level – it does not happen frequently and has no strong impact on the user experience.

After the classification phase, the product team defined what should be changed to improve the interface, basing decisions on test participants' opinions.

4 Results

4.1 Desk Research

The desk research phase was fundamental to gather knowledge and insights by studying similar solutions. Furthermore, its resulting analysis provided the necessary inputs to detect behaviors and navigation flows that could be used as reference in the creation of good practices for project's facial recognition interface (Fig. 5).

A total of 14 products were found. Most of these were only customer service-related kiosks but, among them, a few used facial recognition during the user experience (Table 1).

---

[2] CPF is an individual taxpayer identification number given to people living in Brazil, both native Brazilians and resident aliens, who pay taxes.

Fig. 5. A few face recognition-related products currently available in the market

Table 1. Benchmarking analyzed solutions

Type	Product	Links
Self Service Kiosk	McDonald's	https://youtu.be/wJsfKNx_-Ew
Self Service Kiosk	Supermarket	https://youtu.be/wJsfKNx_-Ew
Face Recognition	User experience while buying coffee	https://youtu.be/iTl7iMYPfW8
Face Recognition	LA Airport	https://youtu.be/iTl7iMYPfW8
Face Recognition	Baidu Headquarter	https://youtu.be/iTl7iMYPfW8
Face Recognition	Alipay	https://youtu.be/iTl7iMYPfW8
Self Service Kiosk	KFC	https://youtu.be/iTl7iMYPfW8
Face Recognition	ZENUS	https://youtu.be/iTl7iMYPfW8
Face Recognition	Baidu and KFC facial recognition	https://youtu.be/iTl7iMYPfW8
Face Recognition	Apple smartphone	https://youtu.be/gRRKu6PZr_M
Face Recognition	MIT Media Lab Research	https://youtu.be/gRRKu6PZr_M
Self Service Kiosk	Nike	https://youtu.be/rzmrY_jzwlo
Self Service Kiosk	Timberland	https://youtu.be/5TZmQPdhpak
Self Service Kiosk	Bob's	https://youtu.be/QoS8UApYUo8

Through the obtained results it was possible to understand a few basic user needs and behaviors, as well as to define visual and interaction parameters for developing these types of interfaces. Defined parameters were (a) Language/Text, (b) Iconography, (c) Feedback and (d) User instructions.

4.2 User Interface

After interface parameters were defined, the ideation phase began. In this stage, design sketches with the first system flows and wireframes were defined through co-creation (Fig. 6).

Fig. 6. Design sketches created during the ideation phase

Then, after defining the information structure, a visual guideline was established based on the client's visual identity. This guideline was applied to the facial recognition kiosk through a first version of the interface, used to collect user feedback during user testing (Fig. 7).

Fig. 7. Facial registration interface – first version

4.3   Interaction Patterns

With the developed prototype, user tests were conducted in order to evaluate the face registration flow's usability, visual language, chosen iconography and semiotics (Fig. 8).

Fig. 8. Facial registration interface used for user testing

Tests resulted in issues categorized in distinct severity levels, as described below (Table 2):

Table 2. Issues with its severity levels

Level	Type	Details
High	Capture angle is too complex	The lower movements were uncomfortable, users had to make 5 or more attempts
High	Fast body/facial movement	Users' facial and body movements made it difficult to complete the registration – the warning message ("move slowly according to the arrow") was not clear
High	Orientation icons	The icon's (arrow) direction made users confused as to which was the correct movement to be performed

(continued)

Table 2. (*continued*)

Level	Type	Details
Medium	Wrong button was selected	Proximity between buttons caused doubts and errors
Medium	*Continue* button was selected	Users did not realize the button was inactive
Medium	Confusing tutorial phase	Some participants thought that the registration was already taking place while going though the tutorial
Medium	Close keyboard action is unclear	After typing the CPF number, a participant took a long time trying to close the keyboard
Medium	Animation-related doubts	Users did not understand what movement to make
Low	Positioning face on the defined area	Four participants could not position themselves correctly and that increased the registration's difficulty

Users took about 1 min and 20 s in test activities. For a better understanding of the test findings, the table below demonstrates which activities the users had difficulties in and related severity levels (Table 3):

Table 3. Activities and its severity levels

Activities	Levels
1. Select the button to register face	Medium
2. Type CPF number and date of birth	Medium
3. Tutorial	High
4. Position face in the circular area	Low
5. Registration (step 1)	High
6. Position face in the circular area	Low
7. Registration (step 2)	Medium
8. Follow interface instructions	Low

During tests, the following improvements and positive feedbacks were also collected (Table 4):

Table 4. Improvements and positive findings list

Improvement points
Capture steps should be faster
Improve instructions and display which movements should be made
Make it clear that there are different registration phases
Feedback message display time is not adequate
Positive points
Users had confidence in the process
Increased security while accessing users sensitive data
Ease and speed during login

After the full data collection and debriefing process, a few changes were made to the product:

- Summarized registration steps;
- Increased typography size;
- Increased the amount of time the process' feedback messages remain on screen.

These minor changes improved not only the product's visual but also made registration faster (the whole process takes an average of 30 s).

Moreover, understanding the interface's visual elements, command phrases and interaction flows was a difficulty faced by several users while using the prototype. Trying to mitigate this issue, an appropriate communication language was identified through user feedback and applied, while a more minimalist approach to the interface was implemented to avoid information conflicts, by using only the necessary interface elements (Fig. 9).

Fig. 9. Facial registration interface – reviewed version

In addition to interface improvements, the project's design thinking approach and research-oriented process resulted in a number of interaction patterns that can be used for the development of solutions that have facial recognition as a part of the user experience (Table 5):

Table 5. Research defined interaction patterns

Interaction patterns
1 – Face registration needs to be as fast and clear as possible, especially taking into consideration the fact that users need to move their head to complete the action. If the process is slow, it can be a cause for dissatisfaction and/or weariness
2 – Improving each step's clarity with screen titles is fundamental so that users have the exact notion of what is happening in each stage of the process
3 – The presented data needs to be evident and have an appropriate size to facilitate reading. It is also necessary to provide a greater amount of time for its interpretation and understanding
4 – While information is being displayed, there should not be any peripheral noise in the interface that compromises the user's attention
5 – The information available in error messages and instructions needs to have a more personal and less technical language

Uncovered interaction patterns served as reference for changes in the developed product's user interface and it is expected that these findings can contribute with the development of future facial recognition interface projects.

5 Conclusions

The present document introduced a study to identify interaction patterns for facial recognition interfaces using exploratory research, ideation techniques, prototyping and validation through usability tests. The study was driven by information design concepts and Design Thinking techniques. Desk research, ideation, prototyping and user testing phases were used to identify interaction patterns to improve user experience.

The research phase provided theoretical basis on the concepts of facial recognition and the advancement of biometrics in the Brazilian market. Desk research provided information about products already on the market. The ideation stage then allowed ideas to be sketched alongside the client while focusing on a new product for a varied audience (in age and technology familiarity). Consequently, these ideas were developed so that they could be tested with real users. Finally, through user testing it was possible to understand the users' difficulties, to identify improvement points and to define interaction patterns for facial recognition interfaces.

Next steps include installing the resulting product in the retail store actual kiosks and performing additional usability tests, now with a greater number of participants and data.

Acknowledgements. Samsung funded this research through resources from the Information Technology Law and other incentive laws.

References

1. Silva, A., Cintra, M.: Reconhecimento de padrões faciais: Um estudo. In: Encontro Nacional de Inteligência Artificial e Computacional 2015, Proceedings ENIAC, pp. 224–231 (2015)
2. About Face ID advanced technology. https://support.apple.com/en-gb/HT208108. Accessed 21 Feb 2020
3. Shedroff, N.: Information interaction design: a unified field theory of design. Inf. Des. 267–292 (1999)
4. De Souza Quintão, F., Triska, R.: Design de informação em interfaces digitais: origens, definições e fundamentos. InfoDesign - Revista Brasileira de Design da Informação **11**(1), 105–118 (2014)
5. Agner, L.: Ergodesign and Information Architecture – Working with the User. Quartet (2009)
6. Vianna, M.: Design Thinking: inovação em negócios. Design Thinking (2012)
7. Schneider, J., Stickdorn, M.: This is Service Design Thinking: Basics, Tools, Cases. Wiley, Hoboken (2011)

8. Unger, R., Chandler, C.: A Project Guide to UX Design: For User Experience Designers in the Field or in the Making. New Riders, Indianapolis (2012)
9. Rocha, H., Baranauskas, M.: Design and Evaluation of Human Computer Interfaces. Nied, Brazil (2003)
10. Severity Ratings for Usability Problems. https://www.nngroup.com/articles/how-to-rate-the-severity-of-usability-problems. Accessed 21 Feb 2020

The Impact of Expectation and Disconfirmation on User Experience and Behavior Intention

Xiaorui Wang[1,2], Ronggang Zhou[1(✉)], and Renqian Zhang[1]

[1] Beihang University, 37 Xueyuan Road, Beijing 100191
People's Republic of China
cecily_wong@126.com, {zhrg, zhangrenqian}@buaa.edu.cn
[2] Beijing Materials Handling Research Institute,
52 Yonghe Road, Beijing 100007, People's Republic of China

Abstract. Satisfaction and behavior intention are crucial elements of system and product success, and are also positive results of user experience (UX). Most existing UX studies focus on perception aspects, and employ models with linear and symmetric assumptions. Expectation-confirmation theory (ECT) points out that people's expectation and confirmation/disconfirmation are vital factors in generating satisfaction. Moreover, the prospect theory (PT) describes people's asymmetric attitude to positive and negative disconfirmation. Based on ECT and PT, the current study proposed hypotheses to explore how users' expectation and disconfirmation affect their satisfaction and behavior intention, as well as the asymmetric impact of different valenced disconfirmation. The hypotheses were tested using data from a retrospective designed e-banking application UX study. Results show that both utility and emotion expectations and their disconfirmation impact user satisfaction and behavior intention. The disconfirmations show negative asymmetric impacts. Besides, satisfaction mediates the impact of expectation and disconfirmation on behavior intention, and it also moderates the asymmetric impact of disconfirmation. Apart from the limitations, conclusions from this study confirmed the application potential of ECT and PT in future UX researches.

Keywords: User experience · Satisfaction · Expectation-confirmation theory · Prospect theory · Asymmetric impact

1 Introduction

Satisfaction plays an essential role in achieving critical business or product goals, including developing behavior intention and cultivating loyalty, which are recognized as vital factors in business competitiveness and success [1]. As an antecedent of user satisfaction and behavior intention, user experience (UX) has been studied a lot and emerged as an increasingly important component in various fields [2]. UX originates from the conception of usability in human-computer interaction, and goes beyond to contain affective aspects such as feelings in the interaction, and desire to reuse or recommendation [3, 4]. A widely accepted opinion is what Hassenzahl et al. proposed,

A. Marcus and E. Rosenzweig (Eds.): HCII 2020, LNCS 12200, pp. 464–475, 2020.
https://doi.org/10.1007/978-3-030-49713-2_32

that pragmatic and hedonic value is what drives UX evaluation and behavior intention [5]. Pragmatic value, including utility and usability, is what users need to achieve behavioral goals and answer the question "what to do". In contrast, hedonic value, such as stimulation and identification, is related to users' self and answers the question "how to do" [6].

The existing UX studies usually collect data using questionnaires or in experiments, and employ linear and symmetric models such as multiple regression and structural equation. Moreover, these studies focus more on the perception aspects of users' interacting with products, systems, or services. The evaluation and prediction of UX satisfaction and behavior intention are based on these collected perception data. However, in consumer satisfaction research, Oliver pointed out that expectation before real experience, and the comparison results of the expectation and real experience are predicting factors of satisfaction [7]. The difference between expectation and real experience is defined as disconfirmation. In contrast, the comparability is confirmation. Thus, consumer satisfaction can be expressed as the function of expectation and disconfirmation. This theory is the expectation-confirmation theory (ECT) [8]. ECT has been widely adopted in various satisfaction researches to describe how satisfaction forms and proved to be correct. However, in the UX field, there are only very limited numbers of similar studies. Kahneman and Tversky [21] also found the impact of disconfirmation in decisions. They published their findings in 1979 and proposed the prospect theory (PT). PT points out that humans behave differently in contexts of loss and gain, because of their difference in weighing gain and loss based on preset reference points [9]. The asymmetric attitude is caused by the value evaluation process.

Similarly, before their real interaction, users may have formed an expectation of experience based on the information they gathered actively or passively [10]. Thus, including expectation and disconfirmation in UX, and exploring how their impact on the formation of satisfaction and behavior intention is practical [11]. Furthermore, according to PT, disconfirmation may arouse users' feelings of gain and loss, and induce asymmetric results. However, models employed in most existing studies include potential linear and symmetric relationship assumptions, which have been challenged both in theory and practice [12]. Thus, we can take a closer look at whether different valenced disconfirmation makes different impacts.

Based on ECT and PT, the current study aims to examine the effect of users' expectation and disconfirmation, as well as the asymmetric effect of positive and negative disconfirmation. Hypotheses were tested using data collected in a retrospectively designed mobile e-banking application (App) UX research. Conclusions from this study confirmed the impact of expectation and disconfirmation on UX satisfaction and behavior intention. Furthermore, we found negative disconfirmation generally had a slightly larger influence than positive disconfirmation, primarily for utility disconfirmation, which is the same as what described in PT. Besides, we found satisfaction moderates the asymmetric impact of disconfirmation on behavior intention. Based on these conclusions, we suggest considering expectation and disconfirmation, as well as asymmetry of disconfirmation in future UX studies.

2 Theories and Hypotheses Development

2.1 Expectation-Confirmation Theory

Olive [7] initially proposed the expectation-confirmation theory to undercover consumer's psychological process in establishing satisfaction. Different from previous satisfaction theories, ECT theorizes expectation as an additional determinant of satisfaction. The ECT framework is illustrated in Fig. 1. According to ECT, satisfaction formation process includes four steps, as is shown in the dashed frame of Fig. 1. The first step is an expectation generation step. Before the real experience of a product, service, or system, people may have obtained related information from the external environment and previous internal experience. For example, advertisements or similar previous experience. The second step is the real experience. In this step, people perceive the actual performance of the object. The third step is confirmation/disconfirmation concluding. People make a comparison between expectation and perception to determine to what extent their initial expectation is confirmed. If their expectation fails to be confirmed, then the failure induces disconfirmation. As disconfirmation is the difference between perception and expectation, it can be either positive or negative. When the experience is better than what has been expected, the disconfirmation is positive; and if the experience is worse than what has been expected, the disconfirmation is negative [11]. In the fourth step, people generate satisfaction based on the confirmation level and primal expectation. According to the satisfaction formation process in this theory, we can see expectation acts as a baseline or reference point in the evaluation of perception.

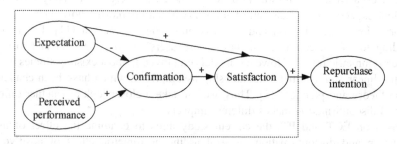

Fig. 1. The framework of expectation-confirmation theory.

ECT has been adopted in vast consumer behavior researches to study their satisfaction and behavior, such as repurchase or recommendation. It showed fairly good explanative and predictive ability in these studies [13, 14]. In the UX field, Bhattacherjee [15] is the first to adapt the ECT to his research on cognitive beliefs and affect influencing users' intention to continue using information systems (IS). Involving user expectation, confirmation, and perceived usefulness, he proposed and tested a post-acceptance model of IS continuance [15]. A series of following UX studies also affirmed the feasibility of involving expectation and confirmation/disconfirmation, such as studies of Lee et al. [16], Eveleth et al. [17], Hsu and Lin [18], and Tam et al. [19]. However, none of these studies made a comparison of the pragmatic and hedonic aspects of UX, or the asymmetric impact of different valenced disconfirmation. Thus, as a further examination, the current study firstly proposed the following hypotheses to examine and compare the effects of utility and emotion expectation and disconfirmation:

H1a: Utility expectation positively impacts UX satisfaction
H1b: Emotion expectation positively impacts UX satisfaction
H2a: Utility disconfirmation positively impacts UX satisfaction
H2b: Emotion disconfirmation positively impacts UX satisfaction

Furthermore, according to the ECT framework, behavior intention is a direct result of satisfaction. However, vast studies have found that attribute performance also impacts behavior intention, and satisfaction acts as a mediation [20]. Thus, we proposed the following hypotheses:

H1c: Utility expectation positively impacts behavior intention
H1d: Emotion expectation positively impacts behavior intention
H2c: Utility disconfirmation positively impacts behavior intention
H2d: Emotion disconfirmation positively impacts behavior intention.

2.2 Prospect Theory

Prospect theory was proposed by Kahneman and Tversky in 1979 to explain people's irrational behaviors in risk decision making contexts [9]. Taking people's bounded rationality and psychological status into consideration, PT describes how people process decision information and finally make a decision. Especially, PT holds the opinion that it is the gains and loss people assess, rather than the final outcome of a decision that acts as a value evaluation criterion in decision making. People base their gain or loss in a decision on a reference point. Expectation is one of the factors influencing the reference point, and other factors include the status quo and aspiration level [21]. When the final outcome of a decision exceeds this point, it induces a feeling of gain; if the outcome is lower than this point, it induces a feeling of loss. When the reference point is anchored by expectation, we can say the gain and loss in PT is what is described as positive and negative disconfirmation, respectively. Moreover, the feeling of loss induced by a certain objective value cannot be made up by the gain feeling induced by the same objective value gain, as is shown in Fig. 2. Thus, people hold a negative asymmetric attitude toward gain and loss.

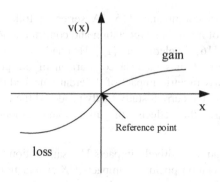

Fig. 2. People's negative asymmetric attitude to gain and loss.

In satisfaction studies, Mittal et al.'s study in 1998 is the first to introduce PT into consumer satisfaction research and to inspect the asymmetric influence of disconfirmation. With the symmetric and linear assumptions being challenged more and more in practice, a series of following studies in wide ranges such as supermarkets [22], bicycles [23], and auto insurance [24], also examined the asymmetric influence. As what has been introduced previously, though some UX studies involve expectation and disconfirmation, methods employed in these studies have linear and symmetric potential assumptions. Few of UX studies considered the asymmetry of different valenced disconfirmations. Thus, we proposed hypotheses related to the asymmetric influence of utility and emotion disconfirmation:

H3a: Utility disconfirmation has a negative asymmetric impact on UX satisfaction
H3b: Emotion disconfirmation has a negative asymmetric impact on UX satisfaction
H3c: Utility disconfirmation has a negative asymmetric impact on behavior intention
H3d: Emotion disconfirmation has a negative asymmetric impact on behavior intention.

3 Data Description

Data used in the hypotheses testing were collected with a questionnaire initially designed to study UX of mobile e-banking App. The study was designed following a retrospective method [25]. By asking peoples' experience at some time in the past, retrospective approaches extract measurement data from people's memories [26, 27]. Though retrospective methods are usually used in studies of UX changing over time, it is also reasonable to measure users' pre-using expectations in this way [28]. Using a structured self-report questionnaire, this study measured users' expectations before using and their perception after using e-banking App, both in several dimensions, including utility and emotion. Utility means how the App helps in business handling, such as improving effectiveness, and emotion means positive feelings when using the App, such as their excitement. Besides, users' overall pre-using expectation, post-using satisfaction, and their willingness of continuance were also measured. All of these items were scored on 7-point Likert scales. Totally, we called back 216 responses in the survey. After excluding incomplete questionnaires, respondents who reported having no mobile e-banking App using experience, and respondents aged 18 or below, we finally got 172 (79.6%) valid questionnaires. And 80 (46.5%) of them were male.

The present research focuses on the effect of user expectation and disconfirmation, and further to examine the effect of positive and negative disconfirmation. Thus, measures of utility (4 items) and emotion (3 items), overall expectation (3 items), UX satisfaction (2 items), and behavior intention (2 items) were involved. The total Cronbach α of the scale is 0.963, and Cronbach α for a single dimension range from 0.845 to 0.863, indicating that the scale is valid. The dimensional average variance extracted (AVE) ranges from 0.560 to 0.783, and composite reliability (CR) ranges from 0.792 to 0.915. The scale is convergent validity. Besides, the square root of the CR value for each construct is larger than its correlation coefficients with other constructs. Discrimination validity was also confirmed. In general, the scale is reliable and valid.

The average score of a dimension measurement was calculated to get a respondent's general evaluation of the dimension. The following equations were employed to calculate disconfirmation increments:

$$dis\_U = UP - UE$$
$$dis\_E = EP - EE \tag{1}$$

UP, UE, EP, and EE donate utility perception, utility expectation, emotion perception, and emotion expectation, respectively. Variables with the prefix "dis_" indicate disconfirmations. The dis_U and dis_E are utility disconfirmation and emotion disconfirmation. The disconfirmation calculation results are summarized in Table 1:

Table 1. Summary of utility and emotion disconfirmation.

	Numbers of disconfirmation (percentage)			Average disconfirmation increment (variance)		
	Positive	Zero	Negative	Positive	Zero	Negative
dis_U	48 (27.9%)	45 (26.2%)	79 (45.9%)	0.708 (0.288)	0 (0)	−0.829 (0.645)
dis_E	59 (34.3%)	56 (32.6%)	57 (33.1%)	0.836 (0.368)	0 (0)	−0.825 (0.469)

4   Analyses and Results

4.1   Impact of Expectation and Disconfirmation on UX Satisfaction

In this section, H1a, H1b, H2a, H2b, H3a, and H3b were tested. Like Olive, we first expressed UX satisfaction as a linear and symmetric function of utility expectation, emotion expectation, and the corresponding disconfirmation, as is shown by Eq. (2):

$$UXS = c + \alpha_1 * UE + \alpha_2 * EE + \beta_1 * dis\_U + \beta_2 * dis\_E \tag{2}$$

The regression results of Eq. (2) are summarized in Table 2. Estimation results show that the model is significant ($F = 62.16$, $p < 0.001$) with adjusted $R^2 = 0.589$. Compared with expectation (0.548 and 0.574), disconfirmation (0.202 and 0.228) plays a minor role in the model. Coefficients for the four variables indicate a significant and positive impact on the dependent variable, i.e., UX satisfaction. Therefore, hypotheses H1a, H1b, H2a, and H2b were supported.

Table 2. Estimation results of Eq. (2) and (3).

Equation (2)		Equation (3)	
UE	0.548^{***}	UE	0.422^{***}
EE	0.574^{***}	EE	0.345^{***}
dis_U	0.202^{**}	Pdis_U	-0.022
		Ndis_U	0.470^{***}
dis_E	0.228^{**}	Pdis_E	0.400^{***}
		Ndis_E	0.463^{***}
$F = 62.16$, $p < 0.001$, $R^2 = 0.589$		$F = 44.14$, $p < 0.001$, $R^2 = 0.602$	

$^*p < 0.05$; $^{**}p < 0.01$; $^{***}p < 0.001$

To test H3a and H3b, we divided disconfirmation into positive and negative to replace the corresponding variables in Eq. (2). As a result, Eq. (3) was constructed to explore asymmetry of different valenced disconfirmation:

$$UXS = c + \alpha_1 * UE + \alpha_2 * EE + \beta_1 * Pdis\_U + \beta_2 * Pdis\_E + \gamma_1 * Ndis\_U + \gamma_2 * Ndis\_E \quad (3)$$

The prefixes "Pdis_" and "Ndis_" mean positive and negative disconfirmation, respectively. Once more, Eq. (3) was estimated. Results show the model is significant ($F = 44.14$, $p < 0.001$, $R^2 = 0.602$) and holds better explanation ability than Eq. (2) ($F = 3.85$, $p < 0.05$). Again, the significant coefficients of expected utility and emotion supported H1a and H1b. Then we made comparisons between coefficients of positive and the corresponding negative disconfirmation. As is shown by the estimation results, the coefficient for negative utility disconfirmation is significant ($\beta = 0.470$, $p < 0.001$), but not for positive disconfirmation ($p > 0.05$). They are significantly different in statistics ($F = 6.21$, $p = 0.014$). It means negative utility disconfirmation has a more substantial impact on UX satisfaction than positive utility disconfirmation, which is consistent with PT. Thus, H3a was supported. As for the emotion disconfirmation, both coefficients for positive and negative emotion disconfirmation are significant (0.400 and 0.463). Though negative disconfirmation has slight larger impacts than positive disconfirmation (0.463 vs. 0.400), they show no significant difference in statistics ($p = 0.728$). Thus, hypothesis H3b was rejected.

In general, apart from H3b, all hypotheses related to impacts of utility and emotion on UX satisfaction were supported. Results are consistent with ECT and PT. Users' expectation before using mobile e-banking App and their disconfirmation do affect their UX satisfaction. Moreover, as is described in PT, negative utility disconfirmation plays a more critical role in predicting UX satisfaction. However, for emotion disconfirmation, the difference is not significant.

4.2 Impact of Expectation and Disconfirmation on Behavior Intention

Behavior intention is generally recognized as a result of satisfaction, and the antecedent of actual behavior. Moreover, in vast studies, satisfaction has been confirmed to mediate the relationship between attribute quality and behavior intention. Thus, in UX, expectation and disconfirmation may also play roles in predicting behavior intention, and the relationship may be mediated by satisfaction. This is another aim of the current study. In this section, by testing H1c, H1d, H2c, H2d, H3c, and H3d, we took a closer look at the relationship. Similarly, a linear and symmetric model (Eq. (4)) was estimated to test H1c, H1d, H2c, and H2d; and Eq. (5) was estimated to test H3c and H3d:

$$BI = c + \alpha_1 * UE + \alpha_2 * EE + \beta_1 * dis\_U + \beta_2 * dis\_E + \varepsilon * UXS \quad (4)$$

$$BI = c + \alpha_1 * UE + \alpha_2 * EE + \beta_1 * Pdis\_U + \beta_2 * Pdis\_E + \gamma_1 * Ndis\_U + \gamma_2 * Ndis\_E + \varepsilon * UXS \quad (5)$$

In Eq. (4) and Eq. (5), BI represents behavior intention, and variables with the prefixes "Pdis_" and "Ndis_" mean positive and negative disconfirmation, respectively. Two-step hierarchical regression analyses were performed to estimate the two equations. In the second steps, UXS was added to the estimation to examine its mediation effect. Estimation results of Eq. (4) and Eq. (5) are summarized in Table 3.

Table 3. Estimation results of Eq. (4) and (5).

	Equation (4)			Equation (5)	
	Step 1	Step 2		Step 1	Step 2
1. UE	0.416^{***}	0.316^{**}	1. UE	0.425^{***}	0.332^{***}
EE	0.540^{***}	0.444^{***}	EE	0.498^{***}	0.423^{***}
dis_U	0.306^{**}	0.232^{*}	Pdis_U	0.045	0.049
			Ndis_U	0.448^{***}	0.345^{**}
dis_E	0.581^{***}	0.470^{***}	Pdis_E	0.590^{***}	0.502^{***}
			Ndis_E	0.536^{***}	0.434^{**}
2. UXS		0.242^{**}	2. UXS		0.220^{*}
R^2	0.630	0.646	R^2	0.633	0.646
ΔR^2	0.630	0.016	ΔR^2	0.633	0.013
F_{change}	73.732^{***}	8.589^{**}	F_{change}	50.194^{***}	6.755^{*}

$*p < 0.05; **p < 0.01; ***p < 0.001$

Equation (4) is linear and symmetric, and Eq. (5) is asymmetric. According to the estimation results of Eq. (4), the model is significant, with a variance explanation percent of 64.6%. Besides, utility and emotion expectation and disconfirmation significantly impact behavior intention, indicating H1c, H1d, H2c, and H2d were supported. When UXS was added to the estimation, the estimation ability was significantly improved (F_{change} = 8.589, p = 0.004), and UXS showed significant predicting ability. Besides, in step 2, all coefficients for the expectation and disconfirmation are smaller, indicating UX satisfaction mediates the relationship between the four predictors in step 1 and behavior intention. Then Eq. (5) was estimated to test H3c and H3d. Similarly, a two-step hierarchical regression analysis was executed. Again, H1c, H1d, H2c, and H2d were supported by the results in this analysis. According to the regression coefficients, negative utility disconfirmation seems to have a larger impact on intention behavior, whereas negative emotion disconfirmation seems to have a smaller impact on behavior intention. We made a comparison between the positive and the negative disconfirmation impact. In step 1, negative utility disconfirmation has significantly larger impact under the confidence level 0.90 (F = 3.42 P = 0.066), but the difference is not significant for emotion disconfirmations (F = 0.08 P = 0.7834). Then UXS was added into the estimation. Though the explanation ability was slightly improved (F_{change} = 6.755, p = 0.010), the differences of both disconfirmation pairs are not significant (F = 1.82, p = 0.179; F = 0.12, p = 0.726). It seems that UXS not only mediates the impact of expectation and disconfirmation on behavior intention but also moderates the asymmetric effect of disconfirmation. Thus, H3c was partially supported, and H3d was rejected.

In general, conclusions drawn from this section confirmed the impact of utility and emotion expectation and disconfirmation on behavior intention. As for the asymmetry, utility disconfirmation partly shows negative asymmetric impact, but emotion disconfirmation shows no significant asymmetric impact. However, when UXS is taken into consideration, the asymmetry is moderated. Conclusions from analyses in this section are consistent with what described in ECT and partially consistent with PT.

5   Conclusions and Discussion

Though vast previous studies have affirmed the positive relationship between UX, satisfaction, and behavior intention, further investigation is necessary. Because user expectation and disconfirmation may play vital roles in the formation of UX satisfaction, as has been found in literature based on expectation-confirmation theory. Furthermore, according to the prospect theory, gain and loss hold different influences. Thus, users' disconfirmation impact may not be symmetric, which is not considered in analyzing methods like multiple regression or structural equation model. Using data from a UX study of mobile e-banking App, the current study explored the impact of user expectation and disconfirmation on UX satisfaction and behavior intention.

Analyzing results in this study confirmed the application potential of ECT and PT in UX research. Firstly, we found that users' expectation and disconfirmation has predicting ability on users' satisfaction and behavior intention in the mobile e-banking App UX context, indicating ECT could be adapted to UX studies. Second, the asymmetric impact of negative and positive utility disconfirmation was confirmed, which is consistent with the asymmetric attitude toward gain and loss described in PT. Nevertheless, the asymmetric assumption was not supported for the emotion disconfirmation in the current study. This indicates that PT can be employed in explaining UX issues. Moreover, the conclusions have practical implications. The reference point in PT is an important issue that fails to attract enough discussion in related researches. Though there are many factors in the formation of reference points, it is reasonable to say in UX users anchor expectation as one of the most crucial factors affecting the reference points. Their expectation plays a vital role in their formation of experience satisfaction and behavior intention, and all the exposed information is the origin of users' expectations. Though inferior information is unfavorable in good UX, overstatement may be harmful, too. Because negative disconfirmation induces results that equivalent positive disconfirmation cannot make up. This conclusion is meaningful in improving UX satisfaction and behavior intention, and PT could provide a psychological explanation.

Several limitations should be addressed. Firstly, respondents of the current study have different levels of experience in using mobile e-banking App. However, UX has been found evolving over time in many previous studies [25]. Experience or time factors could be involved in future researches. Secondly, the current study conveniently took utility and emotion as a typical pragmatic and hedonic dimension. However, there are many other UX dimensions influencing satisfaction and behavior intention. Future researches could examine more UX dimensions. Thirdly, according to PT, the disconfirmation has diminishing sensitivity, which was not explored in the current study. Finally, conclusions of the current study were drawn from the specific context of mobile e-banking App. Thus, the generalization of the conclusions should be cautious. Similar studies can be carried out in other more UX contexts.

Acknowledgment. This work was supported by the National Natural Science Foundation of China [grant number: 71640034].

References

1. Cox, J., Dale, B.G.: Service quality and e-commerce: an exploratory analysis. Manag. Serv. Qual.: Int. J. **11**(2), 121–131 (2001)
2. Zhou, R., Wang, X., Zhang, L.: Who tends to answer open-ended questions in an e-service survey? The contribution of closed-ended answers. Behav. Inf. Technol. **36**(12), 1274–1284 (2017)
3. Law, L.C., Schaik, P.V.: Modelling user experience - an agenda for research and practice. Interact. Comput. **22**(5), 313–322 (2010)
4. Hassenzahl, M., Tractinsky, N.: User experience-a research agenda. Behav. Inf. Technol. **25**(2), 91–97 (2006)
5. Hassenzahl, M.: The interplay of beauty, goodness, and usability in interactive products. Hum.-Comput. Interact. **19**(4), 319–349 (2004)

6. Hassenzahl, M.: The thing and I: understanding the relationship between user and product. In: Blythe, M.A., Overbeeke, K., Monk, A.F., Wright, P.C. (eds.) Funology. Human-Computer Interaction Series, vol. 3, pp. 31–42. Springer, Dordrecht (2003). https://doi.org/10.1007/1-4020-2967-5_4

7. Oliver, R.L.: A cognitive model of the antecedents and consequences of satisfaction decisions. J. Mark. Res. **17**(4), 460–469 (1980)

8. Oliver, R.L., Linda, G.: Effect of satisfaction and its antecedents on consumer preference and intention. Adv. Consum. Res. **8**(1), 88–93 (1981)

9. Kahneman, D., Tversky, A.: Choices, values, and frames. Am. Psychol. **39**(4), 341–350 (1984)

10. Hartmann, J., De Angeli, A., Sutcliffe, A.: Framing the user experience: information biases on website quality judgement. In: Proceedings of the SIGCHI Conference on Human Factors in Computing Systems, pp. 855–864. ACM, Florence (2008)

11. Zhang, Z., Cheng, W., Gu, Z.: User experience studies based on expectation disconfirmation theory. In: Marcus, A. (ed.) DUXU 2016. LNCS, vol. 9747, pp. 670–677. Springer, Cham (2016). https://doi.org/10.1007/978-3-319-40355-7_65

12. Mittal, V., Ross Jr., W.T., Baldasare, P.M.: The asymmetric impact of negative and positive attribute-level performance on overall satisfaction and repurchase intentions. J. Mark. **62**(1), 33–47 (1998)

13. Khalifa, M., Liu, V.: Satisfaction with internet-based services: the role of expectations and desires. Int. J. Electron. Commer. **7**(2), 31–49 (2002)

14. Raita, E., Oulasvirta, A.: Too good to be bad: favorable product expectations boost subjective usability ratings. Interact. Comput. **23**(4), 363–371 (2011)

15. Bhattacherjee, A.: Understanding information systems continuance: an expectation-confirmation model. MIS Q. **25**(3), 351–370 (2001)

16. Lee, Y., Kwon, O.: Intimacy, familiarity and continuance intention: an extended expectation–confirmation model in web-based services. Electron. Commer. Res. Appl. **10**(3), 342–357 (2011)

17. Eveleth, D.M., Baker-Eveleth, L.J., Stone, R.W.: Potential applicants' expectation-confirmation and intentions. Comput. Hum. Behav. **44**(C), 183–190 (2015)

18. Hsu, J.S.C., Lin, T.C., Fu, T.W.: The effect of unexpected features on app users' continuance intention. Electron. Commer. Res. Appl. **14**(6), 418–430 (2015)

19. Tam, C., Santos, D., Oliveira, T.: Exploring the influential factors of continuance intention to use mobile apps: extending the expectation confirmation model. Inf. Syst. Front. 1–15 (2018)

20. Zhou, R., Wang, X., Shi, Y., Zhang, R., Zhang, L., Guo, H.: Measuring e-service quality and its importance to customer satisfaction and loyalty: an empirical study in a telecom setting. Electron. Commer. Res. **19**(3), 477–499 (2019)

21. Kahneman, D., Tversky, A.: Prospect theory: an analysis of decision under risk. Econometrica **47**(2), 363–391 (1979)

22. Ting, S.C., Chen, C.N.: The asymmetrical and non-linear effects of store quality attributes on customer satisfaction. Total Qual. Manag. **13**(4), 547–569 (2002)

23. Lin, F.H., Tsai, S.B., Lee, Y.C.: Empirical research on Kano's model and customer satisfaction. PLoS One **12**(9), e0183888 (2017)

24. Burböck, B.: Prospect theory and SERVQUAL. Management **9**(2), 155–168 (2014)

25. Kim, H.K., Han, S.H., Park, J.: How user experience changes over time: a case study of social network services. Hum. Factors Ergon. Manuf. Serv. Ind. **25**(6), 659–673 (2015)

26. Hassenzahl, M., Sandweg, N.: From mental effort to perceived usability: transforming experiences into summary assessments. In: CHI 2004 Extended Abstracts on Human Factors in Computing Systems, pp. 1283–1286. ACM, Vienna (2004)

27. Karapanos, E., Martens, J.B.O., Hassenzahl, M.: On the retrospective assessment of users' experiences over time: memory or actuality? In: CHI 2010 Physiological User Interaction Workshop, pp. 4075–4080. Association for Computing Machinery, Inc., Atlanta (2010)
28. Hassenzahl, M., Ullrich, D.: To do or not to do: Differences in user experience and retrospective judgments depending on the presence or absence of instrumental goals. Interact. Comput. **19**(4), 429–437 (2007)

Usability Oriented New Baren Product Design and Test Practice

Ke Zhang, Zhen Liu⬛, Yan Wang$^{(\boxtimes)}$, and Xiaoli Dong

School of Design, South China University of Technology,
Guangzhou 510006, People's Republic of China
yanw@scut.edu.cn

Abstract. In this paper, we will carry out the design practice of usability-based baren product, that is, the design of product form. The external form design of the product needs to start from the shape, color and material of the product, find the corresponding points of the factors affecting the usability, get specific design elements, and truly transform baren product usability requirements into product language to complete the design practice. The use of curve shape in the form design of the product can better meet the demand for hand semi-clenched fist and hand comfort, which is not only fashionable with modern sense but also warm with simple life, and more in line with the modern society's pursuit of spiritual and emotional level, but also better meet the hand comfort demand. In the baren product design, the selection of materials follows several key principles: 1) Aesthetic principle: consider whether the sensory characteristics of materials conform to the emotional transmission of products to users. 2) Principle of usability: the function of baren determines that the material should be wear-resistant material. In order to maximize the transmission of the operator's arm power to the tool, it is necessary to consider how to avoid the skid resistance of the interactive interface and reduce the pressure of the operator's hand muscles. 3) Principle of technology: in this study, the plastic forming process and the injection molding process of silicone are relatively mature production processes in the market, and the connection between the plastic and silicone is a breakthrough point. And 4) Economic principle: try to choose materials with low price but good processing performance, so as to produce products with good texture, and the price positioning is more suitable for the consumption level of college students. Through the above analysis and review of the literature related materials, it is finally determined that the baren chassis is made of ABS plastic which supports various processing methods, good surface gloss, heat resistance and wear resistance. Then, the surface of the baren handle can be designed with a non-slip pattern or a handle sleeve, and the handle sleeve is made of a soft rubber material, which can enhance the product feel and increase the operation comfort.

Keywords: Print rubbing tools · Baren · Product design · User experience · Ease of use

© Springer Nature Switzerland AG 2020
A. Marcus and E. Rosenzweig (Eds.): HCII 2020, LNCS 12200, pp. 476–487, 2020.
https://doi.org/10.1007/978-3-030-49713-2_33

1 Introduction

In this practical research that is a further study of 'A Study of Usability Design of Baren Products' [1], a design practice of baren product usability has been conducted, which is the design of product form. The external form design of the product needs to start from the shape, color and material of the product, find the corresponding points of the factors affecting the usability, get specific design elements, and truly transform baren product usability requirements into product language to complete the design practice. The use of curve shape in the form design of the product can better meet the demand for hand semi-clenched fist and hand comfort, which is not only fashionable with modern sense but also warm with simple life, and more in line with the modern society's pursuit of spiritual and emotional level [2], but also better meet the hand comfort demand.

In baren product design, the selection of materials follows several key principles.

1) Aesthetic principle: consider whether the sensory characteristics of materials conform to the emotional transmission of products to users.
2) Principle of usability: the function of baren determines that the material should be wear-resistant material. In order to maximize the transmission of the operator's arm power to the tool, it is necessary to consider how to avoid the skid resistance of the interactive interface and reduce the pressure of the operator's hand muscles.
3) Principle of technology: in this study, the plastic forming process and the injection molding process of silicone are relatively mature production processes in the market, and the connection between the plastic and silicone is a breakthrough point.
4) Economic principle: try to choose materials with low price but good processing performance, so as to produce products with good texture, and the price positioning is more suitable for the consumption level of college students.

Through the above analysis and review of the literature related materials, it is finally determined that the baren chassis is made of ABS plastic which supports various processing methods, good surface gloss, heat resistance and wear resistance. Then, the surface of the baren handle can be designed with a non-slip pattern or a handle sleeve, and the handle sleeve is made of a soft rubber material, which can enhance the product feel and increase the operation comfort.

2 Baren Product Design Practice

The design of the scheme integrates the ease of use attributes summarized in the previous article 'A Study of Usability Design of Baren Products' [1], the factors affecting the usability, and the specific design elements reflected in the product design, etc. The main design factors summarized in the previous article should be referred to at any time in the design of the product scheme as follows:

1. The hand is the most comfortable when it is half held. When designing the shape of the handle, try to consider the most comfortable shape when the hand is operated;
2. How to make the modeling simple and soft with a certain flowing curve.

3. The shape of the product can intuitively guide the user's holding and make the area with more muscles in the hand become the main application point of man-machine contact surface.

Following these design elements, the drawn design scheme is as shown in Fig. 1.

Fig. 1. Baren product design concept renderings.

The innovative features of the new baren products are as follows, as shown in Fig. 2:

1. The handle structure changes the way of holding the existing engraving rubbing tool. The inclined handle is adopted to make the hand in a semi-clenched state. It eliminates the pain caused by the back of finger contact with the chassis;
2. Since the application point is placed on the thenar and hypothenar muscles, it reduces the contact force on sensitive parts of the hand, such as the palm of the hand, and reduces the local pain intensity of the hand;
3. The upper surface of the baren chassis was made into an inclined surface, where the upper surface of the force applying end close to the wrist was of a high vertical height, making the bending angle between the forearm and the palm of the wrist joint become smaller when rubbing, reducing the pressure on the wrist joint and improving the hand comfort in the rubbing process;
4. Change the curvature of the edge of the chassis, compared with the existing plastic baren, reduce the chance of puncture the paper and poke the finger;
5. The large area connection structure between the handle and the chassis makes the pressure distribution at the bottom of the chassis more even than the existing plastic baren;
6. The contact area between thumb and pinky is covered with silicone pads to improve the anti-skid and comfort performance;
7. Baren is generally divided into two parts: the main body of the handle and the main body of the chassis.

The two parts are bonded by the special adhesive for ABS engineering plastics, wherein the structure of the upper and lower buckles increases the stability of the component connection.

Fig. 2. Interaction diagram of baren product design concept.

In the previous research 'A Study of Usability Design of Baren Products' [1], by referring to the hand size of Chinese people and combining with the relevant product size calculation formula, the optimal recommended length range of baren product holding area is 97 mm to 103 mm. The value of handle holding area of this product scheme is 100 mm, which is within the recommended range and meets the requirements. The recommended width range of the massage chassis of baren product should be greater than 92 mm and less than 105 mm. The width size of the chassis of this scheme should be set at 100 mm. Baren chassis length need to be in 105 mm to 174 mm, if given the length and width of the golden ratio relations will be more conform to the requirements of the beautiful, the golden ratio is 0.618:1, as shown in Fig. 3, through calculation, it is concluded that conform to the golden ratio chassis size is about 162 mm in length, with a value within the scope of the suggested size, so the baren product with such size more in line with the size characteristics of the hand.

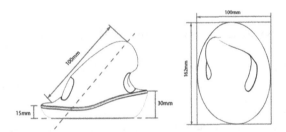

Fig. 3. Product specification of baren product design concept.

The processing technology of baren product adopts injection molding. In order to facilitate processing and production, the product is designed as two big shell structures, the handle body and the chassis body, as shown in Fig. 4. The shell structure is about 2.5 mm thick, which not only saves structural materials, but also has good spatial force transfer performance and pressure bearing performance, as shown in Fig. 5.

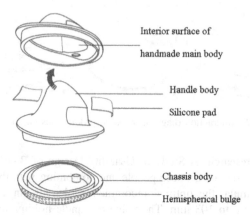

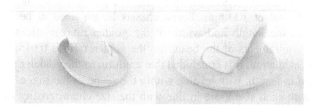

Fig. 4. Structure exploded view of baren product design concept.

Fig. 5. 3D printing model diagram of baren product design concept.

3   Usability Test of the New Design of Baren Product

The baren product used as a comparative test is ABS plastic disc baren and wood mushroom made in China. It is the most commonly used baren product for primary printmaking students, and the plastic baren is a representative product that causes longitudinal bending of the wrist when rubbing, the wood mushroom is a representative product that causes the lateral bending of the wrist joint when rubbing. The two gripping methods caused by these two products are relatively representative, so they are selected as research objects.

Ten college students with experience in lithography were recruited. The student testers had no diseases or injuries in their hands, no muscle fatigue before the experiment, and all had the experience of using baren lithography. The participants are numbered from No. 1 to No. 10, with measuring and recording the participants of the hand basic human body size, in the process of use baren print version. The main human palm size have hands long, wide, so in accordance with the requirements of surveying, testing and record these indicators, which conforms to China's national per capita 10 adult body size standards.

3.1 Comparative Test Analysis of Hand Joint Activity

When the arm applies the same force to the wrist, the new bare and plastic bare, their product chassis has the same pressure on the imprinted board, but the smaller the angle between the wrist and its bearing plane, the less laborious the wrist joint. Obviously the angle A is smaller than the angle C, so the new baren is slightly better than the plastic baren in terms of the longitudinal joint degree of the wrist. Therefore, if the same force is applied to the product, the pressure and damage of the wooden mushroom's wrist joints are greater, as shown in Fig. 6.

Fig. 6. Hand joint activity test diagram.

3.2 Right Arm Fatigue Test

The printing of printmaking is divided into multiple processes. The most tiring one is the process of engraving. After the engraving is completed, it needs to be painted with pigments, and the final color is followed by the process of rubbing. Then, during the process of engraving, the muscles will continue to contract. As the marking time continues, the muscles will enter a state of fatigue and begin to fail to output the required force [3]. By calculating the reduction of the right arm grip strength to understand the user's right arm fatigue change, the right arm fatigue index is used to evaluate whether the new baren product handle is easier to grasp.

In the right arm fatigue test of this subject, the tester needs to use the dynamometer to measure the maximum grip force value and record it before using the different baren products for rubbing, and then start the baren rubbing process for 10 min, and the rest interval of each experiment is 30 min. The subject needs to be rubbed along the provided rubbed road map during the experiment. The length and width of the rubbing path are the same as the A4 layout size, as shown in Fig. 7. A horizontal rubbing action or a vertical rubbing action is required every second, and a total of 600 rubbings are completed. After finishing the rubbing, you need to immediately measure the maximum grip strength with a dynamometer and record. Finally, the reduction of the right arm grip strength is calculated, and the experimental results are compared and analyzed. The brand of electronic grip dynamometer for testing is Xiangshan, model EH101. When the subject continues to apply force for three times, it can automatically give the maximum grip strength after three grips, as shown in Fig. 8.

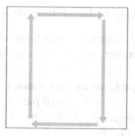

Fig. 7. Roadmap for rubbing operation.

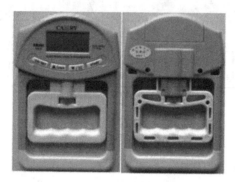

Fig. 8. Electronic grip dynamometer for testing.

Figure 9 lists the amount of grip reduction of the experimenter after 600 rubbing actions. Before the start of the experiment, the average value of the maximum right arm grip strength of the 10 subjects was 28.3 kg, and the standard deviation was 8.33 kg. After 600 rubbing movements, the average reduction of the right arm grip force (8.25%) caused by the new bare solution is much smaller than the average of the grip strength of the original ordinary plastic baren and wood mushrooms, indicating that the new baren handle design is more suitable for users, indirectly verified that the research framework based on usability analysis is effective in the design of new baren products. The specific test results are shown in Table 1.

3.3   Subjective Comfort and Satisfaction of Users

In addition to the objective fatigue index test, users who participate in the test are required to score the comfort of the new baren product to comprehensively analyze and evaluate whether the handle of the new baren product is easy to hold. The overall score is above 8 points, as shown in Table 2, indicating that the product basically meets the user's recognition of the need of easy grip. There are a few individual users who are not very satisfied with the comfort of the rubbing process. The reason is that although it feels very good to use, it is psychologically uncomfortable, because it feels that the appearance of the product changes greatly, and the psychological needs to adapt. Based on these questions, we will discuss how to improve at the end of the article.

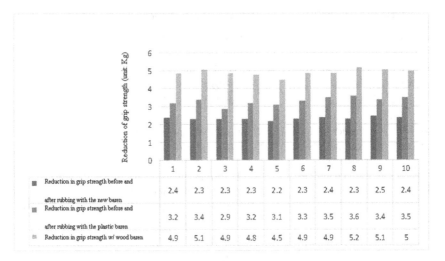

Fig. 9. Comparison of the reduction of grip strength before and after the user uses different baren.

Table 1. Right arm grip analysis of users using different types of baren.

The type of baren		Fatigue of the right arm		
		Average grip strength before rubbing/kg	Average reduction in grip strength/kg	The average reduction rate of grip strength/%
New baren		28.33	2.34 (0.08)	8.25
Existing baren	Plastic baren	28.31	3.31 (0.21)	11.6
	Wood mushroom	28.34	4.93 (0.19)	17.4

3.4   Subjective Psychological Preference of Users

Table 3 lists the experimental participants' psychological preference for the three bare products. Quantitative assessment of the participants' psychological preference for each type of bare product requires the experimenter to choose the type they like (multiple choices are possible) and to justify their reasons. Analysis of these reasons can be drawn: most of the experimenters are very fond of the new plastic baren, because the new product looks more fashionable, people are willing to use, more personalized curve modelling, in use process, easy to grasp and more labor-saving. Individuals who are not optimistic think that they are worried about low product awareness and have a sense of disengagement from other tools of printmaking. There are also very few users who have large palms and long fingers, which makes the hand ball muscle unable to grip on the handle groove comfortably. Some users with long fingers simply do not

Table 2. Evaluation results of users' subjective comfort and satisfaction.

Test issues	Environmental factors	Comfort assessment criteria	Evaluation results
Subjective comfort test	The handle is easy to hold	Handle static holding comfort (1–10)	8.45
		Comfort of handle rubbings (1–10)	8.15
Subjective satisfaction test	Product interaction is clear and easy to understand	1. Can you quickly understand how to grasp?	Can (90%)
	Good emotional experience	2. Scoring the first impression of the new baren product (1–10)	9.25
		3. Is the baren attractive to you to understand and use it?	Yes (100%)
		4. After initial use, do you feel better?	Yes (80%)
		5. Do you feel any fun during use?	Yes (90%)
		6. Use words to describe the feelings of use	Fashion, cool, artistic, high-end

bend their fingers to grasp, can also achieve the requirements of comfort. Half of the users are not very fond of the original plastic baren products (50%). The main reason is that compared with the new baren, there will be more problems in the process of use, such as fatigue, clenching, etc., in short, it is not very useful. Only a small number of users like wood mushrooms, because first of all, the quality of wood mushrooms on the market is not uniform, and some magic mushrooms look very textureless, the surface is not smooth, and the function is relatively simple. The main reasons why the experimenters like the new baren product are as follows: compared with the original baren product, the holding part of the baren product is designed in a more reasonable way, which is more consistent with manual operation, the product interaction is improved, and the product form is more attractive. This is consistent with the conclusion in the second chapter that the handle of baren product is easy to hold, the product interaction is clear and easy to understand, and the good emotional experience, which verifies the effectiveness of the usability attribute.

Table 3. Results of psychological preference survey.

The type of baren		Percentage of subjects selected (rank)	Psychological preference assessment score
New plastic baren		95% (1)	7.4
Existing baren	Plastic baren	50% (2)	6.2
	Wood mushroom	20% (3)	3.0

3.5   Assessment Revision and Outcome Transformation

In summary, the new baren overall usability evaluation result was good, but some users with larger palms reflect the unreasonable groove design of the new baren product handle, the groove depth and width cannot meet the finger comparison. In order to make the products more universal and better meet the needs of more people, the long user has further optimized the handle parts of the baren product solution. The overall recess depth of the groove portion of the bare product handle in the original solution is reduced, making it more suitable for users of different finger lengths. The new bare model was used for retesting, as shown in Fig. 10. The results of the evaluation showed that users of different hand lengths reflected the grip comfort and could well meet the grip requirements of different users.

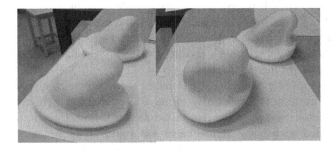

Fig. 10. The final baren design product.

4   Conclusion

After the research of the subject, the follow-up will try to promote this new type of baren and put it into the market. In order to protect the research results, it has applied for a utility model patent. Before the marketization of the product, the production cost needs to be estimated. The previous interview results on the price show that the highest price range acceptable to the primary users is 30–60 yuan; the highest price range acceptable to the senior students is 50–200 yuan. As both the new baren main material and the existing plastic baren material are made of ABS engineering plastics and the

486   K. Zhang et al.

processing technology is injection molding, the price of the new baren can be estimated by referring to the amount of materials. The existing plastic baren weighs about 87 grams, and the new plastic baren model weighs about 225 grams, with a weight ratio of about 1:2.5. The market price of the existing plastic baren is about 9 yuan. Considering that the new baren will use a small amount of silicone. Therefore, the price ratio is estimated to be 1:3, and the new baren price is about 30 yuan, which is consistent with the previous price survey results.

In this paper, the research and design of baren products innovatively introduces usability analysis into the design research of baren. Focusing on the usability of plastic baren, redesigning a new baren that meets the needs of usability and has a good product interaction experience is of great significance for the theoretical innovation of baren products and the development of new markets.

This topic introduces the concept of usability for the design and research of new baren products, and has the following results:

(1) Through market research, pre-interview and observation method, the problems of baren products at home and abroad are summarized. After analysis, the user's usability for baren products is summarized.
(2) Multi-dimensional analysis of the factors affecting the usability of baren products, combined with the basic design elements of the product, summed up the product design practice process framework based on usability.
(3) Through the induction of the usability requirements, the factors affecting the usability are analyzed, and finally a new baren product that satisfies the target users is designed.

The target users of this project are university students, so the new baren designed is mainly aimed at the university market. However, the age distribution of baren's user groups is relatively broad, and the needs of different age groups are also different. Therefore, when designing baren's products, designers should conduct targeted and systematic analysis of the target users.

In the design investigation stage, the elements of easy storage, universality and easy cleaning analyzed from the perspective of the use environment were not expanded in depth in the following text, which led to the feedback from users in the evaluation stage, feeling that the newly designed baren was a little abrupt in the engraving tool. There is also a need for a systematic redesign of the entire printmaking tool, or for them to come up with something to store.

This research mainly considers the operation habits of most right-handed users, and does not consider the situation that some users are left-handed. Generally speaking, there is little difference in the use of power between the left hand and the right hand, except that the ways of holding the product and the direction of movement during operation are different. If baren products are to be industrialized with the printmaking industry, these unique factors need to be considered in the development process, and thoughtful and in-depth research or individual design is needed.

Acknowledgements. This research is supported by "South China University of Technology Central University Basic Scientific Research Operating Expenses Subsidy (project approval no. 2019PY24)".

References

1. Zhang, K., Dong, X.: A study of usability design of baren products. In: Marcus, A., Wang, W. (eds.) HCII 2019. LNCS, vol. 11586, pp. 630–644. Springer, Cham (2019). https://doi.org/10.1007/978-3-030-23535-2_45
2. Wang, J.C.: Ergonomics in Product Design. Chemical Industry Press, Beijing (2004)
3. Zunben, C.: User Experience and Usability Testing. People's Posts and Telecommunications Press, Beijing (2015)

Emotional Design

How Motion Graphics Affect Emotional Quality: In the Context of an In-Vehicle Information System

Meen Jong Kim, Gui Young Kim, Jae Moon Sim, and Yong Gu Ji[(⊠)]

Yonsei University, Seoul, South Korea
{mjkim67,yongguji}@yonsei.ac.kr

Abstract. This study examines the relationship between motion graphic properties and emotional factors which are desirable in IVIS user interface. Three emotional factors, energetic, fluid, simple, which are composed of 11 emotional adjectives are used for the rating and three motion properties are manipulated for the experiment: duration, easing type and time interval. 24 participants evaluated twelve stimuli with eleven bi-polar emotional adjectives in the simulated vehicle environment. With MANOVA and multiple regression analysis, the study found that the emotion 'fluid' and 'energetic' can be evoked through the motion graphic. 'energetic' is strongly influenced by the time interval, shorter interval seems more energetic, in our study, 50 ms condition marked highest rating. On the other hand, 'fluid' is stimulated by the easing type and duration, easing type of acceleration with motion duration 400 ms was the most fluid in our study. To develop detailed guideline for UI designers and UX practitioners in IVIS domain, further work is needed considering more motion properties and tighten the interval between the level.

Keywords: Motion graphic · Emotional quality · IVIS system · User interface

1 Introduction

Autonomous vehicle is expected to arrive near future. Numerous manufacturers are planning to launch fully automated vehicle within 2030 [1]. Fully autonomous cars can be defined as activity spaces beyond the concept of transportation [2, 3]. It is expected that the appearance and interior space of the car will be greatly changed in the future and interior design will be one of factor that attract users to adopt autonomous vehicle [4, 5]. Keep pace with this emerging advancement in the technology, the study on user experience (UX) within the vehicle need to get higher attention.

As Panasonic proposes [6], In-vehicle Information system (IVIS) will be key component in user experience. Therefore, the design elements on IVIS User Interface (UI) also have a role to elicit certain emotional responses.

These days, designers are deeply focused on using graphic design properties to promote positive emotions. Designers have been modifying design elements such as color, layout, and texture to achieve positive emotional reactions [7–9]. However, in the context of human-computer interaction, one additional element should be

© Springer Nature Switzerland AG 2020
A. Marcus and E. Rosenzweig (Eds.): HCII 2020, LNCS 12200, pp. 491–500, 2020.
https://doi.org/10.1007/978-3-030-49713-2_34

considered: motion. Motion refers to the way an object in the user interface changes its properties in UI space in the principle of informative and expressive [10].

The objective of this study is as follows: 1) to examine how different durations, intervals, and easing types of motion graphics (transition effects) affect emotional quality. 2) to present proper values of each transition metric to achieve a positive emotional quality in a 10.3-in. IVIS.

2 Literature Review

2.1 Emotion Measurement

There have been several researches that aims to find the emotional elements in industrial design [11, 12]. There are several ways to measure the user's perception on emotional or affective qualities. According to Desmet [13], there are two categories in research method: the non-verbal and verbal. Non-verbal methods provide an objective measure to emotion. Behavioral reactions, such as facial expression [14], and physiological reaction such as blood pressure responses, skin responses, pupillary responses, brain waves, and heart responses [15, 16]. It has advantage that they are unobtrusive, but these are only reliable limited set of basic emotions, such as anger and surprise [17]. On the other hand, the verbal method methods ask users to report how they feel on a set of adjective interval scales. It provides a quick and clear measure of perceived emotion.

In engineering field, there is method so called Kansei engineering, which translates human emotions into physical design elements and designs products suitable for emotions [18]. It is characterized by using statistical and mathematical techniques to stay connected to physical design elements and to use them in design or to predict emotional responses to new products. In kansei engineering, multiple regression analysis is widely used for identifying the design characteristics of the product from the consumer's emotion [19]. In this study, we'll define motion properties which contribute to user's subjective emotion with self-report method.

2.2 Emotion in Motion

Several studies exist on movement related to emotion in the industrial design field. Prior researchers investigate the emotion arousal by physical movement of interactive product [20, 21], data visualization [22], transition effect on mobile user interface [23, 24]. However, several studies are limited to evaluate emotion in two dimensions of valence and arousal, or generalized feeling of animated interaction. Emotional feeling could be differed by the domains [25], it is needed to explore emotions which are related to in-vehicle UX.

3 Methodology

We conducted an experiment to investigate the relationship between motion properties and emotional quality. Three properties of motion (duration, interval, easing type) were the independent variables in this experiment, while the eleven adjectives of emotional response were the dependent variables.

3.1 Emotional Factors

We collected 438 emotional adjectives related to car interior design from literature, research, and automobile magazines [26–31]. Based on these adjectives, a domain expert survey was conducted to derive adjectives related to IVIS user interface. Finally, 11 adjectives related to motion were selected. To derive emotional factors, participants were asked to evaluate the user interface using a 7-point Likert scale for each adjective. A factor analysis was then performed on the scores assigned to the scores given to the adjectives. Three factors were identified and defined as fluid, energetic, and simple. Table 1 shows the result.

Table 1. Three Emotional factors and 11 adjectives related to motion on user interface.

Emotional factors	Adjectives
Fluid	Delicate, Elegant, Fluid, Natural
Energetic	Lively, Rhythmical, Agile, Sporty
Simple	Understated, Tidy, Simple

3.2 Motion Properties

The context of user interaction provided to each subject in the study was pressing a button on the screen to bring up a list. Subjects were shown fade effect for object transition. Staggered animation, which refers to sequential or overlapping animations, was used within each object. In this context, we can derive three motion properties: duration, time interval, and easing.

Duration – Duration refers to the total animation time of each object. Two different durations were considered in this experiment: 200 ms and 400 ms.

Time interval – refers to time between each sequential animation within a given object. (depicted in Fig. 1) Three different time intervals were considered: 50 ms, 100 ms, and 150 ms.

Easing – According to Google material design [32], easing is a way to adjust an animation's rate of change. Easing allows transitioning elements to speed up and slow down. In this study, we used two easing types: acceleration and deceleration.

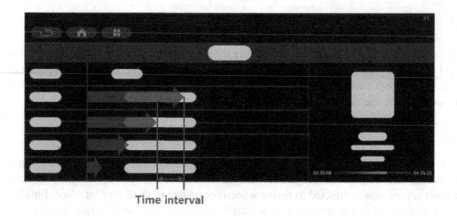

Fig. 1. User interface graphics in the experiment. There are five objects in main space. As participants tap left white oval button, five object fade in, which means that the value of opacity changes 0% to 100%. Time interval is the time between objects start to change.

3.3   Prototype

A prototype interface was developed using Principle™ to show motion via screen transition. The interface was designed with minimal graphics to help the users focus on motion only (Fig. 1). This interface is presented on a 12.3-in. iPad Pro, allowing users to view the motion on direct tapping of the object. A total of 12 stimuli (Duration (2 level) X Time interval (3 level) X Easing (2 type)) are generated.

3.4   Procedure

24 participants, 12 male and 12 female, age from 20 to 35, participated in the experiment. The experiment was conducted in the following process. First, the procedure was explained to the participants before starting the experiment. Then, participants were placed in the driver seat and put into a situation of the car parked on the shoulder of the road (created with STISIM™). During the simulation, the subjects were instructed to operate the user interface. With each tap of the button, the participant viewed one object transition (Fig. 2). After experiencing each motion, a survey was conducted to evaluate emotional response. The survey was designed in 7-point Likert scale giving bipolar adjective pairs on the scale (Table 2). Twelve motion graphic stimuli were presented to each participant in random order.

Fig. 2. Experiment environment

Table 2. Eleven bipolar emotional adjectives. The order of adjectives was rearranged on survey

1. Delicate – Tough	2. Elegant – Not elegant	3. Fluid – Rough
4. Natural – Awkward	5. Lively – Calm	6. Rhythmical – Monotonous
7. Agile – Dull	8. Sporty – Not Sporty	9. Understated – Exaggerated
10. Tidy – Not Tidy	11. Simple – Complicated	

4   Result

The participant's ratings for emotion level of motion graphic stimuli were statistically analyzed. The mean ratings are used for each emotional factor score. Fluid score is the mean of 4 emotional adjectives, 'Delicate', 'Elegant', 'Fluid' and 'Natural'. Energetic score is the mean score of 'Lively', 'Rhythmical', 'Agile' and 'Sporty'. Simple score is the average of 'Understated', 'Tidy', and 'Simple'. Multivariate analysis of variance (MANOVA) and multiple regression method are used for the analysis.

4.1   MANOVA Analysis

MANOVA analysis is conducted to examine the association between motion properties (duration, time interval, and easing type) and emotional factors (fluid, energetic, and simple). The value of Box's M was 71.445 (p-value = .418), which means equality of covariance assumption is satisfied.

From the Multivariate test, there was a statistically significant difference in emotional factors based on all motion properties. All Wilk's Lambda test p-value was below .05 (Table 3). To determine how the emotions differ for the motion properties, Test of between-subject effects is investigated.

Table 3. Multivariate test result

Effect	Wilk's Lambda value	F	Hypothesis df	Error df	Sig.	Partial eta squared
(Intercept)	.028	3214.36	3	274	.000	.972
Easing	.764	28.27	3	274	.000	.236
Duration	.962	3.63	3	274	.014	.038
Time interval	.491	39.04	6	548	.000	.299

We cannot find significant result with the emotion factor 'simple' and motion properties (p-value > 0.05). On the other hand, all motion properties affect the feeling of 'fluid'. Only the time interval has effect on 'energetic' (Table 4). From the Partial Eta squared, Easing with Fluid, and Time interval with Energetic are only showing strong relationship.

Table 4. Test of between-subject effects

Source	Dependent variable	Type III sum of squares	Df	Mean square	F	Sig.	Partial eta squared
Easing	Energetic	.018	1	.018	.016	.900	.000
	Fluid	93.674	1	93.674	77.038	.000	.218
	Simple	4.417	1	4.417	3.728	.055	.013
Duration	Energetic	2.042	1	2.042	1.825	.178	.007
	Fluid	5.080	1	5.080	4.178	.042	.015
	Simple	.852	1	.852	.719	.397	.003
Time interval	Energetic	280.939	2	140.469	125.530	.000	.476
	Fluid	16.227	2	8.113	6.673	.001	.046
	Simple	5.669	2	2.834	2.392	.093	.017

Tukey Post-hoc test revealed that interval 50 ms arouse energetic feeling the most. The Figure below shows that for mean scores for 'energetic' were statistically significantly different between three level of time interval ($p < 0.000$).

Also, significant interaction effect (Easing type X duration) are observed in energetic factor. Participants feel 'energetic most on duration 200 ms with easing type acceleration, but it drastically drops on duration 400 ms (Fig. 3). This interaction effect might cause insignificant result of two motion properties with energetic (Fig. 4).

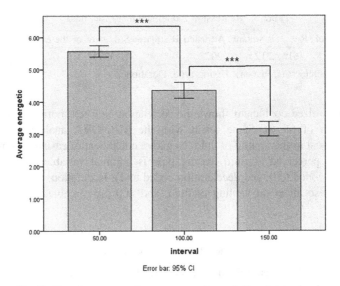

Fig. 3. Bar chart energetic mean score in each time interval value

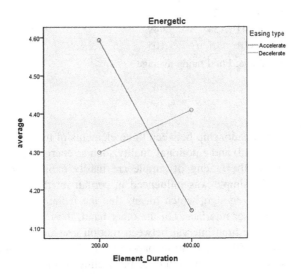

Fig. 4. Mean ratings of energetic according to duration and easing type

4.2 Multiple Regression Analysis

For further investigation, multiple regression analysis was conducted. It can reveal the extent to which each motion property contributes to an explanation of the emotional factor, 'fluid'. From stepwise multiple regression, one variable was deleted: time interval. Statistical measure of fit R-squared was .212 (Table 5).

Table 5. Regression model summary for 'fluid'

Model	R	R square	Adjusted R square	Std. error of the estimate
1	.461ᵃ	.212	.207	1.13375

a. Predictors: (Constant), Easing type, Duration

The Standardized coefficient shows the correlation between motion properties and 'fluid' emotion (Table 6). Same result with the MANOVA analysis, easing type influence the most to the feeling of fluid. Negative coefficient of easing type refers that acceleration is perceived as fluid (easing type is nominal variable, so easing type: acceleration is coded to 0, and deceleration coded to 1). In duration, the result showed that duration also affect the feeling of fluid, and 400 ms perceived more fluid than 200 ms,

Table 6. Regression coefficients

Model	Unstandardized coefficients		Standardized coefficients	t	Sig.
	B	Std. error	Beta		
(Constant)	4.364	.222		19.694	.000
Easing	−1.141	.134	−.449	−8.537	.000
Duration	.001	.001	.105	1.998	.048

Dependent variable: Fluid rating average

5 Conclusion

This study investigated relationship between three elements of motion graphic (easing type, duration, time interval) and emotional quality such as energetic, fluid and simple. The study revealed that the feeling of simple are hardly evoked by our variables. According to Park [23], simple was influenced in certain interaction type, our push button interface is simple enough, which means that the feeling might be associated with design element on user interface. On the other hand, the feeling of energetic are strongly influenced by the time interval between motion graphic, no matter what the duration or easing type is. 50 ms condition marked the highest score. Other two motion properties, easing type and duration influence the feeling of fluid. Acceleration with 400 ms show the best for 'fluid' motion.

This study was exploratory research, to find an evidence of relationship between desirable emotion in in-vehicle domain and motion graphic properties. Despite of findings on our study, it has several limitations. First, the level of properties are limited, so it's hard to say our proposed value are optimal. In future work, tighten the interval between the level is needed. Also, we only explored three motion properties, but there are several properties which are good to be investigated. One example can be transition effect, in this study, we fixed transition effect to fade, but there are several types in fade: cross-fade and fade through [33]. Further study is needed for the detailed guideline for the in-vehicle UI designers.

References

1. Walker, J.: The self-driving car timeline – predictions from the top 11 global automakers, 24 December 2019. https://emerj.com/ai-adoption-timelines/self-driving-car-timeline-themsel ves-top-11-automakers/
2. Lynn, M.: Self-driving cars will kill the auto industry, 6 January 2016. https://www.marketwatch.com/story/self-driving-cars-will-kill-the-auto-industry-2016-01-06
3. Sweet, M.N., Laidlaw, K.: No longer in the driver's seat: how do affective motivations impact consumer interest in automated vehicles? Transportation 1–34 (2019)
4. Pettersson, I., Karlsson, I.M.: Setting the stage for autonomous cars: a pilot study of future autonomous driving experiences. IET Intell. Transp. Syst. 9(7), 694–701 (2015)
5. Jorlöv, S., Bohman, K., Larsson, A.: Seating positions and activities in highly automated cars–a qualitative study of future automated driving scenarios. In: International Research Conference on the Biomechanics of Impact (2017)
6. Panasonic Homepage. https://panasonic.net/design/works/car-future/. Accessed 23 Feb 2020
7. Schenkman, B., Jonsson, F.: Aesthetics and preferences of web pages. Behav. Inf. Technol. 19, 367–377 (2000)
8. Kim, J., Lee, L., Choi, D.: Designing emotionally evocative homepages: an empirical study of the quantitative relations between design factors and emotional dimensions. Int. J. Hum Comput Stud. 59, 899–940 (2003)
9. van der Heijden, H.: Factors influencing the usage of web sites: the case of a generic portal in the Netherlands. Inf. Manag. 40, 541–549 (2003)
10. Google Material Design Homepage. https://material.io/design/motion/understanding-motion.html. Accessed 23 Feb 2020
11. Jordan, P.W.: Designing Pleasurable Products: An Introduction to the New Human Factors. CRC Press, London (2002)
12. Norman, D.A.: Emotional Design: Why We Love (or Hate) Everyday Things. Basic Books, New York (2004)
13. Desmet, P.: Measuring emotion: development and application of an instrument to measure emotional responses to products. In: Blythe, M., Monk, A. (eds.) Funology 2. HIS, pp. 391–404. Springer, Cham (2018). https://doi.org/10.1007/978-3-319-68213-6_25
14. Ekman, P., Friesen, W.V.: Unmasking the Face: A Guide to Recognizing Emotions from Facial Cues. Prentice-Hall, Englewood Cliffs (1975)
15. Ark, W., Dryer, D.C., Lu, D.J.: The emotion mouse. In: Proceedings of HCI International 1999, Munich Germany, August 1999
16. Picard, R.W.: Towards computer that recognize and respond to user emotion. IBM Syst. J. 39(3/4), 705–719 (2000)
17. Cacioppo, J.T., Berntson, G.G., Larsen, J.T., Poehlmann, K.M., Ito, T.A.: The psychophysiology of emotion. In: Lewis, M., Haviland-Jones, J.M. (eds.) Handbook of Emotions, 2nd edn, pp. 173–191. The Guilford Press, New York (2001)
18. Nagamachi, M.: Kansei engineering: a new ergonomic consumer-oriented technology for product development. Int. J. Ind. Ergon. 15, 3–11 (1995)
19. Jindo, T., Hirasago, K.: Application studies to car interior of Kansei engineering. Int. J. Ind. Ergon. 19(2), 105–114 (1997)
20. Lee, J.-H., Park, J.-Y., Nam, T.-J.: Emotional interaction through physical movement. In: Jacko, Julie A. (ed.) HCI 2007. LNCS, vol. 4552, pp. 401–410. Springer, Heidelberg (2007). https://doi.org/10.1007/978-3-540-73110-8_43
21. Vaughan, L.C.: Understanding movement. In: Proceedings of the SIGCHI Conference on Human Factors in Computing Systems (CHI 1997), pp. 548–549. ACM, New York (1997)

22. Heer, J., Robertson, G.: Animated transitions in statistical data graphics. IEEE Trans. Vis. Comput. Graph. **13**(6), 1240–1247 (2007)
23. Park, D., Lee, J.H., Kim, S.: Investigating the affective quality of interactivity by motion feedback in mobile touchscreen user interfaces. Int. J. Hum Comput Stud. **69**(12), 839–853 (2011)
24. Merz, B., Tuch, A.N., Opwis, K.: Perceived user experience of animated transitions in mobile user interfaces. In: Proceedings of the 2016 CHI Conference Extended Abstracts on Human Factors in Computing Systems, pp. 3152–3158, May 2016
25. Schindler, I., et al.: Measuring aesthetic emotions: a review of the literature and a new assessment tool. PloS One (2017)
26. Hassenzahl, M., Platz, A., Burmester, M., Lehner, K.: Hedonic and ergonomic quality aspects determine a software's appeal. In: Proceedings of the SIGCHI Conference on Human Factors in Computing Systems, pp. 201–208. ACM, April 2000
27. Karlsson, B.S., Aronsson, N., Svensson, K.A.: Using semantic environment description as a tool to evaluate car interiors. Ergonomics **46**(13–14), 1408–1422 (2003)
28. Hsiao, K.A., Chen, L.L.: Fundamental dimensions of affective responses to product shapes. Int. J. Ind. Ergon. **36**(6), 553–564 (2006)
29. Wellings, T., Williams, M., Tennant, C.: Understanding customers' holistic perception of switches in automotive human–machine interfaces. Appl. Ergon. **41**(1), 8–17 (2010)
30. Park, D., Lee, J.H., Kim, S.: Investigating the affective quality of interactivity by motion feedback in mobile touchscreen user interfaces. Int. J. Hum. Comput. Stud. **69**(12), 839–853 (2011)
31. Chang, Y.M., Chen, C.W.: Kansei assessment of the constituent elements and the overall interrelations in car steering wheel design. Int. J. Ind. Ergon. **56**, 97–105 (2016)
32. Google Material Design Homepage. https://material.io/design/motion/speed.html#easing. Accessed 23 Feb 2020
33. Google Material Design Homepage. https://material.io/design/motion/choreography.html#sequencing. Accessed 23 Feb 2020

Designing a Multimodal Emotional Interface in the Context of Negotiation

Fabian Pelzl[1,2(✉)], Klaus Diepold[1], and Jan Auernhammer[2]

[1] Chair for Data Processing, Technical University Munich, Munich, Germany
{fabian.pelzl,kldi}@tum.de
[2] Center for Design Research, Stanford University, Stanford, USA
jan.auernhammer@stanford.edu

Abstract. This paper examines whether a virtual assistant with emotional intelligence improves the Human-Machine Interaction (HMI) in the specific use case of price negotiations. We propose a schema for an Emotional Interface, which we derive from the Skills-Rules-Knowledge (SRK)-Model and the Four Branch Model of Emotional Intelligence. According to this schema, a prototype of a virtual assistant with emotional intelligence is constructed. An avatar is used for representing the respective emotions by means of prosody and facial expression. The prototype is compared to a conventional digital assistant in a within-subject design study regarding user experience and trust building. The findings show that emotions animated in the mimic of the avatar cannot be clearly identified and attributed. Nevertheless, the User Experience of the prototype outperforms the conventional digital assistant, which is mainly due to the hedonic quality dimension. The study did not find any difference in trust between the emotional and the conventional digital assistant. This provides several interesting future research directions which are outlined in this paper.

Keywords: Embodied conversational agents · Affective computing · Intelligent interaction · Negotiation · Chatbots · Neurocognition design · User experience · Trust · Virtual human · Emotion recognition · Emotional intelligence

1 Introduction

Emotions play an important role in our everyday life influencing our thinking and behavior. In interpersonal communication emotions can be expressed through different means, such as gestures (movements of the arms, hands and head), facial expressions, the speech content as well as the prosody (intonation, tone and rhythm). Speech controlled systems are on the rise, thanks to popular applications such as Amazon Alexa and Google Assistant. However, these

---

Supported by organization BaCaTec.

A. Marcus and E. Rosenzweig (Eds.): HCII 2020, LNCS 12200, pp. 501–520, 2020.
https://doi.org/10.1007/978-3-030-49713-2_35

state-of-the-art agents do only consider the speech content of the user. Gestures, prosody or facial expressions are not yet taken into account. Emotion recognition based on facial expressions is a very active field in the artificial intelligence community [27,60]. In challenges such as the Emotion Recognition in the Wild Challenge (EmotioW), the emotion recognition in unconstrained conditions improve each year [12,31,52]. In addition to facial emotion recognition the research on other emotional cues such as on gestures, on posture and on linguistic parameters is advancing at a slower speed [1,26,46]. With these advancements in emotion recognition, a key question is how emotions should be incorporated in the human-machine dialogue. The consideration of emotions in HMI will only be successful, if it leads to a more valuable User Experience (UX). In taking this human-centered perspective, the improvement of UX must be a crucial factor when designing novel interfaces, which are capable of emotional processing.

One of the biggest challenges in designing an emotional interface is to find a consistent definition of emotions. Emotional psychology provides different and sometimes conflicting theories for the emotion concept [14]. One of the most prominent theories is the theory of basic emotions which was proposed by Ekman and Friesen [15] in 1971. They proposed, that there are six different basic emotions (Happiness, Sadness, Anger, Surprise, Disgust, Fear) and even today most databases in the Artificial Intelligence (AI) community utilize these basic emotions. However, most of the promising emotion concepts and processing models are based on different theories, such as appraisal and constructionist theories [3,51,54]. The selected theory not only has an impact on the emotional synthesis within a technical system, but also on the emotion labeling with either discrete values, such as the basic emotions, or with dimensional emotion classification, such as pleasure (often referred to as valence), arousal or dominance [4,61].

This paper proposes a schema for an emotional interface for the HMI, which is capable of embodying different perspectives of emotions. Following this schema we created a prototype for a chat bot, which can be applied for a negotiation use case, where emotions play a crucial role [10,45]. In this prototype we used an Embodied Conversational Agent (ECA) in order to display emotions. In addition we conducted an online user study with 50 valid responses, where we compared this interface with a conventional speech interface.

2   Related Work

In affective computing human characteristics, such as emotions, are applied to robots and machines [47]. The aim is to create an interface that is natural and comfortable for the user. Affective Computing research includes both, physical interfaces, such as robots or hardware devices and purely digital interfaces, such as virtual avatars - also referred to as ECAs. ECAs are often modeled after humans and find applications in a variety of fields, such as in clinical psychology [48], in education [59] and in cognitive science [58]. Pioneering work in affective ECA communication such as Rea [5] and Greta [11] enabled current research in this field. Today, the benefits of ECAs, such as creating standardized research conditions while being flexible and affordable in development, leads to further research in various disciplines. This shifts the focus from feasibility towards the question, how humans perceive these virtual agents [6]. However, it remains an open question whether the consideration of emotions in the human-agent dialog improves communication with the currently available systems [33].

Don Norman assumes that emotions do not only improve the HMI, but also technical systems themselves [41]. For humans, emotions play a crucial role in thinking, sense-making and decision making [19]. For this reason Mayer also considers "Using Emotions to Facilitate Thought" in his Four Branch model for Emotional Intelligence [34]. This understanding of human emotions is already transferred to machines and led to research applying emotions to autonomous agents and AI systems. This holds the promise to improve autonomous decision making, learning efficiency and communicative capabilities in AI systems [38].

In order to use emotions in *emotional intelligent* systems, they have to be synthesized. How to synthesize or generate emotions for ECAs is an active field of research. Thereby, most systems and frameworks are based on the appraisal theory. One framework for emotion synthesis would be the Ortony, Clore, Collins (OCC) model [44]. This model assumes that emotions primarily arise through the positive or negative evaluation of events, actions and the environment [16]. The model has five different processes (classification, quantification, interaction, mapping and expression) which are capable of generating 22 different emotions. The OCC model can be implemented as a decision tree, which lead to the popularity of this model. Based on the OCC model, A Layered Model for Affect (ALMA) was developed during the Virtual Human Project and differentiates emotions on a time dimension [20]. The system simulates three temporally different emotional states: short-term emotions, mood and personality. The short-term emotions are generated with the help of the OCC model and are therefore related to a specific event. In contrast, the system's mood is more inherent to the system and not related to a specific event, which results in a longer lasting and stable state.

The influence of emotions in negotiation and decision making has already been investigated with ECAs and virtual avatars [10,22]. DeMelo et al. [9] showed, that test participants give greater concessions with angry ECAs than with happy ECAs. More recent, they also investigated the willingness of people to cooperate with ECAs, which take on cooperative facial features (smiling after a compromise) and competing facial features (laughing after taking advantage of the negotiating partner) [10]. The finding showed that volunteers were more likely to cooperate with ECAs that were willing to cooperate. These findings influenced the design of our prototype and avatar, which is initialized in a positive and cooperative mood.

3   Schema and Prototype

In this section the paper discusses the schema and prototype of an emotional interface. An emotional interface is defined as an input-output system that can recognize, analyze, process, reproduce and display emotions. In the context of HMI this describes a technical system with three main components: Emotion recognition, emotion synthesis and emotion display. The contextual and environmental influences play a crucial role at every level of an emotional interface and must always be taken into account. Most chat bots, ECAs and social robots in previous research, which can be considered as emotional interfaces, are normally limited to one specific context. Examples of these contextual limitations are tutorial systems [20,40], social robots as toys [24,53], digital and virtual assistants [28,29] and negotiation agents [10,22].

However, digital assistants such as Amazon Alexa are increasingly used in different contexts. Therefore, we proposed a schema for an Emotional Interface for HMI, which finds its application across various contexts. Nevertheless, we needed to design the prototype and experiment for a specific context to test this schema and generate valid and reliable results.

3.1   Schema for an Emotional Interface

In order to design emotions within a technical system, we reviewed the literature on emotion and cognition in psychology. From this literature research we deducted a schema for an emotional interface, which is influenced by the SRK model [49] and by the Four Branch Model of emotional intelligence [34]. In addition, the proposed schema is based on the constructionist theory [3]. Hence, an instance of emotion is constructed by the technical system, which is influenced by past experiences, which is collected in previous interactions, and results in emotional concepts.

As with humans, emotions must also be understood, analyzed, interpreted and reproduced in a technical system. These characteristics correspond with the definition of the Four Branch Model [34]. Therefore, the schema of an Emotional Interface includes all four branches and arranges them in a temporal and logical sequence (Fig. 1). This sequence is deducted from the SRK model, which was originally designed to model human reliability, cognitive processing, and decision making. Like the SRK model we divide the schema into three different levels of emotion processing, which we call the *reaction*, *routine*, and *reflection level* [16,41].

The *reaction level* is similar to the skill-based level of the SRK model, which requires little resources and is the fastest to react. Emotions generated at this level are inspired by physical and reflexive reactions. The generation of these emotions is automated and consists of highly integrated behavior patterns (emotional concepts), just like in skill-based human behavior. This could be incorporated as mimicry of an ECA towards the human user [58]: If the user smiles at the interfaces the ECA smiles back. This kind of feedback has to happen very quickly, because a time delay prevents the desired effect of building rapport.

In contrast to the *reaction level*, emotional concepts are less profound in the *routine level*. Due to the lack of mature emotional concepts, more resources and time are needed for the processing of emotions. For this processing, context, internal and external events are assessed and associated with system inherent

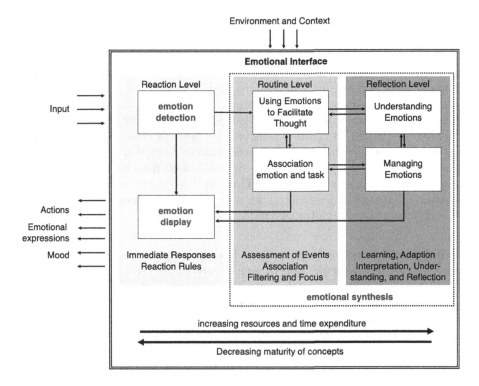

Fig. 1. Schema of an emotional interface

goals and intentions. An example can be described in the context of the Virtual Human Project [20], where the tutor system detects frustration and annoyance of the user who fails a task. In case of a supporting tutor, positive and stimulating emotions would be generated to achieve the tutor's goal: supporting the user. This decision is influenced by several concepts that can both classify the emotion and assign the right response.

The last and deepest level of the technical system with emotional intelligence is the *reflection level*. Here, emotional concepts are not yet existing and thus must be created. Therefore, the *reflection level* comes at the cost of using most system resources, which results in a very slow response time. For this reason, a typical output would be a certain mood, which can bee seen as a long-term emotion [42]. However, also short-term expressions can be generated on this level in case they are novel and concepts are not yet available. Due to the absence of emotion concepts, historical data is taken into account for the creation of emotional responses.

3.2   Designing a Prototype of an Emotional Interface

In order to test the proposed schema for emotional interfaces, we developed a speech-controlled prototype, which was evaluated in an online user study. The requirements of an online study are met with a web-based application consisting of a backend with web server and database, and a frontend with website, webcam and microphone. For development, we use several frameworks such as MongoDB, Express, React, Node.js (MERN stack) and Unity. Most of the negotiation and emotional logic is processed and mapped on the server. The conversation and detected emotion parameters are stored in a database. The frontend consists of a React chat component and an embedded Unity WebGL component. The later component is needed to create a human-like avatar, which is used to express emotions. We chose a human-like representation of emotions, since users are already used to this type of emotional communication from their daily interactions. For the speech synthesis we used Google's Text-to-Speech service [21]. For the natural language understanding, we used Microsoft's Speech-to-Text service [37] and Natural Language Understanding Module [36].

Setting the Context to Negotiation. In order to conduct a controlled experiment, we had to design the interface for a certain use case. Since we did not want to induce emotions from the outside (e.g. through emotional videos [57]), we searched for an emotional context in which emotions occur in a natural way. Due to the fact, that emotions play a very important role in the decision-making process and are omnipresent in a negotiation situation [30,45], we created a emotional interface for a negotiation use case. Here, the user has the task to negotiate the price of an old-timer with the sales agent, who is embodied as human-like avatar. In order to ensure some negotiation rounds, the starting selling price of the old-timer is set to 34,900 Euro, while the user is instructed to spend less than 30,000 Euro.

Design of the Avatar. The avatar (see Fig. 2) is created in the Daz3D software environment using the provided Genesis 8 character [8]. In the next step, the avatar is exported to the Unity development environment. In Unity, the avatar is animated to enable him for an emotional interaction. The features of the avatar can be summarized as lip sync and various methods to express moods and emotional expressions. The avatar is designed with the goal to ensure that the avatar seems realistic and human-like, but not too realistic. A very anthropomorphic avatar could lead to the uncanny valley phenomenon [39]. This phenomenon is likely to result in poor user ratings and in a higher expectation of the user regarding the quality of the emotions shown [32]. Further, we are only designing a male version of the avatar in order to reduce the construction effort. In the best case, the avatar should be adapted to the gender of the user [10].

The emotional communication of the avatar is mediated through different facial expressions and an adapted prosody. According to the schema of an emotional interface, we differentiate three modalities for the facial expression: longer-term mood, short-term expression and emotional reflexes. The avatar is capable of expressing six different facial expressions and five different moods. Besides these eleven facial expressions and the neutral state of the avatar, there are also emotional reflexes, such as smiles and nodding. While those reflexes are triggered

Fig. 2. A screenshot of the prototype for an emotional interface

and processed on the user's front end, the remaining facial expressions were synthesized on server side and are therefore slower in processing and reaction time.

Prosody, pitch, volume, duration, and voice quality play a very important role in synthesizing an emotional voice [2]. With the aim to develop a uniform standard for the emotional synthesis of language, the Speech Synthesis Markup Language (SSML) standard was developed by World Wide Web Consortium (W3C) [63]. Unfortunately, the speech synthesis provided by Google does not yet support each of these parameters. For example, the pitch range can not be adjusted. Nevertheless we modeled the SSML according to the table provided by Crumpton et al. [7] in order to model the language emotionally.

Synthesis of Emotions. Following the schema for an emotional interface, the synthesis of emotions happens on different levels. Since the interface is applied in the context of negotiation, the negotiation logic of the sales agent plays a crucial role in the emotion generation. The developed prototype is created for analyzing the interaction with the user and therefore lacks in learning capabilities. However, we assume, that in using reinforcement learning (like in [17]) the same model could be applied.

Reaction Level. Autonomous emotional reactions, which can be generated quickly and with little computing resources are computed on the reaction level. To prototype this level we create two reaction rules: reciprocal smiling and active listening. When a smile of the user is detected, the avatar smiles back. Research showed, that this mimicking behavior creates rapport [43]. In addition to this mimicry, there are three animations in which the avatar simulates active listening by nodding his head. For fast processing both animations are handled in the frontend of the web application, which results in a fast reaction, since no communication with the server is needed.

Routine Level. Familiar situations and events are assessed on the routine level and further processed into short-term emotional reactions. The OCC-Model provides a framework for this assessment and is compatible with both appraisal and constructionist emotion theory. Emotions synthesized on this level usually dissolve shortly after they have been generated, but may also interact with processes on the reflection level.

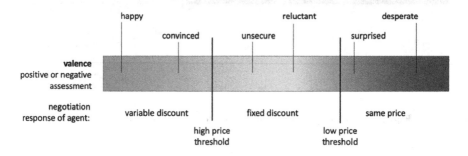

Fig. 3. Synthesis of emotional responses on the routine level

In total six discrete emotions are used for the negotiation dialogue (see Fig. 3). In each round, a Zone of Possible Agreement (ZOPA) is calculated as difference between the agent's price and the user's offer. The low price threshold (20% of ZOPA) and the high price threshold (50% of ZOPA) are derived from this zone. Depending on the bid of the user the agent responses with a different emotional expression (see Fig. 4).

Reflection Level. Due to the various interactions between the routine and reflection level, the borderline between those deeper levels is imprecise and blurred. Therefore, we are using mood in order to prototype this level. Mood embodies a longer term perspective and is influenced by previous events.

In the prototype the mood is reflected as a mood index (see Fig. 4) ranging from one (low valence) to five (high valence). The agent is initialized with a friendly mood with a positive expectation to sell the car. If the user strains the agent's patience with very low and unrealistic offers, the agent's mood gets worse. If the user's bid is acceptable the mood stays the same. In contrast, the mood index increases, if user and agent are about to agree on a deal.

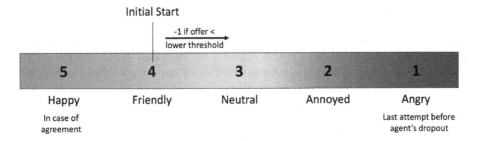

Fig. 4. Mood index on the reflection level

4   Methods

For evaluating the prototype of an emotional interface we conducted an online user study in a within-subject design. In this design every participant tests both independent variables: the emotional version of the chat bot (*emotion-Bot*) and a conventional speech interface (*conventional-Bot*), which does neither provide an avatar nor does it consider emotions. This type of setup is often used in HMI research and comparable to a A/B tests, in which two interfaces are evaluated by the same person. As dependent variables we used the UX and the trustworthiness of each version, which were collected with the User Experience Questionnaire - Short (UEQ-S) and the Trustworthiness Factor (TwF) provided by the Source Credibility Measures (SCM) [35,56].

4.1   Procedure

A call for participation for the online study was spread through the university email lists. Following high research standards, participants were asked to sign a consent form before being forwarded to a setup screen. Here, users have to confirm that they are using a laptop with camera and microphone, that they have a internet connection faster the 15 mbps and they have to grant access rights to use microphone and camera. After receiving background information about the car, users are tasked to negotiate the price of an old-timer. In order to enable a vivid negotiation, the starting price of the old-timer is 34,900 Euro and the participants' budget only 30,000 Euro.

After finishing the instructions the negotiation starts with randomly choosing one version of the agent. In the dialog workflow, both agent versions are exactly the same: Each interaction begins with the agent greeting the user and asking for the user's name. Afterwards the agent starts a welcome dialog, in which he presents some information about the car leading to the final price negotiation. During the interaction, the user can cancel the experiment at any time. After the termination of the negotiation (with or without agreement) the participant has to evaluate the interface in a post-interaction survey, before the second version started. After the second version the participant evaluates the interface with a second post-interaction survey, before he finishes the study with a final survey.

4.2 Measures

The post-interaction survey after the conventional-Bot consists of the UEQ-S and the TwF, which are both standardized questionnaires. UEQ-S is the short version of the UEQ and only consists out of eight opposing pairs of adjectives to assess the UX. In the setting of an online study, we want to keep the number of questions as low as possible in order to prevent premature discontinuation. One half of the questions is assigned to the pragmatic quality dimension, which is comparable to usability. The other half of the questions is attributed to the hedonic quality dimension. The mean value of both dimensions describes the overall UX rating of the product.

The complexity of trust assessment in the context of HMI was already shown previously [50]. Due to the lack of standardized questionnaires for the assessment of trust in the HMI context, this study used SCM from communication science [35]. Like the UEQ-S, the TwF consists of opposing pairs of adjectives that are answered on a seven-level Likert scale.

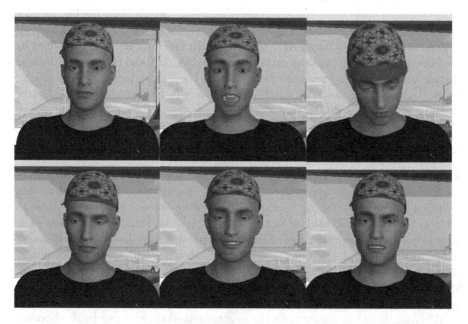

Fig. 5. Screenshots from the six emotion videos - emotions from left to right and from top to bottom: neutral, surprised, desperate, uncertain, happy, angry

The emotional-Bot had a slightly extended version of the post-interaction survey: After UEQ-S and TwF it included a self constructed survey to evaluate the recognition of the emotions displayed through the mimics of the avatar (see

Fig. 5). Following previous work by DeMelo et al. [9] six videos with different emotion categories are displayed in random sequence. These videos start automatically and repeat until one out of six binary emotion categories is selected. The following emotions were used for this test: happy, angry, surprised, insecure, desperate and neutral (for control).

After completion of both post-interaction surveys, the participants were shown a final survey to collect demographic data, their preference between both versions and their Affinity for Technology Interaction (ATI) score [18]. The ATI scale assesses the participants affinity for technology and was chosen because of it's focus on HMI. The study was open until we received 50 valid responses. A response is characterized as valid, if it was finished completely, if there were at least five interactions with each chat bot version and if there was no technical issue during the study. Responses who do not meet all conditions are excluded from further data analysis.

5   Results

In total, 50 participants (15 female and 35 male) finished the study successfully. The average age of the subjects was 28.58 years, the youngest 15 years and the oldest 62 years. The mean (m) of the ATI score was 4.59 with a standard deviation (sd) of 0.88. This can already be rated as an above-average value for technology affinity [18].

5.1   Recognition of Emotions Displayed Through Avatar's Mimics

The six different emotion videos were shown to all 50 test persons. It should be noted that in these videos the emotions should only be mediated through facial expressions. Thus, a total of 300 emotion videos were assigned to an emotion category. Since every participant watched these videos in six rounds in a different order, it can be expected that emotions are better recognized in later rounds, since learning effects occur and the number of remaining emotions decreases. The precision of the participant's emotion recognition per category can be found in Fig. 6. Graphical analysis reveals that the emotions annoyed, surprised and happy were recognized best. According to Ekman, these three emotions are basic emotions [15], while the remaining two emotions (desperate and uncertain) as well as neutral were less well recognized.

As statistical analysis we conducted a logistical regression using emotions and the round as predictors to analyze the probability of a correct assigned emotion. This regression model became significant ($\chi^2 = 104.69; p < .001; n = 300$). As Table 1 shows, only three out of six emotions become significant as predictors with a positive coefficient: angry ($p < .001$), happy ($p = .027$) and surprised ($p < .001$). The emotion insecure became significant ($p < .001$), but with negative coefficient, which means, that it was not recognized. The remaining emotions and the predictor round count did not become significant.

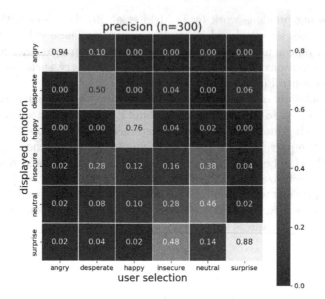

Fig. 6. Precision of emotion recognition of avatar's mimics.

Table 1. Coefficients and p values of the logistic regression for emotion recognition of avatar's mimics

Predictors	coef (β)	std err	z	$P > |z|$	[0,025 0,975]
Angry	2,4531	0,627	3,912	0,000	1,224 3,682
Desperate	−0,2781	0,344	−0,807	0,419	−0,953 0,397
Happy	0,8555	0,388	2,207	0,027	0,096 1,615
Insecure	−1,9365	0,436	−4,445	0,000	−2,790 −1,083
Neutral	−0,4763	0,361	−1,319	0,187	−1,184 0,232
Surprised	1,6969	0,478	3,547	0,000	0,759 2,634
Round	0,5999	0,419	1,432	0,152	−0,221 1,421

5.2   User Experience and Trust Evaluation

User Experience. The results of the user evaluation carried out with the UEQ-S are shown in Fig. 7. The hedonic quality dimension of the emotional-Bot ($m = 5.21, sd = 1.08$) received a higher score than the one of the conventional-Bot ($m = 4.49, sd = 1.34$). In contrast, the evaluation of the pragmatic quality dimension between the emotional-Bot ($m = 4.57, sd = 1.22$) and the conventional-Bot ($m = 4.42, sd = 1.19$) are comparable. Hence, the prototype for an emotional interface was better evaluated than the conventional chat bot version. This is also reflected in a higher UX evaluation of the emotional-Bot ($m = 4.98, sd = 1.00$) in comparison to the conventional-Bot ($m = 4.48, sd = 1.13$).

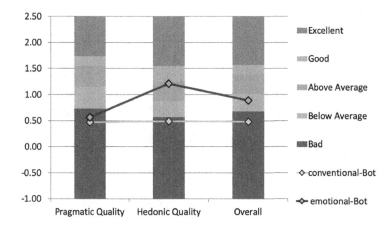

Fig. 7. UEQ-S benchmark comparison of both versions.

Statistical analysis revealed a significant difference between the variants ($t = 2.321; p = .024; n = 50$). Thus, the emotional-Bot ($m = 4.89; sd = 1.00$) performed better in the total UX assessment than the conventional-Bot ($m = 4.48; SD = 1.13$). In summary, the emotional-Bot performs better in the total UX assessment, which is above all due to the hedonic UX dimension.

Trustworthiness. Trustworthiness was measured with the TwF. The descriptive analysis of the data did not suggest any difference in TwF between emotional-Bot ($m = 4.43, sd = 0.94$) and conventional-Bot ($m = 4.34, sd = 0.93$). Even with looking at the individual questions, there is only little difference between the two variants. In addition, also graphical analysis of the box-plots did do not suggest a significant difference between the two interface variants. In statistical analysis, t-test did not show statistically significant influence of the interface variant on the TwF ($t = -0.712; p = 0.480; n = 50$). Therefore, the finding suggests, that the emotional interface is not perceived as more trustworthy than a conventional chat interface.

Final Survey Results. Participants were also asked in the final survey which version they preferred. In the process, 19 test participants clearly opted for the emotional-Bot, while only eight participants opted clearly for the conventional-Bot. Five people did not choose either of the two interface variants. A total of ten people had a slight to strong tendency to the conventional-Bot and eight people had a slight to strong tendency to emotional-Bot. In the analysis, we discovered, that the order of the experiment might have had an influence on this evaluation. Participants who first interacted with the avatar were more likely to

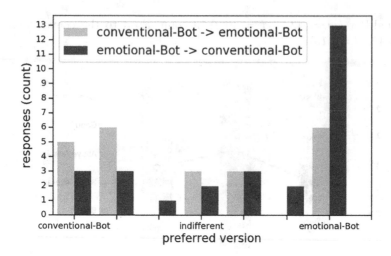

Fig. 8. Participant preference on the sequence of the experiment.

prefer the avatar. Participants, who started with the conventional-Bot, did not seem to have been influenced (Fig. 8).

To understand the reasoning of the participants choice, we also asked them for the reason of their choice. The responses for choosing the conventional-Bot can be summarized into three main reasons: First, the implementation of the avatar for some participants was not ideal and thus unrealistic, less trustworthy and sometimes even scary. Participants, were describing an uncanny valley effect. Secondly, the personal attitude ("I don't like video chats") was given as an explanation. Participants did not see any additional value in using an avatar in negotiation. Third, the missing text representation in the avatar was criticized, which caused that users could not read what the avatar had said. Participants who preferred the emotional-Bot mainly mentioned two reasons: The interaction with the avatar was perceived as more natural and human-like. Some of the participants even mentioned the use of emotions directly: "An avatar gives you a good feeling in the negotiation. You can see emotions to the spoken words, which makes it easier to interpret". Based on the responses, the second reason is the entertainment factor of the avatar. Participants stated that the emotional-Bot was more innovative and interesting, and therefore more fun to use.

6   Discussion

The results of this study suggest, that an emotional ECA increases the UX in the negotiation context. A schema for an emotional interface was introduced, to model emotions for this use case. However, it may be used for applications in different HMI contexts. Expressing emotions in conventional user interfaces remains a challenge for user interface designers. The post-interaction survey of this study suggests that emotions, which are only expressed through the facial expressions of the avatar, cannot be clearly assigned. This underlines the importance of a multimodal emotion expression for ECAs.

Emotion Recognition of Avatar's Mimics. Only three emotions (angry, happy and surprised), which are basic emotions according to Ekman [15], were recognized correctly. However, these findings also go along with the constructionist emotion theory [3]: It can be assumed, that the emotional concepts of these emotions were more distinct and dominant in the perception of the study participants and hence led to a better recognition. In contrast, the emotional concepts of uncertainty and desperation were less distinct for the participants.

The videos in the experiment only displayed the facial expressions, without giving the participant some context for the assignment. This indicates that remaining emotions are more context dependent and also mediated through different means such as prosody. Future research may want to investigate this direction.

User Experience Evaluation. The prototype for an emotional interface received a better UX evaluation, which is mainly due to the better rated hedonic quality dimension. Theory already suggests, that emotions have an influence on the hedonic UX dimension: After all, this dimension determines the extent to which a product is stimulating and provides pleasure and new challenges to the user [25]. According to Hassenzahl et al. [25], the hedonic dimension determines the UX of products to a great extent and should therefore be given particular attention by UX designers. The results of this study are consistent with this view: Emotions that are represented with the help of an avatar can generate a better UX in chat bots and digital assistants.

However, both versions were evaluated with a similar pragmatic product quality, which primarily describes the usability of a product. Compared to the benchmarks offered by the UEQ-S [55], the usability of both versions must be described as poor. Moreover, the benchmark was mainly developed with data from complex business software and web shops [55], which limits the transferability to chat bots. In addition, almost all data is based on ready-developed products, whereas in this study only two prototypes were evaluated. A reason for the poor evaluation of the pragmatic dimension in comparison to the benchmark could be the faulty speech recognition. In 19 cases a poor speech recognition was reported as a technical problem. This led to a very poor usability of a speech controlled interface.

Trust Evaluation. A surprising finding of this study was that the interface variants did not differ in terms of trust. Two reasons can provide an explanation. First, the interaction time during the study could have been too short, so that no trust between user and avatar could be established. Building trust may require a long period of time. Second, anthropomorphism tends to reduce initial expectations of trustworthiness [62]. This result is also consistent with the automation bias [13], which describes that people have higher expectations (in terms of performance and authority) of machine-like agents. This effect could also apply to trust in this negotiation use case. Further research can examine if increasing the interaction time significantly would lead to a different evaluation of trust.

6.1 Limitations

In this study a conventional chat bot was compared with an emotional chat bot, which differed not only in it's emotional interactions but also in using an ECA as additional form of presentation. This could have lead to a bias in the user evaluation. The user may be influenced by the display of an avatar and evaluated not only on the basis of emotional interactions. This "entertainment factor" could have lead to a certain bias in the data and could have been controlled through comparing both, an avatar with emotions and an avatar without emotions. In this study we put emphasis on the comparison to an conventional chat bot, and consequently did not analyze a third version.

In addition, UX designers must always be aware of different or unexpected user behavior. In the negotiation context users might tend to hide emotions completely or even show misleading emotions. In interpersonal negotiations, one party might be rewarded by influencing the other party with pretended emotions [23]. The study design did not allow for controlling whether and to what extent this effect occurred in the negotiation. Specific unexpected use behavior is another area future research can explore and develop emotional interactions in HMI.

6.2 Future Work

This paper has introduced a schema for an emotional interface for the HMI. It's practicability and application to other application contexts still has to be validated in future studies. Another interesting direction would be to investigate the influences on the UX and negotiation outcomes by improving the representation of the avatar or its small knowledge base. Utilizing this kind of a web hosted architecture allows to replicate the study and can potentially generate large amounts of interaction data. This data could be used for both, a better understanding for emotional interaction as well as for further improving AI systems.

References

1. Alex, S.B., Babu, B.P., Mary, L.: Utterance and syllable level prosodic features for automatic emotion recognition. In: Intergovernmental Panel on Climate Change (ed.) 2018 IEEE Recent Advances in Intelligent Computational Systems (RAICS), vol. 53, pp. 31–35. IEEE, Cambridge (2018). https://doi.org/10.1109/RAICS.2018.8635059
2. Bänziger, T., Hosoya, G., Scherer, K.R.: Path models of vocal emotion communication. PLoS One **10**(9), 1–29 (2015). https://doi.org/10.1371/journal.pone.0136675
3. Barrett, L.F.: Solving the emotion paradox: categorization and the experience of emotion. Pers. Soc. Psychol. Rev. **10**(1), 20–46 (2006). https://doi.org/10.1207/s15327957pspr1001_2

4. Buechel, S., Hahn, U.: Emotion representation mapping for automatic lexicon construction (mostly) performs on human level. Technical report, Jena University Language & Information Engineering (JULIE) Lab, Jena, Germany, June 2018. http://arxiv.org/abs/1806.08890

5. Cassell, J., et al.: Embodiment in conversational interfaces: rea. In: Conference on Human Factors in Computing Systems - Proceedings, pp. 520–527 (1999). https://doi.org/10.1145/302979.303150

6. Ciechanowski, L., Przegalinska, A., Magnuski, M., Gloor, P.: In the shades of the uncanny valley: an experimental study of human-chatbot interaction. Future Gener. Comput. Syst. **92**, 539–548 (2019). https://doi.org/10.1016/j.future.2018.01.055

7. Crumpton, J., Bethel, C.L.: A survey of using vocal prosody to convey emotion in robot speech. Int. J. Social Robot. **8**(2), 271–285 (2016). https://doi.org/10.1007/s12369-015-0329-4

8. Daz Productions: Genesis 8—3D Models and 3D Software by Daz 3D (2019). https://www.daz3d.com/genesis8

9. De Melo, C.M., Carnevale, P., Gratch, J.: The effect of expression of anger and happiness in computer agents on negotiations with humans. In: The 10th International Conference on Autonomous Agents and Multiagent Systems, vol. 3, pp. 2–6 (2011)

10. De Melo, C.M., Gratch, J., Carnevale, P.J.: Humans versus computers: impact of emotion expressions on people's decision making. IEEE Trans. Affect. Comput. **6**(2), 127–136 (2015). https://doi.org/10.1109/TAFFC.2014.2332471

11. De Rosis, F., Pelachaud, C., Poggi, I., Carofiglio, V., De Carolis, B.: From Greta's mind to her face: modelling the dynamics of affective states in a conversational embodied agent. Int. J. Hum. Comput. Stud. **59**(1–2), 81–118 (2003). https://doi.org/10.1016/S1071-5819(03)00020-X

12. Dhall, A., Ramana Murthy, O.V., Goecke, R., Joshi, J., Gedeon, T.: Video and image based emotion recognition challenges in the wild: EmotiW 2015. In: ICMI 2015 - Proceedings of the 2015 ACM International Conference on Multimodal Interaction, pp. 423–426 (2015). https://doi.org/10.1145/2818346.2829994

13. Dzindolet, M.T., Peterson, S.A., Pomranky, R.A., Pierce, L.G., Beck, H.P.: The role of trust in automation reliance. Int. J. Hum. Comput. Stud. **58**(6), 697–718 (2003). https://doi.org/10.1016/S1071-5819(03)00038-7

14. Ekman, P.: What scientists who study emotion agree about. Perspect. Psychol. Sci. **11**(1), 31–34 (2016). https://doi.org/10.1177/1745691615596992

15. Ekman, P., Friesen, W.V.: Constants across cultures in the face and emotion. J. Pers. Soc. Psychol. **17**(2), 124–129 (1971). https://doi.org/10.1037/h0030377

16. Feldmaier, J.: Perspectives on the connection of psychological models of emotion and intelligent machines. Ph.D. thesis, Technical University of Munich (2017)

17. Feldmaier, J., Diepold, K.: Path-finding using reinforcement learning and affective states. In: The 23rd IEEE International Symposium on Robot and Human Interactive Communication, pp. 543–548. IEEE, August 2014. https://doi.org/10.1109/ROMAN.2014.6926309

18. Franke, T., Attig, C., Wessel, D.: Assessing affinity for technology interaction - the affinity for technology assessing affinity for technology interaction (ATI). Technical report, Unpublished manuscript (2017). https://doi.org/10.13140/RG.2.2.28679.50081

19. Gazzaniga, M., Ivry, R.B., Mangun, G.R.: Cognitive Neuroscience: The Biology of the Mind, 4th edn. W. W. Norton, New York (2014)

20. Gebhard, P.: ALMA - a layered model of affect. In: Proceedings of the International Conference on Autonomous Agents, pp. 177–184 (2005)
21. Google: Cloud Text-to-Speech (2019). https://cloud.google.com/text-to-speech/
22. Gratch, J., DeVault, D., Lucas, G.: The benefits of virtual humans for teaching negotiation. In: Traum, D., Swartout, W., Khooshabeh, P., Kopp, S., Scherer, S., Leuski, A. (eds.) IVA 2016. LNCS (LNAI), vol. 10011, pp. 283–294. Springer, Cham (2016). https://doi.org/10.1007/978-3-319-47665-0_25
23. Gratch, J., Nazari, Z., Johnson, E.: The misrepresentation game: how to win at negotiation while seeming like a nice guy. In: Proceedings of the International Joint Conference on Autonomous Agents and Multiagent Systems, AAMAS, pp. 728–737 (2016)
24. Hanson, D., et al.: Zeno: a cognitive character. AAAI Workshop - Technical report, pp. 9–11 (2008)
25. Hassenzahl, M., Diefenbach, S., Göritz, A.: Needs, affect, and interactive products - facets of user experience. Interact. Comput. 22(5), 353–362 (2010)
26. Huang, K.Y., Wu, C.H., Hong, Q.B., Su, M.H., Chen, Y.H.: Speech emotion recognition using deep neural network considering verbal and nonverbal speech sounds. In: ICASSP, IEEE International Conference on Acoustics, Speech and Signal Processing - Proceedings, vol. 2019-May, pp. 5866–5870 (2019). https://doi.org/10.1109/ICASSP.2019.8682283
27. Kahou, S.E., Michalski, V., Konda, K., Memisevic, R., Pal, C.: Recurrent neural networks for emotion recognition in video. In: ICMI 2015 - Proceedings of the 2015 ACM International Conference on Multimodal Interaction, pp. 467–474. Association for Computing Machinery, Inc., November 2015. https://doi.org/10.1145/2818346.2830596
28. Kim, K., Boelling, L., Haesler, S., Bailenson, J., Bruder, G., Welch, G.F.: Does a digital assistant need a body? The influence of visual embodiment and social behavior on the perception of intelligent virtual agents in AR. In: Proceedings of the 2018 IEEE International Symposium on Mixed and Augmented Reality, ISMAR 2018, pp. 105–114 (2019). https://doi.org/10.1109/ISMAR.2018.00039
29. Kowalczuk, Z., Czubenko, M.: Emotions embodied in the SVC of an autonomous driver system. IFAC-PapersOnLine 50(1), 3744–3749 (2017). https://doi.org/10.1016/j.ifacol.2017.08.573
30. Lerner, J.S., Li, Y., Valdesolo, P., Kassam, K.S.: Emotion and decision making. Ann. Rev. Psychol. 66(1), 799–823 (2015). https://doi.org/10.1146/annurev-psych-010213-115043
31. Li, Y., Tao, J., Schuller, B., Shan, S., Jiang, D., Jia, J.: MEC 2017: multimodal emotion recognition challenge. In: 2018 1st Asian Conference on Affective Computing and Intelligent Interaction, ACII Asia (2018). https://doi.org/10.1109/ACIIAsia.2018.8470342
32. MacDorman, K.: Subjective ratings of robot video clips for human likeness, familiarity, and eeriness: an exploration of the uncanny valley. In: ICCS/CogSci-2006 Long Symposium: Toward Social Mechanisms of Android Science (2006)
33. Mavridis, N.: A review of verbal and non-verbal human-robot interactive communication. Robot. Auton. Syst. 63(P1), 22–35 (2015). https://doi.org/10.1016/j.robot.2014.09.031
34. Mayer, J.D.: What is emotional intelligence? Technical report, UNH Personality Lab (2004)
35. McCroskey, J., Teven, J.: Source credibility measures. Meas. Instr. Database Soc. Sci. (2013). https://doi.org/10.13072/midss.536

36. Microsoft: Luis - Language Understanding (2019). https://azure.microsoft.com/en-us/services/cognitive-services/language-understanding-intelligent-service/
37. Microsoft: Speech-to-Text (2019). https://azure.microsoft.com/en-us/services/cognitive-services/speech-to-text/
38. Moerland, T.M., Broekens, J., Jonker, C.M.: Emotion in reinforcement learning agents and robots: a survey. Mach. Learn. **107**, 443–480 (2018). https://doi.org/10.1007/s10994-017-5666-0
39. Mori, M., MacDorman, K.F., Kageki, N.: The uncanny valley. IEEE Robot. Autom. Mag. **19**(2), 98–100 (2012). https://doi.org/10.1109/MRA.2012.2192811
40. Mudrick, N.V., Taub, M., Azevedo, R., Rowe, J., Lester, J.: Toward affect-sensitive virtual human tutors: the influence of facial expressions on learning and emotion. In: 2017 7th International Conference on Affective Computing and Intelligent Interaction, ACII 2017, vol. 2018-Janua, pp. 184–189. IEEE, October 2018. https://doi.org/10.1109/ACII.2017.8273598
41. Norman, D.A., Ortony, A., Russell, D.M.: Affect and machine design: lessons for the development of autonomous machines. IBM Syst. J. **42**(1), 38–44 (2003). https://doi.org/10.1147/sj.421.0038
42. Oatley, K., Johnson-Laird, P.N.: Cognitive approaches to emotions. Trends Cogn. Sci. **18**(3), 134–140 (2014). https://doi.org/10.1016/j.tics.2013.12.004
43. Oh, S.Y., Bailenson, J., Krämer, N., Li, B.: Let the Avatar Brighten your smile: effects of enhancing facial expressions in virtual environments. PLOS One **11**(9), e0161794 (2016). https://doi.org/10.1371/journal.pone.0161794. http://dx.plos.org/10.1371/journal.pone.0161794
44. Ortony, A., Clore, G.L., Collins, A.: The Cognitive Structure of Emotions. Cambridge University Press, New York (1990)
45. Phelps, E.A., Lempert, K.M., Sokol-Hessner, P.: Emotion and decision making: multiple modulatory neural circuits. Annu. Rev. Neurosci. **37**(1), 263–287 (2014). https://doi.org/10.1146/annurev-neuro-071013-014119
46. Piana, S., Staglianò, A., Odone, F., Camurri, A.: Adaptive body gesture representation for automatic emotion recognition. ACM Trans. Interact. Intell. Syst. **6**(1), 1–31 (2016). https://doi.org/10.1145/2818740
47. Picard, R.: Affective computing. Technical report 321, MIT Media Laboratory Perceptual Computing, Cambridge, Mass. (1995). https://affect.media.mit.edu
48. Provoost, S., Lau, H.M., Ruwaard, J., Riper, H.: Embodied conversational agents in clinical psychology: a scoping review (2017). https://doi.org/10.2196/jmir.6553
49. Rasmussen, J.: Skills, rules, and knowledge; signals, signs, and symbols, and other distinctions in human performance models. IEEE Trans. Syst. Man Cybern. **3**, 257–266 (1983)
50. Riedl, R., Mohr, P., Kenning, P., Davis, F., Heekeren, H.: Trusting humans and avatars: behavioral and neural evidence. In: ICIS 2011 Proceedings, pp. 1–23 (2011)
51. Russell, J.A.: Core affect and the psychological construction of emotion. Psychol. Rev. **110**(1), 145–172 (2003). https://doi.org/10.1037/0033-295X.110.1.145
52. Salah, A.A., Kaya, H., Gürpınar, F.: Video-based emotion recognition in the wild. In: Multimodal Behavior Analysis in the Wild, pp. 369–386. Elsevier (2019). https://doi.org/10.1016/b978-0-12-814601-9.00031-6
53. Saldien, J., Goris, K., Vanderborght, B., Vanderfaeillie, J., Lefeber, D.: Expressing emotions with the social robot probo. Int. J. Soc. Robot. **2**(4), 377–389 (2010). https://doi.org/10.1007/s12369-010-0067-6
54. Scherer, K.R., Moors, A.: The emotion process: event appraisal and component differentiation. Ann. Rev. Psychol. **70**(1), 719–745 (2019). https://doi.org/10.1146/annurev-psych-122216-011854

55. Schrepp, M., Hinderks, A., Thomaschewski, J.: Construction of a benchmark for the user experience questionnaire (UEQ). Int. J. Interact. Multimed. Artif. Intell. **4**(4), 40 (2017). https://doi.org/10.9781/ijimai.2017.445

56. Schrepp, M., Hinderks, A., Thomaschewski, J.: Design and evaluation of a short version of the user experience questionnaire (UEQ-S). Int. J. Interact. Multimed. Artif. Intell. **4**(6), 103 (2017). https://doi.org/10.9781/ijimai.2017.09.001

57. Soleymani, M., Asghari-Esfeden, S., Fu, Y., Pantic, M.: Analysis of EEG signals and facial expressions for continuous emotion detection. IEEE Trans. Affect. Comput. **7**(1), 17–28 (2016). https://doi.org/10.1109/TAFFC.2015.2436926. http://iee explore.ieee.org/document/7112127/

58. Stevens, C.J., Pinchbeck, B., Lewis, T., Luerssen, M., Pfitzner, D., Powers, D.M.W., Abrahamyan, A., Leung, Y., Gibert, G.: Mimicry and expressiveness of an ECA in human-agent interaction: familiarity breeds content!. Comput. Cogn. Sci. **2**(1), 1–14 (2016). https://doi.org/10.1186/s40469-016-0008-2

59. Tanaka, H., Negoro, H., Iwasaka, H., Nakamura, S.: Embodied conversational agents for multimodal automated social skills training in people with autism spectrum disorders. PLoS One **12**(8), 1–16 (2017)

60. Valstar, M., et al.: AVEC 2016 - depression, mood, and emotion recognition workshop and challenge. In: AVEC 2016 - Proceedings of the 6th International Workshop on Audio/Visual Emotion Challenge, co-located with ACM Multimedia 2016, pp. 3–10. Association for Computing Machinery, Inc., October 2016. https://doi.org/10.1145/2988257.2988258

61. Verma, G.K., Tiwary, U.S.: Affect representation and recognition in 3D continuous valence-arousal-dominance space. Multimed. Tools Appl. **76**(2), 2159–2183 (2017). https://doi.org/10.1007/s11042-015-3119-y. http://dx.doi.org/10.1007/s11042-01 5-3119-y

62. de Visser, E.J., et al.: Almost human: anthropomorphism increases trust resilience in cognitive agents. J. Exp. Psychol.: Appl. **22**(3), 331–349 (2016). https://doi.org/10.1037/xap0000092

63. W3C: Speech Synthesis Markup Language (SSML) Version 1.1 (2010). https://www.w3.org/TR/speech-synthesis11/

Multimodality, Naturalness and Transparency in Affective Computing for HCI

Sónia Rafael$^{(\boxtimes)}$ ⓘ

ITI – Interactive Technologies Institute/LARSyS,
Faculdade de Belas-Artes, Universidade de Lisboa, Lisbon, Portugal
s.rafael@belasartes.ulisboa.pt

Abstract. Post-industrial society, aligned with the model of the Fourth Industrial Revolution, has been providing technological advances in advanced robotics, IoT, self-driving vehicles, non-biological sentient life development, artificial intelligence (AI), machine learning or cognitive computing, among others. This fact determines the understanding that in the near future humans and machines will have a joint role to play.

Multimodality is one of the most important challenges in the field of human-computer interaction (HCI), as it provides an extension of the sensorimotor capabilities of computer systems so that they should replicate the processes of natural communication between humans.

There is a need for the development of increasingly intelligent interfaces, defined as those that promote naturalness, adding the benefits of adaptability, context-fitness and support for task development. There is also a growing desire for interface transparency as a mediator for HCI to make interactions that are truer and closer to reality. On the other hand, current research has been emphasizing the importance of affection and emotions, particularly, in the user's experience with computer systems.

This paper proposes to understand the importance of multimodality, naturalness and transparency for affective computing and how they can synergistically contribute to the anthropomorphization of HCI. Through this understanding, we present design requirements for engineers, designers and IT professionals, and other interveners, for the development of multimodal interfaces.

Keywords: Affective computing · Multimodality · HCI

1 Introduction

Over the years, the area of human-computer interaction has focused primarily on cognitive factors. However, in the last decade there has been a growing interest in imminently emotional factors. In addition, studies in the field of psychology have recognized the importance of emotions for human cognition, motivation, learning and behavior. This understanding of emotions has inspired many researchers to build machines that can recognize, express, model, communicate and respond to human emotions.

© Springer Nature Switzerland AG 2020
A. Marcus and E. Rosenzweig (Eds.): HCII 2020, LNCS 12200, pp. 521–531, 2020.
https://doi.org/10.1007/978-3-030-49713-2_36

Computer systems can display emotions, language and communication patterns, and their conversational and cognitive abilities can be equated to some extent with those of human beings.

Rosalind Picard's *Affective Computing* was published in 1997 [1] and laid the foundation for equipping machines with emotional intelligence. Thus, a new area of research called affective computing has emerged, concerned with the emotional side of computers and their users. The term can be defined as computation that relates to, raises, or deliberately influences emotions. However, the definition may not be consistent since the goal is the automatic recognition of emotion by computer systems. Yet, for a natural and effective HCI that approaches an affective dimension, computers still need to look intelligent [1] and for intelligent interaction the reference should be human-human interaction. In this regard, Wiener [2] defends that human-to-human communication should be the model for human-machine interaction (as well as machine-machine interaction), arguing that communication between humans and machines should not be distinguished from natural communication between humans, and it is irrelevant that a communicative signal is processed by a machine and not by another human.

One of the main limitations of affective computing is that most previous research has focused on recognizing emotions from a single sensory source, or modality. However, as HCI is multimodal, researchers have tried to use various modalities for the recognition of emotions and affective states.

2 Multimodality in HCI

In an HCI, the sender translates concepts (symbolic information) into physical events that are transmitted to the appropriate receiver and the receiver interprets the received signal in terms of abstract symbols. These processes involve the user's senses and motor skills and symmetrically the input and output mechanisms of the system.

The purpose of a multimodal system is to provide an extension of sensorimotor capabilities so that they should replicate the processes of natural communication between humans [3]. This mode of communication involves the simultaneous use of various modalities, so a computer system should be able to support them in interaction with the user.

For this to happen, a multimodal computer system must be equipped with hardware that should enable the acquisition and/or transmission of multimodal expressions (at a time compatible with the user's expectations), be able to choose the output mode appropriate to the content to be streamed, and be able to understand multimodal input expressions [4].

With the increasing complexity of computer applications, a single modality will not be able to ensure effective and emotionally expressed interaction across all tasks and environments. Thus, over the years, there has been an investment in the processing of natural language, computational vision and gesture analysis within HCI. This investment has sought integration into traditional interfaces by giving them a higher functionality potential.

Multimodal interfaces have represented another direction for computing, and there is a great potential for integrating distinct synergistic modalities, supported by the myriad technologies that have been made available. In fact, they present both potentialities and constraints, and each of the sensory modes of interaction should be selected according to the communication effectiveness promoted by it. This effectiveness is conditioned by numerous variables, namely the characteristics of the content to be transmitted, the sender, the receiver, the input and output mechanisms, the cognition systems (human and computational), among others.

2.1 Contribution of the Cognitive Sciences

Multimodality is a research route that requires the contribution of cognitive sciences in the context of human perception and the use of coexistent modalities in a natural context of interaction – for example, speech, gesture, look and facial expressions.

Cognitive sciences have evolved over the course of the twentieth century from a model of atomistic (unimodal) perception – the view of the construction of the whole through the joining of individual parts – to the perceptual (multimodal) model of Gestalt theory – the view that the whole is different from the sum of its constituent parts [5].

Recent studies suggest increasing evidence that our bodies are activated for multiple input mode, although the classical theory of neurological sensory processing favors the single modality model and the primary sensory areas of the cortex are unisensory [6].

Ghazanfar and Schroeder [7] consider that the integration of the different qualities of information from the various sensory organs (combined in the brain to produce a unified and coherent representation of the external world) does not occur at the level of the most specialized, higher level areas of the neocortex after its individualized processing in less specialized lower-level areas (as traditionally suggested). On the contrary, they attest that much (if not all) of the neocortex is multisensory and processes the various qualities of information in an integrated manner, practically from the beginning of its capture. In this context, human perception results from a unified representation of the set of sensory inputs received from the outside world.

Instead of analyzing sensory modalities autonomously with eventual later integration, researchers began to consider the role of multisensory integration in the perceptual process by demonstrating that there are transmodal effects on human perception (i.e., the senses influence each other) and that temporal synchrony also takes over a relevant role in these effects [5]. Indeed, while on the one hand the concept of multisensory data fusion can hardly be considered recent, as humans and animals have evolutionarily developed the ability to use multiple senses in order to increase their survival possibilities, advances in computing and Sensors provided the ability to emulate, through hardware and software, the natural information fusion capabilities of humans and animals [8]. Dumas et al. [9] highlight the fact that research in cognitive psychology has revealed that:

- the working memory of humans dedicated to the different modalities (and consequent processing power) is partially independent of each other, so the presentation of information through different modal channels increases the total memory used by the human in information processing, promoting the expansion of their capabilities and better performance;

- humans tend to reproduce their interpersonal interaction patterns when they multimodally interact with a computer system;
- The way human perception, communication and memory work leads to improved performance when they interact multimodally with a computer system.

It is an understanding also defended by Anthony et al. [10] who stated that it is natural and convenient for humans to communicate with the computer using modal channels to aid thought processing, concept visualization and establishing an affective relationship. Also, Tzovaras [11] argues that the "interface" between the human and the environment, as well as between humans, is multimodal, and all senses (even if some are dominant) participate in the operations of perception, action and interaction. In this regard, Landragin [12] mentions that the way we view an object determines the discourse and gestures we use to refer to it, while the gestures we produce structure our visual perception. This understanding corresponds to the realization that visual perception, language and gesture establish multiple interactions with each other. On the other hand, Aran et al. [13] recall that speech components, such as lip movements, hand-based sign languages, head and body movements, in addition to facial expressions, constitute available multimodal information sources that are integrated into communication by the hearing impaired. Thus, real-world behavior and perception are dominated by the integration of information from multiple and diverse sensory sources.

In recent years, also in the field of linguistics, researchers have become aware that a theory of communication describing real human-human interactions must encompass a diversity of dimensions. This is why multimodality has been considered a better representation of the complexity of discourse [14] than unimodality.

2.2   Potentialities and Constraints of Multimodal Interfaces

Multimodal interfaces are a class of multimedia systems that integrate artificial intelligence and have gradually gained the ability to understand, interpret and generate specific data in response to analytic content, differing from classical multimedia systems and applications that do not understand data semantics (sound, image, video) they manipulate [15, 16].

Although both types of systems may use similar physical input and output (acquiring, storing and generating visual and sound information), each serves a different purpose: in the case of multimedia systems information is subject to the task and is handled by the user; in the case of multimodal systems, information is a resource for performing the task control processes themselves. Martin et al. [17] argue that, in the context of a computer system, the option for multimodal solutions will only be convenient if it has been ratified by usability criteria. They refer, for example, to the following:

- allow faster interaction;
- allow selective adaptation to different environments, users or usage behaviors;
- enable a shorter learning curve or be more intuitive;

- improve the recognition of information in a noisy environment (e.g. sound, visual or tactile aspects);
- allow the linking of information presented to a more global contextual knowledge (allowing for easier interpretation);
- and allow the translation of information between modalities.

This is also the understanding of Ferri and Paolozzi [18], when they state that the choice of a multimodal interface, instead of a unimodal solution, depends on the type of action to be developed by the user and its increased usability potential. In fact, the various input and output channels usable with HCI (keyboard, mouse, touchscreen, microphone, motion sensor, monitor, speaker, haptic receivers, etc.) have their own benefits and limitations, so multimodal interaction is often used to compensate for the limitations of one modality by making another available [19]. Each input modality must be adapted to a set of interaction contexts, not being ideal or even being inappropriate in others [20]; therefore, the selection of interaction modality is a matter of extreme relevance in a multimodal system.

2.3   Development Requirements, Limitations and Constraints

System designers are increasingly using more and more different (often alternative) input/output modalities to exchange information between systems and their users. For this to happen the design of multimodal interfaces must be based on the following principles: selection of content to transfer; assignment of appropriate modalities to the content; and functional implementation of the modality ensuring the transfer of content.

Also Bernsen [21] presents a similar logic of procedures that an interface designer should consider: identifying the information to be exchanged between users and the system; performing a good match between the information and the available input/output modalities in terms of functionality, usability, naturalness, efficiency, etc.; and designing, implementing and testing the interface. The usability of multimodal interfaces can generally be facilitated if users are familiar with this mode of interaction. There are interfaces that place an excessive cognitive burden on their users, although this is a problem that can be circumvented by their "disappearance" and naturalness so that users can focus exclusively on the activity.

In recent years, research on multimodal HCIs has been focused on analyzing and designing mainstream interfaces. In turn, Bernsen and Dybkjær [22] warn against the danger of exaggerating the promotion of multimodal interaction, especially when the aggregation of modalities does not promote any efficiency increase in human-computer communication and point out that the interaction results should always be valued. In this regard, they criticize, for example, the trivialization of research in more or less elaborate animated conversational agents, when they occupy valuable screen space and processing resources, compared to the mere discursive output.

Although empirical studies show that users change their attitude and expectations towards the computer system when confronted with a more or less realistic animated conversational agent, assuming the posture of an interaction closer to human communication, i.e. more affective, multimodal interactive systems are sometimes contaminated by the desire of designers to apply new technologies which do not amount to a real increase in usability and the success of the interface tends to be evaluated by empirical approaches.

3 Naturalness in Multimodal HCI

The flexibility of a multimodal interface should accommodate a wide variety of users, tasks and environments that are beyond the possibilities of interaction through a single mode. In this regard, Ferri and Paolozzi [18] claim that there is a growing demand for user-centered system architectures with which the user can interact through the natural modalities of human-human communication. This should be developed in a natural enough way so that adaptation to the computer system should not be necessary, the opposite being favored. Such an interface will be one that appeals to the user's intuition, supported by the transfer of skills and knowledge acquired in previously experienced environments and contexts. In this regard, Maybury and Wahlster [23] emphasize the need for the development of increasingly intelligent interfaces, defining them as those that promote the efficiency and naturalness of HCI by aggregating the benefits of adaptability, context fitness and task development support. Bernsen and Dybkjær [22] present two possible lines of analysis, constituted around two interaction paradigms:

1. paradigm of natural multimodal interaction sustained in the strict use of the modes of communication that individuals use to communicate with each other;
2. paradigm of functional multimodal interaction in which any modality (natural or not) should be used if it leads to the promotion of more efficient interactions.

For example, Yin [24] defines natural human-computer interaction as the multimodal interaction that occurs in a cognitively transparent and effortless manner, leading the computer system to understand what the user is doing or communicating without letting him alter the pattern of natural behavior he would develop with another person. In this regard, the production of more natural interfaces should involve the use of the sensory modality(ies) that most effectively accomplish the task. He also argues that computer systems have sensory modalities that may have, in some cases, higher usability than those currently used in human-human communication, defining the naturalness of an interaction from the point of view of greater ease of interaction and superior usability rather than from the perspective of its mere parallelism with the interaction between human individuals.

4 Transparency of Interfaces

Advances in technology, in addition to the objectives of ease, learning, use and naturalness, are allowing both computers and interfaces to be transparent. Norman [25] argued that the computers of the future should be invisible. In this context, Bolter and Grusin [26] approach the concept of transparency (as a characteristic of immediacy; i.e., the absence of mediation or representation) that occurs when the human user forgets (or does not have knowledge) of the means by which information is being transmitted, thus being in direct contact with the content. They state that "virtual reality, three-dimensional graphics and interface design are, together, seeking to make digital technology 'transparent'" so that the user may feel that he is a part of the system it integrates.

Within the scope of HCI and in accordance with the above, the interface development processes must ensure their standardization, consistency and transparency, in order to satisfy the user's needs and facilitate human action. There is also a growing desire for the "disappearance" of the interface as a mediator of an HCI in order to make interactions more real and closer to reality.

5   Aspects for the Anthropomorphization of HCI

Human beings tend to attribute anthropomorphic characteristics, motivations and behaviors to animals, artifacts and natural phenomena.

For a computer system to promote an affective relationship with the user, it must promote anthropomorphization, which, in turn, may be the result of particular characteristics such as the promotion of multimodality, the naturalness of interaction and the transparency of the interface (see Fig. 1). Anthropomorphization and also personification seek to inculcate human characteristics to computer systems through the interface, as well as to promote their transition from technological object to subject. Thus, the technological interfaces that, being anthropomorphic, resort to multimodality, naturalness and transparency must become, simultaneously, a representation (of the human) and a device (tool). When this simulation is able to reconstruct the idea of human relationship in human-computer interaction, it achieves its concrete objective: the machine moves from being an object to being a subject. [27] The passage from object to subject, achievable due to the embodiment of physical and psychological aspects of the human being, is indicative of the anthropomorphization of the entire object or machine.

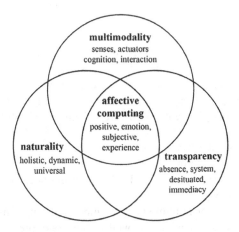

Fig. 1. Aspects for the anthropomorphization of HCI

6 Conclusion

Aspects such as multimodality, naturalness and transparency, which, in synergy, contribute to affective computing, can also contribute to the anthropomorphization of HCI. The whole design of the interaction between humans and computer systems is dependent on the options taken by a series of specialists who intervene in its planning, development and implementation in particular by a variety of ethical decisions involved in the development of an interaction technology. The challenge of approaching affective systems is growing, but the lack of tools to support interface designers and other interveners is a constraint that needs to be resolved. To this end, it is important to develop standards across all interfaces that seek to promote affectivity through multimodality, naturalness and transparency, although this is not, in fact, an easy objective to pursue.

One question that can be asked is whether emotions can be designed so that affective computing should be a design requirement. Emotions are a result of many different aspects and designers may not be able to control and bring together all the conditions necessary to create specific emotions. They may, eventually, establish the context of an emotion and not the emotion itself since it is difficult to generate affective responses in judgments, for example, of questions of aesthetics, of taste, behavior, etc., as well as in how these judgments influence later decision making. Nevertheless, some guidelines are presented that facilitate the design of mainstream, natural, transparent multimodal systems, as the issue of affective computing is taken as an objective to be achieved, and some steps are described that may be determinant for its success and general acceptance:

Terminology – Use of consistent terminology for the presentation and operation of the interface.

Feedback – Constant feedback to the user from the interface, so that the user is aware of the point of use at which he finds himself and knows the possibilities and channels of interaction available at all times.

Error Prevention – Prevention and proper management of errors by the system and its user, providing ways for them to be consciously corrected.

Accessibility – Clear specification of requirements for the interface with particular attention to the imperative that it should cover the maximum number of users, contexts of use and possible applications, in order to ensure flexibility for users with skill limitations and in situations that impose restrictions or different possibilities of use.

Imperceptible Tutorial – Idea that the users accidentally access information, but, actually, it is an occurrence designed to integrate them into the system and indicate the principles for its use.

Personalization – The interface adapts to the user's needs after an analysis of his behavior and interaction patterns.

Privacy – Concern with the necessary flexibility in the decision by users as to how their privacy and security will be managed.

Multimodality – Option for multimodality of input and output in order to maximize the cognitive and physical capacities, as well as the usage preferences of the various users.

Interaction Starting – The interface initiates the interaction and encourages the users by calling their attention to relevant and timely information, instead of waiting for them to start interaction.

Predictive Interface – The interface tries to predict the user's intention, offers possible results and suggestions that go beyond the user's immediate intentions.

Unpredictability – The interface uses randomness as a way to induce the feeling of randomness expressed through interaction and access to the system from multiple points, without a defined hierarchy.

Automation – Common and repetitive tasks are automated to simplify interaction. Generative potential of the interface is based on flexible rules that cause a certain degree of autonomy, without user interaction.

Visible Information – Quick observation and gathering of information at opportune moments are allowed, increasing the relevance of accessory information placed on the periphery of the interface in the user's focus and at the appropriate time.

Natural Interaction Modalities – The use of sensory channels (actuators) that are natural to the equivalent modes of communication in a human-human or human-environment context and, cumulatively, the procedure for using these sensory channels is developed in a way equivalent to the way they would be developed in this context.

Transparency – Disappearance of the interface, placing the user in direct contact with the information through one or more modes of interaction.

These design requirements seek to promote the development of more affective, effective, simpler and more natural interactions by promoting superior accessibility and usability. This effectiveness is conditioned by numerous variables, namely the characteristics of the content to be transmitted, the sender, the receiver, the input and output mechanisms, the cognition systems (of the human and of the computer), among others.

References

1. Picard, R.W.: Affective Computing. MIT Press, Cambridge (1997)
2. Wiener, N.: The human use of Human Beings: Cybernetics and Society. Houghton Mifflin, Boston (1954)
3. Dutoit, T., Nigay, L., Schnaider, M.: J. Signal Process. **86**(12), 3515–3517 (2006). Special issue on "Multimodal Human-computer Interfaces"
4. Coutaz, J., Caelen, J.: A taxonomy for multimedia and multimodal user interfaces. In: First European Research Consortium for Informatics and Mathematics Workshop on Multi-modal Human-Computer Interaction, Lisbon, Portugal (1991)
5. Besson, P.: A multimodal pattern recognition framework for speaker detection, Ph.D. thesis. École Polytechnique Fédérale de Lausanne, Lausanne, Suisse (2007)
6. DeWitte, A.E.: Investigation of Dynamic Three-dimensional Tangible Touchscreens: Usability and Feasibility. Rochester Institute of Technology, Rochester (2008)
7. Ghazanfar, A.A., Schroeder, C.E.: Is neocortex essentially multisensory? TRENDS in Cogn. Sci. **10**(6), 278–285 (2006)
8. Hall, D.L., Llinas, J.: An introduction to multi-sensor data fusion. In: Proceedings of the 1998 IEEE International Symposium on Circuits and Systems, vol. 6, pp. 6–23. IEEE, Monterey, CA, USA (1998)

9. Dumas, B., Lalanne, D., Oviatt, S.: Multimodal interfaces: a survey of principles, models and frameworks. In: Lalanne, D., Kohlas, J. (eds.) Human Machine Interaction. LNCS, vol. 5440, pp. 3–26. Springer, Heidelberg (2009). https://doi.org/10.1007/978-3-642-00437-7_1

10. Anthony, L., Yang, J., Koedinger, K.R.: Evaluation of multimodal input for entering mathematical equations on the computer. In: van der Veer, G.C., Gale, C. (eds.) CHI 2005 Extended Abstracts on Human Factors in Computing Systems, pp. 1184–1187. ACM, Portland (2005)

11. Tzovaras, D.: Introduction. In: Tzovaras, D. (ed.) Multimodal User Interfaces: from Signals to Interaction, pp. 1–4. Springer, Leipzig, Germany (2008)

12. Landragin, F.: Physical, semantic and pragmatic levels for multimodal fusion and fission. In: Proceedings of the Seventh International Workshop on Computational Semantics (IWCS-7), pp. 346–350. Tilburg, Netherlands (2007)

13. Aran, O., Burger, T., Akarun, L., Caplier, A.: Gestural interfaces for hearing-impaired communication. In: Tzovaras, D. (ed.) Multimodal user interfaces: from signals to interaction, pp. 219–250. Springer, Leipzig, Germany (2008). https://doi.org/10.1007/978-3-540-78345-9_10

14. Blache, P., Bertrand, R., Ferré, G: Creating and exploiting multimodal annotated corpora. In: Proceedings of the Sixth International Conference on Language Resources and Evaluation (LREC 2008), pp. 1773–1777. European Language Resources Association (ELRA), Marrakech (2008)

15. Nigay, L., Coutaz, J.: A design space for multimodal systems. In: B. Arnold (ed.), Proceedings of the INTERACT 1993 and CHI 1993 Conference on Human Factors in Computing Systems, pp. 172–178. ACM, New York (1993)

16. Bourguet, M.-L.: An overview of multimodal interaction techniques and applications. In: Zaphiris, P., Ang, C.S. (eds.) Human Computer Interaction: Concepts, Methodologies, Tools, and Applications, pp. 95–101. Information Science Reference, New York, NY, USA (2009)

17. Martin, J.C., Veldman, R., Béroule, D.: Developing multimodal interfaces: a theoretical framework and guided propagation networks. In: Bunt, H., Beun, R.-J., Borghuis, T. (eds.) CMC 1995. LNCS, vol. 1374, pp. 158–187. Springer, Heidelberg (1998). https://doi.org/10.1007/BFb0052318

18. Ferri, F., Paolozzi, S.: Analyzing multimodal interaction. In: Grifoni, P. (ed.) Multimodal Human Computer Interaction and Pervasive Services, pp. 19–33. IGI Global, Hershey (2009)

19. James, F., Gurram, R.: Multimodal and federated interaction. In: Zaphiris, P., Ang, C.S. (eds.) Human Computer Interaction: Concepts, methodologies, Tools, and Applications, pp. 102–122. Information Science Reference, New York, USA (2009)

20. Oviatt, S., et al.: Designing the user interface for multimodal speech and pen-based gesture applications: state of the art systems and future research directions. Hum.-Comput. Interact. 15(4), 263–322 (2000)

21. Bernsen, N.O.: Modality theory in support of multimodal interface design. In: Hayes-Roth, B., Korf, R.E. (eds.) AAAI Spring Symposium on Intelligent Multi-Modal Systems, pp. 37–44. AAAI Press, Menlo Park (1994)

22. Bernsen, N.O., Dybkjær, L.: CLASS Natural and Multimodal Interactivity Deliverable D1.5+6. Best practice in natural and multimodal interactivity engineering. NISLab, University of Southern Denmark (2003)

23. Maybury, M., Wahlster, W.: Intelligent user interfaces: an introduction. In: Maybury, M., e Wahlster, W. (eds.) Readings in intelligent user interfaces, pp. 1–13. Morgan Kaufmann Publishers, San Francisco (1998)

24. Yin, Y.: Toward an Intelligent Multimodal Interface for Natural Interaction. Thesis submitted to The Massachusetts Institute of Technology for the degree of Master of Sciences, Massachusetts, USA (2010)
25. Norman, D.: Why Interfaces Don't Work. In: Laurel, B. (ed.) The Art of Human-Computer Interface Design, pp. 209–219. Addison-Wesley Professional, Massachusetts (1990)
26. Bolter, J.D., Grusin, R.: Remediation: Understanding New Media. The MIT Press, Cambridge (2000)
27. Draude, C.: Computing Bodies: Gender Codes and Anthropomorphic Design at the Human-Computer Interface. Springer, Kassel, Germany (2017). https://doi.org/10.1007/978-3-658-18660-9

palmScape: Calm and Pleasant Vibrotactile Signals

Sang-Won Shim[1,2] and Hong Z. Tan[1(✉)]

[1] Purdue University, West Lafayette, IN 47907, USA
{shim36, hongtan}@purdue.edu
[2] Samsung Electronics Co., Ltd., Seoul, Korea

Abstract. The goal of the present study was to design vibrotactile signals that support a more engaging and delightful user experience. Using a four-tactor display called *palmScape*, custom-designed signals were created to capture the essence of natural phenomena such as *breathing*, *heartbeat*, and *earthquake*. A key insight was the use of slow motions to convey aliveness in a calm manner. Fourteen participants evaluated twenty vibrotactile signals by providing valence and arousal ratings. Our custom-designed patterns were consistently rated at higher valence levels than reference signals from the literature at similar arousal levels. Eight of the sixteen custom signals occupied the fourth quadrant of the valence-arousal space that corresponds to *calm* and *pleasant* ratings, a space that is rarely occupied by other studies of vibrotactile signals. In this article, we share our design approach, signal parameters, and affective rating results. Our work will hopefully encourage more research on affective haptics.

Keywords: Design · Vibrotactile signals · Tactor array display · Affective rating · Calm · Pleasant · palmScape

1 Introduction

As vibrotactile alert signals become ubiquitous on mobile devices, the question arises as to how to devise alert signals that are rich in meaning, carry natural or intuitive messages and are generally more pleasant than a mere "buzz." In the cases of smartwatches and phones that are mostly worn on the wrist or held in the hand, the device is in frequent if not constant contact with the skin. While a somewhat annoying "buzzing" alert may be effective at getting the user's attention, it is also desirable to provide other options that engage the user in a gentler and richer manner by, for example, using broadband tactors (tactile stimulators) to optimize the sensations for each usage and context.

Studies on vibrotactile alerts tend to focus on its functional benefits (e.g., Fukumoto & Sugimura [1], Gordon and Zhai [2]) or its information contents (e.g., Brown et al. [3], Tan et al. [4]). More recently, many researchers have studied emotional responses to vibrotactile stimulation that imitate human touch. Rantala et al. [5] showed that squeeze-like signals were judged to be unpleasant and high in arousal, and signals that felt like finger touch were found to be pleasant and relaxing. Pradana et al. [6] demonstrated that vibrotactile signals can prime the valence of text messages received

© Springer Nature Switzerland AG 2020
A. Marcus and E. Rosenzweig (Eds.): HCII 2020, LNCS 12200, pp. 532–548, 2020.
https://doi.org/10.1007/978-3-030-49713-2_37

on a mobile device. In general, signals at low intensities tend to lead to neutral valence and most signals at high intensities feel annoying (low valence). It thus appears difficult to design vibrotactile signals that can lead to high valence ratings, especially at low arousal levels, by varying signal amplitude, frequency, duration, rhythm, envelope, etc. (e.g., Seifi and MacLean [7], Yoo et al. [8]). Recently, Culbertson et al. [9] and Huisman et al. [10] have investigated stroking-like signals in an attempt to stimulate the C-fibers to evoke pleasant sensations (see [11]), and Korres et al. [12] created an alarm system for pleasant awakening.

A common characteristic of tactile alert signals is that they feel "buzzy" (although Google has made it a priority to remove buzzing from its Pixel 2 and Pixel 3 phones). A major strategy in creating natural and pleasant tactile sensations is to move away from the typical high-frequency "buzzing" signals and instead use lower frequencies for slow motions, gentle roughness, and flutter sensations. The need for richer haptic displays was well recognized by researchers developing haptic devices for sensory substitution. For example, Leotta et al. [13], Rabinowitz et al. [14] and Reed et al. [15] built an artificial mechanical-face around a plastic skull, Eberhardt et al. [16] built the OMAR system for the hand, and Tan and Rabinowitz [17] and Tan et al. [4] built and tested a multi-finger tactual display. These devices were designed to deliver kinesthetic (large-amplitude, low-frequency) motions, tactile (small-amplitude, high-frequency) vibrations, and the sensations associated with the intermediate frequencies and amplitudes, to one or more digits. Bolanowski et al. [18], Mountcastle et al. [19, 20] and Tan [21] have shown that along the frequency continuum, signals on the order of a few Hertz are perceived as slow motions, those within 10–70 Hz feel fluttery (at small amplitude) or rough (at large amplitude), and those above 150 Hz are perceived as smooth vibrations. The dominant frequency of many natural phenomena, such as breathing (12–20 breaths per minute) and heartbeat (60–100 beats per minute), fall into the low-frequency, slow-motion range of 1.67 Hz or slower. Incorporating signals at very low frequencies into our vibrotactile design is an important strategy of the present work.

Russell [22] proposed the circumplex model for subjective affective ratings which is used by most studies on affective haptics. The higher (or lower) the valence, the more pleasant (or unpleasant) the emotion is. The higher (or lower) the arousal, the more exciting (or calm/relaxing) the signal is perceived to be. While some studies use only positive integers for valence and arousal ratings (e.g., Bradley and Lang [23] and Lang et al. [24] used 1 to 9), others use a symmetric positive/negative scale (e.g., Yoo et al. [8] and Bradley and Lang [25] used −4 to 4). Since affective ratings are relative in nature, ratings along a [1, 9] scale can be converted to a [−4, 4] scale and vice versa. The present study uses the circumplex model for validation of the vibrotactile signals we have designed, and compare our results to the findings from published studies.

The present research asks the question of how to delight a user with calm and pleasant vibrotactile alerts. Our work focuses on vibrotactile stimulation, the most common form of haptic alerts. We use multiple tactors in order to expand the spatial contents of the tactile experience. We choose the palm to be the stimulation site due to the relatively large size of the broadband tactors used in our research and the ease with which one can simply place the palm on the tactor array (Fig. 1). Our goal is to explore the possibility of designing vibrotactile signals that are judged to be in the fourth quadrant of the valence-arousal space – *calm* and *pleasant*.

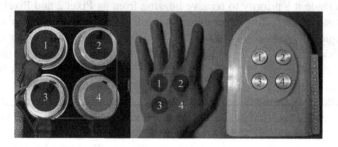

Fig. 1. *palmScape*: (left) the experimental apparatus, (middle) tactor locations under the left palm, and (right) a wireless prototype for demonstration

2 Design Approach

This section outlines the design principles and guidelines that we have followed during the present research. Our work draws inspiration from Cohen et al. [26], Israr et al. [27] and MacLean [28] that outline strategies for designing signals that are explicitly paired with linguistic phrases, and/or associated with natural events, in addition to heuristics. Our signal design follows three design principles and five guidelines, as outlined below.

2.1 Design Principles

I. *Beyond Simple Vibration*

As discussed above, a key strategy of the present research is to introduce low-frequency components into the design of vibrotactile signals to enrich their *expressiveness*. Purely vibrational signals are homogeneous, monotonic, narrow in its expressiveness, and neutral in emotional content. They correspond to a narrow range of sensations we experience in our everyday lives. To overcome the limitations, tactors that move at very low frequencies with sufficient torque are needed to render soft and gentle motions in the z-direction (i.e., perpendicular to the skin) to express deformations and movements such as breathing and heartbeat.

II. *Natural and Delightful*

We are exposed to frequent vibrotactile feedback from smartphones and wearable devices in our daily lives. It is imperative that the vibrotactile feedback on our skin be comfortable, informative and pleasant. To achieve this goal, we take a design approach that is based on natural metaphors to maximize the natural expressiveness of our haptic signals and invite empathy from the users, bringing pleasure and delight to people.

III. *Simple and Distinctive*

We want to achieve simple and distinctive signal patterns that are unique, recognizable and easily learned. By distilling the essence of natural phenomena and simplifying our signals to carry the minimum information required for expressing the physical characteristics of natural events, we can maximize the consensus of users' interpretations of our custom-designed vibrotactile icons. The result is a collection of vibrotactile signals that are easily distinguishable, quickly learned and highly recognizable.

2.2 Design Guidelines

i. *Natural Metaphors*

We sought to understand the physical characteristics of natural phenomena, and designed haptic signals that matched their features. For example, we focused on the *aliveness* of heartbeat, breathing, and pulsation. We applied *randomness* in creating twinkles, bubbles, and raindrops. We incorporated *repeatability* in ripples, cicadas, (horse) galloping, and frog (croaking). For earthquake and thunder, we used *gradualness* to build up or dissipate energy.

ii. *Richness Through Dimensions*

Findings from research on tactile icons (see Azadi and Jones [29], Barralon et al. [30], Brown et al. [31] and MacLean and Enriquez [32]) and tactile speech communication (see Rabinowitz et al. [33] and Tan et al. [4]) have clearly established the use of multiple signal dimensions to enrich the tactile experience. Figure 2 illustrates the progression from a single-point display to a 2-tactor linear display, to a 2-by-2 planar display, and then to our palmScape display that incorporates slow motions along the z-axis.

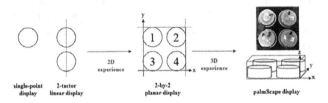

Fig. 2. Expanding the spatial richness of a tactile display from a single-point vibration to a truly 3D experience

In addition to expanding the spatial dimension of a display, we also broadened the use of frequency by (1) lowering the *carrier frequency* (to ≤ 3 Hz) to create slow motions along the z-axis (e.g., breathing), and (2) lowering the *amplitude-modulation frequency* (to ≤ 1 Hz) to express a gradual change of intensity (e.g., earthquake). Figure 3 provides a few examples.

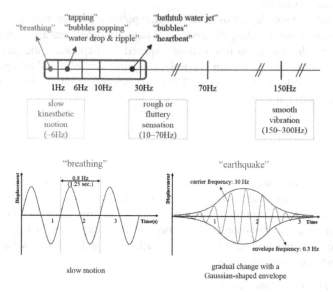

Fig. 3. Top: Illustration of the use of lower frequencies for designing vibrotactile icons. Bottom: Waveforms for "breathing" that evokes the sensation of holding a small puppy in the palm (bottom-left panel), and "earthquake" that conveys a gradual built-up and dissipation of rough, rumbling sensations on the skin (bottom-right panel).

iii. *Parts and Whole*

When dealing with a complex physical phenomenon, we approached the design of vibrotactile icons by dividing one phenomenon into multiple events. The heartbeat signal was created by first identifying the four main events (e.g., expansion of the left atrium) during one cycle of a heartbeat. Then, we found a good representation of each event, and combined them into one composite vibrotactile icon with proper temporal offsets of the four events (Fig. 4).

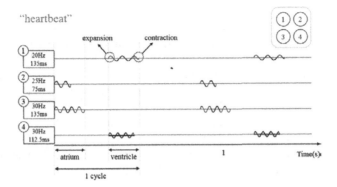

Fig. 4. Illustration of "heartbeat." Shown are the four main events making up a heartbeat and the tactors used to represent each event. The upper-right corner shows tactor numbering.

iv. *Simplicity*

When it comes to designing distinctive and memorable vibrotactile icons, less is more. This is because of factors such as temporal and intensive masking, limited spatial attention span, poor haptic numerosity judgment, and finite temporal-order judgment capability (see Verrillo and Gescheider [34]). Therefore, care should be taken to remove signal components that are redundant, can potentially mask other components, or otherwise do not contribute much to the overall perception. Parameters should be judiciously chosen and used sparingly. For example, the "cicadas" signal consists of a high-pitched 120-Hz background noise with a 32-Hz amplitude modulation for added roughness, and a few bursts of a 60-Hz signal modulated at 2 Hz (Fig. 5). The latter cuts in four times and then fades out.

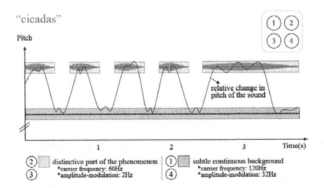

Fig. 5. Illustration of "cicadas"

v. *Randomness*

While some natural phenomena such as heartbeat and breathing carry a regular rhythm, others exhibit a less predictable pattern. When designing the vibrotactile icons for the latter, the multiple parameters making up the haptic signal were varied to represent the randomness of the phenomenon. In the case of a "raindrop" (Fig. 6), for example, the inter-stimulus interval between two adjacent "drops" varied from 70.4 to 316.8 ms, the frequency varied randomly within 80 to 120 Hz, and the stimulation location was randomized among the four tactors (see also Israr et al. [27]). Although we kept the signal amplitude constant, the perceived intensity varied due to frequency variations. We found it important to limit the range of frequency variations in order to create a subtle and natural fluctuation in perceived vibrotactile intensity and pitch.

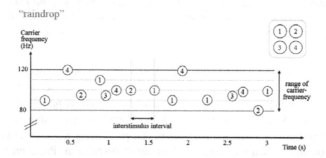

Fig. 6. Illustration of "raindrop"

In addition to the aforementioned design guidelines, we also employed other design considerations. For example, the musical elements of rhythm were used to promote a sense of familiarity with the user. Starting the design process with a sound analysis was found to be conducive to accessing the expression of the vibrotactile phenomenon in a more straightforward manner. We also focused on barely detectable or low-intensity signals to create subtle sensations (e.g., "twinkle"). For "thunder," an intense and short beginning ($\sim$10 ms) led to the feeling of a strong impact. And a satisfying "knock" was achieved with a fast drop ($\sim$5 ms) from its peak amplitude.

3   Custom-Designed Vibrotactile Signals

A total of 16 custom-designed vibrotactile signals were created using the design approach described so far. They were inspired by a wide range of natural phenomena. The parameters for the 16 signals vary along many dimensions in ways that depend on the characteristics of the corresponding natural phenomenon. Table 1 shows the key parameters of the 16 signals (#1–16) and 4 other signals (#17–20, explained in Sect. 4.1, Stimuli, on p.10).

Table 1. The 20 Stimuli used in the present study

No.	Stimulus name	Carrier [Envelope] frequency (Hz)	Expression [applied design guidelines]
1	Breathing	0.8	Extremely slow motion [i, ii]
2	Earthquake	30 [0.3]	Gradualness [i, ii]
3	Heartbeat	20–30	Smooth beating [i, ii, iii]
4	Raindrop	80–120	Subtle pulse [i, v]
5	Elephant trod	20	Deep pounding sensation [i, ii]
6	Tapping	2	Tapping sensation [i, ii]
7	Thunder	30, 135, 150 [0.3]	Strong spatial impact [i, ii, iii]
8	Twinkle	300	Tickling sensation [i, iv, v]
9	Bubbles	20	Soft pushing [i, ii]
10	Water drop & ripple	5–10, 180, 300 [10]	Wavy sensation [i, ii, iii, v]
11	cicadas	60, 120 [0.5, 2, 32]	Roughness [i, ii, iii, iv]
12	Bathtub water jet	10 [0.3]	Medium-soft pushing [i, ii, iv]
13	Frog	50, 120 [1.7, 16]	Roughness [i, ii, iii, iv]
14	(horse) Galloping	3–7, 180, 300	Rhythm/hard tapping [i, ii, iii]
15	Knock	30, 300	Knocking sensation [i, ii]
16	Bubbles popping	2	Slow push/subtle popping [i, ii, iii]
17	*Alarm [12]*	60–200	Co-varying frequency and location
18	*Notification 1 [8]*	300	Strong vibration (1 s, 1.4 g)
19	*Notification 2 [8]*	60	Soft vibration (1 s, 0.12 g)
20	*Notification 2 [8]*	150	Medium vibration (1 s, 0.39 g)

Breathing (#1) is a slow motion in the z-direction with a 2-mm displacement at 0.8 Hz to express the aliveness of a small creature (see Fig. 3). *Earthquake* (#2) is a 30-Hz vibration modulated with a 3.3-s Gaussian-shaped envelope to convey a gradual build-up and dissipation of energy (see Fig. 3). *Heartbeat* (#3) consists of pumping-like 20-30 Hz vibrotactile pulses corresponding to the contractions of the four chambers of the human heart (Fig. 4). *Raindrop* (#4) expresses the feeling of a sprinkle of rain with infrequent and sporadic gentle pulses (Fig. 6). *Elephant trod* (#5) is a 20-Hz vibration delivered to all 4 tactors simultaneously to express a deep pounding effect. *Tapping* (#6) consists of a carrier frequency of 2 Hz with a rapidly-falling envelope from its peak amplitude for the tapping sensation. *Thunder* (#7) stresses the initial impact from rumbling and lightning using 135-Hz and 150-Hz vibrations at high amplitudes, then attenuates the signal amplitude gradually following a 3.3-s Gaussian-shaped envelope. *Twinkle* (#8) expresses the feeling of small particles spreading in space with 300-Hz vibrotactile pulses at low intensities at random tactor locations. *Bubbles* (#9) delivers the sensation of bubbles rising from a water surface with soft 20-Hz vibrations at varying tactor locations. *Water drop & ripple* (#10) mimics a water droplet hitting a water surface, resulting in waves that expand spatially. It starts with a gentle 180-Hz pulse on tactors #1 and #4 for "water drop," followed by 5-Hz or 10-Hz "ripples" delivered to all four tactors. *Cicadas* (#11) expresses the roughness of crying cicadas, as illustrated in Fig. 5. *Bathtub water jet* (#12) is a 10-Hz vibration with a 0.3-Hz amplitude modulation delivered randomly to one of the tactors. It simulates a continuous water flow with soft and variable pressure on the palm. *Frog* (#13) uses two superimposed frequencies of 50 and 120 Hz with amplitude modulations at 1.7 Hz and 16 Hz to characterize the croaking sound and the movement of the frog's vocal sac. *Galloping* (#14) consists of multiple carrier frequencies at 3, 5, 7, 180, and 300 Hz to express rhythmic, rigid tapping on the ground. *Knock* (#15) contains short vibrotactile pulses with superimposed components at 30 Hz and 300 Hz to realize the feel of knocking by knuckles. *Bubbles popping* (#16) uses a 2-Hz vibration with a fast-decaying amplitude to represent slow pushing and popping.

4 Affective Rating Experiment

To assess the emotional response to our custom-designed vibrotactile signals, an affective rating experiment was conducted based on Russell's circumplex model of affect [22].

4.1 Methods

Participants. Fourteen participants (P01–P14; 7 males and 7 females; age range 19–38 years old, average age 24.4 ± 4.4 years old) took part in the affective rating experiment. All but one (P12) are right handed. None had known sensory or motor impairments with their hands. Three of the participants are native English speakers and the others speak English fluently as a second language. All reported prior haptic experience with smart phones, game consoles and controllers, smart watches, electric toothbrushes, or massage devices. Each participant signed an IRB-approved informed consent form, and received 15 USD in compensation of their time.

Apparatus. The *palmScape* device consists of a 2-by-2 tactor array placed on a round plate filled with silicone rubber (see left panel of Fig. 1). The tactors (Tectonic Elements, Model TEAX13C02-8/RH) are wide-bandwidth speakers with a constant impedance of 8 Ω in the frequency range of 50 to 2,000 Hz, except for a peak near 600 Hz. Each tactor measures about 30 mm in diameter and 9 mm in thickness. A MATLAB program generated four independent waveforms that were synchronously converted to four analog audio signals by a MOTU 24Ao device. The signals were then amplified to drive the four tactors, respectively. We verified with an accelerometer (Kistler 8794A500) that the tactor responses followed the signal waveforms from about 300 Hz down to <1 Hz.

Calibration and Equalization of Intensity. Prior to the main experiment, the detection threshold for each participant was estimated and the perceived intensities of the four tactors were equalized. Individual detection thresholds were measured at 150 Hz for tactor #4 under the left thenar eminence (Fig. 1, middle panel). The detection thresholds were measured using a three-interval, two-alternative, one-up two-down adaptive forced-choice procedure with trial-by-trial correct-answer feedback (see Jones and Tan [35]). The vibration was presented with equal *a priori* probability in one of three temporal intervals, and no signal was presented during the remaining two intervals. Each interval was cued visually on a computer monitor. The participant's task was to identify the interval containing the vibration. The level of the vibration was adjusted adaptively using the one-up, two-down rule to estimate the stimulus level required for 70.7% correct detection. Each time the participant made a mistake with the response, the vibration level was increased (i.e., one-up). After two consecutive correct responses from the participant, the vibration level was decreased (i.e., two-down). The adaptive procedure is an efficient way to place vibration levels near detection thresholds on most of the trials.

The perceived intensity of the four tactors was equalized using a method of adjustment (see Jones and Tan [35]). The reference vibration was played on tactor #4. The level of each of the three remaining tactors was then adjusted by the participant so that its strength matched that of the reference tactor. This continued until the participant was satisfied that the reference and test signals were at equal perceived intensity. The results were saved in a level-adjustment table for each participant.

The results from the two steps were used to ensure that the perceived signal intensities, defined in dB above individual detection thresholds, were similar for each participant.

Stimuli. The stimuli included the 16 custom-designed vibrotactile signals (#1–16) and 4 reference signals (#17–20), for a total of 20 stimuli (see listing in Table 1). The reference signals were selected from two earlier studies by Korres et al. [12] and Yoo et al. [8]. Signal #17 was modified from a vibrotactile alarm signal that was rated as the most pleasant (highest valence) in Korres et al.'s study [12]. It consisted of six 300-ms long pulses with a 120-ms overlap that moved over the tactors while the magnitude increased from 0.25 to 1.25 g and the frequency co-varied from 60 to 200 Hz. Signals #18 to #20 were the same as the three signals in Yoo et al.'s study [8] associated with the highest valence ratings at the highest intensity (300-Hz, 1000-ms at 1.4 g), the lowest intensity (60-Hz, 1000-ms at 0.12 g) and an intermediate intensity (150-Hz, 1000-ms at 0.39 g), respectively. The valence and arousal ratings for signal #20 were located in a neutral region near the origin of the valence-arousal space as reported by Yoo et al. [8].

4.2 Procedures

The participants were asked to place their left palm gently on *palmScape* with tactor #4 right under the thenar eminence and the other three tactors covered by the palm (Fig. 7). The participants were asked to maintain a light contact and avoid pressing down too hard on the tactors. They were introduced to the graphic icons adopted from Bradley and Lang [25] and the 9-point integer scale marked under the icons (see Fig. 8). The experimenter then explained the circumplex model, and asked the participants to familiarize themselves with two example stimuli: one at a high intensity and roughness (250-Hz carrier, 32-Hz

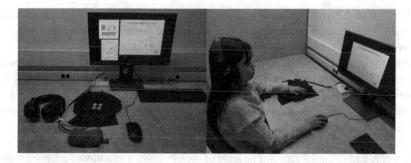

Fig. 7. Experimental setup: (left) noise-reduction headset, the *palmScape* display, elbow support, computer monitor, and mouse; (right) a participant in the middle of the affective rating experiment.

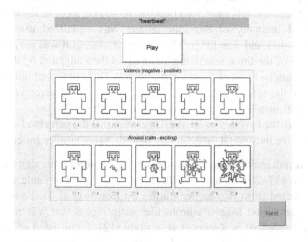

Fig. 8. Computer screen as seen by the participants

amplitude modulation envelope, 1000-ms duration, peak at 4.19 g) and the other at a lower intensity (25-Hz carrier, no modulation, 25-ms duration, peak at 1.17 g).

The main task required the participants to rate the valence and arousal of the 20 vibrotactile signals using integers between 1 and 9. Each signal was presented 5 times, and the signal sequence was randomized for each participant. On each trial, the participant saw the text label for the vibrotactile signal presented, felt the signal, and entered the two integers corresponding to the perceived valence and arousal of the signal (Fig. 8). The participant completed 4 blocks of 25 trials, with a 3-min mandatory break between the blocks to prevent fatigue. The affective rating experiment lasted between 19 min to 55 min per participant.

5 Results and Discussion

The affective ratings for all stimuli are shown in Fig. 9 as filled dots for the custom-designed signals #1–16 and filled squares for the reference signals #17–20. The position of each filled dot or square corresponds to the (valence, arousal) coordinates averaged over all 70 pairs of ratings (14 participants × 5 rating pairs per stimulus). The boxed number next to each filled symbol corresponds to the stimulus number as listed in Table 1. The two blue lines connect the 4 reference signals #17–20. Across the 14 participants, the standard deviations of valence ratings for the 20 stimuli (not shown) ranged from 1.1 to 2.3 with a mean of 1.7. The standard deviations of arousal ratings (not shown) ranged from 1.1 to 1.8 with a mean of 1.4.

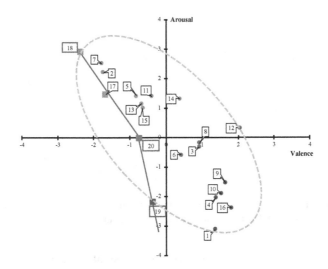

Fig. 9. Experimental results from the present study. The yellow ellipse encloses all data points. (Color figure online)

Three observations can be made from Fig. 9. When appropriate, we compare our results to the studies by Wilson and Brewster [36] and Yoo et al. [8] that used sinusoidal vibrations that varied in amplitude, frequency, duration and modulation envelope (only Yoo et al. used modulation [8]). In contrast, the present study employed complex and custom-designed waveforms. Firstly, 8 out of the 16 signals in the present study successfully landed in the fourth quadrant that corresponds to signals that are *calm* and *pleasant*. In comparison, 4 to 6 signals out of 18 from Wilson and Brewster [36] had affective ratings in the fourth quadrant (2 of the signals were near the origin of the valence-arousal space). Seven (7) out of 85 signals in Yoo et al. [8] were in the fourth quadrant.

Secondly, the 20 filled symbols cluster around a line with a slope of −1, indicating a negative correlation of valence and arousal ratings from the present study. The signals with higher arousal levels tend to be perceived as less pleasant, and those with lower arousal levels more pleasant. The affective ratings from Wilson and Brewster [36] show a similar trend of clustering around a line of negative slope. However, the data from Yoo et al. [8], reproduced in Fig. 10 below, show a very different pattern. The three red circles show the valence-arousal coordinates of signals #18–20 obtained in Yoo et al. [8]. At low arousal levels, the range of valence is quite small. At high arousal levels, valence ratings skew slightly towards the negative values.

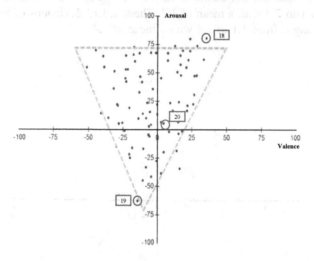

Fig. 10. Results from Yoo et al. [8], redrawn to show all the affective ratings and the (yellow) triangle enclosing most of the data points. (Color figure online)

Thirdly, it can be seen in Fig. 9 that given similar arousal ratings, the four reference signals received the lowest valence ratings. The four colors of the filled symbols encode the four stimulus groups according to the arousal ratings of the four reference signals: purple = low arousal (#19); green = medium arousal (#20); orange = medium-high arousal (#17); and blue = high arousal (#18). The 16 stimuli designed in the present study all felt more pleasant than the reference signals. The differences in valence ratings between the filled dots and the filled square in each color group are shown in Fig. 11 below. Our custom-designed signals were rated more positively along the valence axis by an overall average of 1.41 when compared to the data from Korres et al. [12] and Yoo et al. [8]. The averages according to color groups were, in descending orders, 1.91 (purple), 1.82 (green), 1.01 (orange), and 0.31 (blue).

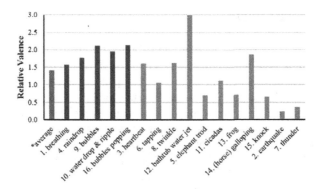

Fig. 11. Increase in valence ratings for stimuli #1–16 as compared to the reference stimuli #17–20 at similar arousal ratings, calculated from the blue lines in Fig. 9. (Color figure online)

The signals that are most calm (low arousal) and pleasant (high valence) are the purple filled dots. They consist of signal #1 (breathing), #4 (raindrops), #9 (bubbles), #10 (water drop & ripple) and #16 (bubbles popping). These signals all contain some form of slow motions except for #4, confirming our design approach of using slow motions to achieve calm and pleasant vibrotactile icons. Among the green-filled dots, #12 (bathtub water jet) has the highest valence rating, followed by #3 (heartbeat) and #8 (twinkle). Again, #3 and #12 contain low-frequency movements. Stimuli #4 (raindrops) and #8 (twinkle) are both light and slightly irregular, another winning combination for a delightful vibrotactile experience.

Note that we used text labels for the natural phenomena corresponding to our custom-designed vibrotactile icons during the experiment. Unlike the study by Yoo et al. [8] where signal parameters for vibrotactile stimuli were systematically varied and the resultant signals were rated by the participants without additional cues, the vibrotactile signals in the present study were inspired by the natural phenomena that they represent. Therefore, we provided our participants with text labels to set the proper context for the interpretation of the vibrotactile signals. This approach allowed us to explore a broader range of emotions through custom-designed vibrotactile feedback with spatial representation to engage users in an authentic and natural experience. Our daily experience is always multisensory and multimodal, and sensory signals presented in isolation can be difficult to interpret without a context. Our approach is similar to the selection of auditory ring tones on mobile and handheld devices. We first select a word or phrase from a list, listen to the auditory alert associated with it, and then select the best ring tone. The word or phrase serve to set the context for the ring tones so they can be remembered and recognized later. We envision the vibrotactile icons developed in the present study to be used in a similar manner in the future.

Anecdotal comments collected after the experiment through a debriefing questionnaire indicated that most participants found the text labels and the respective vibrotactile signals to match well except for two cases. Two participants found a weak connection between "frog" and the signal it represents, and another two participants preferred the "earthquake" signal to be stronger.

6 Concluding Remarks

The present research set out to broaden the expressive range of vibrotactile icons by creating a more realistic and natural vibrotactile experience. We believe that users of mobile devices will be more receptive to calm and pleasant alerts that engage the user in a gentler manner. This will help reduce "buzzing" and the stress associated with the constant reminder and alerts from our daily living. As smaller actuators with wide bandwidth become available, multiple tactors can be installed in game controllers, computer mice, mobile phones, tablets, arm bands, wrist bands, and even smart watches. Users of the devices will be able to select a tacton (tactile icon) from a list, just like we are able to choose a ring tone from a pull-down menu. We envision a day when people shop for handheld and mobile devices for their delightful haptic effects, and calm and pleasant haptic alerts become an integral part of our digital life.

The most significant finding of the present study is that we succeeded in creating eight vibrotactile stimuli that reside in the fourth quadrant of the valence-arousal space, a region that has rarely been occupied by similar attempts before (although see Wilson and Brewster [36] and Yoo et al. [8]). These signals often brought a smile to the person experiencing it for the first time. Some signals such as #12 (bathtub water jet) helped people relax. Others, for example, #1 (breathing), were "controversial." Some people loved the signal because it made them think of their favorite pets, and others found it "creepy" because it felt eerily alive even though it was relatively low in arousal ratings. The anecdotal notes are good indications that the emotional responses to some of our signals are visceral, and not based merely on the text labels or arbitrary and abstract mapping of signals and their meanings.

Our experimental results validated our design approach based on natural and familiar physical phenomena. It appears that systematically varying the parameters that make up a sinusoidal waveform may not be sufficient for creating pleasant-feeling signals (although it is difficult to directly compare the affective ratings from different experiments due to the relative nature of the ratings). In the future, we will compare the affective ratings of the same twenty custom-designed vibrotactile signals with or without text labels to investigate the effect of text labels on our vibrotactile stimulus set. Then, we will expand the range of affect that can be expressed with vibrotactile signals through further design exercises. We will also explore the affective ratings of vibro-tactile patterns designed with one or two tactors to be more compatible with the requirements of mobile and handheld devices.

Acknowledgements. This research was partly funded by Samsung Electronics Co., Ltd. and tangerineX LLC. The authors thank Gina Clepper for comments on an earlier manuscript.

References

1. Fukumoto, M., Sugimura, T.: Active click: tactile feedback for touch panels. In: Proceedings of CHI 2001 (Extended Abstracts), pp. 121–122 (2001)
2. Gordon, M.L., Zhai, S.: Touchscreen haptic augmentation effects on tapping, drag and drop, and path following. In: Proceedings of CHI 2019, vol. 373 (2019)

3. Brown, L.M., Brewster, S.A., Purchase, H.C.: Tactile crescendos and sforzandos: applying musical techniques to tactile icon design. In: CHI 2006 Extended Abstracts on Human Factors in Computing Systems, pp. 610–615 (2006)
4. Tan, H.Z., Durlach, N.I., Reed, C.M., Rabinowitz, W.M.: Information transmission with a multifinger tactual display. Percept. Psychophys. **61**(6), 993–1008 (1999). https://doi.org/10. 3758/BF03207608
5. Rantala, J., Salminen, K., Raisamo, R., Surakka, V.: Touch gestures in communicating emotional intention via vibrotactile stimulation. Int. J. Hum. Comput. Stud. **71**(6), 679–690 (2013)
6. Pradana, G.A., Cheok, A.D., Inami, M., Tewell, J., Choi, Y.: Emotional priming of mobile text messages with ring-shaped wearable device using color lighting and tactile expressions. In: Proceedings of the 5th Augmented Human International Conference (AH 2014), Article no. 14 (2014)
7. Seifi, H., MacLean, K.E.: A first look at individuals' affective ratings of vibrations. In: Proceedings of the IEEE World Haptics Conference, pp. 605–610 (2013)
8. Yoo, Y., Yoo, T., Kong, J., Choi, S.: Emotional responses of tactile icons: Effects of amplitude, frequency, duration, and envelope. In: Proceedings of the IEEE World Haptics Conference, pp. 235–240 (2015)
9. Culbertson, H., Nunez, C.M., Israr, A., Lau, F., Abnousi, F., Okamura, A.M.: A social haptic device to create continuous lateral motion using sequential normal indentation. In: Proceedings of IEEE Haptics Symposium (HAPTICS 2018), pp. 32–39 (2018)
10. Huisman, G., Frederiks, A.D., van Erp, J.B., Heylen, D.K.: Simulating affective touch: using a vibrotactile array to generate pleasant stroking sensations. In: Bello, F., Kajimoto, H., Visell, Y. (eds.) EuroHaptics 2016. LNCS, vol. 9775, pp. 240–250. Springer, Cham (2016). https://doi.org/10.1007/978-3-319-42324-1_24
11. Liljencrantz, J., Olausson, H.: Tactile C fibers and their contributions to pleasant sensations and to tactile allodynia. Front. Behav. Neurosci. **8**(37), 1–6 (2014)
12. Korres, G., Jensen, C.B.F., Park, W., Bartsch, C., Eid, M.: A vibrotactile alarm system for pleasant awakening. IEEE Trans. Haptics **11**(3), 357–366 (2018)
13. Leotta, D.F., Rabinowitz, W.M., Reed, C.M., Durlach, N.I.: Preliminary results of speech-reception tests obtained with the synthetic Tadoma system. J. Rehabil. Res. Dev. **25**(4), 45–52 (1988)
14. Rabinowitz, W.M., Henderson, D.R., Reed, C.M., Delhorne, L.A., Durlach, N.I.: Continuing evaluation of a synthetic Tadoma system. J. Acoust. Soc. Am. **87**(1), 88 (1990)
15. Reed, C.M., Rabinowitz, W.M., Durlach, N.I., Braida, L.D., Conway-Fithian, S., Schultz, M.C.: Research on the Tadoma method of speech communication. J. Acoust. Soc. Am. **77** (1), 247–257 (1985)
16. Eberhardt, S.P., Bernstein, L.E., Barac-Cikoja, D., Coulter, D.C., Jordan, J.: Inducing dynamic haptic perception by the hand: system description and some results. In: Radcliffe, C.J. (ed.) Proceedings of the ASME Dynamic Systems and Control Division, pp. 345–351 (1994)
17. Tan, H.Z., Rabinowitz, W.M.: A new multi-finger tactual display. Proc. Haptics Symp. **58**, 515–522 (1996)
18. Bolanowski Jr., S.J., Gescheider, G.A., Verrillo, R.T., Checkosky, C.M.: Four channels mediate the mechanical aspects of touch. J. Acoust. Soc. Am. **84**(5), 1680–1694 (1988)
19. Mountcastle, V.B., Talbot, W.H., Darian-Smith, I., Kornhuber, H.H.: Neural basis of the sense of flutter-vibration. Science **155**(3762), 597–600 (1967)
20. Mountcastle, V.B., Talbot, W.H., Sakata, H., Hyvarinen, J.: Cortical neuronal mechanisms in flutter-vibration studied in unanesthetized monkeys: neuronal periodicity and frequency discrimination. J. Neurophysiol. **32**, 452–484 (1969)

21. Tan, H.Z.: Information Transmission with a Multi-Finger Tactual Display. Ph.D. dissertation, Department of Electrical Engineering and Computer Science, Massachusetts Institute of Technology, Cambridge, MA (1996)
22. Russell, J.A.: A circumplex model of affect. J. Pers. Soc. Psychol. **39**(6), 1161–1178 (1980)
23. Bradley, M.M., Lang, P.J.: The international affective digitized sounds (IADS-2): affective ratings of sounds and instruction manual. In: Technical Report B-3, University of Florida, Gainesville, FL (2007)
24. Lang, P.J., Bradley, M.M., Cuthbert, B.N.: International affective picture system (IAPS): affective ratings of pictures and instruction manual. In: Technica Report A-8, University of Florida, Gainesville, FL (2008)
25. Bradley, M.M., Lang, P.M.: Measuring emotion: the self-assessment manikin and the semantic differential. J. Behav. Ther. Exp. Psychiatry **25**(1), 49–59 (1994)
26. Cohen, D.J., Barker, K.A., White, M.R.: A standardized list of affect-related life events. Behav. Res. Methods **50**(5), 1806–1815 (2018)
27. Israr, A., Zhao, S., Schwalje, K., Klatzky, R., Lehman, J.: Feel effects Enriching storytelling with haptic feedback. ACM Trans. Appl. Percept. **11**(3), 1–17 (2014)
28. MacLean, K.E.: Foundations of transparency in tactile information design. IEEE Trans on Haptics **1**(2), 84–95 (2008)
29. Azadi, M., Jones, L.A.: Evaluating vibrotactile dimensions for the design of tactons. IEEE Trans. Haptics **7**(1), 14–23 (2014)
30. Barralon, P., Ng, G., Dumont, G., Schwarz, S.K.W., Ansermino, M.: Development and evaluation of multidimensional tactons for a wearable tactile display. In: Proceedings of the International Conference on Human Computer Interaction with Mobile Devices and Services (MobileHCI), pp. 186–189 (2007)
31. Brown, L.M., Brewster, S.A., Purchase, H.C.: Multidimensional tactons for non-visual information presentation in mobile devices. In: Proceedings of the Eighth Conference on Human-Computer Interaction with Mobile Devices and Services, pp. 231–238 (2006)
32. MacLean, K.E., Enriquez, M.: Perceptual design of haptic icons. Proc. EuroHaptics **2003**, 351–362 (2003)
33. Rabinowitz, W.M., Houtsma, A.J.M., Durlach, N.I., Delhorne, L.A.: Multidimensional tactile displays: identification of vibratory intensity, frequency, and contactor area. J. Acoust. Soc. Am. **82**(4), 1243–1252 (1987)
34. Verrillo, R.T., Gescheider, G.A.: Perception via the sense of touch (Chap. 1). In: Summers, I. R. (ed.) Tactile Aids for the Hearing Impaired, pp. 1–36. Whurr Publishers, London (1992)
35. Jones, L.A., Tan, H.Z.: Application of psychophysical techniques to haptic research. IEEE Trans. Haptics **6**(3), 268–284 (2013)
36. Wilson, G., Brewster, S.A.: Multi-moji: combining thermal, vibrotactile & visual stimuli to expand the affective range of feedback. In: Proceedings of the 2017 CHI Conference on Human actors in Computing Systems, vol. 17, pp. 1743–1755 (2017)

Visualizing a User's Cognitive and Emotional Journeys: A Fintech Case

Marianne Veilleux[1]([✉]), Sylvain Sénécal[1], Bertrand Demolin[1],
Frédérique Bouvier[1], Marie-Laure Di Fabio[2],
Constantinos Coursaris[1], and Pierre-Majorique Léger[1]

[1] HEC Montréal, Montréal H3T 2A7, Canada
marianne.veilleux@hec.ca
[2] Mouvement Desjardins, Montréal H5B 1B4, Canada

Abstract. In this article, we propose a visualization approach that presents the user's cognitive and emotional states in conjunction with the actual journey of the user on a web interface. Specifically, we have designed a new visualization method which contextualizes the user's physiological and behavioral data while interacting with a web-based information system in the financial services industry. The proposed approach brings together the user's behavior with his/her cognitive and emotional states to produce a rich overview of his/her experience. Combining these methods produces key insights into the user experience and facilitates an understanding of the evolution of the experience since it highlights where the user was on the interface when s/he experienced a given cognitive and emotional state. Results from an illustrative case suggest that the proposed visualization method is useful in conveying where participants deviate from the optimal path and facilitates the identification of usability issues on web interfaces.

Keywords: Interface design · Web design · Cognitive effort · Affective responses · Consumer behavior

1 Introduction

Customer experience (CX) has become a central concept for many businesses. Experience became a critical element when purchasing a product or service [1, 2]. Hence, creating positive experiences allows brands to attract and retain customers [3]. The measurement of customer experience plays a key role in making insights actionable for firms and helps them remain competitive. Practitioners and academics have developed several tools and methods to understand and manage the customer experience [4]. These tools and methods focus mainly on the development of visualization and prototyping techniques as well as the implementation of measurement tools [4, 5]. The practice of CX management is characterized by the processes used to monitor and organize the series of interactions between the organization and its customers. Thus, visualization and prototyping methods allow to identify key moments of the customer experience that, once addressed, will provide a more valuable global experience.

© Springer Nature Switzerland AG 2020
A. Marcus and E. Rosenzweig (Eds.): HCII 2020, LNCS 12200, pp. 549–566, 2020.
https://doi.org/10.1007/978-3-030-49713-2_38

Customer journey mapping [6, 7], service blueprinting [8, 9] and customer experience mapping [10] are among the most frequently used visualization methods. These techniques are used to visualize and structure the process that the consumer works through during their interaction with the firm [8]. Most studies use the service blueprint methodology, and few go beyond this approach in order to analyze the customer journey [8, 11, 12]. There is a need to improve customer experience measurement tools by focusing on qualitative techniques, such as narrative data collection, to seek more detailed insights [13]. All in all, progress is needed in customer journey mapping in order to identify key opportunities to influence customer experience.

By deepening the understanding of the customer experience, it strengthens the understanding of overall customer satisfaction. New technologies and data represent interesting assets to be integrated in the mapping process. Researchers have begun to incorporate neuroscientific measures (e.g., emotions and cognitive load) in order to track more precisely concurrent measures of customer experience [14–16]. Scholars and practitioners commonly agree that the customer experience includes cognitive, emotional, behavioral, sensorial, and social dimensions [17–19]. Measures such as biometrics, eye tracking and Electrocardiography (ECG) help to better understand how the customer experience is formed and the series of events that led to the overall level of satisfaction [14]. By understanding how affective and cognitive variables influence the customer in his/her journey, it contributes to identifying key drivers to overall customer satisfaction. Our study aims to propose an approach that presents, in conjunction with the actual journey of a user on a web interface, his/her implicit cognitive and emotional states along this journey. Users can deviate from the predicted path, and identifying these deviations can help select the source of intervention or influence needed on a given interface to prevent users from deviating [11]. To illustrate the relevance of the developed method, we present a methodology based on a case study of a given task and the results obtained using the visualization technique. The proposed method is discussed and validated by a group of User Experience (UX) experts to ensure its relevance and usefulness.

2   Literature Review

2.1   The Customer Journey

The analysis of a customer's journey was first used in the areas of service management and multichannel management [8, 20]. Customer journeys are the most popular visualization techniques within the domain of service design [21]. It refers to a series of events that the consumer goes through in order to be informed, to buy or to interact with a given organization [22]. It is a visual and chronological representation of the events experienced by the user [23]. The purpose of such approach is to simulate a "walk in the customer's shoes" [24]. The customer journey analysis allows to identify critical touch points throughout the customer journey that have the most significant impact on customer outcomes [11, 25]. The goal of such technique is to improve customer interaction by enhancing each touch point between the customer and the organization. A study by Lemon & Verhoed [11] states that the understanding the customer journey leads to better insights about the customer experience. Indeed, the customer experience encompasses the customer journey with a given organization over time through multiple touch points [11]. Thus, the customer journey approach allows analyzing the touchpoints between the organizations and its customers.

Customer journey mapping (CJM) is among the most frequently used visualization methods of the customer experience [6, 7]. This method is a visual representation of the customer experience using a given service [5, 26]. This map is a consolidated overview of all sequences of events through which customers must pass through to complete their purchase [12]. CJM establishes all touch points between the firm and its customer during a given purchasing process. The aim of such technique is to improve the quality of the overall customer experience by improving the customer experience associated with each touch point [12]. Mapping the customer experience offers information from the customer's perspective and represents a great way toward operational improvements [27].

Mapping is a commonly used tool in the service design methodology [26]. However, A study by Rosenbaum [12] mentions that CJM assumes that all customers of a given organization experience the same touch points and assigns the same importance to each of these touch points. Hence, the understanding of the participants' overall experience does not necessarily reflect discreet experiences with specific phases, events, or activities. Currently, there is a lack of methods that combine the users' behaviors with their affective and cognitive states. To date, some studies have incorporated neuroscientific data into the analysis of the customer journey in order to have a richer understanding [14–16].

2.2   Measuring Emotional and Cognitive Responses

Psychophysiological data are physical signals measured in real time, which are generated due to psychological changes [28]. These measures allow researchers to assess the user's reaction to a specific stimulus [29]. Several tools are available to measure psychophysiological measures, such as electrocardiography (ECG), skin-based measures including electrodermal activity (EDA), ocular measures, brain measures including electroencephalogram (EEG), respiration rates, and blood pressure (Charles & Nixon [79]). Furthermore, psychophysiological measures are unobtrusive, which allows collecting data about the user's experience without affecting their decision-making [28, 30–32]. These measures therefore allow for more natural reactions from the user while also offering uninterrupted reports of emotions [31, 33, 34]. The advantage of having an uninterrupted report of emotions is that it gives access to the unconscious emotional reactions of users [35]. Indeed, research has shown that interrupting users while they are completing a task often leads to biased results [34, 36–38]. Psychophysiological measures offer a more complete view of the human-computer interaction and allow to assess events of cognitive and emotional relevance to the users [39–42].

In the UX literature, emotions are often defined according to two complementary dimensions, namely valence and arousal [43, 44]. The circumplex model of affect is a very popular dimensional approach to defining several emotional states according to these two psychophysiological constructs [45]. In addition, valence varies from pleasure to displeasure [30, 46, 47], which is equivalent to a variation from positive to negative emotions [48, 49]. Valence can be defined as "what a user feels" and the most reliable way to measure such constructs is with facial coding [50]. Individuals tend to express their emotions with micro-movements of the facial muscles [51]. Arousal is the second and complementary dimension to the circumplex model of affect. This construct refers to "level of arousal which ranges from calm to excited" [46, 49]. Thus, psychophysiological measures translate emotions into measurable constructs.

Moreover, cognition, which refers to the process of reasoning and the mental effort required to understand and complete a given task [52] is also a measurable physiological construct [53]. Several studies have shown that pupil dilation is a significant measure of cognitive load [54–59]. Indeed, the degree of the pupil's dilation correlates with the workload of the task [54]. Hence, pupil size offers an immediate measure of cognitive effort.

A study by Gentile et al. (2007) suggests that customers interpret information from the interface from a cognitive and affective point of view which leads to a personal impression of the given website. Epstein's Cognitive Experiential Self-Theory (CEST) suggests that there are two systems which operate in parallel when exposed to a stimulus event. These two systems are affective and cognitive. Thus, combining cognitive and emotional measures provides a comprehensive understanding of the user's experience. The customer journey map illustrates every touchpoint the consumer has with the company in order to complete a given task [60]. Hence, by adding affective and cognitive measures to the customer journey, it allows UX researchers to identify critical interface elements influencing the user's journey. Thus, the convergence of these three perspectives (i.e., emotions, cognition and behavior) affords a complete view, which few methods allow for [61]. Therefore, we pose the following proposition:

P1: Enriching customer journey visualizations with information about the cognitive and emotional states of the user facilitates the identification of critical touch points shaping customer experience.

3 Method

The study is presented in two phases and consists of a collection of user tests and a focus group. The user tests were performed to collect data for the purpose of developing an illustrative case of the customer experience of all users. The focus group was conducted to validate the research proposal. First, we collected psychophysiological data about each user's experience in order to track their cognitive and emotional responses during an e-commerce interaction. The goal was to develop a method which triangulates behavioral data with psychophysiological data in order to gain key insights into the user journey and to produce a complete overview of the user's experience. Thus, we present a new visualization method that contextualizes the user's physiological and behavioral data while interacting with a web-based information system in the financial services industry, an example of FinTech. We illustrate the methodology by presenting in detail one task and the results obtained using the visualization method. Second, the new visualization method is reviewed by a group of experts in order to confirm whether it enriches contemporary understanding of critical touch points shaping customer experience, and therefore offers support for the research proposition.

Phase 1

3.1 Participants

A total of 38 participants (42% female) were recruited in this study and their age ranged from 23 to 62 years old. Prior to the study, participants were asked to rate the financial institution on the Net Promoter Score (NPS) Scale [62]. NPS is a one-question metric used to assess a customer's overall perception of a brand using a Likert scale from 0 to 10, with 0 being not at all likely to recommend the brand, and 10 being extremely likely to. To reduce the potential influence of brand equity (either extremely high or low) on the participants' experience, only participants who rated the financial institution between a score of 3 to 8 were invited to participate in our study. Each participant received a moderate financial compensation to participate. To participate, users needed normal vision and were screened-out for glasses, laser eye surgery, astigmatism, epilepsy, neurological and psychiatric diagnoses.

3.2 User Test Procedure

The test sessions took place in a university usability laboratory based on standard practice for UX enriched with psychophysiological measures [63]. Upon arrival, participants were asked to complete a consent form, after which they were informed about the purpose of the study and fitted with physiological sensors. Participants were told that their participation was requested in order to evaluate a financial website. Each key segment of the financial institution (e.g., early retirees, midlife adults, youth, and entrepreneurs) was assigned a set of tasks specific to their group. To control the task type, each participant was assigned to a total of nine tasks completed frequently on the website. The nine tasks were grouped evenly into three main categories representing frequent actions taken by users: searching for specific information on the website, using a tool to find answers, and find ways to contact the financial institution. This approach minimizes the effect of the task type by having a varied number of different tasks. Participants were asked to complete tasks for which an optimal navigation path was first established by the authors vis-à-vis the smallest number of clicks necessary to complete a task.

3.3 Measures

For the user test, data were collected using a variety of non-intrusive tools. Behavioral data were captured from the recording of the screen interface allowing the user's actions to be monitored. A Tobii X-60 eye-tracker (Stockholm, Sweden) sampled at 60 Hz was used to capture participant eye movements and Tobii Studio was used to record the experience. The screen recording along with the eye-tracking device allows having the user's perspective by identifying precisely where the participant was looking at every second [64]. Moreover, pupil size measurement allowed for tracking each user's cognitive load [65, 66]. Arousal was measured using electrodermal activity (EDA) [46, 67, 68] with the AcqKnowledge software at MP150 sampled at 500 Hz (BIOPAC, Goleta, USA). EDA represents an indication of the variation of physiological arousal [69]. In fact, it measures the skin conductance, which measures current flow between two points of skin contact after an electrical potential has been applied to them [68]. Hence, it indicates cognitive and emotional stimulation throughout the experience [70]. Furthermore, valence was measured using facial expressions [51, 71] performed with the FaceReaderTM Software (Noldus, Wageningen, Netherlands). Indeed, this tool is used to observe facial reaction and assess emotional valence with a score ranging from -1 (most negative emotions) to +1 (most positive emotions) and a temporal precision of 30 inferences per second [51, 71]. More specifically, the valence score is calculated as the intensity of a happy score minus the intensity of the highest negative responses [72]. Then, Observer XT and CubeHX [73, 74] were used to synchronize all the signals between Acknowledge and FaceReader (Noldus, Wageningen, Netherlands) as recommended by Léger et al. [44].

3.4 Preparation of Visualization Models

In order to triangulate collected data, webpages visited are first grouped and assembled to construct each user's journey consisting of its various navigation paths. Using the eye-tracking device and Tobii Studio, these tools help contextualize the behavioral data of users and group all the webpages used for a given task. This compilation leads to a visual representation of all paths used by the sample for a given task. Moreover, using the complete psychophysiological dataset generated by all users, an average of each measure (i.e., arousal, valence, and cognitive load) was calculated for each webpage; this generated an overview of the page-by-page evolution of the users' cognitive and emotional states. Moreover, the averages for each measure are grouped by webpage, tasks and segments to get an overview of an average customer journey for a given segment.

In order to facilitate the understanding of all collected data, the averages obtained from both cognitive and emotional measures are translated into symbols and visual codes according to pre-established thresholds. Arousal, emotional valence and cognitive load are rescaled to (-1 to $+1$) and adjusted to the baseline. The baseline allows distinguishing the user's psychophysiological sensitivity since each participants' emotional reaction to a stimulus does not have the same direction and intensity [34]. Hence, the baseline allows participants' emotional responses to be standardized on the same scale.

First, the user's emotional responses are translated into four main categories of the circumplex model: enthusiasm, frustration, serenity and tolerance [75]. Indeed, all affective states are characterized by two fundamental neurophysiological constructs which are valence and arousal [45]. Consequently, Russell (1989) proposed the Affect Grid, which is a scale based on the circumplex model of affect in order to describe emotions according to the crossing of the dimensions of valence on the horizontal axis and arousal on the vertical axis (see Fig. 1). The center of the grid represents a neutral valence and a medium level of arousal. For example, when the valence value is below 0, it refers to the lower part of the Affect Grid (i.e., tolerance and serenity). Moreover, when the arousal is below 0, it refers to the left side of the Affect Grid (i.e., frustration and tolerance). Thus, when the arousal and emotional valence are below 0, the user ends up in the quadrant of tolerance. With the Affect Grid, it is possible to analyze whether the participant feels pleasant/unpleasant or active/inactive. Hence, the symbolization of emotions on the visualization models respects the coding of the Affect Grid. Therefore, each quadrant (i.e. frustration, enthusiasm, tolerance and serenity) is represented by an icon of a facial expression. Hence, it is easy to visually recognize what emotion is felt on average by users for each webpage.

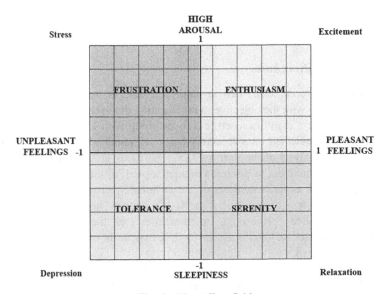

Fig. 1. The Affect Grid

Second, cognitive loads are categorized into three levels such as easy, moderate or difficult and these levels are represented using a gear icon (e.g., one gear symbolizes a relatively easy task whereas three gears represent a difficult task). Since the arousal variable varies from −1 to 1, the difference is divided into three equal parts to distinguish the different levels of difficulty. Given that the arousal values are rescaled between −1 and 1, a cognitive load value of less than zero (i.e., inferior to the baseline) means that cognitive effort is low. Thus, cognitive loads were divided into three main categories which are low cognitive load (< −0.3), moderate cognitive load (between 0.3 and −0.3) and high cognitive load (>0.3) (See Table 1).

The thresholds for cognitive loads and emotional responses are presented in the table below (see Table 1). Such visual codes allow simplifying the visualization of the page-by-page evolution of the user's cognitive and emotional states.

Table 1. Thresholds for Psychological Data.

Cognitive load	Low cognitive load	Medium cognitive load		High cognitive load
	<−0.3	Between −0.3 and 0.3		>0.3
Circumplex model of affect	Frustration	Enthusiasm	Tolerance	Serenity
	EDA > 0 Valence < 0	EDA > 0 Valence > 0	EDA < 0 Valence < 0	EDA < 0 Valence > 0

Phase 2

3.5 Focus Group Procedure

Once all tasks were completed, two visualization models were created using psychophysiological data with the objective of representing the overall experience of users. These two models were then discussed in a focus group with UX experts. Experts are impartial individuals selected on a voluntary basis, who understand usability and have experiences in the analysis of the user journey. The focus group is a collective interview where participants meet to discuss a defined topic [76]. Since our approach aims at facilitating the UX expert's analysis of the customer journey, the focus is on the acceptance of this system by ensuring it meets UX experts' needs. The type of focus group selected is called "prioritizing functionalities", as the main objective is to identify the most attractive functionalities for UX experts in order to guide and optimize the method design.

The focus group procedure lasted 90 min from the reception to the closing of the interview. A total of six (6) UX experts participated. The number of participants in a focus group is recommended to be between six and 10 individuals [77], as a smaller number of participants promote interdependence among members [78]. First, participants were informed about the purpose of the focus group, the activities planned and their roles as UX experts. Then, UX experts had to evaluate two visualization models for which they were asked a series of questions. UX experts used the technique of associating ideas to express what first comes to mind when looking as the visualization model [77]. UX experts were then asked to state their analysis of the customer journey. By stating their understanding, it would reveal whether the model represents an appropriate and relevant analysis tool. Afterwards, UX experts were asked to elicit both strengths and weaknesses for each visualization scheme in order to identify which features to keep or remove. Lastly, following the evaluation of both visualization models, UX experts were asked to define what an ideal visualization scheme should be according to the two models shown previously. Once the focus group was finished, the visualization model chosen by UX experts as the best option is modified according to their recommendations and sent back to UX experts in order to obtain their final impressions.

4 Method

4.1 Customer Journey Visualization

Two models were designed and discussed in this study. Each model is a distinctive visual representation of a task using a variety of pre-established visual codes and symbols. This study aims at comparing both models in order to define the optimal approach to understand the concurrent user experience. Through the representation process, there are seven key elements found in each model which support the representation of customer journeys. These elements are presented in the table below and the visual representation of some elements vary between both models (see Table 2). Indeed, the representation of the optimal path, which refers to the optimal navigation vis-à-vis the smallest number of clicks necessary to complete a task, is represented differently between the two models. The optimal path layout varies across models. It is not aligned or centered in the first model but is in the second model. Also, individual customer journeys are displayed on the second model while the first model does not distinguish between each customer journey.

Table 2. Elements found in each visualization model.

	Model 1 (see Fig. 2)	Model 2 (see Fig. 3)
Optimal path	The desired path is **colored** to highlight the path that users are supposed to follow	The desired path is **colored, aligned and centered** to highlight the path that users are supposed to follow
Physiological data	Physiological data are represented by icons and placed at the top of the webpage	
Action	The place where the user clicked is highlighted with a dot	
Traffic	Traffic is highlighted and the size of the circle is proportional to the number of users who have used this avenue	
Success and failures	The endpoints are illustrated with circles: **green** (if the user ends on the desired page) or **red** (if the user does not end on the desired page)	
Customer journey	No distinction is made for individual paths, only shows all webpages visited	Colored pastilles help to distinguish individual customer journeys

The first visualization scheme is presented in Fig. 2. All pages are aligned in order to provide a structured representation of the different pages used. The most problematic pages can be identified with the indicators of emotional value and cognitive effort. Indeed, these pages are shown in red and represent frustration (key located in top-left box) and high cognitive effort (top-right box) respectively. Moreover, traffic and used paths are indicated in blue to emphasize this information. In short, this model aims to highlight travel and psychophysiological data.

TASK NAME
Total number of users
Demographic data

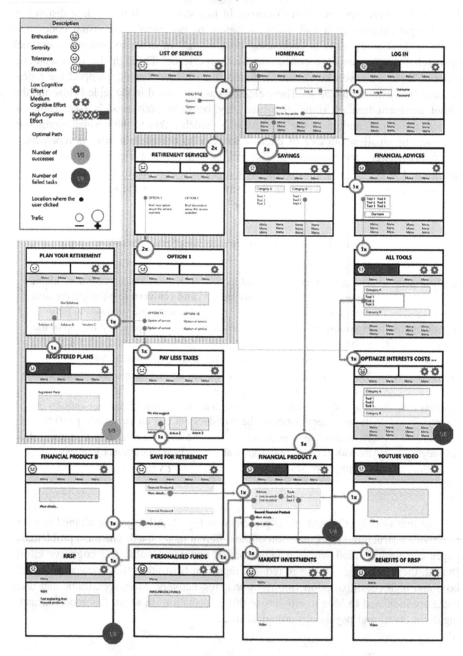

Fig. 2. First Visualization Model. (Color figure online)

The second visualization model is presented in Fig. 3. Unlike the first model, the journeys are represented in the form of swim lanes, where psychophysiological data (i.e., cognitive load, emotional valence, and arousal) are associated to each webpage visited. The most problematic areas are identified using the same indicators of emotional valence and cognitive effort. Indeed, the problematic areas are illustrated by the red zones and represent frustration (left zone) and high cognitive effort (right zone). In Fig. 3, several pages seem to be problematic regarding negative emotional valence. However, no page seems to require high cognitive effort. Since the paths are linear, it is possible to see where participants have deviated from the original goal and where problems have emerged. For example, most users used the link at the bottom of the homepage to go to the "Savings" page, deviating from the expected route.

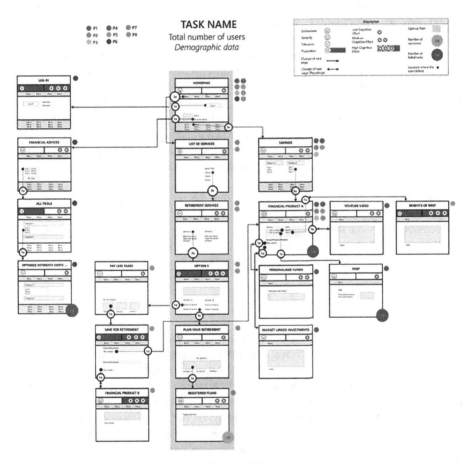

Fig. 3. Second Visualization Model. (Color figure online)

4.2   Results of the Focus Group

Regarding the first visualization model, the UX experts mentioned that the beginning of the experiment is not clearly indicated and thus, the starting point is difficult to identify. Moreover, the fact that the optimal path is not aligned and centered makes the reading of the customer journey less intuitive. In general, UX experts find this model not sufficiently refined and the understanding of the users' experience is not obvious. According to the participating UX experts, this model seems suitable for client reporting through a matrix format. This first visualization model allows to identify problematic areas on the interface.

Regarding the second visualization model, the UX experts mention that the model allows for a better understanding of the sequence experienced by users. Indeed, as mentioned previously, the first model does not distinguish between each journey. Thus, UX experts are more likely to be interested in physiological data than in the context surrounding the use of the webpage. In short, the second method allows us to have more context around the physiological data in order to prioritize the source of intervention on the interface to improve the overall experience. For example, the "log in" page seems problematic according to the first model, because it indicates frustration. However, looking through the second model, it is possible to see that this page has only been viewed by one participant. Hence, this frustration can be caused by several factors and the "log in" page may not be a priority when updating the website. Therefore, UX experts suggest that model 2 represents a good tool to have a summary of the situation and can also serve as a benchmark to measure progress through improvements made on the website.

The results of the Focus Group suggest that the research proposition be accepted since the experts mention that the visualization models facilitate the identification of problematic areas on the interface. Indeed, by bringing together the cognitive and emotional data of the users, it allows for an enriched customer journey and a more complete understanding of the associated experience.

5   Method

Our results suggest, through an illustrative case, that the use of the proposed method facilitates the identification of critical touch points to customer experience. This model is useful in order to have an overview of the experience and different paths taken by users. It allows one to see the problematic webpages when diagnosing the customer journey. Following the focus group, the UX experts agreed that the second model is the more appropriate tool for customer journey analysis. The visual representation has been described as clear and simple to use. A UX expert mentioned that "the red color makes it easier to read problematic pages and the optimal path is well highlighted without cluttering up the parallel paths" (UX expert 5). Moreover, this model has been selected because it has several strengths. First, this model is self-supporting, which means that it presents a "simple and quick visualization, without the need for explanation" (UX expert 3). Secondly, the information presented is clear, thanks to "a clear legend and the use of icons and colors that are easy to understand" (UX expert 2). It is easy to identify successes and failures as well as areas of frustration or high cognitive load. Finally, this model also allows to follow the customer journey of each user thanks to the color tablets. It gives an overview of the experience while differentiating the various paths. This model is also useful for understanding the main errors made during experience sequence (i.e., to understand where participants deviated from the optimal path). Simply put, the model allows to quickly identify where participants are getting lost.

However, the model also has a limitation. Indeed, it is easy to analyze for a certain number of participants. The visual representation represents the paths of 8 participants. However, the larger the number of participants, the more complex the visual representation becomes. The use of color tablets allows the distinction between participants, but leads to limits in terms of sample size.

Our study contributes to the UX literature by presenting a comprehensive method allowing for the visualization of a user's emotions and behaviors during his/her navigation on a website. Thus, this study adds to the literature which focuses on the modelling of the consumer decision journey [12]. Additionally, it provides more precision into the analysis and the interpretation of results, aiding to reveal problematic areas on the interface. This method serves as a complementary approach to other methods available such as questionnaires and interviews that enable collection of self-reported data and adding the convergence of these three perspectives (i.e., emotions, cognition, and behaviors), which few methods allow for [61]. The relative simplicity of this method, which enables the visual representation of the evolution of a user's cognitive and emotional states throughout their online journey and experience, should be particularly useful to both UX researchers and practitioners. Modelling service delivery from the customer's perspective is an important topic for service providers seeking to improve their services [23].

Our method allows contrasting several user journeys against the planned journey. We contend that most customer journey maps can potentially be critically flawed. They assume all customers of an organization experience the same organizational touchpoints and view these touchpoints as equally important [12]. In contrast, our method provides an accurate report of several user journeys. The results also pose managerial implications. First, this new method allows both practitioners and researchers to identify psychophysiological pain points on a webpage easily and the visualization helps to analyze and interpret results more efficiently [79]. Moreover, our method is useful for comparing user experiences on various interfaces, which can be used to compare the user experience of a specific task on competing interfaces.

Furthermore, some limitations need to be acknowledged. First, the method focuses on one section of the website. Hence, the evaluation of the customer experience does not reflect that of the entire website but depends on the selected task. Second, this model is limited to a certain number of users. As there were only 8 individuals user journey studied, this is not a large-scale study, mostly due to the high cost of obtaining the data. As the number of users studied increases there will be different user journeys. In this way, the visualization becomes more complex to analyze due to the large amount of information. Thus, it would be interesting to study the possibility of creating segments from user navigation when the sample size is too large to distinguish each path using a colored pad.

6 Conclusion

Our results show that the models proposed adequately identified and interpreted psychophysiological data supporting an understanding of the user's experience. By representing the various customer journeys through the webpages visited, it makes it possible to have a real report of the experience lived by users. Using this new visualization method generates a complete overview of users' experience and produces key insights. Indeed, it facilitates the understanding of the evolution of the experience since it shows critical touch points of the interface where the user experienced a given cognitive and emotional state. It also helps to identify the main differences between the planned customer journey and the user's decision-making. This method serves as a complementary approach to other methods available such as questionnaires and interviews that enable the collection of self-reported data and adds the convergence of these three perspectives (i.e., emotions, cognition, and behaviors), which few methods allow for [61].

References

1. Rust, R.T., Lemon, K.N.: E-service and the consumer. Int. J. Electron. Commer. 5(3), 85–101 (2001)
2. Gopalani, A.: The service-enabled customer experience: a jump-start to competitive advantage. J. Bus. Strategy 32(3), 4–12 (2011)
3. Pine, B.J., Gilmore, J.H.: The Experience Economy. Harvard Business Press, Cambridge (2011)
4. De Keyser, A., et al.: A framework for understanding and managing the customer experience. Mark. Sci. Inst. Working Pap. Ser. 15(121), 1–48 (2015)
5. Stickdorn, M., et al.: This is Service Design Thinking: Basics, Tools, Cases, vol. 1. Wiley, Hoboken (2011)
6. Rawson, A., Duncan, E., Jones, C.: The truth about customer experience. Harvard Bus. Rev. 91, 90–98 (2013)
7. Browne, J.: Customer Journey Mapping: What Is It For?. F.R. Inc., Editor (2012)
8. Bitner, M.J., Ostrom, A.L., Morgan, F.N.: Service blueprinting: a practical technique for service innovation. Calif. Manag. Rev. 50(3), 66–94 (2008)
9. Patrício, L., Fisk, R.P., Falcão e Cunha, J.: Designing multi-interface service experiences: the service experience blueprint. J. Serv. Res. 10(4), 318–334 (2008)
10. Verma, R., et al.: Customer experience modeling: from customer experience to service design. J. Serv. Manag. 23(3), 362–376 (2012)
11. Lemon, K.N., Verhoef, P.C.: Understanding customer experience throughout the customer journey. J. Mark. 80(6), 69–96 (2016)
12. Rosenbaum, M.S., Otalora, M.L., Ramírez, G.C.: How to create a realistic customer journey map. Bus. Horiz. 60(1), 143–150 (2017)
13. Helkkula, A., Kelleher, C., Pihlström, M.: Characterizing value as an experience: implications for service researchers and managers. J. Serv. Res. 15(1), 59–75 (2012)
14. Venkatraman, V., et al.: New scanner data for brand marketers: how neuroscience can help better understand differences in brand preferences. J. Consum. Psychol. 22(1), 143–153 (2012)
15. Lewinski, P.: Automated facial coding software outperforms people in recognizing neutral faces as neutral from standardized datasets. Front. Psychol. 6, 1386 (2015)

16. Plassmann, H., et al.: Consumer neuroscience: applications, challenges, and possible solutions. J. Mark. Res. **54**, 427–435 (2015)
17. Schmitt, B.: Experiential marketing. J. Mark. Manag. **15**(1–3), 53–67 (1999)
18. Verhoef, P.C., et al.: Customer experience creation: determinants, dynamics and management strategies. J. Retail. **85**(1), 31–41 (2009)
19. Vom Brocke, J., Hevner, A., Léger, P. M., Walla, P., Riedl, R.: Advancing a Neurois Research Agenda with Four Areas of Societal Contributions. Eur. J. Inf. Syst. **29**(1), 9–24 (2020)
20. Neslin, S.A., et al.: Challenges and opportunities in multichannel customer management. J. Serv. Res. **9**(2), 95–112 (2006)
21. Segelström, F.: Stakeholder Engagement for Service Design: How Service Designers Identify and Communicate Insights. Linköping University Electronic Press, Linköping (2013)
22. Norton, D.W., Pine, B.J.: Using the customer journey to road test and refine the business model. Strategy Leadersh. **41**(2), 12–17 (2013)
23. Halvorsrud, R., Kvale, K., Følstad, A.: Improving service quality through customer journey analysis. J. Serv. Theory Pract. **26**(6), 840–867 (2016)
24. Holmlid, S., Evenson, S.: Bringing service design to service sciences, management and engineering. In: Hefley, B., Murphy, W. (eds.) Service Science, Management and Engineering Education for the 21st Century. SSRI, pp. 341–345. Springer, Boston (2008). https://doi.org/10.1007/978-0-387-76578-5_50
25. Temkin, B.D.: Mapping the Customer Journey: Best Practices for Using an Important Customer Experience Tool. Forrester Research Inc., Cambridge (2010)
26. Marquez, J.J., Downey, A., Clement, R.: Walking a mile in the user's shoes: customer journey mapping as a method to understanding the user experience. Internet Ref. Serv. Q. **20**(3–4), 135–150 (2015)
27. Tseng, M.M., Qinhai, M., Su, C.J.: Mapping customers' service experience for operations improvement. Bus. Process Manag. J. (1999)
28. Dirican, A.C., Göktürk, M.: Psychophysiological measures of human cognitive states applied in human computer interaction. Procedia Comput. Sci. **3**, 1361–1367 (2011)
29. Riedl, R., Léger, P.-M.: Fundamentals of NeuroIS. SNPBE. Springer, Heidelberg (2016). https://doi.org/10.1007/978-3-662-45091-8
30. De Guinea, A.O., Webster, J.: An investigation of information systems use patterns: technological events as triggers, the effect of time and consequences for performance. MIS Q. **37**(4), 1165–1188 (2013)
31. De Guinea, A.O., Titah, R., Léger, P.-M.: Explicit and implicit antecedents of users' behavioral beliefs in information systems: a neuropsychological investigation. J. Manag. Inf. Syst. **30**(4), 179–210 (2014)
32. Leger, P.-M., Riedl, R., vom Brocke, J.: Emotions and ERP information sourcing: the moderating role of expertise. Ind. Manag. Data Syst. **114**, 456–471 (2014)
33. Kahneman, D., Riis, J.: Living, and Thinking About It: Two Perspectives on Life in the Science of Well-Being, pp. 285–304. Oxford University Press, Oxford (2005)
34. Lourties, S., Léger, P.-M., Sénécal, S., Fredette, M., Chen, S.L.: Testing the convergent validity of continuous self-perceived measurement systems: an exploratory study. In: Nah, F. F.-H., Xiao, B.S. (eds.) HCIBGO 2018. LNCS, vol. 10923, pp. 132–144. Springer, Cham (2018). https://doi.org/10.1007/978-3-319-91716-0_11
35. Ivonin, L., et al.: Beyond cognition and affect: sensing the unconscious. Behav. Inf. Technol. **34**(3), 220–238 (2014)
36. Zijlstra, F.R.H., et al.: Temporal factors in mental work: effects of interrupted activities. J. Occup. Organ. Psychol. **72**, 163–185 (1999)

37. Bailey, B.P., et al.: A framework for specifying and monitoring user tasks. Comput. Hum. Behav. **22**(4), 709–732 (2006)
38. Bailey, B.P., Konstan, J.A.: On the need for attention-aware systems: measuring effects of interruption on task performance, error rate, and affective state. Comput. Hum. Behav. **22**(4), 685–708 (2006)
39. Picard, R.W.: Affective Computing, in M.I.T Media Laboratory Perceptual Computing Section (1995)
40. Ward, R.D., Marsden, P.H.: Physiological responses to different WEB page designs. Int. J. Hum. Comput. Stud. **59**(1–2), 199–212 (2003)
41. Bentley, T., Johnson, L., von Baggo, K.: Evaluation using Cued-Recall Debrief to Elicit Information about a user's affective experiences. In: OZCHI. Canberra, Australia (2005)
42. Giroux-Huppé, C., et al.: Impact d'une expérience psychophysiologique négative sur la satisfaction des consommateurs dans un contexte d'épicerie en ligne, in Marketing. HEC Montréal, Montréal (2019)
43. Guinea, A.O., Markus, L.: Why break the habit of a lifetime? Rethinking the roles of intention, habit, and emotion in continuing information technology use. MIS Q. **33**(3), 433–444 (2009)
44. Léger, P.-M., et al.: Neurophysiological correlates of cognitive absorption in an enactive training context. Comput. Hum. Behav. **34**, 273–283 (2014)
45. Russell, J.A.: A circumplex model of affect. J. Pers. Soc. Psychol. **39**(6), 1161–1178 (1980)
46. Boucsein, W.: Electrodermal Activity. Springer, Heidelberg (2012). https://doi.org/10.1007/978-1-4614-1126-0
47. Forne, M.: Physiology as a Tool for UX and Usability Testing, in KTH Computer Science and Communication. Royal Institute of Technology, Stockholm (2012)
48. Colombetti, G.: Appraising valence. J. Conscious. Stud. **12**(8–10), 103–126 (2005)
49. Maia, C.L.B., Furtado, E.S.: A Study about psychophysiological measures in user experience monitoring and evaluation. In: Proceedings of the 15th Brazilian Symposium on Human Factors in Computing Systems (2016)
50. Burton-Jones, A., Gallivan, M.J.: Toward a deeper understanding of system usage in organizations: a multilevel perspective. MIS Q. **31**(4), 657–679 (2007)
51. Den Uyl, M.J., Van Kuilenburg, H: The facereader: online facial expression recognition. In: Proceedings of Measuring Behavior (2005)
52. Haapalainen, E., et al.: Psycho-physiological measures for assessing cognitive load. In: Proceedings of the 12th ACM International Conference on Ubiquitous Computing. ACM (2010)
53. Charland, P., et al.: Assessing the multiple dimensions of engagement to characterize learning: a neurophysiological perspective. JoVE J. Visualized Exp. **101**, e52627 (2015)
54. Beatty, J., Lucero-Wagoner, B.: The pupillary system. Handb. Psychophysiol. **2**, 142–162 (2000)
55. Wilson, G.F.: An analysis of mental workload in pilots during flight using multiple psychophysiological measures. Int. J. Aviat. Psychol. **12**(1), 3–18 (2002)
56. Ikehara, C.S., Crosby, M.E.: Assessing cognitive load with physiological sensors. In: Proceedings of the 38th Annual Hawaii International Conference on System Sciences. IEEE (2005)
57. Iqbal, S.T., et al.: Towards an index of opportunity: understanding changes in mental workload during task execution. In: Proceedings of the SIGCHI Conference on Human Factors in Computing Systems. ACM (2005)
58. Léger, P.-M., Charland, P., Sénécal, S., Cyr, S.: Predicting properties of cognitive pupillometry in human–computer interaction: a preliminary investigation. In: Davis, F.D., Riedl, R., vom Brocke, J., Léger, P.-M., Randolph, A.B. (eds.) Information Systems and

Neuroscience. LNISO, vol. 25, pp. 121–127. Springer, Cham (2018). https://doi.org/10.1007/978-3-319-67431-5_14

59. Desrochers, C., et al.: The arithmetic complexity of online grocery shopping: the moderating role of product pictures. Ind. Manag. Data Syst. **119**(6), 1206–1222 (2019)

60. Richardson, A.: Using customer journey maps to improve customer experience. Harvard Bus. Rev. **15**(1), 2–5 (2010)

61. Coursaris, C.K., Kim, D.J.: A meta-analytical review of empirical mobile usability studies. J. Usability Stud. **6**(3), 117–171 (2011)

62. Reichheld, F.F., Markey, R.: The Ultimate Question 2.0 How Net Promoter Companies Thrive in a CustomerDriven World. Harvard Business Review Press, Boson (2011)

63. Alvarez, J., et al.: Towards Agility and Speed in Enriched UX Evaluation Projects, in Human-Computer Interaction. IntechOpen, London (2019)

64. Vasseur, A., P.-M. Léger, Sénécal, S.: Eye-tracking for information systems research: a literature review. In: SIGHCI, vol. 8 (2019)

65. Van Gerven, P.W., et al.: Memory load and the cognitive pupillary response in aging. Psychophysiology **41**(2), 167–174 (2004)

66. Hyönä, J., Tommola, J., Alaja, A.-M.: Pupil dilation as a measure of processing load in simultaneous interpretation and other language tasks. Q. J. Exp. Psychol. Sect. A **48**(3), 598–612 (2007)

67. Hassenzahl, M., Tractinsky, N.: User experience - a research agenda. Behav. Inf. Technol. **25**(2), 91–97 (2006)

68. Braithwaite, J.J., et al.: A Guide for Analysing Electrodermal Activity (EDA) & Skin Conductance Responses (SCRs) for Psychological Experiments. U.o.B. Behavioural Brain Sciences Centre, Editor (2015)

69. Hassenzahl, M., Burmester, M., Koller, F.: AttrakDiff: Ein Fragebogen zur Messung wahrgenommener hedonischer und pragmatischer Qualität. In: Szwillus, G., Ziegler, J. (eds.) Mensch & Computer 2003. BGCACM, vol. 57, pp. 187–196. Springer, Heidelberg (2003). https://doi.org/10.1007/978-3-322-80058-9_19

70. Stern, R.M., et al.: Psychophysiological Recording. Oxford University Press, USA (2001)

71. Ekman, P., Friesen, W.V.: Unmasking the face: A Guide to Recognizing Emotions from Facial Clues. M. Books, Editor (2003)

72. Lojiens, L., Krips, O.: FaceReader Methodology Note. N.I. Technology, Editor (2018)

73. Courtemanche, F., et al.: Method of and system for processing signals sensed from a user. Google Patents (2019)

74. Léger, P.-M., Courtemanche, F., Fredette, M., Sénécal, S.: A cloud-based lab management and analytics software for triangulated human-centered research. In: Davis, F.D., Riedl, R., vom Brocke, J., Léger, P.-M., Randolph, A.B. (eds.) Information Systems and Neuroscience. LNISO, vol. 29, pp. 93–99. Springer, Cham (2019). https://doi.org/10.1007/978-3-030-01087-4_11

75. Posner, J., Russell, J.A., Peterson, B.S.: The circumplex model of affect an integrative approach to affective neuroscience, cognitive development, and psychopathology. Dev. Psychopathol. **17**(3), 714–734 (2005)

76. Lallemand, C., Gronier, G.: Focus Group, in Méthodes de design UX. Eyrolles, Paris (2016)

77. Debus, M.: Handbook for excellence in focus group research. Academy for Educational Development, Durham (2007)

78. Anzieu, D., Martin, J.-Y.: La dynamique des groupes restreints. Presses Universitaires de France, Paris (1968)

79. Lamontagne, C., et al.: User test: how many users are needed to find the psychophysiological pain points in a journey map? In: Ahram, T., Taiar, R., Colson, S., Choplin, A. (eds.) IHIET

2019. AISC, vol. 1018, pp. 136–142. Springer, Cham (2020). https://doi.org/10.1007/978-3-030-25629-6_22

80. Gentile, C., Spiller, N., Noci, G.: How to Sustain the Customer Experience: An Overview of Experience Components That Co-Create Value with the Customer. Eur. Manage. J. **25**(5), 395–410 (2007)

81. Russell, J. A., Weiss, A., Mendelsohn, G. A.: Affect Grid: A Single-Item Scale of Pleasure and Arousal. J. Pers. Soc. Psychol. **57**(3), 493 (1989)

A Comparative Research on Designer and Customer Emotional Preference Models of New Product Development

Tianxiong Wang[1(✉)], Liu Yang[2], Xian Gao[2], and Yuxuan Jin[2]

[1] School of Art Design and Media,
East China University of Science and Technology,
No. 130, Meilong Road, Xuhui District, Shanghai 200237, China
wangtx_2018@163.com
[2] School of Machinery and Electrical Engineering, Anhui Jianzhu University,
No. 292, Ziyun Road, Shushan District, Hefei 230601, China
yelanyi@126.com, micanov@163.com,
King820289182@163.com

Abstract. The intelligent electric bicycle, as a means of transportation, is characterized by low pollution, low noise and energy saving. Hence, how to actively research, develop and promote electric bicycle is an important topic. Meanwhile, as consumer groups vary in psychology and behavior, they show differences in functional preference of smart electric bicycle, how to understand and identify the differences between designers and users in electric bicycle preference, and then to reduce the uncertainties of electric bicycle manufacturers on the market becomes an imperative topic which is of great significance. In order to analyze the emotional preference differences between designers and users in terms of electric bicycle in the qualitative and quantitative manner, this study conducts the kansei evaluation of designers' and users' visual and emotional feelings for electric bicycle products. The emotional preference model adopts semantic differential to carry out quantitative analysis of surveyed designers and users. In order to standardize the cognitive description related to product shape style, the abstract psychological perception of cognitive subjects for physical shape characteristics is extracted from customers' natural language. Then, the key emotional vocabulary can be extracted via factor analysis and focus group. The experiment outcome contains 3 typical emotional words which are combined with their antonyms to form 3 adjective clusters. The sample mean statistics approach is employed to calculate the average value of subjects' scores for the cognitive adjectives regarding the sample style. To compare the differences between designers and customers in preference for electric bicycle products, this study uses two statistical research methods, that is, T-test and the correlation analysis. The experiment results could explain that users and designers demonstrate obvious statistical differences in two kansei words. Furthermore, as a result, the product design form for which the emotional image of designers highly matches with users' emotional image is concluded and comes up with the product form that reflects strong correlation between users' emotional demand and experts' emotional cognition. Accordingly, a new and effective theoretical framework is provided for the development of electric bicycle products. This research results of this experiment could not only help

© Springer Nature Switzerland AG 2020
A. Marcus and E. Rosenzweig (Eds.): HCII 2020, LNCS 12200, pp. 567–581, 2020.
https://doi.org/10.1007/978-3-030-49713-2_39

designers understand customers' views but also significantly increase the efficiency of interaction and communication between designers and users, and then to help with quick and accurate product orientation.

Keywords: Users' emotional preference · User's need · Semantic differential · T-test · Production design

1 Introduction

As competitions in the automotive industry overheats, more attention has been paid not only to the improvements of the mechanical performances and designs but to the satisfaction of preferences and affective facets of customers [1]. Under the background of dynamic customer demand (demand driven) and rapid technological progress (supply driven), enterprises are urged to develop and launch various products in the extremely crowded market [2], which makes the product market competitive environment more intense and dynamic. Product development enterprises can effectively use resources to develop a wide range of products to maintain their competitiveness [3]. Meanwhile, users are faced with a variety of product choices in consumer products and they may become more concerned about their emotional needs than ever before, and then to hope that the products can reflect their own personality, preferences, identity, values and other factors, which makes the traditional product's functional (technical) characteristics may no longer meet user needs [4], so that the emotional characteristics become more important to meet different customer needs [5]. In fact, the product form is the material carrier of the product, which could convey the material and spiritual functions of the product and it is an important medium for users and designers to communicate. Thus, product form design activity starts from the expression of designer's intention and ends with the user's feeling and understanding so that its core lies in expression and communication. Furthermore, user demand information, designer coding process and user decoding process could constitute product form design intention. At present, most of the researches focus on the treatment and acquisition of users' emotional needs from the perspective of users' needs. However, there are differences in the emotional cognitive characteristics between users and designers. The specific causes of cognitive differences can be summed up as: occupation, age, gender, physiological characteristics, education, economic status, society culture and popular factors. More significantly, the subjective and objective meaning of designers has been built into product design, which is different from the meaning of products in the eyes of users. Unfortunately, this contradiction will lead to the failure of product design. In addition, general users may not appreciate the beauty of the product, so it is necessary to study how the emotional conceptual model of designers and users can be related according to the emotional characteristics of the production [6, 7]. Therefore, it is very important to understand the affective experiences by both the designers and the customers of production preference in the electric bicycle [8]. Accordingly, it is necessary to pay attention to the cognitive differences between users and designers, and then through to use the scientific emotional image mining tools, this kind of implicit information can be externalized so as to complete the product development quickly and accurately. Therefore, this study explores the formation mechanism of user's perceptual image affected by product shape characteristics through natural language and factor analysis, and then conducts the independent T-test analysis and correlation analysis of statistical analysis to explore the different factors of designer and user emotional awareness of product shape.

2 Literature Review

Some scholars have also verified the emotional different factors between experts and customers' preferences in their previous studies. These studies mainly involve the following aspects: tacile comparisons of textile specials [9], wine aroma [10], pearl quality [11], aesthetic features in works of art [12] and so on. At the same time, some researches in many fields have carried out the emotional differences between experts and customers' preferences, especially in sensory and emotional evaluation, these studies shows that the emotional perception and evaluation vocabulary in these fields vary with the difference of professional level. For example, Bahn et al. [6] analyzed the luxury elements in vehicle crash pad design, and studied the significant difference between designers and customers in visual and tactile evaluation. Kanai et al. [13] studied the basic factors of fabric aesthetics, different evaluation of the same material by expert groups and untrained customers based on vision and touch, and the research on senses other than vision or touch also shows interesting differences between experts and novices. According to these research results, it can be inferred that experts and customers have different methods and opinions about evaluating the modeling of E-bike. Therefore, when to develop and design E-bike productions, it is very important to understand the differences and take appropriate methods. However, there are still limitations in the systematic research of preference priority and product design elements of E-bike products. In particular, few studies which probe into the differences between designers and customers in emotional preference touch upon the development of electric bicycle.

In order to systematically discuss the inner real emotional cognition of users and designers, a Japanese scholar Nagamachi developed a new product technology of Kansei Engineering for consumers, which is defined as a transformation technology that transforms consumers' feelings and imagination of products into design elements [14]. Kansei Engineering is a user-oriented technology for new product research and development. Kansei is a Japanese word that expresses users' psychological feelings and imagination for new products. Kansei Engineering technology can integrate customers' imagination and feelings for new products into the development of new products. When Kansei engineering is used as a design method, we will pay attention to people's behavior of perceiving images or objects for productions, and then to study the effect of their personal preferences or cultural favor factors based on their psychological feelings. What's more, KE can identify the emotional attributes of customers and associate them with design elements [3]. The commonly used the semantic difference method (SD) [15] in Kansei Engineer can accurately obtain the user's image perception. In many previous literatures, it can be found that some scholars have widely used SD method to quantify users' emotional preferences and many sophisticated methods and models have been established based on the conventional SD method in Kansei engineering. However, the user's perception and preferences are complex and changeable, which are difficult to grasp and extract. Hence, this is the key problem faced by design researchers in the design and development work. To this end, some scholars try to extract the kansei words from users' natural language [16] in order to standardize the cognitive description of product modeling style image, which has the positive research value for accurately obtaining users' emotional semantic space. Therefore, the natural language plays an important role in our highly intelligent thinking and reasoning activities. There have been many related researches in this field [17]. Most of the researches in artificial intelligence including natural language processing adopt a symbolic processing approach to treat knowledge [18], and some scholars and experts used the natural language in the field of Kansei Engineering. For example, Yao et al. [19] used natural language to extract the key semantic features of coach styling in order to standardize the cognitive description of product modeling style image, which made the extracted perceptual image semantic space vocabulary more effective and reasonable. Therefore, in this study, we used natural language to extract the user's perceptual words about the semantics of E-bike products. However, due to the semantic overlap of the extracted adjectives, their importance to the description of E-bike modeling style is also different, and there is a certain correlation relationship of these perceptual semantic spatial variables. The systematic discussion of the whole vocabulary set will undoubtedly increase the calculation difficulty, which is not conducive to the storage and reuse of knowledge. Therefore, it is necessary to reduce the dimension of the description of modeling style through the cognitive test of the image of E-bike style, which can use less comprehensive indicators to replace all kinds of information existing in all variables. Through to utilize the factor analysis method, the key semantic word are screened out, so as to extract the key semantic space which could satisfy perceptual needs of users and experts. Then, we discussed the different factors of emotional preference between designers and users based on the key semantic space. Some scholars adopted factor analysis method to study human emotional semantic space in perceptual design. Guo et al. [20] put forward two color gamut contrast modes and used the method to generate three color scheme, and then designed 368 three color schemes of representative baby carriage, and combined with correlation analysis and factor analysis to determine five sensory characteristics of color design. Ding et al. [21] proposed a product color emotional design method that adapts to the change of product shape features in research, and he used factor analysis and semantic difference method to clarify the formation mechanism of user color image perception space affected by product shape features, and then to build a product color image evaluation model that adapts to the change of product shape features. Finally, a case study of a thermos bottle designed for children is put forward in the study to prove this method can effectively help designers in decision-making. Therefore, this study explores the formation mechanism of user's perceptual image affected by product shape characteristics through natural language and factor analysis, and then to utilize the independent T-test analysis to compare the scores of all samples from designers and customers on the emotional image so as to determine the difference between users and design's emotional cognition. Then, we adopted the correlation analysis to select Pearson's correlation analysis and further compare the preferences between experts and users, and these products with strong correlation coefficient are selected so as to obtain high-quality product sample form that can meet the preferences of users and designers. Hence, this study provides an innovative solution for product innovation development and improve consumer satisfaction.

3 Method

In this study, first of all, the semantic difference method and statistical method are used to evaluate the emotional different factors between designers and users for productions so as to explore the method to eliminate the cognitive and emotional difference between users and designers. This method is applicable to the research of intelligent electric bicycle shape, which is based on the fact that such products are interesting from the perspective of semantics and aesthetics. There is almost no difference in material, structure or even function between these products. Therefore, the shape design attribute have a significant impact on human perception. The evaluation process consists of two stages. First of all, the semantic cognitive space of users is extracted by natural language and the semantic difference method experiment is used to further quantify semantics. Then, we use factor analysis to reduce the dimension of perceptual words in semantic space, and then the key words that can cover the whole semantic space for further research are selected. Then, through T-test and correlation analysis, these differences between users and designers on E-bike products are evaluated and analyzed, and then to explore the product modeling design features that meet the needs of users and designers.

3.1 Obtaining Kansei Vocabulary of Users and Designers

In recent years, with the development of economy, traditional manual work has been unable to meet the needs due to the needs of industry and commerce. Therefore, automatic machines are needed to replace manual work. The development of artificial intelligence and machine learning has enabled computers to have the ability of independent analysis and prediction. In language analysis process, based on statistical analysis, language phenomena or statistical laws are extracted from words that can represent the laws of natural language. This method focuses on the statistics of language phenomena in corpus, which is actually used by people. The essence of this method is to discuss the processing and application of machine to language based on artificial intelligence and linguistics. In this study, through the use of natural language science to extract the user's psychological perception of the emotional image of the electric bicycle, and selected the semantic words and combine the use of the semantic words of the customer's description of the product modeling style, and then to construct the product modeling style description semantic lexicon, so that the semantic words of the customer's original modeling style description language are extracted, which makes the semantic extraction more natural.

3.2   User Semantic Evaluation Experiment

The semantic difference method (SD) [22] is an experimental method to study the psychological image of the subject created by American psychologists. This method could get people's cognitive dimension of something by using scientific methods such as experiment, statistics, calculation, etc., which make people's abstract emotional image datalized. The SD method is used to evaluate products, the representative product are evaluated by survey participants according to each perceptual label. Firstly, an evaluation form showing the product and all perceptual marks should be prepared for all representative products. If there are n representative products need to be evaluated, these different evaluation forms are required. This step uses 7-point scale, which uses a unified bipolar system to evaluate antonym pairs of perceptual markers. In this system, one extreme of scale represents a very strong sense (sensibility) corresponding to this extreme image. Next, participants use forms to evaluate representative products. Then, the evaluation results are collected and organized in the form of matrix so as to carry out simple processing in the following steps, and then excavate the emotional image cognition of designers and users respectively through the way of questionnaire. The specific calculation formula of SD is as follow, where I represents the number of representative samples, and J represents the number of target emotional image lexical pairs, and Y represents the number of subjects.

$$\bar{A}_{ij} = \sum_{Y=1}^{Y} A_{ij}^{Y} / Y \tag{1}$$

3.3   Analyzing Kansei Semantic Words

Factor analysis method, which was originally developed by Spearman in 1904. The factor analysis reduces a variable with mutual correlation to one of the latent factors. The most important function of factor analysis is to simplify a small number of different observation factors into a few mutually exclusive factors. In fact, these factors still have a high ability to explain the original problems so as to reduce the complexity and calculation difficulty in analyzing problems or evaluating schemes. Furthermore, we hope to find out the potential factors that have influence from the observation factors, and these factors could not be directly observed and measured, nor can we use regression analysis to solve the problem at this time, so the factor analysis is adopted to achieve this key purpose. Based on the fixed scale semantic difference method and the main component analysis method of factor analysis, these common factors are extracted. The principle is to select those whose eigenvalue is greater than 1, and then further analyze the characteristics and meanings of each factors style surface, and then to classify and name them so as to find out the key factors of users' perceptual semantic space of E-bike.

3.4   The Statistical Analysis

The statistical analysis plays an important role in the system of Kansei Engineering. In order to determine the perception and kansei difference between designers and customers, the independent T-test analysis and correlation analysis were performed. For independent T-test analysis, the cognitive scores from the designer and the user for perceptual imagery for all samples were compared. For the correlation analysis, the pearson's correlation analysis was selected to analyze the product samples and screen out the high quality products which can meet the user and designer perceptual needs or market conditions. Therefore, such productions are high-quality products on the market.

4   Case Study

4.1   Extracting Semantic Features of the Product

Firstly, we need to collect the popular E-bike products in the market to study the attractive factors of the product. Through the online shopping platform, magazines and related book channels, we search 58 products of the user's favorite E-bike products as test samples, and then process the samples as A4 size through the computer plane processing software PS, and then to set the resolution to a unified format. At the beginning of the experiment, a team composed of 36 experienced product designers and users of e-bikes needs to participate in the research of attractive factors of the products, including 18 males and 18 females. The age of the research population is between 21–46 yrs old, and then the users can make a perceptual evaluation and description of the product samples. At the same time, we use the natural language to extract the perceptual semantic words of user and designers' evaluation of products. Finally, 60 kansei image words are obtained (Table 1).

Table 1. The preliminary kansei vocabulary of user evaluation

Modern	Compact	Thick	Dynamic	Detail
Simple	Sport	Perceptual	Agile	Light
Amooth	Sunlight	Lightweight	Sturdy	Tasteful
Rhythmic	Beautiful	Shapely	High-grade	Bulky
Convenient	Flavorful	Smooth	Round	Delicate
⋮	⋮	⋮	⋮	⋮
Mechanical	Restrained	Personality	Stylish	Cute
Affectionate	Gentle	Steady	Innovation	Warm
Contemporary	Classic	Young	Abrupt	Technological
Soft	Fashionable	Safe	Beautiful	Speed

Then, through the focus group method, a total of 8 researchers were selected, including 4 senior experts with more than 15 yrs of experience in the industrial design and 4 students which major is industrial design. Finally, 15 classic image semantic space of smart electric bicycles were selected (Table 2), and then to use adjective antonyms to aggregate them with antonyms to form a pair adjectives. Thus, we obtained 15 pairs of kansei image adjectives about smart electric bicycles.

Table 2. Screening out kansei vocabulary

Modern	Elegant	Dynamic	Fashionable
Simple	Avant-garde	Technological	Tasteful
Gorgeous	Light	Personality	Convenient
Mellow	Soft	Delicate	/

4.2   Analyzing Kansei Words

If we investigate the cognition of users and experts on these 15 groups of adjectives, the cognitive fatigue factors of experts and users will increase. Meanwhile, the 15 perceptual vocabulary will also partially overlap in word meanings, while modeling styles of electric bicycle are described as a vector with 15 dimensions so as to increase the difficulty of data calculation, and then it is also not conducive to obtaining valid results. Therefore, it is necessary to conduct cognitive test experiments on the image styles of electric bicycles and implement dimensionality reduction processing, in order to dig out the key semantic adjectives which affect the cognitive description of image styles of intelligent electric bicycles.

Then, samples was further filtered to 16 samples by the focus group method, and 68 students with a design background were selected. Based on 15 sentimental semantics screened out, the 7-level Likert scale was used to perform adjective semantics scale division. The experiment requires the subjects to score image scales for each sample, the 0 means that the two semantic scales are equal, and the 3 is to the left, and then the −3 is to the right. The reliability analysis of the experiment was performed to test the effectiveness and stability of the experimental results. The Cronbach's a coefficient method is used in this article, which is the most commonly used method for the psychological attitude test. Moreover, Cronbach's a coefficient is defined as Formula (2) [23].

$$\alpha = \frac{K}{K-1}\left(1 - \frac{\sum_{i=1}^{K}\sigma_{Y_i}^2}{\sigma_X^2}\right) \tag{2}$$

Where K is the number of items in a scale and σ_X^2 is the variance of the total score of the observed questionnaire, and $\sigma_{Y_i}^2$ is the variance of all respondents' scores of the observed item i. Cronbach's a value is usually between 0 and 1.

In order to facilitate the import of the data into SPSS software, the 68 participants who participated in the experiment used the sample mean statistic method to calculate the mean value of the style image cognitive adjective score. Finally, the 16×15 matrix datas are obtained. Then, through KMO sampling suitability test and Barlett spherical test to determine whether the kansei semantic meaning is suitable for factor analysis. Then, the result of KMO is 0.665, and Barlett's test value is 248.065, degrees of freedom is 105, significance is 0.000. According to the research results, it can be found that the value of KMO exceeded than 0.5, which represents a reasonable result. The significance is 0.000 that it is less than 0.05, which indicates the significant difference is existed (see Table 3). Therefore, this data can be further factor analyzed.

Table 3. The KMO and Barlett test

Adequacy Kaiser-Meyer-Olkin of sampling		0.665
Bartlett sphericity test	Approximate chi-square	248.065
	Degrees of freedom	105
	Significance	0.000

After verification, the common factors are extracted by the main component analysis method in factor analysis. The principle is that when the eigenvalue is larger than 1, and then three main factors are selected, and the maximum variance axis method makes the representative meaning of each factor become more obvious and easier to explain. Then, the maximum variance method in the main component analysis method is used to rotate the factors directly to get the rotation component matrix (see Table 4) and gravel fig (Fig. 1), and then to further analyze the characteristics and meanings of various facets and classifies them.

In this study, three factors (Fig. 1) are extracted according to the extraction criterion of initial feature value greater than 1, which can explain 83.828% of all factor variables. Accordingly, these three factor features can better describe the modeling style features of the experimental sample cases. Among them, the load of the first factor is between 0.905 and 0.671, and the explanatory variation is 33.055%. According to Table 4, it can be found that the first factor is composed of six variable semantic words with high degree of correlation: simple, light, convenient, exquisite, modern and soft semantics. Therefore, it is named as delicate and simple perceptual semantics. The load of the second factor is between 0.945 and 0.663, and the explanatory variation is 26.075%. According to Table 4, it is found that the second factor is composed of four variables with high correlation degree, elegant, mellow, tasteful and gorgeous. Therefore, it is named gorgeous and tasteful perceptual image. The load of the third factor is between 0.645 and 0.939, and the explanatory variation is 24.699%. According to Table 4, it is found that the third factor is composed of five variables with high degree of correlation: fashion, avant-garde, personality, technological and dynamic. Therefore, it is named as the perceptual image of technology and fashion.

Table 4. Component Matrix after Facet Load Scale Rotation

Kansei images	Ingredients		
	Factor 1	Factor 2	Factor 3
Simple	**0.905**	0.246	0.076
Light	**0.888**	−0.103	0.305
Convenient	**0.869**	0.032	0.162
Exquisite	**0.778**	0.391	0.331
Modern	**0.735**	0.465	0.379
Soft	**0.671**	0.271	0.26
Elegant	0.16	**0.945**	0.026
Mellow	−0.118	**0.91**	0.198
Tasteful	0.249	**0.778**	0.455
Gorgeous	0.313	**0.663**	−0.055
Fashion	0.37	0.594	**0.645**
Avant-garde	0.489	0.503	**0.634**
Personality	0.287	0.106	**0.907**
Technological	0.574	0.09	**0.697**
Dynamic	0.107	0.068	**0.939**
Explainable variance (%)	33.055	26.075	24.699
Cumulative explanatory variance (%)	33.055	59.13	83.828

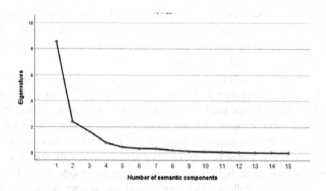

Fig. 1. Factors gravel

4.3   Comparison of Cognitive Preferences Between Designers and Users

Based on the above, while this study uses three factor dimensions to discuss the perception differences between designers and users of product samples. Through to utilize the delicate and simple, gorgeous and tasteful and technology and fashion three kansei image factors to understand the characteristics of consumers and designers' preferences for products. First of all, through SD semantic difference method, 48 designers and 48 users were investigated to quantify the kansei vocabulary of 16 samples in these three semantic spaces words. For the two groups of participants in the experiment, the method of sample mean statistics is used to calculate the results, and further T-test is carried out to investigate whether there is significant difference in statistics between designers and customers according to the average value of perceptual image for each product. Accordingly, take the delicate and simple perceptual image as an example, and then to conduct independent sample T-test, and the results are shown in Table 5. According to Table 5, it can be seen that P = 0.312 > 0.05, so it is found that 95% confidence level between designers and customers has no significant difference on the kansei image of delicate and simple, but in these two kansei images of gorgeous and tasteful (P = 0.015) and technology and fashion (P = 0.021), it is found that 95% confidence level between designers and customers is significantly different, which the p value of both images is less than 0.05.

Table 5. The independent sample T-test of delicate and simple

Kansei images		F	Significance	Degrees of freedom	Sig. (Two tail)	95% Confidence interval	
						Lower limit	Upper limit
Delicate and simple	Assumed equal variance	0.105	.071	30	.312	−1.306	.431
	Not assume equal variance			28.977	.312	−1.307	.432

4.4 Designer and User Emotional Associate Analysis

In order to study the correlation factors between the emotional response of electric bike products perceived by designers and customers, the correlation analysis was performed. If the consumers' feeling aroused by the design of E-bike products is consistent with the emotional feeling of the designer promoting the products. Hence, the design program has a high matching quality, which can effectively reduce the cognitive differences between designers and users. Firstly, the electric bicycle could be promoted by the designers are classified by five design experts with more than 10 yrs of rich design experience. According to their suggestions, all kinds of electric bicycle products are classified into four categories, which could cover the most popular and typical electric bicycle products in the current market (see Table 6).

Table 6. Typical electric bicycle categories

Number of categories	Category styler	Description
1	C_1	Sports electric bike
2	C_2	Lightweight electric bicycle
3	C_3	Folding electric bicycle
4	C_4	Heavy-duty electric bicycle

In view of four types of electric bicycle products, the SD method was used to quantify the semantic preference of experts for four types of products based on two perceptual image words of the gorgeous and tasteful and the technology and fashion, and then to obtain the corresponding perceptual values. If the consumer feeling inspired by a single electric bicycle design is consistent with that promoted by experts, this design is considered to have high matching quality. Therefore, in order to quantify the quality of emotional match level between designers and users, the correlation analysis between the data of previous user surveys and the cognitive data of experts is carried out. Then, the correlation between the user's score and the expert's score is calculated. Thus, the Pearson's correlation coefficient (Pearson's r) is obtained, which represents the correlation strength and the quality of emotional matching between the designer and the user, as well as the quality of the affective matching. A positive correlation means that the consumers' feeling is consistent with that promoted by the design strategy, whereas a negative correlation represents the opposite; a correlation approaching zero is considered as irrelevant. The results are shown in Table 7.

Table 7. The correlation analysis result

Sample	Product description				High Related Category
	C_1	C_2	C_3	C_4	
1	**0.5**	−0.24	0.264	−0.756	C_1
2	−0.945	**0.999**	0.897	0.786	C_2
3	−0.982	**0.996**	0.825	0.866	C_2
4	−0.655	0.419	−0.077	**0.866**	C_4
5	−0.982	0.891	0.556	**0.99**	C_4
6	−1	**0.961**	0.703	0.945	C_2
7	−0.5	0.721	**0.967**	0.189	C_3
8	−0.381	0.623	**0.925**	0.058	C_3
9	−1	**0.961**	0.703	0.945	C_2
10	0	−0.277	−0.711	**0.327**	C_4
11	−0.756	0.908	**0.997**	0.5	C_3
12	−0.5	0.24	−0.264	**0.756**	C_4
13	−0.381	0.623	**0.925**	0.058	C_3
14	−0.277	0.533	**0.878**	−0.052	C_3
15	−0.866	**0.971**	0.965	0.655	C_2
16	0.189	0.091	**0.565**	−0.5	C_3

According to Table 7, it shows the product design sample cases with strong correlation between the consumer feelings aroused by the electric bicycle products and the emotional cognition of the products promoted by the designers, so as to obtain the market categories of the designer experts divided. In fact, in order to define the threshold value of correlation coefficient, some experts have proposed that a correlation greater than 0.8 is generally described as strong, whereas a correlation less than 0.5 is generally described as weak [24]. Accordingly, we classify the design of each type of electric bicycle product form: (1) The design with correlation analysis coefficient above 0.8 is high quality; (2) The design with correlation coefficient between 0.5 and 0.8 is medium quality; (3) The design with correlation coefficient below 0.5 is low quality. Finally, by comparing their shape design, the factors that affect the matching quality are discussed. Table 8 and Table 9 respectively list the detailed electric bicycle information of high matching and low matching perceptual cognition between users and designers. Then, through the comparison and analysis of this production shape design, and to discusses the characteristics of factors which could affect the matching quality. Therefore, this study may help industrial designers and manufacturers reevaluate product design to improve consumer satisfaction.

Table 8. The result of the strong correlation on design samples

Sample number	2	5	11
Pearson's r	0.999	0.99	0.997
Category	C_2	C_4	C_3

Table 9. The result of the weak correlation on design samples

Sample number	1	10	16
Pearson's r	0.5	0.327	0.565
Category	C_1	C_4	C_3

In the high matching design scheme shown in Table 8, the correlation analysis of sample 2 shows that $r = 0.999$, so the highest evaluation is obtained. Then, the related product is Jingdong and Xinri XC1. This electric bicycle is light and fast, and it has a zigzag line, which makes the form have the modern feeling. In addition, through the front round headlamp design, the car has a lively and dynamic kansei image feature. Therefore, the overall model makes the consumer's impression of the product consistent with the target feeling promoted by the designers. Then, in order to study the reason for the success of the product design, the morphology of the real product is studied and discussed, and some obvious details are found, which may enhance the consumers' perception. For example, in terms of the front structure of the electric bicycle, the Y-shaped structure is adopted to let the car convey the perceptual characteristics of lightness and flexibility. At the same time, the appearance of XC1 product is simple and may remove complex decoration, and then to return to the product itself, which could make the whole XC1 more delicate. Therefore, the user image of this product is highly related to the market demands of product designers, so as to make this product become high-quality in the market.

According to Table 9, the first sample of electric bicycles is designed with a square pedal, and the front structure is designed with a rectangular front panel so as to gives the user a sense of calm and firm image. However, the designer's design requirements for this product are sports type, which obviously has no obvious correlation with the original emotional intention of users. Thus, there is only 0.5 correlation coefficient. In

580   T. Wang et al.

addition, the 10th electric bicycle in samples conveys a full and powerful emotion through its raised shape. Hence, there are some gaps between user kansei image and the heavy perceptual image promoted by experts, and then the relevant coefficient is only 0.327, so it can only be used as the low-quality product design. The 16th electric bicycle in the experimental samples conveys light image through the small body line and mini wheel hub design, but the folding structure on the main parts is not obvious, so the emotional image correlation with the folding type promoted by experts in the market is not very strong, so it can only be used as the medium quality design.

5 Conclusion

This study uses electric bicycles as an application case to extract the perceptual image factors of the product, and combines 60 perceptual image items to form 15 perceptual image words, and further condenses the 15 product kansei images by factor analysis, and then through the T-test of statistical methods to explore the emotional and cognitive differences between designers and users based on the shape of electric bicycle products. Furthermore, the high-quality product with high correlation through correlation analysis is further analyzed. After determining the matching quality, the reasons for these samples to obtain a high-quality perceptual match or a low-quality match were explored, so that the styling design principles for electric bicycles were proposed. Moreover, this research method can help product developers to more accurately explore the different factors in kansei needs between designers and consumers, and then to help industrial designers and manufacturing businesses re-evaluate their design work to reduce the possibility of emotional dissonance.

Acknowledgements. This research was financial supported by the Natural Science Foundation of Anhui Province (No. KJ2019JD23).

References

1. Helander, M.G., Khalid, H.M., Lim, T.Y., Peng, H., Yang, X.: Emotional needs of car buyers and emotional intent of car designers. Theor. Issues Ergon. Sci. **14**(5), 455–474 (2013)
2. Wang, C.H., Hsueh, O.Z.: A novel approach to incorporate customer preference and perception into product configuration: a case study on smart pads. Comput. Stand. Interfaces **35**(5), 549–556 (2013)
3. Shahin, A., Javadi, M.H.M., Shahrestani, H.V.: Integrating Kansei engineering and revised Kano model with a case study in the automobile industry. Int. J. Product. Qual. Manag. **13**(2), 201–218 (2014)
4. Guo, F., Liu, W.L., Liu, F.T., Wang, H., Wang, T.B.: Emotional design method of product presented in multi-dimensional variables based on Kansei engineering. J. Eng. Des. **25**(4–6), 194–212 (2014)
5. Chien, C.F., Kerh, R., Lin, K.Y., Yu, A.P.I.: Data-driven innovation to capture user-experience product design: an empirical study for notebook visual aesthetics design. Comput. Ind. Eng. **99**, 162–173 (2016)

6. Bahn, S., Lee, C., Nam, C.S., Yun, M.H.: Incorporating affective customer needs for luxuriousness into product design attributes. Hum. Factors Ergon. Manuf. **19**(2), 105–127 (2009)
7. Krippendorff, K.: On the essential contexts of artifacts or on the proposition that design is making sense (of things). Des. Issues **5**(2), 9–38 (1989)
8. Kim, W., Lee, Y., Lee, J.H., Shin, G.W., Yun, M.H.: A comparative study on designer and customer preference models of leather for vehicle. Int. J. Ind. Ergon. **65**, 110–121 (2018)
9. Atkinson, D., Baurley, S., Petreca, B.B., Bianchi-Berthouze, N., Watkins, P.: The tactile triangle: a design research framework demonstrated through tactile comparisons of textile aterials. J. Des. Res. **14**(2), 142–170 (2016)
10. Torri, L., Dinnella, C., Recchia, A., Naes, T., Tuorila, H., Monteleone, E.: Projective mapping for interpreting wine aroma differences as perceived by naïve and experienced assessors. Food Qual. Prefer. **29**(1), 6–15 (2013)
11. Tani, Y., Nagai, T., Koida, K., Kitazaki, M., Nakauchi, S.: Experts and novices use the same factors - but differently - to evaluate pearl quality. PLoS One **9**(1), e86400 (2014)
12. Van Paasschen, J., Bacci, F., Melcher, D.P.: The influence of art expertise and training on emotion and preference ratings for representational and abstract artworks. PLoS One **10**(8), 1–21 (2015)
13. Kanai, H., Morishima, M., Nasu, K., Nishimatsu, T., Shibata, K., Matsuoka, T.: Identification of principal factors of fabric aesthetics by the evaluation from experts on textiles and from untrained consumers. Text. Res. J. **81**(12), 1216–1225 (2011)
14. Nagamachi, M.: Kansei engineering: a new ergonomic consumer-oriented technology for product development. Int. J. Ind. Ergon. **15**(1), 3–11 (1995)
15. Huang, Y., Chen, C.H., Khoo, L.P.: Products classification in emotional design using a basic-emotion based semantic differential method. Int. J. Ind. Ergon. **42**(6), 569–580 (2012)
16. Zhiwei, F.: Formal Models of Natural Language Processing. Press of University of Science and Technology of China, Hefei (2010)
17. Sagara, T., Hagiwara, M.: Natural language neural network and its application to question-answering system. Neurocomputing **142**, 201–208 (2014)
18. Manning, C.D., Schütze, H.: Foundations of Statistical Natural Language Processing. MIT Press, Cambridge (1999)
19. Yao, G., Xue, C., Wang, H., Yan, B.: Design method for coach styling design based on image cognition. Dongnan Daxue Xuebao (Ziran Kexue Ban)/J. SE Univ. (Nat. Sci. Ed.) **46**(6), 1198–1203 (2016)
20. Guo, F., Li, F., Nagamachi, M., Hu, M., Li, M.: Research on color optimization of tricolor product considering color harmony and users' emotion. Color Res. Appl. **45**(1), 1–16 (2019)
21. Ding, M., Bai, Z.: Product color emotional design adaptive to product shape feature variation. Color Res. Appl. **44**(5), 811–823 (2019)
22. Tanaka, Y., Osgood, C.E.: Cross-culture, cross-concept, and cross-subject generality of affective meaning systems. J. Pers. Soc. Psychol. **2**(2), 143–153 (1965)
23. Dou, R., Zhang, Y., Nan, G.: Application of combined Kano model and interactive genetic algorithm for product customization. J. Intell. Manuf. **30**, 2587–2602 (2016). https://doi.org/10.1007/s10845-016-1280-4
24. Das, P., Bhattacharyya, D., Bandyopadhyay, S.K., Kim, T.H.: Person identification through IRIS recognition. Int. J. Secur. Appl. **3**(1), 129–148 (2009)

Systematic Review on Using Biofeedback (EEG and Infrared Thermography) to Evaluate Emotion and User Perception Acquired by Kansei Engineering

Jiayu Zeng, Marcelo M. Soares, and Renke He[✉]

School of Design, Hunan University, Hunan 410000, People's Republic of China
jiayuzeng@163.com, soaresmm@gmail.com, renke8@163.com

Abstract. KANSEI Engineering (KE) [1] was created at Hiroshima University about 30 year ago and it is well known in the world at present as an ergonomic customer-oriented product development technology. It is a method for translating sensations and impressions into product parameters. The objective of KE is to study the relationship between product forms and KANSEI images. However, the KE method is based on the analysis of human subjective factors, customer's psychological feelings and needs, which is transformed in product design parameters. The customer's psychological feelings and needs are usually acquired by subjective tools. The questions which arises is if these subjective tools reflect the real customer needs. Nowadays, some scholars have recently started using biofeedback to evaluate the emotions of human interaction with products. Some studies have shown that EEG and Infrared Thermography measurements can help reduce subjective interpretation in data and improve user perception in their interactions with products. This systematic literature review aims to search the references on EEG, Infrared Thermography, Kansei Engineering and emotion. It will serve as a support for further researches to check if is possible to include biofeedback tools to contribute to subjective analyzes.

Keywords: Consumer product · Emotion · Kansei Engineer · EEG · Infrared Thermography · Product design · Affective engineering · Emotional design

1 Introduction

Nowadays, emotion plays a fundamental role in consumer product design. Thus, design process must include tools to evaluate emotions in interactions with objects in the world. Normally, researchers usually measure human emotion by subjective evaluation and objective usability evaluation, like questionnaires [2], Self-Assessment-Mannequin (SAM) [3], Emotional Engagement Scale (EES) [4], Cognitive Engagement Scale (CES) [5], System Usability Scale (SUS) [6], Lickert Scale [7], Kansei engineering and other design method, like user observation [8], interview [9], focus groups [10], cultural probes [11], etc. However, sometimes these kinds of method fails to reflect the real emotions of the user and even cause erroneous interpretations. What the customer

A. Marcus and E. Rosenzweig (Eds.): HCII 2020, LNCS 12200, pp. 582–593, 2020.
https://doi.org/10.1007/978-3-030-49713-2_40

says is really what do they feel? So, it is necessary for researchers to do some more studies on this field.

To be mentioned, some scholars have recently started using physiological parameter evaluate the emotions of human interaction with products, such as: Oliveira et al. [12] who evaluated the subjective emotion (valence, arousal and dominance) and heart rate responses, when the participants interact with two immersive Virtual Reality (VR) environment; Trindade et al. [13] who used a face-reading tool to measure the emotional participants reactions, when they play a digital game. They studied the sensitivity of the tool to measure the emotional reactions at the different moments of the game, and the relation with the emotion reactions and the usability problems of the game.

Some studies have shown that EEG, infrared thermography, eye tracking, the face reading and some other technology measurements can help reduce statistical errors in data and improve user perception in their interactions with products. Slobounov et al. [14] used EEG to exams the effect of fully immersive 3Dstereoscopic presentations and less immersive 2D VR environments on brain functions and behavioral outcomes. The study shows that using EEG may be a promising approach for performance enhancement and potential applications in clinical/rehabilitation settings; Guo et al. [15] designed Thirty-two 3D prototypes of LED desk lamp to simulate an aesthetic appreciation flow. The study aims to integrate eye-tracking metrics and EEG measurements to distinguish and quantify the visual aesthetics of a product. The quantification method can help designers measure the visual aesthetics of their products and reduce errors in design; Soares et al. [16] use a subjective evaluation scale and the infrared thermography to measure what the user felt when he was handling a product control device; Barros et al. [7] conducted a usability evaluation of how users manually handle PET bottles for soft drinks by using Lickert scale, eye tracking and EEG.

This paper introduces a systematic review on emotion including Kansei Engineering and biofeedback, such as neuroergonomics and neurodesign tools (Eletroencephalography-EEG and Infrared Thermography).

2   Method

2.1   Systematic Review and Data Mining

Nowadays, a large number of scientific literature and various research results have emerged. The growth rate of journal literature and various monographs has far exceeded the scope of people's reading ability. In order to save reading time and obtain the most relevant information it is possible to carry out a systematic review.

Systematic review can provide a lot of information and knowledge for a certain field and specialty. Systematic review, as a relatively new comprehensive evaluation method of literature, has been widely used in many disciplines, especially the medical field in recent years.

Cook and Deborah (1997) [17] defined a systematic review as a secondary literature research method that aggregates information, critically evaluates the information, and synthesizes the results of the initial research from multiple perspectives. They point out three characteristics that an excellent systematic review should possess, namely:

Precise, explicit definition and statement of the research question to be treated; Reproducible search strategy (for this reason, the systematic review article should include the database, terms, and restrictions on the initial study year, language, etc.), emphasizing the repeatability of the research; use pre-set initial research inclusion and exclusion criteria.

This data mining process uses a visual method to conduct systematic review based on the concept of data mining [18], the data was subdivided into three main moments: problem identification, preprocessing and transformation. In this context, explain the Data Mining process by subdividing it into five steps (Fig. 1): (i) knowledge of the domain; (ii) preprocessing; (iii) pattern extraction; (iv) post-processing; (v) use of knowledge.

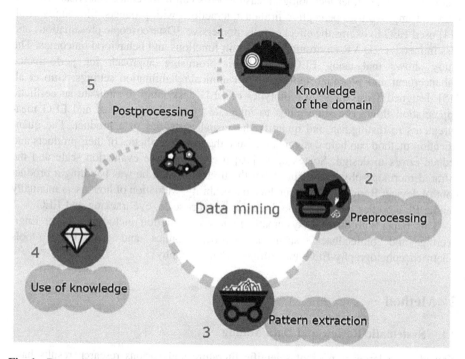

Fig. 1. Data mining process: definition of graphic signals based on the organization. Source: Blum, A.; Merino, E.A.D; Merino, G.S.A.D.

2.2   Research

(i) **Knowledge of domain.** The first step resulted from the choice of databases according to their scope and availability description. And this review is based on human emotions when users interact with products. Thus, the research was applied to Web of science [19], Elsevier [20], ACM [21], SpringerLink [22] and Scopus [23], as they are multidisciplinary in scope and encompass the major areas of interest of the case study, especially Applied Social Sciences (where Design fits) and Health (focus on human and biofeedback).

(ii) **Preprocessing.** Then, we proceeded to step preprocessing, when the period in which the data were to be retrieved, the type of material to be searched, the target areas of the research and the establishment of the descriptors were defined. As data retrieval period, we searched the publications made from the year 2000.

As a type of material to be searched, the search for complete articles was determined within the major areas of interest: Applied Social Sciences, Health and the like- these as main. Some bases, however, allowed to point out the areas of interest of the research more specifically and, according to the indicated ranges and the relationship with the intended focus, were selected as follows: Social Sciences, Social Technology and Arts Humanities at Web of science; Full-Text collection of the ACM; Full-Text collection of SpringerLink; Social Sciences & Humanities, Health Sciences and Life Sciences at Scopus.

It is the processing that data receives in order to be used in later steps. And on this step, the descriptors (keywords) was defined as Product design, EEG, Infrared Thermography, Kansei Engineer and Emotion (Fig. 2).

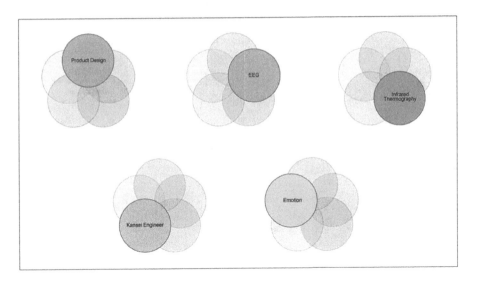

Fig. 2. Descriptors defined in step (ii) preprocessing. Source: the authors.

Subsequently, they were organized, in a combined manner, in step (iii) pattern extraction, when the Boolean operators "AND" were used. The terms, in English, were combined to promote the collection of data that covered from macro to micro approach, as the research interests.

(iii) **Pattern extraction.** The use of Boolean operators allowed an organized approach in the following fields: (A) Use EEG and Infrared Thermography to test product design; (B) Use EEG, Infrared Thermography and Kansei Engineer method to test product design; (C) Use EEG, Infrared Thermography and Kansei

Engineer method to measure user emotion by testing product design; (D) Use Infrared Thermography and Kansei Engineer method to test product design; (E) Use EEG to measure user emotion by testing product design; (F) EEG, Infrared Thermography and Kansei Engineer methodology; (G) Use EEG, Infrared Thermography and Kansei Engineer method to measure user emotion.

For better visualization to help the search process, these fields were organized using symbols and colors that acted as a query scheme throughout the search. Figure 3 shows the representation of fields A, B and C; D and E; F and G.

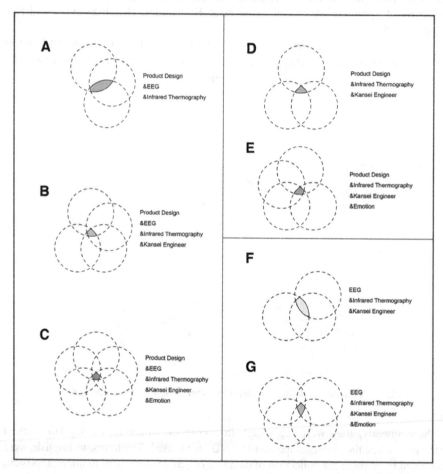

Fig. 3. Combination of descriptors in step (iii) pattern extraction. Source: the authors.

Fields A through C brought together terms focused on "using EEG and Infrared Thermography test product" and were structured as follows: A = [(product design) AND (EEG) AND (Infrared Thermography)]; B = [(A) AND (Kansei Engineer)]; C = [(B) AND (emotion)]. Likewise, the fields D and E - which brought together terms focusing on "using Infrared Thermography and Kansei engineer test product" - followed the same logic: D = [(product design) AND (Infrared Thermography) AND (Kansei Engineer)]; E = [(D) AND (emotion)];

Similar to the organizations in the previous fields, F to G have put together terms that focus on "EEG, Infrared Thermography and Kansei Engineer": F = [(EEG) AND (Infrared Thermography) AND (Kansei Engineer)]; G = [(F) AND (emotion)].

The combination and division by fields allowed the extraction of patterns that resulted in a quantitative survey of articles. Table 1 shows the results of the survey conducted between January 10–15th, 2020. The highlighted numbers correspond to the articles that were analyzed in more detail in the subsequent step.

Table 1. Table indicating the number of articles raised in the bases from the application of step (iii) pattern extraction. Source: the authors.

	Web of Science	Elsevier	ACM	SpringerLink	SCOPUS
A	1	42	241	61	2
B	0	1	0	1	0
C	0	1	0	1	0
D	0	0	3	3	0
E	0	0	1	3	0
F	0	0	234	3	0
G	0	0	140	2	0

(iv) **Post-processing.** Considering Data Mining by grouping, post-processing step further analyzed the numerical results obtained. The results over one hundred were again mined from title and keyword analysis.

As can be seen from Table 1, in the field A, there only one paper-Comparing Thermographic, EEG, and Subjective Measures of Affective Experience During Simulated Product Interactions [24]-from Web of science related to the field A; Two papers from Scopus, one is same as the one from Web of science, another is "Comparison of thermographic, EEG and subjective measures of affective experience of designed stimuli [25]".

The field B and C have same papers: (i) One is from the 23rd annual meeting of the Japan neuroscience society and the 10th annual meeting of the Japanese neural network society [26]. (ii) And one paper - Proposal for Indices to Assess Attractiveness on Initial Use of Mobile Phones [27]-is form SpringerLink.

The field D and E have one same papers from ACM: It is "A system for embodied social active listening to sound and music content [28]." from ACM; To be mentioned, the field D has two more related papers from ACM than field E from ACM: (i) one is "Kansei: a testbed for sensing at scale [29]"; (ii) another one is "Implementing an autonomic architecture for fault-tolerance in a wireless sensor network testbed for at-scale experimentation [30]".

The field D and E have three same papers from SpringerLink: One is "Using Digital Thermography to Analyse the Product User's Affective Experience of a Product [31]"; Another one is "Application of Digital Infrared Thermography for Emotional Evaluation: A Study of the Gestural Interface Applied to 3D Modeling Software [16]"; And one paper same as the one from (iii) of field B and C.

The field F has 234 papers from ACM and three from SpringerLink: (i) One related paper is "Dynamic analysis of dorsal thermal images [32]"; (ii) And another one is "Analysis of Product Use by Means of Eye Tracking and EEG: A Study of Neuroergonomics [7]"; (iii) The last one is same as the one from (iii) of field B and C.

The field G has 140 papers from ACM and two papers from SpringerLink: one is same as the one from (ii) of field B and C; and another one is same as the one from (ii) of field F.

Subsequently, the articles were appreciated through the abstract and framed in "related topics". Of these, those that dealt with subjects directly related to the research theme were classified as "direct relation" (Table 2).

Table 2. Table indicating the number of articles on the subject of interest from the application of step (iv) post processing. Source: the authors.

Post-processing of collected data						
	Web of Science	Elsevier	ACM	SpringerLink	SCOPUS	
Total step 3	1	1	141	6	2	Total
New mining	1	0	34	5	1	
Related topics	1*	0	24	4	1*	30
Direct relationship	1*	0	2	4	0	7
Similarity of approach	0	0	0	0	0	0

*papers obtained from more than one database

(v) **Use of knowledge.** As a result of the applied process, the papers listed under "Related topics", two were available on more than one basis. The "related topics" totaled 30 papers. Of these, seven were directly related to the research theme, that is, studies involving elements of product design, measure emotion by using biofeedback or EEG or Infrared Thermography or Kansei engineer. They are: Jenkins, Brown and Rutterford (2009) [24]; Lennart (2010) [33]; Jaichandar, Elara and Edgar (2012) [34]; Yamagishi et al. (2011) [27].

3   Findings

This study have found 740 related papers from thousands of articles, and selected 151 related topic papers by title and keywords. Further read the content and output of these 151 papers, and finally select 30 papers related to "Using biofeedback (EEG And Infrared Thermography) to evaluate emotion And user Perception acquired by Kansei Engineering".

From the data of Table 2, the number of papers related to the research topic is relatively small (30 papers), which indicates that there are relatively few studies focus on emotion recognition by using the biofeedback (EEG and Infrared Thermography) and Kansei Engineer method. From the content of the papers, the majority of emotion measurement is performed by using EEG or Infrared Thermography (16 papers. To be mentioned there are only two related papers using EEG and Infrared Thermography measure participants' recognition or emotion. And seven papers mentioned other biofeedback measure method. There are five papers that use the combination of physiological data and subjective data measurement method; And any paper that uses Kansei engineer method and physiological data measurement to study user emotions.

Seven Directly Related Papers

(i) "Comparing Thermographic, EEG, and Subjective Measures of Affective Experience During Simulated Product Interactions". In this paper, Jenkins, Brown and Rutterford [24] using Affective Self Report (ASR), EEG and Infrared Thermography measure cognitive work and affective state of Sixteen male volunteers (mean age = 21.75 years)' cognitive.

(ii) "Proposal for Indices to Assess Attractiveness on Initial Use of Mobile Phones". In this study, Yamagishi et al. [27] measured physiological indices of attractiveness during participants initial use of a mobile, including measurements of the automatic nervous system, nasal skin temperature, pupil diameter, EEG, blinking and electrocardiography. This study measured Nasal Skin Temperature and Pupil Diameter of Eleven undergraduate and graduate participants (six men and five women, mean age = 22.1 years, SD = 1.30); tested Ten undergraduate and graduate participants (eight men and two women, mean age = 21.7 years, SD = 0.67) participated in the EEG experiment; and Ten undergraduate and graduate participants (10 men, mean age = 21.2 years, SD = 0.63) participated in the experiment to measure blinks and ECG.

(iii) "Using Digital Thermography to Analyse the Product User's Affective Experience of a Product". This study conducted a usability evaluation of users during manual handling of soda PET packaging by comparing the user-reported experience and the actual experience felt measured through usability analysis techniques and thermography. Barros et al. [31] proved that thermography has proven to be effective to measure users' satisfaction (felt experience) in handling consumer products. There are two field studies: Field Study I, 12 participants (8 female and 4 male) and Field Study II, 11 volunteers were selected (7 female and 4 male).

(iv) "Application of Digital Infrared Thermography for Emotional Evaluation: A Study of the Gestural Interface". In this paper, Soares, Vitorino and Marçal [16] studied the application of infrared digital thermography as a tool to evaluate the level of emotional stress during the use of a computer system. They using a subjective evaluation scale and the infrared thermography to measure what the user felt when he was handling a product control device. In the usability evaluation, a test was developed with a sequence of tasks performed by 12 volunteers.

(v) "Analysis of Product Use by Means of Eye Tracking and EEG: A Study of Neuroergonomics". Barros et al. [7] measured user satisfaction with soft drinks PET packaging by using Lickert scale assess, eye tracking and EEG. This study comprising 12 participants for the usability study who are from different age groups and are higher education students.

(vi) "Wii remote vs. controller: electroencephalographic measurement of affective gameplay interaction". In this paper, Lennart [33] studied the influence of interaction modes (Playstation 2 game controller vs. Wii remote and Nunchuk) on subjective experience and brain activity measured with Electroencephalographic measures and survey measures-a game experience questionnaire (GEQ). This study measured Thirty-six Swedish undergraduate university students and employees participated in this experiment. Their age ranged between 18 and 41, having an average (M) age of 24 (Standard Deviation [SD] = 4.9).

(vii) "Investigation of facial infrared thermography during interaction with therapeutic pet robot during cognitive training: a quantitative approach". Jaichandar et al. [34] using thermography validate the functional process involved in temperature and correlation between cognitive task. The participants were mainly students from the bioengineering option (Singapore Polytechnic), with a total of 11 students of ages from 18 to 21 years old with an average of 19.6 years old and a standard deviation of 1.2.

From the information above, we can see clearly that most of the experiments are focus on electronic products: three different models of mobile phones, gesture computer system, Wii mote, controller, and pet robots. The participants of the experiments were all young people with average ages between 19.6 to 24.

4   Conclusion

Purpose of this research is searching the related references on EEG, Infrared Thermography, Kansei Engineering and emotion. To achieve this aim, this study selected papers from five databases through a visual method to conduct systematic review based on the concept of data mining. Searching for the combination of five keywords "product design, EEG, Infrared Thermography, Kansei Engineer and emotion".

Through the selection and reading of related topic papers, it is found that currently there are some research papers on biofeedback measurement of user emotions; but there are fewer articles combining physiological data measurement and psychological data measurement methods; Moreover, there is no research use biofeedback and Kansei engineer methods to study user emotions. This also reveals that this field is still in the preliminary research stage and is worth further research and discussion in the future.

There are some limitation of this research, because the database is too large, so this research set the following conditions: (i) The papers must be written in English; (ii) The search resources are limited to the selected five databases; (iii) The papers must be published from January 01, 2000 to January 15, 2020. It results the papers are relatively limited. Follow-up work, in future research, it is necessary to expand more databases, choose more language types, and extend the time. To ensure that the research is comprehensive and accurate.

References

1. Schütte, S.T.W., Eklund, J., Axelsson, J.R.C., et al.: Concepts, methods and tools in Kansei engineering. Theor. Issues Ergon. Sci. 5(3), 214–231 (2004)
2. Lietz, P.: Research into questionnaire design. Int. J. Market Res. 52(2), 249–272 (2010)
3. Bradley, M.M., Lang, P.J.: Measuring emotion: the self-assessment Manikin and the semantic differential. J. Behav. Ther. Exp. Psychiatry 25(1), 49–59 (1994)
4. Karsaklian, E., Sorbello, C., Sorbello, A.: Mapping the pathway to emotional engagement a methodology to create the emotional engagement model. J. Acad. Bus. Econ. 17, 47–56 (2017)
5. Greene, B.A.: Measuring cognitive engagement with self-report scales: reflections from over 20 years of research. Educ. Psychol. 50(1), 14–30 (2015)
6. Barros, R.Q., Santos, G., Ribeiro, C., Torres, R., Barros, M.Q., Soares, M.M.: A usability study of a brain-computer interface apparatus: an ergonomic approach. In: Marcus, A. (ed.) DUXU 2015. LNCS, vol. 9186, pp. 224–236. Springer, Cham (2015). https://doi.org/10.1007/978-3-319-20886-2_22
7. Barros, R.Q., et al.: Analysis of product use by means of eye tracking and EEG: a study of neuroergonomics. In: Marcus, A. (ed.) DUXU 2016. LNCS, vol. 9747, pp. 539–548. Springer, Cham (2016). https://doi.org/10.1007/978-3-319-40355-7_51
8. Wimmer, K., Stiles, J.: The observational research handbook: understanding how consumers live with your products. J. Advert. Res. 41(1), 91–93 (2001)
9. Creusen, M., Hultink, E.J., Eling, K.: Choice of consumer research methods in the front end of new product development. Int. J. Market Res. 55(1), 81–104 (2013)

10. Bruseberg, A., McDonagh-Philp, D.: Focus groups to support the industrial/product designer: a review based on current literature and designers' feedback. Appl. Ergon. 33(1), 27–38 (2002)
11. Gaver, W.W.: Cultural probes and the value of uncertainty. Interactions 11(5), 53–56 (2004)
12. Oliveira, T., Noriega, P., Rebelo, F., Heidrich, R.: Evaluation of the relationship between virtual environments and emotions. In: Rebelo, F., Soares, M. (eds.) AHFE 2017. AISC, vol. 588, pp. 71–82. Springer, Cham (2018). https://doi.org/10.1007/978-3-319-60582-1_8
13. Trindade, Y., Rebelo, F., Noriega, P.: Potentialities of a face reading tool to a digital game evaluation and development: a preliminary study. In: Rebelo, F., Soares, M. (eds.) AHFE 2017. AISC, vol. 588, pp. 371–381. Springer, Cham (2018). https://doi.org/10.1007/978-3-319-60582-1_37
14. Slobounov, S.M., Ray, W., Johnson, B., et al.: Modulation of cortical activity in 2D versus 3D virtual reality environments: an EEG study. Int. J. Psychophysiol. 95(3), 254–260 (2015)
15. Guo, F., et al.: Distinguishing and quantifying the visual aesthetics of a product: an integrated approach of eye-tracking and EEG. Int. J. Ind. Ergon. 71, 47–56 (2019)
16. Soares, M.M., Vitorino, D.F., Marçal, M.A.: Application of digital infrared thermography for emotional evaluation: a study of the gestural interface applied to 3D modeling software. In: Rebelo, F., Soares, M.M. (eds.) AHFE 2018. AISC, vol. 777, pp. 201–212. Springer, Cham (2019). https://doi.org/10.1007/978-3-319-94706-8_23
17. Cook, D.J.: Systematic reviewes: synthesis of best evidence for clinical decisions. Ann. Intern. Med. 126(5), 376 (1997)
18. Blum, A., Merino, E.A.D., Merino, G.S.A.D.: Visual method for systematic review in design based on concepts of Data Mining. Eugenio Andrés Díaz Merino DAPesquisa 11(16), 124–139 (2016)
19. Web of Science (2020). www.isiknowledge.com. Accessed 16 Jan 2020
20. Elsevier (2020). https://www.sciencedirect.com. Accessed 16 Jan 2020
21. ACM (2020). https://dl.acm.org. Accessed 16 Jan 2020
22. LNCS (2020). http://www.springer.com/lncs. Accessed 16 Jan 2020
23. Scopus (2020). https://www.scopus.com. Accessed 16 Jan 2020
24. Jenkins, S., Brown, R., Rutterford, N.: Comparing thermographic, EEG, and subjective measures of affective experience during simulated product interactions. Int. J. Des. 3(2), 53–65 (2009)
25. Jenkins, S., Brown, R., Rutterford, N.: Comparison of thermographic, EEG and subjective measures of affective experience of designed stimuli. In: Proceedings from the 6th Conference on Design and Emotion (2008)
26. Abstract of the joint meetings of the 23rd annual meeting of the Japan neuroscience society and the 10th annual meeting of the Japanese neural network society, 4–6 September 2000, Yokohama, Japan. Plenary Lecture. Neurosci. Res. 38(Suppl. 1), pp. S1–S189 (2000)
27. Yamagishi, M., Jingu, H., Kasamatsu, K., Kiso, H., Fukuzumi, S.: Proposal for indices to assess attractiveness on initial use of mobile phones. In: Marcus, A. (ed.) DUXU 2011. LNCS, vol. 6769, pp. 696–705. Springer, Heidelberg (2011). https://doi.org/10.1007/978-3-642-21675-6_79
28. Volpe, G., Camurri, A.: A system for embodied social active listening to sound and music content. J. Comput. Cult. Heritage 4(1), 1–23 (2011)
29. Ertin, E., Arora, A., Ramnath, R., et al.: Kansei: a testbed for sensing at scale. In: Proceedings of the 5th International Conference on Information Processing in Sensor Networks (IPSN 2006), pp. 399–406. ACM, New York (2006)

30. Sridharan, M., Bapat, S., Ramnath, R., et al.: Implementing an autonomic architecture for fault-tolerance in a wireless sensor network testbed for at-scale experimentation. In: Proceedings of the 2008 ACM Symposium on Applied Computing (SAC 2008), pp. 1670–1676. ACM, New York (2008)
31. Barros, R.Q., Soares, M.M., Maçal, M.A., et al.: Using digital thermography to analyse the product user's affective experience of a product. In: Rebelo, F., Soares, M. (eds.) Advances in Ergonomics in Design. Advances in Intelligent Systems and Computing, vol. 485, pp. 97–107. Springer, Cham (2016). https://doi.org/10.1007/978-3-319-41983-1_10
32. Nozawa, A., Takei, Y.: Dynamic analysis of dorsal thermal images. Artif. Life Rob. **16**(2), 147–151 (2011)
33. Nacke, L.E.: Wiimote vs. controller: electroencephalographic measurement of affective gameplay interaction. In: Proceedings of the International Academic Conference on the Future of Game Design and Technology (Futureplay 2010), pp. 159–166. ACM, New York (2010)
34. Jaichandar, K.S., Elara, M.R., García, E.A.M.: Investigation of facial infrared thermography during interaction with therapeutic pet robot during cognitive training: a quantitative approach. In: Proceedings of the 6th International Conference on Rehabilitation Engineering & Assistive Technology (i-CREATe 2012), Article 28, pp. 1–4. Singapore Therapeutic, Assistive & Rehabilitative Technologies (START) Centre, Midview City (2012)

Author Index

Printed in the United States
By Bookmasters